Henry Edwin Barnes

Handbook to the birds of the Bombay presidency

Henry Edwin Barnes

Handbook to the birds of the Bombay presidency

ISBN/EAN: 9783337731892

Printed in Europe, USA, Canada, Australia, Japan

Cover: Foto ©ninafisch / pixelio.de

More available books at **www.hansebooks.com**

HANDBOOK

TO THE

BIRDS

OF THE

BOMBAY PRESIDENCY.

BY

Lieut. H. EDWIN BARNES, D.A.C.,

BOMBAY COMMISSARIAT DEPARTMENT,

MEMBER OF THE BRITISH ORNITHOLOGICAL UNION AND BOMBAY NATURAL HISTORY SOCIETY.

Calcutta:

PUBLISHED BY THE CALCUTTA CENTRAL PRESS CO., LD.,

5, Council House Street.

1885.

CALCUTTA:
PRINTED BY A. ACTON, AT THE CALCUTTA CENTRAL PRESS CO., LD.,
5, COUNCIL HOUSE STREET.

To

COLONEL CHARLES SWINHOE, F.L.S., F.Z.S.,

THIS WORK

Is Respectfully Dedicated

BY HIS GRATEFUL

AND

OBEDIENT SERVANT

THE

AUTHOR.

Fam. Vulturidæ
Vulturinæ
Neophroninæ
Gypaetinæ
Fam. Falconidæ
Falconinæ 2d. quill
Accipitrinæ 4th. "
Aquilinæ 4th. "
Buteoninæ 3d. "
Milvinæ
Fam Strigidæ
Striginæ
Syrniinæ
Asioninæ
Buboninæ
Surniinæ

Insessores
Fam Hirundinidæ
Hirundininæ
Cypselinæ
Fam Caprimulgidæ
Caprimulginæ
Fam Trogonidæ
Fam. Meropidæ
Fam Coraciadæ
Fam Halcyonidæ
Halcyoninæ
Alcedininæ
Fam. Bucerotidæ
Scansores
Fam. Psittacidæ
Palæorninæ
Loriinæ
Fam Picidæ
Picinæ
Campephilinæ
Gecininæ
Yunginæ
Fam Megalaimidæ
Fam Cuculidæ
Cuculinæ
Phænicophainæ
Centropodinæ

Nectarininæ
Dicæinæ
Certhinæ
Sittinæ
Fam Upupidæ
Fam Laniadæ
Laniinæ
Malaconotinæ
Campephaginæ
Dicruninæ
Artaminæ
Fam. Muscicapidæ
Myiag[illegible]inæ
Muscicapinæ
Fam Merulidæ
Myotherinæ
Turdinæ
Timalinæ
Fam Brachypodidæ
Pycnonotinæ
Phyllornithinæ
Ireninæ
Oriolinæ
Fam Sylviadæ
Saxicolinæ
Ruticillinæ
Calamoherpinæ
Drymoicinæ
Phylloscopinæ
Sylvinæ
Motacillinæ
Fam Ampelidæ
Leiotrichinæ
Parinæ
Tribe Conirostres
Fam Corvidæ
Corvinæ
Dendrocittinæ
Fam Sturnidæ
Sturninæ
Lamprotorninæ

PREFACE.

T IS with extreme reluctance that I have been induced to publish the following unpretentious volume, and I could have wished that the task had fallen into more able hands; but, believing that a work of this kind is much needed, and no one else apparently being willing to undertake it, I venture with some diffidence to place it before the public, hoping that it will meet with a favorable reception.

Its object is to place, at a cost within the reach of all, a book that will enable them to identify any bird they may meet with.

When I first commenced taking an interest in ornithology, I was much hindered by the difficulty experienced in obtaining works dealing with the subject, those extant being so costly as to be quite beyond my means; and it was only by practising rigid economy, and the exercise of much self-denial, that I obtained them. Even then my difficulties were not ended; the information was scattered throughout so many volumes, and I met with so many perplexing contradictions that the books were often a hindrance rather than a help to me. I conceived the idea of compiling a hand-book for private use, dealing exclusively with that portion of India proper garrisoned by Bombay troops. Many friends, to whom I showed the compilation, expressed a wish to have a similar one, and strongly urged me to publish it; it is in deference to these wishes that the book appears.

I have followed Jerdon as closely as possible, and have deviated from his descriptions only when such appeared really necessary; and for these alterations I am mainly indebted to Mr. A. O. Hume, whose numerous works on Indian Ornithology are so well known.

The Bombay Presidency falls naturally into three divisions,—Sind, Rajputana, (including Guzerat, Kutch, and portions of Central India), and the Deccan.

For information relating to the Birds of Sind, I am indebted to many papers scattered throughout "Stray Feathers," and also to Mr. Murray's valuable work on the Vertebrate Zoology of Sind.

For similar information regarding Rajputana, I am mainly indebted to Major Butler, whose able papers on the "Avifauna of Northern Guzerat and Mount Aboo" appeared in "Stray Feathers," Volumes III, IV, and V.

I am again indebted to this gentleman for his exhaustive resume of the "Birds of the Deccan," compiled from papers by various authors published in "Stray Feathers," and supplemented to a great extent by his own researches.

I have quoted largely from the above authors, and trust that this general acknowledgment will be deemed sufficient.

I would add, in conclusion, that my long residence in India, embracing a period of 20 years (during which time I have been located at most of the military stations in the Bombay Presidency) has afforded me ample opportunities for the careful study of bird-life in all its various phases.

Grallatores
Pressirostres
Fam Otididae
Fam Cursoridae
Fam Glareolidae

Fam. Charadriidae
Charadriinae
Vanellinae
Esacinae
Fam Haematopodidae
Strepsilinae
Dromadinae

CONTENTS.

Jerdon's Number.	POPULAR NAME.	SCIENTIFIC NAME.	Page.
1	The Cinereous Vulture ...	Vultur monachus, *Lin.* ...	2
2	The Indian King Vulture.	Otogyps calvus, *Scop.* ...	3
3*bis.*	The Bay Vulture ...	Gyps fulvescens, *Hume* ...	4
4*bis.*	The Long-billed Pale Brown Vulture ...	„ pallescens, *Hume* ...	5
5	The White-backed Vulture	Pseudogyps bengalensis, *Gm.*	6
6	The White Scavenger Vulture	Neophron ginginianus, *Lath.*	7
7	The Lammergeyer ...	Gypætus barbatus, *Lin.* ...	8
8	The Peregrine Falcon ...	Falco peregrinus, *Gm.* ...	9
9	The Shaheen Falcon ...	„ peregrinator, *Sund.* ...	11
10	The Saker Falcon ...	„ sacer, *Gm.* ...	12
11	The Laggar Falcon ...	„ jugger, *J. E. Gr.* ...	12
12	The Red-cap Falcon ...	.. babylonicus, *Gurn.*	13
			16
			16
			17

ERRATA.

Page 204, line 13, *for* "tringi" *read* "Kingi."

„ 307 „ 29 „ "Setraonidæ" *read* "Tetraonidæ."

Jerdon's Number.	POPULAR NAME.	SCIENTIFIC NAME.	Page.
17	The Kestril ...	Cerchneis tinnunculus, *Lin.* ...	18
18	The Lesser Kestril ...	„ naumanni, *Fleisch.*	19
18*bis.*	....	„ pekinensis, *Swinh.*	20
19	The Red-legged Falcon ...	„ vespertina, *Lin.* ...	20
19*bis.*	....	„ amurensis, *Radde*	21
22	The Crested Goshawk ...	Astur trivirgatus, *Tem.* ...	22
23	The Shikra ...	„ badius, *Gm.* ...	22
24	The Sparrow Hawk ...	Accipiter nisus, *Lin.* ...	24
25	The Jungle Sparrow Hawk	„ virgatus, *Reinw.* ...	24
26	The Golden Eagle ...	Aquila chrysaëtus, *Lin.* ...	25
27	The Imperial Eagle ...	„ mogilnik, *S. G. Gm.*	26
28	The Spotted Eagle ...	„ clanga, *Pall.* ...	28
29	The Tawny Eagle ...	„ vindhiana, *Frankl.* ...	29
31	The Dwarf Eagle ...	Hieraëtus pennatus, *Gm.* ...	30
32	The Black Eagle ...	Neopus malayensis, *Reinw.*	31
33	The Crestless Hawk Eagle.	Nisaëtus fasciatus, *Vieill.* ...	32
35	The Crested Hawk Eagle.	Limnaëtus cirrhatus, *Gm.* ...	33
37	The Rufous-bellied Hawk Eagle	„ kieneri, *Gerv.* ...	35
38	The Common Serpent Eagle	Circaëtus gallicus, *Gm.* ...	36
39	The Crested Serpent Eagle	Spilornis cheela, *Lath.* ...	37

I have followed Jerdon as closely as possible, and have deviated from his descriptions only when such appeared really necessary; and for these alterations I am mainly indebted to Mr. A. O. Hume, whose numerous works on Indian Ornithology are so well known.

The Bombay Presidency falls naturally into three divisions,—Sind, Rajputana, (including Guzerat, Kutch, and portions of Central India), and the Deccan.

For information relating to the Birds of Sind, I am indebted to many papers scattered throughout "Stray Feathers," and also to Mr. Murray's valuable work on the Vertebrate Zoology of Sind.

For similar information regarding Rajputana, I am mainly indebted to Major Butler, whose able papers on the "Avifauna of Northern Guzerat and Mount Aboo" appeared in "Stray Feathers," Volumes III, IV, and V.

I am

tive resı

papers b,

and supplemented to a great extent by his own researches.

I have quoted largely from the above authors, and trust that this general acknowledgment will be deemed sufficient.

I would add, in conclusion, that my long residence in India, embracing a period of 20 years (during which time I have been located at most of the military stations in the Bombay Presidency) has afforded me ample opportunities for the careful study of bird-life in all its various phases.

Ord Grallatores
Tribe Pressirostres
Fam Otididae
Fam Cursoridae
Fam Glareolidae

Fam. Charadridae
Charadrinae
Vanellinae
Esacinae
Fam Haematopodidae
Strepsilinae
Dromadinae

CONTENTS.

Jerdon's Number.	POPULAR NAME.	SCIENTIFIC NAME.	Page.
39*bis.*	The Southern Harrier Eagle ...	... Spilornis melanotis, *Jerd.* ...	37
40	The Osprey	... Pandion haliaëtus, *Lin.* ...	38
41	The White-tailed Sea Eagle ...	... Polioaëtus ichthyaëtus, *Horsf.* ...	39
42	The Ring-tailed Sea Eagle.	Haliaëtus leucoryphus, *Pall.*	39
42*bis.*	The European White-tailed Sea Eagle ...	„ albicilla, *Lin.* ...	40
43	The Gray-backed Sea Eagle	„ leucogaster, *Gm.*	42
45	The Long-legged Buzzard.	Buteo ferox, *S. G. Gm.* ...	42
48	The White-eyed Buzzard.	Butastur teesa, *Frankl.* ...	44
51	The Pale Harrier	... Circus macrurus, *S. G. Gm.*	45
52	Montagu's Harrier ...	„ cineraceus, *Mont.* ...	49
53	The Pied Harrier ...	„ melanoleucos, *Forst.*	52
54	The Marsh Harrier ..	„ æruginosus, *Lin.*. ...	52
55	The Brahminy Kite	... Haliastur indus, *Bodd.* ...	54
56	The Pariah Kite	... Milvus govinda, *Sykes.* ...	54
56*bis.*	The Large Pariah Kite ...	„ melanotis, *Tem. and Schl.* ...	57
57	The Honey Buzzard	... Pernis ptilorhynchus, *Tem.*...	57
59	The Black-winged Kite ...	Elanus cæruleus, *Desf.* ...	59
60	The Indian Screech Owl ...	Strix javanica, *Gm.* ...	60
61	The Grass Owl ...	„ candida, *Tick.* ...	61
63	The Brown Wood Owl ...	Syrnium indranee, *Sykes.* ...	62
65	The Mottled Wood Owl ...	„ ocellatum, *Less.* ...	62
67	The Long-eared Owl	... Asio otus, *Lin.* ...	63
68	The Short-eared Owl ...	„ accipitrinus, *Forst.* ...	64
69	The Rock-horned Owl	... Bubo bengalensis, *Frankl.* ...	65
70	The Dusky-horned Owl ...	„ coromandus, *Lath.* ...	66
72	The Brown Fish Owl	... Ketupa ceylonensis, *Gm.* ...	68
74	The Indian Scops Owl	... Scops pennatus, *Hodgs.* ...	70
74*sept.*	The Striated Scops Owl ...	„ brucii, *Hume.* ...	71
75*ter.*	....	„ bakkamuna, *Forst.* ...	72
75*quat.*	The Malabar Scops Owl ...	„ malabaricus, *Jerd.* ...	74
76	The Spotted Owlet	... Carine brama, *Tem.* ...	75
77	The Jungle Owlet	... Glaucidium radiatum, *Tick.*	76
78	The Malabar Owlet ...	„ malabaricum, *Bly.* ...	76
81	The Brown Hawk Owl	... Ninox lugubris, *Tick.* ...	77
82	The Common Swallow	... Hirundo rustica, *Lin.* ...	79
84	The Wire-tailed Swallow	„ filifera, *Steph.*. ...	79
85	The Red-rumped Swallow	„ erythropygia, *Sykes*	80
86	The Indian Cliff Swallow	„ fluvicola, *Jerd.* ...	81
87	The European Sand Martin	... Cotyle riparia, *Lin.* ...	82
89	The Indian Sand Martin	„ sinensis, *J. E. Cr.* ...	82
90	The Dusky Crag Martin	Ptyonoprogne concolor, *Sykes.* ...	83
91	The Mountain Crag Martin	„ rupestris, *Scop.* ...	83

Jerdon's Number.	POPULAR NAME.	SCIENTIFIC NAME.	Page.
91*bis*.	The Pallid Crag Martin	Ptyonoprogne obsoleta, *Cab.*	83
92	The English House Martin	Chelidon urbica, *Lin.* ...	84
95	The White-rumped Spinetail	Chætura sylvatica, *Tick.* ...	85
98	The Alpine Swift ...	Cypsellus melba, *Lin.* ...	85
99	The European Swift ...	„ apus, *Lin.* ...	85
100	The Common Indian Swift	„ affinis, *J. E. Gr.*	86
101	The White-clawed Swift	„ leuconyx, *Tick.* ...	86
102	The Palm Swift ...	„ batassiensis, *J. E. Gr.* ...	87
103	The Indian Edible-nest Swiftlet ...	Collocalia unicolor, *Jerd.* ...	87
104	The Indian Crested Swift	Dendrochelidon coronata, *Tick.*	88
107	The Jungle Night Jar ...	Caprimulgus indicus, *Lath.*	89
108	The Neilgherry Night Jar	„ kelaarti, *Bly.*	89
109	The Large Bengal Night Jar	„ albonotatus, *Tick.* ...	90
111	The Ghat Night Jar ...	„ atripennis, *Jerd.* ...	90
111*bis*.	Unwin's Night Jar ...	„ unwini, *Hume.*	90
112	The Common Indian Night Jar ...	„ asiaticus, *Lath.*	91
113	Sykes' Night Jar ...	„ mahrattensis, *Sykes* ...	92
114	Franklin's Night Jar ...	„ monticolus, *Frankl.* ...	92
115	The Malabar Trogon ...	Harpactes fasciatus, *Forst.*	93
117	The Common Indian Bee-eater	Merops viridis, *Lin.* ...	93
118	The Blue-tailed Bee-eater	„ philippinus, *Lin* ...	94
119	The Chesnut-headed Bee-eater ...	„ swinhoii, *Hume.* ...	95
120	The Egyptian Bee-eater	„ persicus, *Pall.* ...	95
121	The European Bee-eater	„ apiaster, *Lin.* ...	95
122	The Blue-necked Bee-eater	Nycticornis athertoni, *Jard. and Selb.*	96
123	The Indian Roller ...	Coracias indica, *Lin.* ...	97
125	The European Roller ...	„ garrula, *Lin.* ...	98
127	The Brown-headed Kingfisher	Pelargopsis gurial, *Pears.* ...	98
129	The White-breasted Kingfisher	Halcyon smyrnensis, *Lin.* ...	99
130	The Black-capped Purple Kingfisher ...	„ pileata, *Bodd.* ...	100
132	The White-collared Kingfisher	„ chloris, *Bodd.* ...	100

Jerdon's Number.	POPULAR NAME.	SCIENTIFIC NAME.	Page.
133	The Three-toed Purple Kingfisher ...	Ceyx tridactylus, *Pall.* ...	101
134	The Common Indian Kingfisher ...	Alcedo bengalensis, *Gm.* ...	101
134*bis.*	The European Kingfisher	„ ispida, *Lin.* ...	102
135*quat.*	Beavan's Kingfisher ...	„ beavani, *Wald.* ...	102
136	The Pied Kingfisher ...	Ceryle rudis, *Lin.* ...	103
140	The Great Hornbill ...	Dichoceros cavatus, *Shaw.* ...	104
141	The Malabar Pied Hornbill	Hydrocissa coronata, *Bodd.*	105
144	The Common Grey Hornbill	Ocyceros birostris, *Scop.* ...	106
145	The Jungle Grey Hornbill	Tockus griseus, *Lath.* ...	106
147	The Alexandrine Paroquet	Palæornis eupatria, *Lin.* ...	108
148	The Rose-ringed Paroquet	„ torquatus, *Bodd.*	108
149	The Rose-headed Paroquet	„ purpureus, *P.L.S. Müll.* ...	109
151	The Blue-winged Paroquet	„ columboides, *Vig.*	110
153	The Indian Loriquet ...	Loriculus vernalis, *Sparr.* ...	111
158	The Sind Woodpecker ...	Picus sindianus, *Gould.* ...	112
160	The Yellow-fronted Woodpecker	„ mahrattensis, *Lath.* ...	112
164	The Southern Pigmy Woodpecker ...	Yungipicus nanus, *Vig.* ...	113
165	The Heart-spotted Woodpecker	Hemicercus cordatus, *Jerd.*	114
166*bis.*	The Southern Large Golden-backed Woodpecker	Chrysocolaptes delesserti, *Malh.* ...	114
167	The Black-backed Woodpecker	„ festivus, *Bodd.*	115
169	The Great Black Woodpecker	Thriponax hodgsoni, *Jerd.*...	116
171	The Small Green Woodpecker	Gecinus striolatus, *Bly.* ...	116
175	The Southern Yellow-necked Woodpecker ...	Chrysophlegma chlorigaster, *Jerd.* ...	117
178	The Bengal Rufous Woodpecker	Micropternus phæoceps, *Bly.*	118
179	The Madras Rufous Woodpecker	„ gularis, *Jerd.*...	118
180	The Golden-backed Woodpecker	Brachypternus aurantius, *Lin.* ...	118
181	The Lesser Golden-backed Woodpecker ...	„ puncticollis, *Malh.* ...	119
188	The Common Wryneck ...	Yunx torquilla, *Lin.* ...	120

Jerdon's Number.	POPULAR NAME.	SCIENTIFIC NAME.	Page.
193	The Common Green Barbet	Megalaima caniceps, *Frankl.*	121
193*bis.*	The Western Green Barbet	Megalaima inornata, *Wald.*	121
194	The Small Green Barbet	„ viridis, *Bodd.* ...	122
197	The Crimson-breasted Barbet	Xantholæma hæmacephala, *Müll.* ...	122
198	The Crimson-throated Barbet	„ malabarica, *Bly.*	123
199	The Cuckoo ...	Cuculus canorus, *Lin.* ...	124
201	The Small Cuckoo ...	„ poliocephalus, *Lath.*	124
202	The Banded Bay Cuckoo	„ sonnerati, *Lath.* ...	125
203	The Indian Cuckoo ...	„ micropterus, *Gould.*	125
205	The Common Hawk Cuckoo	Hierococcyx varius, *Vahl.* ...	126
208	The Indian Plaintive Cuckoo	Cacomantis passerinus, *Vahl.*	127
210	The Drongo Cuckoo ...	Surniculus lugubris, *Horsf.*	128
211	The Emerald Cuckoo ...	Chrysococcyx maculatus, *Gm.*	128
212	The Pied Crested Cuckoo	Coccystes jacobinus, *Bodd.*	129
213	The Red-winged Crested Cuckoo	„ coromandus, *Lin.*	130
214	The Indian Koel or Black Cuckoo	Eudynamis honorata, *Lin.* ...	130
216	The Small Green-billed Malkoha	Rhopodytes viridirostris, *Jerd.* ...	131
217	The Common Coucal ...	Centropus rufipennis, *Ill.* ...	132
217*quint.*	The Large Crow Pheasant	„ maximus, *Hume.*	133
218	The Lesser Indian Coucal	„ bengalensis, *Gm.*	133
219	The Southern Sirkeer ...	Taccocua leschenaulti, *Less.*	134
220	The Bengal Sirkeer ...	„ sirkee, *Gray.* ...	134
224	The Little Spider Hunter	Arachnothera longirostra, *Lath.* ...	135
226	The Violet-eared Red Honey-Sucker ...	Æthopygia vigorsi, *Sykes.*	135
232	The Amethyst-rumped Honey-Sucker ...	Cinnyris zeylonica, *Lin.* ...	136
233	The Tiny Honey-Sucker	„ minima, *Sykes.* ...	136
234	The Purple Honey-Sucker	„ asiatica, *Lath.* ...	137
235	The Large Purple Honey-Sucker	„ lotenia, *Lin.* ...	137
238	Tickell's Flower-Pecker ...	Dicæum erythrorhynchus, *Lath.* ...	138
239	The Neilgherry Flower-Pecker	„ concolor, *Jerd.* ...	138
240	The Thick-billed Flower-Pecker	Piprimosa agile, *Tick.* ...	139
246	The Spotted Grey Creeper	Salpornis spilonota, *Frankl.*	139
250	The Chesnut-bellied Nuthatch	Sitta castaneiventris, *Frankl.*	140

Jerdon's Number.	POPULAR NAME.	SCIENTIFIC NAME.	Page.
253	The Velvet-fronted Blue Nuthatch	Dendrophila frontalis, *Horsf.*	140
254	The European Hoopoe ...	Upupa epops, *Lin.* ...	141
255	The Indian Hoopoe ..	„ ceylonensis, *Reich.* ..	142
256	The Indian Grey Shrike	Lanius lahtora, *Sykes.* ...	143
257	The Rufous-backed Shrike	„ erythronotus, *Vig.* ...	143
259	The Black-headed Shrike	„ nigriceps, *Frankl.* ...	144
260	The Bay-backed Shrike...	„ vittatus, *Val.* ...	144
260*bis.*	The European Red-backed Shrike	„ collurio, *Lin.* ...	145
261	The Brown Shrike ...	„ cristatus, *Lin.* ...	145
262	The Pale Brown Shrike...	„ isabellinus, *Hemp. & Ehr.* ...	146
264	The Malabar Wood-Shrike	Tephrodornis sylvicola, *Jerd.*	147
265	The Common Wood-Shrike	„ pondicerianus, *Gm.* ...	147
267	The Little Pied Shrike ...	Hemipus picatus, *Sykes.* ...	148
268	The Black-headed Cuckoo Shrike	Volvocivora sykesi, *Strickl.*	148
269	The Dark Grey Cuckoo-Shrike	„ melaschista, *Hodgs.*	149
269*quat.*	....	Hypocolius ampelinus, *Bp.*	149
270	The Large Cuckoo Shrike	Graucalus macii, *Less.* ...	150
271	The Large Minivet ...	Pericrocotus speciosus, *Lath.*	151
272	The Orange Minivet ...	„ flammeus, *Forst.*	151
273	The Short-billed Minivet	„ brevirostris, *Vig.*	152
276	The Small Minivet ...	„ peregrinus, *Lin.*	152
277	The White-bellied Minivet	„ erythropygius, *Jerd.* ...	153
278	The Kingcrow ...	Buchanga atra, *Herm.* ...	154
280	The Long-tailed Drongo Shrike	„ longicauda, *Hay.*	154
281	The White-bellied Drongo	„ cærulescens, *Lin.*	155
282	The Bronzed Drongo ...	Chaptia ænea, *Vieill.* ...	155
284	The Large Racket-tailed Drongo	Dissemurus grandis, *Gould.*	156
285	The Malabar Racket-tailed Drongo	„ paradiseus, *Lin.*	156
286	The Hair Crested Drongo	Chibia hottentota, *Lin.* ...	157
287	The Ashy Swallow Shrike	Artamus fuscus, *Vieill.* ...	157
288	The Paradise Flycatcher	Muscipeta paradisi, *Lin.* ...	158
290	The Black-necked Blue Flycatcher ...	Hypothymis azurea, *Bodd.*	159
291	The White-throated Fantail	Leucocerca albicollis, *Vieill.*	160
292	The White-browed Fantail	„ aureola, *Vieill.*...	160
293	The White-spotted Fantail	„ leucogaster, *Cuv.*	161

Jerdon's Number.	POPULAR NAME.	SCIENTIFIC NAME.	Page.
295	The Grey-headed Flycatcher ...	Culicicapa ceylonensis, *Sws.*	162
297	The Southern Brown Flycatcher ...	Alseonax latirostris, *Raffl.*...	163
299*bis*.	The Cherry Chopper ...	Butalis grisola, *Lin.* ...	163
301	The Verditer Flycatcher	Stoporala melanops, *Vig.*	164
304	The Blue-throated Redbreast ...	Cyornis rubeculoides, *Vig.*...	164
306	Tickell's Blue Redbreast	„ tickelli, *Bly.* ...	164
307	The Rufous-tailed Flycatcher	„ ruficaudus, *Sws.* ...	165
309	The White-bellied Blue Flycatcher ...	„ pallipes, *Jerd.* ...	165
310	The White-browed Blue Flycatcher ...	Muscicapula superciliaris, *Jerd.*	166
323	The White-tailed Robin Flycatcher ...	Erythrosterna albicilla, *Pal.*	167
323*bis*.	The European White-tailed Flycatcher ...	„ parva, *Bechst.*	167
326	The Little Pied Flycatcher	„ maculata, *Tick.*	167
342	The Malabar Whistling Thrush	Myiophoneus horsfieldi, *Vig.*	168
345	The Yellow-breasted Ground Thrush ...	Pitta brachyura, *Lin.* ...	169
351	The Blue Rock Thrush..	Monticola cyaneus, *Lin.* ...	169
353	The Blue-headed Chat Thrush	„ cinclorhynchus, *Vig.*	170
354	The White-winged Ground Thrush	Geocichla cyanotis, *Jard. & Sel.* ...	171
355	The Orange-headed Ground Thrush	„ citrina, *Lath.* ...	171
356	The Dusky Ground Thrush	„ unicolor, *Tick.*...	171
357	Ward's Pied Blackbird ...	Turdulus wardi, *Jerd.* ...	172
359	The Black-capped Blackbird	Merula nigropilea, *Lafr.* ...	173
365	The Black-throated Thrush	„ atrogularis, *Tem.*	173
385	The Yellow-eyed Babbler	Pyctoris sinensis, *Gm.* ...	174
386*ter*.	The Grey-throated Babbler	„ griseogularis, *Hume*	174
389	The Neilgherry Quaker Thrush	Alcippe poiocephala, *Jerd.*...	175
390	The Black-headed Wren Babbler	„ atriceps, *Jerd.* ...	175
395	The Yellow-breasted Wren Babbler	Mixornis rubricapillus, *Tick.*	176
397	The Rufous-bellied Babbler	Dumetia hyperythra, *Frankl.*	176
398	The White-throated Wren Babbler	„ albogularis, *Bly.*...	177

Jerdon's Number.	POPULAR NAME.	SCIENTIFIC NAME.	Page.
399	The Spotted Wren Babbler	Pellorneum ruficeps, *Sws.*...	177
404	The Southern Scimitar Babbler	Pomatorhinus horsfieldi, *Sykes* ...	178
404*ter.*	Hume's Scimitar Babbler	„ obscurus, *Hume.*	178
432	The Bengal Babbler ...	Malacocercus terricolor, *Hodgs* ...	179
433	The White-headed Babbler	„ griseus, *Lath.*	179
434	The Jungle Babbler ...	„ malabaricus, *Jerd.* ...	180
435	The Rufous-tailed Babbler	„ somervillii, *Sykes.*	180
436	The Large Grey Babbler	„ malcolmi, *Sykes*	180
437	The Rufous Babbler ...	Layardia subrufa, *Jerd.* ...	181
438	The Striated Bush Babbler	Chatarrhæa caudata, *Dum.*	181
439	The Striated Reed Babbler	„ earlii, *Bly.* ...	182
441	The Grass Babbler ...	Chætornis striatus, *Jerd.* ...	183
442	The Broad-tailed Reed Bird	Schœnicola platyurus, *Jerd.*	183
443	The Long-tailed Reed Bird	Laticilla burnesi, *Bly.* ...	184
446	The Ghat Black Bulbul	Hypsipetes ganesa, *Sykes* ..	185
450	The Yellow-browed Bulbul	Criniger ictericus, *Strickl.*	185
452	The White-browed Bush Bulbul	Ixus luteolus, *Less.* ...	185
455	The Ruby-throated Bulbul	Rubigula gularis, *Gould.* ...	186
457	The Grey-headed Bulbul	Brachypodius poiocephalus, *Jerd.*	186
459	The White-eared Crested Bulbul	Otocompsa leucotis, *Gould.*	187
460*bis.*	The Southern Red-whiskered Bulbul ...	„ fuscicaudata, *Gould.*	187
461	The Common Bengal Bulbul	Pycnonotus pygæus, *Hodgs.*	188
462	The Common Madras Bulbul	„ hæmorrhous, *Gm.*	188
463	The Common Green Bulbul	Phyllornis jerdoni, *Bly.* ...	189
464	The Malabar Green Bulbul	„ malabaricus, *Gm.*	190
468	The White-winged Iora	Iora tiphia, *Lin.* ...	190
468*bis.*	The Western Iora ...	„ nigrolutea, *Marsh.* ...	191
469	The Fairy Blue Bird ...	Irena puella, *Lath.* ...	192
470	The Indian Oriole ...	Oriolus kundoo, *Sykes.* ...	193
470*bis.*	The Golden Oriole ...	„ galbula, *Lin.* ...	194

Jerdon's Number.	POPULAR NAME.	SCIENTIFIC NAME.	Page.
471	The Black-naped Indian Oriole	Oriolus indicus, *Jerd.* ...	195
472	The Bengal Black-headed Oriole	„ melanocephalus, *Lin.*	195
473	The Southern Black-headed Oriole ..	„ ceylonensis, *Bp.* ...	196
475	The Magpie Robin ...	Copsychus saularis, *Lin.* ...	197
476	The Shama ...	Kittacincla macroura, *Gm.*	197
479	The Indian Black Robin	Thamnobia fulicata, *Lin.* ...	198
480	The Brown-backed Indian Robin	„ cambaiensis, *Lath*	198
481	The White-winged Black Robin	Pratincola caprata, *Lin.* ...	199
483	The Indian Bushchat ...	„ indica, *Bly.* ...	200
484	The White-tailed Bushchat	„ leucurus, *Bly.* ...	200
485*bis.*	Stoliczka's Bushchat ...	„ macrorhyncha, *Stol.* ...	201
488	The Indian White-tailed Stonechat ...	Saxicola opistholeuca, *Strickl.*	201
489	The Pied Stonechat ...	„ picatus, *Bly.* ...	202
489*bis.*	Hume's Pied Stonechat ...	„ alboniger, *Hume* ..	202
490	The White-headed Stonechat	„ morio, *Hemp. & Ehr.*	203
490*bis.*	The Hooded Stonechat ...	„ monachus, *Rüpp.* ...	203
491	The Wheatear ...	„ isabellinus, *Rüpp.* ...	203
491*bis.*	The Red-tailed Wheatear	„ kingi, *Hume* ...	204
492	The Black-throated Wheatear ...	„ deserti, *Rüpp.* ...	205
492*ter.*	The Grey-backed Warbler	Ædon familiaris, *Méné.* ...	205
493	The Black-tailed Rockchat	Cercomela melanura, *Rüpp.*	206
494	The Brown Rockchat ...	„ fusca, *Bly.* ...	206
497	The Indian Redstart ...	Ruticilla rufiventris, *Vieill...*	207
507	....	Larvivora superciliaris, *Jerd.*	208
512	The Common Ruby-throat	Calliope camtschatkensis, *Gm.* ...	209
514	The Indian Blue-throat...	Cyanecula suecica, *Lin.* ...	209
515	The Large Reed Warbler	Acrocephalus stentorius, *Hemp. & Ehr.*	210
516	The Lesser Reed Warbler	„ dumetorum, *Bly.*	210
517	The Paddy Field Warbler	„ agricolus, *Jerd.*	211
518*bis.*	The Moustached Grass Warbler	Lusciniola melanopogon, *Tem.*	211
	Hume's Grass Warbler ...	„ neglecta, *Hume* ...	212
518*ter.*	Cetti's Bush Warbler ...	Cettia cetti, *Marm.* ...	212
520	The Streaked Reed Warbler	Locustella hendersoni, *Cass.*	213
530	The Indian Tailor Bird ...	Orthotomus sutorius, *Forst.*	214

Jerdon's Number.	POPULAR NAME.	SCIENTIFIC NAME.	Page.
532	The Yellow-bellied Wren Warbler	Prinia flaviventris, *Deless*....	215
533	The White-bellied Wren Warbler	„ adamsi, *Jerd.* ...	215
534	The Dark Ashy Wren Warbler	„ socialis, *Sykes* ...	215
535	Stewart's Wren Warbler	„ stewarti, *Bly.* ...	216
536	Franklin's Wren Warbler	„ gracilis, *Frankl.* ...	216
538	The Malaber Wren Warbler	„ hodgsoni, *Bly.* ...	217
539	The Rufous Grass Warbler	Cisticola cursitans, *Frankl.*	217
543	The Common Wren Warbler	Drymoipus inornata, *Sykes*	218
544*bis.*	The Great Rufous Wren Warbler	„ rufescens, *Hume*	219
545	The Jungle Wren Warbler	„ sylvaticus, *Jerd.*	220
546	The Allied Wren Warbler	„ neglectus, *Jerd.*	220
549*quint.*	....	Blanfordius striatulus, *Hume*	221
550	The Streaked Wren Warbler	Burnesia gracilis, *Licht.* ...	221
550*bis.*	The Streaked Scrub Warbler	Scotocerca inquieta, *Rüpp*....	222
551	The Rufous-fronted Wren Warbler	Franklinia buchanani, *Bly.*	223
553	Sykes' Tree Warbler ...	Hypolais rama, *Sykes* ...	224
553*bis.*	The Booted Tree Warbler	„ caligata, *Licht.* ...	224
553*ter.*	The Pale Tree Warbler...	„ pallida, *Hemp. & Ehr.* ...	225
553*quat.*	....	„ languida, *Hemp. & Ehr.* ...	225
	The Desert Tree Warbler	„ obsoleta, *Sev.* ...	226
554	The Brown Tree Warbler	Phylloscopus tristis, *Bly* ...	227
554*bis.*	Hume's Tree Warbler ...	„ neglectus, *Hume*	227
556	The Large-billed Tree Warbler	„ magnirostris, *Bly.*	228
558	The Dull Green Tree Warbler	„ lugubris, *Bly.* ...	228
559	The Bright Green Tree Warbler	„ nitidus, *Lath.* ...	228
560	The Greenish Tree Warbler	„ viridanus, *Bly.*	229
561	Tickell's Tree Warbler ...	„ affinis, *Tick.* ...	229
562	The Olivaceous Tree Warbler	„ indicus, *Jerd.* ...	229
	The Sind Tree Warbler...	„ sindianus, *Brooks.*	229
563	The Large Crowned Warbler	Reguloides occipitalis, *Jerd.*	230
565	The Crowned Tree Warbler	„ superciliosus, *Pall.*	230

Jerdon's Number.	POPULAR NAME	SCIENTIFIC NAME.	Page.
565*bis*.	The Brown-headed Willow Warbler ...	Reguloides humii, *Brooks* ...	231
570	The Lesser Black-browed Warbler	Abrornis cantator, *Tick.* ...	231
581	The Large Black-capped Warbler	Sylvia jerdoni, *Bly.* ...	232
582	The Allied Grey Warbler	„ affinis, *Bly.* ...	232
582*bis*.	Hume's Lesser White-throat	„ minuscula, *Hume* ...	232
582*ter*.	The Himalayan Lesser White-throat ...	„ althea, *Hume* ...	233
582*quat*.	The Grey Warbler ...	„ rufa, *Bodd.* ...	233
583*bis*.	The Desert Warbler ...	„ nana, *Hemp. & Ehr.*	234
589	The Pied Wagtail ...	Motacilla maderaspatensis, *Gm.* ...	234
590	The White-faced Wagtail	„ leucopsis, *Gould*....	235
591	The Black-faced Wagtail	„ personata, *Gould*....	236
591*bis*.	Sykes' Grey and Black Wagtail ...	„ dukhunensis, *Sykes*	236
591*ter*.	The European White-faced Wagtail ...	„ alba, *Lin.* ...	237
592	The Grey and Yellow Wagtail ...	Calobates melanope, *Pall.* ...	237
593	The Slaty-headed Field Wagtail ...	Budytes cinereocapilla, *Savi.*	238
593*bis*.	The Black-cap Field Wagtail	„ melanocephala, *Licht.*	239
593*ter*.	The Grey-headed Field Wagtail	„ flava, *Lin.* ...	239
594	The Yellow-headed Wagtail	„ calcarata, *Hodgs.* ...	240
594*bis*.	The Grey-backed Yellow Wagtail	„ citeola, *Pall.* ...	241
595	The Black-breasted Wagtail	Limonidromus indicus, *Gm.*	241
596	The Indian Tree Pipit ...	Anthus maculatus, *Hodgs.*...	242
597	The European Tree Pipit	„ trivialis, *Lin.* ...	242
605*ter*.	The Water Pipit ...	„ spinoletta, *Lin.* ...	243
605*quat*.	Blakiston's Pipit ...	„ blakistoni, *Swinh.* ...	244
600	The Indian Titlark ...	Corydalla rufula, *Vieill.* ...	244
601	The Large Titlark ...	„ striolata, *Bly.* ...	245
602	Tho Stone Pipit ...	Agrodroma campestris, *Lin.*	245
603	The Rufous Rock Pipit...	„ similis, *Jerd.* ...	246
604	The Brown Rock Pipit ...	„ sordida, *Rüpp.*...	246
631	The White-eyed Tit ...	Zosterops palpebrosa, *Tem.*...	247
645	The Indian Grey Tit ...	Parus nipalensis, *Hodgs.* ...	248
646	The White-winged Black Tit	„ nuchalis, *Jerd.* ...	248

Jerdon's Number.	POPULAR NAME.	SCIENTIFIC NAME.	Page.
647	The Yellow-cheeked Tit...	Machlolophus xanthogenys, *Vig.* ...	249
648	The Southern Yellow Tit	„ aplonotus, *Bly.*	249
657*bis.*	The Indian Raven ...	Corvus lawrencii, *Hume* ...	250
660	The Indian Corby ...	„ macrorhynchus, *Wagl.*	250
660*bis.*	The Brown-necked Raven	„ umbrinus, *Hedenb* ...	251
663	The Common Indian Crow	„ splendens, *Vieill.* ...	251
674	The Common Indian Magpie	Dendrocitta rufa, *Scop.* ...	252
681	The Common Starling ...	Sturnus vulgaris, *Lin.* ...	253
681*bis.*	The Lesser Starling ...	„ minor, *Hume* ...	254
684	The Common Myna ...	Acridotheres tristis, *Lin.* ...	254
685	The Bank Myna ...	„ ginginianus, *Lath.*	255
686*bis.*	The Southern Dusky Myna	„ mahrattensis, *Sykes* ...	255
687	The Black-headed Myna	Sturnia pagodarum, *Gm.* ...	256
688	The Grey-headed Myna...	„ malabarica, *Gm.* ...	256
689	The White-headed Myna	„ blythi, *Jerd.* ...	257
690	The Rose-colored Pastor	Pastor roseus, *Lin.* ...	257
692	The Southern Hill Myna	Eulabes religiosa, *Lin.* ...	258
694	The Common Weaver-Bird	Ploceus philippinus, *Lin.* ...	259
695	The Striated Weaver-Bird	„ manyar, *Horsf.* ...	260
696	The Black-throated Weaver-Bird ...	„ bengalensis, *Lin.* ...	261
697	The Black-headed Munia	Amadina malacca, *Lin.* ...	262
698	The Chesnut-bellied Munia	„ rubronigra, *Hodgs.*	262
699	The Spotted Munia ...	„ punctulata, *Lin.* ...	262
700	The Rufous-bellied Munia	„ pectoralis, *Jerd* ...	263
701	The White-backed Munia	„ striata, *Lin.* ...	263
703	The Plain Brown Munia	„ malabarica, *Lin.* ...	263
704	The Red Waxbill ...	Estrelda amandava, *Lin.* ...	264
705	The Green Waxbill ...	„ formosa, *Lath.* ...	265
706	The House Sparrow ...	Passer domesticus, *Lin.* ...	265
707	The Willow Sparrow ...	„ hispaniolensis, *Tem.*	266
709	The Rufous-backed Sparrow	„ pyrrhonotus, *Bly.* ...	266
711	The Yellow-throated Sparrow	„ flavicollis, *Frankl.* ...	267
716	The Grey-necked Bunting	Emberiza buchanani, *Bly.* ...	268
718	The White-capped Bunting	„ stewarti, *Bly.* ...	269
719	The Grey-headed Bunting	„ fucata, *Pall.* ...	269
720*bis.*	The Striolated Bunting ...	„ striolata, *Licht.* ...	269
721	The Black-headed Bunting	Euspiza melanocephala, *Gm.*	271
722	The Red-headed Bunting	„ luteola, *Sparr.* ...	271

Jerdon's Number.	POPULAR NAME.	SCIENTIFIC NAME.	Page.
724	The Crested Black Bunting	Melophus melanicterus, *Gm.*	272
732*bis.*	The Desert Bull-finch ...	Bucanetes githagineus, *Licht.*	273
738	The Common Rose Finch	Carpodacus erythrinus, *Pall.*	274
756	The Red-winged Bush-Lark	Mirafra erythroptera, *Jerd.*...	274
757	The Singing Bush-Lark	„ cantillans, *Jerd.* ...	275
758	The Rufous-tailed Finch-Lark	Ammomanes phœnicura, *Frankl.* ...	276
759	The Pale Rufous Finch-Lark	„ deserti, *Licht.* ...	276
760	The Black-bellied Finch-Lark	Pyrrhulauda grisea, *Scop.* ...	277
760*bis.*	The Black-necked Finch-Lark	„ melanauchen, *Cab.*	277
761	The Social Lark ...	Calandrella brachydactyla, *Leisl.* ...	279
761*ter.*	....	Melanocorypha bimaculata, *Méné.* ...	279
762	The Indian Sand-Lark ...	Alaudula raytal, *Bly.* ...	280
762*ter.*	The Little Sand-Lark ...	„ adamsi, *Hume* ...	280
765	The Small Crown-crest Lark	Spizalauda deva, *Sykes* ...	281
765*bis.*	The Large Crown-crest Lark	„ malabarica, *Scop.*	282
767	The Indian Sky-Lark ...	Alauda gulgula, *Frankl.* ...	282
769	The Large Crested Lark	Galerida cristata, *Lin.* ...	283
770	The Desert Lark ...	Certhilauda desertorum, *Stan.*	284
772	The Bengal Green Pigeon	Crocopus phœnicopterus, *Lath.* ...	285
773	The Southern Green Pigeon	„ chlorigaster, *Bly.* ..	285
775	The Grey-fronted Green Pigeon	Osmotreron malabarica, *Jerd.*	286
780	The Green Imperial Pigeon	Carpophaga ænea, *Lin.* ...	287
784	The Himalayan Cushat ...	Palumbus casiotis, *Bp.* ...	287
786	The Neilgherry Wood-pigeon	„ elphinstonii, *Sykes*	288
787	The Indian Stock Pigeon	Palumbœna eversmanni, *Bon.*	288
788	The Blue Rock Pigeon ...	Columba intermedia, *Strickl.*	289
788*bis.*	The Rock Dove ...	„ livia, *Bp.* ...	289
792	The Ashy Turtle Dove ...	Turtur pulchratus, *Hodgs.*	290
793	The Rufous Turtle Dove	„ meena, *Sykes* ...	290
794	The Little Brown Dove...	„ senegalensis, *Lin.* ..	291
795	The Spotted Dove ...	„ suratensis, *Gm.* ...	291
796	The Common Ring Dove	„ risorius, *Lin.* ...	291
797	The Ruddy Ring Dove ...	„ tranquebaricus, *Herm.*	292
798	The Bronze-winged Dove	Chalcophaps indica, *Lin* ...	293
799	The Large Sand Grouse	Pterocles arenarius, *Pall.* ...	294

Jerdon's Number.	POPULAR NAME.	SCIENTIFIC NAME.	Page.
800	The Painted Sand Grouse	Pterocles fasciatus, *Scop.* ...	295
800*bis.*	The Close-barred Sand Grouse	„ lichtensteini, *Tem.*	296
801	The Large Pin-tailed Sand Grouse ...	„ alchata, *Lin.* ...	297
801*bis.*	The Spotted Sand Grouse	„ senegallus, *Licht.*	297
801*ter.*	The Coronetted Sand Grouse	„ coronatus, *Licht.*	299
802	The Common Sand Grouse	„ exustus, *Tem.* ...	300
803	The Common Peacock ...	Pavo cristatus, *Lin.* ...	302
812	The Red Jungle Fowl ...	Gallus ferrugineus, *Gmel.* ...	303
813	The Grey Jungle Fowl ...	„ sonnerati, *Tem.* ...	304
814	The Red Spur Fowl ...	Galloperdix spadiceus, *Gm.*	305
815	The Painted Spur Fowl...	„ lunulatus, *Val.*	306
818	The Black Partridge ...	Francolinus vulgaris, *Steph.*	307
819	The Painted Partridge ...	„ pictus, *Jard. & Selb.* ...	308
820	The Chukar Partridge ...	Caccabis chukar, *J. E. Gr.*	309
821	The Seesee Partridge ...	Ammoperdix bonhami, *Gray.*	310
822	The Grey Partridge ...	Ortygornis pondiceriana, *Gm.*	311
826	The Jungle Bush Quail..	Perdicula asiatica, *Lath.* ...	312
827	The Rock Bush Quail ...	„ argoondah, *Sykes.*	313
828	The Painted Bush Quail	Microperdix erythrorhynchus, *Sykes*	314
829	The Large Grey Quail ...	Coturnix communis, *Bon.* ...	315
830	The Black-breasted Quail	„ coromandelica, *Gm.*	316
832	The Black-breasted Bustard Quail ...	Turnix taigoor, *Sykes* ...	317
834	The Large Button Quail	„ joudera, *Hodgs.* ...	318
835	The Small Button Quail	„ dussumieri, *Tem.* ...	319
836	The Indian Bustard ...	Eupodotis edwardsi, *J. E. Gr.*	320
837	The Houbara Bustard ...	Houbara macqueeni, *J. E. Gr.*	321
839	The Lesser Florican ...	Sypheotides aurita, *Lath.* ...	322
840	The Indian Courier Plover	Cursorius coromandelicus, *Gm.*	324
840*bis.*	The Cream-colored Courser	„ gallicus, *Gm.* ...	324
842	The Large Swallow Plover	Glareola orientalis, *Leach.* ...	325
842*bis.*	The Collared Pratincole...	„ pratincola, *Lin.* ...	326
843	The Small Swallow Plover	„ lactea, *Tem.* ...	326
844	The Grey Plover ...	Squatarola helvetica, *Lin.* ...	327
845	The Indian Golden Plover	Charadrius fulvus, *Gm.* ...	328
845*bis.*	The European Golden Plover	„ pluvialis, *Lin.* ...	328
845*quat.*	The Caspian Sand Plover	Ægialitis asiatica, *Pall.* ...	329
846	The Large Sand Plover...	„ geoffroyi, *Wag.* ...	329
847	The Lesser Sand Plover	„ mongola, *Pal.* ...	330
848	The Kentish Ringed Plover	„ cantiana, *Lath.* ...	330

Jerdon's Number.	POPULAR NAME.	SCIENTIFIC NAME.	Page.
849	The Indian Ringed Plover	Ægialitis dubia, *Scop.* ...	330
850	The Lesser Ringed Plover	„ minuta, *Pall.* ...	331
851	The Crested Lapwing ...	Vanellus vulgaris, *Bechst.* ...	332
852	The Black-sided Lapwing	Chettusia gregaria, *Pall.* ...	332
853	The White-tailed Lapwing	„ villotæi, *And.* ...	333
854	The Grey-headed Lapwing	„ cinerea, *Bly.* ...	333
855	The Red-wattled Lapwing	Lobivanellus indicus, *Bodd.*	334
856	The Yellow-wattled Lapwing	Lobipluvia malabarica, *Bodd.*	335
857	The Spur-winged Lapwing	Hoplopterus ventralis, *Cuv.*	335
858	The Large Stone Plover...	Æsacus recurvirostris, *Cuv.*	336
859	The Stone Plover ...	Œdicnemus scolopax, *S. S. Gm.* ...	337
860	The Turnstone ...	Strepsilas interpres, *Lin.* ...	338
861	The Crab Plover ...	Dromas ardeola, *Payk.* ...	339
862	The Oyster Catcher ...	Hæmatopus ostralegus, *Lin.*	339
863	The Sarus	Grus antigone, *Lin.* ...	340
864	The Snow-wreath ...	„ leucogeranus, *Pall.* ...	341
865	The Common Crane ...	„ communis, *Bechst.* ...	341
866	The Demoiselle Crane ...	Anthropoides virgo, *Lin.* ...	342
867	The Woodcock ...	Scolopax rusticola, *Lin.* ...	343
868	The Woodsnipe ...	Gallinago nemoricola, *Hodgs.*	344
870	The Pin-tailed Snipe ...	„ sthenura, *Kuhl.* ...	344
871	The Common Snipe ...	„ gallinaria, *Gm.* ...	345
872	The Jack Snipe ...	„ gallinula, *Lin.* ...	346
873	The Painted Snipe ...	Rhynchæa bengalensis, *Lin.*...	347
875	The Black-tailed Godwit	Limosa ægocephala, *Lin.* ...	348
875*bis.*	The Bar-tailed Godwit ...	„ lapponica, *Lin.* ...	349
876	The Avocet Sandpiper ...	Terekia cinerea, *Gm.* ...	351
877	The Curlew... ...	Numenius lineatus, *Cuv.* ...	351
878	The Whimbrel ...	„ phæopus, *Lin.* ...	352
880	The Ruff	Philomachus pugnax, *Lin.*...	352
881*bis.*	Temminck's Knot ...	Tringa crassirostris, *Tem & Schl.* ...	353
882	The Curlew Stint ...	„ subarquata *Gm.* ...	354
883	The Dunlin ...	„ alpina, *Lin.* ...	354
884	The Little Stint ...	„ minuta, *Leisl.* ...	355
885	The White-tailed Stint ...	„ temmincki, *Leisl.*...	355
886	The Broad-billed Stint ...	Limicola platyrhyncha, *Tem.*	356
888	The Sanderling ...	Calidris arenaria, *Tem.* ...	356
890	The Red-necked Phalarope	Lobipes hyperboreus, *Lin.*...	357
891	The Spotted Sandpiper ...	Rhyacophila glareola, *Gm.* ...	357
892	The Green Sandpiper ...	Totanus ochropus, *Lin.* ...	358
893	The Common Sandpiper	Tringoides hypoleucos, *Lin.*...	359
894	The Green-Shanks ...	Totanus glottis, *Lin.* ...	359
895	The Little Green-Shanks	„ stagnatilis, *Bech.* ...	359
896	The Spotted Red-Shanks	„ fuscus, *Lin.* ...	360
897	The Red-Shanks ...	„ calidris, *Lin.* ...	360
898	The Stilt	Himantopus candidus, *Bp.*...	361
899	The Avocet ...	Recurvirostra avocetta, *Lin.*	362
900	The Bronze-winged Jacana	Parra indica, *Lath.* ...	363

Jerdon's Number.	POPULAR NAME.	SCIENTIFIC NAME.	Page.
901	The Pheasant-tailed Jacana ...	Hydrophasianus chirurgus, *Scop.*	364
902	The Purple Coot ...	Porphyrio poliocephalus, *Lath.*	365
903	The Coot	Fulica atra, *Lin.* ...	366
904	The Water Cock ...	Gallicrex cinereus, *Gm.* ...	367
905	The Water Hen ...	Gallinula chloropus, *Lin.* ...	368
907	The White-breasted Water Hen ...	Erythra phœnicura, *Penn.* ...	368
908	The Brown Rail ...	Porzana akool, *Sykes.* ...	369
909	The Spotted Crake ...	„ maruetta, *Leach.* ...	370
910	Baillon's Crake ...	„ bailloni, *Vieill.* ...	370
910*bis.*	The Little Rail ...	„ parva, *Scop.* ...	371
911	The Ruddy Rail ...	„ fusca, *Lin.* ...	372
913	The Blue-breasted Banded Rail ...	Hypotænidia striata, *Lin.*	372
914	The Indian Water Rail ...	Rallus indica, *Bly.* ...	373
915	Tho Adjutant ...	Leptoptilus, argalus, *Lin.* ...	374
916	The Hair-crested Stork...	„ javanicus, *Horsf.*	374
917	The Black-necked Stork	Xenorhynchus asiaticus, *Lath.*	375
918	The Black Stork ...	Ciconia nigra, *Lin.* ...	376
919	The White Stork ...	„ alba, *Bechst.* ...	376
920	The White-necked Stork	Dissura episcopa, *Bodd.* ...	376
923	The Blue Heron ...	Ardea cinerea, *Lin.* ...	377
924	The Purple Heron ...	„ purpurea, *Lin.* ...	378
924*bis.*	The Large White Heron	Herodias alba, *Lin.* ...	379
925	The Large Egret ...	„ torra, *B.-Ham.* ...	379
926	The Smaller Egret ...	„ intermedia, *Hass.*	379
927	The Little Egret ...	„ garzetta, *Lin.* ...	380
928	The Ashy Egret ...	Demi-egretta gularis, *Bosc.*	380
929	The Cattle Egret ...	Bubulcus coromandus, *Bodd.*	381
930	The Pond Heron ...	Ardeola grayii, *Sykes* ...	381
931	The Little Green Heron	Butorides javanica, *Horsf.*...	382
932	The Black Bittern ...	Ardetta flavicollis, *Lath.* ...	383
933	The Chesnut Bittern ...	„ cinnamomea, *Gm.*	384
934	The Yellow Bittern ...	„ sinensis, *Gm.* ...	384
935	The Little Bittern ...	„ minuta, *Lin.* ...	385
936	The Bittern ...	Botaurus stellaris, *Lin.* ..	385
936*bis.*	The Malayan Tiger Bittern	Goisakius melanolophus, *Raffl.*	386
937	The Night Heron ...	Nycticorax griseus, *Lin.* ...	387
938	The Pelican Ibis ...	Tantalus leucocephalus, *Forst.*	387
939	The Spoonbill ...	Platalea leucorodia, *Lin.* ...	388
940	The Shell Ibis ...	Anastomus oscitans, *Bodd.*	389
941	The White Ibis ...	Ibis melanocephala, *Lath.* ...	390
942	The Black or Warty-headed Ibis ...	Inocotis papillosus, *Tem.* ...	390
943	The Glossy Ibis ...	Falcinellus igneus, *Gm.* ...	391
944	The Flamingo ...	Phœnicopterus antiquorum, *Tem.* ...	392

Jerdon's Number.	POPULAR NAME.	SCIENTIFIC NAME.	Page.
944*bis.*	The Lesser Flamingo ...	Phœnicopterus minor, *Geof.*	393
944*ter.*	The Mute Swan ...	Cygnus olor, *Gm.* ...	394
945	The Grey Goose ...	Anser cinereus, *Meg.* ...	394
947	The White-fronted Goose	„ albifrons, *Scop.* ...	395
949	The Barred-headed Goose	„ indicus, *Lath.* ...	395
950	The Black-backed Goose	Sarcidiornis melanonotus, *Penn.* ...	396
951	The Cotton Teal ...	Nettopus coromandelianus, *Gm.* ...	397
952	The Whistling Teal ...	Dendrocygna javanica, *Horsf.* ...	398
953	The Large Whistling Teal ...	„ fulva, *Gm.* ...	399
954	The Ruddy Shieldrake ...	Tadorna casarca, *Pall.* ...	400
956	The Shieldrake ...	„ cornuta, *S. G. Gm.*	400
957	The Shoveller ...	Spatula clypeata, *Lin.* ...	401
958	The Mallard ...	Anas boschas, *Lin.* ...	402
959	The Grey Duck ...	„ pœcilorhyncha, *Forst.*	403
960	The Pink-headed Duck ...	Rhodonessa caryophyllacea, *Lath.* ...	404
961	The Gadwall ...	Chaulelasmus streperus, *Lin.*	405
961*bis.*	The Marbled Teal ...	„ angustirostris, *Méné.* ...	406
962	The Pintail Duck ...	Dafila acuta, *Lin.* ...	407
963	The Widgeon ...	Mareca penelope, *Lin.* ...	408
964	The Common Teal ...	Querquedula crecca, *Lin.* ...	409
965	The Blue-winged Teal ...	„ circia, *Lin.* ...	410
966	The Clucking Teal ...	„ formosa, *Geor.*	411
967	The Red-crested Pochard	Fuligula rufina, *Pall.* ...	412
968	The Red-headed Pochard	„ ferina, *Lin.* ...	412
969	The White-eyed Pochard	„ nyroca, *Güld.* ...	413
970	The Scaup Pochard ...	„ marila, *Lin.* ...	413
971	The Crested Pochard ...	„ cristata, *Ray.* ...	414
971*bis.*	The Golden Eye ...	Clangula glaucium, *Lin.* ...	415
972	The Merganser ...	Mergus merganser, *Lin.* ...	416
972*bis.*	The Red-breasted Merganser ...	„ serrator, *Lin.* ...	416
973	The Smew ...	Mergellus albellus, *Lin.* ...	417
974	The Crested Grebe ...	Podiceps cristatus, *Lin.* ...	418
974*bis.*	The Black-necked Grebe	„ nigricollis, *Sund.* ...	419
975	The Little Grebe ...	„ minor, *Gm.* ...	420
976	Wilson's Petrel ...	Oceanites oceanica, *Kühl.* ...	421
976*bis.*	The Persian Shearwater	Puffinus persicus, *Hume* ...	421
977*ter.*	The Skua ...	Stercorarius asiaticus, *Hume*	422
978*bis.*	The Yellow-legged Herring Gull ...	Larus cachinnans, *Pall.* ...	423
978*ter.*	The Lesser Herring Gull	„ affinis, *Reinw.* ...	424
979	The Great Black-headed Gull ...	„ ichthyaëtus, *Pall.* ...	424
980	The Brown-headed Gull	„ brunneicephalus, *Jerd.*	425
981	The Laughing Gull ...	„ ridibundus, *Lin.* ...	425

Jerdon's Number.	POPULAR NAME.	SCIENTIFIC NAME.	Page.
981*ter*.	The Sooty Gull ...	Larus hemprichi, *Bp.* ...	426
981*quat*.	" ...	" gelastes, *Licht.* ...	426
982	The Caspian Tern ...	Sterna caspia, *Pall.* ...	428
983	The Gull-billed Tern ...	" anglica, *Mont.* ...	428
984	The Small Marsh Tern ...	Hydrochelidon hybrida, *Pall.*	427
985	The Large River Tern ...	Sterna seena, *Sykes* ...	429
987	The Black-bellied Tern ...	" melanogastra, *Tem.*	429
987*bis*.	The White-cheeked Tern	" albigena, *Licht.* ...	430
988*ter*.	Saunder's Little Tern ...	" saundersi, *Hume* ...	430
989	The Large Sea Tern ...	" bergii, *Licht.* ...	431
990	The Smaller Sea Tern ...	" media, *Horsf.* ...	432
990*bis*.	....	" cantiana, *Gm.* ...	432
992	The Brown-winged Tern	" anætheta, *Scop.* ...	433
992*bis*.	The Sooty Tern ...	" fuliginosa, *Gm.* ...	433
993	The Noddy ...	Anous stolidus, *Lin.* ...	433
995	The Indian Skimmer ...	Rhynchops albicollis, *Sws.*...	434
999*bis*.	The Indian Tropic Bird...	Phæton indicus, *Hume* ...	434
996*bis*.	The White Booby ...	Sula cyanops, *Sund.* ...	436
1003	The Lesser White Pelican ...	Pelecanus javanicus, *Horsf.*	437
1004	The Grey Pelican ...	" philippensis, *Gm.*	438
1004*bis*.	The White Pelican ...	" crispus, *Bruch.*...	436
1005	The Large Cormorant ...	Phalacrocorax carbo, *Lin.* ...	438
1006	The Lesser Cormorant ...	" fuscicollis, *Steph.* ...	439
1007	The Little Cormorant ...	" pygmæus, *Pall.* ...	439
1008	The Indian Snake Bird ...	Plotus melanogaster, *Pen.* ...	440

APPENDIX.—List of birds collected or observed in Khandesh by J. Davidson... ... 442

INDEX

TO THE

ABBREVIATIONS OF THE NAMES OF AUTHORITIES CITED.

—o—

And.	J. V. Andouin.
Banks.	Sir Joseph Banks.
Bechst.	J. M. Bechstein.
B. Ham.	Fr. Ham. Buchanan-Hamilton
Bly.	Edward Blyth.
Bodd.	M. Boddaert.
Boie.	H. Boie.
Bonn.	L'Abbe Bonnaterre.
Bosc.	L. A. G. Bosc.
Bp.	Prince Charles Lucian Bonaparte.
Briss.	Brisson.
Brooks.	William Edwin Brooks.
Bruch.	Bruch.
Cab.	Dr. Jean Cabanis.
Cas.	John Cassin.
Cuv.	George L. C. F. D. Cuvier.
Daud.	W. M. Daudin.
Deless.	Adolphe Delessert.
Desf.	R. L. Desfontaines.
Dum.	A. M. C. Dumeril.
Ehr.	C. G. Ehrenburg.
Eversm.	Dr. Edouard Eversman.
Fleisch.	E. G. Fleischer.
Forst.	John Reinhold Forster.
Frankl.	James Franklin.
Geor.	J. G. Georgi.
Gerv.	Paul Gervais.
Gm.	Jo. Fred. Gmelin.
Gm. S. G.	S. G. Gmelin.
Gould.	John Gould.
Gr. G. R.	George Robert Gray.
Gr. J. E.	John Edward Gray.
G. St. Hill.	Isodore Geoffrey St. Hillaire.
Güld.	Ant. J. Güldenstädt.
Gurn.	J. H. Gurney.
Hardw.	General Hardwicke.
Hass.	Van Hasselt.
Hay.	Lord Arthur Hay. *Afterwards Lord Walden and later Marquess of Tweeddale.*
Heden.	Hedenborg.
Hem.	F. G. Hemprichi.
Herm.	J. Hermann.
Hodgs.	Brian H. Hodgson.
Hors.	Dr. Thomas Horsfield.
Hume.	Allan Oscar Hume.
Ill.	C. Illiger.
Jard.	Sir William Jardine.
Jerd.	Dr. T. C. Jerdon.
Kaup.	J. J. Kaup.
Kuhl.	Heinrich Kuhl.
Lace.	B. G. Lacepede.
Lafr.	Baron Frederic de Lafresnaye
Lath.	John Latham.
Leach.	William Elford Leach.
Leisl.	J. P. A. Leisler.
Less.	Rene Primevere Lesson.
Licht.	Heinrich Lichtenstein.
Lin.	Carl v. Linne.
Malh.	Alfred Malherbe.
Marm.	Alb. de la Marmoree.
Marsh.	Capt. G. F. L. Marshall, R. E.
Ménétr.	Ed. Ménétries.
Mey.	Bern. Meyer.
Mont.	George Montagu.
Müll., P. L. S.	Ph. L. St. Müller.
Müll., S.	S. Müller.
Pall.	P. S. Pallas.
Payk.	Gust. Paykull.
Pears.	Dr. J. T. Pearson.
Penn.	Thomas Pennant.
Radde.	Professor Gustav Radde.
Raffl.	Sir Thomas Stamford Raffles.
Reich.	H. G. L. Reichenbach.
Reinh.	Professor J. Reinhardt.
Reinw.	Reinwardt.
Rüpp.	Dr. Edward Rüppell.
Sav.	J. Ces. Savigny.
Savi.	P. Savi.
Schl.	Dr. Herman Schlegel.
Scop.	J. Ant. Scopoli.
Selb.	Prideaux John Selby.
Sharpe.	Robert Bowdler Sharpe.
Shaw.	G. Shaw.
Sparr.	Anders Sparrman.
Stanl.	Edward Stanley.
Steph.	James Francis Stephens.
Stol.	Dr. Ferdinand Stoliczka.
Storr.	C. T. Storr.
Strickl.	H. E. Strickland.
Sund.	Carl. J. Sundevall.
Swinh.	Robert Swinhoe.
Sws.	William Swainson.
Sykes.	Col. W. H. Sykes.
Tem.	C. J. Temminck.
Tick.	Col. S. R. Tickell.
Tunst.	Tunstalt.
Vahl.	Mart. Vahl.
Valenc.	A. Valenciennes.
Vieill.	L. P. Vieillot.
Vig.	N. A. Vigors.
Wagl.	Dr Joannes Wagler.
Wald.	Viscount Walden. *Earlier Lord Arthur Hay; later Marquess of Tweeddale.*

LIST OF REFERENCES.

The Birds of India, by T. C. Jerdon.

Stray Feathers, Vols. I to X, edited by A. O. Hume.

Game Birds of India, Burmah and Ceylon, by Messrs. Hume and Marshall.

My Scrap Book, by Allan O. Hume.

The Vertebrate Zoology of Sind, by J. A. Murray, Curator, Frere Hall Museum, Karachi.

Nests and Eggs of Indian Birds, by A. O. Hume.

Birds Nesting in India, by Capt. G. F. L. Marshall, R. E.

Ibis, 1885, edited by Messrs. Sclater and Saunders.

HANDBOOK

TO THE

BIRDS OF THE BOMBAY PRESIDENCY.

INTRODUCTION.

THE Animal Kingdom consists of five divisions, the first of which, the Vertebrates, falls naturally into four classes :—

I.—MAMMALIA.
II.—AVES.
III.—REPTILIA.
IV.—PISCES.

The second of these only comes within the scope of this work; it has been divided into the following orders :—

I.—RAPTORES.
II.—INSESSORES.
III.—GEMITORES.
IV.—RASORES.
V.—GRALLATORES.
VI.—NATATORES.

This arrangement is considered by many to be far from perfect, but it is the system adopted by Jerdon in his Birds of India, in accordance with which nearly every collection in India is arranged, and it has at least the merit of being simple and easily understood.

ORDER, Raptores.

Bill strong, covered at the base with a cere or naked membrane, strongly hooked at the tip; nostrils open; legs strong and muscular; toes four, three in front and one behind, on the same plane, more or less rough beneath, and with strong, generally well-curved, and sharp claws.

FAMILY, Vulturidæ.

Bill rather long, compressed, straight at the culmen, curved towards the tip, upper mandible never toothed, sometimes sinuate; cere very large; tarsus reticulated with small scales, somewhat short, stout, usually feathered at the knee, sometimes slightly elevated; middle-toe long; outer-toe joined to the middle one by a membrane; hind-toe short; claws rather blunt, strong, not much curved.

SUB-FAMILY, **Vulturinæ.**

Bill large, thick, strong, higher than broad, hooked only at the tip; cere large; nostrils naked, transverse; head and upper part of neck naked, or covered only with down; wings long, first quill short, third and fourth quills sub-equal, fourth longest; tail moderate or rather short, with twelve or fourteen tail feathers; tarsus reticulated, with some large scutæ near the claws.

GENUS, **Vultur**, *Lin.*

Tail with twelve feathers; bill rather short, strong, deep, curving from the end of cere; nostrils round or oval; tarsus feathered from more than half its length; claws strong, rather acute.

The neck ruff advances upwards towards the hinder part of the head, and there is a transverse occipital crest of down; otherwise as in the characters of the sub-family.

Vultur monachus, *Lin.*

1.—Jerdon's Birds of India, Vol. I, p. 6; Butler, Guzerat; Stray Feathers, Vol. III, p. 441; Murray's Vertebrate Zoology of Sind, p. 62; Swinhoe and Barnes, Central India; Ibis, 1885, p. 53; Hume's Scrap Book, p. 1.

THE CINEREOUS VULTURE.

* Length, 42 to 45; expanse, 96 to 118; wing, 29·5 to 32; tail, 13 to 16; tarsus, 4·8 to 5·5; bill from gape, 3·6 to 4.

Bill horny, dusky black at tip, paler at base of upper mandible; cere pale-mauve; naked part of neck delicate bluish-white, occasionally shaded pink; irides brown; legs creamy-white.

The whole body, including the wings, is a rich, very dark, chocolate-brown, beneath darker; quills and tail nearly black; ruff conspicuous, dense, feathers lengthened and lanceolate, rather lighter in color than the back; lores, cheeks, chin, throat, and crown covered with dark-brown fur-like feathers, sparse below but dense and soft on the upper parts of the head.

This fine Vulture is comparatively rare; it has not as yet been recorded from the Deccan or South Mahratta country. Butler only observed a single specimen in Guzerat, Murray states it to be a winter visitant to Sind, and Jerdon notes its occurrence in Central India, where I have myself occasionally met with it.

Of its nidification in this country nothing appears to be known.

GENUS, **Otogyps**, *Gray.*

Head and neck bare, sides of neck with a wattle of skin; bill

* All dimensions are in English inches.

very thick and strong; crown of the head flat; cranium very large, otherwise as in *Vultur*.

Otogyps calvus, *Scop.*

2.—Jerdon's Birds of India, Vol. I, p. 7; Butler, Guzerat; Stray Feathers, Vol. III, p. 441; Deccan and South Mahratta country; Stray Feathers, Vol. IX, p. 369; Murray's Vertebrate Zoology of Sind, p. 62; Swinhoe and Barnes, Central India; Ibis, 1885, p. 53; Hume's Scrap Book, p. 8.

THE INDIAN KING VULTURE.
Lal Siri Gidh, Hin.

Length, 30 to 33; expanse, 80 to 88; wing, 22·5 to 24; tail, 9·8 to 11; tarsus, 4·3 to 4·6; bill from gape, 2·6 to 3.

Bill black; cere naked; head and neck deep yellowish-red, more or less spotted with black; irides red-brown; legs dull-red.

Dark brown-black, lighter on lower back and rump, brownish on scapulars and some of the secondaries; quills black; tail black, shaded with brown; crop-patch black, a zone of white downy feathers across the breast; beneath deep-black; inner side of thigh bare, with a patch of white above the joint.

The Indian King Vulture, or, as Jerdon prefers to call it, the Black Vulture, has been recorded from all parts of the region. It is not uncommon as a rule, but only occurs singly or in pairs, rarely more than two being seen together. It is of a very pugnacious disposition, and admits of no companionship, more especially when feeding. I have often seen a score or more of *Gyps fulvescens*, or other Vulture, patiently waiting until his kingship had gorged himself on a dead cow or other carcass before they dared approach. It is, I believe, a permanent resident, breeding wherever found. Jerdon states that "it is said to breed usually on inaccessible cliffs." Murray also states that "it is said to do so in Sind." This is contrary to my experience, and it may perhaps be noticed that neither of them speak from their own personal knowledge. I found a nest near Deesa in February; it was a large, compact, cup-shaped structure, composed of twigs, placed in a thick thorny ber-bush, about ten feet from the ground. Later I found two others in similar situations. The locality where I found these nests was a rather extensive plain, studded with ber-bushes, with occasional high trees dotted here and there, and on one side was a range of hills, offering splendid sites to a cliff building bird, which however they did not avail themselves of. In Central India I have found the nests on lofty trees. The egg—there is only one—is pale greenish-white when first laid, but after a time, as incubation proceeds, it becomes more or less stained by the droppings of the parent birds. The texture is moderately fine; the egg lining is green. They vary from a long oval shape to one nearly spherical, but generally speaking they are broad ovals. They average 3·4 inches in length by 2·6 in breadth.

GENUS, **Gyps**, *Sav.*

Tail with twelve or fourteen feathers; bill more lengthened than in *Vultur*; culmen more gradually curving, much rounded and compressed beyond the cere; nostrils oblong, oblique, or transverse; head and neck clothed with soft down; the bottom of the neck with a ruff of lengthened feathers.

Gyps fulvescens, *Hume.*

3 *bis.*—Butler, Guzerat; Stray Feathers, Vol. III, p. 442; Murray's Vertebrate Zoology of Sind, p. 63; Swinhoe and Barnes, Central India; Ibis, 1885, p. 53; Hume's Scrap Book, p. 19.

THE BAY VULTURE.

Length, 41 to 47; expanse, 94 to 106; wing, 27 to 29·5; tail (of 14 feathers), 12 to 13·5; tarsus, 3·88 to 4·2; bill from gape, 3 to 3·2; weight, 12 to 18 lbs.

The top of the head, cheeks, chin and throat are covered with dingy yellowish-white hair-like feathers, so closely set upon the top of the head, chin and throat, and with such an admixture of brown that the dark skin, which in the hill bird (*G. himalayensis*) shows so plainly through the scant covering, is, in this species, completely hidden. The nape and the whole of the neck (except the back and side of the basal one-fifth or less, which are bare or nearly bare), are closely covered with dense, short, fur-like white or dingy yellowish-white down. The crop-patch is about the same color as in the hill bird, but somewhat more rufous, and the whole of the rest of the plumage is a far more rufous, and deeper fawn or buffy-brown than in *G. himalayensis*. The lower plumage is in the adult of a rich rufous-brown, bay, or even dull-chesnut, conspicuously white shafted, whilst the mantle is a warm sandy-brown, unlike the coloring of any of our other Indian Vultures. The feathers of the ruff are almost linear, (the web not so much separated as in the hill bird) usually of a warm wood-brown or rufous-fawn, the feathers conspicuously paler centred. The upper back, the whole of the upper wing-coverts and all but the longest scapulars are a warm wood-brown, or brownish rufous-fawn, yellower and sandier, in some deeper and more of a bay color in others. The secondaries, tertials and longer scapulars, umber (but not dark-umber) brown; the latter (*viz.* the longer scapulars) more or less tipped with the rufous or sandy color of the upper back, which color, in some specimens, more or less extends to the tips and outer webs of the tertiaries. Lower back, rump, and upper tail-coverts the same color as the upper back, but of a considerably lighter tint, in some mingled with brown, and in some altogether of a pale pure bay. The primaries and tail-feathers are very dark brown; in some not so dark as the corresponding feathers in *G. himalayensis*, but in others of an intense chocolate-brown. Lower parts a rich sandy or rufous, or even a deep bay, (the tint varies in different stages of plumage) each feather conspicuously paler shafted, and most of them (in the younger birds) conspicuously, though narrowly, paler centred.—*Hume,* " *Rough Notes.*"

The Bay Vulture does not occur in the Deccan or South Mahratta country, but is not uncommon in Central India, Guzerat, and Sind. Of its nidification, little appears to be known: it is said to breed during January and February, building a large platform nest on lofty trees, and laying a single white egg, larger than either *calvus* or *bengalensis.*

Gyps pallescens, *Hume.*

4 *bis.*—Butler, Guzerat; Stray Feathers, Vol. III, p. 442; Deccan and South Mahratta country; Stray Feathers, Vol. IX, p. 369; Swinhoe and Barnes, Central India; Ibis, 1885, p. 54.

THE LONG-BILLED PALE-BROWN VULTURE.

Length, 36 to 39; expanse, 85 to 90; wing, 23 to 25·5; tail from vent, 10 to 11; tarsus, 3·5 to 4; bill from gape, 2·65 to 2·95; weight, 11 to 14 lbs.

Bill and cere pale greenish, yellowish horny on culmen and blackish towards tips of mandibles; bare skin of head and face dusky ashy-leaden; irides brown; legs and feet dingy ashy-leaden; margins of scales whitish; claws creamy-horny.

In the perfect adult brownish-white hair-like feathers are thinly sprinkled over the head, nape, cheeks, and throat; the upper half of the back and sides of the neck are perfectly bare; the crop-patch is closely covered with silky tight-fitting, dark hair-brown feathers; the whole of the rest of the lower surface is a pale whity-brown, becoming almost a pure white towards the vent and lower tail-coverts; the ruff is full, soft, and pure white, of very downy feathers, the webs much disintegrated; the whole mantle is pale earthy-brown, the centres of the lesser, and all but the tips and margins of the larger scapulars being dark hair-brown.

The lower back, rump and upper tail-coverts white, tinged with pale earthy brown, many of the feathers, however, especially of the longer tail-coverts, being brown at the base, but so broadly tipped and margined with the paler color that little of the brown shows; the primaries and tail-feathers are deep chocolate-brown; the secondaries and tertiaries hair-brown, more or less suffused on their outer webs with pale dingy earthy or fulvous-brown.

A quite young bird has the top and back of the head, and upper part of the back of the neck, thickly covered with white down; the rest of the head and neck, as in the adult; the crop-patch much lighter than in the adult, is covered with pale, dove-colored brown feathers; the rest of the lower surface is pale brown, becoming albescent towards the vent, each feather broadly centred (most conspicuously so on the sides and breast), with dingy white; the ruff, of long, linear lanceolate feathers, is a very pale fulvous-white, faintly margined with brown; the mantle a somewhat pale hair-brown, every feather narrowly, but conspicuously, centred with fulvous-white; the quill-feathers and tail-feathers chocolate-brown, darkest on the primaries and rectrices; the lower back, rump, and upper tail-coverts are nearly pure white, only a few of the longest being tinged with brown.

In an intermediate stage the crop-patch is intermediate in color between that of the adult and of the young, as is also the color and character of the ruff, and indeed of the whole plumage.

This bird differs at all ages from *bengalensis* in having fourteen instead of twelve rectrices.—*Hume*, "*Rough Notes.*"

With the exception of Sind, this Vulture is common throughout the Presidency. It breeds on cliffs during December and January; the egg is usually very pale greenish-white, but is occasionally spotted and blotched with pale-reddish or faint purplish-brown. They average 3·61 in length by 2·72 in breadth.

GENUS, **Pseudogyps**, *Sharpe.*

Tarsus shorter than middle toe; tail of twelve feathers.

Pseudogyps bengalensis, *Gm.*

5.—Jerdon's Birds of India, Vol. I, p. 10; Butler, Guzerat; Stray Feathers, Vol. III, p. 442; Deccan and South Mahratta country; Stray Feathers, Vol. IX, p. 369; Murray's Vertebrate Zoology of Sind, p. 63; Swinhoe and Barnes, Central India; Ibis, 1885, p. 54; Hume's Scrap Book, p. 26.

THE WHITE-BACKED VULTURE.
Gidh, Hin.

Length, 33 to 37; expanse, 83 to 88; wing, 22 to 24; tail, 9 to 11; tarsus, 3·5 to 3·9; bill from gape, 2·65 to 2·9; weight, 9 to 13 lbs.

Bill horny, dusky on cere; irides red-brown; legs dusky-black.

Adult: above cinereous-black; back and rump white, beneath dark-brown; the feathers centred lighter; the short feathers of the crop deep-brown; ruff whitish, the feathers short and downy; head and neck nearly bare, with a few scattered hair-like feathers.

The young is paler, with the head and neck more or less clothed with whitish down; bill and cere horny-black; legs black; irides brown.

The White-backed is the commonest Vulture we have; it occurs in great numbers all over the country; they breed during December, January, and February, choosing lofty trees in the neighbourhood of villages, in the tops of which they make huge platform nests, sometimes as many as twelve or fourteen in a single tree. Jerdon says: "It breeds by preference on rocky cliffs." I doubt this, as I have found the nests on trees, adjacent to cliffs, in every way suitable. I have never found more than a single egg, or a single nestling, in a nest; this would seem conclusive, but others state that they lay one or two eggs.

The color of the egg is white, with a greenish tinge, and is generally much discolored; they are often spotted and blotched, with various shades of reddish-brown. The texture is moderately fine, the shell thick and strong, and the lining a deep green. They vary much in size and shape, some being moderately long ovals, while others are nearly spherical. They average 3·26 inches in length by 2·42 in breadth.

SUB-FAMILY, **Neophroninæ**.

Bill lengthened, slender, straight, hooked suddenly at the tip; cere very long, occupying nearly two-thirds of the whole bill; nostrils longitudinal, nearly in the middle of the bill; part of the head and face naked; neck with acuminated feathers; wings ample, pointed, the third quill longest; tail moderate, wedge-shaped, of twelve or fourteen feathers; legs moderate, toes much united at base by membrane.

GENUS, **Neophron**, *Sav.*

The characters are the same as those of the sub-family.

Neophron ginginianus, *Lath.*

6.—Jerdon's Birds of India, Vol. I, p. 12; Butler, Guzerat; Stray Feathers, Vol. III, p. 442; Deccan and South Mahratta country; Stray Feathers, Vol. IX, p. 369; Murray's Vertebrate Zoology of Sind, p. 64; Swinhoe and Barnes, Central India; Ibis, 1885, p. 54; Hume's Scrap Book, p. 31.

THE WHITE SCAVENGER VULTURE.

Length, 26 to 29; wing, 19; tail, 9 to 10; tarsus, 3; bill from gape, 2·5.

Bill horny-brown; cere and face turmeric-yellow; irides reddish-brown; legs and feet yellowish-white.

Adult: yellowish or creamy-white; quills black; neck feathers long, lanceolate, and tinged rusty; secondaries dark brown, ashy-white at base.

The young bird has the plumage dirty-brown, with the quills blackish-brown; the back and rump albescent or tawny; the inner edge of the secondaries and of some of the primaries cinereous; the nude parts of head and cere greyish; feet cinereous.

In an intermediate stage the birds are mottled-brown and white.

The White Scavenger Vulture is another very common species, and is found throughout the whole district; it breeds during March and April, generally on trees but occasionally on rocky cliffs, old buildings and such like places. It makes a large nest of twigs, lined with old rags and rubbish; straggling, if built on a cliff or a building—rather more compact if on a tree. In the latter situation, the nest is generally placed at the junction of a large limb with the trunk, but sometimes on a horizontal branch, very rarely in a fork. The eggs, two in number, are very handsome; they are somewhat chalky in texture, greyish-white in color, richly blotched and clouded with deep brownish-red. They vary much in shape, size and color.

They average 2·6 inches in length by 1·98 in breadth.

SUB-FAMILY, **Gypaetinæ,** *Bonn & Gray.*

Bill strong, lengthened, compressed, straight; upper mandible ascending in front of cere, then curved, with the tip much hooked; nostrils oval, vertical, covered with dense rigid recumbent bristles; lower mandible with a beard, or tuft of rigid setaceous bristles directed forward; head closely feathered; wings very long, the first quill rather shorter than the second, the third longest; feet short, stout; the tarsus hirsute to the toes; the thigh-coverts lengthened; the three front toes slightly united by membrane, middle-toe very long, hind-toe short; claws strong, moderately curved; tail cuneate, long.

GENUS, **Gypaetus,** *Storr.*

The characters are the same as those of the sub-family.

Gypaetus barbatus, *Lin.*

7.—Jerdon's Birds of India, Vol. I, p. 12; Murray's Vertebrate Zoology of Sind, p. 64; Hume's Scrap Book, p. 35.

THE LAMMERGEYER.

Length, 44 to 49; expanse, 99 to 110; wing, 30 to 34; tail, 21 to 25; tarsus, 3·9 to 4·7; bill from gape, 4 to 4·7.

Bill bluish-horny, dusky at tip; irides pale-orange or straw color; sclerotic membrane blood-red; feet plumbeous; claws black.

Head whitish with dark stripes, tinged rufous; cheek-stripe and supercilium black; feathers of the nape lengthened, creamy-white, tinged wiih bright tawny; upper parts black; the back and rump paler, with white shafts, and the coverts with white streaks; greater-coverts, wing and tail ashy-black, with darker edges and white shafts to the feathers; beneath dull orange or ferruginous, with a more or less marked black pectoral collar (not always present), paling below the breast, and becoming albescent or nearly white on the lower belly and under tail-coverts.

The Lammergeyer or Bearded Vulture only occurs in the northern parts of Sind.

Family, Falconidæ.

Bill usually short and compressed, tip elongated, curved, and sharp; margin of upper mandible toothed or festooned; wings more or less pointed; tail various, generally rather long; legs and feet strong; tarsus bare, or feathered; toes generally unequal, with the claws long, sharp, and well curved; head and neck are always feathered; eyes sunk, shaded above by a bony projection or brow.

Sub-family, Falconinæ.

Bill short, strongly curved and hooked, the upper mandible with a sharp tooth (or sometimes two) over-lapping the lower one, which is short, truncated and slightly notched to receive the tooth of the upper mandible.

The wings are long, with the second quill usually longest, sometimes the third nearly equal to it, and one or two of the first quills are usually notched on their inner webs; the tail is moderately long, even, or very slightly rounded, and broad; the legs are short, muscular, and reticulated; the toes lengthened, with the outer and inner one generally very unequal in length; the claws sharp, well-curved, and somewhat retractile.

Genus, Falco, *Lin.*

Bill with the upper mandible furnished with one strong tooth; nostrils round, with a central tubercle; wings long and pointed, reaching nearly to the end of the tail, the first one or two quills notched internally, the second quill longest; the tail rather short; tarsus short, strong, reticulated, feathered at the knee; toes long, scutellated, the middle-toe very long, outer-toe longer than the inner; claws long and sharp; inner fore and hind-claw very large.

Falco peregrinus, *Gm.*

8.—Jerdon's Birds of India, Vol. I, p. 21; Butler, Guzerat; Stray Feathers, Vol. III, p. 442; Deccan and South Mahratta country; Stray Feathers, Vol. IX, p. 370; Murray's Vertebrate Zoology of Sind, p. 65; Hume's Scrap Book, p. 49.

THE PEREGRINE FALCON.

Bhyri, HIN.

♀. Length, 18 to 20·25; expanse, 35 to 39; wing, 13 to 14·5; tail, 6 to 6·75; tarsus, 2 to 2·2; bill from gape, 1·3.

♂. Length, 16; wing, 12·25; tail, 5·75.

Bill, pale blue at base of upper mandible, greenish at base of lower mandible, bluish-black at tips of both; cere dingy-yellowish; irides deep brown; legs and feet pale yellowish-brown; claws black.

Adult: above deep bluish-grey, most of the feathers with some dark markings; head, nape, and moustache darker; rump and upper tail-coverts much lighter; wings blackish-brown, more or less spotted or barred with white on the inner web; tail grey, with some dark bands, and a pale tip; beneath chin and throat pure white; breast, white, with a few narrow longitudinal streaks, almost disappearing in old individuals; abdomen with some small heart-shaped spots; flanks and thigh-coverts with dark transverse bars; inner wing-coverts white, with numerous well-marked dark cross bars.

Young bird: above dark brown, most of the feathers edged with paler and somewhat rufous brown; head more edged with whitish, especially the hind head; cheek-stripe brown; wings darker brown than the back, with pale rufous spots or bars on the inner webs; the tail dusky-cinereous, with numerous interrupted pale rufous or rufous-white bars; beneath white or creamy, with brown oval spots, longitudinal and narrow on the throat and breast, wider and ovate on the abdomen.

The following extract from Mr. Hume's "*Rough Notes*" will assist in discriminating the various species of Falcons:—

"First, the *Sacer* so far exceeds all the others in size that this alone would be sufficient to identify it. The wings average from 15 to 16 inches, against 14 in *F. juggur* and *F. peregrinus*, and 13 in *perigrinator* and *babylonicus*. Then, while the central tail-feathers of *peregrinus, perigrinator*, and *babylonicus* are all barred, (in different stages according to age) and those of *juggur* are unbarred, those of *Sacer*, in most of the specimens I have seen, are marked with roundish spots (more or less broad ovals on the laterals). Then, again, the *Sacer* never has much, and commonly shows scarcely any sign of a cheek-stripe, while in all the others it is well marked. Further, the *Peregrine* is distinguished at all times from the *Juggur*, by its huge, broad cheek-patch, which in the *Laggar* is at most about a quarter of an inch broad, and by the entire absence of barring on the centre tail-feathers in *F. juggur*, which absence equally distinguishes this later from both *perigrinator* and *babylonicus*.

From *babylonicus*, both *perigrinator* and *peregrinus* differ in the cheek-stripe, which is narrow in the former, as in the *juggur*, but very broad and strongly marked in the two latter; but *babylonicus*, as far as my experience goes, is not of the *juggur* type of brown plumage, the old birds becoming slaty or greenish-blue as do both *peregrinus* and *perigrinator*, whilst the oldest *juggur* is never more than slaty-brown.

Then, as to *perigrinator* and *peregrinus*, the comparatively rich rufous coloring at all ages of the under parts, and the very dark head and nape of the former, at once separate the two species.

The Peregrine, though it occurs throughout the district, is nowhere common. It is also called the Duck-hawk, from its habit of preying on the duck tribe; so long as they (the ducks) remain on the water, they are safe, and the ducks seem instinctively to know this, for immediately a Peregrine appears in sight, they betake themselves to the water with the utmost speed they are capable of, the hindmost generally falling a victim to the Peregrine's superior powers of flight.

Nothing certain appears to be known concerning its nidification in this country, but it is strongly suspected to breed on the banks of the Cabool and Swat rivers. I have myself seen young birds offered for sale at Kotri, Sind: these birds were said to have been obtained from nests on the banks of the Indus.

Falco perigrinator, *Sund.*

9.—Jerdon's Birds of India, Vol. I, p. 25; Butler, Guzerat; Stray Feathers, Vol. III, p. 443; Deccan and South Mahratta country; Stray Feathers, Vol. IX, p. 370; Swinhoe and Barnes, Central India; Ibis, 1885, p. 55; Hume's Scrap Book, p. 55.

THE SHAHEEN FALCON.

Shahin, Hin.

♂. Length, 14·87; wing, 11·49; tail, 6; tarsus, 1·85; bill from gape, 1·1.

♀. Length, 18; wing, 13·5; tail, 6·25.

Bill bluish, black at tip; irides brown; cere, orbits, legs and feet yellow; claws, black.

Young bird with the upper parts and cheek-stripe very dark cinereous, or dusky-blackish, darkest on the head, hind-neck and cheek-stripe, most of the feathers narrowly edged with rufous, those of the back and rump more broadly so; occasionally the forehead is somewhat rufous, and there is always a patch on the nape, where it forms a sort of crucial mark; tail paler than the rest of the body, faintly barred with rufous, and tipped with the same; chin and throat pale rufous-yellow, almost white in some birds and unspotted; cheeks the same, with narrow dark stripes; the rest of the body beneath bright rufous or chesnut, with longitudinal dark-brown stripes on the lower breast and the middle of the abdomen; oblong spots on the sides, and arrow-shaped markings on the lower abdomen, vent and under tail-coverts; under wing-coverts rufous, with dark brown bars; the quills barred with rufous on their inner webs.

The old bird has the head, nape, and cheek-stripe almost black; back and upper parts slaty, light on the rump, and almost without any markings; chin, throat, and upper breast white; the rest of the plumage beneath rufous or chesnut, almost unspotted.

The changes of plumage from the young bird consists in the head, gradually becoming darker; the back (and the rump more especially) becoming lighter and more slaty-blue, and in the markings of the lower surface gradually disappearing from the crop downwards with each successive moult. Individuals vary a good deal in the amount of white on the chin and throat, and in its intensity; in some it is well marked, in others always a creamy or rufous-white.

The Shaheen Falcon occurs sparingly throughout the country, with the exception of Sind, from whence it has not yet been recorded. Dr. Jerdon says that it breeds on inaccessible cliffs, and that he has seen three eyries. One, at the large waterfall in Mhow, is within our district, and I have myself seen, during the cold season of 1881, a pair of Shaheens frequenting this spot. Major Butler had reason to believe that a pair bred annually at Khandalla.

Falco sacer, *Gm.*

10.—Jerdon's Birds of India, Vol. I, p. 29; Murray's Vertebrate Zoology of Sind, p. 66; Hume's Scrap Book, p. 62.

THE SAKER.
Chargh, Hin.

♂. Length, 19·81; wing, 15; tail, 9·2; tarsus, 2·13; bill from gape, 1·42.

♀. Length, 22; wing, 15·5; tail, 10·75; tarsus, 2·13; bill from gape, 1·45.

Young bird with the top of the head yellowish-white, brown streaked; upper parts brown, with slight pale edgings to some of the feathers; beneath white, with large oval brown spots; legs and feet pale bluish; bill and cere bluish-black at tip. The adult has the upper parts rather pale slaty-brown, almost slaty in old birds; cheek-stripe indistinct; top of the head reddish-ash color with fine black streaks; chin white; breast and lower parts white, with oblong, slaty spots; cere greenish-white; feet lemon-yellow.

The Saker Falcon or Cherrug has only been obtained from Sind, where it is stated to be not common and only occurring in the cold weather. Those obtained were all in the immature phase.

Falco juggur, *J. E. Gray.*

11.—Jerdon's Birds of India, Vol. I, p. 30; Butler, Guzerat; Stray Feathers, Vol. III, p. 443; Deccan and South Mahratta country; Stray Feathers, Vol. IX, p. 370; Murray's Vertebrate Zoology of Sind, p. 67; Swinhoe and Barnes, Central India; Ibis, 1885, p. 55; Hume's Scrap Book, p. 70.

THE LAGGAR.
Laggar, Female, Hin.
Juggur, Male, Hin.

♂. Length, 15 to 16·5; expanse, 37 to 41; wing, 12 to 13; tail, 7 to 8; tarsus, 1·7 to 1·9; bill from gape, 1 to 1·12.

♀. Length, 17·5 to 19; expanse, 42 to 45; wing, 13 to 15; tail, 8 to 9; tarsus, 1·75 to 2; bill from gape, 1·15 to 1·37.

In the young, the color of the legs and feet vary from pale plumbeous to dull greenish-grey; in the adult from full wax-yellow to a bright almost orange-yellow. The claws are blackish-horny; the cere is dingy greenish-grey or plumbeous in the young, bright yellow in the adult; the orbit greenish-yellow in the former, bright yellow in the latter; the bill varies at base from greenish-horny to greyish-blue and even blue, and at tip from dark horny-blue to bluish-black; the irides are brown.

Adult Male.—Above dusky-ashy or slate color; crown of head dull rufous with central ashy-black striations; lores, forehead, chin, throat and eyebrow white; moustachial stripe black; wing-coverts concolorous with the back, the carpal margin white; the breast white with a few brown spots; lower abdomen, flanks and thighs ashy brown; tail clear ashy-grey with pale rufous bars on the inner webs and a white tip.

Young of a chocolate-brown above and below; wing-coverts with rufous margins; head yellowish-fawn; or pale rufous; forehead and eyebrow whitish; chin and throat white; under tail-coverts dirty-white with faint brown markings.

The Laggar is the commonest of the larger Falcons, and occurs throughout the region. It is a permanent resident, and breeds during the first three months of the year, the majority of them laying in Fabruary. It is by no means particular in the choice of a site for its nest; a hole in the face of an old building, a ledge on a rocky or clayey cliff, a fork in a tree, or even a deserted crow or other nest, are all made use of. The eggs, three or four in number, are oval in shape, of a fine but chalky texture, reddish or yellowish-white in color, so closely freckled and stippled with reddish-brown, as to leave little or none of the ground color discernible. At such times the egg, unless looked at closely, appears to be a uniform brick-red. Sometimes the color is whiter and the egg blotched, clouded or capped with reddish-brown, not however very distinct. They are at times very beautiful.

They average 2 inches in length by 1·55 in breadth.

Falco babylonicus, *Gurney.*

12.—Jerdon's Birds of India, Vol. I, p. 32; Hume's Scrap Book, p. 79; Murray's Vertebrate Zoology of Sind, p. 67.

THE RED-CAP FALCON.

Length, 16; expanse, 38; weight, 12ozs; wing, 11·87; tail, (of 12 feathers), 6; tarsus, (feathered for 0·5 in front) 1·87; bill from gape, 1·19.

Legs and feet bright yellow, whitish at the joints of the reticulated scales of the tarsus; soles with large pads, very conspicuous under second joint of middle and exterior toe; claws horn black; middle-toe very slender and elongated; irides dark brown; edges of the lids greenish-yellow, with tiny dark lashes; membrane of the orbits pale greenish.

Forehead buffy-white, feathers dark shafted; line over the

eye continued round the back of the head, whitish or fulvous-white; feathers dark shafted; whole crown of the head brown, a few feathers in centre towards the front very broadly margined, the rest very narrowly margined, with fulvous or buffy-white; the nape below the white stripe darkish-brown in the centre, the feathers margined with buffy-white, and with a patch of white on either side the feathers of which have dark spots towards the tip; the whole of the rest of the back of the neck, upper back, scapulars, and wing-coverts a nearly uniform brown with a faint tinge of slaty, and all the feathers tipped and margined with fulvous-white, very narrowly towards the head, and more broadly towards the points of the scapulars; the hue of the back of the neck is slightly darker; the quills are much the same color, but somewhat more bluish; all the quills have a number of incomplete bars, or oval spots of rufous-white on the inner web; the last five primaries, the secondaries and the tertiaries have each two or three tiny rufous-white spots on the outer webs also; and the greater-coverts of the secondaries and tertiaries have similar small inconspicuous spots on both webs; and all the secondaries and tertiaries, and the last few primaries, are narrowly tipped with buffy-white; the rump and lower back are a somewhat paler and more sandy-brown, margined with pale rufous; the upper tail-coverts are a still more sandy-brown, tipped and margined with dingy-white, and with one or more incomplete bars of fulvous-white; the tail-feathers are brown, paler and sandier on the centre feathers, and darker, and more slaty on the outer feathers, all narrowly tipped with dirty-white, and all with six or seven one-quarter-inch broad transverse bars on both webs, fulvous white on the centre feathers, and rufous-white on the exterior feathers; the bars are scarcely visible on the outer web of the exterior feather; chin, and upper part of throat, pure white; a dark-brown cheek-stripe from under the eye, margined with pale rufous; ear-coverts mingled pale brown and rufous-white.

Hinder portion of the cheeks white, some of the feathers tinged pale-rufous; an ill-defined brown stripe (the feathers slightly tipped fulvous-white) running backwards from the posterior angle of the eye, and dividing the white of the hind-cheeks from the white of the sides of the nape; the lower throat and upper portion of breast fulvous-white, each feather dark shafted, and with a narrow somewhat pear-shaped streak of dark brown towards the tip; the rest of the breast, sides and upper abdomen fulvous-white, each feather with a well marked central stripe of brown, narrowest in front, broadest towards the sides.

Lower abdomen and vent white, slightly tinged with fulvous, a few of the feathers dark shafted; lower tail-coverts (which do not reach within two inches of the end of the tail) white, with two or three transverse, somewhat wavy bars, of pale brown; interior thigh-coverts white; exterior thigh-coverts white, tinged with fulvous, each feather dark shafted, and with a central lanceolate stripe of brown, the bars above mentioned showing through; the lower wing-coverts, all reddish-brown, conspicuously margined at the tip, and the longer ones barred with somewhat fulvous-white.

Mr. Hume in his "*Rough Notes*" gives the measurements and description of a fine female, shot by him in the Punjaub:—

Dimensions.—Length, 17·95; expanse, 4·1, tail from vent, 7·25; foot, greatest length, 4·5, greatest width 4; wing, 13; wings, when closed, reach to within 1·87 of end of tail; tarsus, 1·75; mid-toe to root of claw, 1·9; weight, 1·87 lbs.

Description.—The irides were deep brown; the cere, gape, and orbital skin, as well as the legs and feet, were bright yellow; the claws were black, and the corneous portion of the bill was blue, changing to horny-black at the tip.

The forehead and the centre of the top of the head were sandy-rufous, each feather with a dark-brown shaft; the sides of the top and the back of the head were a somewhat ashy or slaty-brown, the feathers more or less margined with sandy-rufous; a broad, rufous, half collar ran round the back of the neck, a little mottled behind the ear-coverts, and again in the centre of the back of the neck, with dusky-slaty; the whole mantle was slaty-grey, dark and dusky towards the base of the neck, and paling towards the rump and upper tail-coverts; most, if not all, of the feathers were narrowly margined paler, those towards the nape with rufous, and those lower down with greyish-white; most of the feathers also were somewhat conspicuously darker shafted, and all exhibited broad, transverse somewhat ill-defined, dusky-slaty, bands; the rump and upper tail-coverts were pale slaty, or French-grey, with brown shafts, and transverse arrow head, dusky bars; the tail-feathers were pale slaty-grey, tipped with rufous, and with numerous broad transverse, well defined, slaty-brown bars, broadest towards the tips; there was a blackish line under the eye, continued downwards for about an inch and a quarter, as a narrow cheek-stripe; the two cheek-stripes nearly meet on the throat, about an inch and a half below the base of the lower mandible; the whole of the lower parts were a rich rufous-salmon color, somewhat paler on the chin and centre of the throat, and deeper on the ear-coverts, sides of neck, and centre of the abdomen; the breast, chin and throat are perfectly spotless; the abdomen, flanks, lower tail-coverts and tibial plumes were regularly, but rather widely barred with slaty-brown; the bars, everywhere narrow, being nearly obsolete in the centre of the abdomen, and best marked on the flanks; the under wing-coverts were of a pale salmon color, conspicuously barred with brown.

The Red-headed Falcon or Lanner has only been recorded from Sind. With regard to its nidification nothing certain seems to be known, but Mr. Hume had reason to believe that it bred in the Peshawar Valley and in Cashmere.

Falco barbarus, *Lin.*

12 *bis.*—Murray's Vertebrate Zoology of Sind, p. 68.

THE BARBARY FALCON.

♂. Length, 14; wing, 10·8; tail, 5; tarsus, 1·6.

♀. Length, 15·5; expanse, 36·4; wing, 11·4; tail, 6·4; tarsus, 1·8; bill from gape, 1·1.

The base of the beak is yellow, but the point is blue; the cere and feet beautiful yellow, and the orbital skin orange.

The forehead presents a mixture of rufous and dull white. This part of the head is encircled by a black (or dark slaty) horse-shoe-shaped band, of which the lateral branches pass over the eyes, their extreme points joining in front of the eyes, the moustachial stripes which extend along the sides of the neck; the occiput and nape are covered by a rufous half-collar marked with three black spots, of which the centre one forms a band on the nape; the back and wings are a light bluish-grey, with large spots and irregular bars of bluish-black; the tail, which is a lighter grey than the back, is barred transversely with black bands, very narrow towards the bases of the feathers, but widening gradually towards their ends, the tips of which are white; the chest is pure isabeline; the flanks, vent, and abdomen of the same color, but the feathers bear very narrow longitudinal striæ and little triangular black spots.

This Falcon only occurs as a rare visitant, Sind being the only part of the region with which I am dealing, in which it has occurred.

Falco subbuteo, *Lin.*

13.—Jerdon's Birds of India, Vol. I, p. 33; Butler, Aboo; Stray Feathers, Vol. III, p. 443; Deccan, Stray Feathers, Vol. IX, p. 370; Murray's Vertebrate Zoology of Sind, p. 69; Hume's Scrap Book, p. 85.

THE HOBBY.

♂. Length, 10·75; wing, 9·4; tail, 5·25.

♀. Length, 12·5; wing, 10·4; tail, 5·5.

Cere and legs greenish-yellow.

Adult: blackish-slaty above, rusty-white beneath; throat and neck unspotted; breast and abdomen with dark brown streaks, narrow on the centre of the abdomen, wider on the flanks; thigh-coverts and under tail-coverts pure ferruginous; tail dark slaty, with dark bands; frontal line and narrow stripe over the eye pale rusty-whitish; cheek-stripe black, distinctly separated from the dark cheeks and ear-coverts; quills barred internally with light rufous.

Young bird: dark brown above, the feathers edged with ferruginous; cheek-stripe darker, beneath whitish, with a rusty tinge, and all the feathers with broad blackish-brown spots or streaks; the lower abdomen, thigh-coverts, and under tail-coverts ferruginous, with a few brown streaks.

The European Hobby is a somewhat rare winter visitant to the greater part of the region; at Aboo it is not uncommon, but has not as yet been recorded from Central India.

Falco æsalon, *Tunst.*

15.—*Hypotriorchis æsalon*, Gm.—Jerdon's Birds of India, Vol. I, p. 35; Murray's Vertebrate Zoology of Sind, p. 7; Hume's Scrap Book, p. 89.

THE MERLIN.

♂. Length, 11·25; wing, 8; tail, 5.

♀. Length, 13·5; wing, 9; tail, 5·5.

Above, fine blackish-grey, darkest on the crown, and reddish, mixed with white, on the nape; ear-coverts yellowish-grey; quills blackish-brown; tail grey, with a broad black band, white-tipped at the end; chin and throat white, the same tinged with ochrey on the breast and with reddish-orange on the abdomen, with dark brown spots. The female is browner than the male, with the markings more rufous, and the lower parts ochrey-white, tinged with rufous on the breast, and the spots larger and more numerous.

The young bird has the head rufous, with dark streaks; and the rest of the plumage above brown, tinged grey, with dark shafts, and pale rufous edges; quills dark brown; tail ashy-brown, barred with rufous; the chin is white, the rest of the plumage beneath pale ochrey-white, with broad brown marks reduced to lines on the thighs and under tail-coverts.

The Merlin is another very rare visitant to Sind.

Falco chiquera, *Daud.*

16.—*Hypotriorchis chiquera*, Daud.—Jerdon's Birds of India, Vol. I, p. 36; Butler, Guzerat; Stray Feathers, Vol. III, p. 444; Deccan and South Mahratta country, Stray Feathers, Vol. IX, p. 370; Murray's Vertebrate Zoology of Sind, p. 70; Swinhoe and Barnes, Central India; Ibis, 1885, p. 55; Hume's Scrap Book, p. 91.

THE RED-HEADED MERLIN.
Turumti, Hin.

♂. Length, 11 to 12; expanse, 26; wing, 8 to 8·25; tail, 4·75 to 6; tarsus, 1·5.

♀. Length, 13 to 14; wing, 8·5 to 9; tail, 5·5 to 6; tarsus, 1·5.

Cere, orbitar skin, and legs, bright yellow.

Adult: head, nape, and cheek-stripe bright rufous; the rest of the plumage above fine pale grey; quills dark slaty; tail light grey, with a broad black terminal band, white tipped at the end; beneath white, unspotted to the breast; all the rest of the lower parts with narrow cross bands of dusky grey; quills with the inner webs banded dusky and whitish; tail with narrow cross bars, conspicuous beneath, not seen above.

Young bird: head, nape, and moustache dark dusky-rufous, with dark mesial lines; the upper parts grey, with dark markings to all the feathers; quills darker; tail with numerous bars, and a broad black terminal band; beneath white, more or less tinged rusty, with some streaks on the neck and breast, and broadish bars on the abdomen and thigh-coverts.

The Turumti is more or less common throughout the region. It frequents open country in the vicinity of cultivation, and I have often obtained its nest within village enclosures. It commences to breed in January, and nests may be found quite up to the end of March. They prefer rather high trees, such as tamarind and peepul, and in a fork near the top, they construct rather a neat cup-shaped nest of twigs, lined with grass, roots, &c. It would be rather a difficult nest to find were it not for the fussy habit the bird has of darting out, attacking, and driving away any bird that may happen to come near the tree. Jerdon says that they do not hesitate to attack the Tawny Eagle. The usual number of eggs is four, but I have occasionally found only three, well incubated. They are rather longish ovals, somewhat chalky in texture, of a yellowish or reddish-brown color, closely stippled, blotched, mottled and clouded with darker shades of the same color.

They average 1·65 inches in length by about 1·25 in breadth.

Genus, **Cerchneis.**

Tarsi long, strong, with transverse hexagonal scales; rest as in *Falco.*

Cerchneis tinnunculus, *Lin.*

17.—*Tinnunculus alaudarius*, Brisson.—Jerdon's Birds of India, Vol. I, p. 38; Butler, Guzerat; Stray Feathers, Vol. III, p. 444; Deccan and South Mahratta country; Stray Feathers, Vol. IX, p. 370; Murray's Vertebrate Zoology of Sind, p. 71; Swinhoe and Barnes, Central India; Ibis, 1885, p. 56; Hume's Scrap Book, p. 96.

THE KESTRIL.
Narzi, Hin.

♂ Length, 13 to 14; expanse, 30; wing, 10; tail, 6·25; bill from gape, 0·85; tarsus, 1·53.

♀ Length, 15; wing, 10·75; tail, 7.

Bill yellowish at the base, bluish-black at tips and on culmen; irides brown; cere and orbits bright yellow; legs and feet bright orange-yellow; claws blackish-horny.

Male: forehead yellowish; head, nape and tail fine ashy-grey, the latter with a broad black band, and the former sometimes tinged black; mantle and wing-coverts vinaceous, with some heart-shaped black spots; beneath creamy or rusty with spots of brown, linear on the breast, oval on the abdomen, and heart-shaped on the sides; the under tail-coverts are unspotted; quills brown, with white bands or spots on the inner webs.

Female (and young male): above of a ruddy vinaceous color, with long dark stripes on the head and neck, broadish bars on the back and wing-coverts; tail with numerous dark bands, and a broader one at the end, white-tipped; cheek-stripe dark, of small extent; ears hoary; plumage beneath reddish-ochraceus, with numerous and close brown spots.

To the above description, which is Dr. Jerdon's, must be added, that the tail is tipped with white, and that the centre tail-feathers have at times linear black spots on their inner webs; the quills are also often narrowly edged and tipped with white.

The young male is not exactly like the female; it is always more rufous.

The Kestril is common throughout the country, but only as a winter visitant. It arrives in September and does not take its departure until April. It does not breed anywhere within our limits; but is known to do so on the Himalayan, Suleiman, and Neilgherry ranges. I obtained a good series of eggs on the Khoja Amran Hills, between Quetta and Kandahar.

Cerchneis naumanni, *Fleish.*

18.—*Erythropus cenchris*, Maum.—Jerdon's Birds of India, Vol. I, p. 40; Butler, Deccan and South Mahratta country; Stray Feathers, Vol. IX, p. 371; Hume's Scrap Book, p. 103.

THE LESSER KESTRIL.

Total length, 12·5 inches; culmen, 0·75; wing, 9·5; tail, 6; tarsus, 1·2.

Bill lightish-blue, yellow at base, and blackish at tip; cere, orbits, and feet beautiful yellow; the claws generally white, very rarely inclining to blackish; iris dark brown.

Adult male: upper surface of body rich cinnamon-rufous; entire head and hind-neck, lower back, rump, upper tail-coverts, and tail blue-grey, the latter tipped with white, and crossed by a broad subterminal band of black; lores and a few streaks on the cheeks whitish; lesser and medium wing-coverts cinnamon-rufous, like the back, a few of the outer ones of the latter series washed with blue-grey; the greater-coverts and inner secondaries blue-grey washed with rufous externally; primaries dark brown; throat deep fulvous-white; breast pale cinnamon or vinous, with a few blackish spots on the breast, becoming larger on the sides of the body; thighs paler rufous, unspotted; abdomen and under tail-coverts yellowish-white; under wing-coverts white, with a few tiny black oval spots, larger on the axillaries.

Adult female: dissimilar to the male. Above tawny-rufous, transversely crossed by bars of blackish-brown, narrower and more obscure on the lower back, rump, and upper tail-coverts, the latter of which are strongly inclined to grey; tail rufous, barred with black, tipped with whitish, before which a broad subterminal band of black; head and neck rather paler rufous, the former broadly, the latter more narrowly, streaked with blackish shaft stripes; forehead and a distinct eye-brow whitish; cheeks and ear-coverts silvery-white, with narrow shaft lines of black; primaries dark-brown, barred on the inner web with rufous; secondaries colored like the back, the outer ones narrowly margined with white at the tip; throat, vent and under tail-coverts fulvous-white, unspotted; breast inclining to rufous-fawn color; all the feathers mesially streaked with blackish, these stripes being broader on the flanks, and very tiny on the sides, which are also paler rufous. Total length, 12·5 inches; culmen, 0·7; wing, 9·3; tail, 5·9; tarsus, 1·2.

Young male: like the old female, but somewhat paler rufous. The blue tail is assumed by a moult, the blue head being, on the other hand, gained by a change of feather. Birds in intermediate stages are often thus seen.—*Sharpe's Catalogue.*

The Lesser Kestril has been recorded from the Deccan by several observers, but Mr. Hume remarks that it is doubtful whether the form that occurs there may not be the closely allied *Cerchneis pekinensis.* I therefore add a description of the latter.

18 *bis.*—**Cerchneis pekinensis,** *Swinh.*

Adult male: very similar to *C. naumanni,* but darker and more vinous-red above; underneath also darker colored and unspotted when adult. The principal distinction is in the wing-coverts, which are almost entirely blue-grey, only the very innermost being slightly washed with rufous. Total length, 12 inches; culmen, 0·8; wing, 9·6; tail, 5·8; tarsus 1·45.—*Sharpe's Catalogue.*

Cerchneis vespertina, *Lin.*

19.—Jerdon's Birds of India, Vol. I, p. 41.

19 *bis.*—Butler, Deccan; Stray Feathers, Vol. IX, p. 371; Hume's Scrap Book, p. 106.

The Red-legged Falcon.

♂. Length, 11; wing, 8·75.

♀. Length, 11·5; wing, 9·25; expanse, 27; tail, 5.

Bill fleshy-red, with a dusky tip; cere and legs deep orange-red; claws fleshy; orbitar skin orange-yellow.

Young bird: above dark slaty-grey, some of the feathers centred and tipped darker; tail light grey, obsoletely barred; ocular region and cheek-stripe nearly black; narrow frontal band, supercilium, lores, ear-feathers, and sides of neck and throat white; breast and abdomen rusty-white, with blackish-brown marks, longitudinal on the breast, heart-shaped on the sides, and arrow-like on the centre of the abdomen; vent, under tail-coverts, and thigh-coverts pale unspotted rusty.

The adult male has the whole upper plumage unspotted ashy, pale ashy beneath; chin and throat whitish; wings dusky-black; thigh-coverts, and under tail-coverts, bright rusty-red.

Dr. Jerdon remarks that the Red-legged Falcon is not common in India, but that he has killed it in Central India; it is nearly certain that he mistook it for 19 *bis*, *Cerchneis amurensis*, Radde. This latter Major Butler procured at Belgaum. The points of difference are as follows:—

VESPERTINA.	AMURENSIS.
ADULT ♂.	
Under wing-coverts and axillaries.	
Bluish-grey.	Pure white.
Breast.	
Bluish-grey.	Grey.
ADULT ♀.	
Under surface.	
Rufous, either uniform or with slight remains of blackish shaft lines.	Creamy-white; the breast broadly streaked and the flanks barred with black; abdomen, thighs, and under tail-coverts uniform pale rufous.
JUV.	
Head.	
Rufous with narrow shaft lines of black; forehead whitish; under surface of body buff, streaked down the centres of the feathers with brown; no bars on the flanks; tail bluish.	Dark bluish, with black shaft streaks; forehead fulvous; under surface of body buff, broadly streaked with black on the chest and barred on the flanks with the same color; tail bluish.

SUB-FAMILY, **Accipitrinæ.**

Bill short and stout, curving from the base, with a blunt tooth or festoon in the upper mandible; wings short, rounded; tail longish, ample, and rounded; tarsus long, scutellate in front, or nearly smooth in some; toes long; claws long, curved and acute, unequal; inner-claw large.

GENUS, **Astur,** *Lac.*

Bill short, stout, curved from the base, compressed, with a prominent festoon or rounded tooth in the upper mandible, near the middle; nostril large, oval, oblique, near the culmen; lores thickly clad with minute feathers; wings short, rounded; first quill short, fourth and fifth quills usually equal and longest; tail long, far exceeding the points of the wings, nearly even or slightly rounded; tarsus moderate, or shortish, plumed below the knees for nearly half the length of the tarsus, stout, with large scutæ in front and behind; near the knee, posteriorly, the scales are small and reticulated; toes strong, outer-toe longer than the inner one, joined to the middle-one; middle-toe moderately long; claws well curved, unequal; inner claw very large, about equal to that of the hind-toe.

Astur trivirgatus, *Tem.*

22.—Jerdon's Birds of India, Vol. I, p. 47; Hume's Scrap Book, p. 116.

THE CRESTED GOSHAWK.
Gor besra, Hin.

♂. Length, 16; wing, 8·5; tail, 7; tarsus, 2·2.

♀. Length, 17·5; wing, 9·5; tail, 8; tarsus, 2·5; irides bright yellow; legs pale yellow; cere lemon-yellow.

The young bird is brown above, with pale edgings to the feathers; eyebrows white, and some white or rufous about the nape; below white, more or less spotted on the breast, abdomen and flanks with dark brown spots, least numerous in the male; tail pale ashy-brown, with four or five dark broad bands; thigh-coverts with transverse brown bands; a narrow dark line down the centre of the chin and throat; and two more, one on each side of the neck, not very distinct in the male, but becoming more so with age; an occipital crest of several elongated feathers; under wing-coverts white, with brown spots; quills and tail beneath light cinereous, with dark bands.

The adult bird has the upper plumage glossy dark brown, in some with an olivaceous tinge, in older birds with a dark slaty hue, especially when freshly moulted; wings and tail banded, the latter with four distinct dark bands; beneath white, the throat and upper part of the breast, with pale yellow-brown oval spots; the rest of the plumage beneath barred with rich yellow-brown, the bars broad on the breast, belly and flanks; narrow on the thigh-coverts, but all becoming more narrow by age.

The *Gor-besra* is one of the rarest winter visitants we have. As yet it has only been doubtfully recorded from the hilly wooded regions near Mhow; outside our limits, on the Neilgherries, it is not uncommon.

With regard to its nidification nothing definite seems to be known, but it is strongly suspected to breed in the more southern parts of India.

Astur badius, *Gm.*

23.—*Micronisus badius,* Gm.—Jerdon's Birds of India, Vol. I, p. 49; Butler, Guzerat; Stray Feathers, Vol. III, p. 445; Deccan and South Mahratta country; Stray Feathers, Vol. IX,

p. 371; Murray's Vertebrate Zoology of Sind, p. 72; Swinhoe and Barnes, Central India; Ibis, 1885, p. 56; Hume's Scrap Book, p. 117.

THE SHIKRA, *Hin.*

♂. Length, 12 to 12·5; expanse, 23; wing, 6·8 to 7·5; tail, 5·5 to 5·9; bill from gape, 0·78; weight, 5 to 6 ozs.

♀. Length, 14 to 15; wing, 8·25; tail, 7; tarsus, 1·9; weight, 8½ to 9½ ozs.

Bill bluish, dusky at tip; irides pale yellow; cere yellow; legs and feet yellow.

The young bird is dark reddish, or dusky-brown above; the feathers edged with rufous, most broadly so in the male; back of the head and nape a good deal variegated with white; tail light ashy-brown, with six dark bands, beneath white, with a central dark chin line; the breast and abdomen with large oval brown spots, longer on the breast, rounded on the abdomen; the thigh-coverts rufescent-white, with smaller spots; under tail-coverts with a few faint stripes. The male has usually fewer spots than the female.

The adult bird is pale ashy-grey above, darkest on the head, and with a dusky-reddish nape, only conspicuous when the head is bent forwards; tail with the two centre feathers and the two outer ones not barred, the others only barred on their inner webs; quills blackish-grey, with some dark narrow bands on the inner webs; beneath white, with a faint chin-stripe, not always present; breast and upper abdomen closely barred with pale rufescent, fawn-colored, transverse marks; the lower abdomen, thigh-coverts, and under tail-coverts pure white; irides deep orange color; cere bright yellow; feet dark buff-yellow.

As this plumage is not assumed before the fourth or fifth year, intermediate stages are common, and consist in the upper plumage becoming more uniform; in the bars of the tail becoming gradually indistinct; and in the longitudinal drops beneath changing to bars, gradually disappearing in some parts.

The Shikra is common throughout the region, frequenting gardens, cultivated ground, and open jungle. It is a permanent resident, breeding during April and May. It takes a very long time to make its nest, which is generally placed in a fork near the top of a tree; it is composed of twigs and is not very compact, scarcely so large as that of the *Turumti.* The eggs, three or four in number, are oval in shape and of a pale delicate bluish-white color, indistinctly spotted with very faint grey; the shell is smooth and glossless. They average from 1·56 inches in length to 1·21 in breadth.

GENUS, **Accipiter**, *Briss.*

Bill very short, curving from the base, compressed, with a very prominent festoon in the middle of the edge of the upper mandible; nostrils oval, oblique; wings rounded, the fourth and fifth quills nearly equal; tail long, slightly rounded or even slender; tarsi long, slender; the scutæ very smooth, and scarcely perceptible; toes long, slender; the inner toe considerably shorter than the outer one, but longer than the hind-toe; claws well curved.

Accipiter nisus, *Linn.*

24.—Jerdon's Birds of India, Vol. I, p. 51; Butler, Guzerat; Stray Feathers, Vol. III, p. 445; Deccan, Stray Feathers, Vol. IX, p. 371; Murray's Vertebrate Zoology of Sind, p. 73; Swinhoe and Barnes, Central India; Ibis, 1885, p. 56; Hume's Scrap Book, p. 124.

THE SPARROW HAWK.
Basha, Hin.

♂. Length, 12 to 13; wing, 8·5; tail, 6; tarsus, 2·25.

♀. Length, 15 to 16; wing, 9·5; expanse, 25; tail, 7·5; tarsus, 2·5.

Young bird yellowish-brown above, the feathers edged with ochrey, not much so in female; the quills banded on their inner webs; and the tail with four bands; beneath ochrey-white, with broad longitudinal streaks on the chin and throat, changing to bars on the breast, lower abdomen, and thigh-coverts.

The adult is blackish or brownish-grey above, white on the eyebrow and nape; the quills brown banded, and tail more ashy and lighter, with four bands, the last widest and with a white tip, the others somewhat indistinct in very old birds; the chin and throat pale ochrey-white, with brown stripes; the rest of the plumage beneath white, the feathers with brown shafts, and densely banded with reddish ochrey, in some specimens quite rusty; under tail-coverts pure white.

The adult female differs somewhat from the male in being paler and browner above, and in the lower parts being whiter, with the bars and markings more narrow.

The Sparrow Hawk occurs sparingly throughout the region, but only as a cold weather visitant.

Accipiter virgatus, *Reinw.*

25.—Jerdon's Birds of India, Vol. I, p. 52; Butler, Guzerat; Stray Feathers, Vol. III, p. 445; Swinhoe and Barnes, Central India; Ibis, 1885, p. 56; Hume's Scrap Book, p. 132.

THE JUNGLE SPARROW HAWK.
Besra, Hin.

♂. Length, 11; wing, 6·75; tail, 5; tarsus, 2; weight, 5¼ ozs.

♀. Length, 14·5; wing, 8·5; tail, 6·5; tarsus, 2·25; weight, 7 ozs.

Irides pale yellow; cere pale lemon-yellow; legs and feet pale greenish-yellow.

The young bird is dark brown, above the feathers edged paler and rufous, tinged with dusky on the cheeks and ears; tail light brown, with dark bars; beneath white, with a mesial throat stripe, and brown oval drops on the breast and abdomen, most numerous in the female.

The adult bird has the plumage above deep glossy olive-brown, with a blackish or slaty tint; the head and neck dusky-black; ears and face light dusky; the tail light greyish, with four dark bands on the centre tail-feathers, and six on the outer ones; throat white, with a mesial blackish stripe, and a few streaks of the same; the rest of the lower parts white, very closely banded with bright ferruginous-brown, mixed with dusky-brown; under tail-coverts pure white. With increasing age the brown of the upper parts become dark slaty-blackish on the head, and light on the tail, and the transverse bands of the breast tend to coalesce, and the lower belly to become whiter. In the female, after the first moult, the breast is marked with oval light yellow-brown drops, and the abdomen with broadish bars. The adult male differs from the female in being more grey on the upper parts; in the breast and flanks being almost ferruginous, and in the bands on the lower belly and thigh-coverts being fewer and lighter in tint.

The Besra has only been recorded from the Deccan and Central India. In both it only occurs as a rather rare winter visitant.

Sub-family, Aquilinæ.

Bill strong, more or less lengthened, straight at first, curved towards the point; wings moderate or long, 4th quill usually the longest; tail moderate or rather long, tarsus rather long, stout, bare or feathered; toes moderate, strong; claws well curved; of large size and robust make.

Genus, Aquila.

Bill strong, more or less lengthened, straight at base, arching downwards towards the tip, which is moderately hooked; upper mandible with the margin somewhat sinuate; nostrils oblique, oblong; wings long, with the fourth and fifth quills sub-equal and longest; tail moderate or long, rounded or graduated; tarsus moderately long, feathered to the toes; toes with reticulated scales, with some large scutæ near the claws, which are of moderate size and curvature; the hind-toe and claw powerful; the outer-toe joined by a small web to the middle-toe.

Aquila chrysaëtus, *Lin.*

26.—Jerdon's Birds of India, Vol. I, p. 55; Murray's Vertebrate Zoology of Sind, p. 74; Hume's Scrap Book, p. 139.

THE GOLDEN EAGLE.

Length, 36 to 40; expanse, 95 to 100; wing, 28; tail, 17; tarsus, 4·25; bill at gape, 2·5.

Irides clear orange-brown; cere and feet yellow.

Adult rich dark umber-brown, glossed with purple on the back and wings; the feathers of the hind-head and nape lanceolate, pale orange-brown, having a golden appearance in the sunshine; shoulders, thigh-coverts in front, and leg-coverts, with a tinge of the same; quills blackish-brown, white towards the base on the inner webs, and clouded with greyish-black; tail nearly square, the centre feathers somewhat elongated and narrowed, greyish-brown, with numerous dark markings and cloudings, or dusky-brown with numerous grey mottlings on the inner web, especially towards the base, almost white on the base in young birds.

The Golden Eagle is very rare, and only occurs within our limits, on the hills that separate Sind from Khelat.

Aquila mogilnik, *S. S. Gm.*

27.—*A. imperialis*, Bechst.; Jerdon's Birds of India, Vol. I, p. 57 (in part); Butler, Deccan; Stray Feathers, Vol. IX, p. 372; *Aquila heliaca*, Sav.; Murray's Vertebrate Zoology of Sind, p. 74; Hume's Scrap Book, p. 142.

THE IMPERIAL EAGLE.

♂. Length, 28·5 to 30·5; expanse, 69 to 76; wing, 20·75 to 23; tail, 10·5 to 12·5; tarsus, 3·38 to 4; bill from gape, 2·13 to 2·63.

♀. Length, 30 to 32·63; expanse, 70 to 85; wing, 23 to 24·5; tail, 12 to 14; tarsus, 3·75 to 4·06; bill from gape, 2·75 to 3·13.

Bill pale bluish-grey, bluish-horny at tip; cere, gape and base of lower mandible deep yellow, tinged green near nostril; legs and feet dingy-yellow; claws black.

This bird has two well marked stages of plumage:—

1*st.*—The general character of this stage is lineated. The under parts with broader or narrower pale centres to the feathers, and the upper parts with pale central stripes. What I take to be the earliest form of this stage has the head and nape brown, the feathers tipped and margined with pale yellowish-brown; the upper back, scapulars, and lesser wing-coverts darker brown, most of them showing faint traces of paler centres and tips, and some faintly margined slightly paler.

The lower back is buffy, a patch on the rump being mottled with brown, the upper tail-coverts being fulvous-white; the tail-feathers pale wood-brown, much abraded with dirty fulvous tips, and showing towards the bases traces of a mottled, paler, and darker barring.

The primary quills are dark-brown, almost black; the secondaries and tertiaries paler and dingier brown, with a mere trace of a fulvous-white tipping, but the tertiaries are a good deal mottled with fulvous-white; the median and greater wing-coverts are, here and there, tipped with fulvous-white, but many are not so; the chin, throat, sides of the neck, breast, and abdomen are pale buffy-brown; the feathers margined with darker-brown, which latter, however, is very narrow, and almost wanting on most of the throat feathers, while it occupies the greater portion of the feathers on the lower breast and abdomen; the tibial plumes, vent, and lower tail-coverts are dingy reddish-buff; the lesser and median lower wing-coverts are reddish-buff, more or less centred with brown, and the greater lower wing-coverts are mingled white and blackish-brown; the lineation of the lower surface is more obscure and ill-defined than in what I take to be later forms of this same stage. In the next form of this stage every feather of the head, nape, and upper back is brown (a soft hair brown), darker than the form above described, with a conspicuous narrow, fulvous, central stripe. All the wing-coverts and scapulars are tipped with fulvous or fulvous-white, the lesser ones narrowly, in fact with a mere spot at the tip—the larger ones more broadly; the rump, back and upper tail-coverts are as above described; but the tail is a dingy wood-brown, without any trace of bars, and broadly tipped with fulvous-white.

The secondaries are conspicuously tipped with white or fulvous white; the chin, throat, and ear-coverts are unstreaked fulvous; the breast and upper two-thirds of the abdomen are a warm, somewhat purplish-brown, with conspicuous, well defined, narrow, central fulvous stripes; the lesser and median lower wing-coverts are more mingled with brown than in the specimen above described, and the larger lower-coverts are greyish-white, mottled with blackish-brown, and the axillaries, which, in the form first described, were reddish-buff, mottled with brown, are in this one similar to the feathers of the breast. In another form of this stage the head and back resemble the form first described; the tail and wings the second; while the chin, throat and ear-coverts are very pale buff, and the breast and abdomen are of the same color, each feather narrowly margined with the warm purplish-brown.

Specimens in this stage vary greatly, independently of the points noted above; in the color of the thighs, vent and lower tail-coverts (which in some are nearly white, in others rufous buff), and in the extent and purity of the white, or fulvous-white tipping, to the tail and secondaries. The difficulty is, that these various differences do not go together. If the birds be arranged in a series, with reference to the comparative width of the central stripes of the breast feathers, which width varies, as above noticed, from less than one-fifth to nearly four-fifths of the total width of the feathers, and then turned back upwards, no corresponding progression in the lineation of the upper surface is observable, and, in order to obtain a regular series, according to the extent and amount of the lineations of the upper feathers, a totally different arrangement will be necessary. Adopting either of these arrangements, we shall still have no regular progression in the extent or purity of the white tipping of the tail, or secondaries, or in the color of the lower abdomen, vent, and leg-feathers.

Two birds, whose heads, necks, and upper backs correspond, differ entirely where the lower plumage, or perhaps tail-feathers, are concerned, and *vice versâ*. It is clear, therefore, that some birds change first below, others above; some earlier on the heads and others on the tails; thus rendering the determination of the comparative priority of the various forms doubly difficult.

The adult stage is well-known. The whole head, nape, cheeks, ear-coverts, and sides of the neck, buff or orange-buff; the back, scapulars (except a few which are pure white), upper tail-coverts, wing-coverts, primaries, and secondaries, chin, throat, breast, abdomen, leg-feathers, sides, axillaries, and wing-lining, deep blackish-brown; the lesser wing-coverts margined, and the upper tail-coverts tipped with fulvous-white; the lower tail-coverts white, and a good deal of white mottling about the tertiaries, which are a pale-brown; the tail grey, with a very broad terminal black band, occupying fully two-fifths of its visible surface, and above this, a number of more or less broad, irregular mottled, and imperfect transverse dark brown bands, which sometimes do, and sometimes do not, coincide exactly at the shaft.

This is what I take to be the perfect adult. In less advanced examples of this stage, the forehead, and more or less of the crown, are blackish-brown; the feathers of the chin and throat, as well as the upper breast, are margined, more or less broadly, with the same orange-buff as the head and nape.

The axillaries and lower wing-coverts are more or less mottled with rufous; the lower tail-coverts with rufous-brown; and the ground color of the tail, above the black tip, is pale yellowish-stone color rather than grey; the upper tail-coverts likewise are paler brown, and more broadly tipped with fulvous-white. In this stage, too, the changes are not synchronous; birds most advanced about the head being often least so about the tail; those most advanced on the upper, least so on the under surface, and *vice versâ*.

The amount of white on the scapulars, too, varies greatly; some have only a single feather, others nearly the whole scapulars white, and I have some specimens, perfect adults, as regards the plumage on every other point, but exihibiting no trace whatsoever of white on the scapulars.—*Hume*, "*Rough Notes.*"

The Imperial Eagle is by no means common. It occurs throughout the region, excepting perhaps Guzerat.

Aquila clanga, *Pall.*

28.—*Aquila nævia*, Gm.—Jerdon's Birds of India, Vol. I, p. 59; Butler, Guzerat; Stray Feathers, Vol. III, p. 445; Deccan, Stray Feathers, Vol. IX, p. 372; Murray's Vertebrate Zoology of Sind, p. 75; Swinhoe and Barnes, Central India; Ibis, 1885, p. 56; Hume's Scrap Book, p. 162.

THE SPOTTED EAGLE.

♂. Length, 25 to 26·5; expanse, 60 to 64; wing, 19 to 20; tail, 10·6 to 11; tarsus, 4; bill from gape, 2·3 to 2·7.

♀. Length, 27 to 28·5; expanse, 68 to 73; wing, 20 to 21; tail, 11·5 to 12; tarsus, 4 to 4·25; bill from gape, 2·3 to 2·5.

Cere, orbits, and feet dark yellow; irides deep brown.

Adult: richly empurpled brown on the scapulars, inter-scapulars, and lesser wing-coverts; the lanceolate feathers of the head and neck somewhat lighter brown, streaked paler, and the under parts generally lighter brown than the upper plumage; some larger and pure white spots on the greater wing-coverts, and two white bars tipping the secondaries and greater-coverts, as in *A. mogilnik;* the tibial plumes similarly spotted; the under tail-coverts, and generally the short tarsal plumes, are white; and the abdomen is more or less streaked with fulvous.

Young birds are pale brown throughout, lighter beneath; and in the intermediate plumage the feathers are dark, centred with pale brown; some have the plumage dark dull brown, with dingy-white markings.

The Spotted Eagle occurs throughout the district, frequenting tanks and marshes, more especially the well-wooded parts.

It is often seen in the early morning sitting in a slouching kite-like attitude, half way up a tree. Its favorite food appears to be frogs, but it does not disdain carrion.

It breeds about May; the nest is a large platform-like structure, built generally in a fork, near the top of a high tree, in the vicinity of water, and is composed of sticks and twigs. The eggs, one or two in number, are blunt oval in shape, of a slightly yellowish glossless white color, profusely spotted and blotched with faint yellowish and purplish-brown. They measure 2·75 by 2.

Aquila vindhiana, *Frankl.*

29.—*A. fulvescens,* Gray.—Jerdon's Birds of India, Vol. I, p. 60; Butler, Guzerat; Stray Feathers, Vol. III, p. 446; Deccan, Stray Feathers, Vol. IX, p. 372; Murray's Vertebrate Zoology of Sind, p. 76; Swinhoe and Barnes, Central India; Ibis, p. 57; Hume's Scrap Book, p. 173.

THE TAWNY EAGLE.

Wokhab, Hin. *Dholwa,* Wagree.

♂. Length, 24 to 26; expanse, 60 to 66·5; wing, 18 to 21; tail, 10 to 11; bill at gape, 2 to 2·25.

♀. Length, 27 to 28·5; expanse, 69 to 73·5; wing, 20 to 22·5; tail, 11 to 12; bill from gape, 2·25 to 2·5.

Cere deep yellow; irides hazel-brown; feet yellow.

Young bird, light fulvous, brightest on the head and throat, changing to pale dingy-brown on the back and scapulars, and to whitish-yellow beneath, with dark shafts; shoulders and lesser-coverts pale whity-brown; quills black; tail dusky, with faint dark bars.

At a later stage the bird is uniform fulvous-brown throughout. In an intermediate state, the abdomen is marked with fulvous streaks, and there are many specks and streaks of the same on the head and back of the neck. The adult bird is tawny-brown, with the head and throat dusky, or almost black; the feathers of the crown, and the neck-hackles, tipped with pale brown; the wings, breast, and lower parts deep fuscous brown; the breast slightly speckled, and the belly and wings spotted more or less with light tawny-brown; two wing bars, and the tip of the tail also light.

The Tawny Eagle is very common everywhere, and is frequently to be seen soaring with Kites, or perched on the top of a tree, even within cantonments. They breed from December to March, or even later; the nest, composed of sticks, is placed rather high up in a lofty tree, as a rule, near a village; the eggs, two in number (very rarely three), are broad greyish-white ovals, thinly spotted with yellowish-brown; unspotted varieties frequently occur.

They average 2·63 inches in length, by 2·1 in breadth.

Genus, Hieraëtus, *Kaup.*

Bill small, slightly curving from the base; commissure perfectly straight; wings not reaching to the end of the tail; tarsus short, stout; toes short, inner claw very large. Birds of small size, with a tendency to an occipital crest. The inner edge of the centre claw is somewhat dilated as in *Pernis.*

Hieraëtus pennatus, *Gm.*

31.—*Aquila pennata,* Gm.—Jerdon's Birds of India, Vol. I, p. 63; Butler, Deccan and Southern Mahratta country; Stray Feathers, Vol. IX, p. 372; Murray's Vertebrate Zoology of Sind, p. 78; Hume's Scrap Book, p. 182.

THE DWARF EAGLE.

♂. Length, 18·75 to 22; expanse, 49 to 53; wing, 15 to 16·5 tail, 8·25 to 9; tarsus, 2·3 to 2·5; bill from gape, 1·4.

♀. Length, 19 to 24; wing, 15·5 to 16·5; tail, 9 to 9·25; tarsus, 2·8.

Bill bluish-black, pale blue at base; cere bright yellow; irides pale brown; legs and feet pale wax-yellow.

Head and neck pale orange-brown; the feathers lanceolate, and streaked in the centre with dark brown; some of the feathers lengthened, entirely brown, forming a rudimentary crest; a narrow superciliary stripe, and a band from the angle of the mouth below the ears, and a central stripe on the chin, dark brown; the rest of the upper plumage sepia-brown; the middle wing-coverts, and some of the scapulars, broadly edged with whitish-brown, forming a conspicuous light band on the wings; tail dark brown, with a pale tip, the inner webs of the feathers barred indistinctly; plumage beneath reddish-brown, palest on the feathers of the tarsi, and the feathers streaked with dark-brown.

The young bird is white beneath, head and neck also with white edges to the feathers and the brown of the upper parts lighter, and the white markings on the wing more distinct; the upper tail-coverts also are whitish, and the tail distinctly barred on both webs. There is very generally a white shoulder spot at all ages, and the forehead is white in some.

The Dwarf Eagle occurs sparingly throughout the district. It is, perhaps, less uncommon in the Deccan than elsewhere. The nest, composed of twigs, is generally built on a high tree; the eggs, two in number, are similar to those of *Milvus govinda*, but are perhaps more highly colored. They may be looked for in February.

GENUS, **Neopus**, *Hodgson.*

Bill rather small, slight, bending from the base, much hooked at tip, with a slight festoon in the upper mandible; cere rather large; nostrils ovoid, oblique; wing very long, equal to or exceeding the long tail; fourth and fifth quills equal and longest; first quill short; second nearly equal to the third; the larger quills strongly emarginate; tail long, slightly rounded; tarsus feathered, somewhat feeble, of moderate length; toes short, unequal, the outer-toe very short, and the claw small; inner-toe very large, nearly as long as the central one, and stouter, and the claw much larger, longer than the hind-claw; all the claws moderately curved.

Neopus malayensis, *Rein.*

32.—Jerdon's Birds of India, Vol. I, p. 65; Butler, Deccan and South Mahratta country; Stray Feathers, Vol. IX, p. 372; Hume's Scrap Book, p. 187.

THE BLACK EAGLE.

♂. Length, 27·5; wing, 22; tail, 14.

♀. Length, 30·5; wing, 23; tail, 14; tarsus, 4.

Cere, gape, and feet deep yellow; bill greenish-horny, black at tip; irides dark brown.

Of an uniform brown-black, paler and duller beneath; upper tail-coverts barred with white; tail with some light bars; quills faintly barred with grey on their inner webs.

The Black Eagle occurs sparingly along the Western Ghats, but has not as yet been recorded from any other part of the district.

The very peculiar feet of this bird make it a very easy one to identify. The genus consists of this one species only.

GENUS, **Nisaetus**, *Hodgs.*

Bill moderately long, strong, deep, much hooked at the tip, moderately compressed; cere large; nostrils large, elliptic; upper mandible strongly festooned; wings moderate, fifth quill longest, tail long, nearly even; tarsi long, strong, but not thick, feathered to the toes; toes large, unequal; claws very large, sharp and well curved; the inner-toe and claw, and hind-toe and claw, especially very large.

Nisaetus fasciatus, *Vieill.*

33.—*Nisaetus bonelli*, Tem.—Jerdon's Birds of India, Vol. I, p. 67; Butler, Deccan, &c.; Stray Feathers, Vol. IX, p. 373; Guzerat, Stray Feathers, Vol. III, p. 446; Murray's Vertebrate Zoology of Sind, p. 77; Hume's Scrap Book, p. 189.

THE CRESTLESS HAWK EAGLE.

Length, 27 to 29; expanse, 64 to 68; wing, 18·5 to 20; tail, 11 to 13; tarsus, 3·75 to 4; bill from gape, 2·1 2·2.

Bill greenish-horny, black at tip; irides bright yellow, pale brown in the young bird; feet pale greenish-yellow.

Adult: above dark hair-brown, with usually some white about the head and back of neck; quills dusky-black; tail slaty-greyish, with about seven narrow dark bars, and a broad subterminal one; beneath white, with dark brown mesial streaks on the feathers of the lower part of the abdomen; thigh-coverts, tarsal feathers and vent nearly brown, the feathers centred darker, and the thigh-coverts, tarsal feathers, and under tail-coverts more or less banded with white, or with rufous in some In some old birds the entire ground color of the lower parts is rufous-brown.

The young bird is pale brown above, pale rufous or ferruginous beneath, in some nearly white; tail pale greyish-brown, with dark bars.

With each successive moult the white or ferruginous becomes purer white and the dark central stripe to each feather increases in size, more especially on the lower part of the abdomen.

The Crestless Hawk, or as some prefer to call it, Bonelli's Eagle, occurs throughout the region, but is nowhere common. It nests on ledges of rocky cliffs, which are often very difficult of access, owing to their choosing a site under a projecting crag. Th e nest is a huge affair composed of sticks, sometimes measuring four or five feet in diameter; the egg cavity is lined with green leaves; the eggs, two in number, are moderately broad ovals, measuring 2·75 by 2; they are of a pale greyish-white color, sometimes unspotted, but are generally thinly marked with yellowish or reddish-brown spots. They are seldom, if ever, richly marked.

GENUS, **Limnaetus**, *Vigors.*

Bill short, high at the base, curved, hooked at the tip, with a prominent festoon in the upper mandible; wing short; tail long, square; tarsi long, moderately strong, feathered to the base;

toes unequal, large ; claws large, strong and much curved ; head usually crested.

Limnaetus cirrhatus, *Gm.*

35.—*Limnaetus cristatellus*, Tem.—Jerdon's Birds of India, Vol. I, p. 71 ; Butler, Deccan, &c. ; Stray Feathers, Vol. IX, p. 373 ; Guzerat, Stray Feathers, Vol. III, p. 446 ; Hume's Scrap Book p. 206.

The Crested Hawk-Eagle.

♂. Length, 24 ; wing, 16 ; tail, 11 ; tarsus, 4.

♀. Length, 29 ; wing, 17·5 ; tail, 12·5.

Irides yellow, dun-brown in the young birds ; cere and feet pale yellow.

Young : pale brown above ; head and neck fulvous ; long occipital crest black, with white tip ; feathers of the head and neck white-edged ; beneath, white, with some small light fulvous or brown spots on the breast and lower parts.

There is less white on the wing-coverts than in the young of the last, and the bars on the tail are wider.

The adult bird has the occipital crest sometimes five inches long, and of as many as twelve feathers of different lengths, deep black, tipped with white ; the head and neck fulvescent-brown, with dark mesial streaks ; upper plumage glossy hair-brown ; the scapulars, interscapulars, and tertiaries, more or less black ; the wing-feathers banded more or less distinctly ; tail light greyish-brown, with three or four dark bands, the last one broader ; beneath, the foreneck and breast pure white, with a broad dark mesial streak to each feather, and three dark lines on the white throat, not so distinct, however, as in the last, from all the feathers being more or less streaked ; belly, flanks, vent, and under tail-coverts dark brown ; thighs the same, only a little freckled with whitish ; tarsal feathers mottled white and fulvous-brown.

The above is Jerdon's description, to which I will add an extract from *Stray Feathers*, Vol. IV, p. 356, by Mr. Hume :—

"The youngest birds of *cirrhatus*, when they first issue from the nest, have the entire head, neck all round, chin, throat and entire under parts white ; only on the crown and sides of the neck is there a slight fulvous tinge, and a few of these feathers have linear brown shaft stripes, and the flanks and the upper portion of the tibia have a pinkish fawn-colored tinge ; the entire chin, throat, breast, and abdomen, absolutely pure spotless white ; the crest black, with usually very little white tipping ; the tertiaries and secondary greater-coverts, conspicuously margined with white ; the tail with six or seven transverse darker brown bars, besides the subterminal one which is not wider than the others. A little later a buffy fawn-colored tinge spreads over the whole head and sides of the neck, a few of the feathers of the breast get a faint tinge of the same color, and these exhibit a linear shaft stripe; on the abdomen many of the feathers get a fawn-colored spot towards their tip, and a tint of the same color pervades portions of the vent-feathers and lower tail-coverts.

"Later, again, the whole head, nape, and sides of neck become a warm fawn brown, all the feathers now showing narrow, blackish shaft stripes. The lower parts are still chiefly white, but almost all the feathers of the breast and abdomen have a more or less triangular brownish, fawn-colored spot at the tip, and show a tendency to a dark shaft stripe; and in some birds at this time several of the feathers of the lower throat have conspicuous narrow black shaft-stripes.

"The sides become fawn-brown, though the feathers still are mottled white at the bases and the shafts are darker; the thighs, vent-feathers, and lower tail-coverts are now a warm, but brownish fawn color, somewhat irregularly barred with white; the tail has now only four bands besides the subterminal one, which has become conspicuously broader. (Sometimes the young bird, before exhibiting any black streaks on the side of the neck or on the throat, become nearly uniform warm fawn color on the entire lower surface, and even retains this plumage until it has acquired the adult tail.)

"Then (to return to the normal stage of progression) the black striping of the head, back, and sides of the neck, becomes more conspicuous; a black central throat stripe begins to be indicated, the warm fawny tint of thighs and vent becomes replaced by a wood-brown, the black shaft stripes of the breast become more oval, and the tail begins to approach the normal type with only three transverse bars besides the subterminal one.

"Gradually the brown of the vent and flanks creeps up to the lower breast; the breast spots grow larger and larger, and ultimately the white margins of the feathers almost wholly assume the brown tint of the abdomen. The entire white chin and throat have the feathers so broadly striped, centrally, with black, that only just enough white peeps through to give indications of separation between a black throat stripe, and two broad black moustachial stripes.

"The brown of the head and sides of the neck, though still warm, has lost the fawny tinge of the younger stages, and the black centres of the feathers have greatly increased in size.

"The tail has a very broad terminal band, of say 1·8 and inter space of 2, and three other bands each about an inch broad. The crest, quite black and untipped, grows to a great length. While these changes have been going on the whole upper plumage has been growing darker.

"As to the white tipping to the crest this is very irregular, the youngest birds and the oldest generally want it; birds of intermediate stages generally have it."

The Crested Hawk Eagle is confined to the hilly tracts of the

Deccan, where it is not uncommon; it is more plentiful at Ratnagiri. It is a permanent resident, but nothing certain is known in regard to its nidification. It has been observed at and near Aboo, but has not yet been recorded from Sind.

Limnaetus kienerii, *Gerv.*

37.—Jerdon's Birds of India, Vol. I, p. 74; Hume's Scrap Book, p. 216.

THE RUFOUS-BELLIED HAWK EAGLE.

Length, 22 to 29; expanse, 50; wing, 15 to 17·5; tail, 10 to 12·5; bill from gape, 1·5; tarsus, 3.

Bill leaden-blue; cere yellow; irides brown; feet yellow; claws black.

"The whole of the top and sides of the head, including the lores, cheeks, and ear-coverts, the back and sides of the neck, the back, scapulars, rump, and upper tail-coverts, and lesser and median wing-coverts, a nearly uniform blackish brown; the feathers all with more or less of metallic reflections, some greenish, some purplish; in some lights the whole of these parts appear to be almost, if not quite, black. The tail-feathers are a dark chocolate brown; the central ones, with two or three faint irregular paler patches, traces of where bars may have been; the lateral ones, with broad, but faint and irregular, paler and mottled transverse bars. The under surface of the tail-feathers, a sort of silver-grey; the shafts white, a broad ill-defined dusky terminal patch, and in all, but the exterior feathers, four or five somewhat narrow transverse dusky bars above this; the quills are of two colors, the one set which appear to be older, dingy hair-brown; the others, almost blackish-brown, with faint green or purple reflections. The inner webs in *all* are paler, except quite at the tips; and above these, there are dim transverse darker bars. The first five quills are conspicuously notched on the inner web, and the second to the fifth are emarginate on the outer web. The chin, throat, and breast are white; the feathers tinged towards the tips with pale rufous, and most of them with narrow, blackish-brown lanceolate shaft stripes. The whole of the wing-lining, (except the lower greater primary-coverts), axillaries, sides, flanks, abdomen, tarsal and tibial plumes, vent and lower tail-coverts, bright ferruginous; most of the feathers dark shafted, and many of those of the wing-lining, abdomen and sides with a conspicuous narrow, black, shaft stripe, and a few of the feathers just above the base of the tibia, very broadly tipped with blackish-brown, forming a very conspicuous patch." —*Hume's Stray Feathers, Vol. I, p.* 311.

Jerdon remarks in his Birds of India, that "this beautiful Hawk Eagle has been found in Central India, and in the Himalayas, but appears very rare. No other observer appears to have met with it within the district.

GENUS, Circaëtus, *Vieillot.*

Bill rather short, gently curving from the base, much hooked at the tip; culmen rounded, compressed at the sides; commissure nearly straight; nostrils oval, oblique; wings long, the third quill longest, or second and third sub-equal, fourth nearly as long, the first three quills emarginate; tail long, nearly even; tarsi long, plumed below the heel, clad with small, hexagonal scales; feet small; toes short, scutellate at the base of the claws; the lateral toes about equal; claws tolerably curved, rather short, of nearly equal length.

Circaëtus gallicus, *Gm.*

38.—Jerdon's Birds of India, Vol. I, p. 76; Butler, Guzerat; Stray Feathers, Vol. III, p. 446; Deccan, &c., Stray Feathers, Vol. IX, p. 373; Murray's Vertebrate Zoology of Sind, p. 79; Swinhoe and Barnes, Central India; Ibis, 1885, p. 57; Hume's Scrap Book, p. 217.

THE COMMON SERPENT EAGLE.
Jean le Blanc.
Sampmar, Hin.

♂. Length, 25·75; expanse, 70; tail, 11·75; wing, 20·8; tarsus, 3·7.

♀. Length, 29; expanse, 76; tail, 13·25; wing, 22.

Bill pale greyish-blue at the base, blackish horny at the tips; cere small, whitish, with a tinge of bluish-grey in places; irides deep yellow; legs dirty pale yellow; claws black.

Young: head and nape whitish; the feathers brown streaked; back and wings pale earthy-brown, lightest on the wing-coverts; quills dusky-black; tail pale ashy-brown, with darker bands, and the inner webs almost white; beneath chin to breast fulvous, with narrow longitudinal brown streaks; from the breast to the vent white, with a pale brown streak on the centre of each feather.

The adult is darker brown above and on the head; and the lower parts white; the feathers all marked with brown stripes, or spots, tending to form a denser zone on the throat and breast.

The head is large, full and puffy; the feathers of the head and neck rounded, not lanceolate; the wings reach to the end of the tail; the inner edge of the centre claw is conspicuously dilated into a cutting edge.

This Eagle is known by several trivial names, one of the best known being *Jean-le-Blanc;* it was called the Common Serpent Eagle, by Jerdon, on account of its penchant for snakes, to which habit also it owes its Hindustani appellation; it is also called the Short-toed Eagle.

It is found throughout the region, frequenting open plains, but eschewing the more densely-wooded districts. It breeds during the first three months of the year; the nest is generally built on trees, and is a large, loose, straggling structure, composed of sticks and twigs. The egg, there is only one, is a broadish oval, of a pale bluish-white color; the egg lining is a peculiar bright sap-green. The size of an average egg is 3 inches by 2·35.

GENUS, **Spilornis**, *Gray*.

Bill straightish at the base; wings short; head crested; otherwise as in *circaëtus*.

Spilornis cheela, *Lath*.

39.—Jerdon's Birds of India, Vol. I, p. 78; Butler, Deccan, &c.; Stray Feathers, Vol. IX, p. 373; Murray's Vertebrate Zoology of Sind, p. 80; Hume's Scrap Book, p. 222.

THE CRESTED SERPENT EAGLE.

♂. Length, 26 to 28; expanse, 58 to 63; wing, 18·5 to 20; tail, 12 to 13; tarsus, 3·9 to 4·3; bill from gape, 1·9.

♀. Length, 29 to 32; expanse, 67·5 to 73; wing, 19·5 to 21; tail, 14 to 15; tarsus, 4·15 to 4·5; bill from gape, 2·12.

Cere and orbits deep yellow; irides bright yellow; legs dirty yellow.

Adult: head black, the feathers white on their basal portion, and for nearly two-thirds their length, showing a conspicuous full black and white crest; above hair-brown; shoulders and lesser wing-coverts with small white spots, the quills with broad dusky bands; tail brown, mottled and clouded with white, and with two broad blackish bands; beneath chin to breast unspotted brown; thence to under tail-coverts pale brown, with whitish faint bars, and white ocelli.

The young bird has the upper plumage brown, edged with pale rufous, the crest feathers having more white than the adult; the tail hoary-brown, with three broad bars; quills brown, with darker bands, and the quills and medial wing-coverts tipped white; beneath pale whity-buff; the feathers of the breast darkest, and centred with brown; ear-coverts, and stripe beneath the eyes, deep black.

The Crested Serpent or Indian Harrier Eagle is very rare; one was obtained at Savantvadi by Mr. Crawford, and another in Sind by Mr. Blanford. These are, I believe, the only recorded instances of its occurrence within our limits.

Spilornis melanotis, *Jerd*.

39*bis*.—Butler, Deccan, &c.; Stray Feathers, Vol. IX, p. 373; Hume's Scrap Book, p. 230.

The Southern Harrier Eagle differs perceptibly from *S. cheela* of Upper India; the wings of the latter vary in the males from 18·5 to nearly 20 inches, and in the females from 19·5 to nearly 21; while in this present species they vary in the males from 17 to barely 18 inches, and in the females from 18 to 18·5 inches; the lower parts also are somewhat less conspicuously ocellated, and the barring on the breast, so conspicuous in adult *cheela*, is almost entirely wanting.

The Southern Harrier Eagle is a permanent resident and is not uncommon in the hilly tracts and jungles along the Western Ghats, but has not been recorded from elsewhere within our limits.

Genus, **Pandion**, *Savigny*.

Bill short, curved from the cere, rounded above; tip produced and much hooked; margin of upper mandible sinuated; nostrils small, narrow, obliquely transverse; wings long, reaching beyond the end of the tail, second quill longest, or second and third nearly equal; tail moderate, nearly even; the tarsus moderate, entirely covered with reticulated scales; toes quite free, outer-toe versatile, longer than the inner-toe; claws large, much curved, rounded below, nearly of equal size; soles of the feet covered with sharp pointed scales.

Pandion haliætus, *Lin*.

40.—Jerdon's Birds of India, Vol. I, p. 80; Butler, Guzerat; Stray Feathers, Vol. V, p. 40; Deccan, Stray Feathers, Vol. IX, p. 373; Murray's Vertebrate Zoology of Sind, p. 81; Hume's Scrap Book, p. 234.

The Osprey.

♀. Length, 26; wing, 20; tail 9; tarsus, 2·25; bill at gape 1·6; mid toe, 3·5.

♂. Length, 23·5; wing 19; tail, 8·5.

The bill black; gape and base of lower mandible pale lavender plumbeous; cere dark lead-color; irides bright yellow; legs and feet delicate sea-green; claws black.

Above, head and nape white, the feathers of the forehead and crown with dark brown stripes; upper plumage rich hair-brown; quills blackish; tail pale brown, with dark bars, whitish on the inner web; a dark brown band from the eyes over the ears; beneath pure white, with some brown spots on the breast, longitudinal in youth, broader in advancing age, and tending to coalesce in the fully adult.

The Osprey or Fish Hawk occurs throughout the region, but is nowhere abundant; it frequents the backwaters and lagoons on the coast, also the larger tanks and lakes inland, and is found occasionally along the courses of the larger rivers; it is perhaps more common along the sea coast. It probably breeds within the district, but there is no record of its eggs having been taken.

Genus, **Polioætus**, *Kaup*.

Bill somewhat lengthened, straight at the base, compressed, with a prominent sharp festoon; wings short; tail rather short, slightly rounded; tarsus feathered in front for one-third of its length, stout, covered in front with large transverse scales, posteriorly with some large, somewhat irregular scales, externally and internally with very small scales; feet large, toes nearly covered above with large scutæ; lateral toes nearly equal; middle and outer-claws about equal, less than the hind-claw; claws rounded.

Polioætus ichthyætus, *Horsf.*

41.—Jerdon's Birds of India, Vol. I, p. 81; Hume's Scrap Book, p. 239.

THE WHITE-TAILED SEA EAGLE.

Length, 27 to 29; wing 19; tail, 8·5; tarsus, 3·5; weight, 4 lbs. Bill and cere blackish; irides brown.

Adult with the head, lores, ears, chin, and throat light grey, the rest of the plumage light wood-brown, darkest above, lighter beneath, and deepening on the scapulars and wings; lower abdomen, vent, thigh-coverts, and tail white, the latter with a broad terminal dark brown band.

The young bird is lighter brown above, all the feathers edged and tipped with whitish; beneath pale reddish-brown with pale mesial streaks, and albescent on the under tail-coverts; tail mottled and clouded with light cinereous and brown.

Dr. Jerdon says: "This Fish-Eagle is found over a considerable part of India, but is rare towards the south. Mr. Elliot met with in it Dharwar. I never observed it myself south of the Nerbudda." And again: "I found its nest on several occasions; once near the Nerbudda, in a large tree."

GENUS, Haliaetus, *Savigny.*

Bill straight at base, longish, compressed, curved towards the tip, which is much hooked; upper mandible with the margin strongly sinuate; nostrils somewhat oblong, transverse; wings long, fourth and fifth quills sub-equal and longest; tail moderate or rather short; tarsus moderate, strong, plumed for nearly half its length, the lower half with large transverse scutæ in front and a short and more irregular series behind; or with a few and irregular ones in front above, and the whole of the rest reticulated with small scales, hexagonal, or irregular; toes large, covered with scutæ; outer-toe scarcely mobile; claws large, unequal, squared beneath, well curved.

Haliaëtus leucoryphus, *Pall.*

42.—*Haliaëtus fulviventer*, Vieill.—Jerdon's Birds of India, Vol. I, p. 82; *H. Macei*, Cuv.; Butler, Guzerat; Stray Feathers, Vol. III, p. 447; Murray's Vertebrate Zoology of Sind, p. 82; Hume's Scrap Book, p. 242.

THE RING-TAILED SEA EAGLE.

♂. Length, 29 to 31; expanse, 75 to 79; wing, 21 to 22; tail, 11 to 12; tarsus, 3·75 to 4; bill from gape, 2·25 to 2·43.

♀. Length, 32 to 34·25; expanse, 82 to 85; wing, 23 to 24; tail, 13 to 14; tarsus, 4 to 4·5; bill from gape, 2·65 to 2·88.

Cere pale bluish-green; nostrils, gape, and base of lower mandible bluish; upper mandible greenish-horn color; irides pale brownish-yellow; feet greyish-white.

Adult: whole head and neck pale fulvous, brownish on the head and nape; feathers of the neck long and lanceolate; interscapulars, back and rump rich brown; scapulars and wings dark brown, blackening on the quills; tail ashy-black, or dark cinereous, with a broad white central band; beneath, from the throat, reddish-brown, darkest on the lower abdomen, thigh-coverts, and under tail-coverts.

The young bird has the head and hind neck light brown; ear-coverts dusky-brown; the upper plumage brown, with the quills dark; tail black throughout; lower plumage pale brown; the wings reach to the end of the tail, which is very slightly rounded.

The Ring-tailed Sea Eagle occurs sparingly in Guzerat, but is far more common in Sind, where it breeds during November, December, and January. The nests are huge platforms, composed of stout sticks and are placed near the top of a high tree in the vicinity of water; the eggs, generally three (occasionally only two, more seldom four), in number, are greyish-white in color and measure about 2·75 inches, in length by 2·2 in breadth.

Haliaëtus albicilla, *Lin.*

42*bis.*—Murray's Vertebrate Zoology of Sind, p. 83; Hume's Scrap Book, p. 253.

THE EUROPEAN WHITE-TAILED SEA EAGLE.

♂. Length, 36; expanse, 72; wing 24; tail, 11·5; tarsus, 4.

♀. Length, 40; expanse, 80; wing, 27·5; tail, 12; tarsus, 4·5.

Male.—The cere and bill are pale yellow; the irides bright yellow; the tarsi and toes gamboge; the claws black with a tinge of greyish-blue; the plumage of the head, neck, forepart of the back and breast, with the upper wing-coverts greyish-yellow; the feathers all greyish-brown at the base, of the other parts greyish-brown, edged with yellowish-grey; the scapulars and feathers of the rump glossed with purple, those of the abdomen, tibiæ, and subcaudal region inclining to chocolate-brown; the quills and alular feathers brownish-black, with a tinge of grey; the inner secondaries inclining to greyish-brown; the shafts of all white towards the base; the lower surface of the quills and the larger coverts tinged with greyish-blue; upper tail-coverts and the tail are white, (generally freckled with dusky grey at the base); the down on the breast is pale grey, that on the sides darker.

Female.—The female does not differ from the male in color, and her superiority in size is often not remarkable.

Young.—The bill is brownish-black; the cere greenish-yellow; the feet yellow; the claws black; the bases of all the feathers are brownish-white; their middle parts light reddish-brown; their tips only blackish-brown; the head and nape are dark brown; each feather with a minute brownish-white spot on the tip; on the middle of the back and on the wings light reddish-brown is the prevalent color; the black tips of comparatively small extent; on the third part of the back there is much white, that color extending further from the base; the quills and larger wing-coverts are blackish-brown, with a tinge of grey; the tail feathers brownish-white in the centre, black towards the margins, with irregular white dots; the lower parts are of the same color as the back, or are pale reddish-brown, marked with longitudinal streaks and spots of dark brown; the lower wing-coverts brown; the tail-coverts white, with light-brown tips.

Progress towards Maturity.—In the second year the young exhibits little difference, being, however, of a darker tint on the back and wings. An individual at this age has the bill brownish-black, tinged with blue; its base and the cere greenish-yellow; the iris hazel-brown; the feet gamboge; the claws brownish-black; the head and nape are dark brown; the base of all the feathers, on the upper parts, is white; on the hind-neck and foreparts of the back that color, tinged with yellowish-brown, prevails, a lanceolate or obovate deep brown spot, being on each feather towards the end; on the middle of the back the brown prevails, on the hind part white, and the rump and upper tail-coverts are light brown, tipped darker; the scapulars are dark brown with a purplish tinge; the wing-coverts dark brown at the end, but most of the larger pale brown in the greater part of their extent; the quills black, with a purplish-grey tinge, the secondaries gradually becoming more brown, and all faintly variegated with light grey and brown on the inner webs; the tail is brownish-black, with a tinge of grey, and more or less finely mottled with whitish; the lower parts may be described as brownish-white, longitudinally streaked with dark brown, there being a lanceolate patch of the latter on each feather; the lower wing-coverts and feathers of the legs dark brown; the lower surface of the quills bluish-grey; the lower tail-coverts white, tipped with brown; the down on the breast pure white.

Remarks.—In this species the bill and iris change from dusky-brown to pale yellow, and the plumage, at first white at the base, and dark brown at the end, gradually loses its white, while the dark parts become paler and more extended, the final coloring being more uniform.

The tail forms no exception, for its basal white also diminishes but the white, which is gradually substituted for the brownish-black, spreads from near the end to the base.—*Macgillivray.*

The European White-tailed Sea Eagle occurs along the banks of the Indus; they are mostly immature specimens.

Haliaëtus leucogaster, *Gm.*

43.—Jerdon's Birds of India, Vol. I, p. 84; Butler, Deccan and South Mahratta Country; Stray Feathers, Vol. IX, p. 373; Hume's Scrap Book, p. 259.

THE GREY-BACKED SEA EAGLE.

Female.—Length, 30; expanse, 84; tail, 11·5; wing, 23; tarsus, 4; bill from gape, 2·65.

Male.—Length, 26·75; expanse, 74; tail, 9·8; wing, 21; tarsus, 4; bill from gape, 2·4.

Bill, upper mandible pale leaden-brown, bluish at junction with cere; lower mandible pale blue, brownish at tip; irides brown; cere and gape pale leaden color; legs and feet white, tinged more or less greenish-brown.

Adult: head, neck and entire under parts pure white; mantle and wing pale blue-grey; quills and tail cinereous black, the latter broadly tipped with white.

The young bird has the mantle and wing-coverts brown, the white parts fulvous-white, tinged with rusty-brown, and dusky, especially on the head, breast and middle of the abdomen; and the tail is dark with spots and speckles.

Wings reach beyond the end of the tail, which is much rounded or somewhat wedge-shaped. Its talons have trenchant inner edges, and the feet are rough beneath.

The Grey-backed Sea Eagle is not uncommon on the Sea-coast. A large colony frequents and breeds upon Pigeon Island.

They appear to subsist chiefly upon sea snakes, as the ground beneath their nests (which are generally built upon high trees) is strewed with their bones. It is also called the White-bellied Sea-Eagle.

SUB-FAMILY, Buteoninæ.

Bill small or moderate, rather weak; wings long or moderate; tail short, or moderately long in a few; tarsi rather long, with scutæ both in front and behind; feet short; hind-toe short.

GENUS, Buteo, *Cuvier.*

Bill short, sloping from the base, tip hooked, margin of the upper mandible very slightly festooned; nostrils large, oval, transverse; gape, wide; lores clothed with hair-like feathers; wings long, with the third and fourth quills sub-equal and longest, fifth quill nearly as long; the inner web of the first four quills strongly notched; tail moderate, or short, even or rounded; tarsi rather long, feathered on the upper third or further; tarsal scales broad, transverse; toes with four or five large scales at their extremity only; lateral toes very unequal; all toes short.

Buteo ferox, *S. G. Gmelin.*

45.—*Buteo canescens,* Hodgs.—Jerdon's Birds of India, Vol. I,

p. 88; Butler, Guzerat; Stray Feathers, Vol. III, p. 447; Deccan, Stray Feathers, Vol. IX, p. 374; Murray's Vertebrate Zoology of Sind, p. 85; Swinhoe and Barnes, Central India; Ibis, 1885, p. 57; Hume's Scrap Book, p. 274.

THE LONG-LEGGED BUZZARD.

Chuhamar, Hin.

♂. Length, 20·75 to 23·5; expanse, 50·25 to 59; wing, 16 to 17·6; tail, 9·25 to 10·5; tarsus, 3·2 to 3·75; bill from gape, 1·8 to 2.

♀. Length, 22·75 to 25; expanse, 56·25 to 62; wing, 18·2 to 19·75; tail, 10·18 to 19·75; tarsus, 3·2 to 3·8; bill from gape, 1·9 to 2·08.

Cere greenish-yellow; irides pale dun; legs pale yellow.

Young: head, neck, throat, breast, and belly white, some of the feathers streaked with brown, and dashed with buff; back and wing-coverts pale yellowish-brown, some of the feathers edged with rufous; quills dusky-brown, whitish on their inner webs, and the secondaries barred; tail with the outer webs reddish-white, inner webs dirty-whitish, barred with brown.

In a more advanced state of plumage the head and neck are rufescent-brown, with a whitish eye-streak; back and wing-coverts darker brown, with a tinge of purple in the freshly-moulted bird, and many of the feathers edged with rufous; quills greyish on their outer web, with a dusky tip, and whitish internally, except at the tip, which is black; tail pale rufous, or rufous-grey, with a darker subterminal band, and some indistinct bars, and ashy-white below; beneath, the throat is white, with dusky streaks, and the rest of the under parts fulvous-white, with dusky and rufous blotches, forming a sort of gorget on the breast and a more or less dark abdominal band; tibial feathers dusky-rufous.

The adult bird is yellowish-brown above, and on the throat and breast, purest on the head and breast, and many of the feathers, especially of the back, with dark centres, where the lighter tint indeed is nearly lost; quills, with the outer webs, greyish, the inner webs blackish from the tip to the deep sinuosity, white beyond; wings with a large white patch beneath, formed chiefly by the inner webs of the quills; tail reddish or cinnamon-grey, indistinctly barred; belly, vent, thigh-coverts, and under tail-coverts deep auburn-brown; the line of demarcation between this and the lighter tint of the breast abrupt and strongly marked.

The plumage of this handsome Buzzard varies considerably in all its different stages, and this has led to its being described under numerous synonyms. It still remains a *vexata quæstio* as to which is its adult plumage. The difficulty, as Mr. Hume observes in his Scrap Book, is the changes of the upper and lower surfaces vary in different specimens, some change first on the upper surface others on the lower, so that it is difficult to assign any chronological value to these changes.

The Long-legged Buzzard occurs, as a cold weather visitant,

throughout the region with which I am dealing, but is nowhere very common. It feeds on rats, mice and lizards, and occasionally small birds which, however, it always seizes on the ground.

GENUS, Butastur.

Bill, short edge of mandible scarcely festooned; nostrils small, oval, with a superior membrane; wings reaching nearly to the end of the tail; third and fourth quills sub-equal and longest; the first four emarginate.

Butastur teesa, *Frankl.*

48.—*Poliornis teesa,* Frank.—Jerdon's Birds of India, Vol. I, p. 92; Butler, Guzerat; Stray Feathers, Vol. III, p. 447; Deccan, Stray Feathers, Vol. IX, p. 374; Murray's Vertebrate Zoology of Sind, p. 86; Swinhoe and Barnes, Central India; Ibis, 1885, p. 57; Hume's Scrap Book, p. 286.

THE WHITE-EYED BUZZARD.

Teesa, Hin.

Length, 16 to 18·2; expanse, 36 to 39; wing, 11 to 12·5; tail, 6·5 to 7·5; tarsus, 2 to 2·5; bill at gape, 1·2 to 1·4.

Bill yellowish-white, dusky at tip; irides stone-white, pale brown or dun in the young bird; legs and feet yellowish-white.

Upper plumage rufescent-brown, feathers dark shafted; forehead white; a conspicuous white nuchal mark; wing-coverts mottled light brown and whitish, feathers dark shafted; quills pale brown with narrow dark bars, and dark tip; winglet dark brown; tail pale rufous with indistinct bars, plainer towards the tip; beneath chin and throat fulvescent, with a central dark chin-stripe, and a lateral one on each side, bounding the light chin; the rest of the lower parts hair-brown, banded on the abdomen, less so on the breast, with white bars; thigh-coverts faintly barred with rufous, and the under tail-coverts unspotted fulvescent-white.

The young bird is brown above, paler and rufescent on the head, with a white eyebrow, and a nuchal spot; wing-coverts much mottled with white, forming a light wing-spot; quills pale brown, banded darker and white beneath; tail pale rufescent, with dark bars on the inner webs, and on both near tip; beneath, white or fulvescent, some of the feathers streaked with brown, especially on the breast and flanks.

The Teesa is very common, and is a permanent resident, breeding principally in April. The nest is usually placed high up in a fork in an umbrageous tree, often a mango forming one of a small clump, generally an outer one; it is a loose structure of sticks and twigs, unlined; the eggs, from two to four (but most often three) in number are pale bluish-white, unspotted; they are oval in shape and measure about 1·8 in length by 1·5 in breadth.

GENUS, **Circus**, *Lacepede.*

Bill short, weak, high at the base, compressed, sloping, moderately hooked at tip, a slight festoon in the middle of the margin of upper mandible; cere large, covered with setaceous curved plumes; lores covered with small feathers and bristles; ears large; the coverts and the lower parts of the face partly surrounded by a ruff of small thick-set feathers forming an imperfect disc; wings long, third and fourth quills longest; tail long, slightly rounded; tarsi long, slender, well plumed at the knee, smooth, with large transverse scutæ in front; toes rather short, not very unequal; talons sharp, well curved; hind-toe short.

Circus macrurus, *S. G. Gm.*

51.—*Circus swainsoni*, A. Smith.—Jerdon's Birds of India, Vol. I, p. 96; Butler, Deccan, &c.; Stray Feathers, Vol. IX, p. 374; Murray's Vertebrate Zoology of Sind, p. 88; Swinhoe and Barnes, Central India; Ibis, 1885, p. 57; Butler, Guzerat; Stray Feathers, Vol. III, p. 447; Hume's Scrap Book, p. 298.

THE PALE HARRIER.

♂. Length, 17·6 to 18·5; expanse, 41 to 42·25; wing, 13·5 to 14; tail, 9 to 10; bill from gape, 1 to 1·2; tarsus, 2·6 to 2·8.

♀. Length, 18·65 to 20·65; expanse, 40 to 47·5; wing, 13·75 to 15·15; tail, 9·5 to 11·25; bill from gape, 1·2 to 1·38; tarsus, 2·65 to 2·92.

Male, above pale grey; wings and back darker; beneath greyish-white; rump white, banded with greyish; tail-feathers, except the two centre ones, banded grey and white; 3rd, 4th and 5th quills dusky.

The female is brown above, the feathers of the head and neck edged with rufous; beneath dark ochraceous with brown streaks continued on to the lower tail-coverts; upper tail-coverts banded whitish-brown; tail with the centre feathers greyish, the outer ones pale rufous, all with dark bands.

The above is Dr. Jerdon's description which is very meagre. I therefore add Mr. Hume's description, extracted from *Rough Notes* which is more voluminous:—

Description.—Legs and feet bright orange to lemon-yellow, according to age; claws black; irides bright yellow in adults, dark brown in the young; orbits yellow, dingier in the young; bill, cere greenish or dusky-greenish in the adult, somewhat yellower in the young, specially on the culmen, and hidden at sides by the bristles of the lore; gape and base of lower mandible blue, or sometimes greenish-blue; upper mandible and tip of lower mandible bluish or horn-black.

Plumage, male.—Lores closely clothed with tiny white feathers, with elongated, naked, black-brown, hair-like shafts; forehead, and streak above eyes, and feathers of orbits greyish-white, slightly paler than surrounding parts; the whole of the rest of the top of the head and nape to where the ruff joins in, grey, tinged with brown, most strongly so on nape feathers and with dark shafts; cheeks and ear-coverts grey, the feathers broadly edged with greyish-white, so as to produce a striated appearance. Feathers of ruff, which, as regards color, is very conspicuous, greyish-white with narrow, central, grey streaks; back of the neck, below, brownish-grey; patch of nape greyish-white, the feathers slightly darker shafted and some of them with the greyish traces of faint, brownish-grey, transverse, subterminal spots; the whole of the base of the neck behind, upper back and scapulars, a sort of ash-grey, more or less tinged towards the tips with brownish-grey, and the longer scapulars frosted with a purer grey; the middle and lower back a shade lighter grey, the white bases of the feathers showing through, more or less; upper tail-coverts pure white, with regular, broad, transverse, grey or slightly brownish-grey bars; the whole of the wing-coverts, winglet, tertials, and outer webs of secondaries and last four primaries grey, more silvery on quills, and browner on lesser-coverts; the median-coverts narrowly pale margined, and most of the other feathers of the corners narrowly, paler tipped; the second and last four primaries have the central halves of the inner webs pure grey, and the marginal halves white; the first primary is silver-grey on the outer web, dusky-grey on the inner, as far as the notch, and above this chiefly white; the next four are nearly black, with a good deal of silver-grey, however, on the outer webs of the first two, and of white, more or less mottled with dusky, on the inner webs of all towards the base; the sixth is dusky-grey on the outer web and tip, and paler and browner-grey on inner web, which has a broad marginal stripe, broadest towards base, where it occupies nearly the whole web of white irregularly mottled with grey; the central tail-feathers are a uniform silver-grey, slightly shaded with dusky on the terminal half; the next feather, on each side, is similar, but there are five or six white patches on the shafts, and traces of corresponding paler bars on the inner webs, which are very narrowly, paler margined; in each succeeding feather, the white patches on the shaft are better marked, and extend further and further across the outer webs, while the corresponding broad pale bars on the inner webs, at first only mottled with white, become pure white and larger, and at the same time the white margin of the inner webs spreads inwards, so that the two exterior feathers have the inner webs pure white, with only four or five, somewhat narrow bars of grey, or brownish-grey, (which do not extend to the margin), and here and there a little freckling, chiefly towards the base of the same color; chin, throat and front of the neck pearl-grey, whitish on chin; breast, abdomen, vent, sides, wing-lining and thigh-coverts pure white with just the faintest possible grey mottling or freckling in places on sides, and base of thighs; lower tail-coverts white, with rather brownish-grey, broad, incomplete, rather wavy, transverse bars, about one or two on each feather; inner surface of the wings mingled white and very pale grey, only the terminal one-third to one-half of the second to the fifth primaries blackish-brown; the first to the third quills are conspicuously notched on their inner webs, the second to the fourth emarginate on outer webs.

Female.—The lores dusky, covered with black bristle-like hairs, as is also the point of the chin; a patch (scarcely noticeable in some specimens) over the eye, and in front of it, white, tipped with brownish; below the eye, and front of the ear-coverts, somewhat purer, while a band, inside the ruff, from the base of the lower mandible over the ear-coverts to the sides of the nape, dark umber-brown, usually darkest towards the nape, the feathers narrowly edged with rufous, and centred darker; a dark streak from the posterior corner of the eye, meeting the top of this band; forehead, and a line from the forehead over the eye, and the last mentioned dark streak, nearly unstriated rufous-brown; the rest of the forehead, and top and back of the head, and nape, where the ruff joins in, and back and sides of the neck, rufous, the feathers all more or less broadly centred with umber-brown; the centres being larger, proportionably, at the base of the neck; upper back and smaller scapulars umber-brown, most of the feathers usually tipped with rufous; the longest scapulars somewhat lighter colored, with scarcely a trace of the rufous tipping; middle back often of a somewhat lighter brown than the upper back, and the feathers with conspicuous rufous tips or margins; rump feathers slightly darker, and with somewhat less conspicuous rufous tips; upper tail-coverts pure white, with only a spot or incomplete bar of dark or pale brown, or rufous, towards the tips; centre tail-feathers dark umber-brown, inconspicuously tipped with grey, scarcely perceptible in some and with four or five transverse grey bars, the broadest bars towards the tip; the next feather darker brown, conspicuously tipped with white or rufous-white, and with one broad, and two or three narrow, pale rufous, and greyish transverse bars, the rufous being chiefly next the shaft; the next feather much the same, but the white or rufous (some are whiter, some more rufous) of the bar, and tipping, purer, and a considerable patch at the base, on the outer web, mingled white and rufous, with only a tinge of brown; the second, exterior feather, nearly pure white, or a pale rufous, as the case may be, with subterminal, central, and basal bands of brown, which are more or less rufous in the two latter on the outer web; the exterior feather has almost the whole outer web rufous-white, and the interior more or less rufous-white, with traces of a subterminal and two other bands of mingled darkish rufous and brown; the whole of the lesser wing-coverts umber-brown, broadly margined with rufous or rufous-white;

the median-coverts the same color, in some conspicuously, in some faintly tipped with the same rufous-white tint; the greater-coverts of the secondaries, and the tertials themselves, still the same umber-brown, but only very narrowly (in some not at all) tipped with rufous-white; the winglet, primaries and their greater-coverts and secondaries, slightly darker brown, all but the first four primaries, and most of the secondaries, with a very narrow, whitish tipping, and the outer webs of the first primary, and the next three, which are conspicuously marginate, below the margination more or less silvered with grey; the inner webs of all the primaries above the tips, more or less white or rufous-white, with conspicuous, broad, dark brown bars. In some specimens the brown bars are so broad that the ground of the web appears brown, and the rufous interspaces appear like pale bars; there are traces of similar markings on the secondaries, most conspicuous in those nearest the primaries, and less so in those adjoining the tertials; chin white or rufous-white; the ruff in front, and on either side towards the nape, white or rufous-white; the feathers centred darkish brown; the whole of the front of the throat, breast and abdomen white or fulvous or pale rufous-white, the feathers all broadly or conspicuously centred with brown and rufous; the feathers of the vent, lower tail-coverts, and external thigh-coverts, pure white or pale rufous-brown, shafted, and with two or more irregular spots of pale rufous along the shafts; the axillaries mostly rufous-brown, with indistinct incomplete fulvous-white bars; the lesser under wing-coverts fulvous, or pale rufous-white, the feathers mostly darker centred; the greater lower wing-coverts mostly a brown or rufous-brown, and for the most part edged and tipped with fulvous-white or pale rufous; the longest of the lower tail coverts are rather conspicuously tipped with pale rufous.

Females differ considerably in the amount of rufous on the top and back of the head, back and sides of neck, etc. in some, the prevailing line is rufous, there being only very narrow brown centres to the feathers, but in others, the brown much predominates, the feathers having only somewhat narrow rufous margins; the extent and amount of the rufous tippings to the feathers of the back and rump varies much, as also the extent and depth of rufous in the tail, and on the lower parts.

Young.—Lores, forehead, a patch under the eyes, a streak over the eyes, to upper corner of the ruff, and a broad patch on the nape, (which latter has several of the central feathers brown tipped) white; bristles of the lores black; a patch in the interior corner of the eye, under the white line, and beyond the posterior angle of the eye, backwards, till it joins the top of the ear-coverts, dark umber-brown; the whole top of the head warm umber-brown, faintly margined with rufous, where it infringes on the white supercilium and white nape-patch; the whole of the nape, upper back, scapulars, and wings (except in some specimens some of the median-coverts) nearly uniform umber-brown, but the quills with a trace of darker banding, most of the median wing-coverts in some specimens so broadly edged with pale ferruginous or buff as to show but little of the brown, these edgings entirely wanting in others; the winglet, greater-coverts, secondaries, and most of the primaries very narrowly paler tipped; feathers of the lower back and rump the same brown as the rest of the upper parts, but each feather distinctly tipped with buff; the upper tail-coverts often pure white, one or two of them only with an ill-defined brown patch; in other cases marked as in adult female; two centre tail-feathers dark umber-brown, with four bars of lighter greyish-brown; the next four feathers the same dark-brown, but tipped and barred with ferruginous or buff, which is brighter and more extensive, as the feathers recede from the centre; exterior tail-feather almost entirely rufous-buff with two irregular, dark-brown bars, and a trace of a third; patch from the lower mandible, over the cheeks, and embracing the ear-coverts rich dark umber-brown; round this posteriorly, the ruff uniform pale rufous-buff, except just where it separates the white eye-streak from the white nape-patch, where the feathers are mingled with dark brown; sides of the neck, below the ruff, which is thus clearly defined, dark umber-brown; chin whitish, with black bristles at the tip; whole lower parts of the body, including lower tail-coverts, uniform rufous fawn or pale ferruginous; the lining of the wing the same, but paler, and the largest of the lower wing-coverts mottled with brown; the lower surface of the quills greyish-brown; the primaries very distinctly-barred and with more or less white replacing the brown; the first three primaries conspicuously emarginate on the inner webs, and the third and fourth on their outer webs; lower surface of the tail exterior feathers nearly uniform pale fawn, with only an indistinct trace of three ill-defined bars; the four next feathers umber-brown, with fulvous-white tips, and two well marked, fulvous-white, broad bars; the two centre feathers with scarcely a trace of paler tipping, and with three narrower greyish bars.

The Pale Harrier is a very common cold weather visitant to all parts of the district; it arrives in October, and leaves about the end of March, and does not therefore breed anywhere within our limits.

Circus cineraceus, *Mont.*

52.—Jerdon's Birds of India, Vol. I, p. 97; Butler, Deccan; Stray Feathers, Vol. IX, p. 374; Murray's Vertebrate Zoology of Sind, p 88; *Circus pygargus*, Lin.; Swinhoe and Barnes, Central India; Ibis, 1885, p. 57; Hume's Scrap Book, p. 303.

Montague's Harrier.

♂. Length, 16·5 to 17 7; expanse, 40 to 43·5; wing, 14·5 to 15·3; tail, 9·3 to 10·2; tarsus, 2·17 to 2·35; bill from gape, 1 to 1·12.

♀. Length, 18·6 to 19·5; expanse, 41·8 to 43·9; wing, 15 to 16; tail, 9·87 to 10·5; tarsus, 2·28 to 2·46; bill from gape, 1·07 to 1·2.

Male: above throat and breast darkish blue-grey, darkest on the back; the first six quills black, the next one lighter, changing to grey; secondaries grey, with a black bar; tail grey, the outer two feathers barred on their inner webs with bright rufous, the other three with dusky; belly, vent, under tail-coverts, and under wing-coverts white, with bold dashes of rich chestnut or reddish-brown.

The female chiefly differs from the female of the last in color, by the lower parts being whiter, and the streaks much larger, and more rufous-brown.

Such is Jerdon's description. To this I add Mr. Hume's description, which is much more detailed and is taken from his "*Scrap Book.*"

Description.—Legs and feet yellow; claws black; irides bright yellow in the adult, sometimes brownish-yellow in the female, almost white in one young one examined; bill black, dusky in the young; cere greenish-yellow, yellower in the young.

Plumage, Adult Male.—The whole head, chin, throat, neck all round, breast, back, scapulars, wings, (except the first seven primaries which are blackish), and central tail-feathers grey, of different shades; the neck, cheeks, and ear-coverts bluish; crown of the head and occiput (below which there is a white mottled nape-patch, owing to the white bases of the feathers showing through), here and there tinged with rufous brown; the scapulars infuscated and brownish; the back darker and more ashy, and the wings and centre tail-feathers more silvery; the secondaries have a broad, blackish, transverse band across both webs, forming a conspicuous wing-band (not unlike that of the common pigeon *C. intermedia*), and with traces of another, or in some specimens, two other bands on the inner webs; the central tail-feathers unbarred, the laterals with four very broad, transverse, dark bars on the inner webs, and traces of the same on the outer webs of some of the feathers, the grey fading as the feathers recede from the central ones, and to pure white on the exterior ones, and the dark brown bands changing gradually to dull chesnut on the latter; a broad circle round the eye whitish; the lower parts from the breast downwards, and the whole wing-lining (except a few of the longer lower-coverts, which are ashy-grey with large white spots), pure white; the feathers of the abdomen with narrow, rather pale chesnut central streaks; there are lanceolate chesnut dashes in the wing-lining; the axillaries are broadly and irregularly barred with blotches, and lower tail and thigh-coverts have the shafts of the same color, a few faint streaks of which are also generally to be seen mingling with the blue-grey of the breast.

Adult Female.—Forehead, and a band round the eye, slightly rufous-white; crown and occiput rufous-brown, streaked with dark hair-brown; a streak from the base of the lower mandible, widening so as to involve the whole ear-coverts, darkish brown, in some very dark; some of the feathers, commonly, very narrowly margined rufous; back, wings, scapulars, and central tail-feathers dark umber-brown; the quills and central tail-feathers darkest; the lateral tail-feathers paling as they recede from the central ones, which are unbarred, with four or five broad transverse, lighter and generally more rufous-brown bars, often more or less obsolete on the outer webs; the whole of the lower parts are light rufous-buff, with narrow, deeper rufous, shaft stripes; rump and upper tail-coverts mingled white, rufous-buff, and reddish-brown.

"*Young male* of the *second year* killed while undergoing his second moult."

The top of the head, and the feathers round the cheeks, a mixture of brown and rufous; ear-coverts grey; occiput varied with white; the nape, back, scapulars, tertials, and upper tail-coverts lead-grey; upper surface of all the tail-feathers, except the two in the middle, barred with shades of brown and rufous; middle tail-feathers, with the outer webs, uniform pearl-grey; the inner webs with fine dark brown bands on a greyish ground; wing primaries and secondaries blackish-brown; greater wing-coverts dark brown; lesser wing-coverts lighter brown, varied with rufous and two or three grey feathers; chin, and front of neck, pearl-grey; breast, belly, thighs, and under tail-coverts white, with a longitudinal rufous stripe on the centre of each feather; under surface of tail-feathers barred with greyish-white and brown; legs, toes, and claws, as in the adult male.

A *young male* of the *year*: a narrow frontal band, a line above, and a patch below and behind the eye, and two broad patches on either side of the nape white, the feathers of the latter with brown shafts; chin and throat whitish, bristles, at point of chin, black; the top of the head rusty-rufous; the feathers with more or less narrow, lanceolate or linear, dark brown shaft stripes; ear-coverts and a line extending to them from the base of the lower mandible dark brown, the feathers mostly narrowly margined with ferruginous; wings, back, and scapulars rich brown of different shades, palest on the upper back; rump, and lesser wing-coverts, more umber on the secondaries and longer scapulars, and greyer, except at the extreme tips, on the primaries; all the quills, the primary greater-coverts, back, rump, and scapulars, narrowly but conspicuously margined at the tips with rufous buff, or faintly rufous-white; the lesser and most of the median-coverts more broadly margined with brighter rufous.

The first few primaries silvered on their outer webs towards their bases, and with three or more irregular, dark, transverse bars on the inner webs, (which are mostly brownish-white above the notches), and faint traces of these on the grey-brown, outer webs, above the emarginations; all the tail-feathers tipped with pale rufous, most broadly on the external feathers; the central tail-feathers deep brown, with four broad, transverse, greyish-brown bars, greyer at the bases and broader towards the tips; the lateral tail-feathers similar in character, but the grey-brown bars change, as the feathers recede from the central ones, to rufous-grey, rufous, and rufous-white; and the deep brown inter-spaces change similarly to nearly pure cinnamon-rufous; the upper tail-coverts are absolutely pure white in some, in others with very narrow, rufous-brown, shaft stripes. From the throat, the whole lower parts, including the wing-lining, are pure, pale cinnamon-rufous; some of the feathers of the sides of the breast, with linear, dark-brown shaft stripes, and all the feathers with the shafts slightly deeper colored than the webs.

Montague's Harrier occurs throughout the Deccan, Rajpootana and Sind. I did not meet with it in Guzerat; it is of course a seasonal visitant only.

Circus melanoleucus, *Forst.*

53.—Jerdon's Birds of India, Vol. I, p. 98; Hume's Scrap Book, p. 307.

The Pied Harrier.

Length, 17 to 18; wing, 14; tail, 8; tarsus, 2·9; mid-toe and claw, 1·6.

Bill and cere black; irides yellow; legs yellow.

Whole head, neck, breast, back, upper scapulars, middle wing-coverts and primary quills black; the greater-coverts and secondaries, and some of the scapulars, beneath the others, pale grey; the lesser-coverts and shoulders partially white mixed with some grey; upper tail-coverts mixed white and grey; beneath from the breast pure white; tail pure grey, unbarred, paling on the outer feathers.

The wings reach nearly to the end of the tail. Sexes alike.

Dr. Jerdon remarks that the Pied Harrier is rare in the Deccan and Central India, but common in Bengal.

Circus æruginosus, *Lin.*

54.—Jerdon's Birds of India, Vol. I, p. 99; Butler, Guzerat; Stray Feathers, Vol. III, p. 447; Deccan, Stray Feathers, Vol. IX, p. 374; Murray's Vertebrate Zoology of Sind, p. 89; Swinhoe and Barnes, Central India; Ibis, 1885, p. 58; Hume's Scrap Book, p. 314.

The Marsh Harrier.

♂. Length, 19 to 21·7; expanse, 47 to 50; wing, 15·6 to 16·75; tail, 9·4 to 10·2; tarsus, 3·4 to 3·86; bill from gape, 1·4 to 1·5.

♀. Length, 21 to 24; expanse, 50 to 54; wing, 16·2 to 17·1; tail, 9·75 to 10·22; tarsus, 3·55 to 3·9; bill from gape, 1·5 to 1·68.

Legs and feet rich yellow, dingy or pale greenish-yellow in the young; the claws brownish-black; the irides are orange-yellow, sometimes with a pink tinge, deep brown, or brownish-yellow in the young; the bill is blackish or brownish-black, yellowish at the base, and bluish there in the young; the cere is greenish-yellow, or sometimes pale-greenish, in the young.

The young bird is uniform dark reddish umber-brown; in a further stage the head and throat are yellowish, or rufous-white, with dark stipes on the crown; in some the head is pure white, and the upper tail-coverts and base of the outer tail-feathers are pale reddish.

In the fully adult the head, neck, and breast are pale rufous, with dark brown stripes, deepening to dark red-brown on the belly and thigh-coverts; upper tail-coverts marked with red, white, and brown; the shoulders, secondaries, and tail pure silvery-grey; back, scapulars and tertiaries deep brown; primaries black.

To this Mr. Hume adds that, as the young bird advances towards maturity, there first appears a large rufous-fawn, or rufous-white patch upon the breast; then the rufous, or yellowish-white of the head and nape begins to run down the back of the neck, and margins of a similar color begin to make their appearance on the feathers of the upper back and the smaller wing-coverts; the color of the upper parts slightly fades, and a greyish tinge begins to overspread the outer webs of the primaries.

It is probable that the adult plumage, in which the shoulders, secondaries, and tail are silver grey, is only assumed by the male.

The Marsh Harrier is generally spread throughout the district, and (although a few may possibly remain to breed) is a cold weather visitant only. It frequents marshes, rivers, and lakes, and feeds chiefly on frogs, rats, and water insects.

It often carries off wounded duck and teal.

It seems instinctively to know sportsmen, and not infrequently follows them round a tank or jheel, with a view to dinner. I have often, by their help, retrieved wounded birds that would otherwise have been lost to me.

SUB-FAMILY, **Milvinæ**.

Bill typically small and weak, occasionally stout, rather straight at the base, and suddenly hooked, or curved from the base, and much hooked at the tip, rounded at the sides and compressed only at the tip; the margin sinuated or toothed; wings long; tail short and even, or long and forked; tarsi short, rather thick; toes short, broad; claws moderate, not very unequal.

GENUS, **Haliastur**, *Selby*.

Bill rather stout, straight over the cere, curved and hooked beyond margin of the upper mandible, festooned (as is very prominently seen in young birds); nostrils oval, oblique; wings very long, the 4th quill longest; tail moderate, broad, and slightly rounded; tarsi short, moderately stout, with a large plume of feathers at the knee, covered anteriorly and posteriorly with large scutæ; lateral scales small, reticulate; feet small, lateral toes unequal; claws not very unequal, grooved beneath, inner and hind-claws about equal; toes rough beneath, with sharp points.

Haliastur indus, *Bodd.*

55.—Jerdon's Birds of India, Vol. I, p. 101; Butler, Guzerat; Stray Feathers, Vol. III, p. 448; Deccan, Stray Feathers, Vol. IX, p. 374; Murray's Vertebrate Zoology of Sind, p. 90; Swinhoe and Barnes, Central India; Ibis, 1885, p. 58; Hume's Scrap Book, p. 316.

THE BRAHMINY KITE.
Brahmani Chil, Hin.

Length, 18 to 21; expanse, 54 to 57; wing, 15 to 16·75; tail, 6·5 to 7·5; tarsus, 2 to 2·25; bill at gape, 1·4 to 1·5.

Adult: head, neck, and body below, as far as the middle of the abdomen, white, with longitudinal narrow streaks of dark brown; the rest of the plumage rich chesnut-rufous, darkest on the interscapulars and back; quills black, chesnut internally towards the base; tail paling towards the tip.

The young bird is pale brown; the feathers of the head, neck, and lower parts lighter streaked, and the upper feathers spotted with fulvous or whitish; the tail is dusky, with a tinge of maroon.

The Maroon-backed Kite is found throughout the region, abundantly in Sind, but more rarely in Guzerat and Rajputana. It is a permanent resident, breeding on trees in February and March. The eggs, two in number, are oval in shape, greyish white in color, sparingly spotted with dull brownish-red; they average 2 inches in length by about 1·64 inches in breadth.

GENUS, Milvus, *Cuvier.*

Bill short, somewhat straight at the base, tip well curved and hooked, upper mandible with a rounded obsolete tooth, or festoon; nostrils oval, oblique; wings long, 4th quill, or 3rd and 4th, longest; tail lengthened, forked or emarginate; tarsus short, plumed above in front, with scutæ in front below; posteriorly naked to the knee, reticulate; toes rather short; claws moderate, unequal, and moderately curved; outer-toe slightly mobile.

Milvus govinda, *Sykes.*

56.—Jerdon's Birds of India, Vol. I, p. 104; Butler, Guzerat; Stray Feathers, Vol. III, p. 448; Deccan, Stray Feathers, Vol. IX, p. 374; Murray's Vertebrate Zoology of Sind, p. 90; Swinhoe and Barnes, Central India; Ibis, 1885, p. 58; Hume's Scrap Book, p. 320.

The Pariah Kite.

Chil, Hin.

Length, 22 to 25; expanse, 51 to 60; wing, 17 to 19; tail, 11 to 13·75; tarsus, 2 to 2·25; bill from gape, 1·5 to 1·8.

The males are generally the smallest, but large males exceed small females in size, so I have not given the measurements of the sexes separately.

Legs and feet from pale lemon-yellow in young birds to wax-yellow in older ones, pale greenish-grey in very young birds; claws black; irides varying from deep brown to pale or yellowish-brown; bill blackish-horny; cere and gape vary from greenish-grey in the young to yellow in the old bird.

Adult: top of the head, back and sides of the neck dingy or pale umber-brown; the feathers with a narrow dark shaft stripe, and a narrow stripe, towards the tips, on each side of this; the rest of the upper parts brown, darker on the first few primaries, paler on the tertials and lesser wing-coverts; tail tinged grey, and with obscure traces of transverse darker bars; some of the lesser-coverts, tertials, upper tail-coverts, and tail-feathers are narrowly but obscurely tipped paler; chin and throat whity-brown; the shafts darker; the breast, abdomen, lower tail-coverts, and tibial plumes, dull hair-brown, dark shafted; those of the breast with narrow, pale stripes on each side of the shaft stripes; the rest, in most birds, with a pale spot towards the tips.

Young bird: head, neck, breast, abdomen, and sides umber-brown, each feather broadly streaked fulvous-yellow or buff; chin and throat dingy-fulvous, some of the feathers inconspicuously darker shafted; back, scapulars, upper tail-coverts, and wing, (except the first few primaries which are almost black) a more or less rich umber-brown, glossed in many cases with purple, and every feather more or less narrowly tipped with fulvous or fulvous-white; the tail and lower tail-coverts much as in the preceding; in some specimens the light streaks are almost pure white, in others rufous-buff.

All intermediate stages are met with; the changes are not regular, and have no chronological value, and even amongst adult birds considerable variations occur.

The Pariah Kite is common everywhere, and is a most important feature in an Indian landscape. To visitors from England, on their first arrival in Bombay Harbour, (which is literally swarming with these birds) they must appear strange and their numbers incredible, unaccustomed as they (the visitors) are to the presence of birds of prey. They hang round the ships on the eager look-out for scraps of food, which sailors and others amuse themselves by throwing to them; long before the scrap reaches the water, it is pounced upon by one of the kites, who rarely misses a fair chance. If the scrap be small, it is devoured upon the wing; if large, the kite perches upon the rigging, but is not allowed to consume the morsel in peace as the other kites try to get it from him, and it, in general, changes hands, or rather feet, several times before it is finally disposed of. Garbage washed through the scupper holes, if at all eatable, is eagerly pounced upon; in fact, they are excellent scavengers, inland as well as in the harbour. The kite is fearless and venturesome in the pursuit of food; it has been known to swoop down on, and snatch food from the hand of a child, or even a grown up person; meat or other food in a plate, carried in hand, is not safe from their attacks, and it would be the height of folly to carry anything eatable on the head (the usual custom with natives in this country), unless it was well covered over. They are easily caught, by placing a light blanket on the ground and throwing a piece of meat upon it. The kite swoops down on the meat, its claws become entangled in the blanket, and the bird can be secured before it can release itself. Soldiers often amuse themselves in this way, and after cutting the webs of the quills and tail-feathers into fantastic shapes, let them go.

Kites, although far more numerous near the haunts of man, are by no means uncommon elsewhere. A camp is sure to be infested by some scores of them; they seem to know instinctively when a meal is under preparation, and show increased activity at these times. They have a peculiar habit of assembling together in some favorite spot at the close of the day before retiring to roost.

All writers on the subject seem to agree that they breed during the first three months in the year, and a nest taken on Christmas day has been spoken of as exceptionally early. I have taken nests from October to April, not in one year, or in one district only, but habitually, as the following extracts from my nesting memoranda will show:—

	From.	To.
Aboo	7th October, 1876	8th April, 1877.
Deesa	20th October, 1876	7th April, 1877.
"	25th October, 1877	25th March, 1878.
Hyderabad, Sind ...	5th November, 1878	10th March, 1879.
" " ...	8th November, 1880	5th April, 1881.
Mhow	15th October, 1881	
Poona	25th October, 1881	20th March, 1882.
Neemuch	4th December, 1883	9th April, 1884.
"	5th October, 1884	31st March, 1885.

Most of these nests were observed inside cantonment limits; indeed, in the breeding season, there is scarcely a compound, containing a suitable tree, that is not tenanted by a pair of these birds; in fact, they have a decided penchant for breeding in the vicinity of man. This, considering the persecution they receive at times, on account of the havoc they make in a brood of chickens, is not a little to be wondered at. A pair of kites with their hungry brood are not desirable neighbours near a poultry yard. I am inclined to think that they have two broods in a year; more especially as I notice in Poona that a nest in a *neem* tree in my garden was occupied twice in the same season, whether by the same birds or not I cannot say. The nests are more numerous in the months of November and February than at other times; this also points to two broods in the year.

The nests are clumsy structures, often of large size, built generally in a stout fork, or junction of the limbs, but occasionally on a horizontal bough of a tree. The eggs are usually two (rarely three) in number, broad oval in shape, greyish-white in color, boldly and handsomely blotched, streaked, and spotted bright red-brown. They vary much in coloring. In size they average 2·2 inches in length by about 1·8 in breadth.

Milvus melanotis, *Tem & Schl.*

56*bis.*—*Milvus major*, Hume.—Sind, Stray Feathers, Vol. I, p. 160; Butler, Bombay; Stray Feathers, Vol. IX, p. 375; Murray's Vertebrate Zoology of Sind, p. 91; Hume's Scrap Book, p. 326.

THE LARGE PARIAH KITE.

Length, 26·75, 27·75; wing, 21, 21·5; tail, 13·3, 13·75; tarsus, 2·5, 2·4; bill at gape, 1·75, 1·78.

Adult Female.—Bill and claws horny-black; legs dull yellow; toes mingled dingy-greenish and yellow.

Plumage.—General plumage much as in the common kite.

There appears to be a set controversy regarding the distinctness of this from *M. govinda.* I have never met with the bird myself, although I have constantly been on the look-out for it. Mr. Hume saw several specimens in the *dhunds* of Upper Sind, and obtained one in Bombay Harbour.

GENUS, Pernis, *Cuvier.*

Bill rather small, gently curving from the base, the tip very slightly hooked; margin of the upper mandible almost straight, or very feebly sinuated; nostrils narrow, oblique; the lores covered with small scale-like feathers; wings moderate, fourth quill longest, the second to the sixth sinuate internally; tail rather long, slightly rounded; tarsi short, half plumed in front, covered with small reticulated scales; toes with transverse scales, entire at the roots of the nails, elsewhere divided; lateral toes about equal, free, or barely united to the mid-toe; nails unequal, only moderately curved; middle-claw dilated internally.

Pernis ptilorhynchus, *Tem.*

57.—*Pernis cristata,* Cuv.—Jerdon's Birds of India, Vol. I, p. 108; Butler, Guzerat; Stray Feathers, Vol. III, p. 448;

Deccan, Stray Feathers, Vol. IX, p. 375; Swinhoe and Barnes, Central India; Ibis, 1885, p. 58; Hume's Scrap Book, p. 330.

THE HONEY BUZZARD.

♂. Length, 24 to 25·5; expanse, 49 to 54; wing, 15·5 to 16; tail, 10·3 to 11; bill from gape, 1·4 to 1·45.

♀. Length, 26 to 28; expanse, 55 to 57; wing, 15·75 to 17·25; tail, 11·5 to 12·75; bill from gape, 1·63 to 1·76.

Young bird: brown above, the feathers more or less edged lighter; head and neck usually paler, sometimes rufous-brown, at other times whitish, with central dark streaks, more or less developed; beneath white, sometimes only faintly streaked, at times with large streaks, more rarely with large oval brown drops, and with or without a dark central chin-stripe, and two lateral ones.

In some birds, especially those from Southern India, there is a well marked occipital crest of several graduated feathers, generally deep brown or almost black.

In a further stage the brown above becomes darker and more uniform; and the lower parts assume a pale rufous brown tinge, with the central streak more or less developed, according as it was in the young bird, and the incomplete tail bands are more clouded.

The adult has the plumage above rich brown; the head and lores generally, but not always, suffused with ashy-grey, and the lower parts uniform darkish-brown, with the dark streak almost obliterated; the tail is brownish-ashy, faintly clouded with dusky, and with two wide dark black bars, and a third, almost concealed by the upper tail-coverts; the terminal bar is tipped white or greyish.

The wings reach to about three inches from the end of the tail; the gape is short, only reaching to the anterior part of the eye.

In most birds in a transition state the feathers of the lower parts are banded brown and white, especially on the lower abdomen, thigh-coverts, &c., and some of these feathers are generally to be found at all ages.

Mr. Hume, after giving very detailed descriptions in his "*Scrap Book*," adds: "Almost every possible combination of the varying plumage, and shades of color, of different parts, above described, may be met with."

Jerdon omits giving the colors of the soft parts; the omission has been well supplied by Mr. Hume, whom I now quote:—

"The legs and feet, which are very full and puffy, vary from dingy yellowish-white in the young to bees wax-yellow in old adults; scutellation well marked and reticulate (the plates somewhat concave, especially at back of tarsus), except about three or four transverse scutæ at the tip of all the toes; a mere trace of a connecting membrane between the central and outward toes at the base; claws black, and except the mid-toe claw, compressed; hind-claw much curved, and mid-claw with the interior margin usually much dilated, especially towards the tip; irides brilliant yellow, duller or slightly brownish in younger birds; cere black, greenish at nostrils and towards commissure; gape and two-thirds of the commissure from gape, and greater portion of lower mandible, pale blue; greater portion of upper mandible and tip of lower black; a small dingy-greenish patch on each side of the lower mandible towards the base; tongue moderate, obtuse, entire, rather stiff and membraneous towards the tip (where it is slightly emarginate) and margins."

With the exception of Sind, the Honey Buzzard is more or less common throughout the region; it occurs more plentifully in well-wooded districts; it is a permanent resident, and breeds during May and June. The nest is generally placed at some height in a fork of a tree, and is composed of twigs, lined with dead leaves; the eggs, two in number, are very broad oval or nearly spherical in shape; they are white, or buffy-white, in color, thickly clouded, blotched, or capped with deep reddish-brown or blood-red; they measure 2 inches in length, by about 1·7 inches in breadth.

GENUS, **Elanus**, *Savigny.*

Bill very small, wide at the base, compressed at the tip, which is much hooked and lengthened; edge of upper mandible slightly sinuated; cere short; nostrils large, oval, longitudinal; wings very long, pointed, second quill longest, the first emarginate near the tip; tail short, almost even, or emarginate; tarsi short, thick, weak, plumed above, covered with reticulated very small roundish scales beneath; toes thick, soft, free, unequal; outer toe shorter than the inner one; claws rather large, middle one keeled, others rounded.

Elanus cœruleus, *Desf.*

59.—*Elanus melanopterus*, Daud.—Jerdon's Birds of India, Vol. I, p. 112; Butler, Guzerat; Stray Feathers, Vol. III, p. 449; Deccan, Stray Feathers, Vol. IX, p. 375; Murray's Vertebrate Zoology of Sind, p. 92; Swinhoe and Barnes, Central India; Ibis, 1885, p. 58; Hume's Scrap Book, p. 338.

THE BLACK-WINGED KITE.

Length, 12 to 13; expanse, 34 to 35; wing, 10 to 11·75; tail, 5·25 to 5·75; tarsus, 1·1 to 1·3; bill from gape, 0·95 to 1·15.

Legs and feet bright yellow; claws black; bill black, cere and base of lower mandible yellow; irides bright crimson in the adult, yellowish-pink or bright yellow in the young.

Plumage.—Adult: forehead a narrow streak above the dark supercilium; the anterior portion of the lores, the chin, cheeks, ear-coverts, throat and whole lower parts, wing-lining, edge of the wing, and all but the central tail-feathers white; the external webs of all, but the two exterior on each side of these, more or less faintly tinged grey; posterior portion of lores, a narrow supercilium, a small patch of coverts just at the origin of the primaries, nearly hidden by the winglet, (which is grey and not black, as Dr. Jerdon gives it), and the whole of the lesser-coverts, and the median, secondary, and tertiary coverts black; the wing patch more or less glossy, with the browner bases of the feathers showing through, and usually with more or less of a greyish bloom most conspicuous over the forearm; the rest of the upper plumage grey, (of very different shades in different individuals, but always darkest on the primaries, scapulars and interscapulary region) which varies from a full slate-grey to a pale almost pearl-grey.

The Black-winged Kite is more or less common throughout the whole district; it is a permanent resident, but I have been unable to ascertain anything in regard to its breeding, and the published accounts are at present misleading.

Family, **Strigidæ**.

Head large, densely feathered; eyes surrounded with a radiating circle of feathers, forming the facial disc, which is bounded in some by a ruff of close set feathers; eyes large, directed forwards; bill short, usually covered by recumbent setæ; ears large; feet usually feathered to the toes; outer-toe reversible, generally shorter than the inner one.

Sub-family, **Striginæ**.

Head very large, disc complete, occupying the whole face; ear-conch very large; ears operculated; wings long; tail short; tarsus long, more or less plumed; toes reticulated, with one or two scutæ at the root of the claws.

Genus, **Strix**, *Linnæus*.

Bill rather long, straightish at base, curved at the tip, somewhat shallow and feeble, with large nasal fossæ, and long lunated nostrils; operculum somewhat tetragonal; wings reaching beyond the tail, which is short, and nearly even, or slightly rounded; second quill longest, first nearly equal to it, third only a little shorter; tarsi long and slender, rather scantily feathered; toes moderate, scutellate above, slender; nails sub-equal, large, well curved, middle one pectinated; outer-toe shorter than the inner, united to the middle one by a membrane, and reversible.

Strix javanica, *Gm.*

60.—Jerdon's Birds of India, Vol. I, p. 117; Butler, Guzerat; Stray Feathers, Vol III, p. 449; Deccan, Stray Feathers, Vol. IX, p. 375; Murray's Vertebrate Zoology of Sind, p. 101; *Strix indica*, Blyth; Hume's Scrap Book, p. 342.

The Indian Screech Owl.

Length, 13 to 15; expanse, 37 to 43; wing, 11 to 12; tail, 5·75 to 6·2; tarsus, 2·5 to 2·8; bill from gape, 1·5 to 1·75.

Above, pale yellow-buff, beautifully mottled with light grey, each feather tipped with a white spot, edged darker; quills and tail darker and somewhat fulvous, with distinct mottled bands and specks between them; disc white, with a patch of rufous at the inner corner of the eye; ruff yellow and brown; all beneath, including the under wing-coverts, white in some, pale yellowish-buff in others; the feathers of the breast and abdomen with small black specks and spots.

The tarsus is feathered to the feet, but the feathers become very sparse and bristly towards the latter, and are little more than bristles at the foot; the toes are fleshy or dirty white, or light-brown with a pinkish tinge, thinly covered on the whole upper surface with whitish bristles; the claws horny-brown, tinged only with brown on the ridges; bill slightly yellowish-white, faintly tinged with pinkish towards the cere, which is fleshy; irides brown, sometimes almost black.

The Indian Screech Owl occurs throughout the region, but is nowhere common, except perhaps in the Deccan.

It is a permanent resident, and breeds from February to June, in holes of trees, rocks, and similar situations; the eggs, three or four in number are less spherical than those of Owls usually are, measuring 1·75 inches in length by 1·3 in breadth; they are white with a creamy tinge.

Sub-family, **Syrniinæ**.

Head not so large as in the last family and the disc incomplete above; no ear-tufts; wings moderate, somewhat rounded; the first four or five quills emarginate; tarsus short, stout, well feathered; mid-toe longer than the inner one; claw dilated internally, as are the toes also partially; tail slightly lengthened, and rounded or graduated.

Strix candida, *Tick.*

61.—Jerdon's Birds of India, Vol. I, p. 118; Hume's Scrap Book, p. 345.

The Grass Owl.

Length, 14; wing, 14; tail, 4·5; tarsus, 3·5.

Bill horny; irides very dark brown; legs livid, above tawny yellow; the feathers brown, yellowish at base and with a terminal white spot; the quills fulvous-yellow, with distinct brown bars; tail pale yellow, with four dark brown bars, the terminal one mottled at the ending; disc fulvous-white, with a dark brown spot at the inner angle of the eye; ruff dark fulvous; beneath yellowish-white, with small brown specks; tarsus and toes with a few scattered bristles, scarcely plumed at the knee; the wings reach three inches beyond the tail; the claws are blunter and less curved than in the last.

Dr. Jerdon procured the Grass Owl in Central India, as did

also Colonel Tickell. Neither Colonel Swinhoe or myself met with it there.

GENUS, **Syrnium**, *Savigny*.

The characters are the same as those of the sub-family.

Syrnium indranee, *Sykes*.

63.—Jerdon's Birds of India, Vol. I, p. 121; Butler, Deccan; Stray Feathers, Vol. IX, p. 375; *Bulaca indranee*, Sykes; Hume's Scrap Book, p. 347.

THE BROWN WOOD OWL.

Length, 19 to 21; wing, 13 to 14; tail, 8 to 9; tarsus, 2·4. Toes feathered for three-quarters of their length, and with strong scutæ beyond; the inner claw is the largest, the outer one about equal to the hind-claw; the wings reach nearly to the end of the tail.

Above, hair-brown, darkest on the head and neck, the greater-coverts, scapulars, and tertiaries banded with white, the outer scapulars being almost white with brown bars; rump and upper tail-coverts also faintly barred with fulvous; quills brown, barred with pale fulvous on both webs and with narrow whitish bars and a white tip; disc, black round the eye, with a pale whitish upper edge or supercilium, rufous externally; ruff brown with some white markings; throat below the ruff white; body beneath pale rufous-white, narrowly and closely barred with brown; quills and tail beneath dusky-brown, with white bars; bill pale greenish; irides deep brown; claws horny-reddish.

The Brown Wood Owl appears to be very uncommon, and is confined to the Western Ghats and forests in the vicinity. It has been procured at Ratnagiri and at Mahableshwar. Nothing appears to be known in regard to its nidification; in fact, Mr. Hume and others seem somewhat to doubt the distinctness of this and *S. newarense*, but as Jerdon points out the present is a considerably smaller bird.

Syrnium occellatum, *Less*.

65.—*S. sinense*, Lath.—Jerdon's Birds of India, Vol. I, p. 123; Butler, Guzerat; Stray Feathers, Vol. V, p. 208; Deccan, Stray Feathers, Vol. IX, p. 376; Hume's Scrap Book, p. 353.

THE MOTTLED WOOD OWL.

Length, 17·9 to 19·2; expanse, 45 to 50·5; wing, 13 to 15; tail, 7 to 8·5; tarsus, 2 to 2·4; bill from gape, 1·6 to 1·7.

Bill black, paler, and greyish on lower mandible; eyelids orange; irides brown, deep in some, lighter in others; claws sharp, slightly curved, middle claw dilated on inner edge.

General plumage: above, rich tawny-yellow, the feathers of the head and nape spotted with black and white, each plume having a blackish tip, and crossed by an interrupted white band; feathers of the back, scapulars, wing-coverts, and upper tail-coverts beautifully mottled and speckled with dusky and white; quills tawny at their base, dusky at the tip, with pale mottled bands; inner webs tawny, with brown bands; tail much the same, the mottled bars on both webs of the centre tail-feathers, but on the outer web and tip only of the others; disc mottled white, brown, and fulvous; the ruff dark-brown, beneath the chin whitish; the rest of the body beautifully banded white and brown, each feather being white, with numerous narrow bars of brown; tarsal feathers the same; the toes clad nearly to the end. Some specimens are much tinted with fulvous beneath.

The Mottled Wood Owl is not uncommon in the Deccan, and it has been obtained in Guzerat. I procured it at Neemuch in Central India, but it has not, as yet, been recorded from Sind.

It is a permanent resident where found, and breeds during the month of March; the eggs, two in number, are deposited in a cavity in a tree, or in the depression at the fork of two large branches. There is no nest to speak of, except, perhaps, a few dead leaves that appear to have fallen there by accident; the eggs are rather roundish ovals, white in color, occasionally with a faint tinge of cream; they measure 2 inches in length by about 1·7 in breadth.

SUB-FAMILY, **Asioninæ.**

Head large, with two aigrettes, or plumes of lengthened feathers on each side of the forehead; orifice of the ears large, lunate, operculate; wings long, second quill longest, and third quill sub-equal to it; tail moderate, or longish, nearly even; facial disc nearly perfect; bill short, strong, curved from the base; upper mandible sometimes festooned, well protected by bristles; tarsus stout, moderate, or short, feathered, as are the toes as far as the scales in front of the nails, which are sub-equal.

GENUS, **Asio**, *Strick.*

The characters are the same as those of the sub-family.

Asio otus, *Lin.*

67.—*Otus vulgaris*, Flem.—Jerdon's Birds of India, Vol. I, p. 125; Murray's Vertebrate Zoology of Sind, p. 99; Hume's Scrap Book, p. 361.

THE LONG-EARED OWL.

Length, 14 to 16; expanse, 36 to 40; wing, 11 to 12·5; tail, 5·5 to 6; tarsus, 1·4 to 1·6; bill, 1·1.

Bill blackish-brown or dark-horny; cere fleshy; claws blackish-horny; irides from bright yellow to orange.

Above: the forehead finely mottled, dusky and tawny; the ear-tufts, about 1·75 inches long, deep brown, edged with tawny; the disc pale tawny, with a narrow black stripe along the inner side of the eye; the ruff blackish; the head, neck, and breast dark-brown; the feathers edged tawny-yellow, broadly so on the neck and upper part of the breast; rest of the plumage above brown, mottled whitish, the feathers tawny at the base; the quills tawny, with a few dark brown bars, changing to mottled fulvous-white, and dusky towards the tip; tail pale tawny with brown bands, mottled at the tip; beneath, from the breast, tawny with dark brown dashes, and a few cross stripes; vent and under tail-coverts and tarsal feathers unmarked.

At present, within our district, this Owl has only been recorded from Hyderabad, Sind, where it was obtained by Captain Butler, Mr. Doig, and myself. It is by no means common.

Asio accipitrinus, *Pall.*

68.—*Otus brachyotus*, Gmel.—Jerdon's Birds of India, Vol. I, p. 126; Butler, Guzerat; Stray Feathers, Vol. III, p. 449; Deccan, Stray Feathers, Vol. IX, p. 377; Murray's Vertebrate Zoology of Sind, p. 100; Hume's Scrap Book, p. 354.

THE SHORT-EARED OWL.

♂. Length, 14·5 to 15; expanse, 36·5 to 40; wing, 11·75 to 12·5; tail, 6 to 6·8; tarsus, 1·4 to 1·8; bill from gape, 1 to 1·25.

♀. Length, 15 to 16; expanse, 40 to 42; wing, 12 to 13·3; tail, 6·25 to 7; tarsus, 1·4 to 1·8; bill from gape, 1 to 1·25.

Bill blackish; irides yellowish.

Above: head and neck brown, the feathers broadly margined with pale tawny; wings and back the same, but more tawny on the scapulars and back, and the brown more irregular, tending to become narrow in parts, and to extend into bars in other parts; quills deep tawny, with broad brown bars; tail light fulvous, also brown banded, and light tipped; the disc pale fulvous, much streaked blackish; the ruff mottled tawny and brown, beneath pale fulvous, with narrow long stripes, wider on the throat and breast; the under tail-coverts and the tarsal plumes unspotted.

The Short-eared Owl occurs during the winter months, throughout the region, but is nowhere very common.

SUB-FAMILY, Buboninæ.

Head moderate, furnished with two long ear-tufts on the forehead; orifice of the ears rather small or moderate, without an operculum; wing moderate or longish; tarsus short, usually feathered; toes and nails strong.

GENUS, Bubo, *Auct.*

Bill slightly lengthened, scarcely arched from the base, compressed, strong, black; nostrils ovoid, transverse; wings long, 3rd quill longest aud 4th quill sub-equal to it; tail rather long, nearly even; tarsi and toes feathered; tarsi moderate, fairly strong, and claws sub-equal.

Bubo bengalensis, *Frankl.*

69.—*Urrua bengalensis*, Franklin.—Jerdon's Birds of India, Vol. I, p. 128; Butler, Guzerat; Stray Feathers, Vol. III, p. 450; Deccan, Stray Feathers, Vol. IX, p. 376; Murray's Vertebrate Zoology of Sind, p. 93; Swinhoe and Barnes, Central India; Ibis, 1885, p. 58; Hume's Scrap Book, p. 366.

THE ROCK-HORNED OWL.

Ghugu, Hin.

Length, 20 to 23; expanse, 44 to 58; wing, 14 to 16; tail 8·25 to 9; tarsus, 2·4 to 3·25; bill from gape, 1·5 to 1·75.

Bill horny black; irides intense orange-yellow; legs and feet feathered.

Above: the feathers of the head and neck are tawny, fading into white, each with a broad stripe of rich dark-brown; forehead brown-black, with a few tawny and white spots; aigrettes rich black-brown, edged on the inner sides with fulvous; back, shoulders, and greater coverts are varying shades of dark-brown, with pairs of mottled or freckled spots or incomplete bars of white, buff, or whity-buff; the tertiaries are similar, but have a lighter or more rufous ground-color; the primaries are a rich rufous-buff, tipped dusky-brown, gradually diminishing in extent inwards; the outer webs of the first two are banded brown and rufous-buff, freckled with brown, but in the succeeding ones the rufous-buff above the tips is nearly pure, except for two or three narrow, irregular spots, or incomplete bars; the dusky tips are themselves a good deal freckled and banded, more especially towards the secondaries, which latter want the dusky tips, and have four or five brown bars on the outer, and three or four much narrower ones on the inner webs, the buff between the bars being freckled with brown and dashed with white; the inner webs are clear salmon color, inclining to white on the outer edges; the wing-lining is pale buff, mottled with white, the lesser lower-coverts being banded with faint, wavy, zigzag, brown lines or bars; the two centre tail-feathers resemble the outer webs of the secondaries, aud the lateral ones their inner webs; the lores and sides of the upper mandibles are occupied with dense tufts of white bristly feathers, having the webs much disunited, with the extreme tips black and prolonged, and a broad band of similar feathers, tinged with pale buffy-brown, bounded posteriorly by a narrow dark brown band, from the base of the aigrettes, behind and below the eye; the under parts are rufous-buff (whitish on the throat and neck), the breast with conspicuous dark-brown stripes, and the abdomen, sides and lower tail-coverts with numerous narrow, transverse, wavy, rufous-brown bars, darkest and closest on the sides, and almost wanting on the vent; the thigh-coverts, tarsi, and toe-feathers are buffy or sullied white, unspotted.

The Rock-horned Owl is fairly common in all parts of the presidency.

It frequents, by preference, rocky hills, ravines, and river banks, particularly if the latter are partially covered with brushwood. As noticed by Jerdon, it may frequently be seen in the early morning, seated on the ledge of a rock, looming large against the sky. It breeds during February, March and April, but eggs are occasionally found both earlier and later. The eggs, three or four in number, are deposited on the bare ground, either in a small cave or on a projecting edge of a cliff generally near water. A favorite breeding place is the precipitate bank of a river facing westward, where the sun seldom or never penetrates; the eggs, though rarely, have been found on the level ground. They are broad oval in shape, and white in color, with a faint creamy tinge, fairly glossy, and average 2·1 inches in length by 1·73 in breadth.

Bubo coromandus, *Lath.*

70.—*Urrua coromanda*—Jerdon's Bird's of India, Vol. I, p. 130; Butler, Guzerat; Stray Feathers, Vol. III, p. 450; Murray's Vertebrate Zoology of Sind, p. 94; Swinhoe and Barnes, Central India; Ibis, 1885, p. 58; Hume's Scrap Book, p. 371.

THE DUSKY-HORNED OWL.
Jangli Ghugu, Hin.

♂. Length, 22 to 23·5; expanse, 54 to 57; wing, 15·75 to 16·5; tail, 8 to 9; tarsus, 2·2 to 2·4; bill from gape, 1·9 to 1·7.

♀. Length, 23 to 25; expanse, 56 to 60; wing, 17 to 17·5; tail, 8·75 to 9·25; tarsus, 2·3 to 2-6; bill from gape, 1·6 to 1·7.

Bill greyish at base, horny-yellow on culmen and tip; irides deep yellow; feet sparsely feathered; claws horny-brown.

Upper parts, except primaries and tail-feathers, earthy-brown; in some specimens greyer, in others more umber, often considerably darker on the head; lesser scapulars, and interscapulary region, and often many of the scapulars and lesser-coverts with narrow, ill-defined, dark-brown shaft stripes; all the feathers more or less vermicellated very finely with excessively narrow, irregular, imperfect wavy bars of a paler color, producing a freckled appearance. This pale color is, in some, a dull fulvous-white, in others grey, in others pale greyish-brown; in some, this marking is very conspicuous; in others it is almost obsolete, especially about the shoulders; the long ear-tufts, which in some specimens are fully 2·75 inches long, are of the same dark-brown as the narrow, central shaft stripes, which brown varies much in shade, in different specimens, being in some very dark, almost black, in others a moderately dark hair-brown. There are large white or pale yellowish white patches on the outer webs of the exterior scapulars, and towards the tips of most of the larger and median-coverts; the tail is a dull rufous-fawn, nearly pure white towards the tip, with four, and on the central feathers, generally five, broad, transverse, umber-brown bands, darker in some, lighter in others, and the pale inter-spaces on the central tail-feathers are much freckled, and in some cases entirely suffused with the same color; this freckling, occurs, though in a less degree, on the succeeding feathers, the interspaces growing clearer and brighter as they recede from the centre; the primaries are similar to the tail-feathers, the tips infuscated or freckled like the central ones, and the interspaces clearer and brighter towards the bases.

The lower parts are greyish-white, with a faint yellow tinge everywhere, expect on the middle of the throat, each feather with a narrow dark shaft stripe, and with numerous very fine wavy and freckled transverse greyish-brown bars, or vermicil-lations; the extent and depth of color of these delicate markings vary much in different specimens, in some almost entirely obscuring the ground color on the breast and abdomen.

Tibial and tarsal plumes yellowish or pale fulvous-white, in some specimens with faint longitudinal, dark-brown streaks and in others with narrow, clouded, imperfect, transverse bars of the same color.

The Dusky-horned Owl is abundant in Central India, and in parts of Rajpootana; it is not uncommon in Sind, but occurs more rarely in Guzerat, and has not yet been recorded from the Deccan or South Mahratta country.

It greatly affects the clumps of trees and mango topes that occur so abundantly in the vicinity of villages and along the banks of rivers and canals. It breeds during the months of December and January, and occasionally later. The nest composed of sticks is often of enormous size, owing to its being used for several successive seasons; it is generally placed in a fork of a large tree, but occasionally on a horizontal branch, or in the depres-sion at the junction of three or four large branches. The eggs, generally two in number, are coarse in texture, creamy-white in color, and average about 2·33 inches in length by about 1·9 in breadth.

A fresh and an incubated egg will often be found in the same nest, so that they must begin to sit as soon as the first egg is laid. I think this habit is somewhat general amongst the Owls, as I have noticed the same fact with *Bubo bengalensis* and *Carine brama*.

GENUS, **Ketupa**, *Lesson*.

Bill large, strong, deep, moderately long, straight at base, gradually curving beyond the cere, moderately compressed and hooked; nares elliptic, partially exposed; large ear-tufts; disc indis-tinct; ears moderate; wings rather short, reaching not quite to end of tail; 4th quill longest; tail moderate; tarsus rather long, or moderate, stout, naked, reticulate; toes naked, finely reticulate, with three or four scales at the base of the nails, moderately long, nervous, compressed; the hind-toe rather large; soles of the feet aculeate; talons subequal, compressed, cultrated below, (except the middle one) sharp; inner claw the largest.

Ketupa ceylonensis, *Gmel.*

72.—Jerdon's Birds of India. Vol. I, p. 133; Murray's Vertebrate Zoology of Sind, p. 92; Butler, Deccan and South Mahratta Country; Stray Feathers, Vol. IX, p. 376; Hume's Scrap Book, p. 379.

THE BROWN FISH OWL.

Amrai ka Ghugu. Hin.

♂. Length, 21 to 22; expanse, 54 to 56; wing, 15 to 15·75; tail, 7·6 to 8; tarsus, 2·8 to 3·1; bill from gape, 2.

♀. Length, 22 to 23·5; expanse, 56 to 59; wing, 16·5 to 18; tail, 7·8 to 8·5; tarsus, 2·8 to 3·25; bill from gape, 2·1.

Bill greenish-dingy; point of upper mandible blackish-horny; of the lower mandible yellowish; irides bright yellow; cere greenish-grey; legs and feet partly feathered, bare parts dingy greenish-grey, sometimes plumbeous; claws bluish-grey at the base, horny black at tip, mid-claw with two sharp edges developed one on the inner side, and one beneath.

Lores with a huge patch of bristle-like feathers, with greatly elongated bare black shafts, overhanging the commissure, and meeting over the base of the cere, some of them almost, if not quite, as long as the bill itself; the whole of the forehead, top and back of the head, are a somewhat pale pinkish-brown, each feather centred darker; the feathers above the ear-coverts on each side, behind the eye, lengthened so as to form aigrettes or ear-tufts, from an inch and a half to two inches in length; the feathers of the back of the neck are often of a somewhat darker shade, more broadly shafted with a still darker brown, and most of the feathers with a trace of wavy mottling, or obscure bars, especially towards the tips on the lighter-brown portion; upper back and scapulars much the same hue, and dark, centred in the same manner as the feathers of the back of the neck, but most of the exterior feathers of the scapulars, where they overhang the lesser wing-coverts, with nearly the whole outer webs white, and the lighter brown of the scapulars, and in a less degree of the feathers of the upper back, very much mottled and variegated with tiny wavy lines, and small irregular blotches of fulvous-white; lower back, rump, and upper tail-coverts much the same hue as the upper back, but with only a central line of dark-brown, and very feebly mottled with fulvous-white; all the lesser wing-coverts, the same brown as the upper back, with similar broad dark brown centres with a few spots of fulvous-white on some of the longest; the median-coverts mostly dark-brown towards the shafts, and on the inner webs, with one or two well-marked spots of white or fulvous-white on the latter and the outer webs mostly white or fulvous-white, freckled or mottled with paler brown; the winglet and primary-coverts chiefly dark-brown, with two or more imperfect transverse bars of fulvous-white or paler brown; the greater-coverts of the secondaries much the same as the preceding, but the outer webs much tinged with pale fulvous-brown, and there is more white and more mottling about them than the preceding; the primaries are dark-brown, tipped with fulvous-white, and with four or five ½ to ¾-inch transverse bars of white, fulvous, or rufescent white, on the outer, and pale brown across the inner webs; the secondaries have much the same character as the primaries, but the bars are closer and larger in proportion, and are more conspicuously mottled, and as a whole generally appear to have more white upon them than the primaries; the tertiaries and their coverts, like the greater-coverts of the secondaries, are a paler and more fulvous-brown, and much marked with imperfect bars or blotches of fulvous-white, mottled with brown; the tail-feathers are dark, somewhat umber-brown, tipped with rufous or fulvous-white, and with three or four comparatively narrow transverse bars of the same hue, most of the bars showing marks of faint mottling with a darker color; under the eyes and ear-coverts is a conspicuous patch of elongated, bristle-like feathers, with elongated, bare, black, pointed shafts, which curl up round, and are nearly as long as the lower mandible; the feathers of the rest of the chin, and a patch on the throat immediately below it, pure white, with, towards the tips, a dark-brown central streak, and three or four narrow, wavy bars of reddish-brown; the feathers on each side of this patch on the sides and front of the neck, breast, abdomen and flanks, a somewhat rufous or pinkish-brown, each feather with a narrow well-defined central streak of very dark-brown, and closely barred throughout its whole length on both webs, with narrow, transverse, wavy bars of a somewhat darker-brown than the ground color, though much lighter than the central streaks; thigh-coverts and vent-feathers uniform fulvous, streaked and barred like the body feathers; the bars are closer and more numerous on the breast, and the general tint is more vivacious, and the reverse of this on the flanks and lower tail-coverts; the wing-lining somewhat similar to the body feathers, but much less narrowly banded, and altogether lighter; the greater lower-coverts, however, of the primaries are pure white, broadly tipped with blackish-brown; lower surface of the quills glossy-brown, darkest on the primaries, tipped with greyish white and with three or four transverse bars of greyish-white, growing yellower as they approach the bases, where the inner webs are mostly yellowish-white.

The Brown Fish Owl is found throughout Sind, but has not yet been recorded from Guzerat, neither did I meet with it in Rajputana or Central India. It reappears in the Deccan and

South Mahratta Country, but is nowhere numerically common. It is a permanent resident where found, breeding from December to March. It is by no means choice in the selection of a site for a nest. A cavity in an old tree, a cleft in a rock overhanging a stream, a broad shelf on the clayey cliff of some river, or even an old nest of the Fishing Eagle, are all at times made use of by this very accommodating bird. The nest is seldom well made; a few sticks mingled with feathers, if on a cliff; or merely a few dead leaves and feathers if in a hole of a tree; but, when they appropriate an old nest of a Fishing Eagle, they generally line it carefully with grass, fine twigs, and feathers; the eggs, two in number, are broad perfect ovals in shape, and are white in color; the shell close grained and pitted all over but still more or less glossy. They average 2·3 inches in length by about 1·88 in breadth.

Genus, **Scops**, *Savigny*.

Of small size; head rather large; large ear-tufts; orifice of ears moderate; bill moderate, lateral margin somewhat curved; nostrils round on margin of the cere; disc imperfect; wings long and pointed, third and fourth quills longest; tail rather short, even, or slightly rounded; tarsus moderate, feathered; toes naked and scaled, inner toe nearly equal to the middle one; claws moderate.

Scops pennatus, *Hodgs.*

74.—*Ephialtes pennatus*, Hodgs.—Jerdon's Birds of India, Vol. I, p. 136; Butler, Deccan; Stray Feathers, Vol. IX, p. 376; Murray's Verebrate Zoology of Sind, p. 95; Swinhoe and Barnes, Central India; Ibis, 1885, p. 59; Hume's Scrap Book, p. 386.

THE INDIAN SCOPS OWL.

Length, 7·5 to 8·25; expanse, 15·5 to 19; wing, 5 to 6; tail, 2·5 to 3; tarsus, 1; bill from gape, 0·8.

Bill dusky-greenish, yellowish beneath; irides pale yellow; legs and feet fleshy-grey or dingy fleshy.

Above ashy-grey, more or less tinged with rufous or rufous-grey; the feathers dark shafted, finely mottled with brown, and with a white subterminal spot; wings more rufescent, and without the white spots, except on the outer scapulars, as usual and on some of the greater-coverts; quills rufescent, with darkish double bars, the interval between the bars dusky or mottled, and the light spaces, or ground color, on some of the outer primaries rusty-white in some specimens; or, it may be said, that the quills are dusky-rufescent, mottled with pale bands; the tail rufescent, with double bars, in some mottled almost throughout; beneath the feathers streaked dark-brown and banded with white, and mottled rufous-grey and brown, mostly grey on the upper part, and white on the lower part of the abdomen; tarsal feathers barred and mottled; disc ashy-white, with a few darker specks, and the shafts of the frontal bristles white; ruff marked with dull brown and rufous.

In the rufous phase, the upper parts are uniform bright golden chesnut-red, with black shafts, inconspicuous on the back, more distinct on the forehead, ear plumes, and shoulders of the wings; outer edges of scapulars whitish; disc rufous with some of the feathers white shafted; ruff deep brown, with the outer feathers black tipped or black; beneath deeply tinged with the hue of the back, but with more or less white on the belly and under tail-coverts; the breast and sides of the belly with brownish central black streaks, the latter with transverse pencillings; four faint bars on the inner webs of the tail-feathers, and the primaries also indistinctly barred with dusky, or mottled brown. The young bird has all the feathers duller red, more black shafted, and there is much white on the lower surface, and the disc has a good deal of white; the scapulars are white externally, with black tips; and the bars on the quills and tail-feathers are more distinct, brown, and mottled.

The Indian Scops Owl occurs sparingly throughout the district, excepting, perhaps, Guzerat; it is of retiring habits, frequenting forests and well-wooded districts; it is, I believe, a permanent resident, but I am not aware of its eggs ever having been taken anywhere within our limits.

Scops brucei, *Hume.*

74. *Sept.*— Butler, Deccan and South Mahratta Country; Stray Feathers, Vol. IX, p. 376; Murray's Vertebrate Zoology of Sind, p. 95.

THE STRIATED SCOPS OWL.

Length, 9; expanse, 22; wing 6·4; tail, 3·25; tarsus, 1·45; bill from gape, 0·73.

Bill dusky; irides bright yellow; legs and feet densely feathered; claws black, well curved, slender and very sharp.

Cheeks and feathers under the eye greyish-white, excessively finely and indistinctly barred with brown; the lores and a stripe running up from them to the top of the eye creamy-white; the longer ones that meet over the base of the upper mandible tinged brownish; a few tiny dark-brown feathers on the eyelids; chin and throat creamy-white, with very narrow central shaft stripes towards the tips, and excessively finely vermicellated with brown; feathers of the ruff, (which is inconspicuous), very pale buff, narrowly edged with dark-brown; the whole of the forehead, crown, back of head, back and sides of neck, back, scapulars, wing-coverts, rump and upper tail-coverts, very pale buff or creamy-white, so minutely and closely powdered with pale-brown that looked at from a very little distance the feathers appear to be a uniform pale earthy-brown.

Every feather has a narrow central dark-brown stripe; some of the outer scapulars have inconspicuous patches of buff on their outer webs, and the ground color of the feather on each side of the crown, immediately above the eye, is slightly paler; but, beyond this, the whole of the upper plumage above described is singularly uniform in tint and appearance, and is absolutely devoid of those white spots and blackish-brown or buff dashes and streaks so characteristic of the other Indian species; the primaries are pale dingy-buff, with broad transverse brown bars, which, towards the tips, are with the ground color, mottled and freckled over, the ground color with brown and the bars with dingy-fulvous; nearer the base of the feather, the light bars are on the exterior webs pure pale buff, while the dark bars continue freckled as already described; on the inner webs, the dark bars are nearly uniform and unmottled, while the light bars are pure and unmottled towards the edge of the webs, and suffused with brown towards the shafts; the tertiaries and the tips of the secondaries approximate closely to the plumage of the back and coverts; of the breast and abdomen, the ground color is similar to that of the upper parts, but the brown powdering is coarser, so that more of the ground coloring is seen, and the dark-brown central shaft stripes are somewhat broader towards the vent; on the flanks and lower tail-coverts, the ground color becomes almost pure white, and the brown powdering very sparse, while the shafts stripes are reduced, as on the back and wing-coverts, to well marked dark lines; the short, dense tibial and tarsal plumes are brownish-white, each little feather with its dark central shaft stripe; the axillaries and wing-lining are cream colored, or yellowish-white, entirely unstreaked and unmottled.

Not much is known concerning the Striated Scops Owl. It was named by Mr. Hume, after the Revd. H. Bruce, that gentleman having procured the first specimen near Ahmednagar; others have since been procured in different parts of the Deccan. Messrs. Blandford, Doig and myself procured it in Sind, the former at Oomercote, Mr. Doig and myself at Hyderabad, where it frequents dense plantations of young babool trees. I found it nesting on the Khoja Amran mountains in South Afghanistan. It will doubtless turn up both in Rajpootana and Guzerat.

Scops bakkamuna, *Forst.*

75*ter*.—Butler, Sind; Stray Feathers, Vol, VII, p. 175; Aboo, Stray Feathers, Vol. III, p. 450.

Length, 7·88 to 9; expanse, 20·5 to 21·5; wing, 5·6 to 6·75; tail from vent, 2·5 to 3·37; tarsus, 1·06 to 1·19; bill from gape, 0·88 to 0·94.

Toes and claws very pale greyish-brown, the latter darker at the points, and not much curved; soles creamy-white; pads and papillæ much developed and soft, scutellation obscure; three or four transverse quasi-scales at the end of each toe; interior ridge of mid-claw slightly dilated; irides, in some brownish-yellow, in others, dark-brown; in one nearly pure yellow; bill, upper mandible, dark-brown, lower mandible paler, especially towards the chin; cere dusky-greyish.

A prominent tuft of disunited, webbed, bristly, white feathers (with dark naked tips to the shafts, and traces on those nearest the eye of dark cross bars), on each side of the upper mandible at its base; a faint tinge of buffy at the anterior angle of the eye; rest of lores, feathers below and behind eye, including ear-coverts, loose, webbed, silky, greyish-white, with traces of faint minute transverse brown bars; chin white, the feathers of the extreme tip somewhat bristly and curving upwards round lower mandible; across the throat and upwards immediately behind the ear orifice, as far as the base of the aigrettes, a band of creamy or pale buff feathers, with numerous minute, transverse, wavy brown pencillings and bars; those from the aigrettes to the sides of the throat with conspicuous dark-brown tippings, which form the defining line of the disc, and a few of those in the centre of the throat with similarly colored spots at the tips; forehead and a broad supercilium running up the inside webs of the aigrette feathers, and a curved band at the back of the head, extending from the point of one aigrette, to the point of the other (when laid flat on the head) a silvery-grey or greyish-white, the feathers with dark brown shafts, and numerous minute, transverse pencillings of that color, and some of them with terminal spots; centre of forehead and top of head, and a triangular space surrounded by this grey band, a rich dark brown; purest on the centre of the forehead, with small twin spots or imperfect transverse bars and mottlings, to a greater or lesser extent, of pale buff; the outside webs of the aigrettes are similar, as are the feathers of the band outside, and contiguous to the curved grey band, which latter seems continuous with the dark line of the outer webs of the aigrette, while the former seems to start immediately above the centre of the eye; below the dark band, at the base of the neck, is another band of very similarly marked feathers, but whereas the dark brown predominates in the former, the buff much predominates in the latter; the back, rump, upper tail-coverts, scapulars, wing-coverts, (except the greater ones of the primaries) a mixture of pale brownish-grey and pale buffy, with dark brown central streaks, and numerous transverse, wavy brown pencillings and mottlings.

In the outside line of the scapulars, the buff is very pure, and in some positions conspicuous, and while the rump, upper tail and lesser wing-coverts, are dingier and greyer, the centre of the upper back and the median and secondary wing-coverts show more of a pale buff; the primary greater-coverts are very dark-brown, with broad transverse buffy mottled bars; the quills are darkish-brown, with numerous broad transverse greyish, more or less dingy white bars, much more conspicuous on the outer webs; with the exception of a few bars on the upper portion of the outer webs of the earlier primaries, (which are unmottled and slightly tinged with cream); all the rest of these bars are closely mottled and pencilled with brown; the second, third, and fourth primaries are just perceptibly emarginate on the outer webs, and the first to the fourth are conspicuously notched on the inner webs; the sides of the neck behind the dark line, the breast, sides, abdomen, thigh-coverts, a sort of creamy-grey, very soft and silky; the feathers with narrow rich brown central streaks and numerous minute, irregular, wavy, transverse pencillings; greater portion of wing-lining, vent-feathers, and lower tail-coverts, silky greyish-white, the latter, some of them, with dark central streaks towards the tips; tarsus-feathers silky greyish-white, with a faint buffy tinge towards the joint, and with several narrow, somewhat irregular, transverse, brown bars; tail-feathers greyish-brown, with imperfect, transverse, mottled bars of very pale dingy-buff, and with the interspaces, too, more or less mottled with the same color.

Other specimens answer well to the above description, except that in some specimens the whole of the colors are dingier, while the white of the lower abdomen, vent, lower tail and thigh-coverts is purer; the tarsal plumes in some are entirely unbarred, and generally the markings are less pronounced and clear than in the first described specimen. In most birds the tarsal plumes are entirely unbarred.

Only some specimens shew the silvery half collar on the neck described above; in most the deep brown of the top of the head is continuous down to the broad buffy collar, at most a few feathers on the nape being greyish towards the tips.

On the whole, however, the coloration of specimens from the most distant localities differs but little.—*Hume's "Scrap Book."*

This Scops Owl is very rare, a single specimen was obtained at Aboo, by Dr. King, and a pair nesting at Hyderabad by Captain Butler; those, I believe, are the only recorded instances of its occurrence within our limits.

Scops malabaricus, *Jerdon.*

75*quat.*—Butler, Deccan; Stray Feathers, Vol. IX, p. 377; Murray's Vertebrate Zoology of Sind. p. 97; Hume's Scrap Book, p. 402.

THE MALABAR SCOPS OWL.

Length, 8 to 8·24; expanse, 10·5; wing, 5·95; tail, 2·75; exterior tail-feathers, 0·25, shorter than the centrals; tarsus, 1·05 to 1·08; bill from gape, 0·8.

Bill yellowish horny, darker above; irides dark yellow; feet yellow.

The full description of *S. bakkamuna* already given renders any minute description unnecessary.

Generally it may be said that only the point of the forehead, and a narrow streak over the eye, is white; and these parts instead of being silvery-white, as in *bakkamuna*, are fulvous; again, the chin, throat, ruff-feathers, abdomen, and breast, instead of being white or creamy-white, as in *bakkamuna*, are a rich buffy-fawn. Altogether the bird is a good deal smaller, and the lower parts conspicuously more buffy than in any specimen of *S. bakkamuna*.

The Malabar Scops Owl is said to be a permanent resident in Ratnagiri, and it also occurs in Sind, but is uncommon in both districts; it has not been recorded from any other part of the Presidency. It is often confounded with the preceding *S. bakkamuna*.

Sub-family **Surniinæ**, *Kaup*.

Ear orifice small, oval, no operculum; disc incomplete, or nearly obsolete; no ear-tufts.

Genus, **Carine**, *Kaup*.

Cere swollen; first primary much lengthened; fifth scolloped on the outer web like the fourth; hind tarsus plumed; nostrils pierced near the anterior margin of the cere; bill short, curved from the base, hooked; lower mandible notched.

Carine brama, *Tem*.

76.—*Athene brama*, Tem.—Jerdon's Birds of India, Vol. I, p. 142; Butler, Guzerat; Stray Feathers, Vol. III, p. 450; Deccan, Stray Feathers, Vol. IX, p. 377; Murray's Vertebrate Zoology of Sind, p. 99; Swinhoe and Barnes, Central India; Ibis, 1885, p. 59; Hume's Scrap Book, p. 404.

The Spotted Owlet.

Length, 8 to 9·5; expanse, 20·05 to 22·5; wing, 6·15 to 6·65; tail, 2·75 to 3·5; tarsus, 1 to 1·1; bill from gape, 0·78 to 0·84.

Bill horny-green; cere dusky; irides bright or golden pale-yellow; feet dingy-greenish.

Above earthy grey-brown, each feather with two white spots; beneath white, broadly barred, or with cordate brown bars; tarsal feathers not spotted; wing with five or six white interrupted bars, and tail with five; disc white, edged externally with brown; a dusky-brown patch outside the eye, and a small dark spot at the inner canthus; ear-coverts barred.

The Spotted Owlet is spread universally throughout India, and is exceedingly common in all parts of the Bombay Presidency, with the exception of the hills, which it does not ascend to any great height, its place there being taken by one of the next two species; it is a permanent resident, and breeds during March and April. Eggs are occasionally found in February, but the majority of them are laid in March. It is not particular in its choice of a site for a nest; an old decayed tree will afford a lodging to several pairs; in fact, holes in trees are their most favorite to nesting places, and they may often be seen peeping out of holes in trees during the daytime, but holes in walls are not neglected.

If they can effect an entrance beneath the tiles of a bungalow, they do so, and there they will rear their families; in such cases (by no means uncommon) they become an almost intolerable nuisance, as they are such noisy disagreeable birds; they are familiar and not easily driven away when once they have made a lodgment, the only sure method is extermination; nothing less seems to have any effect; if one of a pair be shot the survivor obtains another mate in a very short time. I have found the eggs in holes in hay stacks, and very frequently in holes in the sides of wells. They do not make an elaborate nest, a few dead leaves and feathers quite sufficing for their requirements. The eggs, four or five in number, are frequently found in different stages of incubation, owing to the bird commencing to sit as soon as the first egg is laid. Another curious fact in connection with this bird is, that three or four adults are occasionally found sitting on one clutch of eggs.

The eggs are white in color, broad ovals in shape, and average 1·25 inches in length, by about one inch in breadth.

GENUS, **Glaucidium**, *Boie.*

Nostrils in the middle of a swollen cere, prolonged and tubular; wing short, first quill shorter than the next four, emarginate, fourth and fifth quills about equal; tarsus and toes well developed; plumage distinctly banded.

Glaucidium radiatum, *Tick.*

77.—*Athene radiata*, Tickell.—Jerdon's Birds of India, Vol. I, p. 143; Butler, Mount Aboo; Stray Feathers, Vol. III, p. 450; Hume's Scrap Book, p. 409.

THE JUNGLE OWLET.

Length, 8 to 8·5; expanse, 17·5 to 21; wing, 5; tail, 2·6 to 2·9; tarsus, 0·92; bill from gape, 0·7.

Bill yellowish-horny; irides bright yellow; feet yellow.

Above brown, uniformly barred with close rays of rufescent whitish and dusky; wings more rufous, especially the primaries, and barred with dusky brown; some of the greater-coverts and scapulars with white spots; beneath, throat white, the rest of the body barred transversely with dusky and whitish; under tail-coverts white.

Within our limits, the Jungle Owlet, has only been recorded from Mount Aboo, where it breeds during April and May.

Glaucidium malabaricum, *Bly.*

78.—*Athene malabarica*, Blyth.—Jerdon's Birds of India, Vol. I, p. 144; Butler, Deccan; Stray Feathers, Vol. IX, p. 377; Hume's Scrap Book, p. 413.

THE MALABAR OWLET.

Length, 7·6 to 8·25; expanse, 17·5 to 18; wing, 5 to 5·25; tail, 2·58 to 2·62; tarsus, 0·9 to 1; bill from gape, 0·7·

Irides bright yellow.

Head, neck, and interscapulars uniform lightish rufous, with narrow close dusky rays; wing the same, but the color deeper, and the bands broader; primaries deep rufous, the first three barred throughout with dusky, the rest mostly unspotted, or obscurely banded at the base, distinctly barred at the tip; secondaries with broad bands throughout of rufous and dusky; the tertiaries and scapulars barred rufescent-whitish and dusky; the outermost scapulars with large white spots; the lower parts are barred throughout with dusky, and white on the belly and flanks, and with rufous and dusky on the breast; the vent and lower tail-coverts pure white; tail dusky, with eight or nine whitish bars, somewhat broader than those of the last species.

The Malabar Owlet is common all along the Western Ghats, in the adjacent forests and also at Ratnagiri, but does not occur on the plains; it is a permanent resident where found; its call, considering the size of the bird, is extraordinarily loud and disagreeable.

GENUS, **Ninox**, *Hodgson.*

Head small; disc obsolete; bill short; cere large; nostrils tumid; wings long, firm; third quill longest, first and second moderately graduated; tail long, firm, nearly even; tarsi rather short, feathered; toes long, thinly clad with bristles, and bordered laterally by stiff bristles; lateral toes equal.

Ninox lugubris, *Tick.*

81. (in part)—Jerdon's Birds of India, Vol. I, p. 147; Butler, Deccan; Stray Feathers, Vol. IX, p. 377; Hume's Scrap Book, p. 420.

THE BROWN HAWK OWL.

Length, 11 to 12·1; expanse, 27 to 29; wing, 8·6 to 9·25; tail, 5·1 to 5·4; bill from gape, 0·9 to 1.

Bill blackish, pale horny-yellow on culmen; cere greenish; irides bright yellow.

Legs and feet vary from yellow to reddish-yellow, and in young birds greenish-grey.

Lores, forehead, and chin white; the elongated bristle-like shafts of some of the feathers blackish; ear-coverts brown, ashy at the base; top of the head, back and sides of the neck ashy-brown; throat and front of the neck slightly more rufous-brown, streaked with fulvous; in some specimens the fulvous greatly predominates, and these parts may then be said to be light fulvous, streaked with greyish-brown; back, scapulars, lesser, median, and greater secondary wing-coverts, tertiaries, and most of the secondaries, rump, and upper tail-coverts brown, varying much in shade in different individuals, some being a greyer and more dove-brown, others more rufous, but always more rufous on the coverts, and generally palest or clearest on the tertiaries; the exterior scapulars with larger or smaller pure white bars, sometimes on both and sometimes upon one web only, in some specimens conspicuous even when the bird is at rest, in others only visible by lifting the feathers; the tertiaries are barred on both webs with white; the tail is pale grey, greyish-brown, or pale brown, white at the extreme tip, with five regular, transverse, brown bars, darker or lighter in different individuals, the basal one of which is more or less completely hidden by the upper tail-coverts, and which average about 0·4 inches in breadth; the primaries, their greater-coverts, and the winglet are generally somewhat darker-brown than the rest of the wing, but the former are paler on the outer webs; all the quills are banded paler, somewhat obsoletely towards the tips and on the outer webs, but very conspicuously on the inner webs above the tip; the breast, abdomen, sides, flanks, vent and lower tail-coverts are pure white the breast with broad, rufous-brown stripes, and the flanks and abdomen with large, more or less heart-shaped, spots of the same color towards the tips of the feathers; the lower tail-coverts sometimes spotless, and sometimes with traces of a few pale-brown arrow-head, transverse bars; tarsal and tibial plumes mottled white, pale fulvous and brown, one or other of these colors, in some specimens the white, in others the fulvous or the brown, greatly predominating; axillaries white, or pale fulvous, more or less imperfectly but broadly barred with brown, or pale fulvous-brown; edge of the wing just above the base of the primaries white; wing-lining mingled white, brown, and pale fulvous.

The Brown Hawk Owl only occurs as an occasional straggler in some parts of the Deccan. It may perhaps be rather more common than is generally supposed, but owing to its very shy nature it must often escape notice.

Order, **Insessores**, *Vigors.*

Bill very varied in form; feet either with three toes in front and one behind, on the same plane, or with two before and two behind; in some few the hind-toe reversible, so that all four can be brought to the front, and in a few cases one toe is wanting.

Family, **Hirundinidæ.**

Bill short, broad at the base, depressed, compressed at the tip, more or less curved, not notched; gape very wide; wings long, pointed; tarsi short; feet feeble; hind-toe short.

Sub-family, **Hirundininæ.**

The bill is short, flat, nearly triangular, compressed at the tips, with a slight emargination; the culmen gently bent at the tip, but not hooked; the gape is large, without any rictal bristles;

the wings are long and pointed; the two first quills generally equal, sometimes the first longest; the primary quills are nine in number, the secondaries moderate, covered at the base only by short coverts; the tail is various, even in some, or only slightly emarginate, deeply forked in others; the tarsi are short; the feet small; the middle-toe lengthened, the lateral toes nearly equal, and the claws short, slightly curved, acute and slender. The tarsus is occasionally feathered, and in some the toes also; these last, like the Swifts, have a tendency to revert the posterior toe; their plumage is soft, dense, and glossy.

GENUS, **Hirundo**, *Lin.*

Bill rather large, very broad at the base, triangular, compressed at the tip; tail long and forked, or short and square, or sub-furcate; tarsus naked; feet moderate.

Hirundo rustica, *Lin.*

82.—Jerdon's Birds of India, Vol. I, p. 157; Butler, Guzerat; Stray Feathers, Vol. III, p. 451; Deccan and South Mahratta Country; Stray Feathers, Vol. IX, p. 377; Murray's Vertebrate Zoology of Sind, p. 102; Swinhoe and Barnes, Central India; Ibis, 1885, p. 59.

THE COMMON SWALLOW.

Length, 5·25 to 8·9; expanse, 13 to 14; wing, 4·3 to 5; tail, 2·75 to 4·5; the middle tail-feathers are only two inches in length.

Bill dusky-black; irides deep brown; legs dusky-black.

Male.—Above glossy blue-black; the chin, throat, and a narrow band on the forehead deep ferruginous; a slightly glossed black pectoral band; beneath, from the breast, rufescent-white; tail with all, except the mesial feathers, having a large white spot on their inner web.

The female has the outer tail feathers shorter, and the under parts whiter. The young may be known by the pale ferruginous hue of the throat, and by the dull color of the upper plumage, as also by the shorter outer tail-feathers.

The European Swallow is a common cold weather visitant, arriving early in August, and leaving towards the end of March, but stragglers are occasionally seen, both earlier and later; they do not appear to breed anywhere within our limits, but in the Bolan Pass, Quetta, Chaman, and Kandahar I found them breeding freely.

Hirundo filifera, *Steph.*

84.—Jerdon's Birds of India, Vol. I, p. 159; Butler, Guzerat; Stray Feathers, Vol. III, p. 451; Deccan, Stray Feathers, Vol. IX, p. 377; Swinhoe and Barnes, Central India; Ibis, 1885, p. 59; Murray's Vertebrate Zoology of Sind, p. 102.

The Wire-tailed Swallow.

Leishra, Hin.

Length, to end of middle tail-feathers, 4·75; outer tail-feathers, 5 inches longer; expanse, 12; wing, 4·12 to 4·7; tail, except the outer two feathers, 1·5; tarsus, 0·5; bill at gape, 0·5; bill at front, 0·25.

Bill black; irides very dark brown; legs and feet black.

Above, very glossy steel-blue; top of head deep ferruginous; lores deep black; beneath pure white, with white spots on all, except the four central tail-feathers, the outermost prolonged in the form of a thin wire; the female differs in having the outer tail-feathers much less developed.

The Wire-tailed Swallow occurs throughout the district, but is nowhere numerically common; it is a permanent resident, and breeds from February to August, rearing at least two broods in the year; the nest is deep half saucer-shaped, and is composed of pellets of mud, well lined with soft feathers, and is usually placed in the immediate vicinity of water; under the cornices of bridges, arches of culverts, sides of wells, where there are projections under which they can build, niches in buildings overhanging water, or under projecting ledges of rock, it is always placed against the side and a little below the roof or projection, just enough space being left for the ingress and egress of the bird.

The eggs, generally three in number, are long, narrow ovals, in shape a good deal pointed towards one end, are fine and delicate in texture, and fairly glossy when fresh, but as incubation proceeds this disappears.

Their color is white, beautifully speckled, spotted, and blotched with various shades of reddish-brown. When fresh and unblown, the ground color is a delicate pink, owing to the yolk showing through. They will not desert the nest, even if the eggs are taken. I have obtained as many as nine eggs from a single nest, but never more than three at any one time.

They vary a good deal in size, but average 0·72 in length by 0·52 in breadth.

Hirundo erythropygia, *Sykes.*

85.—*Hirundo daurica*, Lin.—Jerdon's Birds of India, Vol. I, p. 160; Butler, Guzerat; Stray Feathers, Vol. III, p. 451; Deccan, Stray Feathers, Vol. IX, p. 377; Murray's Vertebrate Zoology of Sind, p. 103; Swinhoe and Barnes, Central India; Ibis, 1885, p. 59.

The Red-rumped Swallow.

Length, 6·5 to 7; expanse, 12·25 to 13; wing, 4·1 to 4·5; tail, 3 to 3·35; (the tail is forked to the extent of about 1·5 inches); tarsus, 0·46; bill from gape, 0·58; bill at front, 0·3.

Bill black; irides brown; legs black.

Above, blue-black; narrow supercilium; sides of the head, behind the ear-coverts, and rump ferruginous; beneath rufescent-white, with dusky streaks; terminal half or third of under tail-coverts abruptly black. Young more dull in its tints merely.

The Red-rumped Swallow occurs generally throughout our limits, but is more common in hilly districts (such as Mount Aboo) than in open country; most of them retire to the hills to breed about April, but a few remain; and nests are occasionally found in the plains. The nest, constructed of pellets of mud lined with feathers, is affixed to the under-surface of a ledge of rock, the roof of a cave, the arch of a bridge, or some such similar place; it is retort-shaped, having a bulb-like chamber at one end, with a tubular passage, sometimes seven or eight inches long at the other; they continue to lengthen this passage, even after the eggs are laid. I have never myself found nests of any other type than this, but Mr. Blewitt remarks that "they are eccentric to a degree in the selection of a suitable place for a nest, the form and material of which mainly depends on the locality; in a hole, a simple collection of feathers answers, &c.," and is disposed to believe that these retort-shaped nests are merely intended for winter residences. I have many times watched the building of the nest and the rearing of the young in these same retort-shaped nests.

The eggs, three in number, are pure white in color, long ovals in shape, and average 0·78 in length by 0·55 in breadth.

Hirundo fluvicola, *Jerd.*

86.—Jerdon's Birds of India, Vol. I, p. 161; Butler, Deccan; Stray Feathers, Vol. IX, p. 378; Guzerat, Stray Feathers, Vol. III, p. 432.

The Indian Cliff Swallow.

Length, 4·5; wing, 3·5; tail, 1·75.

Above, glossy black with some whitish edges to the dorsal feathers; crown dark-rufous; rump brownish; beneath white, with black mesial streaks to the feathers of the throat and breast; the under-surface of the wings pale brown; tail slightly furcate, with a small whitish spot towards the tip of the inner web of each feather.

The Indian Cliff Swallow is not uncommon in some parts of the Deccan, but is very locally distributed. It occurs at Satara and Sholapur in some numbers. Near Aboo and Deesa it is very rare, but at Ahmedabad there are several large colonies. It does not occur in Sind. It is generally a permanent resident where found, breeding against the faces of cliffs, &c., from February to April, and again in July and August; the nests, composed of mud, lined with feathers, are retort-shaped, and occur in clusters of from 30 to 200, or even more; the eggs, generally three in number, are either wholly white, or white, streaked, spotted, blotched, or capped with pale yellowish or reddish-brown. They average 0·76 in length by 0·53 in breadth.

GENUS, Cotyle, *Boie.*

Bill weak, depressed, very broad at base, smaller than in *Hirundo*, barely hooked at tip; wings somewhat longer, first quill longest, longer than the tail; tail, even or slightly notched; tarsus slightly longer; toes weaker, outer toe proportionally longer; claws lengthened; plumage sombre, and barely glossed.

Cotyle riparia, *Lin.*

87.—Jerdon's Birds of India, Vol. I, p. 163; Butler, Deccan, Stray Feathers, Vol. IX, p. 378; Guzerat, Vol. III, p. 432; Murray's Vertebrate Zoology of Sind, p. 103.

THE EUROPEAN SAND MARTIN.

Length, 4·75; wing, 4; tail, 2.

Bill black; legs and feet horny; tarsus feathered on the back, down to the hind-toe.

Plumage above, and the breast, pale dusky greyish-brown; throat, belly, and under tail-coverts white; the tail slightly forked.

The European Sand Martin has been very doubtfully recorded from almost every part of the district. I have myself never met with it.

Cotyle sinensis, *J. E. Gr.*

89.—Jerdon's Birds of India, Vol. I, p. 164; Butler, Guzerat; Stray Feathers, Vol. III, p. 432; Deccan, Stray Feathers, Vol. IX, p. 378; Murray's Vertebrate Zoology of Sind, p. 103; Swinhoe and Barnes, Central India; Ibis, 1885, p. 60.

THE INDIAN SAND MARTIN.

Length, 4 to 4·7; expanse, 9·8 to 10·75; wing, 3·3 to 3·8; tail, 1·6 to 1·8; tarsus, 0·4; bill from gape, 0·42 to 0·47.

Bill black; gape pale fleshy; irides dark-brown; feet brownish or dusky fleshy.

Above earthy grey-brown, darker on the crown; upper tail-coverts somewhat albescent; throat and breast pale-greyish; crown, wings and tail dusky-brown; belly and lower tail-coverts white; tarsus not feathered, but with a small tuft.

The young birds have a more or less rufous tinge.

The Indian Sand Martin is common throughout the district, and breeds in holes in banks of rivers, from November to February, and even later. The nest-holes vary from eighteen to thirty-six inches in depth, according to the nature of the soil in which they are excavated; the nest is composed of fine grass, lined with feathers; the eggs, three in number, are pure white ovals, measuring 0·68 inches in length by about 0·48 in breadth.

Cotyle (Ptyonoprogne) concolor, *Sykes.*

90.—Jerdon's Birds of India, Vol. I, p. 165; Butler, Guzerat; Stray Feathers, Vol. III, p. 453; Deccan, Stray Feathers, Vol. IX, p. 378; Swinhoe and Barnes, Central India; Ibis, 1885, p 60.

THE DUSKY CRAG MARTIN.

Length, 4·6; wing, 4; tail, 2.

Smoky brown, slightly paler, and with a reddish tinge beneath; a round white spot on the inner webs of all the tail-feathers, except the centre and outer pairs; the tail is nearly square.

The Dusky Crag Martin, with the exception of Sind, occurs more or less abundantly throughout our limits. It is somewhat solitary in its habits, rarely more than a single pair nesting in the same vicinity. They have apparently two broods in the year, and lay at different seasons in different parts of the country, but from January to March, and July to September, are perhaps the best months to search for eggs. Its nest, affixed to projecting eaves or ledges of rock, is very like that of *H. filifera*, but is smaller, more cup-shaped, and pointed at the bottom, but, like it, is well lined with feathers; the eggs, three or four in number, are white with numerous spots and specks of various shades of yellowish or reddish-brown, but these markings are neither so bright, or so bold, as those of the Wire-tailed Swallow; they average 0·72 in length by 0·52 in breadth.

Cotyle (Ptyonoprogne) rupestris, *Scop.*

91.—Jerdon's Birds of India, Vol. I, p. 166; Butler, Guzerat; Stray Feathers, Vol. III, p. 456; Deccan, Stray Feathers, Vol. IX, p. 378.

THE MOUNTAIN CRAG MARTIN.

Length, 5·25; expanse, 14·5; wing, 5·5; tail, 2·4; tail nearly square.

Bill black; legs light reddish-brown.

Above, pale ashy-brown, darker on the quills and tail; throat and breast rufous-white; abdomen rufous-ashy; under tail-coverts ashy-brown; a large white spot on the inner webs of all the tail feathers, except the two outer and two centre ones.

The Mountain Crag Martin is a not uncommon winter visitant to the more hilly districts, but it does not occur on the plains, and has not as yet been recorded from Sind, where its place is taken by the next species.

Cotyle (Ptyonoprogne) obsoleta, *Cab.*

91*bis.*—Murray's Vertebrate Zoology of Sind, p. 104; Hume, Stray Feathers, Vol. I, p. 1.

Length, 5·25 to 5·6; expanse, 12·25 to 13; wing, 4·4 to 4·75; tail, 1·8.

Bill black; legs and feet horny-brown.

The whole upper surface a very pale greyish earthy-brown, very much paler than the same parts in *P. rupestris* or *C. sinensis*; the quills only slightly darker, yet sufficiently so to contrast pretty markedly with the scapulars, back, rump, and upper tail-coverts; the lateral tail-feathers, all but the external feather on each side, with a large oval white spot on the inner web, as in *rupestris*, and with dark shafts and a darker tint on the web near the shaft, as in that latter species; lower surface as in *rupestris*, but much paler; the whole of the chin, throat, breast, and abdomen being white with only a faint fulvous or rufous tinge, and the wing-lining and lower tail coverts, which in *rupestris* are a decided dark-brown, are in this species the same pale earthy grey-brown as the upper surface.

Mr. Hume states that the Pallid Crag Martin occurs along the streams that issue from the bare stony hills that divide Sind from Kelat, and also that it is common off the rocky headland of Manora, at the mouth of the Kurrachee Harbour. It is not recorded from any other portion of the district.

GENUS, **Chelidon.**

Bill somewhat shorter than in *Hirundo*, but thicker; first quill longest; tarsi and toes feathered; tail very slightly forked.

Chelidon urbica, *Lin.*

92.—Jerdon's Birds of India, Vol. I, p. 166; Butler, Deccan; Stray Feathers, Vol. IX, p. 378.

THE ENGLISH HOUSE MARTIN.

Length, 5·5; expanse, 12; wing, 4·1; tail, 2·4; legs fleshy-white.

Above glossy blue-black; wing and tail dull black; rump and entire under parts pure white; under parts of shoulders and axillaries greyish-white.

The English House Martin only occurs as a somewhat rare seasonal visitant to some parts of the Deccan.

GENUS, **Chætura**, *Steph.*

Toes three in front, nearly equal; the hallux shorter, opposable, but also reversible to the front; tarsus covered with a naked skin; tail short, even, or wedged, the feathers with the shafts ending in rigid spines.

Chætura sylvatica, *Tick.*

95.—*Acanthylis sylvatica*, Tickell.—Jerdon's Birds of India, Vol. I, p. 170.

THE WHITE-RUMPED SPINE-TAIL.

Length, 4·25; wing, 5; tail, 1·5.

Bill black; irides dark brown; legs and feet livid.

Above, the whole plumage glossy green-black, except the rump, which is pure white, and the upper tail-coverts which are also white, the outermost being tipped black; the throat, cheeks, and breast pale grey, gradually passing into black on the sides of the body; belly and under tail-coverts pure white.

Tickell was the first naturalist who observed this species, and he states that, in Central India, "it haunts open cultivated grounds in the midst of forest; also the cleared patches on the sides and summits of hills."

SUB-FAMILY, Cypselinæ.

Bill very small, much hooked; wings excessively long and pointed; tail usually short, of ten feathers only; hind-toe directed inward but reversible to the front.

GENUS, Cypsellus, *Illiger*.

Wing, with the first quill equal to the second, or the second longest; tail emarginate, or forked; tarsus feathered, in front at all events; toes and claws nearly equal, short, robust; hallux directed inwards and forwards, not opposable.

Cypsellus melba, *Lin.*

98.—Jerdon's Birds of India, Vol. I, p. 175; Butler, Deccan; Stray Feathers, Vol. IX, p. 379; Guzerat, Stray Feathers, Vol. III, p. 453; Murray's Vertebrate Zoology of Sind, p. 104.

THE ALPINE SWIFT.

Length, 9; expanse, 19·5; wing, 8·5; tail (moderately forked) 3. Bill blackish; irides deep-brown; legs and toes livid-purple.

Above wood-brown, glossed with purple on the back; wings somewhat darker; beneath the chin, throat, and abdomen white; a wide pectoral band brown; sides of the rump, tarsal plumes, and under tail-coverts also brown.

The Alpine Swift only occurs as a somewhat rare cold weather visitant to most parts of the region, but is rather more common in the more hilly districts.

Cypsellus apus, *Lin.*

99.—Jerdon's Birds of India, Vol. I, p. 177; Murray's Vertebrate Zoology of Sind, p. 105.

THE EUROPEAN SWIFT.

Length, 7; extent, 15·5; wing, 6·25; tail, 2·62.

The whole plumage, except the chin and throat, which are white, glossy brown-black; the tail is rather more forked than in the last; and the wings extend two inches beyond the tail.

The European Swift only occurs as a cold weather visitant to some parts of Sind. It has not been recorded from any other portion of the district.

Cypsellus affinis, *J. E. Gr.*

100.—Jerdon's Birds of India, Vol. I, p. 177; Butler, Deccan; Stray Feathers, Vol. IX, p. 379; Guzerat, Stray Feathers, Vol. III, p. 454; Murray's Vertebrate Zoo'ogy of Sind, p. 105; Swinhoe and Barnes, Central India; Ibis, 1885, p. 60.

THE COMMON INDIAN SWIFT.
Ababil, Hin.

Length, 5·5; extent, 12; wing, 5; tail, 1·75.

Bill black; irides deep brown, feet dusky.

Above brown-black, darkest on the back, and glossed with green; head brownish, paler on the forehead; chin, throat, and rump white; rest of body beneath brownish-black; the tail is nearly even, with the feathers not pointed.

The Common Indian Swift is abundant throughout the whole district, and is a permanent resident; it has at least two broods in the year, and eggs may be taken, I believe, the whole year through. They are very accommodating in the choice of nesting sites, and I have found them in all the following places:—

In holes in the faces of old walls, mosques, and forts; in these cases the nests are detached, unless the hole happens to be large enough to contain more than one.

On the roofs of caves, they occur in large clusters, containing over fifty or a hundred nests.

Under the eaves of houses, tombs, &c., several nests are found together, with a few detached ones.

In the doorways and roofs of stables, or between closely set beams or rafters.

I never saw so many nests as at Hyderabad, Sind, where the favorite nesting place seemed to be under the roofs of the domed canopies that are built over the Mirs' tombs; almost every one of them had an immense cluster or congeries of nests affixed round the central portion of the dome; these nests are composed of agglutinated saliva of the birds, mixed with feathers and occasional straws; they are of every conceivable shape and size, so as to fit in with each other.

The eggs, two or three in number, are elongated ovals, and glossless white in color; they vary considerably in size, but average 0·87 by 0·57 inches.

Cypsellus leuconyx, *Blyth.*

101.—Jerdon's Birds of India, Vol. I, p. 179; Butler, Deccan and South Mahratta Country; Stray Feathers, Vol. IX, p. 379.

THE WHITE-CLAWED SWIFT.

Length, 6·25; tail, 2·5; wing, 6·75.

Feet small; claws white, or more or less so.

Very similar in color to the last; above glossy blackish-brown, darkest on the head; the rump white; beneath the chin and throat dirty white; the rest of the body glossy brown; the tips of the feathers whitish; the tail is forked, the outer feathers being about one inch shorter than the central ones.

In the *Ibis* for 1871-72, Dr. Jerdon considerably modified the above description. I cannot do better than reproduce the passage:— "Stolickza remarks that in some specimens there was no trace of white on the claws. This character is indeed exceptional, and the name is therefore unfortunate." Dr. S. also states that a slight pale supercilium is generally traceable, and that the head and neck are paler than the back.

Dr. Jerdon obtained a specimen in the western part of the Deccan, and several in Malabar; it does not appear to have been procured by any other naturalist.

Cypsellus batassiensis, *J. E. Gr.*

102.—Jerdon's Birds of India, Vol. I, p. 180; Butler, Deccan; Stray Feathers, Vol. IX, p. 379; Guzerat, Stray Feathers, Vol. III, p. 454.

THE PALM SWIFT.

Tadi ababil, Hin.

Length, 4·92 to 5·25; expanse, 9·50; wing, 4·5; tail, 2·35; tarsus, 0·4; bill from gape, 0·5.

Bill black; irides brown; feet dusky-reddish.

Wholly glossy ashy-brown; darker on the wings and tail, and lighter and somewhat albescent beneath; tail deeply forked.

The Palm Swift is a common and permanent resident in many parts of the Deccan, wherever there are plenty of palm trees, but where there are not, this bird is generally absent. Captain Butler saw a pair at Mount Aboo, but it must be very rare there, as no other observer has noticed it.

They nest twice in the year, in March and again in July; the nest, a tiny, watch-pocket-shaped cup, is made of saliva, incorporated with fine feathers, the down of plants, and such like kindred substances, and is fixed to the under surface of a bent palm leaf; the eggs, generally three in number, are miniatures of those of *C. affinis*, and average barely 0·71 in length by 0·46 in breadth.

GENUS, Collocalia, *Gray.*

Hind toe pointing backwards; second quill longest; tail moderate, even, or slightly forked; bill very small, much hooked; feet very small.

Collocalia unicolor, *Jerd.*

103.—*Collocalia nidifica*, Latham.—Jerdon's Birds of India, Vol. I, p. 183; Butler, Deccan; Stray Feathers, Vol. IX, p. 380.

THE INDIAN EDIBLE-NEST SWIFTLET.

Length, 4·75 to 5; expanse, 11·5; wing, 4·5 to 4·75; tail, 2·25, slightly forked and the feathers very broad.

Of a glossy cinereous-brown or mouse-brown color, darkest on the head, wings, and tail, and tinged with steel-blue or green, paler beneath.

The Edible-nest Swiftlet is a hot weather visitant to the Vingorla Rocks, where it breeds; it has not been recorded from any other part of our district.

GENUS, Dendrochelidon, *Boie.*

Hallux posterior, not reversible; tarsus short, naked, or feathered; wings very long, the first two feathers sub-equal; tail long, forked; head crested.

Dendrochelidon coronata, *Tick.*

104.—Jerdon's Birds of India, Vol. I, p. 185; Butler, Deccan; Stray Feathers, Vol. IX, p. 380; Swinhoe and Barnes, Central India; Ibis, 1885, p. 60.

THE INDIAN CRESTED SWIFT.

Length, 9 to 10; expanse, 14 to 15·7; wing, 6·05 to 6·35; tail, 3·16 to 5·25; tarsus, 0·28; bill from gape, 0·7 to 0·8.

Bill black; irides deep-brown; legs blue-black; soles of feet reddish-white.

Above bluish-grey, somewhat darker on the head, clearer on the back and rump, and glossed throughout with greenish; wings anteriorly with a slight purple gloss; beneath pale ashy, whitening on the middle of the belly and lower tail-coverts; ear-coverts ferruginous in the male, (connected with the chin by a line of the same color), black in the female, with a whitish line bordering the throat.

The Indian Crested Swift is common at and near Mhow in Central India, and has also been obtained along the Sahyadri range; it has not been recorded from any other portion of the region.

FAMILY, Caprimulgidæ, *Vigors.*

Bill small or moderate, (large in a few), weak, curved; gape very wide, extending below the eyes, generally with numerous and strong bristles; wings, and their coverts, long; tail moderate, or long, of ten feathers; tarsus short, scutellate, often feathered in front; feet feeble; hallux in some reversible; head broad, flat; plumage soft, light, mottled; eyes large; of nocturnal habits.

SUB-FAMILY, Caprimulginæ.

Bill small, weak, flexible; nostrils tubular; wings long, usually the second quill longest; tail usually long; lateral toes short, equal or nearly so; middle toe long with the claw pectinated on the inner margin; hallux short, sometimes reversible.

GENUS, Caprimulgus, *Lin.*

Bill very short, flexible, broad at base, compressed and bent at the tip; rictal bristles very strong, numerous, directed forwards; other characters as in the sub-family.

Caprimulgus indicus, *Lath.*

107.—Jerdon's Birds of India, Vol. I, p. 192; Butler, Guzerat; Stray Feathers, Vol. III, p. 454; Deccan, Stray Feathers, Vol. IX, p. 380.

THE JUNGLE NIGHT-JAR.

Length, 12; wing, 7·5 to 7·9; tail, 5·5 to 6.

Prevalent hue light ashy, with dusky pencillings and black streaks to the feathers of the middle of the head, back, scapulars, rump, and upper tail-coverts, and fulvous blotches on the wing-coverts; the quills with dark rufous spots or interrupted bars; the tail cinerascent, more or less dark, and the outer feathers more or less tinged with rufous, with narrow black bars, and numerous dusky mottlings; the lower parts rufescent-ashy with dark bars and mottlings.

Some specimens are darker in their ground color than others, and the rufescent markings are deeper.

The male has the cheek-stripe, throat band, the spots or interrupted bands on the first three primaries, and the tips of all the outer feathers, white, the latter ended by a narrow dusky tip; the female has these marks more or less rufescent, or fulvescent, and wants the white terminations to the tail-feathers; the primaries are strongly mottled towards their tips; the first primary almost equals the fourth; the tail is slightly rounded, and the wings reach to about one inch from its end.

The Jungle Night-jar is not very common; it affects forest and hilly districts in the Deccan, and is fairly common at Mount Aboo; it is believed to be a permanent resident.

It does not occur in Sind.

Caprimulgus kelaarti, *Bly.*

108.—Jerdon's Birds of India, Vol. I, p. 193; Butler, Deccan; Stray Feathers, Vol. IX, p. 380.

THE NEILGHERRY NIGHT-JAR.

Length, 11·5; wing, 7·25; tail, 5·75; tarsus, 0·6.

Plumage generally light cinereous, much mottled with black and dusky, and in parts tinged with light fawn and cream-color; ears black, edged with light rufous; line below the ears extending along the gape and throat spot white; small white marks on the inner webs only of the first four quills; all the tail-feathers, except the four centre ones, tipped with white, with a dusky margin; the primaries are slightly mottled at their tip; the wings do not reach to the end of the tail.

The Neilgherry Night-jar is very rare, and has only been recorded from the Konkan and the forest tract to the west of

Belgaum. It is only doubtfully distinct from *C. indicus*, and might I think with advantage be suppressed.

Caprimulgus albonotatus, *Tick.*

109.—Jerdon's Birds of India, Vol. I, p. 194.

THE LARGE BENGAL NIGHT-JAR.

Length, 13; expanse, 25; wing, 9; tail, 7.

Crown and tertiaries cinerascent, minutely mottled and marked with a stripe of black dashes along the middle of the crown; upper range of scapularies black, more developed in the male, and bordered more broadly externally with rufescent white; a broad white patch in front of the neck, as in several allied species; a double spot, or interrupted band of white on both webs of the first four primaries contracted and rufescent in the female; two outer tail feathers broadly tipped with white in the male, tinged with fulvous, or rufescent, in the female; rictorial bristles white at the base, black tipped; altogether the females are usually paler, more brown, and less ashy than the males.

According to Tickell (quoted by Jerdon) the large Bengal Night-jar is common in the jungles of Central India.

Caprimulgus atripennis, *Jerd.*

111.—Jerdon's Birds of of India, Vol. I, p. 196; Butler, Deccan; Stray Feathers, Vol. IX, p. 380.

THE GHAT NIGHT-JAR.

Length, 10·5 to 11; wing, 6·5 to 7·5; tail, 5·5 to 6.

Males have the crown and nape dark brownish-ashy, minutely mottled with black dashes along the crown; margins of the scapulars and wings white; breast and forepart of the abdomen dark, contrasting strongly with the light buffy tint of the hind part of the belly; vent and lower tail-coverts, which last tend to whitish in some; nape, breast, and back suffused with a russet tinge, not seen in the other species of the group; quills pure black, not mottled at the tip; ear-coverts ferruginous.

In females the quills are mottled at the tips; the Ghat Night-jar has been obtained in the forest tract to the west of Belgaum, but has not been recorded from any other portion of our limits.

Caprimulgus unwini, *Hume.*

111*bis.*—Murray's Vertebrate Zoology of Sind, p. 105.

UNWIN'S NIGHT-JAR.

Length, 9·75 to 10·37; expanse, 20 to 21·5; wing, 6·75 to 7·25; tail, 4·5 to 5·25; bill at front, 0·25 to 0·43; bill at gape, 1·18 to 1·31.

Very similar to *C. europæus*, a description of which I give below:—

Caprimulgus europæus.—Plumage above and that of the throat ashy-grey, thickly streaked and spotted with brown, mostly of a yellowish tinge; head and neck with longitudinal blackish streaks; a white stripe beneath the base of the lower mandilble extends along each side of the lower part of the head, and there is a central patch upon the throat; primaries, secondaries, and tertiaries dark-brown; the outer webs blotched with reddish-brown and the three exterior feathers with a large white patch near the tips of the inner webs; tail irregularly marked amd indistinctly barred with blackish-grey and yellowish-brown; the two external feathers on each side white at their termination; plumage of under parts yellowish-brown; tarsi paler; female like the male, the white spots on the quills and tail feathers absent.

The following is a description of *C. unuini*:—

This species has the upper three-fourths of the tarsus feathered in front.

In both sexes the two outer feathers on each side are tipped with white, but the tippings are about 1·55 and 1·0 broad in the male on the outer and penultimate feathers respectively, and only about 0·75 and 0·44 in the female, and in the latter sex the white is less pure; both sexes have a white spot on the inner webs of the first three, and a corresponding one on the outer webs of the second and third primaries; but here again, while the spots on the inner webs of the male are about one inch broad, those of the female are about half the size.

Within our limits, this Night-jar has only been obtained in Sind, where it is very common.

Caprimulgus asiaticus, *Lath.*

112.—Jerdon's Birds of India, Vol. I, p. 197; Butler, Guzerat; Stray Feathers, Vol. III, p. 455; Deccan, Stray Feathers, Vol. IX, p. 380; Murray's Vertebrate Zoology of Sind, p. 106; Swinhoe and Barnes, Central India; Ibis, 1885, p. 60.

The Common Indian Night-jar.

Length, 9; expanse, 18; wing, 5·5 to 6; tail, 4·5.

Pale rufescent-ashy, the feathers finely mottled with dusky; the top of the head (as usual), marked narrowly with black; a distinct rufescent collar with black marks; the black markings on the scapulars not extended, but they are much edged with buff, as are all the wing-coverts; back not streaked with black; quills with a white spot on each of the first four feathers and mottled at the tip; the outermost feathers are tipped with white, and there is a white spot on the neck; the lower parts are lightly mottled and barred.

The Indian Night-jar is common throughout the district and is a permanent resident, breeding during April and May. The eggs (there is no nest) are two in number, and are laid on the bare ground; they vary from a warm pinkish stone-color to a deep salmon-pink, and are clouded, blotched, and streaked with different shades of pale reddish and purplish brown; they average 1·04 by 0·77 inches.

Caprimulgus mahrattensis, *Sykes.*

113.—Jerdon's Birds of India, Vol. I, p. 198; Butler, Guzerat; Stray Feathers, Vol. III, p. 455; Deccan, Stray Feathers, Vol. IX, p. 381; Murray's Vertebrate Zoology of Sind, p. 107.

SYKES' NIGHT-JAR.

Length, 8·75 to 9·5; wing, 6·75 to 7; tail, 4·5 to 5·5.

Pale ashy-grey, variegated and waved with brown and ferruginous; the breast, the three outer quills in the centre, and the two lateral tail feathers on each side marked with white.

This Night-jar occurs pretty well throughout the district, and is a permanent resident at all events in Sind, where it breeds in February and March, laying two eggs, upon the bare ground.

Caprimulgus monticolus, *Frankl.*

114.—Jerdon's Birds of India, Vol. I, p. 198; Butler, Guzerat; Stray Feathers, Vol. III, p. 455; Deccan, Stray Feathers, Vol. IX, p. 381.

FRANKLIN'S NIGHT-JAR.

Length, 10; expanse, 24; wing, 8; tail, 4·25.

Pale ashy-brown, variegated with rufous and dusky; the abdomen banded with rufous and black; primaries brownish-black, the four outer ones with a broad white band, the six middle tail-feathers with slender black undulations, the two outer ones on each side entirely white, tipped with brown.

The female has a rufous band on the first four primaries, and the tail is all of one color without any white; she is also generally paler than the male.

The general hue of this species is more uniform than in any of the others; tarsus naked.

Franklin's Night-jar is not uncommon in well-wooded portions of the Deccan and South Mahratta country, and it is also common at Mount Aboo, Mhow and Neemuch, but has not been recorded from Sind.

FAMILY, Trogonidæ.

Bill short, stout, somewhat triangular, strong, curved from the base; tip, and sometimes the margin, toothed; gape wide; nostrils and base of bill concealed by long tufts of bristles; wings moderate or short; tarsus short, partially feathered; toes short, feeble, two before and two behind, the inner toe being turned backwards; tail long and broad, of twelve feathers; plumage soft; skin very thin.

GENUS, Harpactes, *Swains.*

Bill strong, broad and deep, conic much curved; margins of the mandibles smooth; nostrils partially covered by tufts of hair-like feathers; tarsus half feathered; anterior toes of equal length, barely joined at the base; a naked skin round the eyes.

Harpactes fasciatus, *Forst.*

115.—Jerdon's Birds of India, Vol. I, p. 201; Butler, Deccan; Stray Feathers, Vol. IX, p. 381.

THE MALABAR TROGON.

Length, 12; expanse, 16; wing, 5; tail, 6; bill at front, 0·5; bill at gape, 1.

Bill deep blue; orbital skin smalt-blue; irides dark-brown; feet light lavender-blue.

Male, entire head and neck black; the rest of the upper plumage castaneous olive-brown; the lesser wing-coverts, tertiaries, and some of the secondaries finely streaked with black and white; breast, belly and lower parts fine crimson red; the tail with the centre feathers the same color as the back but more chesnut; the lateral feathers black and white.

The female wants the black head and neck, which are concolorous with the body; the tertiaries and coverts are finely banded black and brown, and the lower plumage is ochreous-yellow instead of red.

The Malabar Trogon occurs sparingly in the forest tracts of the Deccan and South Mahratta country, but does not occur in any other portion of the district.

FAMILY, Meropidæ.

Bill lengthened, rather slender, slightly curved throughout, sharp pointed; wings long and pointed; tail generally even, moderate or long, with the central-feathers frequently elongated.

GENUS, Merops, *Lin.*

Bill very long, slender, slightly curved, depressed at base, somewhat compressed for the rest of its length; culmen keeled; tip entire, sharp, not bent down; nostrils partially covered by a tuft of bristles; some small rictal bristles at the base of the bill; wings long and pointed; first quill longest; tips of the lesser quills emarginate; tail somewhat lengthened, nearly even, the two centre feathers occasionally lengthened; tarsus very short; feet short with the two lateral toes much syndactyle; outer-toe much longer than the inner one; claws acute, strong, well-curved.

Merops viridis, *Lin.*

117.—Jerdon's Birds of India, Vol. I, p. 205; Butler, Guzerat; Stray Feathers, Vol. III, p. 455; Deccan, Stray Feathers, Vol. IX, p. 381; Murray's Vertebrate Zoology of Sind, p. 107; Swinhoe and Barnes, Central India; Ibis, 1885, p. 60.

THE COMMON INDIAN BEE-EATER.
Hurrial, Hin.

Length, including centre tail-feathers, 8·5; expanse, 10; wing, 3·5; tail, 4; tarsus, 0·36; bill at gape, 1·3; bill at front, 1; the centre tail feathers exceed the others by 1·25 to 2·5 inches.

Bill black; irides blood-red; feet plumbeous,

Plumage, above bright grass-green; the head, nape, and hind neck burnished with golden; a black eye-streak from the base of the bill through the eye to the top of the ear-coverts; quills with a reddish tinge, especially on the inner web, and all tipped dusky; tail duller green, the webs dusky at their inner edge; the two central tail-feathers elongated; chin and throat verdigris-green, and a black collar on the top of the breast; the rest of the lower parts bright green, mixed with verdigris, paler and more cœrulescent on the lower abdomen, and under tail-coverts.

The Common Indian Bee-eater occurs abundantly throughout the district; it is a permanent resident, breeding during April and May.

They usually excavate holes in sand banks or earthy cliffs, but occasionally make them in level ground; these holes vary in depth from 1½ to 5 feet, according to the nature of the soil; the eggs, four or five in number (more rarely six), are spherical in shape, white in color and are highly glossy when fresh, but as incubation proceeds the gloss disappears and they become dead white; they measure 0·78 in length by about 0·7 in breadth.

Merops philippinus, *Lin.*

118.—*Merops philippensis*, Lin.—Jerdon's Birds of India, Vol. I, p. 207; Butler, Guzerat; Stray Feathers, Vol. III, p. 456; Deccan, Stray Feathers, Vol. IX, p. 381; Murray's Vertebrate Zoology of Sind, p. 108.

THE BLUE-TAILED BEE-EATER.

Length, 12 to 12·5; wing 5·25; tail, 5·75; tarsus, 0·5; bill at front, 1·6.

Bill black; irides crimson; feet plumbeous.

Head, neck, back, wing-coverts, and tertiaries dull grass-green, with more or less rufous gloss; rump and upper tail-coverts bright azure-blue; a black eye-streak from the base of both mandibles to the end of the ear-coverts, with a pale blue line beneath; quills dull green-rufous towards the edge of the inner webs, and black tipped; tail dull blue; chin yellow-white; throat dark ferruginous, extending to the sides of the face and neck as far as the end of the ear-coverts; breast and upper abdomen green, glossed with rufous; lower abdomen and vent paler, and with a blue tinge and the under tail-coverts pale blue; the tail is nearly even, with the centre pair of feathers elongate and the pair next them slightly shorter.

The Blue-tailed Bee-eater occurs sparingly throughout the greater portion of our district.

Merops swinhoii, *Hume.*

119.—*Merops quinticolor*, Vieillot.—Jerdon's Birds of India, Vol. I, p. 208; Butler, Deccan; Stray Feathers, Vol. IX, p. 382.

THE CHESNUT-HEADED BEE-EATER.

Length, 8·5; wing, 4·3; tail, 3·25; bill at front, 1·3.

Bill black; irides fine crimson-red; legs and feet plumbeous.

Whole top of the head, nape, hind-neck, and upper part of back rich chesnut; wing-coverts, interscapulars, and tertiaries bight green, the latter tinged with blue; rump and upper tail-coverts pale azure-blue; quills dull green, tending to rufous on the inner web, and black tipped; tail, with the centre feathers, blue on the outer web, all the rest dull green, tipped dusky; tail even, or slightly emarginate, with the centre feathers not elongated; beneath, the chin, throat, and sides of the neck up to the ear-coverts, pale yellow, below which is a band or collar of ferruginous, edged with black; the breast bright green; abdomen, vent, and under tail-coverts the same, tinged with blue; wings within rufous-brown.

The Chesnut-headed Bee-eater occurs sparingly on the Western Ghâts and in the jungles adjoining.

Merops persicus, *Pall.*

120.—*Merops ægyptius*, Vieill.—Jerdon's Birds of India, Vol. I, p. 209; Butler, Guzerat; Stray Feathers, Vol. III, p. 456; Deccan, Stray Feathers, Vol. IX, p. 382; Murray's Vertebrate Zoology of Sind, p. 108; Swinhoe and Barnes, Central India; Ibis, 1885, p. 61.

THE EGYPTIAN BEE-EATER.

Length, 12 to 12·5; expanse, 18·5; wing, 6·21; tail to the end of the central tail-feathers, 5·5; tarsus, 0·44; bill at gape, 2·34; bill at front, 1·6.

Bill black; irides crimson; feet dark-plumbeous.

Above, including wings and tail, green mixed with verdigris-blue on the back, rump, and upper tail-coverts; forehead with a narrow line of yellowish-white, succeeded by a pale blue band, which continues over the eyes; a dark line through the eyes to the ear-coverts, which are mixed greenish blue and dusky; below this from the gape is another narrow white line, edged with pale blue; chin yellow; throat deep chesnut; rest of the lower parts blue-green; tail even, with the two centre tail-feathers elongated.

The Egyptian Bee-eater is a common seasonal visitant to all parts of Sind, but occurs less commonly in Guzerat, Rajpootana and Central India, and is extremely rare in the Deccan.

Merops apiaster, *Lin.*

121.—Jerdon's Birds of India, Vol. I, p. 210; Murray's Vertebrate Zoology of Sind, p. 108.

THE EUROPEAN BEE-EATER.

Length, 10 to 11; expanse, 17 to 18; wing, 5·5 to 6; tail, 3·75 to 4·75; tarsus, 0·5; bill at front, 1·2.

Bill black; irides red; legs reddish-brown; forehead pale whitish-blue; body above maroon-red, passing into rufous-yellow on the rump; a black eye-streak from the base of the bill, through the eye, nearly meeting another black band which crosses the lower part of the throat; chin and throat rich yellow; wings blue-green, or greenish blue, with most of the coverts and the secondaries chesnut, the latter black tipped, as are the primaries, though faintly; tertiaries blue-green; tail dull green, the tips of the centre feathers bluish; lower parts verdigris-blue.

Mr. Murray, in his Vertebrate Zoology of Sind, states that the European Bee-eater "occurs as a bird of passage in Sind, Kutch, Kattiawar, Rajpootana, and the Deccan." I have myself never met with the bird in India, but further north in Afghanistan, I found it very common.

GENUS, **Nycticornis**, *Swainson.*

Bill moderately long, well curved, strong, compressed; ridge flattened towards the base, with a parallel groove on each side; nostrils concealed by setaceous feathers; wings moderate, full, rounded; fourth quill longest; tail longish, nearly even; feet short, much as in *Merops;* plumage lax, soft and dense, with a plume of long stiff pectoral feathers differently colored.

Nycticornis athertoni, *Jard. & Selby.*

122.—Jerdon's Birds of India, Vol. I, p. 211; Butler, Deccan; Stray Feathers, Vol. IX, p. 382.

THE BLUE-NECKED BEE-EATER.

Length, 14; expanse, 18; wings 5·5; tail 6; bill at front, 1·7; tarsus, 0·6.

Bill bluish-plumbeous, with black tip; irides deep yellow; legs and feet dusky-greenish.

General color bright vernal-green, shaded on the belly and vent with buff; forehead blue; gular hackles rich ultramarine-blue, formed of a double series of long drooping plumes, ranged opposite each other or either side of the median line; lining of wings, the wings internally, under tail-coverts, and lower surface of the tail buff.

The Blue-necked Bee-eater was obtained by Mr. Laird in the forests to the west of Belgaum. This seems to be the only recorded instance of its occurrence within the district.

FAMILY, **Coraciadæ.**

Bill moderate or rather long, strong, broad at the base, compressed towards the tip, which is hooked, and sometimes slightly notched; the gape is large, with or without rictal bristles; tarsus short, stout; feet moderate; toes free, or slightly syndactyle;

wings moderate or long, broad; tail variable, sometimes short and even, at other times with very elongated outer tail-feathers.

GENUS, Coracias, *Lin.*

Bill large, moderately thick, lengthened, straight, strong, somewhat broad at the base, compressed towards the tip; culmen sloping, hooked abruptly; the nostrils basal, oblique, linear, apert; gape very wide, with strong rictal bristles; wings tolerably lengthened, the second quill longest, or the second and third sub-equal; tail even or slightly rounded, short; tarsus stout, shorter than the middle-toe; outer-toe nearly free to the base, much longer than the inner-toe; hind-toe shorter than the inner-toe; tarsus and toes strongly scutate.

Coracias indica, *Lin.*

123.—Jerdon's Birds of India, Vol. I, p. 214; Butler, Guzerat; Stray Feathers, Vol. III, p. 456; Deccan, Stray Feathers, Vol. IX, p. 382; Murray's Vertebrate Zoology of Sind, p. 109; Swinhoe and Barnes, Central India; Ibis, 1885, p. 61.

THE INDIAN ROLLER.
Nilkant, Hin.

Length, 12 to 13·5; expanse, 23·3 to 25; wing, 7·25; tail, 5·1; tarsus, 0·98; bill at gape, 1·7; bill at front, 1·1.

Bill dusky-brown; irides dark red-brown; eyelids yellow; legs dusky orange-yellow.

Head above and nape dingy greenish-blue, the forehead tinged with rufous; hind-neck, scapulars, inter-scapulars and tertiaries dull ashy-brown with a green gloss, and tinged with vinous on the hind-neck; back blue; rump and upper tail-coverts deep violet-blue; lesser-coverts and shoulders deep cobalt-blue; the other coverts dingy greenish-blue; the winglet, greater coverts and quills pale sky-blue, with a broad band of violet-blue on the middle of the wings, occupying the terminal half of the secondaries and last two or three primaries; the first seven primaries tipped dark blue; tail, with the two centre feathers, dull green, the others dark violet-blue, with a broad pale-blue band, occupying the greater part of the terminal half of the tail, and widening exteriorly; beneath, chin, throat, and breast, light vinous-purple; the feathers with pale fulvous shafts passing into tawny-isabella, with light streaks on the abdomen; lower abdomen, flanks, vent, and under tail-coverts pale blue; wings beneath entirely pale blue, with a broad violet band.

The Roller, or as Europeans prefer to call it, the Blue Jay, is generally distributed throughout the district; it is a permanent resident, but retires to the better-wooded portions of the country to breed. At and near Hyderabad, Sind, I found many nests and have several times taken them in Central India.

They breed during April, May and June, in holes in trees, old walls and roofs; the size of the nest depends mainly on the size of the hole, and is composed of grass, feathers, and bits of rags, &c.; the eggs, generally four in number, are broad oval in shape, glossy china-white in color, and measure 1·3 in length by 1·06 in breadth.

Coracias garrula, *Lin.*

125.—Jerdon's Birds of India, Vol. I, p. 218; Murray's Vertebrate Zoology of Sind, p. 109.

THE EUROPEAN ROLLER.

Length, 13; wing, 7·75; tail, 5; tarsus, 0·98; bill at front, 1·37.

Bill blackish; irides red-brown; feet yellow-brown.

The whole head, neck, and lower parts pale blue, duller on the head, brighter on the chin and throat, and streaked paler; back, scapulars and tertiaries chesnut-bay; shoulders and lesser-coverts violet-blue; the greater-coverts pale blue; quills deep violet blue; the lower part of the back violet-blue; upper tail-coverts light blue; tail with the two centre tail-feathers dull ashy-blue, the others pale azure, dull dark blue at their base, which color increases in extent towards the centre; the two outer feathers are tipped with dark blue.

The European Roller occurs as an occasional seasonal visitant to Sind; but has not been recorded from any other portion of the district.

FAMILY, Halcyonidæ, *Vigors.*

Bill very long, stout, angular, straight pointed, broadish at base, acute at tip; gape wide; rictus smooth; wings moderate, rounded; tail usually short; tarsus and toes very small, feeble, the latter much syndactyle, especially the outer one to the middle; one toe sometimes wanting.

SUB-FAMILY, Halcyoninæ.

Mostly of large size; bill strong, thick, broad at the base, straight; culmen slightly inclining at the tip; gape smooth; wings short, broad.

GENUS, Pelargopsis.

The characters are the same as those of the sub-family, but the culmen is flattened.

Pelargopsis gurial, *Pears.*

127.—*Halcyon leucocephalus*, Gmel.—Jerdon's Birds of India, Vol. I, p. 222; Butler, Deccan; Stray Feathers, Vol. IX, p. 382; Swinhoe and Barnes, Central India; Ibis, 1885, p. 61.

THE BROWN-HEADED KINGFISHER.

Length, 16; expanse, 22; wing, 6; tail, 4; tarsus, 0·75; bill at gape, 4; bill at front, 3·4.

Bill dark blood-red, dusky at tip, lighter on gonys; irides brown; legs and feet coral-red.

Head: lores, cheeks, and hind-neck in part light olive or fulvous-brown; the sides and lower part of the back of the neck buff; lower part of hind-neck and scapulars dingy brownish-green; the wing-coverts, quills, the sides of the lower part of the back, upper tail-coverts, and tail dull bluish-green; the primary quills tipped dusky-black and the inner webs of all dusky; the back, from the shoulders to the rump, light silky azure-blue; chin and throat pale yellowish-white, passing into the buff of the sides of the neck; rest of the lower plumage orange-buff, deepest on the flanks.

The young has the buff of the lower parts edged with brown, and the colors generally duller.

The Brown-headed Kingfisher occurs as a somewhat rare straggler in the Deccan. I met with it at Neemuch, and Colonel Swinhoe found it near Mhow, Central India. It has not been recorded from Guzerat, neither does it occur in Sind.

GENUS, **Halcyon**, *Swains.*

Bill long, straight, deep, and broad, somewhat quadrangular; culmen, in some, inclining towards the tip, near which the margin is slightly sinuated; lower mandible angulated; gonys ascending towards the tip; wing rather short, third quill longest, fourth and fifth nearly equal; tail short, rounded, or even; feet with the outer toe nearly as long as the middle one, syndactyle for more than half its length; scales of the tarsus obsolete.

Halcyon smyrnensis, *Lin.*

129.—*Halcyon fuscus*, Bodd.—Jerdon's Birds of India, Vol. I, p. 224; Butler, Guzerat; Stray Feathers, Vol. III, p. 456; Deccan, Stray Feathers, Vol. IX, p. 382; Murray's Vertebrate Zoology of Sind, p. 110; Swinhoe and Barnes, Central India; Ibis, 1885, p. 61.

THE WHITE-BREASTED KINGFISHER.

Length, 10·5 to 11·5; expanse, 14·25 to 16·5; wing, 4·5 to 5; tail, 3·2 to 3·7; tarsus, 0·6; bill at front, 2·25; bill at gape, 2·7 to 3.

Bill rich coral-red, dusky at tip; irides brown; feet vermilion-red.

Head: face, sides of neck and body, abdomen, and under tail-coverts, deep rich brown-chesnut; scapulars and tertiaries dul-greenish-blue; back, rump and upper tail-coverts bright cœrulean blue; wings, with the lesser-coverts, chesnut, median-coverts black, and the greater-coverts and winglet dull blue; quills blue, with a broad black tip diminishing to the last primary; and the inner webs of all dusky black, with a broad oblique white bar on the inner webs of the primaries, extending over nearly the whole feather in the last primary, small in extent on the first;

chin, throat, middle of the back, breast and abdomen pure white; tail blue, the centre feathers slightly tinged with greenish.

The White-breasted Kingfisher is generally distributed throughout the district; it is a permanent resident and breeds from March to the commencement of July and even later; it pierces a hole in the bank of a river, or side of a well or tank; there is no nest, and the eggs, five or six in number, are nearly spherical in shape, pure white in color, highly glossy when freshly laid, but becoming discolored and dull as incubation proceeds.

They measure 1·12 inches in length by 1·03 in breadth.

Halcyon pileata, *Bodd.*

130.—*Halcyon atricapillus*, Gmel.—Jerdon's Birds of India, Vol. I, p. 226; Butler, Deccan; Stray Feathers, Vol. IX, p. 382.

THE BLACK-CAPPED PURPLE KINGFISHER.

Length, 11·5 to 12·5; expanse, 18 to 19; wing, 5 to 5·3; tail, 3·25 to 3·75; bill from gape, 3.

Bill coral-red; irides red-brown; legs dusky brownish-red.

Head, lores, face, ear-coverts and nape black; whole upper parts rich violet purple, brighter on the back and rump; wings with the coverts, except those of the primaries, black; quills tipped black, with a white wing-bar on the inner webs, and the inner webs of the rest black; chin, neck, and throat all round white, with a tinge of fulvous; the middle of the breast and abdomen also white; rest of the lower parts, including the under wing-coverts, rich rusty.

This beautiful Kingfisher was obtained by Mr. Vidal at Ratnagiri, and is the only recorded instance of its occurrence within the region.

Halcyon chloris, *Bodd.*

132.—*Todiramphus collaris*, Scop.—Jerdon's Birds of India, Vol. I, p. 228; Butler, Deccan; Stray Feathers, Vol. IX, p. 383.

THE WHITE-COLLARED KINGFISHER.

Length, 10·25; expanse, 14 to 15; wing, 4·25 to 4·5; tail, 2·8 to 3; tarsus, 0·6; bill from gape, 1·6 to 2·3.

Bill black, livid-reddish at base beneath; irides reddish-brown; legs shining greenish-grey.

Head, ears and nape dull bluish-green, darker on the ear-coverts and nape, forming a sort of collar, or coronet, slightly separated from the cap by some white feathers mixed with the others; upper back and scapulars blue-green; the lower back and rump bright pale blue; wings and tail blue, more dull on the coverts, and slightly tinged greenish beneath, and a broad collar all round the neck, white.

The White-collared Kingfisher has been obtained by Mr. Vidal on two or three occasions at Ratnagiri; it has not been observed in any other portion of the district.

GENUS, **Ceyx**, *Lacepede.*

Bill, as in *Halcyon*, large, wide, barely grooved; gonys inclined upwards; culmen flattish; tail very short; feet with only three toes, two in front, one behind, the inner-toe being absent.

Ceyx tridactylus, *Pallas.*

133.—Jerdon's Birds of India, Vol. I, p. 229; Butler, Deccan, Stray Feathers, Vol. IX, p. 383.

THE THREE-TOED PURPLE KINGFISHER.

Length, 5 to 5·5; expanse, 8; wing, 2·25; tail, 0·75; bill at front, 1·25.

Bill fine coral-red; irides brown; legs and feet red.

Head rufous, with a lilac gloss, a violet spot behind the ear, and a white patch below that; a small dark blue patch at the base of the bill; interscapulars and wings deep blue, the quills black; back dark blue, with some lustrous blue streaks; lower back, rump, and upper tail-coverts, rich rufous, with a lilac shine on the middle; cheeks and lower parts ferruginous, paler on lower belly; chin and throat white.

The Three-toed Purple Kingfisher was observed by Major Butler at Khandalla, and has been recorded from other parts of the Deccan, but it is very rare, and only occurs along the banks of the mountain streams that issue from the more densely-wooded parts of the Sahyadri range.

SUB-FAMILY, **Alcedininæ.**

Bill longer, more slender and compressed, acute, grooved near the culmen for the greater part of its length; gonys nearly straight.

GENUS, **Alcedo**, *Lin.*

Bill long, slender, straight, compressed, tip acute; culmen sharp, carinated, not inclined; commissure straight, second and third quills sub-equal, third slightly the longest, first very little shorter; tail very short, even; feet weak; inner-toe very short, equal to the hind-toe, both lateral toes syndactyle.

Alcedo bengalensis, *Gm.*

134.—Jerdon's Birds of India, Vol. I, p. 230; Butler, Guzerat; Stray Feathers, Vol. III, p. 456; Deccan, Stray Feathers, Vol. IX, p. 383; Murray's Vertebrate Zoology of Sind, p. 111; Swinhoe and Barnes, Central India; Ibis, 1885, p. 61.

THE COMMON INDIAN KINGFISHER.

Length, 6 to 6·5; expanse, 9·5 to 10; wing, 2·75 to 2·9; tail, 1·1 to 1·3; tarsus, 0·4; bill from gape, 1·9; bill at front, 1·4.

Bill blackish on culmen, orange beneath towards base; irides dark brown; legs and feet orange-red.

Head and hind-neck dusky, the feathers edged with pale blue; a rufous band from the base of the nostrils to the end of the ear-coverts; below this a dark band, extending down the sides of the neck, followed by a white patch; scapulars dull green; back, rump, and upper tail-coverts pale blue; wings and tail dull green-blue; the wing-coverts speckled with pale blue; quills dusky on their inner edges; chin and throat white, the rest of the lower plumage bright ferruginous.

In young birds a bluish-green tinge is the prevalent tint; in adults a pure blue.

The Indian Kingfisher is commonly distributed throughout the district, but it occurs more rarely in Sind, where it is replaced by the next species; with this exception it is a permanent resident, breeding from March quite to the end of May and occasionally later; the nest-hole is pierced in the bank of a stream, invariably according to my experience over running water; the eggs, five or six in number, are broadish ovals, white and beautifully glossy. They measure 0·8 in length by 0·68 in breadth.

Alcedo ispida, *Lin.*

134*bis.*—Murray's Vertebrate Zoology of Sind, p. 111.

THE EUROPEAN KINGFISHER.

Length, 6·8 to 7·5; expanse, 10 to 11; wing, 2·95 to 3·; bill, at front, 1·4 to 1·6.

Bill above blackish-brown, at base and beneath reddish-orange; irides hazel; legs orange-red.

A broad bright orange stripe from the bill to the ear-coverts margined on the sides of the gape and crossed below the eye by a narrow black streak; sides of the neck with a white patch commencing from behind the ear-coverts; chin and throat white; head, nape, neck behind, a broad streak from the base of the lower mandible and lesser wing-coverts, greenish-blue; the feathers edged with bright light blue, and forming narrow bars or spots of that color; scapulars and exterior webs of the primaries greenish-blue, the inner webs of the latter dusky brown; back, rump, and upper tail-coverts rich azure-blue; tail deep blue; breast and entire under surface of the body bright orange.

The European Kingfisher occurs commonly in Sind, where it takes the place of *A. bengalensis;* the latter, however, is not altogether absent, but only occurs as an occasional seasonal visitant.

Its nesting arrangements are similar to those of its relative, *A. bengalensis.*

Alcedo beavani, *Wald.*

135*quat.*—Butler, Deccan; Stray Feathers, Vol. IX, p. 383.

BEAVAN'S KINGFISHER.

Length, 6·25 to 6·5; expanse, 9·25 to 9·75; wing 2·55 to 2·62; tail, 1·4 to 1·75; tarsus, 0·3 to 0·35; bill from gape, 1·9 to 2·05; bill at front, 1·4 to 1·6·

Bill, ♂, black, orange at gape; ♀, deep red, clouded with dusky.

Chin and throat creamy-white, washed faintly with rufous; remainder of under surface and the under tail-coverts deep bright rufous, paler in some than in others; feathers of the head black, with a penultimate bright blue band, those of the cheeks all bright blue; back and upper tail-coverts bright blue; wing-coverts black, washed with blue, each feather tipped with, bright blue; scapulars and rectrices black, washed with blue.

Major Butler had a specimen in his possession that was shot in the forests west of Belgaum; this is the only record I can find of its occurrence within the region.

GENUS, Ceryle.

Bill long, straight, compressed, acute at tip; culmen obtuse, somewhat flattened, and margined on each side by an indented groove; tail slightly lengthened, rounded; wings long, second and third quills nearly equal; inner-toe longer than the hinder one which is very short.

Ceryle rudis, *Lin.*

136.—Jordon's Birds of India, Vol. I, p. 232; Butler, Guzerat; Stray Feathers, Vol. III, p. 456; Deccan, Stray Feathers' Vol. IX, p. 383; Murray's Vertebrate Zoology of Sind, p. 112; Swinhoe and Barnes, Central India; Ibis, 1885, p. 61.

THE PIED KINGFISHER.

Length, 11 to 11·5; expanse, 18·5 to 20; wing, 5·4 to 5·8; tail, 3; tarsus, 0·5 to 0·7; bill at front, 2·3; bill from gape, 3·1.

Bill black; irides dark brown; legs and feet blackish-brown.

Head and ears black, white-streaked, with also a white supercilium; back, rump, upper tail-coverts, and wings black, white-edged; lower parts and the sides of the neck white, with a streak of black down the sides of the neck from the ear-coverts; breast with a broad interrupted band of black in both sexes, and below this another complete but narrow band in the male only; wings with a white band, formed by the bases of some of the quills, and the greater-coverts; primary-coverts and winglet black; tail white at the base, broadly black at the end, and tipped white.

The Pied Kingfisher is another very common species, generally distributed throughout our limits.

It is a permanent resident and breeds from February to April, in holes pierced in the banks of rivers; the eggs, four to six in number, are broad oval in shape, white in color, and are highly glossy. They measure 1·15 in length by about 0·92 in breadth.

This Kingfisher never resorts to wells and tanks, as *H. smyr-*

nensis and *A. bengalensis* do, but only occurs on rivers and the larger lakes.

FAMILY, **Bucerotidæ.**

Bill enormous, arched or curved, often with an appendage or casque on the upper mandible; nostrils small at the junction of the casque with the bill, or near the culmen, when there is no casque; wings short, rounded; tail long, of ten feathers; tarsus short, stout; feet moderately large, syndactyle; hind-toe short; claws short, thick, well curved.

GENUS, **Dichoceros.**

GENUS, **Homraius.**

Bill with a broad flat casque, extending backwards over the head, for more than half the length of the bill, and descending to meet the bill at a right angle, of large size; plumage black and white.

Dichoceros cavatus, *Shaw.*

140.—*Homraius bicornis,* Lin.—Jerdon's Birds of India, Vol. I, p. 242; Butler, Deccan, &c.; Stray Feathers, Vol. IX, p. 383.

THE GREAT HORNBILL.

♂. Length, 45 to 47; expanse, 63 to 66; tail, 15·5 to 16·75; wing, 18·25 to 19; tarsus, 2·73 to 3; bill from gape, 9·75 to 10·6.

♀. Length, 41·75 to 44; expanse, 54 to 59·28; tail, 14·5 to 17·75; wing, 17·25 to 18·25; tarsus, 2·45 to 2·75; bill from gape, 8·25 to 9.

General color of bill and casque yellow, paler on the lower mandible, but varying much in depth of color.

The upper mandible is more or less tinted with red at the tip and with orange in the medial portion; the sides of the casque have generally an orange tinge, and the flat or rather curved portion of the casque is generally tinged with orange, intermingled with red.

In some specimens the coloration is very bright, in others the whole bill and casque is duller and paler.

In the male, the posterior portion of the casque, a triangular patch on each side of the casque in front, and the truncated portion of the culmen from three to five inches downwards from the anterior margin of the casque, are black.

In the female, the posterior portion of the casque is red; there is no patch on the side of the casque, and the truncated portion of the culmen in front of the casque or more is red.

In the male the irides are blood-red; in the female pearly-white; the orbital region dark fleshy-pink; the eyelids black.

The legs and feet are dull greenish-plumbeous, or pale dingy glaucous-green; claws dark greenish-horny.

Head and base of bill all round, back, wings, and belly, black; neck, ends of upper tail-coverts, tail, thigh-coverts, vent, under tail-coverts, and wing-spot, white, the latter formed by the edges of the greater-coverts; the base of the primaries, and the tips of all the quills, also white; tail with a broad black band towards the terminal third; the neck, and sometimes the wing-spot, are often smeared yellow from the secretion of the uropygial gland.

The Great Hornbill is a permanent resident in the forest-clad portions of the Sahyadri range, where it is not uncommon.

It has not been recorded from any other portion of our limits.

GENUS, **Hydrocissa**, *Bonap.*

Bill with a long, sharp, acute casque, extending from the base of the bill over two-thirds of its length.

Hydrocissa coronata, *Bodd.*

141.—Jerdon's Birds of India, Vol. I, p. 245; Butler, Deccan; Stray Feathers, Vol. IX, p. 383.

THE MALABAR PIED HORNBILL.

Length, 36; expanse, 39; wing, 11·25 to 13; tail, 12 to 14; bill from gape, 6 to 7.

Bill and part of the casque yellowish-white; base of both mandibles black, extending obliquely downwards and forwards, also the hind margin of the casque (in the male only); a large patch of the same color occupies the anterior three-fourths of the casque in old specimens, but never reaches downwards to the upper mandible, as in the next species; casque very large and exceedingly compressed, laterally protruding far backward over the crown and its ridge terminating in an acute angle anteriorly, being prolonged considerably beyond the junction of the casque with the upper mandible; irides crimson; feet dark green.

The female has no black on the hind edge of the casque, and both bill and casque are slightly smaller.

The young have at first no black on the incipient casque, which appears and increases in quantity with the growth of the latter.

Black beneath from the breast; tips of the primaries and secondaries, and the three outer tail-feathers on each side, with more or less of the next pair, pure white.

Permanent resident and not uncommon in the forests near Belgaum and in the Kanara jungles. It also occurs along the Sahyadri range.

It has not been recorded from any other portion of the district.

GENUS, **Ocyceros.**

Bill with a compressed sharp-pointed casque, size small; plumage grey.

Ocyceros birostris, *Scop.*

144.—*Meniceros bicornis*, Scop.—Jerdon's Birds of India, Vol. I, p. 248 ; Butler, Guzerat ; Stray Feathers, Vol. III, p. 457 ; Deccan, Stray Feathers, Vol. IX, p. 384 ; *Lophoceros birostris*, Scop. Swinhoe and Barnes, Central India ; Ibis, 1885, p. 62.

THE COMMON GREY HORNBILL.

Length, 22 to 25 ; expanse, 25 to 32 ; wing, 7·5 to 8·7 ; tail, 10 to 12 ; tarsus, 1·7 ; bill from gape, 3·5 to 4·25.

Bill and casque dusky ; the tips and ridges of both mandibles whitish ; casque low and compressed, the ridge prolonged anteriorly to a very acute angle, and the hind part concealed by the feathers of the forehead (which bend down over it) and not extending backward over the crown.

In the female the casque is lower, more depressed and the sharp pointed horn is wanting ; irides red-brown ; feet dark plumbeous.

Plumage grey, paler below, and from the breast gradually albescent ; ear-coverts darker cinereous, and a light streak over the eye and ear-coverts ; primaries and secondaries dusky black, the latter margined with grey, all except the two first tipped white, with a brownish-white streak on the outer web ; tail black near the end, tipped white.

In the female and in immature bird the first six or seven primaries want the white tips entirely, while on all but the first two, the whitish streaks are much more developed and conspicuous than in the *adult male.*

The Common Grey Hornbill does not occur in Sind, and has only been doubtfully recorded from the Deccan ; it is not uncommon at Mount Aboo and forests at foot, and is very common at and near Mhow and Neemuch ;—indeed, generally speaking, it is not uncommon in all the well-wooded portions of Rajpootana, Guzerat, and Central India.

GENUS, Tockus, *Lesson.*

Bill without a casque, but with the ridge somewhat elevated and much curved ; size small ; plumage grey.

Tockus griseus, *Lath.*

145.—*Tockus gingalensis*, Shaw.—Jerdon's Birds of India, Vol. I, p. 250 ; Butler, Deccan ; Stray Feathers, Vol. IX, p. 384.

THE JUNGLE GREY HORNBILL.

Length, 22 ; expanse, 25 to 27 ; wing, 8·25 ; tail, 8·5 to 9·5 ; tarsus, 1·6 ; bill from gape, 4·25.

Bill horny-yellow, suffused with a brownish-red tinge, except towards the tips ; margin along commissure black ; tips paler ; orbital skin black ; irides red ; tarsi and feet greenish.

Head above, and back, dark cinereous-brown, with a cast of bluish grey ; the greater coverts, secondaries, and primaries, all narrowly edged with whitish, and the latter broadly tipped with white, and with an oblique white line on their outer edge; a pale line over the eyes, extending along the sides of the head; the two centre tail feathers dusky bluish-grey, the rest dusky blackish-grey, broadly tipped with white, except the pair next the centrals; beneath light dusky-grey, the feathers centred paler; rufescent on the lower abdomen, outer thigh-feathers, and under tail-coverts.

A specimen in Mr. Hume's possession, obtained from Travancore does not correspond over well with Dr. Jerdon's description. I therefore quote Mr. Hume's description in full:—"The forehead is greyish-white; a broad superciliary stripe from the nostrils over the eyes extending some distance back, a slightly brownish-white; the feathers of the crown and occiput slaty-grey, the latter conspicuously elongated and with greyish-white shaft-stripes; faint greyish-white tippings to most of the feathers of the crown; the ear-coverts dark brown paler shafted; feathers of the chin whitish; entire throat and sides of the neck grey; the feathers pale, almost white shafted; the whole of the plumage of these parts is dull, as is also that of the lower parts, but all the rest of the upper parts is well glossed; the entire back, rump, upper tail-coverts, scapulars, and wing-coverts, dark greyish-dusky, with a faint greenish reflection on it; the coverts have mostly the faintest possible pale edges, and the shafts of many of the feathers have in certain lights a scarcely perceptible line on either side of them; the quills and tail-feathers are black, with a greenish lustre on them, very conspicuous on the secondaries and tail-feathers except the central pair; the third to the eighth primary inclusive broadly tipped with pure white on both webs, the ninth similarly tipped but on the inner web only.

All the tail-feathers but the central pair broadly tipped with white; breast, flanks, sides, and upper abdomen, greyish-white to white; vent and lower tail-coverts white, tinged with fulvous or dingy pale rufescent.

The Jungle Grey Hornbill is a permanent resident and occurs sparingly all along the Sahyadri range. It does not occur in any other portion of our limits.

TRIBE, **Scansores.**

Toes in pairs; bill, wings, and tail various.

FAMILY, **Psittacidæ.**

Bill short, thick, strong; upper mandible much curved and hooked (sometimes toothed or notched), overhanging the lower one, and with an acute tip; lower mandible short, obtuse; base of bill covered with a cere, in which the round and small nostrils are pierced near the culmen; wings usually moderate or long, the second quill generally the longest; tail various; tarsi short, stout, covered with small tubercle-like scales; toes in pairs; claws well curved.

SUB-FAMILY, **Palæorninæ**, *Vigors.*

Bill moderate; upper mandible moderately hooked; under mandible short; tail very long, wedge-shaped, the feathers narrow and pointed; tarsus moderate.

GENUS, **Palæornis**, *Vigors.*

Bill short; culmen rounded, well curved, toothed, and with the tip acute, not much deeper than it is long; lower mandible short; wings long, with the second and third quills sub-equal and longest; tail very long, cuneate; the feathers narrow, almost linear, with their tips obtuse, and the two middle feathers in general exceeding the others.

Palæornis eupatria, *Lin.*

147.—*Palæornis alexandri,* Lin.—Jerdon's Birds of India, Vol. I, p. 256; Butler, Guzerat; Stray Feathers, Vol. III, p. 457; Swinhoe and Barnes, Central India; Ibis, 1885, p. 62.

THE ALEXANDRINE PAROQUET.

Length, 21; wing, 8·25; tail, 11·5; bill at gape, 1·25.

Bill deep red, yellowish beneath; irides pale yellow; feet plumbeous.

Adult male, green, brilliant emeraldine on the head and face, duller on the back, paler beneath, inclining to dingy on the breast and yellowish on the chin and lower tail-coverts; quills bluish; the inner edge of the inner webs dusky; tail with the two centre feathers bright green at their base, pale bluish-green for the remaining two-thirds, and tipped yellowish; the outer feathers light green on the outer webs, yellowish-green internally; a black stripe from the base of the lower mandible crossing round behind the ears, and a demi-collar of peach-rose color on the nape and sides of the neck; in front of this collar the feathers are glaucous; a dark red spot on the shoulders of the wings, and some of the feathers of the wing-coverts and scapulars narrowly edged with dusky; a narrow line from the nostrils to the eye tinged with black.

The female wants the collar of the male, and is generally less brightly colored.

The Alexandrine Paroquet is not uncommon on the Vindhian range and the jungles adjacent; and it also occurs not infrequently in the better wooded portions of Rajpootana and Central India; one was obtained at Mount Aboo by Captain Butler. It does not occur either in the Deccan or in any part of Sind.

Palæornis torquatus, *Bodd.*

148.—Jerdon's Birds of India, Vol. I, p. 257; Butler, Guzerat; Stray Feathers, Vol. III, p. 457; Deccan, Stray Feathers, Vol. IX, p. 384; Murray's Vertebrate Zoology of Sind, p. 112; Swinhoe and Barnes, Central India; Ibis, 1885, p. 62.

THE ROSE-RINGED PAROQUET.
Tota, Hin.

Length, 16·5 ; wing, 6·5 to 7 ; tail, 9·5 ; bill from gape, 1.

Bill cherry-red ; irides pale yellow ; feet cinereous.

Adult male : head and face emerald-green ; a dark line from the nostrils to the front of the eye, indistinct round the base of the narrow cere ; hind-neck and nape glaucous or light-ashy, succeeded on the sides of the neck by a black demi-collar meeting under the chin and followed by another of a peach-rose color ; back, scapulars, and tertiaries dull-green ; upper tail-coverts emerald-green ; entire under-surface pale green, yellowish towards the vent ; primaries, their coverts and secondaries, dark-green, their inner webs and under-surface dusky ; tail-feathers dark-green, their inner webs and under-surface yellowish, the two centre feathers dark-green at their base, bluish for the remaining two-thirds and tipped yellowish, all black shafted ; under wing-coverts greenish-yellow.

The female wants the rose collar, but has a bright emeraldine narrow green collar in its place.

The Rose-ringed Paroquet occurs in vast flocks, throughout the district ; it is a permanent resident, breeding during February and March, in holes in trees or stone walls, occasionally under roof tiles ; when the nest hole is in a tree, it is often two or three feet in extent.

There is no nest ; the eggs, four in number, are deposited on any chips that may have accidentally fallen whilst the hole was being enlarged ; they are oval in shape, pure glossless white in color, and measure 1·2 in length by 0·95 in breadth.

The absurd attitude and affected manner of the female during the courting season in the endeavour to attract the notice of her mate is highly entertaining ; the male, on the other hand, seems to take little notice of it, beyond rewarding her with an occasional kiss.

Palæornis purpureus, *P. Z. S. Mull.*

149.—*Palæornis rosa*, Bodd.—Jerdon's Birds of India, Vol. I, p. 259 ; Butler, Guzerat ; Stray Feathers, Vol. III, p, 457 ; Deccan, Stray Feathers, Vol. IX, p. 384 ; Swinhoe and Barnes, Central India ; Ibis, 1885, p. 62.

THE ROSE-HEADED PAROQUET.
Tuia-tota, Hin.

Length, 14 to 15 ; wing, 5·25 ; tail, 8·5 ; bill from gape, 0·62 to 0·7.

Bill : upper mandible yellow,. under dusky ; irides, outer circle yellowish-white, inner blue ; legs grey.

Adult male : the whole head and face pale roseate, tinged with plum-bloom posteriorly and inferiorly ; a black spot from the base of the lower mandible, uniting into a narrow complete collar, and meeting its opposite one at the chin, which is thus broadly black ;

behind the collar, the hind-neck verdigris-green; the upper portion of the back and scapulars yellow-green; the lower back, rump, and upper tail-coverts, pale blue-green; the wings green, with a small red spot on the lesser-coverts; shoulders bluish-green; the whole inner webs of most of the quills dusky; tail, with the two centre feathers, cobalt-blue, tipped white; the next pair blue towards the apical portion, also tipped white, the others pale green on their outer webs, yellowish internally; plumage beneath bright siskin, or yellow green; some are less brightly colored, and more of an uniform green color, with less yellow; and the old males have the cap much brighter and deeper colored than their juniors.

The female has the head plum-blue, and wants the black collar, but has a yellow demi-collar in front and on the sides; and the breast is much tinged with oil yellow.

The young birds are green throughout; but the centre tail-feathers are always blue, and there is usually a faint indication of the pale collar of the female.

With the exception of Sind, the Purple-headed Paroquet is generally distributed throughout our limits, but is far less common and is more locally distributed than *P. torquatus.* It is a permanent resident, and breeds in holes in trees about April.

The eggs are miniatures of those of *P. torquatus;* they measure 1 inch in length by 0·8 in breadth.

Palæornis columboides, *Vigors.*

151.—Jerdon's Birds of India, Vol. I, p. 261; Butler, Deccan; Stray Feathers, Vol. IX, p. 384.

THE BLUE-WINGED PAROQUET.

Length, 15; wing, 6; tail, 8·75; bill from gape, 0·7.

Bill, above cherry-red, beneath dusky; legs and feet greenish-plumbeous.

Head: hind-neck, inter-scapularies, and the plumage beneath, generally, pale dove-grey, purest on the head and cheeks; a verdigris-green patch on the forehead, lores, and below the eye; a black collar round the neck, meeting at the chin; and in front of this, there is a verdigris-green collar, which widens on the upper part of the neck; the lower part of the back, rump, and upper tail-coverts, blue-green; wing-coverts and scapulars dark blue-green; the feathers edged pale; the primary-coverts and quills darkish blue, faintly edged with green externally, and dusky on the inner webs; tail, with the centre feathers blue, tipped with yellowish-white; the next pair blue on the outer web, greenish near the base, and tipped yellow; all the others green externally, yellow internally; lower abdomen, vent, and under tail-coverts pale verdigris-green.

The female wants the collar, or has only a faint indication of it, and the bill is black.

The Blue-winged Paroquet is common on the Ghâts to the west of Belgaum, and it also occurs on the Sahyadri range quite as far north as Khandalla.

It does not occur elsewhere within our limits.

SUB-FAMILY, **Loriinæ**.

Bill compressed, small or moderate, slightly curved; the margin of the upper mandible sometimes sinuated, and the notch obsolete; the lower mandible slender, conic, much longer than high.

GENUS, **Loriculus**, *Blyth.*

Bill rather small, gently curving from the base; the upper mandible lengthened, slightly sinuated at the margin, moderately hooked, and tapering to a fine point; lower mandible small; wings nearly as long as the tail; first and second quill longest; tail short, even, or barely rounded.

Loriculus vernalis, *Sparrm.*

153.—Jerdon's Birds of India, Vol. I, p. 265; Butler, Deccan and South Mahratta country; Stray Feathers, Vol. IX, p. 384.

THE INDIAN LORIQUET.

Length, 5·5 to 5·75; expanse, 8·75 to 10·25; wing, 3·4 to 3·75; tail, 1·5 to 1·81; tarsus, 0·3 to 0·35; bill from gape, 0·45 to 0·5.

Bill dark yellow to plumbeous; irides pale yellow; legs and feet leaden to plumbeous.

Above grass-green, darker on the wing-coverts and scapulars, paler and yellowish beneath; the wings and tail blue-green; rump and upper tail-coverts dull deep red; wings and tail beneath pale bluish; chin and throat, in the male, tinged with verdigris-blue.

The Indian Lorikeet is a cold weather visitant to the forests of the Sahyadri Range as far north at least as Khandalla, and it has been observed at Ratnagiri, Dharwar and in the Goa forests, but it is absent from all other portions of the district.

FAMILY, **Picidæ**.

Bill moderate and long, straight, angular, wedge-like; tongue long, extensile; wings moderate, or rather long; tail of twelve feathers, ten of them with shafts, thick and stiff, the outermost pair minute; feet with the toes in pairs, one toe sometimes wanting.

SUB-FAMILY, **Picinæ**, *Gray.*

Bill perfectly wedge-shaped, compressed; culmen straight; the lateral ridge well marked, more or less median; gonys long; the outer posterior toe longer than the anterior one; wings rather long.

Genus, Picus, *Lin.*

Bill moderate, compressed, with the culmen straight and sharp; the lateral ridge distinct, midway between the culmen and margin, and joining the margin about its middle; gonys long, barely angulated; versatile toe longer than the anterior.

Picus sindianus, *Gould.*

158.—Jerdon's Birds of India, Vol. I, p. 273; Murray's Vertebrate Zoology of Sind, p. 113.

THE SIND PIED WOODPECKER.

♂. Length, 8·5 to 8·6; expanse, 14·5 to 15; wing, 4·5 to 4·6; tail, 3·1 to 3·2; bill, 1·25.

♀. Length, 8 to 8·5; expanse, 13 to 15; wing, 4·4 to 4·7; tail, 3 to 3·2.

Bill blackish above, lighter beneath; irides crimson; legs dusky.

Adult male: forehead, lores, sides of the head, ear-coverts, supercilia and breast white, tinged buffy on the forehead, or a soiled white; a very narrow dark line above the supercilia; a dark stripe from the lower mandible extending down each side of the throat, projecting to the lower side of the breast, and joining the back at the shoulder; crown of the head mixed crimson and black; back, rump, upper tail-coverts and centre tail-feathers, glossy black with a dusky tinge; scapulars, and the adjacent wing-coverts, white, the remainder of the wing-coverts black with a few white spots; quills brownish-black, spotted with white on both webs forming white wing-bars, of which there are four on the primaries and three on the secondaries; lateral tail-feathers black, barred and tipped with white; lower parts white, with a few dusky streaks on the flanks and abdomen; middle of abdomen and lower tail-coverts crimson.

The female has the crown black.

This Woodpecker occurs pretty generally throughout Sind, where it is a permanent resident, breeding during March and April. It does not occur in any other portion of the district.

Picus mahrattensis, *Lath.*

160.—Jerdon's Birds of India, Vol. I, p. 274; Butler, Guzerat; Stray Feathers, Vol. III, p. 458; Deccan, Stray Feathers, Vol. IX, p. 385; Murray's Vertebrate Zoology of Sind, p. 114; Swinhoe and Barnes, Central India; Ibis, 1885, p. 62.

THE YELLOW-FRONTED WOODPECKER.

Length, 7·5 to 7·75; expanse, 12·5; wing, 4 to 4·4; tail, 2·5; bill at front, 1.

Bill slaty-plumbeous; irides crimson; legs cinereous.

Plumage above, wings, and tail, black, banded with white; forehead and top of head pale yellow; occiput bright crimson in the male, yellow in the female; lores, around the eyes, ear-coverts, sides of neck behind the throat, and middle of the neck and breast, white, a brown stripe commencing near the nape, down the sides of the neck and breast; breast and abdomen brown, with pale edges to the feathers; a patch of crimson on the centre of the abdomen continued to the vent.

The Yellow-fronted Woodpecker occurs sparingly in Sind, but is common throughout the remaining portion of the district. It is a permanent resident breeding about March; it lays three transparent white eggs, at the bottom of a hole, pierced in a decayed branch of a tree; there is no nest, except a few chips that may have fallen in during the time the hole was being excavated. They measure 0·87 inches in length, by 0·68 in breadth.

GENUS, Yungipicus, *Bonap.*

Of small size; plumage spotted, or banded black and white above; bill barely straight; lateral ridge near the culmen; wings long; tail, with the two central feathers, longest; the outer feathers soft and rounded.

Yungipicus nanus, *Vig.*

164.—*Yungipicus hardwickii*, Jerd.—Jerdon's Birds of India, Vol, I, p. 278; Butler, Deccan; Stray Feathers, Vol. IX, p. 385; Guzerat, Stray Feathers, Vol. III, p. 458.

THE SOUTHERN PIGMY WOODPECKER.

Length, 5 to 5·25; expanse, 9·5; wing 3; tail, 1·5; tarsus, 0·4; bill at front, 0·4.

Bill plumbeous; orbital skin lake; irides pale yellow; legs plumbeous.

Above brownish or sooty-brown, banded with white on the back; head pale rufescent or yellowish-brown, scarcely deepening posteriorly; beneath white, sullied on the abdomen, and with pale brown streaks throughout; a narrow white band from above the eye down the side of the neck; a pale brown band from beneath the eye, below the white band, and another faint line beginning on the sides of the neck and being gradually lost in the markings of the breast. The male has a somewhat long and narrow orange streak, beginning considerably behind the eye.

This Woodpecker occurs sparingly along the Sahyadri Range as far north as Khandalla; it also occurs in the forest to the west of Belgaum, and at Mahableshwar, Savantvadi and Ratnagiri. With the exception of a doubtful specimen from Anadra near Mount Aboo, it has not been recorded from any other portion of the district.

SUB-FAMILY, Campephilinæ.

Bill strong, somewhat wide, nearly straight, or very slightly curving; lateral ridge near the culmen sometimes wanting; gonys short; versatile toe about equal to the anterior, sometimes

8

longer; hind-head generally with a full crest; neck thin; wings and tail various.

Genus, Hemicercus, *Swainson.*

Bill straight, considerably compressed, the lateral ridge slight near the margin; wings long, nearly reaching (when closed) to the end of the tail; tail very short, broad; neck short, very slender; feet very large; versatile toe always longer than the anterior one.

Hemicercus cordatus, *Jerd.*

165.—*Hemicercus canente*, Lesson.—Jerdon's Birds of India, Vol. I, p. 280; Butler, Deccan; Stray Feathers, Vol. IX, p. 385.

THE HEART-SPOTTED WOODPECKER.

♂. Length, 6; expanse, 12; wing, 3·72; tail, 1·25; bill at front, 0·88.

♀. Length, 5·75; expanse, 10·75; wing, 3·6; tail, 1·36; bill at front, 0·67.

Bill bluish-black; irides brownish-red; legs dusky-green.

Female, with the forehead and top of the head a narrow line in the middle of the inter-scapular region, rump, shoulders, lesser wing-coverts, and a stripe from the lower mandible running below the ears of a light whitish-yellow; the wing-coverts and tertiaries with a black heart-shaped spot near the tip of each feather; face, cheeks, long occipital crest, nape, scapulars, quills, upper tail-coverts, and tail, deep black; tertiaries greenish; middle of back dull blackish-green; beneath, chin and throat, whitish-yellow; from throat to vent dull blackish-green; under tail-coverts black.

The male differs from the female in having the forehead and head black, with minute whitish spots. On the centre of the back is a brush of dark sap-green bristly feathers, smeared with a viscid secretion from a gland beneath.

Jerdon (by a slip of the pen probably) has described the male as the female, and *vicê versâ*, but this has been rectified in the text.

The Heart-spotted Woodpecker occurs sparingly in the forests west of Belgaum and on the Sahyadri Range. It has not been recorded from elsewhere within our limits.

Genus, Chrysocolaptes, *Blyth.*

Bill much as in typical *picus*, almost quite straight, strong; the lateral ridge medial at first, afterwards parallel to, and nearer the margin; tail short, square; the four central feathers equal; feet strong; hind-toe longer than the anterior-toe.

Chrysocolaptes delesserti, *Malh.*

166*bis.*—Butler, Deccan; Stray Feathers, Vol. IX, p. 385.

THE SOUTHERN LARGE GOLDEN-BACKED WOODPECKER.

Length, 11·5; expanse, 18·75; wing, 5·75; tail, 4; bill at front, 1·7.

Bill slaty; irides yellow; legs slaty.

Male: top of the head and crest crimson; upper back and greater part of the wings externally golden-yellow; lower part of back shining carmine-red; band from the eyes, surrounding the forehead, ruddy-brown, passing through the eye, and changing into a wide black neck-stripe; above this, between it and the crest is a narrow white line; the dorsal aspect of the neck also white; primaries wholly blackish, with three or four white spots on the inner webs of all the feathers; upper tail-coverts and tail black; beneath the neck is anteriorly white, with five black gular stripes; breast black, more or less brunnescent, with large central drops of white; the rest of the body, below, and lining of the wings, white, transversely barred with black.

The female has the cap black, with a white drop on each feather.

This Woodpecker only differs from *Chrysocolaptes sultaneus*, Hodgs., in its smaller size.

It is a not uncommon permanent resident all along the Sahyadri Range, but has not been recorded from elsewhere within our limits.

Chrysocolaptes festivus, *Bodd.*

167.—*Chrysocolaptes goensis*, Gmel.—Jerdon's Birds of India, Vol. I, p. 282; Butler, Guzerat; Stray Feathers, Vol. III, p. 458; Deccan, Stray Feathers, Vol. IX, p. 385; Swinhoe and Barnes, Central India; Ibis, 1885, p. 62.

THE BLACK-BACKED WOODPECKER.

Length, 12·2 to 12·5; expanse, 19·5 to 20·5; wings, 6 to 6·25; tail, 3·4 to 3·5; tarsus, 1; bill at front, 1·9 to 2.

Bill dusky-blackish; irides crimson; legs and feet horny-plumbeous.

Crown and occiput of the male splendid crimson; forehead mingled black and white; lores white; a white streak begins behind the eye, and is continued to the nape, the entire hind-part of the neck being wholly white, and extending down upon the interscapulars; the rest of the back, scapulars, rump, and tail, are brownish-black, having a slight aureous cast on the scapulars; wings, with their coverts and secondaries, bright golden-yellow; bend of the wing, winglet, and coverts of the primaries, as also the primaries, dusky black, with distant, large, round whitish spots on their inner webs, and similar dull spots on the outer webs; a broad black streak, down the sides of the neck, from the eye, beneath, the throat white, with three black stripes; the rest of the body, beneath, more or less streaked; the feathers of the breast white, with black lateral edges, which last gradually all but disappear on the belly, vent and lower tail-coverts.

The Black-backed Woodpecker is not common; it has been obtained near Aboo, at Mhow in Central India, aud at Ratnagiri; it does not occur in Sind.

GENUS, Thriponax.

Lateral ridge prominent near the culmen, which is sharp and very slightly arched; gonys hardly half the length of the under mandible; toes short; anterior toe longer than the versatile one; claws very large; neck long and slender; head, with a short compact crest; wings and tail long, the latter cuneate.

Thriponax hodgsoni, *Jerdon.*

169.—*Mulleripicus hodgsoni*, Jerd.—Jerdon's Birds of India, Vol. I, p. 284; Butler, Deccan; Stray Feathers, Vol. IX, p. 386.

THE GREAT BLACK WOODPECKER.

Length, 17 to 19; expanse, 24 to 26; wing, 8 to 9; tail, 7·5; bill at front, 2 to 2·3.

Bill black; irides crimson; legs dark plumbeous.

Head, with short thick crest, and stripe running from the base of the lower mandible, crimson; lower part of back, rump and middle of belly, white; the rest of the plumage deep black.

The Great Black Woodpecker has been obtained at Kanara and also in the forests west of Belgaum; there is no other record of its occurrence within the district.

SUB-FAMILY, Gecininæ.

Bill widened, with the culmen more or less curved; lateral ridge very slight or absent altogether; gonys short; feet small; hind-toe shorter than the anterior outer one; the hind-toe, indeed, is always very small, and absent in some.

GENUS, Gecinus, *Boie.*

Bill slightly widened in its whole length, compressed at the tip; upper mandible thickened at the base, with one or more slightly elevated lines (representing the lateral ridge), close to the culmen, which is very slightly arched; gonys very short; wings moderate; anterior and versatile toes nearly equal; hind-head with a narrow pointed crest; neck thick; tail rather long, cuneate.

Gecinus striolatus, *Blyth.*

171.—Jerdon's Birds of India, Vol. I, p. 287; Butler, Guzerat; Stray Feathers, Vol. III, p. 458; Deccan, Stray Feathers, Vol. IX, p. 386.

THE SMALL GREEN WOODPECKER.

Length, 11·5; expanse, 17; wing, 5·25; tail, 3·75; bill at front, 1·2; foot, 2·2.

Bill horny above, yellowish at base and beneath; irides pink with an outer circle of white; feet greenish-slaty.

Above green, the rump and upper tail-coverts tinged with yellowish; forehead and lores whitish, mixed with black; a small white eye-brow, with a black line above it, which is lost on the hind-head; ear-coverts mixed black and white; cheek-stripe inconspicuous, with a white line above it; entire under parts whitish, streaked with dusky-green, more or less dark on the breast, and always greenish-black on the belly; on the throat and foreneck the feathers have each a mesial dusky-black line, widening on the breast, and dividing and becoming scale-like, lower on the abdomen; caudal bars almost obsolete, except on the middle pair, and on the exterior web of the outermost pair in some specimens; head crimson in the male, black in the female.

The Small Green Woodpecker has been observed in the forests west of Belgaum, and is not uncommon in the jungles at the foot of the Aravalli Range; it has not been recorded from any other part of the district.

Genus, **Chrysophlegma**, *Gould.*

Bill similar to that of the last, wider at the base and more compressed at the tip, slightly more curved, and shorter, with the lateral ridge nearly obsolete, only existing close to the base of the bill; the culmen blunt; tail long, cuneate; feet short; the claws very strongly curved.

Chrysophlegma chlorigaster, *Jerdon.*

175.—*Chrysophlegma chlorophanes*, Vieill.—Jerdon's Birds of India, Vol. I. p. 290; Butler, Deccan; Stray Feathers, Vol. IX, p. 386.

The Southern Yellow-naped Woodpecker.

Length, 9; wing, 4·75; tail, 3·9; bill at front, 0·9.

Bill slaty-greenish, yellow beneath; irides reddish-brown; legs dull green.

Male with the whole head and cheek-stripe red, a small occipital crest of the same color, shortly terminated by bright yellow; plumage above bright green; ear-feathers and beneath dull sap or brownish-green; the feathers of the lower abdomen banded and spotted with white; wings greenish with an orange tinge, and the outer web of most of the quill feathers deep orange-red; the inner webs dusky with white spots; tail unspotted, black.

Has several times been obtained in the forests west of Belgaum, but hitherto has not been recorded from any other portion of the district.

Genus **Micropternus**, *Blyth.*

Bill broad at base; culmen arched, the sides slightly rounded; lateral ridge wanting; wing rather short; tail short and broad; feet small; versatile and anterior toes above equal; inner hind-toe and claw minute; the plumage of a peculiar chesnut-bay coloring.

Micropternus phaioceps, *Blyth.*

178.—Jerdon's Birds of India, Vol. I. p. 294.

THE BENGAL RUFOUS WOODPECKER.

Length, 9·5; wing, 4·75 to 5; tail, 2·75; bill at front, 1.

Plumage dark chesnut bay, with black bands; head brown above, paling posteriorly, the feathers faintly streaked, and gradually merged on the hind-neck in the bay color of the back; chin, cheek, and throat, pale, the feathers of this last concolorous with the body, or nearly so, merely having lighter lateral margins; neck in front, breast and upper part of abdomen, bright chesnut-bay; from the middle of the abdomen the same but paler and with dusky cross-bands.

According to Jerdon, the Bengal Rufous Woodpecker is found in some of the forests of Central India.

Micropternus gularis, *Jerd.*

179.—Jerdon's Birds of India, Vol. I, p. 294; Butler, Deccan; Stray Feathers, Vol. IX, p. 386.

THE MADRAS RUFOUS WOODPECKER.

Length, 7 to 9; wing, 4·8; tail, 2·5 to 3; bill at front, 0·9.

Bill blackish; orbital skin slaty; irides brown; legs slaty.

Head dusky-brown; the rest of body rufous-bay, with cross bars of dusky black; a crimson stripe in the *male*; chin, throat, lower sides of neck, dark olive-brown, the feathers edged with white; lower parts unspotted bay; under tail-coverts faintly barred with dusky.

The Madras Rufous Woodpecker is a permanent resident in the forests of the Sahyadri Range, and occurs as far north as Khandalla, where it is not very uncommon. It has not been recorded from any other place within the district.

GENUS, Brachypternus, *Strick.*

Bill distinctly curved, moderately compressed and sloping on the sides; lateral ridge wanting; nostrils apert, but the frontal feathers produced to their base; gonys short; tail cuneate, the two central feathers longest; feet small, outer posterior and mid-toe nearly equal; hind-toe and claw minute.

Brachypternus aurantius, *Lin.*

180.—Jerdon's Birds of India, Vol. I, p. 295; Butler, Guzerat; Stray Feathers, Vol. III, p. 458; Murray's Vertebrate Zoology of Sind, p. 114; Swinhoe and Barnes, Central India; Ibis, 1885, p. 62.

THE GOLDEN-BACKED WOODPECKER.

Length, 11 to 12; extent, 17 to 19; wing, 5·5 to 5·8; tail, 3·5 to 4; bill at front, 1·35; bill from gape, 1·5 to 1·7.

Bill slaty-black; irides red-brown; legs and feet dark green.

Male: head and crest bright crimson; middle of neck, behind, black; upper back and scapulars rich golden-yellow; middle of the back black mixed with olive-yellow; lower back, upper tail-coverts, and tail, black; wing-coverts black at the shoulder, gradually changing to golden olive-yellow, each feather spotted with fulvescent-white; wings the same externally, except the first quills which are black, as all are internally, and marked with large white spots on their inner webs; a stripe through the eyes and ear-coverts mixed black and grey; lores, cheek and sides of neck forming a white stripe below the dark eye-streak; chin, throat, neck below, and breast black, with white marks increasing in size on the breast, all the feathers being edged or scaled with black, diminishing in extent on the lower abdomen, which is almost white, and forming cross-bands on the flanks and thigh-coverts.

The Golden-backed Woodpecker is very common throughout the district, with the exception of the Deccan and South Mahratta country, where it is replaced by the next species.

It is a permanent resident, breeding during March and April and again in June and July; the eggs, there is no nest, are deposited at the bottom of a hole, pierced in a branch of a tree, most frequently a mango; they are three in number, of a polished milk-white color, of an elongated oval shape and measure 1·11 inches in length by 0·8 in breadth.

Brachypternus puncticollis, *Malh.*

181.—*Brachypternus chrysonotus*, Less.—Jerdon's Birds of India, Vol, I, p. 296; Butler, Deccan; Stray Feathers, Vol. IX, p. 386.

THE LESSER GOLDEN-BACKED WOODPECKER.

Length, 11·5; expanse, 17; wing, 5·25; tail, 3·25; bill at front, 1·12.

Bill dark slaty; irides crimson; legs plumbeous-green.

Very similar to the last, but smaller; the frontal feathers are more mixed with black in the male; the black of the nape is continued lower upon the shoulders, contrasting strongly with the golden-orange of the back; the wings are of a duller golden; the eye-streak is narrower, but darker and more strongly defined, and it has the white spots smaller; the white markings of the throat and foreneck are also smaller, and consist of round oval points, being edged on the sides of the neck by unspotted black; and, lastly, the white markings of the under parts are narrower, giving a generally darker hue to the breast and abdomen.

The Lesser Golden-backed Woodpecker only occurs in the

Deccan, where it replaces *B. aurantius*, from which it is only doubtfully distinct.

SUB-FAMILY, Yunginæ.

Bill short, conical, somewhat round, straight, pointed; nostrils basal, approximate, near the culmen, narrow, pierced in the membrane, apert; wings moderate, pointed, second and third quills subequal, but third the longest, first nearly as long, and fourth only a little shorter; tail moderate, flexible, broad, slightly rounded, or nearly even, of twelve feathers, the two outer small, as in the Woodpeckers; tarsus short, with the toes in pairs; posterior (outer) toe long but equal to the anterior outer; hind and inner-toes short; claws well curved and compressed.

GENUS, Yunx, (*Iynx.*)

Similar to the sub-family, of which it is the only genus.

Yunx (Iynx) torquilla, *Lin.*

188.—Jerdon's Birds of India, Vol. I, p. 303; Butler, Guzerat; Stray Feathers, Vol. III, p. 459; Deccan, Stray Feathers, Vol. IX, p. 386; Murray's Vertebrate Zoology of Sind, p. 115; *Iynx torquilla*, Jerd.; Swinhoe and Barnes, Central India; Ibis, 1885, p. 62.

THE COMMON WRYNECK.

Length, 7·5; expanse, 11·5; wing, 3·5; tail, 2·5; tarsus, 0·98; bill at front, 0·5; bill from gape, 0·78.

Biil horny-brown; irides crimson; legs greenish-horny.

Above, a beautiful speckled grey, with a broad irregular line from the crown to the middle of the back, dark brown, with black stripes; lores whitish, and sometimes the chin; sides of the throat, cheeks, and breast, pale buff yellow, with narrow transverse bars; a brown stripe runs from each eye through the ear-coverts, extending along the side of the neck, and another darker and narrower from the base of the lower mandible down the sides of the throat; between these is a buff or isabella band, finally becoming albescent; breast and upper part of the belly fulvous-white with narrow cross lines, pointed anteriorly, and passing into small triangular black linear spots on the lower abdomen, vent, and under tail-coverts, which are whitish; the wings are fulvous-brown, minutely speckled, and with some fulvous spots, and a black longitudinal band on the scapulars; lower part of belly fulvous-white, with narrow cross lines, pointed anteriorly, passing into small triangular black linear spots; the quills are barred with deep brown and isabella; rump and tail speckled grey, the former with black longitudinal streaks, the latter with three darker broad bands, and a fourth subterminal one.

The Wryneck, though not common, occurs throughout our limits as a cold weather visitant.

FAMILY, Megalaimidæ.

Bill stout and somewhat conic, inflated at the sides, moderate in length or short, wide at the base, more or less compressed towards the tip; base of upper mandible continued backward to the gape, and usually furnished at the base with numerous stiff bristles projecting forwards; some have the mandibles denticulated, and grooved at the sides; culmen generally blunt; wings and tail short, the latter even or nearly so; with the feathers soft, only ten in number; toes in pairs, the hind-claws much curved; tongue of ordinary structure.

GENUS, Megalaima, *Gray*.

Bill moderate, about as long as the head, robust, conical, more or less wide at the base and compressed at the tip; culmen tolerably arched; upper mandible somewhat overlapping the lower one; gape wide; nostrils somewhat exposed in a groove at the side of the culmen; wings moderate, rounded; tail short, nearly even; feet truly zygodactyle; conspicuous tufts of bristles surrounding the bill, a series of them above each nostril, a tuft at each angle of the gape, and another growing from the chin.

Megalaima caniceps, *Frankl.*

193.—Jerdon's Birds of India, Vol. I, p. 310; Swinhoe and Barnes, Central India; Ibis, 1885, p. 63.

THE COMMON GREEN BARBET.

Length, 10·5; expanse, 16; wing, 5; tail, 3·5; tarsus, 1·1; bill at front, 1·37.

Bill pale orange-brown; irides orange-brown; orbitar skin dull orange; legs light yellowish-brown.

Above green; paler on the flanks and lower belly; vent and lower tail-coverts yellowish; head, neck, breast, and upper abdomen brownish; throat dusky-brown; the feathers of these parts with narrow pale streaks, continued but gradually diminishing upon the green of the back; each wing-covert and tertiary has a whitish speck on the tip; forehead and neck almost uniform brown, with pale mesial streaks.

Within our limits the Common Green Barbet has only been recorded from the forests on the Vindhian Hills, near Mhow, Central India, its place being taken elsewhere by the next species, with which it is often confounded.

Megalaima inornata, *Wald.*

193*bis*.—Butler, Guzerat; Stray Feathers, Vol. III, p. 459; Deccan, Stray Feathers, Vol. IX, p. 387.

THE WESTERN GREEN BARBET.

Length, 10·5; expanse, 16·5; wing, 5·1; tail, 3·4; tarsus, 1·08; bill at front, 1·35.

Very similar to *M. caniceps*, but the terminal spots to the wing-coverts and tertiaries are almost altogether wanting; the chin, throat, breast, and upper portion of the abdominal region uniform pale-brown; each feather has the shaft very faintly paler; the absence of the pale median streaks on the pectoral feathers readily distinguishes this species.

The Western Green Barbet is common on the Aravelli Hills, and in the jungles below; it occurs on the Western Ghats and all along the Sahyadri Range as far north at least as Khandalla. It is a permanent resident, breeding during April and May. The eggs, four in number, are of a dull white color, and are deposited in a hole, pierced in the branch of a tree, generally at some distance from the ground; there is no nest.

Megalaima viridis, *Bodd.*

194.—Jerdon's Birds of India, Vol. I, p. 311; Butler, Deccan; Stray Feathers, Vol. IX, p. 387.

THE SMALL GREEN BARBET.

Length, 8; wing, 4; tail, 2·75; bill at front, 0·9.

Bill pale horny-brown; irides red-brown; orbitar skin brown; legs plumbeons-brown.

Very similar to *M. caniceps*, but smaller, the brown of the head and nape scarcely lineated, that of the under parts pale, becoming whitish on the throat; there are no pale specks on the wing-coverts, nor any traces of pale streaks on the green of the back.

The Small Green Barbet is common at Satara, Belgaum, and on the Sahyadri Range as far north as Khandalla. It has not been recorded from any other portion of our limits.

GENUS, **Xantholæma,** *Bonap.*

Bill still shorter, wider, and less compressed; wing, with second quill, long, sub-equal to the next three.

Xantholæma hæmacephala, *Mull.*

197.—*Xantholæma indica*, Lath.—Jerdon's Birds of India, Vol. I, p. 315; Butler, Guzerat; Stray Feathers, Vol. III, p. 460; Deccan, Stray Feathers, Vol. IX, p. 387; Murray's Vertebrate Zoology of Sind, p. 116; Swinhoe and Barnes, Central India; Ibis, 1885, p. 63.

THE CRIMSON-BREASTED BARBET.

Length, 6·3 to 6·5; expanse, 10·75 to 11; wing, 3·12 to 3·25; tail, 1·4 to 1·5; bill at front, 0·7; tarsus, 0·75.

Bill black; irides brown; orbits dull crimson; feet coral-red; claws black.

Green above, the feathers of the back and wing-coverts more or less margined with yellowish; beneath, yellowish or greenish-white, streaked with green; the whitish predominating on the middle of the belly, broad frontal space, and wide pectoral gorget, glistening crimson; throat and around the eye pale sulphur-yellow; below the crimson gorget is a narrow crescent of golden-yellow; a band across the crown, continued round to the yellow throat, and a moustachial streak black; a bluish tinge on the occiput and sides of the neck, where the black passes gradually into the green of the back, and also on the margins of the scapulars and tail.

The Crimson-breasted Barbet is very common throughout the Deccan, and in most parts of Rajpootana and Central India; it is not uncommon in Guzerat, but in Sind it only occurs as a somewhat rare visitant. In all other places within our limits it is a permanent resident, breeding from February to the end of May; its eggs, three in number, (there is no nest) are deposited in a hole pierced in a branch of a tree, generally one that is decayed and hollow in the centre; the eggs are dull-white in color, elongated ovals in shape, and measure 0·99 inches in length by 0·69 in breadth.

During the breeding season its monotonous note (from which it gets its name of coppersmith), *took-took-took*, which it utters from the top of a tree, is heard incessantly from early morning till late at night.

Xantholæma malabarica, *Blyth.*

198.—Jerdon's Birds of India, Vol. I, p. 317; Butler, Deccan; Stray Feathers, Vol. IX, p. 387.

THE CRIMSON-THROATED BARBET.

Length, 6·25; wing, 3·2; tail, 1·5; bill at front, 0·5; tarsus, 0·7. Bill black; irides red-brown; legs red.

Above darkish-green, the feathers edged pale, light green beneath; forehead, around the eyes, and chin and throat, crimson, the last margined externally with golden-yellow; occiput black passing into dull blue, which is the color of the cheeks, ear-coverts and sides of the neck.

The Crimson-throated Barbet has been recorded from Savantwadi and from the forests west of Belgaum, but it is rare, and has not been found in any other portion of the region.

FAMILY, **Cuculidæ.**

Bill of moderate size, usually slender, moderately curved and compressed; nostrils exposed; gape wide; toes long, unequal; the outer toe versatile, usually turned back; tail long and broad, with ten feathers, eight only in one group.

SUB-FAMILY, **Cuculinæ.**

Bill slender, somewhat broad at the base, convex above, gently curved at the culmen; nostrils round, membranous; wings pointed; tail rounded, nearly square, sub-furcate in one group; tibial feathers lengthened; tarsus very short, partly feathered;

feet small; outer-toe capable of being directed either backwards or sideways.

Genus, Cuculus.

Bill rather small, broadish at the base, compressed moderately beyond, gently curved, and the culmen convex; tip obsoletely notched; nostrils basal, circular, with a raised tumid margin; wings long, pointed; the third quill usually longest, second and fourth nearly equal; tail lengthened, rounded; tarsus very short, feathered posteriorly, with transverse scutæ in front; feet slender, short; feathers of the rump and upper tail-coverts long, thick set and rigid.

Cuculus canorus, *Lin.*

199.—Jerdon's Birds of India, Vol. I, p. 322; Butler, Guzerat; Stray Feathers, Vol. III, p. 199; Deccan, Stray Feathers, Vol. IX, p. 387; Murray's Vertebrate Zoology of Sind, p. 116; Swinhoe and Barnes, Central India; Ibis, 1885, p. 63.

The Cuckoo.

Length, 14; expanse, 26; wing, 8·75 to 9; tail, 7; tarsus, 0·8; bill at front, 0·78.

Bill black, yellowish at base beneath, and at gape; irides yellow; orbits deeper yellow; legs yellow.

Adult: head and upper parts ashy; throat, underside of neck, and upper part of breast, pale ashy; lower part of breast and belly white, with narrow transverse, undulating black lines; quills dusky, with a faint gloss of green; inner webs barred with oval white spots or incomplete bars; the two central feathers of the tail blackish, dashed with ashy, and tipped white; the others black, with white spots on one or both webs, and the tip white; under tail coverts white, with distinct arrow-shaped markings.

The female has very generally a tawny-brown tinge on the upper parts; and the neck and breast of both sexes are often mingled with rufous, having some dusky-bars.

The young bird is dusky-grey above with white or ferruginous bars; beneath white, with the bars close on the neck and breast, distant and narrower on the abdomen; irides blue-grey, afterwards brown; they vary considerably in this state of plumage.

The European Cuckoo is found throughout the district, but, excepting the hills, it is nowhere common and only occurs during the rains and cold weather.

Cuculus poliocephalus, *Lath.*

201.—Jerdon's Birds of India, Vol. I, p. 324; Butler, Deccan; Stray Feathers, Vol. IX, p. 388.

The Small Cuckoo.

Length, 10 to 10·5; wing, 5·85; tail, 5·12; tarsus, 0·62; bill at front, 0·7.

Male: upper plumage ashy, slightly glossed with green on the back and upper tail-coverts; quills brown, also with a green gloss, and numerous close large white spots; tail deep ashy, almost black, with large white spots on the middle of each feather on the edge of the inner webs, and at the tip; beneath the chin and throat are pale ashy, with some rusty about the breast; the lower parts white, with rather narrow distant bars; under tail-coverts spotless.

Many adults have the upper parts fine rufous-bay, spotless on the forehead, sides of neck, and rump, but elegantly barred with dusky across the scapulars, wings and tail, and faintly on the crown, hind-neck, and interscapulars; throat, foreneck, and breast, whitish along the middle, stained with rufous laterally, and with dark bars more or less distinct; the rest of the lower parts broadly barred, as also are the tail-coverts.

The Small Cuckoo has been obtained in various parts of the Deccan, but is rare; it has not been recorded from elsewhere within our district.

Cuculus sonnerati, *Lath.*

202.—Jerdon's Birds of India, Vol. I, p. 325; Butler, Deccan; Stray Feathers, Vol. IX, p. 388.

THE BANDED BAY CUCKOO.

Length, 10; wing, 5; tail, 5; tarsus, 0·6; bill at front, 0·7.

Above greenish-dusky, numerously crossed barred with rufous (which color, indeed, may be said to predominate), except on the coverts of the primaries; quills dusky-rufous on the edge of the outer web, pale internally; tail rufous, with a broad dusky bar near the end; the outer webs nearly dusky, and the tip white, and the inner webs with narrow bars; the whole under-parts, from the throat, white, very faintly tinged with fulvous on the flanks, and marked with numerous narrow dusky cross bars; sides of head and neck also white, similarly barred; but the ear-coverts are colored like the back, and the frontal feathers are white at the base, showing conspicuously just over the bill.

The young are more coarsely barred than adults, with pale rufescent on a blackish ground, and the breast is white, banded with dusky, and aged individuals have the back and wings very faintly barred, the tail with the central feathers nearly all black, the edges scolloped with rufous, and the outer feathers with dusky.

The Banded Bay Cuckoo occurs sparingly in various parts of the Deccan and South Mahratta country, but only as a seasonal visitant. It does not occur elsewhere within our limits.

Cuculus micropterus, *Gould.*

203.—Jerdon's Birds of India, Vol. I, p. 326; Butler, Deccan; Stray Feathers, Vol. IX, p. 388.

THE INDIAN CUCKOO.

Length, 12 to 12·5; expanse, 23; wing, 7·5; tail, 5·75; tarsus, 0·75; bill at front, 0·96.

Bill blackish, yellow at the base beneath, and at the gape; irides pale dusky, or yellowish-brown; orbits light wax-yellow; legs yellow.

Upper parts darkish-ashy, pure on the head; throat and breast grey; abdomen white, with broad and tolerably distant dark-brown bars; quills brown, the inner webs with wider bars or spots than those of *C. canorus*; tail concolorous with the body, or brownish-ashy; a broad dark band at the end, narrowly tipped with white; in some with a few white spots, successively more developed on the outer tail-feathers.

In old birds the color above is deep-ashy; but in those only once moulted the hue is a bronzed ash-brown, with the head and neck grey, and some slight traces of rufous on the sides of the neck and wings. The young are much mottled with blackish and white, especially on the head, neck, and back; the quills and tail have rufous bars and tips; but they have much less rufous than the young of *C. canorus*, and are much less barred.

The Indian Cuckoo is common along the Sahyadri range and adjacent forests; it has been obtained from other parts of the Deccan and South Mahratta country, and is not uncommon in the jungles on the Vindhian Range, but Major Butler did not meet with it in Northern Guzerat, nor has it been recorded from Sind.

GENUS, Hierococcyx, *Müller*.

Bill stouter, deeper and wider, than in *cuculus*; wing shorter; the fourth quill longest, and the fifth about equal to the second; tail nearly even, broad, with distinct dark bars.

Hierococcyx varius, *Vahl*.

205.—Jerdon's Birds of India, Vol. I, p. 329; Butler, Guzerat; Stray Feathers, Vol. III, p. 205; Deccan, Stray Feathers, Vol. IX, p. 388; Swinhoe and Barnes, Central India; Ibis, 1885, p. 63.

THE COMMON HAWK CUCKOO.

Length, 13·4; expanse, 22·1; wing, 7·5; tail, 7; tarsus, 0·8; bill at front, 0·83; bill from gape, 1·2.

Bill black on the culmen and tip, yellow beneath; orbits orange-yellow; irides dull gamboge-yellow; legs and feet yellow.

Upper parts uniform ash-grey; the winglet and coverts of the primaries darker; foreneck and breast pale rufous, each feather light grey in the centre; belly and flanks white, barred with adjoining lines of grey and rufous, the white hardly visible exteriorly, from the overlapping of the feathers; thighs, vent, and lower-coverts, pure white, the first a little barred; throat grey, and some white at the base of the bill and sides of the throat; tail grey, tipped with faint rufous, and finally whitish, having a broad dusky subterminal band, and five other narrower and undulating zigzag bands (one near the base) composed of a dusky bar, then a whitish one adjoining, with some traces of rufous; quills barred with white on their inner webs for the basal two-thirds of their length.

The young bird has the upper plumage browner and rufous-barred; and the lower parts are whitish, tinged with rusty, and with longitudinal brown drops. In older birds the spots are longitudinal on the neck and breast, transverse and arrow-shaped on the abdomen.

With the exception of Sind, the Hawk Cuckoo is generally spread throughout the district; but there are parts of the Deccan where it is absent or only occurs as a somewhat rare straggler.

GENUS, **Cacomantis**, *Müller*.

Of small size; plumage variable, grey or dusky above; lower plumage not barred in the normal adult state; the tarsi less plumed externally than in *cuculus*.

Cacomantis passerinus, *Vahl.*

208.—*Polyphasia nigra, apud* Blyth.—Jerdon's Birds of India, Vol. I, p. 333; Butler, Guzerat; Stray Feathers, Vol. III, p. 461; Deccan, Stray Feathers, Vol. IX, p. 388.

THE INDIAN PLAINTIVE CUCKOO.

Length, 9; expanse, 14; wing, 4·5; tail, 4·5; tarsus, 0·6; bill at front, 0·6.

Bill blackish, red at base and gape; irides rusty-red; feet reddish-yellow.

Adult, uniform dark-ashy above, with more or less of a green gloss; beneath pale ashy; vent and under tail-coverts pure white; quills dusky, with a broad white band on the inner web of each feather; tail blackish; the inner webs banded with white (except the middle pair), and all tipped white.

A common phase of this species in South India is dusky-cinereous, almost blackish above, with a greenish gloss beneath the same, but less glossed; tail as in the last, but darker and with fewer white spots.

The younger state of this phase is glossy dark-cinereous only on the back and wings, the head and rump being ashy; chin and throat cinereous; breast darker cinereous, banded with rufous and white; belly pale cinereous, faintly marked with pale rufous and white; under tail-coverts white; tail as in the last.

In some states of plumage all the upper parts are bright rufous, with dusky bars; the primaries dusky brown with rufous edges; the tail rufous, all the outer feathers having dark bars and a broader subterminal one, with a white spot at the tip; throat, neck and breast, pale rufous, with dusky bars; and the belly, flanks, and tail-coverts white, also with dusky cross bars tibial feathers rufous barred.

In a more advanced state of the same plumage the bars on the head and rump disappear, and those that remain have a green gloss upon them.

Not uncommon during the rains in many parts of the Deccan, and at Mount Aboo; it probably also occurs at and near Mhow; it has never been recorded from Sind, Cutch, Kattiawar, or Jodhpore.

GENUS, **Surniculus**, *Lesson.*

Tail even or forked, with the two outermost feathers short, the penultimate being slightly the longest, and each lateral half of the tail curling outward towards the tip as in the Drongos; otherwise as in the last; plumage black.

Surniculus lugubris, *Horsf.*

210.—Jerdon's Birds of India, Vol. I, p. 336.

THE DRONGO OR FORK-TAILED CUCKOO.

Length, 10; wing, 5·5; tail 3·75; outermost tail feathers, 1·25 inches less than the penultimate, which is the longest; middle pair 0·5 inch shorter.

Bill black; palate red; irides red brown; legs and feet dusky reddish.

Black, with a changeable blue and green gloss, brightest above; the head sub-crested, and generally two or three white feathers in the centre of the occiput; tibial and tarsal feathers partially white; some white specks on the wing-coverts, and on the upper tail-coverts occasionally; lower tail-coverts marked with white; outermost primary with a round white spot, and all the others with an oblique white mark, causing an oblique streak of white on the inner surface of the wings; outermost tail-feathers obliquely barred or spotted with white.

The young birds are spotted with white on the head, wing-coverts, and lower surface; and the tail has also more white spots.

According to Jerdon, the Drongo or Tork-tailed Cuckoo occurs sparingly in Central India.

GENUS, **Chrysococcyx**, *Boie.*

Bill as in *cuculus*, but a little more depressed at the base. and quite entire at tip; wings pointed; second quill longer than the fourth; third nearly as long; the feathers of the rump and upper tail-coverts soft; and tarsi very short and much plumed.

Chrysococcyx maculatus, *Gm.*

211.—*C. hodgsoni*, Moore.—Jerdon's Birds of India, Vol. I, p. 338.

THE EMERALD CUCKOO.

Length, 6·5 to 7; wing, 4·25; tail, 3; tarsus, 0·5; bill at front, 0·6.

Bill yellow, tipped dusky; irides red brown; feet reddish cinereous.

Above brilliant emerald-green with a rich golden gloss; beneath white with cross bars of shining green; tail, with the outer feathers barred with white externally.

Jerdon in his "Birds of India" states that this lovely Cuckoo has been procured rarely in Central India.

GENUS, Coccystes, *Goger*.

Head crested; bill slender and cuculine, but more compressed, slightly curving at first, suddenly bent down at the tip which is entire; nostrils basal, lengthened and ovate, close to edge of mandible; wings moderate, slightly rounded; third and fourth quills sub-equal, or fourth quill longest; tail long graduated; tarsus longer than in *cuculus*, not feathered; feathers of the rump soft.

Coccystes jacobinus, *Bodd.*

212.—*Coccystes melanoleucos*, Gmel.—Jerdon's Birds of India, Vol. I, p. 339; Butler, Guzerat; Stray Feathers, Vol. III, p. 461; Deccan, Stray Feathers, Vol. IX, p. 388; Murray's Vertebrate Zoology of Sind, p. 117; Swinhoe and Barnes, Central India; Ibis, 1885, p. 63.

THE PIED-CRESTED CUCKOO.

Popiya, Hin.

Length, 13; expanse, 17·5; wing, 5·75; tail, 7; tarsus, 0·98; bill at front, 0·75; bill at gape, 1·1.

Bill black; irides red-brown; legs leaden-blue.

Above, uniform black, with a greenish shine; bases of the primaries white, forming a conspicuous wing-spot; all the tail-feathers tipped white, broadly, except the central pair, which are very narrowly tipped; under-parts dull white; in some, especially the females, slightly tinged with fulvescent.

The nestling plumage is dull black above, and fulvous beneath.

The Pied-crested Cuckoo occurs as a monsoon visitant throughout the district, but is much more common in some places than others; for instance, at Mhow it literally swarms during the rains, while at Neemuch it only occurs as a straggler.

Its eggs resemble somewhat those of *C. caudata*, in whose nests, as well as in those of *M. terricolor* and *malcolmi*, they are generally deposited, but may be distinguished from the former by their somewhat larger size and rounder shape, and from those of the latter by being slightly smaller as well as rounder.

They are deep sky-blue in color, and measure 0·94 inches in length by 0·73 in breadth.

Coccystes coromandus, *Lin.*

213.—Jerdon's Birds of India, Vol. I, p. 341; Butler, Deccan; Stray Feathers, Vol. IX, p. 389.

THE RED-WINGED CRESTED CUCKOO.

Length, 14·5 to 15·5; expanse, 18 to 19; wing, 6·25 to 6·5; tail, 8·5 to 9·8; tarsus, 0·8 to 1·08; bill at front, 1; bill from gape, 1·3.

Bill black; inside of mouth fleshy; irides hazel to red-brown; feet leaden or plumbeous.

Upper parts with the tertiaries black, glossed with green, paler on the tertiaries, and less glossed on the head; a conspicuous half collar of white encircles the nape; wings deep ferruginous, with the tips of the primaries and secondaries dusky; under parts white, a little tinged with fulvous, except the lower tail-coverts, which are green-black, and the throat and foreneck, which are deep ochreous fulvous in some; in others, light fulvous.

Mr. Vidal obtained a specimen at Savantwadi; this is the only recorded instance of its occurrence within our limits.

GENUS, Eudynamis, *Vig. & Horsf.*

Bill strong, thick, vertically deep, much curved at tip, and hooked; the lower mandible nearly straight; gonys slightly undulated upwards; nostrils long, oval; wings with the fourth quill longest; tail lengthened, rounded; rump and upper tail-feathers soft; tarsus strong, not feathered below the joint, flattened in front.

Eudynamis honorata, *Lin.*

214.—*Eudynamis orientalis*, Lin.—Jerdon's Birds of India, Vol. I, p. 342; Butler, Guzerat; Stray Feathers, Vol. III, p. 461; Deccan, Stray Feathers, Vol. IX, p. 389; Murray's Vertebrate Zoology of Sind, p. 117; Swinhoe and Barnes, Central India; Ibis, 1885, p. 63.

THE INDIAN KOEL. THE BLACK CUCKOO.
Koel, Hin.

♂. Length, 15·5; expanse, 23; wing, 7·5; tail, 7·5; tarsus, 1·12; bill at front, 1.

♀. Length, 17·5; wing, 8; tail, 8.

Bill pale greenish; inside of mouth reddish; irides crimson; legs slaty-blue.

Male, glossy greenish-black throughout.

Female, glossy dusky-green, spotted with white above; wings and tail banded white; beneath white, with black spots, longitudinal on the throat and neck, somewhat heart-shaped or arrow-shaped on the breast, and transverse on the abdomen, thigh-coverts, and under tail-coverts.

The young female has the white spots and marks much tinged with rufous; and the young male has a good deal of white on his plumage.

The Indian Koel is very common throughout the district, excepting Sind, where it appears to be somewhat rare. Some of them at least are permanent residents, but during the breeding season they are everywhere more common; at this season, too, they are excessively noisy, so much so as to become a positive nuisance. They lay their eggs in nests of the common crow, sometimes a single egg only, but as often as not two will be found, and I have on two occasions found three Koel eggs in a single nest. I much doubt whether the Koel destroys the crow eggs before depositing her own, as I have always found them intact; they may do so in other districts, but my experience is a wide one, extending through Guzerat, Rajpootana, Central India, Sind, and the Deccan.

The eggs vary surprisingly in color; pale sea-green, dingy stone-color, and olive-green and brown, are all met with; the markings also are diversified; specks, spots, streaks and clouds of olive and reddish-brown and dull purple are all represented. The eggs measure about 1·19 inches in length by 0·92 in breadth. The bird has not inaptly been named the Brain Fever Bird by some waggish godfather.

Sub-family, Phœnicophainæ.

Bill moderate or longish, ridge curved; orbital region generally naked; wings short; tail long, graduated.

Genus, Rhopodytes.

(*Zanclostomus*).

Bill much compressed throughout, curved both at the culmen and lower mandible; nostrils basal, oval, pierced in a slight depression in the horny substance; wing short, rounded, with the fourth, fifth and sixth quills nearly equal and longest; tail much lengthened, graduated; tarsus moderate or longish; hallux very short; claws well curved, sharp.

Rhopodytes viridirostris, *Jerd.*

216.—*Zanclostomus viridirostris.*—Jerdon's Birds of India, Vol. I, p. 346; Butler, Deccan; Stray Feathers, Vol. IX, p. 389.

The Small Green-billed Malkoha.

Length, 15; wings, 5·25; tail, 10; tarsus, 1·3; bill at front, 1.

Bill bright apple green; naked skin around the eyes cobalt-blue; irides blood-red; legs blackish green.

Above, dusky cinereous, with a tinge of glossy green; wings

and tail glossy green-black, the latter tipped with white; beneath light greyish, with a tinge of fawn color mixed with blackish on the chin and throat.

The Small Green-billed Malkoha is not uncommon at Belgaum and Ratnagiri, where it is a permanent resident. I know of no record of its occurrence elsewhere within our limits.

Sub-family, Centropodinæ.

Bill strong, deep, compressed; wings rather short, rounded; tarsus long; feet fitted for walking; hallux lengthened in some, and with the nail straight, in others short and more curved.

Genus, Centropus, *Illiger*.

Bill strong, of moderate length, well curved, high at the base, entire at the tip; nostrils lateral, basal half covered with a scale; wings rounded; tail elongate, graduate, very broad; tarsus long; feet larger; hallux long; claws of the hallux generally lengthened, somewhat straight.

Centropus rufipennis, *Illiger*.

217.—Jerdon's Birds of India, Vol. I, p. 349; Butler, Guzerat; Stray Feathers, Vol. III, p. 461; Deccan, Stray Feathers, Vol. IX, p. 389; Swinhoe and Barnes, Central India; Ibis, 1885, p. 64.

THE CROW PHEASANT.

THE COMMON COUCAL.

Mahoka, Hin.

Length, 19; extent, 23; wing, 7·25; tail, 10; tarsus, 2; bill at front, 1·3.

Bill black; irides crimson; legs black.

Whole head, neck, lower back, upper tail-coverts and all the under parts, richly empurpled black; tail glossed with green; upper part of the back and wings bright deep rufous bay.

The young vary very much; some (females) are barred throughout with rufous and blackish above, and with dusky and whitish beneath; tail barred with pale grey bands; wings also prettily banded.

Others (young males) resemble the adult, but the colors are more dull.

With the exception of Sind, the Crow Pheasant is common throughout our limits. It is a permanent resident, breeding during the monsoon. They build large, globular-shaped, domed nests, in the centre of thick, thorny bushes or trees; the eggs, three in number, are broadish regular ovals, coarse and chalky in texture, of a dull white color, and average 1·44 in length by 1·16 in breadth.

They are subject to great variation in size; eggs of the same clutch even differ.

Centropus maximus, *Hume.*

217*quint.*—Murray's Vertebrate Zoology of Sind, p. 118.

THE LARGE CROW PHEASANT.

Length, 19 to 20; wing, 9 to 10; tail, 10 to 10·5; bill at front, 1·25.

Bill black; irides crimson; legs black.

Head, neck, lower back, upper tail-coverts and entire under parts richly empurpled black, duller towards the vent; feathers of the forehead bristly, and those on the neck and breast with spiny shafts; tail dusky-black, with a greenish gloss; wings deep rufous-bay or dark red.

Only found within our limits, in the Sind district; its habits are similar to those of *C. rufipennis.*

Centropus bengalensis, *Gm.*

218.—*C. viridis*, Scop.—Jerdon's Birds of India, Vol. I, p. 350.

THE LESSER INDIAN COUCAL.

Length, 15; wing, 6·5; tail, 8; tarsus, 1·5; bill at front, 1.

Bill black; irides red; legs plumbeous.

Adult.—Head, hind-neck, upper tail-coverts, tail, and beneath, glossy green black; wings and back rufous, or chesnut, infuscated at the tips of the wings, and often more or less so on the back, scapulars and tertiaries; tail-coverts much elongated.

Young birds are pale rufous above with broadish black bands, the rufous forming narrow bands on the upper tail-coverts and tail, and the black, narrow bands on the back and wings; the head and neck are streaked longitudinally, the feathers being dusky with a pale rufous centre; under-parts flavescent whitish, with only a few dusky specks and rays; bill pale yellow-horny.

In another state, in the adult female, the general color is light rufous, more or less infuscated above, dingy yellowish-white below; the spinous shafts to the feathers of the head, neck, wing-coverts, and breast yellowish-white and showing conspicuously, being set off with blackish, which brings out the contrasts, and the feathers are more or less barred transversely, expecially the scapulars, back, and the long upper tail-coverts.

In a further stage the feathers are black with yellowish-white shafts on the head, back, wing-coverts and breast, to a greater or lesser extent; and to this the fully adult plumage appears to succeed.

Dr. Jerdon remarks that "the Small Indian Coucal is a somewhat rare bird, but spreads more or less through most parts of India," and that he has had it from Central India.

GENUS, Taccocua, *Lesson.*

Bill short or of a moderate length, much compressed, the culmen regularly arching; commissure and gonys straight or slightly concave; nostrils basal, in a slight depression near the gape, with a tuft of bristly feathers bordering their upper edge; wings rounded; third and fourth quills nearly equal and longest; tail long, graduated; tarsus high; feet adapted for walking, of moderate size; the hallux short; claws short and moderately curved.

Taccocua leschenaulti, *Less.*

219.—Jerdon's Birds of India, Vol. I, p. 352; Butler, Deccan; Stray Feathers, Vol. IX, p. 389; Swinhoe and Barnes, Central India; Ibis, 1885, p. 64.

THE SOUTHERN SIRKEER.
Jungli Totah, Hin.

Length, 15 to 15·5; wing, 5·5 to 5·75; tail, 8.

Bill cherry-red, yellowish at the tip; irides reddish-brown; feet plumbeous.

Above, pale earthy-brown; head inclining to ashy; throat whitish; foreneck and breast ashy, tinged with ferruginous; belly dark ferruginous, there being a marked distinction between the two colors; feathers of the head, neck, and breast, with the shafts, black and glistening; upper tail-coverts long; lateral tail-feathers dark brown, broadly tipped with white.

The Southern Sirkeer occurs sparingly in the Deccan, and at Mhow, Central India, and again in Neemuch, Rajpootana; its place in other portions of our district being occupied by *T. sirkee.* It is a permanent resident and breeds in a similar manner to *C. rufipennis.*

Taccocua sirkee, *Gray.*

220.—Jerdon's Birds of India, Vol. I, p. 353; Butler, Guzerat; Stray Feathers, Vol. III, p. 461; Murray's Vertebrate Zoology of Sind, p. 118.

THE BENGAL SIRKEER.

Length, 17; wing, 6; tail, 9·5.

Above, pale satin-brown; beneath ashy-brown on the foreneck and breast, tinged with ferruginous, and passing gradually into the ferruginous of the belly, flanks and tibial plumes; this hue is darker here than in the last, and browner about the vent and under tail-coverts; feathers of the head and neck also black shafted.

The Bengal Sirkeer is not uncommon in Northern Guzerat and Sind; its habits much resemble those of the last.

TRIBE, Tenuirostris.

Bill, in most, slender and long, often curved; in a few short and thick; wings moderate or long.

FAMILY, Nectarinidæ.

Bill of various length, generally long, more or less curved, generally entire; nostrils basal, usually nearly covered by a scale; wings moderate, more or less rounded; nine or ten primaries, third and fourth longest; wing-coverts short; tarsus moderate; hind-claw equal to, or scarcely longer than, that of the middle-toe.

SUB-FAMILY, Nectarininæ.

Bill curved, base broad; nostril small; tail long; outer-toe longer than inner.

GENUS, Arachnothera, *Tem.*

Bill very long, moderately curved; base broad, and somewhat three-sided; tip entire; nostrils small, oval, completely covered by a membrane, which only opens by a lateral slit; wings long; third and fourth quill longest; tail short, broad, even; legs large and strong; lateral toes slightly unequal; hind-toe and claw large.

Arachnothera longirostra, *Lath.*

224.—*A. pusilla*, Blyth.—Jerdon's Birds of India, Vol. I, p. 361; Butler, Deccan; Stray Feathers, Vol. IX, p. 389.

THE LITTLE SPIDER-HUNTER,

Length, 5·75; wing, 2·5; tail, 1·5; tarsus, 0·6; bill at front, 1·5.

Bill dusky; irides brown; legs plumbeous-brown.

Above, olive-green, more or less fulvescent; the crown darker, with scale-like feathers, merely green-edged; a dark streak from the base of the upper mandible; chin and throat white; rest of the under parts dull greenish-albescent, passing into bright pale yellow on the belly; tail-feathers slightly tipped with whitish, chiefly on their inner webs, forming a spot most distinct outwardly.

The Little Spider-hunter is very rare; it has been obtained in the forests west of Belgaum, but does not occur elsewhere within our limits.

GENUS, Æthopyga, *Cabanis.*

Bill of moderate length and curvature; tail graduated, with the central tail-feathers much elongated.

Æthopyga vigorsi, *Sykes.*

226.—Jerdon's Birds of India, Vol. I, p. 363; Butler, Deccan; Stray Feathers, Vol. IX, p. 390.

THE VIOLET-EARED RED HONEY SUCKER.

Male.—Length, 5·5; tail, 2·5.

Female.—Length, 5; tail, 1.

Bill black; irides brown.

Head metallic green; nape, neck above, shoulders, and scapulars, deep sanguineous; lower part of back sulphur-yellow; upper tail-coverts, middle tail-feathers, and outer webs of all the others (except the outermost pair), metallic-green; throat, neck, and breast, scarlet; a stripe on each side from the chin to the breast, shining violet; ear-spot also violet; wings, lateral tail-feathers, sides of the lower part of the back, and a band below the breast, dusky; abdomen grey.

The female is greenish-olive above; wings and tail darker, lighter beneath.

The Violet-eared Red Honey Sucker only occurs within our limits on the Sahyadri Range and in the adjacent forests as far north as Khandalla, where it is a not uncommon permanent resident.

GENUS, Leptocoma (CINNYRIS) *Cabanis.*

Tail square or nearly so; bill moderately curved, most of small size.

Cinnyris zeylonica, *Lin.*

232.—*Leptocoma zeylonica*, Lin.—Jerdon's Birds of India, Vol. I, p. 368; Butler, Deccan; Stray Feathers, Vol. IX, p. 390.

THE AMETHYST-RUMPED HONEY SUCKER.

Length, 4·5; wing, 2·2; tail, 1·5; bill in front, 0·63.

Irides bright ruby-red; bill and legs black.

Head above and angle of the wing bright metallic glossy-green; back, scapulars and wing-coverts, deep maroon-red; wings dusky-brown, the quill edged with cinnamon-brown; tail black; throat, neck, rump, and upper tail-coverts fine metallic amethystine-purple; the rest of the body beneath yellow, divided from the amethyst of the neck by a narrow maroon bar.

The female is dull green above, with a slight tinge of rufous; the quills edged with pale brown; the tail dusky-black; under parts pale yellow, albescent on throat and foreneck.

Young males resemble the females, but have the throat more yellow.

The Amethyst-rumped Honey Sucker is a permanent resident in the Deccan, where it is not uncommon; it does not occur elsewhere within our region.

Cinnyris minima, *Sykes.*

233.—*Leptocoma minima*, Sykes.—Jerdon's Birds of India, Vol. I, p. 369; Butler, Deccan; Stray Feathers, Vol. IX, p. 380.

THE TINY HONEY SUCKER.

Length, 3·5 to 3·75; expanse, 5·25 to 5·75; wing, 1·8; tail, 1 to 1·2; tarsus, 0·5; bill at front, 0·65.

Head and nape fine metallic-green; back, scapulars, and wing-coverts, rich bright sanguine-red; rump the same, but with a fine violet or amethystine gloss; wings and tail dusky-brown; throat and neck fine amethystine; the rest of the lower parts yellow.

The female is olive brown above, with a red rump, and pale yellow beneath.

Major Butler says: "Permanent resident on the Ghâts. Common, as a rule, all along the Sahyadri Range from Goa to Khandalla; extending often to the adjacent forests." He also obtained a specimen or two at Belgaum, where, however, it is only a rare seasonal visitant.

It has not been recorded from elsewhere within our limits.

Cinnyris asiatica, *Lath.*

234.—*Arachnechthra asiatica*, Lath.—Jerdon's Birds of India, Vol. I, p. 370; Butler, Deccan; Stray Feathers, Vol. IX, p. 390; Guzerat, Stray Feathers, Vol. III, p. 462; Murray's Vertebrate Zoology of Sind, p. 119; Swinhoe and Barnes, Central India; Ibis, 1885, p. 64.

THE PURPLE HONEY SUCKER.

Length, 4·5; wing, 2·3; tail, 1·5; tarsus, 0·6; bill at front, 0·75.

Bill and legs black; irides red-brown. In summer, breeding plumage this species has the whole head, neck, throat, breast, and back glossy green-purple; the abdomen purplish-black; wings and tail dull black, the latter faintly white-tipped; a tuft of crimson and yellow feathers at the axillæ of the wings.

After breeding, the fine purple garb is doffed, all except a long stripe from the chin to the vent.

The young bird has the upper parts dull olive-green; beneath bright yellow; shoulders and central stripe beneath brilliant glossy-violet; wings and tail dusky or black.

The female is greenish brown-grey above, greenish-yellow beneath, deepest on the throat and breast, and lighter on the vent and under tail-coverts; quills dusky; tail black.

The Purple Honey Sucker is very common throughout the region and is a permanent resident.

It breeds from March to September, but most nests are found in April and May; the nest is pendant, and resembles a florence-flask in shape; it is attached to a twig, and all sorts of material are made use of in its construction, fine grass, lichens, cobwebs, pieces of straw, dead flowers, and leaves, &c. The entrance is high up on one side, and has a projection or canopy over it to keep out the rain.

The eggs, two or three in number, are dingy little ovals, of a whitish ground color, thickly speckled with brown and greyish-brown. They measure 0·64 in length by about 0·46 in breadth.

Cinnyris lotenia, *Lin.*

205.—*Arachnecthra lotenia*, Lin.—Jerdon's Birds of India, Vol. I, p. 372; Butler, Deccan; Stray Feathers, Vol. IX, p. 390.

THE LARGE PURPLE HONEY SUCKER.

Length, 5·5; wing, 2·3; tail, 1·6; tarsus, 0·6; bill at front, 1.

Bill and legs black; irides dark brown.

Above, brilliantly glossed with metallic green and purple; abdomen dull brownish-black; axillary tuft yellow and red; wings and tail black, the latter slightly glossed purple; throat and breast rich purple; a narrow bright maroon collar separates the purple of the breast from the back of the abdomen.

Within our limits, the Large Purple Honey Sucker only occurs on the Western Ghâts and in the adjacent forests, also in the forests west of Belgaum and perhaps in the Konkan, but it is nowhere common.

Sub-family, Dicæinæ.

Bill short, usually depressed at the base, thick in some; tail short; wings rather long, of very small size.

Genus, Dicæum, *Cuvier.*

Bill short, broad at the base, suddenly compressed beyond, tip entire, culmen curved; nostrils triangular; wings lengthened, with nine primaries, the first three are about equal, the second slightly the longest; tail short, even; feet with the lateral toes unequal, the outer-toe a good deal syndactyle.

Dicæum erythrorhynchus, *Lath.*

238.—*D. minimum*, Tickel.—Jerdon's Birds of India, Vol. I, p. 374; Butler, Deccan; Stray Feathers, Vol. IX, p. 390.

Tickell's Flower-pecker.

Length, 3·12; wing, 1·75; tail, 0 88; tarsus, 0·66; bill at front, 0·38.

Bill pale-fleshy; tip dusky; irides brown; legs leaden-brown.

Above ashy-olive, paler and fulvescent beneath; wings and tail darker.

Tickell's Flower-pecker is locally common in many parts of the Deccan. At Belgaum, where it is very common, it breeds in the hot weather. It occurs along the Sahyadri Range as far north as Mahableshwar and has been procured at Ratnagiri. It has not been recorded from any other portion of our limits.

Dicæum concolor, *Jerdon.*

239.—Jerdon's Birds of India, Vol. I, p. 375; Butler, Deccan; Stray Feathers, Vol. IX, p. 391.

The Neilgherry Flower-pecker.

Length, 4·2; wing, 2·1; tail, 1·1; tarsus, 0·5; bill at front, 0·4.

Bill dusky-brown; irides dark brown; legs cinereous-brown.

Above brownish-olive; beneath greenish-white; wings and tail brown; sexes alike.

Occurs in the same localities as the last, but is somewhat rare.

Genus, Piprisomæ, *Blyth.*

Bill short and sub-conical, acutely triangular as viewed from above; ridge of the upper mandible angulated, and that of the lower slightly so; both of them curved, the lower one perhaps most; tip of the upper over-hanging the lower mandible; nostrils almost closed by the nasal membrane; gape unarmed; feet rather small; tarsus equal to the middle-toe; outer-toe syndactyle; claws moderately hooked; wings long, reaching to the end of tail; tail short, even.

Piprisoma agile, *Tickell.*

240.—Jerdon's Birds of India, Vol. I, p. 376; Butler, Deccan; Stray Feathers, Vol. IX, p. 391.

THE THICK-BILLED FLOWER-PECKER.

Length, 4; wing, 2·25; tail, 1·2; tarsus, 0·5.

Bill and legs leaden; irides orange-yellow.

Above dull olive-ashy, greenish on the rump and upper tail-coverts; wing and tail brownish, the former edged green and the tail slightly edged at tip with whitish, which forms a terminal spot on the inner web of the outermost feathers; beneath dirty greenish-white, with a few faint striæ on the throat, fore-neck, and flanks.

Occurs in the same localities as the last, but as a rule is not very common.

Sub-family, Certhinæ.

Bill generally curved, of moderate length, or rather long, slender; wings moderate or long, ample, rounded, of ten primaries, the first short; wing-coverts short; tail longish in most and with the feathers often stiff and pointed, short in some; toes long and slender, outer-toe longer than the inner, much syndactile; inner-toe slightly so; hind-toe very long, and its claw longer than the middle one; claws long, compressed, and curved and all the toes very mobile.

Genus, Salpornis, *Gray.*

Bill long, curved, broadish at base, much compressed beyond the nostrils; wings reaching to the end of the short tail; pointed; first primary very short, second nearly as long as third and fourth, which are equal and longest; tail short, even, soft and flexible.

Salpornis spilonota, *Franklin.*

246.—Jerdon's Birds of India, Vol. I, p. 382; Butler, Guzerat; Stray Feathers, Vol. III, p. 462.

THE SPOTTED-GREY CREEPER.

Length, 5·75; wing, 3·5; tail, 1·7; tarsus, 1·6; bill at front, 1.

Above fuscous-grey, white-spotted, with narrow white streaks on the head; throat and abdomen whitish, the latter barred with dusky; tail banded and fuscous.

The Spotted-grey Creeper has been obtained at Mount Aboo; it has not been recorded from any other portion of our limits.

SUB-FAMILY, Sittinæ.

Bill of moderate length, nearly straight, stout, compressed at the tip; wings moderate; tail short, even; toes long and slender; outer-toe longest, syndactyle.

GENUS, Sitta, *Lin.*

Bill moderate, straight, wedge-shaped; tip entire, barely deflexed; nostrils basal, rounded, covered by setaceous tufts; wings rather long, first quill short, fourth and fifth equal and longest; tail short, even, soft; feet short, strong; the inner-toe very short; outer nearly equal to the middle one, all cleft to the base; hind-toe long, equal to the tarsus; claws strong, broad and well curved.

Sitta castaneiventris, *Franklin.*

250.—Jerdon's Birds of India, Vol. I, p. 386.

THE CHESNUT-BELLIED NUTHATCH.

Length, 5·5; wing, 3·1; tail, 1·7; bill at front, 0·68.

Bill horny-black; irides brown; legs plumbeous.

Above greyish-plumbeous, lightest on the head and nape; stripe from the gape, through the eyes, to the nape, black; quills, with the inner webs of the feathers, black; throat and face white; breast and under tail-coverts, with the abdomen, deep chesnut bay in the male, dark cinnamon color in the female; the tail has the two central feathers grey, the rest blackish; the outermost three on each side with large white spots on the inner webs near the tip; the outermost of all has also a spot on the outer web near the base; the two next the uropygials are grey at the tip and on the outer web.

The Chesnut-bellied Nuthatch occurs in most of the jungles of Central India; it is much more common on the Vindhian Range.

GENUS, Dendrophila, *Swainson.*

General structure of *Sitta;* nostrils large, oval, open, nearly naked, with a very few incumbent hairs; base of bill widened; tip of the culmen slightly inclined downwards; the foot typical, with the hind-toe, if anything, larger.

Dendrophila frontalis, *Horsf.*

253.—Jerdon's Birds of India, Vol. I, p. 388; Butler, Deccan; Stray Feathers, Vol. IX, p. 391.

THE VELVET-FRONTED BLUE NUTHATCH.

Length, 5; extent, 8·5; wing, 3; tarsus, 0·9; tail, 1·5.

Bill bright coral-red; orbitar skin lemon-yellow; irides light straw-yellow; legs sienna-yellow.

Above fine cœrulean-blue, with a tinge of lilac on the head; forehead deep velvety-black; quills and lateral feathers blackish, the former more or less edged with blue, the latter tipped with white; beneath, delicate lilac-brownish, darkest on the vent and under tail-coverts, and reddish on the flanks; chin and throat white. The male, even in nestling plumage, is distinguished by having a black sincipital streak.

The Velvet-fronted Nuthatch occurs on the Sahyadri Range and in the adjacent forests; it has been found in the jungles west of Belgaum, Savantwadi, and along the Goa frontier; it is very rare, and has not been obtained in any other portion of our limits.

FAMILY, Upupidæ.

Bill long and slender, slightly curved throughout; the tip acute and entire; nostrils small; wings rounded; tail moderate or long, even or rounded; tarsi short and stout; outer toe syndactyle at the base; toes and claws strong.

SUB-FAMILY, Upupinæ.

Tail with ten feathers; wings long; bill keeled at the base; head with a large erectile crest.

GENUS, Upupa, *Lin.*

Bill very long, moderately curved, compressed; gape wide; head with a large crest; nostrils round, slightly removed from the base, destitute of any membrane; wings long, with fourth quill longest; tail even, broad, of ten feathers; tarsus moderate, with transverse scutæ in front, reticulate posteriorly; claws short, that of hallux longer, somewhat straight.

Upupa epops, *Lin.*

254.—Jerdon's Birds of India, Vol. I, p. 390; Butler, Guzerat; Stray Feathers, Vol. III, p. 462; Deccan, Stray Feathers, Vol. IX, p. 391; Murray's Vertebrate Zoology of Sind, p. 120; Swinhoe and Barnes, Central India; Ibis, 1885, p. 64.

THE EUROPEAN HOOPOE.

Length, 12 to 12·5; wing, 5·5; tail, 4; tarsus, 0·8; bill at front, 1·75 to 2.

Bill black, reddish at base; irides red-brown; legs brownish-black.

Head, with the feathers of the crest, pale cinnamon-rufous, tipped with black, and with a white space between the black and rufous on the median and posterior feathers; hind-neck, sides of neck, interscapulars, and shoulders of the wings, pale fawn, passing into brownish-ashy; the middle of the back banded white and black; the upper tail-coverts white at the base, ended with black; wings black; the coverts black, with two large white bars; the primary quills with a white spot or bar near the tip, on the first on the inner web only, on the others upon both webs; the secondaries and tertiaries with three, and finally four, white bands; tail with a broad white oblique band, about the middle; beneath the chin whitish; the throat and breast pale rufous-fawn, ashy on the sides of the breast; abdomen white, with black streaks and dashes; under tail-coverts white.

The European Hoopoe is a common cold weather visitant, throughout our limits.

Upupa ceylonensis, *Reich.*

255.—*Upupa nigripennis*, Gould.—Jerdon's Birds of India, Vol. I, p. 392; Butler, Guzerat; Stray Feathers, Vol. III, p. 462; Deccan, Stray Feathers, Vol. IX, p. 391.

THE INDIAN HOOPOE.

Length, 10·5; expanse, 18; wing, 5 to 5·5; tail, 4; tarsus, 0·87; bill at front, 1·8.

Bill blackish, paler at base; irides brown; legs dusky-plumbeous.

Very similar to the last, but smaller, and distinguished by the generally darker hue of the rufous of the head and crest, and there is no white on the crest, the white wing-bands being also smaller and less conspicuous; the hind-neck and interscapulars are deeper rufous, inclining to brown and less to ashy; the rump is dusky-black, with a downy-white ending to the feathers; the chin is rufous, and this color extends along the abdomen to the vent with only a few dusky streaks on the lower abdomen; vent and under tail-coverts white.

With the exception of Sind, the Indian Hoopoe is a not uncommon permanent resident throughout the district.

They nest from February to May, in holes in trees, banks, or walls under the rafters of houses, and such like places; the eggs are five or six in number, and are of a pale greyish-blue color, sometimes olive-brown or dingy olive-green and intermediate shades; in shape, they are lengthened ovals, occasionally pointed at both ends. They measure 0·97 inches in length by 0·66 in breadth.

FAMILY, **Laniadæ.**

Bill strong or of moderate length, notched or toothed at the tip; gape rather wide with rictal bristles; tarsus short, strong, usually with large scutæ in front and on the toes.

SUB-FAMILY, **Lanianæ.**

Bill strong, deep, more or less abruptly hooked, and the tip strongly notched; wings moderate; tail moderate or long; tarsus rather short, stout; feet short, strong; lateral toes nearly equal; middle-toe short; claws sharp.

GENUS, Lanius, *Lin.* (*in part*)

Bill short, strongly hooked and toothed, much compressed; rictal bristles numerous, rather weak; wings moderate; third and fourth quills about equal and longest; tail somewhat long, graduated; tarsus short; feet short, but strong.

Lanius lahtora, *Sykes.*

256.—Jerdon's Birds of India, Vol. I, p. 400; Butler, Guzerat; Stray Feathers, Vol. III, p. 462; Deccan, Stray Feathers, Vol. IX, p. 391; Murray's Vertebrate Zoology of Sind, p. 120; Swinhoe and Barnes, Central India; Ibis, 1885, p. 64.

THE INDIAN GREY SHRIKE.

Dudeya Latora and *Sufaid Latora*, Hin.

Length, 9·5 to 10; wing, 4·25; tarsus, 1·12; bill at front, 0·62.

Bill black; irides hazel-brown; legs brown-black.

Pale blue-grey; a very narrow frontal streak, continued through the eyes to the nape; the wings and middle tail-feathers black; a large band on the wings, formed by a broad band occupying two-thirds of all the primaries, and the outer webs and tips of the secondaries; the margins of the scapulars, the two external tail-feathers on each side, and the tips of the two following white; also all the lower plumage.

The Indian Grey Shrike is generally distributed throughout the province, but is less common perhaps in the more hilly districts. It is a permanent resident and breeds from February to July, but most nests are found in March, April and May. The nest is large, compact and cup-shaped, and is composed of twigs, coarse grass, pieces of rag, &c., lined with finer grass roots. It is generally placed in the centre of a dense thorny bush or small tree. The eggs, generally four in number, occasionally five, are broad ovals, pointed at one end, of a delicate greenish-white color, spotted and blotched with yellowish, reddish, or purplish brown. The markings are more numerous at the larger end, sometimes forming a zone or cap. They measure about an inch in length by 0·79 in breadth.

Lanius erythronotus, *Vig.*

257.—Jerdon's Birds of India, Vol. I, p. 402; Butler, Guzerat; Stray Feathers, Vol. III, p. 463; Deccan, Stray Feathers, Vol. IX, p. 392; Murray's Vertebrate Zoology of Sind, p. 121; Swinhoe and Barnes, Central India; Ibis 1885, p. 64.

THE RUFOUS-BACKED SHRIKE.

Mattiya Latora, Hin.

Length, 10; wing, 3·5 to 3·75; tail, 4·5 to 5; tarsus, 1·12.

Bill black; irides dark brown; legs black.

Head above, and nape, and upper part of back, pure ashy; narrow frontal streak, continued through the eyes to the end of the ear-coverts, black; scapulars, lower back, rump, and upper tail-coverts ferruginous; wing black; edge of the wing, and a small spot near the base of the primaries, white; tail, with the four central feathers, black, the outer feathers reddish-cineraceous, edged and tipped paler or whitish; beneath white, ferruginous on the flanks and under tail-coverts.

The Rufous-backed Shrike is common throughout the district, and is a permanent resident, breeding from May to August, but occasionally nests are found much earlier; they are generally built in babool trees, and are compact, deep, cup-shaped structures, composed of the same materials as the last.

The eggs, from four to six in number, are miniatures of those of *L. lahtora*. They measure 0·92 inches in length by 0·71 in breadth.

Lanius nigriceps, *Franklin.*

259.—Jerdon's Birds of India, Vol. I, p. 404.

THE BLACK-HEADED SHRIKE.

Length, 9·2 to 10·3; expanse, 11 to 12; wing, 3·6 to 3·75; tail, 4·75 to 5·25; tarsus, 1·16; bill from gape, 1; bill at front, 0·65.

Bill black; irides deep brown; legs brown-black.

Head above, nape, wings and tail, black; upper part of back ashy; lower back, scapulars, rump and upper tail-coverts, rufous; beneath the throat, breast and middle of the abdomen white; sides of abdomen, vent, and lower tail-coverts, rufous.

Jerdon in his Birds of India states: "I have seen it in Goomsoor but not further south; and from this it ranges in land into the northern part of Central India."

Lanius vittatus, *Valenc.*

260.—*Lanius hardwickii*, Vigors.—Jerdon's Birds of India, Vol. I, p. 405; Butler, Guzerat; Stray Feathers, Vol. III, p. 463; Deccan, Stray Feathers, Vol. IX, p. 392; Murray's Vertebrate Zoology of Sind, p. 121; Swinhoe and Barnes, Central India; Ibis, 1885, p. 65.

THE BAY-BACKED SHRIKE.

Length, 7·25 to 8; expanse, 10; wing, 3·25; tail, 3·25 to 4; tarsus, 0·7 to 0·8; bill at front, 0·5.

Bill black; irides hazel-brown; legs black.

The whole forehead, with eye-stripe, continued to the nape, black; top of the head white; back of head, nape and the lower part of the back, whitish-grey, paler and almost white on the upper tail-coverts; middle of the back and scapulars deep chesnut or bay; wings and tail black, the former with a wing-spot on the primaries, and the latter with the two outermost tail-feathers on each side and base, and tips of the others (except the four central) white; body beneath, white, tinged with fulvescent on the breast, and the sides of the abdomen dark ferruginous.

The female sometimes wants the black forehead and stripe over the eyes.

The Bay-backed Shrike is generally spread throughout the district, frequenting low thorny jungle, groves of young babool trees, gardens, hedges, &c.

It is a permanent resident, breeding from April to September, but June and July are the months in which most nests are to be found; they are generally built in forks of small trees, and are firm, compact, deep, well-woven cups, composed of fine twigs, grass roots, wool, rags, &c.

The eggs, four in number, are miniatures of the preceding, but the markings are perhaps paler.

They measure 0·82 inches in length by 0·36 in breadth.

Lanius collurio, *Lin.*

260*bis.*—Butler, Guzerat; Stray Feathers, Vol. III, p. 463.

THE EUROPEAN RED-BACKED SHRIKE.

Length, 7·5; wing, 3·5; tail, 3·5; tarsus, 0·96; bill at front, 0·56; bill from gape, 0·81.

Bill black, paler at base of lower mandible; irides dark brown; legs black.

A conspicuous black streak from the nostrils, widening so as to include the whole of the lores, eyes and ear-coverts; the forehead and the whole top and back of the head, between the black stripes, pale grey, darkening on the occiput and nape; scapulars and interscapulary region brownish-chesnut; lower back duller and more rusty; rump and upper tail-coverts light grey, the feathers just perceptibly darker shafted; wings hair-brown; primaries and their coverts very narrowly, and secondaries and tertiaries very broadly margined with dull pale and bright rusty-chesnut respectively; the tail black, all but the central tail-feathers white at their bases, and the external feathers on each side 0·4 shorter than the others, narrowly tipped white and with nearly the whole of their outer webs white; the entire under parts white, but the breast, abdomen, sides, and flanks with a rich vinaceous tinge.

There is a small white spot at the base of the fourth long primary on the outer web, only visible, however, when the larger-coverts are somewhat deranged.

The European Red-backed Shrike was discovered by Major Butler in the neighbourhood of Deesa, during the latter part of the rains in September, 1874.

This is the only instance on record of the occurrence of the bird within the Indian Empire.

Lanius cristatus, *Lin.*

261.—Jerdon's Birds of India, Vol. I, p. 406; Butler, Guzerat; Stray Feathers, Vol. III, p. 464; Deccan, Stray Feathers, Vol.

IX, p. 392; Murray's Vertebrate Zoology of Sind, p. 122; Swinhoe and Barnes, Central India; Ibis, 1885, p. 66.

THE BROWN SHRIKE.

Length, 7·6 to 8·1; expanse, 9·5 to 11; wing, 3·25 to 3·5; tail, 3·4 to 3·9; bill from gape, 0·84 to 0·86; bill from front, 0·5 to 0·58.

Bill blackish-horny, beneath fleshy; irides brown; legs leaden-blue.

Above rufous-brown with the head, tail and upper tail-coverts, more rufous; streak over the eye, sometimes faintly and narrowly extending over the forehead, white; throat white; the rest of the lower parts whitish, with a fulvous tinge; lores and ear-coverts forming a broad band through the eye, dull brown-black. Female and young much edged with brown bands, and the eye-spot paler and brown.

The Brown Shrike occurs more or less commonly as a cold weather visitant throughout the district.

Lanius isabellinus, *Hemp. & Ehr.*

262.—*Lanius arenarius*, Bly.—Jerdon's Birds of India, Vol. I, p. 407; Butler, Guzerat; Stray Feathers, Vol. III, p. 464; Murray's Vertebrate Zoology of Sind, p. 122.

THE PALE BROWN SHRIKE.

Length, 7·75; wing, 3·75; tail, 3·5.

The race differs from *cristatus* by its much paler hue, being light ashy-brown, barely tinged with rufous on the rump only; lores and superciliary streak pale; ear-coverts dark above, pale beneath; wings pale brown; the primaries narrowly edged, and the coverts and secondaries broadly with rufescent; the central tail-feathers brown; the rest pale rufous-brown; beneath white, smeared all over, but especially on the breast and flanks, with fawn or fulvescent; under tail-coverts white.

The Pale Brown Shrike is a common winter visitant to Sind and Guzerat. It does not occur in the Deccan, nor has it as yet been recorded from Central India.

SUB-FAMILY, Malaconotinæ.

Bill more lengthened and less compressed than in the true Shrikes; wings longer, and tail shorter; tarsus short; feet small.

GENUS, Tephrodornis, *Swainson.*

Bill lengthened, widish at the base, compressed, strong, moderately hooked at the tip, and notched; base of bill and nostrils partially covered with procumbent setaceous feathers; a few moderately long rictal bristles; wings moderate or long, slightly rounded; tail rather short, even, or slightly emarginate; tarsus and toes short; lateral toes unequal; outer-toe the longest, slightly syndactyle.

Tephrodornis sylvicola, *Jerdon.*

264.—Jerdon's Birds of India, Vol. I, p. 409; Butler, Deccan and South Mahratta country; Stray Feathers, Vol. IX, p. 392.

THE MALABAR WOOD SHRIKE.

Length, 8·5; expanse, 14; wing, 4·5; tail, 3·25; tarsus, 0·9; bill at front, 0·7.

Bill blackish; irides wax-yellow; legs plumbeous.

Above slaty-cinereous; rump white; wings, tail, and some of the upper-coverts, dusky-brown; a broad eye streak from the nostrils, through the eye, to beyond the ear-coverts, black; beneath white, reddish-cinereous on the neck, breast, and flanks.

The Malabar Wood Shrike is not common, and has only been recorded from the jungles west of Belgaum.

Tephrodornis pondicerianus, *Gm.*

265.—Jerdon's Birds of India, Vol. I, p, 410; Butler, Guzerat; Stray Feathers, Vol. III, p. 464; Deccan, Stray Feathers, Vol. IX, p. 392; Murray's Vertebrate Zoology of Sind, p. 123; Swinhoe and Barnes, Central India; Ibis, 1885, p. 65.

THE COMMON WOOD SHRIKE.

Length, 6·5 to 7; expanse, 10; wing, 3·5; tail, 2·75; tarsus, 0·75; bill at front, 0·62.

Bill dusky-horny; irides greenish-yellow; legs plumbeous-brown.

Above ashy-brownish; the feathers of the rump edged with white, and the upper tail-coverts deep brown; beneath, chin and throat white, the rest whitish, with a tinge of reddish grey; under tail-coverts white; superciliary streak reddish-white; wings and tail dusky-brown, and with the two outer feathers on each side white at the base and also at the tip; a dark brown band from the nostrils through the eye to the ear-coverts.

The Common Wood Shrike is found in all the principal portions of our limits, but is much more numerous in some places than in others. It is a permanent resident, breeding generally in March and April. The nest, composed of fine roots and grass, and lined with wool and vegetable fibres, is a neat, well made, compact, shallow cup, coated on the exterior with cobwebs, and is built in the fork of a tree. The eggs, three in number, are broadish oval in shape, delicate greenish-white in color, spotted and blotched with different shades of yellowish and reddish-brown. They measure 0·75 in length by 0·61 in breadth.

GENUS, Hemipus, *Hodgson.*

Much as in *Tephrodornis,* but the bill more flat, depressed and wider at the base; rictal bristles small; nostrils concealed; wing moderate, third quill almost equal to fourth; tail narrow, graduated; legs and feet small

Hemipus picatus, *Sykes.*

267.—Jerdon's Birds of India, Vol. I, p. 412; Butler, Deccan; Stray Feathers, Vol. IX, p. 393.

THE LITTLE PIED SHRIKE.

Length, 5·5; expanse, 7·6; wing, 2·3 to 2·5; tail, 2·3 to 2·5; tarsus, 0·5; bill at front, 0·4; bill from gape, 0·7.

Bill black; irides hazel; legs plumbeous-brown.

Male, above black glossed, less so on the back and scapulars, with a white nuchal collar and white rump; band on the wings white; tail with the lateral feathers tipped with white, more broadly so on the outermost feathers; beneath white, tinged with reddish-ashy, purer white on the throat, vent, and under tail-coverts.

The female differs in having the upper parts dull sooty brown-black.

Within our limits the Little Pied Shrike only occurs in various parts of the Deccan and South Mahratta country. I cannot do better than reproduce, *in extenso*, what Major Butler has written concerning its distribution. He says:—

"Locally not uncommon along the Sahyadri Range. Mr. Fairbank obtained it at Nagar; Mr. Laird in the jungles south-west of Belgaum; Mr. Crawford at Savantwadi; and Mr. Vidal mentions it from the south of Ratnagiri; outside of the forests tracts it probably does not occur."

SUB-FAMILY, Campephaginæ.

Bill of moderate length, or rather short, rather deep vertically, broadish at base; culmen arched or curved; rictal bristles few, feeble; nostrils basal, in a fossa, partially covered by short plumules; wings of moderate length; third and fourth or fourth and fifth quills sub-equal and longest; tail rather long, rounded, or graduated; feathers of the back and rump often rigid; tarsus short; feet weak or moderate.

GENUS, Volvocivora, *Hodgson.*

Bill rather short, broadish at base, compressed at tip, where bent down and notched; culmen scarcely keeled; rictal bristles almost wanting; nostrils basal, oval, partly concealed by tufts; wings rather long; third and fourth quills equal and longest; tail moderate or long, rounded; upper tail-coverts long; tarsus short; feet short; outer-toe slightly longer than the inner; claws small, slightly curved.

Volvocivora sykesi, *Strick.*

268.—Jerdon's Birds of India, Vol. I, p. 414; Butler, Guzerat; Stray Feathers, Vol. III, p. 464; Deccan, Stray Feathers, Vol. IX, p. 393; *Lalage sykesi*, Strick.; Swinhoe and Barnes, Central India; Ibis, 1885, p. 65.

THE BLACK-HEADED CUCKOO-SHRIKE.

Length, 7·5 ; wing, 4 ; tail, 3 ; tarsus, 0·8 ; bill at front, 0·5.

Bill black ; irides dark red-brown ; feet black.

Head, neck, and breast deep black ; whole upper plumage pale grey ; tail black, the outer feathers broadly tipped with white ; lower breast and abdomen pale grey, passing gradually to white on the lower abdomen and lower tail-coverts.

The young bird has the head grey like the back ; the throat and entire under parts whitish, with dusky cross rays ; and the rump more or less distinctly rayed.

The Black-headed Cuckoo-Shrike is a not uncommon visitant to most parts of the district, but it has not as yet been recorded from Sind.

Volvocivora melaschista, *Hodgson.*

269.—Jerdon's Birds of India, Vol. I, p. 415 ; Butler, Deccan ; Stray Feathers, Vol. IX, p. 393.

THE DARK-GREY CUCKOO-SHRIKE.

Length, 9·5 to 10 ; expanse, 15 ; wing, 4·6 ; tail, 5·25 ; tarsus, 0·88 ; bill at front, 0·62.

Bill black ; irides hazel-brown ; legs black.

Plumage iron-grey, darker and almost black on the quills and tail, the latter tipped white on all but the central feathers, paler grey beneath.

Young birds are dusky-grey above, paler beneath, with dark bands ; albescent on the under tail-coverts.

The Dark-grey Cuckoo-Shrike has been obtained at Savantvadi, but there is no other record of its occurrence within our limits.

GENUS, **Hypocolius**, *Bp.*

Bill hooked at tip, and notched ; third quill longest ; feet scutellated ; tail long, subcuneate.

Hypocolius ampelinus, *Bp.*

269*quat.*—Murray's Vertebrate Zoology of Sind, p. 123.

Length, 10·25 ; wing, 4·2 ; tail, 4·75 ; tarsus, 1 ; bill from gape 0 9.

Bill horny, dusky at tip ; legs flesh-colored.

Upper parts generally ashy-grey, with a slight rufous tinge on the head, which is more marked on the frontal portion where the feathers are rather lighter and more isabelline in tint ; feathers above the nostrils, lower part of the lores, all round the eyes, and a band round the nape, black, so that there is a black ring all round the head, except in the centre of the forehead ; ear-coverts dark silver-grey, looking black in some lights in the preserved skin ; primary quills black, with rather long white tips, the tip on the first long primary being wholly, and on the second partially dusky ; outer secondaries black with grey edges, the black diminishing in amount, until it disappears completely on the feathers near the body; tail-feathers all the same color as the back, with black tips about three-quarters of an inch long; chin and throat isabelline; breast grey, like the back; abdomen and lower tail-coverts pinkish-isabelline; under wing-coverts light grey.

A single specimen was obtained in Sind, by Mr. Blanford, on the lower hills of the Kirthur Range, which forms the boundary between Sind and Khelat.

It has not been procured elsewhere within our range.

Genus, Graucalus, *Cuvier.*

Bill strong, deep, of moderate length, wide at the base; culmen tolerably curved and hooked, slightly toothed; a few weak rictal bristles; wings rather long, pointed; tail moderate, slightly rounded, or nearly even, with the two outer feathers shorter; tarsus and toes moderate; claws well curved, of rather large size.

Graucalus macii, *Less.*

270.—Jerdon's Birds of India, Vol. I, p. 417; Butler, Guzerat; Stray Feathers, Vol. III, p. 464; Deccan, Stray Feathers, Vol. IX, p. 393; Murray's Vertebrate Zoology of Sind, p. 126; Swinhoe and Barnes, Central India; Ibis, 1885, p. 65.

THE LARGE CUCKOO-SHRIKE.

Length, 12; wing, 6·5; tail, 5; tarsus, 1; bill at front, 0·87.

Bill blackish; irides rich-lake; legs plumbeous.

Whole upper plumage light plumbeous-grey, paling on the rump and upper tail-coverts; tail with the two central feathers grey, the rest dusky-black, the two outer ones on each side tipped white, and the outermost also edged with white; beneath, neck and breast, light grey, slightly tinged with reddish-ash on the breast; abdomen greyish-white, with numerous narrow cross stripes, white on the lower abdomen and under tail-coverts.

Mr. Hume remarks that "Dr. Jerdon does not point out the difference that exists between the adults of the two sexes in all the races of this species. In the young of both sexes, the whole of the lower parts, except the vent and lower tail-coverts, are more or less regularly transversely barred: as the bird grows older, the bars disappear in both sexes from the chin, throat and breast, the whole of which parts become pale grey; more or less barring remains for a time on the abdomen in both sexes, and indeed always remains in the female even in the most perfect plumage. In the male, as time goes on, the chin, throat and breast become a darker grey, and the markings disappear entirely from the abdomen, the upper portions of which become tinged with grey.

Moreover, the black eye-streak becomes much more strongly marked in the male than it ever is in the female, and the points of the forehead, which always remain grey in the female, become quite black, presenting the appearance of a narrow black frontal band.

The Large Cuckoo-Shrike is more or less common throughout the district, and is said to be a resident at Ratnagiri and other localities. It is, however, somewhat uncommon in Sind.

GENUS, **Pericrocotus**, *Boie.*

Bill shorter than the head, moderately broad at the base, rather high; culmen slightly curved; nostrils partially concealed by the frontal plumes; rictal bristles few and feeble; wings moderate, fourth and fifth quills sub-equal and longest; tail long, with three outer feathers on each side graduated, and the four middle ones nearly equal; tarsi and feet short, rather feeble; claws well curved.

Pericrocotus speciosus, *Lath.*

271.—Jerdon's Birds of India, Vol. I, p. 419.

THE LARGE MINIVET.

Length, 9; expanse, 12·5; wing, 4·25; tail, 4·25; tarsus, 0·9; bill at front, 0·5.

Bill black; irides deep-brown; legs black.

Male.—Head, whole neck, upper back, wings and two central tail-feathers, shiny blue-black; lower back broad band on the wing, formed by a large spot on all of the quills and some of the lower-coverts also, some spots on the secondaries, the lateral tail-feathers and beneath from the breast, rich vermilion-red.

Female.—Head, neck, upper back, and central tail-feathers, light ashy-grey, with a tinge of green; forehead, rump and upper tail-coverts greenish yellow; the quills dusky-black, with a deep yellow spot; tail with the four central feathers dusky, the outer pair tipped yellow; the whole of the others deep yellow, with some blackish at the base crossing each feather obliquely; the whole of the lower parts deep king's-yellow.

The two central tail-feathers have sometimes the outer web red for a great part of their length, and the yellow on the forehead of the young male has an orange tinge; otherwise it resembles the adult female.

Jerdon states in his *Birds of India* that "this splendidly colored bird extends from the Himalayas to Central India and Goomsoor, where I obtained it, but it does not appear to go further south."

Pericrocotus flammeus, *Forst.*

272.—Jerdon's Birds of India, Vol. I, p. 420; Butler, Deccan; Stray Feathers, Vol. IX, p. 393.

THE ORANGE MINIVET.

Length, 8·25; wing, 3·8; tail, 4; tarsus, 0·62; bill at front, 0·5.
Bill black; irides dark-brown; legs brown-black.

Male, with the whole head and neck, upper back, scapulars and wings, glossy blue-black; wings with a broad orange-red band, formed by all the quills having the central portion red, and the edges of the lesser wing-coverts also; tail with the two central feathers black, the next pair black, tipped red, and all the others blackish at the base, and orange-red for nearly half their terminal length.

The female has the head, neck, back and wing-coverts ashy; the forehead narrowly tinged with yellow; the lower back, rump and upper tail-coverts, greenish-yellow; the quills and tail dusky-black, the former with a yellow wing spot, and the latter with the lateral tail-feathers yellow.

The Orange Minivet is a permanent resident and is not uncommon all along the Sahyadri Range from Goa to Khandalla. It has not been recorded from any other portion of our province.

Pericrocotus brevirostris, *Vig.*

273.—Jerdon's Birds of India, Vol. I, p. 421; Butler, Guzerat; Stray Feathers, Vol. III, p. 465; Murray's Vertebrate Zoology of Sind, p. 126.

THE SHORT-BILLED MINIVET.

Length, 7·5 to 8; expanse, 11; wing, 3·5; tail, nearly 4; tarsus, 0·6; bill at front, 0·37.

Bill black; irides dark-brown; legs brown-black.

Male.—Head, neck, nape, upper back, wings, and middle tail-feathers, shining blue-black; body beneath, lower back, rump, upper tail-coverts, wing spot, and tips of some of the coverts, and the lateral tail-feathers, fine deep crimson; the latter black at their bases.

The female has the head and back grey; the forehead tinged with yellow; beneath, spots on the wings, rump, and lateral tail-feathers, yellow; wings and tail dusky; the pair next the middle feathers slightly edged with yellow.

The Short-billed Minivet is rare; it has been obtained on Mount Aboo and on the Vindhian Hills near Mhow. It also occurs during the summer months in Sind.

Pericrocotus peregrinus, *Lin.*

276.—Jerdon's Birds of India, Vol. I, p. 423; Butler, Guzerat; Stray Feathers, Vol. III, p. 465; Deccan, Stray Feathers, Vol. IX, p. 394; Murray's Vertebrate Zoology of Sind, p. 125; Swinhoe and Barnes, Central India; Ibis, 1885, p. 65.

THE SMALL MINIVET.

Length, 6·4; wing, 2·7; expanse, 8·5; tail, 3; tarsus, 0·9; bill at front, 0·3.

Bill black; irides brown; legs black.

Male.—Head, nape, and back, ashy; lores, chin, throat, and ears, blackish; wings and tail dusky-black, the former with an orange stripe formed by a central band on all the primaries (except the first three), and the secondaries orange on the outer, yellow on the inner web; tail, with the four outer feathers on each side, widely tipped with orange; breast, upper part of abdomen, flanks, and rump, rich scarlet or aurora-red, fading to yellow on the lower abdomen and under tail-coverts, and whitish on the vent.

The female differs in having the eyestreak, sides of forehead, chin, throat, and lower parts whitish, tinged with yellow on the breast, abdomen, flanks, and under tail-coverts; the wings and tail are dingier black, and the wing-spot is yellow; the under tail-coverts of the wing are yellow in both sexes; tail as in the male, but the colors are not quite so bright.

The Small Minivét is a common permanent resident throughout the region.

It breeds during the months of June, July and August. The nest is placed high up, in a fork in a tree, generally a mango; it is a well made, compact, deepish cup-shaped nest, composed of fine twigs, grass roots, lichens, dead leaves and pieces of bark, which assimilate in color with the bark of the tree, and make it an exceedingly hard nest to find. The eggs are of a rather broad oval shape, pale greenish-white in color, more or less spotted and blotched with brownish-red. They measure 0·67 inches in length by 0·53 in breadth.

Pericrocotus erythropygius, *Jerd.*

277.—Jerdon's Birds of India, Vol. I, p. 424; Butler, Guzerat; Stray Feathers, Vol. III, p. 465; Deccan, Stray Feathers, Vol. IX, p. 394; Swinhoe and Barnes, Central India; Ibis, 1885, p. 66.

THE WHITE-BELLIED MINIVET.

Length, 6·5; wing, 2·7; tail, 3·5; tarsus, 0·5; bill at front, 0·3. Bill black; irides brownish-yellow; legs black.

Male.—Plumage above (except rump), cheeks, and chin, of a glossy blue-black; beneath longitudinal stripe on wings, outer edges and tips of the lateral tail-feathers, white; breast and rump of a fine orange or aurora-red, darkest on the rump.

The female has the parts that are black in the male smoky-ash color (except the tail, which is deep black); the forehead whitish; rump and beneath white, tinged with ashy on the breast.

With the exception of Sind, the White-bellied Minivet is spread throughout the region, but is everywhere rare.

SUB-FAMILY, **Dicrurinæ.**

Bill rather large, wide at the base, thick, more or less curved and keeled at the culmen, and notched at the tip; numerous moderately strong rictal bristles; nostrils basal, rounded, concealed by short plumes; wings lengthened; fourth and fifth quills usually the longest; legs short; feet small; tail usually long, forked; the outer feathers occasionally much lengthened; of ten feathers only.

GENUS, **Buchanga**, *Hodgson.*

Bill moderate or rather long, stout, depressed at the base, moderately hooked, and the culmen more or less keeled, and distinctly notched at the tip; nostrils small, partially covered by short feathers and bristles; rictal bristles strong; wings lengthened; first quill short, second shorter than sixth; tail long, deeply forked; tarsus moderate, strongly scaled in front; outer-toe slightly the longest; claws sharp.

Buchanga atra, *Herm.*

278.—*Dicrurus macrocercus*, Vieill.—Jerdon's Birds of India, Vol. I, p. 427; *B. albirictus*, Hodgs.; Butler, Guzerat; Stray Feathers, Vol. III, p. 465; Deccan, Stray Feathers, Vol. IX, p. 394; Murray's Vertebrate Zoology of Sind, p. 126; Swinhoe and Barnes, Central India; Ibis, 1885, p. 66.

THE COMMON DRONGO-SHRIKE.
THE KING CROW.
Kolsa, Hin.

Length, 11·5 to 13·75; expanse, 17 to 18·75; wing, 5·50 to 5·75; tail, 6 to 7·25; tarsus, 0·9; bill from gape, 1 to 1·25; bill at front, 0·75.

Bill black; irides maroon-red; legs black.

Glossy black, with a small white spot at the gape (not always present), somewhat duller black on the quills and tail, which are brownish-black beneath.

Young with whitish lunules on the abdominal plumage.

The King Crow is a common permanent resident throughout the region, breeding during May, June and July, a few breeding earlier or later according to locality.

The nest is usually built in a fork of a tree, at some height from the ground, and is composed of grass roots and stems neatly woven together, and is of a shallow saucer-shape. The regular number of eggs is four, but occasionally five are found; they are of two very distinct types. The first is a pure white, without markings; the other a pale salmon color, marked with rich red-brown.

Between these types every variety occurs, but all the eggs out of the same nest strongly resemble each other.

They measure 1·01 inches in length by 0·75 in breadth.

Buchanga longicauda, *Hay.*

280.—*Dicrurus longicaudatus*, Hay.—Jerdon's Birds of India, Vol. I, p. 395; Butler, Deccan; Stray Feathers, Vol. IX, p. 394; Swinhoe and Barnes, Central India; Ibis, 1885, p. 66.

THE LONG-TAILED DRONGO-SHRIKE.

Length, 10·8 to 11·8 ; expanse, 16 ; wing, 5·2 to 5·5 ; tail, 6 to 7 ; tarsus, 0·8 ; bill from gape, 1·15.

Bill black ; irides brownish-red ; legs black.

Above glossy bluish-black ; beneath dusky blackish, with a tinge of blue ; wings and tail brownish-black, also with a blue gloss.

The young bird has some white mixed with the black of the abdomen and under tail-coverts.

The Long-tailed Drongo is common on the Western Ghats and in the adjoining forests, also on the Sahyadri Range as far north as Khandalla. Major Butler notes that it is common in Belgaum in the cold weather, but it is a permanent resident in the other places mentioned. Colonel Swinhoe procured it near Mhow, and I have occasionally met with it at and near Neemuch. It does not occur in Sind; neither did Major Butler or myself obtain it in Guzerat.

Buchanga cœrulescens, *Lin.*

281.—*Dicrurus cœrulescens*, Lin.—Jerdon's Birds of India, Vol. I, p. 432; Butler, Guzerat; Stray Feathers, Vol. III, p. 465; Deccan, Stray Feathers, Vol. IX, p. 394; Swinhoe and Barnes, Central India; Ibis, p. 66.

THE WHITE-BELLIED DRONGO.

Length, 9·5; wing, 4·75; tail, 5; tarsus, 0·8; bill at front, 0·7.

Bill black; irides lake; legs black.

Upper plumage, wings, and tail, black, with a blue gloss; chin, throat, and breast, iron-grey; abdomen and lower tail-coverts white.

With the exception of Sind, the White-bellied Drongo occurs sparingly throughout the region.

GENUS, Chaptia, *Hodgson.*

Bill much more depressed and feeble, *muscipeta*-like, wide; the culmen very gently arching, and feebly hooked and toothed; first quill very short, fourth longest, third and sixth equal; tail moderately forked; legs and feet very feeble.

Chaptia ænea, *Vieill.*

282.—Jerdon's Birds of India, Vol. I, p. 433; Butler, Deccan; Stray Feathers, Vol. IX, p. 394.

THE BRONZED DRONGO.

Length, 9 to 9·5; wing, 4·75; tail, 4·5; tarsus, 0·6; bill at front, 0·75.

Bill black; irides deep-brown; legs black.

Plumage throughout richly glossy, bronzed blue-black; quills and tail black, with a faint gloss; abdomen, vent, and under tail-coverts, dull grey-black.

The Bronzed Drongo is not uncommon on the Sahyadri Range, as far north as Khandalla. It does not occur elsewhere within our limits.

GENUS, **Dissemurus**, *Glog.*

Bill lengthened, strong, moderately depressed at the base, compressed towards the tip; the culmen well curved and hooked, and distinctly notched, and the ridge well developed; rictal bristles long, rather weak; a few short frontal plumes cresting the nostrils, but they mostly rise up and fall back over the forehead, forming a fine crest; tail forked; the outermost pair have the inner webs gradually thinning off, and the shaft is bare for some distance, terminating in a web, long and broadish on the outer side, with a narrow and short web on the inner side.

Dissemurus grandis, *Gould.*

284.—*Edolius paradiseus*, Lin.—Jerdon's Birds of India, Vol. I, p. 435.

THE LARGE RACKET-TAILED DRONGO.

Length, to end of ordinary tail, 14; wing, 6·75; tail to middle, 6·5; outer tail-feathers, 12 or 13 inches more; the shaft having the terminal end, for about 3·5 inches barbed externally, but towards the tip only on the inner side, and turning inwards, so that the underside becomes uppermost; bill at front, 1·4 to 1·5; tarsus, 1.

Plumage uniformly black, with a steel-blue gloss; feathers of the crown slightly hackled, those of the nape strongly so, on breast slightly; plumage generally loose and puffy; frontal crest falling backwards over the nape, varying from 1·5 to 2·25 inches in length.

According to Jerdon, the Large Racket-tailed Drongo occurs in Central India.

Dissemurus paradiseus, *Lin.*

285.—*Edolius malabaricus*, Scop.—Jerdon's Birds of India, Vol. I, p. 437; Butler, Deccan, Vol. IX, p. 395.

THE MALABAR RACKET-TAILED DRONGO.

Bhimraj, Hin.

Length, 13; wing, 5·75 to 6·25; tail, 6·5; outer tail-feathers, 12 inches more; bill at front, 0·75.

Plumage uniformly black, with a steel-blue gloss; feathers of crown slightly hackled, those of the nape strongly so, on breast slightly; plumage generally loose and puffy; frontal crest falling backwards over the nape, varying from 0·75 inches to 1·25 in length.

The Bhimraj is a permanent resident all along the Sahyadri

Range, as far north as Khandalla, extending to the forests below. It is very partial to bamboo jungles.

It does not occur elsewhere within our limits.

Genus, **Chibia**, *Hodgson.*

Bill lengthened, compressed, curved both on the culmen and commissure, more slender than in others of the family, slightly hooked at the tip, and obsoletely notched; rictal bristles short and feeble; nostrils denuded; a crest of hair arising from the forehead and falling back over neck; tail forked; outer tail-feathers slightly lengthened, turned up into a sort of scoop; plumage of the head and neck highly lanceolate, especially on the sides of neck.

Chibia hottentota, *Lin.*

286.—Jerdon's Birds of India, Vol. I, p. 439; Butler, Deccan; Stray Feathers, Vol. IX, p. 395.

THE HAIR-CRESTED DRONGO.

Length, 11·9; wing, 6·5; tail, 5; tarsus, 1; bill at front, 1·4.

Bill black; irides red-brown; legs black.

Deep black, with purple and blue reflections on the hind-neck and breast; wings deep glossy bronze-green; tail the same; abdomen deep black.

The Hair-crested Drongo is very rare; it was obtained in Savantvadi by Mr. Vidal, but this is the only record of its occurrence within our limits.

Sub-family, **Artaminæ**.

Bill short or moderate, wide at the base, deep, slightly curved; culmen rounded; commissure gently curved, barely hooked at the tip, and entire; nostrils basal, impended by a minute tuft at their base only; a few inconspicuous rictal bristles; tarsus and toes short, strong; claws well curved, acute; wings long; first quill minute, second longest; tail short or moderate, even or slightly emarginate; lateral toes nearly equal.

Genus, **Artamus**, *Vieill.*

The characters are the same as those of the sub-family.

Artamus fuscus, *Vieill.*

287.—Jerdon's Birds of India, Vol. I, p. 441; Butler, Deccan; Stray Feathers, Vol. IX, p. 395.

THE ASHY SWALLOW-SHRIKE.

Length, 7; expanse, 15; wing, 5·25; tail, 2·2; tarsus, 0·6; bill at front, 0·6.

Bill pale-bluish, dusky at tip; irides dark brown; legs slaty.

Lores black; general hue cinereous, or ashy-grey, purest on the head, and with a tinge of rufous on the back and scapulars; breast, abdomen, under wing-coverts, and under tail-coverts, ashy-white, with a tinge of rufous on the belly; quills and tail blackish ashy-grey, the latter tipped narrowly with pale ashy; upper tail-coverts white beneath, showing a white border next the dark tail.

This is another bird that within our limits has only been obtained by Mr. Vidal. He remarks: "Has been found in the cocoanut gardens round Vingorla."

Family, Muscicapidæ.

Bill rather wide, depressed, shallow; the culmen straight, distinctly hooked and notched at the tip; rictal bristles (typically) numerous and strong; wings moderate; tail generally rather short or moderate; tarsus short, weak; feet moderately small, feeble.

Sub-family, Myiagrinæ, *Bonap.*

Bill broad at base, much depressed, straight, considerably hooked at the tip, and notched; rictal bristles numerous and long; wings rather lengthened; tail moderate or somewhat long, in one genus with the central tail-feathers greatly elongated in the male sex; feet and legs short and feeble.

Genus, Muscipeta, *Cuv.*

Bill lengthened, wide, depressed at base, tolerably stout and deep, narrowing suddenly at the tip, which is moderately hooked and notched; the ridge of the culmen raised; nostrils somewhat in front, protected by a few stout nareal bristles, and plumed at their base; gape wide; rictal bristles numerous, long, and stout; wings rather long, somewhat pointed; the first four quills unequally graduated, fourth and fifth sub-equal and longest; tail rather long, cuneate, with the two central feathers greatly elongated in the male; feet and legs short and feeble; head crested.

Muscipeta paradisi, *Lin.*

288.—*Tchitrea paradisi*, Lin.—Jerdon's Birds of India, Vol. I, p. 445; Butler, Guzerat; Stray Feathers, Vol. III, p. 466; Deccan, Stray Feathers, Vol. IX, p. 395; *Tersiphoni paradisi*, Lin.; Murray's Vertebrate Zoology of Sind, p. 127; Swinhoe and Barnes, Central India; Ibis, 1885, p. 66.

THE PARADISE FLY-CATCHER.

Dood-raj and *Shah Bulbul*, Hin. The white bird.

Sultana Bulbul, Hin. The red bird.

Dimensions.

Sex.	Plumage.	Length.	Expanse.	Wing.	Tail from vent.	Tarsus.	Bill from gape.	Bill at front.
♀	Chesnut ...	8·2	10·2	3 41	3·7	0 62	1	0·58
„	„ ...	8·6	10·6	3·66	6·4	0·62	0·98	0·5
„	„ ...	8·56	10·58	3·66	6·1	0·6	1·04	0·C6
„	„ ...	8·58	10·25	3·44	4·98	0·66	1 04	0·64
♂	„ ...	18·12	10·8	3·8	13·5	0·62	1·18	0·68
„	„ ...	17·78	11·1	3·81	13·5	0 62	1·08	0·62
„	„ ...	19·1	10·5	3 55	14·6	0·62	1·06	0·64
„	White ...	21 75	11 25	3·75	17	0 66	1·2	0·7
„	„ ...	10·42	10·7	3·6	5·8	0·6	1·1	0·64
„	„ ...	13 75	10·8	3·68	9·1	0·62	1·06	0·66
„	„ ...	19·5	11·2	3·81	15·25	0·66	1·16	0·66
„	„ ...	19	10·25	3·7	14·5	0·64	1	0·64

Bill cobalt-blue; irides deep brown; eyelids cobalt-blue; legs pale lavender-blue.

Adult male.—Whole head with the full crest, neck and throat, glossy green-black, the rest of the plumage white, the feathers more or less black shafted; primaries and secondaries black, with the outer webs white, and also the edge of inner webs of the innermost quills; head with a full crest of elongated feathers; two central tail-feathers greatly elongated.

The adult female is similar to the male; its middle tail-feathers are only slightly elongated.

The younger male has the head, neck, and throat, glossy black, the abdomen white, and the rest of the plumage light chesnut. The young female has the same, without the long tail.

In a still younger state, the throat, breast, upper part of abdomen, and the flanks are ashy.

The Paradise Fly-catcher is probably a permanent resident throughout the district, but is very locally distributed. It is somewhat rare in Sind. I found it breeding near Neemuch in Central India.

Genus, Myiagra (*Hypothymis*) *Vigors.*

Bill of moderate length, broad, triangular, suddenly narrowed, straight; tip well hooked and distinctly notched; rictal bristles long, slender, numerous; nostrils small, basal, plumed at the base and overhung by a few fine hairs; wings moderate, broad, fourth and fifth quills about equal and longest; tail rather long, even or slightly rounded; tarsus rather short; feet very small; outer-toe much longer than inner one, much syndactyle.

Hypothymis azurea, *Bodd.*

290.—*Myiagra azurea*, Bodd.—Jerdon's Birds of India, Vol. I. p. 450; Butler, Deccan; Stray Feathers, Vol. IX, p. 395.

THE BLACK-NAPED BLUE FLY-CATCHER.

Length, 6 to 6·5; expanse, 8·5; wing, 2·75 to 2·85; tail, 2·75 to 3; tarsus, 0·6 to 0·75; bill from gape, 0·71 to 0·8; bill at front, 0·4.

Bill dark cobalt-blue, edges and tip black, edges of eyelids blue; eyelids plumbeous; irides deep brown; legs ranging from cobalt-blue to plumbeous.

Above pale lazuline-blue, with the head and neck paler but brighter blue; a large occipital spot of short erectile feathers, and a slender jugular one, silky-black; throat, neck, and breast, pale blue; abdomen, vent, and under tail-coverts, bluish-white.

The female is bluish-ashy above; the head and neck pale blue, and the abdomen white; and it has neither the occipital crestlet nor jugular black streak.

The Black-naped Blue Fly-catcher within our limits is confined to the Ghats region. It has been recorded from Belgaum, Nagar, and Ratnagiri. It occurs sparingly all along the Sahyadri Range as far north as Khandalla.

Genus, Leucocerca, *Swains.*

Bill rather long, depressed, wide throughout, except at tip, which is slightly hooked and notched; nostrils apert, but overhung by some long nareal bristles; rictal bristles very long, slender; wings with the first four quills unequally graduated; fourth and fifth quills sub-equal and longest; tail lengthened, wide, rounded or graduated; tarsus moderate, strong; feet moderate; lateral toes unequal.

Leucocerca albicollis, *Vieill.*

291.—*Leucocerca fuscoventris*, Frankl.—Jerdon's Birds of India, Vol. I, p. 451; Butler, Deccan; Stray Feathers, Vol. IX, p. 395.

THE WHITE THROATED FANTAIL.

Length, 7·5; expanse, 9·25; wing, 3·13; tail, 4·5; tarsus, 0·75; bill at front, 0·3.

Bill black; irides dark-brown; legs black.

Sooty brown-black throughout, tinged with ashy in the abdomen and back, and dusky-brownish on the wings and outer tail-feathers, the three outermost of which are tipped with dirty-white; a very short supercilium; chin and throat white.

The occurrence of the White-throated Fantail within our limits is doubtful.

Franklin is said to have procured it in Central India. Adams, who evidently mistook it for *L. aureola*, says it is common at Poona. Colonel Sykes includes it in the Birds of the Deccan.

Leucocerca aureola, *Vieill.*

292.—*Leucocerca albofrontata*, Frankl.—Jerdon's Birds of India, Vol. I, p. 452; Butler, Guzerat; Stray Feathers, Vol. III,

p. 466; Deccan, Stray Feathers, Vol. IX, p. 396; *Rhipidura albofrontata*, Frankl.; Murray's Vertebrate Zoology of Sind, p. 129; Swinhoe and Barnes, Central India; Ibis, 1885, p. 66.

THE WHITE-BROWED FANTAIL.

Length, 7·5; expanse, 10; wing, 3·3; tail, 3·75; tarsus, 0·7; bill at front, 0·3.

Bill black; irides deep-brown; legs black.

Above the head and neck deep-black; a broad frontal band, extending over the eyes to the nape, pure white; back ashy-black; wings and tail dusky-black, the wing-coverts with some white spots; the tips of all the tail-feathers, except the central ones, broadly white; beneath, the chin and throat black, more or less spotted and lined with white; the breast and abdomen white.

The White-browed Fantail Fly-catcher is common throughout the region, excepting, perhaps, the hilly and more wooded tracts, where it is replaced by the next species. It is a permanent resident and breeds from February to August, but March and July are the months in which most nests are to be found. They have at least two broods in the year, and if undisturbed use the same nest for the second brood. The nest is generally placed on the upper surface of a horizontal bough, and is difficult to find, as it appears to be a mere excrescence on the branch, with which it assimilates in color. In shape it is a rather deep cup, about 1¾ inches in diameter, and rather more than an inch in depth; it is rarely more than one-quarter of an inch thick.

It is generally composed of fine grass or vegetable fibres, coated on the outside with cobwebs.

After their eggs are laid, these little birds become very fussy and courageous, darting out and attacking any bird that approaches the nest, no matter how large. The eggs, three in number, are broad ovals in shape, and vary from white to dingy creamy-white or pale yellowish-brown in color, with a belt of greyish-brown and faint inky-purple specks and spots round the larger end. They average 0·66 in length by about 0·5 in breadth.

Leucocerca leucogaster, *Cuv.*

293.—*Leucocerca pectoralis*, Jerd.—Jerdon's Birds of India, Vol. I, p. 453; Butler, Guzerat; Stray Feathers, Vol. III, p. 293; Deccan, Stray Feathers, Vol. IX, p. 396.

THE WHITE-SPOTTED FANTAIL.

Length, 7; wing, 3; tail, 4; tarsus, 0·38; bill at front, 0·3.

Bill black; irides dark-brown; legs black.

Above, the whole head black, with a narrow white supercilium; the rest of the upper plumage brownish-dusky; wings dusky; the coverts very slightly tipped with albescent; tail dusky, all but the middle feathers passing gradually into dirty-whitish towards their extremity; beneath, the throat and belly white; the under tail-coverts edged with rufous; the sides of the throat, and the whole breast, black, the middle of the latter marked with oval white spots.

The White-spotted Fantail Fly-catcher is found in various parts of the Deccan; it is also common at Mount Aboo; it is a permanent resident, and breeds during March and April. The nest is placed in a fork of some low thick bush, generally a *couranda* bush, and is a neat, well-made cup, composed of grass stems, and coated on the exterior with cobwebs; the sides are nowhere more than a quarter of an inch in thickness, but the bottom is often continued to a point. The eggs, three in number, are broad ovals in shape, of a buffy-white color, with a zone of lavender and brownish spots towards the larger end.

They measure 0·67 inches in length by about 0·52 in breadth.

Genus, Culicicapa.

Bill short, broad, suddenly compressed at tip, and much deflected, barely notched; nareal bristles long and strong; rictal bristles a little shorter; wings, with the first quill shorter, and the third longer, the fourth and fifth very little longer; tail moderate, almost even; tarsus short; feet very feeble.

Culicicapa ceylonensis, *Swains.*

295.—*Cryptolopha cinereocapilla,* Vieill.—Jerdon's Birds of India, Vol. I, p. 455; Butler, Deccan; Stray Feathers, Vol. IX, p. 396; Swinhoe and Barnes, Central India; Ibis, 1885, p. 66.

The Grey-headed Fly-catcher.

Length, 4·5 to 4·75; wing, 2·4; tail, 2·12; tarsus, 0·5.

Bill blackish above, horny-reddish beneath; irides deep-brown; feet dingy-red.

Above, the head, nape, and ear-coverts, dark-ashy; back, wings, and tail light-yellow green; quills and tail-feathers dusky internally; rump and upper tail-coverts tinged yellow; beneath, the chin, throat, neck, and breast, pale-ashy; the rest of the lower plumage dingy-yellow, greenish on the flanks.

The Grey-headed Fly-catcher is a not uncommon cold weather visitant to Satara, and has been recorded from the Ahmednagar district. It is fairly common in Central India, but does not occur elsewhere within our limits.

Sub-family, Muscicapinæ.

Bill depressed, moderately wide, slightly hooked and notched at the tip; rictal bristles moderate; wings moderate; tarsus short or slightly lengthened, moderately strong; feet small or moderate. chiefly of small size.

Genus, Alseonax.

Bill much depressed and very shallow, wide at the base, slender and suddenly narrowed at the tip, and faintly hooked and notched; rictal bristles moderate; wing longish, the third and fourth quills equal and longest.

Alseonax latirostris, *Raffles.*

297.—Jerdon's Birds of India, Vol. I, p. 459; Butler, Deccan; Stray Feathers, Vol. IX, p. 396.

THE SOUTHERN BROWN FLY-CATCHER.

Length, 5·5; wing, 2·75; tail, 2; tarsus, 0·53; bill at front, 0·3.

Bill dusky-yellow at gape and beneath, and dusky at tip; irides deep-brown; legs brown.

Above light brownish-grey, beneath white, tinged with very pale-ashy on the breast, sides of throat, and flanks; eyelids conspicuously white.

The Southern Brown Fly-catcher occurs sparingly throughout the Deccan, but is rather more common at Belgaum and Ratnagiri. It has not been recorded from either Sind or Guzerat.

Butalis grisola, *Lin.*

299*bis.*—Butler, Guzerat; Stray Feathers, Vol. III, p. 467; *Muscicapa grisola*, Lin.; Murray's Vertebrate Zoology of Sind, p. 127.

THE SPOTTED-GREY FLY-CATCHER.

THE CHERRY CHOPPER.

Length, 6 to 6·3; expanse, 10 to 10·5; wing, 3·25 to 3·45; tail from vent, 2·75 to 3; tarsus, 0·6.

Bill black, dark fleshy at base of lower mandible; irides deep-brown; legs and feet blackish-brown.

The lores and feathers immediately above the nostrils dingy fulvous-white; head, nape, cheeks, ear-coverts, back and scapulars, pale-earthy or greyish-brown; the feathers of the head with darker brown central streaks not extending to the tips, and those of the forehead tinged with the fulvous color of the lores; the rump in some uniform with the back, in others slightly darker; wings and tail brown, paler and greyer on the tertials and laterals; all the feathers margined with brownish-white, the greater secondary-coverts and tertials most broadly so; the tail-feathers, except the exterior lateral ones, very inconspicuously so; lower parts white, tinged with fawn-color towards the vent, and with narrrow inconspicuous grey-brown streaks on the breast; axillaries and wing-lining very pale rufous-fawn; sides and flanks tinged faintly with the same color and dull fulvous.

The Cherry Chopper only occurs as a very rare visitant, during August and September, to parts of Sind and Guzerat. It has not been recorded from the Deccan.

GENUS, Stoporala, *Blyth.*

Bill short, depressed, perfectly triangular, short, much hooked at tip; rictal and nareal bristles moderate; wings rather long;

third, fourth, and fifth quills subequal; tail moderate, even; tarsus short, stout; lateral toes nearly equal.

Stoporala melanops, *Vig.*

301.—*Eumyias melanops*, Vig.—Jerdon's Birds of India, Vol. I, p. 463; Butler, Guzerat; Stray Feathers, Vol. III, p 467; Deccan, Stray Feathers, Vol. IX, p. 396; Swinhoe and Barnes, Central India; Ibis, 1885, p. 66.

THE VERDITER FLY-CATCHER.

Length, 6; wing, 3·3; tail, 2·75; tarsus, 0·6.

Bill black; irides deep-brown; legs black.

Plumage generally verditer-blue, brightest on the forehead, sides of head, chin, throat and breast, also on the rump and upper tail-coverts; dull on the back of the neck and interscapulars; lores black; quills dusky internally, dull-blue externally; tail greenish-blue.

With the exception of Sind, the Verditer Fly-catcher occurs as a cold weather visitant throughout the region, but is nowhere very common.

GENUS, Cyornis, *Bly.*

Bill feeble, somewhat lengthened, not very wide at the base, tapering, suddenly narrowing and well hooked at tip; rictal bristles moderate, feeble; nareal bristles rather long; wings moderate; third quill a little shorter; fourth and fifth quills sub-equal and longest; tail moderate, nearly even; tarsus moderate, slender; lateral toes nearly equal; middle-toe long.

Cyornis rubeculoides, *Vig.*

304.—Jerdon's Birds of India, Vol. I, p. 466; Butler, Deccan; Stray Feathers, Vol. IX, p. 397.

THE BLUE-THROATED RED-BREAST.

Length, 5·75; expanse, 9; wing, 2·9; tarsus, 0·7; bill at front, 0·33.

Bill black; irides dark-brown; legs brown.

Male.—The head, neck, body above, dark-blue; forehead and shoulder of the wing bright pale-blue; lores, ear-coverts, and frontal plumes, black; inner webs of quills, and of the tail-feathers (and the whole under surface of these), dusky-black; throat dark-blue; neck and breast bright-rufous; abdomen white.

The female is olive-brown above, with a rufous breast and white belly.

The Blue-throated Red-breast is a very rare cold weather visitant to parts of the Deccan, but does not occur elsewhere within our range.

Cyornis tickelli, *Bly.*

305 ♂.—*Cyornis banyumas*, Horsfield.

306 ♀.—*Cyornis tickelliæ*, Blyth.—Jerdon's Birds of India, Vol. I, pp. 466 and 467; Butler, Guzerat; Stray Feathers, Vol. III, p. 468; Deccan, Stray Feathers, Vol. IX, p. 397; *Siphia tickellæ*, Bly.; Swinhoe and Barnes, Central India; Ibis, 1885, p. 66.

TICKELL'S BLUE RED-BREAST.

Length, 5·75 to 6; expanse, 9; wing, 2·75; tail, 2·5; tarsus, 0·75; bill at front, 0·3.

Bill black; irides deep-brown; legs brownish.

Male.—Above rather dark-blue; forehead, and streak over eye, pale bright-blue; lores and ear-coverts black; beneath, the chin, throat, and breast, yellow-ferruginous, passing to white on the middle of the abdomen, and the under tail-coverts pure white; flanks slightly fulvescent.

Female.—Above dull greyish-blue, brighter on the forehead, shoulders of the wings, and upper tail-coverts; chin white, tinged with fulvescent; throat and breast light ferruginous; belly albescent; under tail-coverts pure white; bill blackish; legs pale.

Tickell's Blue Red-breast does not occur in Sind, but it has been recorded as more or less rare from all other portions of our district. It is probably a permanent resident in the hilly and forest districts, but elsewhere appears to be a seasonal visitant only.

Jerdon in his Birds of India has described the male and female as different species.

Cyornis ruficaudus, *Swains.*

307.—Jerdon's Birds of India, Vol. I, p. 468; Butler, Deccan; Stray Feathers, Vol. IX, p. 469; Guzerat, Stray Feathers, Vol. III, p. 397.

THE RUFOUS-TAILED FLY-CATCHER.

Length, 5·5; wing, 2·8; tail, 2·25; tarsus, 0·6.

Bill dusky; irides deep-brown.

Above, olivaceous-brown; rump and upper tail-coverts ferruginous, and the tail bright dark-ferruginous, the middle pair suffused with dusky, and the outer webs of the other also sullied with fuscous; beneath, the chin whitish, the rest of the plumage below pale greyish-brown, passing to white on the abdomen and under tail-coverts, which last are faintly tinged with ferruginous.

The Rufous-tailed Fly-catcher has been recorded as a very rare cold weather visitant both from Ahmednagar and Sholapur, and also from Mount Aboo. These are the only instances of its occurrence within our limits.

Cyornis pallipes, *Jerd.*

309.—Jerdon's Birds of India, Vol. I, p. 469; Butler, Deccan; Stray Feathers, Vol. IX, p. 397.

THE WHITE-BELLIED BLUE FLY-CATCHER.

Length, 6·5; expanse, 10; wing, 3; tail, 2·5; bill at front, from edge of feathers, 0·5; tarsus, 0·73.

Bill black; irides brown; feet and claws vary from pale whity-brown to pale leaden-grey.

Entirely of a deep indigo-blue, except on the belly and under tail-coverts which are white; wings and tail dusky on their inner webs.

The above is Dr. Jerdon's description which is very brief and not altogether satisfactory. I therefore subjoin Mr. Hume's description:—

The lores and an excessively narrow line across the forehead at the base of the bill black; above this the forehead and two long superciliary stripes are of a perceptibly paler and brighter blue than the rest of the plumage; the belly, abdomen, vent, and lower tail-coverts, and greater portion of wing-lining, pure white; sides and flanks greyish; chin blackish; inner webs of the quills, greater-coverts, and tail-feathers, hair-brown; the rest of the plumage dull blue, indigo in some specimens.

The White-bellied Blue Fly-catcher is probably a rare cold weather visitant to the Ghat range only. It has been obtained on the Goa frontier and on the Ghats west of Belgaum.

GENUS, **Muscicapulæ**, *Blyth*.

Bill feeble, depressed, moderately wide at the base, gradually narrowing and triangular, very slightly hooked and notched at the tip; nareal and rictal bristles rather short; wing moderate; third and fourth quills sub-equal, fifth very little shorter; tail moderate; tarsus slender, slightly lengthened; toes unequal, middle-toe somewhat lengthened.

Muscicapula superciliaris, *Jerd.*

310.—Jerdon's Birds of India, Vol. I, p. 470; Butler, Deccan; Stray Feathers, Vol. IX, p. 397.

THE WHITE-BROWED BLUE FLY-CATCHER.

Length, 4·25; wing, 2; tail, 1·8; tarsus, 0·5.

Bill black; irides deep-brown; legs brown.

Above, and the sides of the head, full prussian blue, some of the feathers of the rump with the shaft, and a bar in the middle of the feather, white; wing and tail black, edged with blue; the base of the tail-feathers except the centrals, white; a broad superciliary stripe extending to some distance behind the eyes, and the plumage beneath snowy-white; a band of blue extending from the sides of the neck more or less across the sides of the breast.

The White-browed Blue Fly-catcher is an extremely rare cold weather visitant to the Deccan, it having been obtained at Nagar by Mr. Fairbank, but this is the only record of its occurrence within our limits.

GENUS, **Erythrosterna**, *Bon.*

Bill moderately wide at the base, depressed, slightly hooked and notched at the tip; rictal and nareal bristles moderate; wings moderate, or rather long, third quill nearly as long as the fourth; tail moderate, even, or emarginate; tarsus slighly lengthened; feet moderate.

Erythrosterna albicilla, *Pall.*

323.—*Erythrosterna leucura,* Gmel.—Jerdon's Birds of India, Vol. I, p. 481.

THE WHITE-TAILED ROBIN FLY-CATCHER.

Length, 5; wings, 2·6; tail, 2; tarsus, 0·7.

Bill dusky-brown; irides dark-brown; legs pale-brown.

Above greyish olive-brown; wings brown; tail blackish-brown; the four outer tail-feathers on each side white for the greater part of their length, broadly tipped with brown; beneath white, tinged with ashy-brown on the breast and flanks.

In spring, by the end of March or the beginning of April, the male by a partial moult assumes a bright orange-rufous chin and throat, and the lores, cheeks, and sides of the neck become tolerably pure ashy. This livery is again cast at the autumnal moult.

The occurrence of the White-tailed Robin Fly-catcher within our limits is very doubtful.

Erythrosterna parva, *Bechst.*

323*bis.*—Jerdon's Birds of India, Supplementary List; Ibis, 1872; Butler, Guzerat; Stray Feathers, Vol, III, p. 469; Deccan, Stray Feathers, Vol. IX, p. 397; *Muscicapa parva,* Bechst; Murray's Vertebrate Zoology of Sind, p. 128; Swinhoe and Barnes, Central India; Ibis, 1885, p. 67.

The EUROPEAN WHITE-TAILED FLY-CATCHER differs only from the last in having the ferruginous coloring spread down the breast, instead of being confined to the neck and throat. It is doubtful if the male ever assumes the garb of the female. It is spread generally throughout the district, but only as a rather common cold weather visitant

Erythrosterna maculata, *Tickell.*

326.—Jerdon's Birds of India, Vol. I, p. 483.

THE LITTLE PIED FLY-CATCHER.

Length, 4·5; expanse, 7·5; wing, 2·4; tail, 1·85; tarsus, 0·9.

Bill black; irides dark-brown; legs red-brown.

Above, with the lores, cheeks, and sides of neck black; a broad white eyebrow extending to the nape; large spot on the wings formed by the greater-coverts, and the edges of the secondaries white, and all the tail-feathers, except the central ones, white for two-thirds of their length; beneath pure white.

The Little Pied Fly-catcher is stated by Tickell to be rare in Central India, and Jerdon surmises that it occurs only during the cold weather.

FAMILY, Merulidæ.

Bill typically moderate, compressed, nearly straight, with the culmen gently curved, and slightly notched or entire; in a few larger and curved, in some thick and deep; tarsus moderate or long; feet strong, fit for progression on the ground.

SUB-FAMILY, Myiotherinæ, *Swains.*

Bill slender, straight, or slightly curved, stout in a few; wings typically short; feet and legs long and strong; tail short in most.

GENUS, Myiophonus, *Temm.*

Bill large, strong, compressed, of moderate length, nearly straight, strongly hooked at tip, and slightly notched; rictal bristles almost wanting; nares round, with some frontal plumes and hairs at their base; wing long, rather pointed; fourth and fifth quills nearly equal; fifth longest; tail moderate, even, or slightly rounded; tarsus long, stout, entire; feet strong; middle-toe long; laterals short, nearly equal; claws strong, well curved.

Myiophonus horsfieldi, *Vig.*

342.—Jerdon's Birds of India, Vol. I, p. 499; Butler, Guzerat; Stray Feathers, Vol. III, p. 342; Deccan, Stray Feathers, Vol. IX, p. 398.

THE MALABAR WHISTLING THRUSH.

Length, 11; wing, 6; tail, 4·75; tarsus, 0·9; bill at front, 1·25.

Bill black; irides dark-brown; legs brown-black.

General plumage black, more or less tinged with deep-blue; a band on the forehead, not extending to the base of the bill, and shoulders fine shining cobalt or smalt-blue; some of the feathers of the breast and abdomen edged with the same.

The Malabar Whistling Thrush is a not uncommon permanent resident along the whole of the Sahyadri range; it occurs also at Mount Aboo. The nest, a large structure composed of roots, moss, &c., is placed under the shelf of a rock, or in some such similar situation. The eggs, three or four in number, are broadish ovals, salmon-pink or whitish-pink in color, speckled and spotted with brownish-pink. They measure 1·22 in length by about 0·96 inches in breadth. It breeds during March and April.

GENUS, Pitta, *Vieill.*

Bill moderate; tip slightly forked; wings moderate; the second and third, or third and fourth quills being the longest; first a little shorter than the fourth.

Pitta brachyura, *Lin.*

345.—*Pitta bengalensis*, Gmel.—Jerdon's Birds of India, Vol. I, p. 503; *P. coronata*, Mull; Butler, Guzerat; Stray Feathers, Vol. III, p. 470; Deccan, Stray Feathers, Vol. IX, p. 398.

THE YELLOW-BREASTED GROUND THRUSH.

Nourang, Hin.

Length, 7; wing, 4·25; tail, 1·7; tarsus, 1·5; bill at front, 0·6. Bill black; irides hazel-brown; legs yellowish-pink.

Head olivaceous-fulvous, with a median black stripe from the base of bill to the back of the neck, meeting another black band that passes through the ears; a white superciliary line extending also to the nape, but not quite meeting its fellow; the whole back, rump, scapulars and wing-coverts, dull blue-green; the lengthened upper tail-coverts pale-blue; a pale azure-blue patch on the shoulder of the wing; quills black, with a white bar on the first six primaries, and the tip of all white or albescent; secondaries blue-green on the outer margin, increasing in extent inwardly; tail black, tipped with dull-blue; beneath, the chin, throat, and the sides of the neck below the ears, white; the rest of the lower parts isabelline or fulvescent, with the middle of the lower part of the abdomen, the vent, and the under tail-coverts, scarlet.

The Yellow-breasted Ground Thrush is not uncommon in the Deccan, during the seasons of migration, *viz.*, April and May, and again in September and October; it also occurs at Mount Aboo, about the same time, and has not unfrequently been obtained at and near Deesa.

It has not been recorded from Sind.

SUB-FAMILY, Turdinæ.

Bill of moderate length, as long as head; nostrils in a groove apert; wings long and broad, somewhat pointed; first quill very short; third and fourth longest, sub-equal; tail moderate; outer-toe longer than inner, and united to middle at base.

GENUS, Monticola.

Bill moderate or long, moderately hooked at tip; nostrils apert; rictal bristles numerous; wings long; third quill longest; tarsus scutellate.

Monticola cyaneus, *Lin.*

351.—*Petrocossyphus cyaneus*, Lin.—Jerdon's Birds of India, Vol. I, p. 511; *Cyanocincla cyana*, Lin.; Butler, Guzerat; Stray Feathers, Vol. III, p. 470; Deccan, Stray Feathers, Vol. IX, p. 398; Murray's Vertebrate Zoology of Sind, p. 129; Swinhoe and Barnes, Central India; Ibis, 1885, p. 67.

THE BLUE ROCK THRUSH.

Length, 8·5 to 9; expanse, 13 to 14·5; wing, 4·5 to 5; tail, 3·1 to 3·8; bill at front, 0·7 to 0·9; bill from gape, 1·25.

Bill black; irides brown; legs black.

Male throughout of a dull indigo-blue, more or less marked with dusky, and the feathers of the abdomen, vent, and under tail-coverts, pale tipped, in some specimens with a tinge of deep ferruginous on the feathers of these parts.

The female is dingy greyish-brown, with a faint blue or ashy tinge, greyish on the tail; some of the feathers edged with whitish, and the under parts fulvescent-greyish, with dusky cross bands, some being rufescent on the lower parts, especially on the vent and under tail-coverts.

The Blue Rock Thrush is a common winter visitant throughout the region, arriving during October and leaving about April; it is very solitary in its habits, and appears to frequent the same locality, not only throughout the season, but for several successive ones Jerdon records that "it is supposed to be the sparrow of our English version of the Scriptures that sitteth alone on the house tops."

Monticola cinclorhynchus, *Vig.*

353.—*Orocetes cinclorhynchus*, Vig.—Jerdon's Birds of India, Vol. I, p. 515; Butler, Guzerat; Stray Feathers, Vol. III, p. 470; *Petrophila cinclorhynchus*, Vig.; Deccan, Stray Feathers, Vol. IX, p. 398; Murray's Vertebrate Zoology of Sind, p. 130; Swinhoe and Barnes, Central India; Ibis, 1885, p. 67.

THE BLUE-HEADED CHAT THRUSH.

Length, 7·5; expanse, 11·5; wing, 3·8 to 4·2; tail, 2·8; tarsus, 0·85; bill at front, 0·6; bill from gape, 1·1.

Bill brownish-black; irides hazel-brown; legs plumbeous.

Male.—Head, nape, and shoulders of the wings, pale-blue; lores, ear-coverts, back and wings, black, tinged with dusky-blue on the back, and on some of the wing-coverts and quills; a white wing spot, formed by a white bar on the outer webs of the secondaries; rump and upper tail-coverts ferruginous; tail black, edged with blue; chin pale-blue; breast, abdomen, and under tail-coverts ferruginous.

Female.—Brownish-olive above, yellowish-white beneath, tinged with rufous on the breast, and barred crosswise with olive-brown.

During the cold weather the Blue-headed Chat Thrush is generally distributed throughout the region, but occurs much more rarely in Sind. It is solitary in its habits.

GENUS, Geocichla, *Kuhl.*

Bill moderate, stout, compressed, straight; culmen gently arched throughout, tolerably hooked at the tip, and slightly notched; nostrils lengthened; a small nude spot behind the eye; wings and tail moderate, or rather short; tarsus slightly lengthened; lateral toes short, nearly equal.

Geocichla cyanotis, *Jard. and Selby.*

354.—Jerdon's Birds of India, Vol. I, p. 517; Butler, Deccan; Stray Feathers, Vol. III, p. 398.

THE WHITE-WINGED GROUND THRUSH.

Length, 7·5 to 8·5; expanse, 12·25 to 14; wing, 4·2 to 4·5; tail, 2·75 to 3; tarsus, 1·25 to 1·5; bill at front, 0·7; bill from gape, 1.

Bill blackish; irides dark-brown; legs fleshy-brown.

Head, nape, hind-neck, and sides of neck, ferruginous; the rest of the plumage above dull-cyaneous or leaden; wings and tail dusky, the former with a white spot on the median wing-coverts, and the outer feathers of the tail also tipped with white; lores white; ear-coverts white in the centre, continued down the sides of the neck, and with a brown spot above and below the latter passing into ferruginous, and bordering the white of the ears; beneath, the chin, throat, and neck, white; the breast, abdomen, and flanks, bright-ferruginous; and the vent and under tail-coverts white.

The colors of the female are less pure than those of the male.

The White-winged Ground Thrush only occurs within our limits on the Sahyadri Range and in the adjoining forests, as far north at least as Khandalla.

It is a permanent resident, but owing to the bird's crepuscular habits, it often escapes observation.

Geocichla citrina, *Lath.*

355.—Jerdon's Birds of India, Vol. I, p. 517; Butler, Deccan; Stray Feathers, Vol. IX, p. 398.

THE ORANGE-HEADED GROUND THRUSH.

Length, 8·12 to 9; expanse, 13·75 to 15; tail, 2·75 to 3·25; wing, 4·4 to 4·82; tarsus, 1·2 to 1·35; bill from gape, 1·05 to 1·2.

Bill horny-black, fleshy-white at base beneath; irides dark-brown; nude patch behind eye, flesh-colored; legs fleshy-white.

The whole head, neck, and lower plumage, pale brownish-orange; the chin and throat paling and albescent; the rest of the upper plumage blue-grey; a small white wing spot on the median-coverts, and the primary-coverts tipped black; lower part of abdomen paling towards the vent, which, with the lower tail-coverts, is white.

The female differs slightly, being tinged with olivaceous on the back, wings and tail.

The occurrence of the Orange-headed Ground Thrush within our limits is very doubtful; if it occurs at all, it can only be as a very rare winter visitant.

Geocichla unicolor, *Tickell.*

356.—Jerdon's Birds of India, Vol. I, p. 519; Butler, Guzerat; Stray Feathers, Vol. III, p. 470; Deccan, Stray Feathers, Vol. IX, p. 399; Murray's Vertebrate Zoology of Sind, p. 131.

THE DUSKY GROUND THRUSH.

Length, 9; expanse, 14·5; wing, 4·5; tail, 3·13; tarsus, 1·12; bill at front, 0·7.

Bill dusky-yellow; eyelids and gape yellow; irides brown; legs yellowish-brown.

Male above uniform dusky slaty ash-color; chin nearly white; throat pale-ashy; breast ashy; abdomen and lower tail-coverts white; under wing-coverts and flanks of abdomen ferruginous.

The female is olive-brown above, ashy about the rump; ear-coverts ashy-brown, with light shafts; beneath the chin and throat albescent or very pale-ashy, bordered by a dark stripe from the base of the lower mandible, and the feathers of the throat and neck streaked with dusky-brown; the breast and sides ashy-brown, tinged with fulvous, or olive-brown on the flanks; belly, vent, and lower tail-coverts, white.

Occurs throughout the district as a rather rare cold weather visitant.

GENUS, Turdulus, *Hodgson*.

Bill rather short, something like that of *Geocichla*, generally yellow; tarsus rather short. Males colored black, and white; females dingy-olive or brown. Otherwise as in *Merula*.

Turdulus wardi, *Jerd*.

357.—Jerdon's Birds of India, Vol. I, p. 520; Butler, Guzerat; Stray Feathers, Vol. III, p. 399.

WARD'S PIED BLACKBIRD.

Length, 8·5 to 9; wing, 4·6; tail, 3·4; tarsus, 1·2; bill at front, 0·75.

Bill yellow; irides brown; legs yellow.

Male, above with the whole head and neck, black; eye-streak, a patch on the shoulders of the wings, tips of all the coverts, especially the medial-coverts white; tertiaries and secondaries also tipped white, the latter slightly, and the primaries narrowly edged with the same; upper tail-coverts also tipped; tail with the central tail-feathers slightly white tipped, the rest of the feathers successively more broadly so, but chiefly on the inner webs, and increasing in amount to the outermost, which has the inner web white for two-thirds of its length; the web black nearly to the tip.

The female is pale-brownish above; the eye-streak, tips of the wing-coverts and of the tertiaries, fulvous-white; upper tail-coverts and tips of the tail-feathers, whitish; beneath fulvous-white, variegated with dusky; under tail-coverts pure white; the feathers of the throat, breast and flanks, with dusky spots; axillaries pure white.

The occurrence of Ward's Blackbird within our limits is very doubtful.

Major Lloyd includes it in his list of the Birds of the Concan.

GENUS, **Merula**, *Leach.*

Bill slightly lengthened, compressed at the tip, and notched; nostrils feathered at the base; rictal bristles short and strong; tarsus of moderate length; feet strong; wings long, second quill shorter than the fifth, which is nearly as long as the third and fourth; tail square or nearly so.

Merula nigropilea, *Lafr.*

359.—Jerdon's Birds of India, Vol. I, p. 523; Butler, Guzerat; Stray Feathers, Vol. III, p. 470; Deccan, Stray Feathers, Vol, IX, p. 399.

THE BLACK-CAPPED BLACKBIRD.

Length, 9·5; wing, 4·9; tail, 3·5; tarsus, 1·2; bill at front, 0·8. Bill orange-yellow, as also are the gape and eyelids; legs brownish-yellow.

Male.—Head, with the lores, cheeks and nape, deep black; back, rump, wings and tail, dark-blackish, tinged with brown on the interscapulars; chin blackish; neck, all round to the nape (contrasting there strongly with the black of the crown) and the lower parts brownish-ashy, paler on the belly, and passing to white on the vent; under tail-coverts mingled white and ashy.

The Black-capped Blackbird is a permanent resident and occurs on the Sahyadri Range as far north as Khandalla, and is also common at Mount Aboo, where it is particularly abundant during the rains at which season it breeds, but its nest does not appear to have been taken.

Merula atrogularis, *Tem.*

365.—*Planestiçus atrogularis*, Gm.—Jerdon's Birds of India, Vol. I. p. 529; Murray's Vertebrate Zoology of Sind, p. 131.

THE BLACK-THROATED THRUSH.

Length, 10·5; expanse, 17; wing, 5·75; tail, 4·4; bill at front, 0·6.

Bill yellow, dusky at tip; orbits yellow; irides dark-brown; legs horny-yellowish-brown.

Male.—Above pale cinereous-brown; wings and tail darker; tail occasionally tinged with rufous; beneath the throat albescent-brownish with some undefined dark markings, the centre of each feather being dark, and lower down these coalesce and form a broad dark-brown, or blackish pectoral gorget; the rest, beneath, pale cinereous-white, a few of the feathers next the breast centred or barred with dusky; under wing-coverts rusty; lower tail-coverts indistinctly barred with brown and rusty.

The female wants the pectoral gorget, but has the breast buff, mixed with dusky, and some brown striæ on the sides of the throat and breast; the abdomen, too, is whiter than in the male, and the lower tail-coverts are buffy-white.

The Black-throated Thrush only occurs as a cold weather visitant to Northern Sind. I found it very common between Kandahar and Quetta during the time of its migration.

SUB-FAMILY, **Simalinæ.**

Legs and feet stout and large ; bill various in form and length, almost always compressed, usually notched; wings short and rounded; tail largish, graduated; plumage often lax.

GENUS, **Pyctorhis,** *Gmelin.*

Bill rather short, strong, deep, arched, entire ; rictus strongly bristled; orbits nude; wings rather short and feeble, fourth and fifth quills longest ; tail long, graduated ; legs and feet stout and large ; claws large, moderately curved.

Pyctorhis sinensis, *Gmelin.*

385.—Jerdon's Birds of India, Vol. II, p. 15 ; Butler, Guzerat ; Stray Feathers, Vol. III. p. 471 ; Deccan, Stray Feathers, Vol. IX, p. 399 ; Murray's Vertebrate Zoology of Sind, p. 132 ; Swinhoe and Barnes, Central India ; Ibis, 1885, p. 67.

THE YELLOW-EYED BABBLER.

Length, 6·5 ; expanse, 7 to 7·8 ; wing, 2·4 to 2·8 ; tail, 3 to 3·5 ; bill at front, 0·45 ; tarsus, 0·9 to 1·1.

Bill black, with the nostrils deep yellow ; irides dark brown, with an outer circle of buff; orbits bright orange ; legs yellow.

Above clear red-brown, rufous or cinnamon color on the wings, and the tail obsoletely banded with dusky ; lores and all the lower plumage white; lower surface of wings and tail dusky-cinereous.

The Yellow-eyed Babbler is a common permanent resident throughout the district, breeding from June to August ; the nest is beautifully made, of a deep cup-shape, and is placed in a slender fork of a bush or small tree ; sometimes it is suspended between stalks of growing corn or reeds ; it is composed of grass, interlaced with vegetable fibre and lined with fine grass; the eggs, four or five in number, vary much in shape, size and color but they are generally rather broad ovals, averaging 0·73 in length by about 0·59 inches in breadth.

Some eggs have a pinkish-white ground, thickly mottled and speckled with bright deep brick-dust red ; others have the pinkish-white ground, but are boldly, though sparingly, blotched with patches and streaks of blood or bright brick-red, interspersed with a few inky-purple spots or clouds ; between these two types every variety is met with ; the eggs are in general finely glossed.

Pyctorhis griseigularis, *Hume.*

386*ter*.—Murray's Vertebrate Zoology of Sind, p. 132.

THE GREY-THROATED BABBLER.

Length, 5·5 ; wing, 2·5 ; tail, 3·4 ; tarsus, 1.

Bill horny or fleshy-brown ; legs pale fleshy-brown.

Forehead, upper part of lores and streak over the eyes deep reddish-brown, each feather streaked with ashy-grey ; crown and occiput deep ferruginous ; cheeks and ear-coverts paler ferruginous ; sides of neck yellowish-rusty ; nape, back, scapulars, rump, and upper tail-coverts, bright rusty-ferruginous, in some lights slightly brownish and most rusty on upper tail-coverts, almost entire visible portion of closed wing bright ferruginous-chesnut, rest of feathers hair-brown ; tail moderately dark-brown, feathers margined strongly on outer webs with ferruginous and most broadly so towards their bases ; chin, throat, and upper breast pale brownish-grey or ashy, rest of lower parts dull rusty, browner and lighter on lower breast, brighter and more ferruginous on flanks and lower tail-coverts.

The Grey-throated Babbler is a rather doubtful species.

Within our limits it has only been procured in Sind, where doubtless it is a permanent resident.

GENUS, Alcippe, *Blyth.*

Bill short, moderately stout and compressed ; culmen slightly curved, hooked and notched ; nostrils slightly impended by some setæ ; rictal bristles moderate ; wings moderate, rounded, fourth and fifth quills equal ; tail moderate or rather short, very slightly rounded ; tarsus stout, moderate ; lateral toes unequal ; claws tolerably curved.

Alcippe poiocephala, *Jerdon.*

389.—Jerdon's Birds of India, Vol. II, p. 18 ; Butler, Deccan ; Stray Feathers, Vol. IX, p. 399.

THE NEILGHERRY QUAKER THRUSH.

Length, 5·9 ; wing, 2·8 ; tail, 2·3 ; tarsus, 0·88 ; bill at front, 0·45.

Bill horny, yellow at gape and edges ; irides greenish-white ; legs pale fleshy.

Head and nape dusky-cinereous ; back and rump greenish-olive, inclining to rufous on the rump, darker and more ferruginous on the wings and tail ; beneath pale rufescent or fulvous, lightest and albescent on the chin and throat.

The Neilgherry Quaker Thrush is a permanent resident on the Sahyadri Range, but has not been recorded from any other portion of our limits.

Alcippe atriceps, *Jerdon.*

390.—Jerdon's Birds of India, Vol. II, p. 19 ; Butler, Deccan ; Stray Feathers, Vol. IX, p. 399.

THE BLACK-HEADED WREN BABBLER.

Length, 5·5 ; expanse, 7 ; wing, 2·3 ; tail, 2 ; tarsus, 0·9 ; bill at front, 0·4.

Bill horny-brown ; irides pale orange or buff ; legs plumbeous.

Head, cheeks, and nape, black ; wings, tail and under tail-coverts, brownish-olive, darkest on the tail and wings ; beneath white, with a tinge of orange-brown on the sides and towards the vent.

The Black-headed Wren Babbler has been obtained in the forest west of Belgaum ; it has not been recorded from elsewhere within the region.

GENUS, **Mixornis,** *Hodgson.*

Bill rather long, compressed, with a tendency to arch ; tip blunt, barely notched ; nostrils ovoid, advanced ; wings moderate, rounded, the first four quills graduated, fifth and sixth sub-equal and longest ; tail moderate or rather short, laterals very unequal ; hind-toe large, nails well curved.

Mixornis rubicapillus, *Tickell.*

395.—Jerdon's Birds of India, Vol. II, p. 23.

THE YELLOW-BREASTED WREN BABBLER.

Length, 5·75 ; wing, 2·38 ; tail, 2 ; tarsus, 0·8 ; bill at front, 0·6.

Bill horny ; irides reddish-hazel ; legs pale horny-brown.

Above dull olive-green, inclining to rufescent or brown ; wings and tail rufescent-brown ; part of the forehead, supercilium, ears, and sides of the neck, yellowish-green, with some dusky streaks ; crown of the head dull ferruginous ; beneath pale yellow, fading to whitish on the lower abdomen and olivaceous on the flanks and vent ; the throat and upper part of the breast with some blackish streaks.

The Yellow-breasted Wren Babbler has been doubtfully recorded from Central India.

GENUS, **Dumetia,** *Blyth.*

Bill moderate, or rather short, compressed, pointed ; culmen slightly curving from the base, and the commissure also slightly curved ; a few small rictal bristles ; wings short, rounded, fourth, fifth, and sixth quills nearly equal ; tail moderate, rounded ; tarsus stout ; middle-toe not elongate, lateral toes about equal, hind-toe and claw moderately large.

Dumetia hyperythra, *Franklin.*

397.—Jerdon's Birds of India, Vol. II, p. 26 ; Butler, Deccan ; Stray Feathers, Vol. IX, p. 399 ; Swinhoe and Barnes, Central India ; Ibis, 1885, p. 67.

THE RUFOUS-BELLIED BABBLER.

Length, 5·25 ; wing, 2·1 ; tail, 3·2 ; tarsus, 0·8.

Bill horny ; irides pale yellow-brown ; legs fleshy-yellow.

Above brownish-olive, the tail obsoletely barred with dusky ; forehead and whole body beneath rufous.

The Rufous-bellied Babbler is a permanent resident in parts of the Deccan, and occurs also in the vicinity of Mhow.

It breeds from June to August; the nest is globular in shape, composed of coarse grass blades, sparingly lined with fine grass. It is frequently placed on the ground amongst coarse grass or dead leaves, with which it is frequently incorporated, but sometimes in low scrub-bushes, only a foot or so from the ground. The eggs, four in number, are broad oval in shape, white in color, spotted, freckled, streaked, and blotched with brownish-red and reddish-purple; the markings are sometimes clearly defined, at others they are smudgy; in others again they are speckly. They measure 0·67 inches in length by about 0·53 in breadth.

Dumetia albogularis, *Blyth.*

398.—Jerdon's Birds of India, Vol. II, p. 26; Butler, Guzerat; Stray Feathers, Vol. III, p. 471; Deccan, Stray Feathers, Vol. IX, p. 400.

THE WHITE-THROATED WREN BABBLER.

Length, 5·62; expanse, 6·2; wing, 2·12; tail, 2·25; tarsus, 0·75; bill at front, 0·4; bill at gape, 0·57.

Like the last, but the chin and throat pure white.

The White-throated Babbler is another species that only occurs within our limits, on the Sahyadri Range and forests adjacent, but turns up again at Mount Aboo. It is probably a permanent resident.

GENUS, Pellorneum, *Swainson.*

Bill moderate, straight, compressed, very gently curving throughout, slightly hooked at tip, and notched; rictal bristles feeble; wings much rounded, fifth, sixth and seventh quills nearly equal; tail moderate, rounded; tarsus moderate; feet large; middle-toe lengthened; laterals barely unequal; hind-toe long; claws tolerably curved.

Pellorneum ruficeps, *Swainson.*

399.—Jerdon's Birds of India, Vol. II, p. 27; Butler, Deccan; Stray Feathers, Vol. IX, p. 400.

THE SPOTTED WREN BABBLER.

Length, 7; expanse, 9; wing, 3; tail, 3; tarsus, 1; bill at front, 0·7.

Bill horny above, yellowish-fleshy beneath; irides brick-red; legs fleshy-yellow.

Above olive-brown; crown and nape deep rusty colored, with a more or less marked white eyebrow from the forehead to the nape; ears dusky-white, or mixed brown and white, or entirely brown; beneath white or fulvous-white, with spots of dark olive on the sides of the breast and belly, olivaceous on the flanks and under tail-coverts.

The Spotted Wren Babbler only occurs within our limits, on the Sahyadri Range, as far north as Mahableshwar.

GENUS, **Pomatorhinus**, *Horsfield*.

Bill long, compressed, pointed, much curved throughout, entire at the tip ; nostrils barely apert, lengthened ; a few very small rictal bristles ; wings short, rounded ; fifth and sixth quills longest ; tail long or moderate, rounded ; tarsi and feet long and stout ; anterior toes not much elongated ; hind-toe large ; claws large, moderately curved, somewhat blunt.

Pomatorhinus horsfieldi, *Sykes*.

404.—Jerdon's Birds of India, Vol. II, p. 31 ; Butler, Deccan ; Stray Feathers, Vol. IX, p. 400.

THE SOUTHERN SCIMITAR BABBLER.

Length, 9·5 ; wing, 3·8 ; tail, 4 ; tarsus, 1·3 ; bill at front, 1.

Bill yellow, dusky above ; irides dark-red ; legs dusky-green.

Above deep olive-brown ; a white superciliary stripe ; neck in front, breast, and middle of abdomen, white ; the flanks, vent, and under tail-coverts olive-brown.

The Southern Scimitar Babbler has the same range as the preceding, but is much more common and is a permanent resident.

Pomatorhinus obscurus, *Hume*.

404*ter*.—Butler, Guzerat ; Stray Feathers, Vol. III, p. 471.

HUME'S SCIMITAR BABBLER.

Length, 9·5 to 10·12 ; expanse, 11 ; wing, 3·5 to 4·15 ; tail, 4 ; bill at front, 1·32 to 1·35 ; bill at gape, 1·4.

Bill ivory-yellow, horny at base of upper mandible or dirty-yellow, blackish on the ridge at base of upper mandible ; irides dark red or reddish-brown ; legs and feet dark, slightly greenish-plumbeous, or olivaceous-slate.

Chin, throat, breast and centre of abdomen, and a long superciliary stripe from forehead to nape, pure white ; the whole of the rest of the plumage a dull smoky earth-brown, rather a purer brown on quills and tail, which are very faintly rufescent ; the tail obsoletely barred ; the lores dark-brown ; the ear-coverts slightly darker-brown than the rest of the body.

Hume's Scimitar Babbler is common at Aboo, and must occur on the hills in the vicinity of Mhow.

GENUS, **Malacocercus**, *Swainson*.

Bill short or moderate, much compressed, rather deep, curving from the base, barely hooked at the tip, entire ; commissure slightly curved ; gonys ascending ; nostrils apert ; a few short pale rictal setæ ; wings short, much rounded, fourth, fifth and sixth quills nearly equal and longest ; tail moderately long, broad ; tarsus stout, scutellate ; feet rather large ; claws moderately curved.

Malacocercus terricolor, *Hodgson.*

432.—Jerdon's Birds of India, Vol. II, p. 59; Butler, Guzerat; Stray Feathers, Vol. III, p. 472; Murray's Vertebrate Zoology of Sind, p. 133; Swinhoe and Barnes, Central India; Ibis, 1885, p. 67.

THE BENGAL BABBLER.
Sat bhai, Hin.

Length, 9 to 10; extent, 13; wing, 4·12; tail, 4·5; tarsus, 1·5; bill at front, 0·75.

Bill horny-brown; irides pale yellow; legs dingy-yellow.

Above brownish-ashy, paler and somewhat cinereous on the head and neck, browner on the back, where the feathers are faintly pale shafted; quills brown, with outer webs paler, and narrowly bordered with ashy; tail reddish-brown, faintly barred, and the outer feathers tipped with pale whity-brown; beneath pale ashy-brown on the throat and breast, the feathers very faintly edged and shafted lighter; abdomen, vent, and under tail-coverts, pale fulvescent.

With the exception of the Deccan, the Bengal Babbler is common throughout our limits; it is a permanent resident and breeds from March to July.

The nests are often found in gardens, in fruit trees, vineries, thick hedges, and in fact almost anywhere; they are of a deep cup-shape, generally loosely constructed, but occasionally they are more neatly made; they are composed of grass stems and roots.

The eggs, three or four in number, are variable both in shape and color, but are typically broad oval in shape and deep blue in color.

They average one inch in length by about 0·78 in breadth.

They are in general highly glossy.

Malacocercus griseus, *Latham.*

433.—Jerdon's Birds of India, Vol. II, p. 60; Butler, Deccan; Stray Feathers, Vol. IX, p. 400.

THE WHITE-HEADED BABBLER.

Length, 9; wing, 4; tail, 4; tarsus, 1·25; bill at front, 0·55.

Bill yellowish; irides yellowish-white; legs fleshy-yellow.

Head, lores and nape, fulvescent or dirty-whitish; plumage above darker brown than the last, the feathers with pale shafts; quills not barred; tail brown, very faintly barred, and the outer feathers tipped pale; beneath the chin and throat are mixed brown and ashy, conspicuously darker than the neighbouring parts, each feather being ashy at the base, and with a dark band, tipped paler; as the pale tip gets worn away, the dark tinge becomes more apparent; from the breast the rest of the lower parts are pale fulvescent, inclining to rufescent.

The White-headed Babbler is common at and near Belgaum, where it is a permanent resident, breeding from April to July.

Malacocercus malabaricus, *Jerdon.*

434.—Jerdon's Birds of India, Vol. II, p. 62; Butler, Deccan; Stray Feathers, Vol. IX, p. 400.

THE JUNGLE BABBLER.

Length, 9; wing, 4·1; tail, 4·5; tarsus, 1·2; bill at front, 0·75.

Bill and gape dark yellow; orbits yellow; irides pale-yellow; legs dirty-yellow, with a fleshy tinge.

Very like *M. terricolor*, but somewhat darker in color, with broader and more distinct pale mesial streaks on the feathers of the back, and especially of the breast; the tertiaries are but very obscurely striated, but the tail is distinctly so.

The Jungle Babbler is rather irregular in its breeding habits, nests having been taken from April to October; it is generally placed in the centre of a thorny bush. The eggs, three or four in number, are similar to those of *M. terricolor*.

They average 0·97 inches in length by about 0·77 in breadth.

The occurrence of the Jungle Babbler within our limit is rather doubtful. Jerdon implies that it occurs along the Malabar coast, and Major Lloyd includes it in his list of Konkan species.

Malacocercus somervillii, *Sykes.*

435.—Jerdon's Birds of India, Vol. II, p. 63; Butler, Deccan; Stray Feathers, Vol. IX, p. 400.

THE RUFOUS-TAILED BABBLER.

Length, 9·5; wing, 4·25; tail, 4; tarsus, 1·13; bill at front, 0·75.

Bill horny-yellow; irides pale-yellow; legs dirty-yellow.

Above ashy-brown, the feathers of the back barely lighter shafted, passing into rufescent on the rump and upper tail-coverts; quills dark-brown on both webs; tail rufous-brown, obsoletely banded; beneath, the chin and throat are mixed dark-brown and ashy as in *griseus;* the upper part of the breast pale whity-brown, the feathers dark at their base; the lower breast, belly, vent, and under tail-coverts, rufescent.

The Rufous-tailed Babbler is a common permanent resident on the Sahyadri Range and the country adjacent. Mr. Hume says it is confined to a belt of country about 60 miles north and south of Bombay. In its breeding habits it resembles, its congeners.

Malacocercus malcolmi, *Sykes.*

436.—Jerdon's Birds of India, Vol. II, p. 64; Butler, Guzerat; Stray Feathers, Vol. III, p. 472; Deccan, Stray Feathers, Vol. IX, p. 401; Murray's Vertebrate Zoology of Sind, p. 133; Swinhoe and Barnes, Central India; Ibis, 1885, p. 67.

THE LARGE GREY BABBLER.

Length, 11; wing, 4·6; tail, 5·75; tarsus, 1·3; bill at front 0·9.

Bill horny; irides light-yellow; legs dirty-yellow.

Above of a pale brownish-grey, lighter and more cinereous on the rump; quills and middle rectrices darker, the latter with some faint cross bands, and the lateral feathers whitish; forehead pale-bluish, the feathers with white shafts; the first three quills with the outer webs pale-yellowish; beneath uniform whitish-grey, with a tinge of fulvescent, or rufescent, most distinct on the breast and upper part of the abdomen.

The Large Grey Babbler is a permanent resident throughout the district, but is much less common in Sind than elsewhere.

It breeds nearly the whole year round, as I have taken eggs from January to the end of October. A small babool tree is generally selected as the site of the nest, and on a low branch, not more than 5 or 10 feet from the ground, it constructs a rather loosely woven, but neat cup-shaped, nest. The materials of which it is composed are generally dried grass and roots intermixed with fine twigs. The eggs, generally four in number, are indistinguishable from those of *Malococercus terricolor.*

GENUS, **Layardia,** *Blyth.*

Similar to *Malacocercus*, but of more decided colors; the bill shorter and deeper; the wings shorter and rounded; the frontal plumes hispid, but of open texture, and *monticolus* in its habits.

Layardia subrufa, *Jerdon.*

437.—Jerdon's Birds of India, Vol. II, p. 66; Butler, Deccan; Stray Feathers, Vol. IX, p. 401.

THE RUFOUS BABBLER.

Length, 9·5; wing, 3·7; tail, 4·25; tarsus, 1·3; bill at front, 0·7.

Above darkish olive-brown; forehead pale bluish-ash, the frontal feathers somewhat rigid; beneath deep-rufous, paler on the chin.

The Rufous Babbler occurs in various parts of the Deccan; it has not been recorded from any other portion of our limits.

GENUS, **Chatarrhœa,** *Blyth.*

Bill longer than in *Malacocercus*, more slender, and very gently curved, both in the commissure and culmen; tail long, narrow; lateral toes about equal; hind-toe very long; claws slightly curved.

Chatarrhœa caudata, *Dumeril.*

438.—Jerdon's Birds of India, Vol. II, p. 67; Butler, Guzerat; Stray Feathers, Vol. III, p. 472; Deccan, Stray Feathers, Vol.

IX, p. 401; Murray's Vertebrate Zoology of Sind, p. 133; Swinhoe and Barnes, Central India; Ibis, 1885, p. 68.

THE STRIATED BUSH BABBLER.

Length, 9; wing, 3; tail, 4·5; tarsus, 1; bill at front, 0·6.

Bill pale brownish-horny; irides red-brown; legs dull-yellow.

Above pale ashy-brown, with numerous dusky striæ, each feather being centred brown; tail pale olive-brown, obsoletely barred with dusky; beneath the chin white, the rest of the plumage rufescent-ashy, darkest on the flanks.

The Striated Bush Babbler is very common throughout the region; it is a permanent resident, and breeds almost the whole year through. I have personally taken eggs in every month except December. The nests are generally placed in thorny bushes, two or three feet from the ground; they are fairly well made, deep, cup-shaped nests, composed of grass stems and roots, occasionally lined with finer grass. The eggs, three or four in number, are of a moderately elongated oval shape, but spheriform varieties are not uncommon. They are of a glossy spotless pale-blue color, and average 0·82 inches in length by about 0·64 in breadth.

Eggs of *Coccystes jacobinus* are often found in these nests, and are distinguished by their more globular shape.

Chatarrhœa earlii, *Blyth.*

439.—Jerdon's Birds of India, Vol. II, p. 68; Murray's Vertebrate Zoology of Sind, p. 134.

THE STRIATED REED BABBLER.

Length, 9·9; expanse, 11; wing, 3·5; tail, 5·5; tarsus, 1·38; bill at front, 0·75.

Bill pale greenish-yellow, dusky above and at the tip; irides bright-yellow; legs dirty greenish-horn.

Above pale ashy-brown, with dark brown streaks on the head and back, fading on the upper tail-coverts; tail concolorous with the back, still paler perhaps, and with no trace of striæ; chin, throat, and upper part of the breast dull reddish-fulvous, edged paler, and with faint dark central lines; the rest of the under parts dingy-fulvous or albescent-brown.

Within our limits, the Striated Reed Babbler only occurs in Sind, where it is a permanent resident, breeding from March to September.

They build a neat but rather massive cup-shaped nest, either in close growing reeds or small bushes. The eggs, three or four in number, closely resemble those of *C. caudata*, but are larger, averaging 0·96 by 0·73.

GENUS, Chætornis, *Grey.*

Bill very short, strong, high, compressed, curved on the culmen, strongly hooked at the tip, and notched; five remarkably strong bristles between the gape and the eyes, forming an almost vertical range curved stiffly outwards; wing somewhat long; third quill longest; fourth and fifth nearly equal to it; second equal to the seventh; feet and legs strong; tarsus moderately long, the middle-toe elongate; laterals unequal; inner-toe very versatile; hind-toe long; all the claws slightly curved.

Chætornis striatus, *Jerd.*

441.—Jerdon's Birds of India, Vol. II, p. 72; Butler, Aboo and Northern Guzerat; Stray Feathers, Vol. V, p. 209.

THE GRASS BABBLER.

Length, 7 to 8·25; expanse, 11; wing, 3 to 3·5; tail, 3·75; tarsus, 1·1; bill at front, 0·48.

Bill dusky-brown above, fleshy brown beneath; irides yellow-brown or dull grey in some; legs brownish-fleshy.

Above olive or yellowish-brown, the feathers all centred with deep brown; tail brownish, banded with dusky externally, and dusky along the centre of each feather, which is tipped fulvous-white, and the outer feathers have further a dark brown sub-terminal band; beneath the color is white, tinged with earthy-brown on the breast, and with a few dark specks.

The Grass Babbler occurs in Central India, and is not uncommon in the neighbourhood of Deesa.

It breeds during the rains, constructing a roundish nest of dry grass, with the entrance on one side near the top, which it places on the ground in the centre of a low bush. The eggs, four in number, are white in color, speckled all over with reddish-brown and pale lavender, more profusely at the large end. They strongly recall eggs of *Franklinia buchanani*, but are much larger, equalling those of *Chatarrhœa caudata.*

GENUS, Schœnicola, *Blyth.*

Bill moderate, rather deep, much compressed, slightly curved on the culmen; a few strong rictal bristles; wings moderate, slightly rounded; fourth quill longest; third quill equal to fifth; tail moderate, very broad, soft; tarsus long; toes grasping; plumage somewhat lax.

Schœnicola platyurus, *Jerdon.*

442.—Jerdon's Birds of India, Vol. II, p. 73; Butler, Deccan; Stray Feathers, Vol. IX, p. 401.

THE BROAD-TAILED REED BIRD.

Length, 5·75; expanse, 8; wing, 2·5; tail, 2·5; tarsus, 0·88; bill at front, 0·4.

Bill horny-yellow; irides yellowish-brown; legs fleshy-yellow.

Above dark olive-brown; the feathers of the tail obsoletely barred; beneath ochrey-yellowish.

The Broad-tailed Reed Bird is very rare. Major Butler found

it breeding at Belgaum amongst long grass in September. It is probably only a seasonal visitant.

GENUS, Laticilla, *Blyth.*

Bill of moderate length, compressed, slender, nearly straight: culmen gently curved, barely hooked at tip; a few distant, short rictal setæ; wings short, rounded; fourth and fifth quills longest; tail long, graduated; the feathers very broad and soft; tarsus long; middle-toe elongated; lateral toes unequal; hind-toe rather short.

Laticilla burnesii, *Blyth.*

443.—*Eurycercus burnesii.*—Jerdon's Birds of India, Vol. II, p. 74; Murray's Vertebrate Zoology of Sind, p. 134.

THE LONG-TAILED REED BIRD.

Length, 6·25; wing, 2·13; tail, 3·75; tarsus, 0·8; bill at front, 0 4.

Bill horny above, yellowish beneath; irides brownish-yellow; legs yellow-brown.

Above brownish-grey, with dark central streaks, mostly on the scapulars and back; tail faintly barred; under parts whitish, tinged with fulvescent on the flanks, and a shade of the same on the side of the neck, where also a few mesial streaks are distinct; under tail-coverts ferruginous.

Within our limits, the Long-tailed Reed Bird has only been recorded from Sind, where in certain localities it is by no means uncommon, especially in reed and tamarisk thickets.

It breeds from March to September; the nest is placed in the centre of a tussock of grass, and is composed of coarse grass, lined with finer grass. The eggs, three or four in number, are of a pale-greenish ground color, covered with irregular blotches of purplish-brown, but they vary a good deal. The eggs in my possession average 0·72 inches in length by 0·53 in breadth.

FAMILY, Brachypodidæ.

Legs and feet very short, only suited for perching; wings moderate or rather long; bill various, long and Thrush-like in some, short and somewhat depressed in others.

SUB-FAMILY, Pycnonotinæ.

Bill generally short, straight and depressed; rictal bristles well developed; nostrils exposed.

GENUS, Hypsipetes, *Vigors.*

Bill moderately strong, lengthened, nearly straight; culmen very slightly arched; nostrils long, with some short tufts and a few hairs at their base; wings long, fourth and fifth quills longest, third nearly as long; tail rather long, square or emarginate; feet and legs very short. The head is sub-crested, the feathers being lanceolate, and the rictal bristles are very few and weak.

Hypsipetes Ganesa, *Sykes.*

446.—Jerdon's Birds of India, Vol. II, p. 78; Butler, Deccan; Stray Feathers, Vol. IX, p. 401.

THE GHAT BLACK BULBUL.

Length, 9·6 to 10·75; expanse, 14 to 15·5; wing, 4·5 to 5; tail, 4·3 to 4·9; tarsus, 6 to 7·5; bill from gape, 1·3.

Bill deep coral-red; irides deep-brown; legs deep coral-red.

Above grey-brown, paler beneath; wings and tail brown; head slightly crested, metallic-black.

The Ghat Black Bulbul is a rare but permanent resident in the more hilly portions of the Deccan. It occurs on the Sahyadri Range as far north as Mahableshwar.

GENUS, Criniger, *Temminck.*

Bill of moderate length, strong and deep; the culmen well curved; rictal bristles distinct, long; tail nearly even, with the outermost feathers distinctly shorter; head more or less crested.

Criniger ictericus, *Strickland.*

450.—Jerdon's Birds of India, Vol. II, p. 82; Butler, Deccan; Stray Feathers, Vol. IX, p. 402.

THE YELLOW-BROWED BULBUL.

Length, 8; wing, 3·7; tail, 3·5; tarsus, 0·8; bill at front, 0·6.

Bill black; irides blood-red; legs dark-plumbeous.

Plumage above bright olive-green; superciliary streak extending to the forehead, and the whole plumage beneath bright-yellow; quills dusky on their inner webs; the shafts of the tail-feathers beneath yellow.

The Yellow-browed Bulbul has a similar distribution to the last, but is locally not uncommon.

GENUS, Ixus, *Temminck.*

Bill rather short, slightly arching on the culmen, the tip bent over, distinctly notched; commissure nearly straight; a few rictal bristles, mixed with some smaller tufts; hairs on the nape distinct, and some of the feathers of the throat bristle-ended; lateral toes nearly equal; hind-toe shorter than middle-toe; fourth, fifth and sixth quills sub-equal and longest; seventh barely shorter; tail slightly rounded in some, almost even in others, with the outer feathers slightly shorter.

Ixus luteolus, *Less.*

452.—Jerdon's Birds of India, Vol. II, p. 84; Butler, Deccan; Stray Feathers, Vol. IX, p. 402.

THE WHITE-BROWED BUSH BULBUL.

Length, 7·5; wing, 3·5; tail, 3·5; tarsus, 0·8; bill at front 0·6.

Bill blackish; irides blood-red; legs dark-plumbeous.

Above dull-brownish olive-green, palest on the head, where it is slightly ashy, and yellowish on the rump; quills and coverts edged with brighter green; over the eye to the ear-coverts, and from the base of the upper mandible extending below the eye, obscure white; chin, and base of lower mandible, pale clear yellow; lower parts whitish-ashy, tinged with pale-yellow; the breast dashed with brownish-grey, and the vent and under tail-coverts pale-yellow.

The White-browed Bush Bulbul is a permanent resident in some portions of the Deccan, but is very local, and appears to avoid the Ghat Range.

GENUS, Rubigula, *Blyth.*

Bill rather short, moderately stout; rictal bristles small or moderate; tail slightly rounded, or almost even; head black, more or less crested; the feathers of the back loose and decomposed; irides yellow.

Rubigula gularis, *Gould.*

455.—Jerdon's Birds of India, Vol. II, p. 87; Butler, Deccan; Stray Feathers, Vol. IX, p. 402.

THE RUBY-THROATED BULBUL.

Length, 6·5; wing, 3; tail, 2·75; tarsus, 0·55; bill at front, 0·4.

Bill black; irides light-yellow; legs greenish-dusky.

Head and cheeks pure glossy-black; plumage above yellowish olive-green; a small chin spot black; throat beautiful shining ruby-red, the feathers much divided and somewhat bristly; the rest of the plumage beneath bright-yellow; quills with a tinge of dusky on the inner webs.

The Ruby-throated Bulbul is very rare. Mr. Laird procured it in the forests west of Belgaum, but this is the only record of its occurrence within our limits.

GENUS, Brachypodius, *Blyth.*

Bill somewhat as in *Rubigula*, short, rather deep at the base but the rictal bristles more feeble; tail more or less rounded.

Brachypodius poiocephalus, *Jerdon.*

457.—Jerdon's Birds of India, Vol. II, p. 89; Butler, Deccan; Stray Feathers, Vol. IX, p. 402.

THE GREY-HEADED BULBUL.

Length, 7; expanse, 9; wing, 3; tail, 2·8; tarsus, 0·25; bill at front, 0·46.

Bill greenish-horny; irides bluish-white; legs reddish-yellow.

Crown of head, occiput and throat, bluish-grey; forehead siskin-green; back, wings, and plumage beneath, oil-green, lighter towards the vent; feathers of the rump light yellowish-green, broadly streaked with black; tail with the centre feathers greenish, broadly edged with grey; lateral feathers black, also grey-edged; under tail-coverts light-grey.

The Grey-headed Bulbul is not uncommon in the forests south-west of Belgaum. It has not been recorded from any other portion of the region.

It is a permanent resident in the locality indicated.

GENUS, **Otocompsa,** *Cabanis.*

Bill short or moderate, slightly curved; rictus bristled; the head black, with an erectile pointed crest; the upper plumage brown, and the under tail-coverts yellow or red.

Otocompsa leucotis, *Gould.*

459.—Jerdon's Birds of India, Vol. II, p. 91; Butler, Guzerat; Stray Feathers, Vol. III, p. 473; Murray's Vertebrate Zoology of Sind, p. 135.

THE WHITE-EARED CRESTED BULBUL.

Length, 7; wing, 3·5; tail, 3·25; tarsus, 0·75; bill at front, 0·45.

Whole head and neck black, passing into rich brown on the neck; ear-coverts, and a patch below them, white, edged black; upper plumage earthy-brown; tail brown at the base, the terminal half blackish-brown, with the edges white, most broadly so on the outer feathers; beneath, from the breast, whity-brown; the under tail-coverts rich saffron yellow.

The White-eared Crested Bulbul is a very common permanent resident in Sind, and is far from being uncommon in Guzerat; it does not occur in the Deccan. They breed from May to August; the nests are usually built in dense tamarisk thickets, (occasionally in babool trees), four or five feet from the ground. The nests are composed of fine twigs and roots, scantily lined with fine grass. They are cup-shaped, slenderly, but compactly built. The eggs, three or four in number, are longish ovals pointed at one end, reddish-white in color, spotted, streaked, and blotched with brownish purplish-red.

They measure 0·82 inches in length by 0·64 in breadth.

Otocompsa fuscicaudata, *Gould.*

460*bis.*—Butler, Guzerat; Stray Feathers, Vol. III, p. 473; Deccan, Stray Feathers, Vol. IX, p. 402.

THE SOUTHERN RED-WHISKERED BULBUL.

Length, 8; expanse, 11; wing, 3·75; tail, 3·9; tarsus, 0·9; bill at front, 0·5.

Head, with crest, black; ear-coverts white, with a tuft of glossy hair-like crimson feathers over the ears, and reaching beyond them; a narrow line of black borders the ear-coverts beneath; plumage above light hair-brown, darker on the quills and on the tail, especially towards the tip; beneath from the chin white, the sides of the breast dark-brown, forming an interrupted gorget.

The Southern Red-whiskered Bulbul is common on the Sahyadri Range and adjacent forests; it is also very common at Aboo.

It is a permanent resident and breeds from March to May. The nests are neatly made, and are of a deep cup-shape, composed of grass roots, with a quantity of dead leaves or dried ferns worked into the bottom and lined with fine grass. The eggs, two or three in number, are reddish-white in color, thickly mottled, freckled, and streaked with rich blood-red, with a few scarcely visible spots of pale inky-purple.

They measure 0·9 inches in length, by 0·66 in breadth.

GENUS, **Pycnonotus**, *Kuhl.*

Bill moderately long, strong, moderately curved, with strongish rictal bristles; legs and feet stout; tail barely rounded, almost square; under tail-coverts red.

Pycnonotus (Molpastes) pygæus, *Hodgs.*

461.—Jerdon's Birds of India, Vol. II, p. 93.

THE COMMON BENGAL BULBUL.

Length, 8·75; expanse, 12·5; wing, 3·85; tail, 3·25; tarsus, 0·88; bill at front, 0·62.

Bill black; irides deep-brown; legs dark-brown.

Head, nape, hind-neck, chin, throat, and breast, glossy black; ear-coverts glossy hair-brown; from the hind-neck dark smoky brown, edged with ashy, which is the color of the rump; the upper tail-coverts white; tail brownish-black, tipped with white, except the central pair; wings as the back; the shoulders and wing-coverts edged with whitish; below, from the breast, dark brown, edged with ashy, passing to ashy on the lower abdomen; vent and under tail-coverts rich crimson.

According to Jerdon, the Bengal Bulbul is found in the jungles of Central India, north of the Nerbudda river.

Pycnonotus hæmorrhous, *Gmelin.*

462.—Jerdon's Birds of India, Vol. II, p. 94; Butler, Guzerat; Stray Feathers, Vol. III, p. 473; Deccan, Stray Feathers, Vol. IX, p. 402; Murray's Vertebrate Zoology of Sind, p. 135; Swinhoe and Barnes, Central India; Ibis, 1885, p. 68.

THE COMMON MADRAS BULBUL.

Length, 8; expanse, 11; wing, 3·6; tail, 3·3; tarsus, 0·8; bill at front, 0·52.

Bill black; irides deep-brown; legs greenish-slaty.

Head, chin, and throat, black; nape and back smoky-brown

more or less edged paler, and the pale edging often extends to the darker feathers of the hind-head and nape, giving it a speckled appearance; rump somewhat cinerascent; upper tail-coverts white; beneath, from the top of the breast, brown, edged with ash, paling posteriorly, and becoming albescent on the lower abdomen and vent; under tail-coverts crimson; wings smoky-brown; tail brownish-black, tipped with white, except the central pair.

The Common Madras Bulbul is very abundant throughout the region, except in Upper Sind, where it is very rare; it is a permanent resident and breeds from April to October, rearing at least two broods in the year. The nest is generally built on a low bush or fruit tree, rarely at any great height from the ground. It is neatly but lightly made, cup-shaped, and is composed of grass stems, lined with finer grass, and occasionally with hair. The eggs, three or four in number, are rather longish ovals in shape, pinkish-white in color, speckled, blotched, streaked and clouded with red and purplish-red. They average 0·9 inches in length by 0·68 in breadth.

SUB-FAMILY, **Phyllornithinæ.**

Bill slightly lengthened, more or less curved, of variable strength; wings moderate; tail short; tarsus and feet short, stout. Of a beautiful grass-green color, more or less adorned with various glistening blue patches on the throat and shoulders of the wings.

GENUS, **Phyllornis**, *Boie.*

Bill moderate or rather long; culmen keeled, and more or less curved; tip bent down and notched; nostrils basal, lengthened; wings moderately long, with the fourth and fifth quills sub-equal, or the fourth longest; tail moderate, or rather short, even; tarsus short, smooth.

Phyllornis jerdoni, *Blyth.*

463.—Jerdon's Birds of India, Vol. II, p. 97; Butler, Deccan; Stray Feathers, Vol. IX, p. 403.

THE COMMON GREEN BULBUL.

Length, 7·25; wing, 3 5; tail, 2·75; tarsus, 0·78; bill at front, 0·69.

Bill dusky; irides light-brown; legs plumbeous.

Male, pale grass-green; shoulder-patch pale shining-blue; quills dusky internally; chin, throat and gorget, deep-black, surrounded by a greenish-yellow band, which extends through the eyes to the forehead; maxillary streak hyacinth-blue, short.

The female has the parts that are black in the male light bluish-green, surrounded by the yellowish band, and the maxillary streak light-azure.

The Common Green Bulbul is a not uncommon permanent resident on the Sahyadri Range, occurring as far north as Khandalla.

Phyllornis malabaricus, *Gmelin.*

464.—Jerdon's Birds of India, Vol. II, p. 98; Butler, Deccan; Stray Feathers, Vol. IX, p. 403.

THE MALABAR GREEN BULBUL.

Length, 7·9; expanse, 11; wing, 3·5; tail, 3; bill at front, 0·75; tarsus, 0·7.

Bill dusky-blackish; irides light yellowish-brown; legs plumbeous.

Male, bright grass-green; forehead golden-yellow; chin and throat black, with a small blue moustachial streak; flexure of wing verdigris-blue.

The female wants the golden forehead of the male, and has the black gorget and blue maxillary streak somewhat smaller.

The Malabar Green Bulbul is a permanent resident on the Sahyadri Range, from Goa to Khandalla.

GENUS, (Ægithina) Iora, *Horsfield.*

Bill moderate, or rather long, somewhat compressed, very slightly curving; culmen rounded, slightly hooked at tip, and notched; rictal bristles almost wanting; nostrils apert; wings rather short, with fourth, fifth and sixth quills sub-equal and longest; secondaries long, nearly equal to the primaries; tail even, short; tarsus rather short with scales divided; toes short; middle-toe very little longer than the outer, which is slightly syndactyle; claws slightly curved; hind-toe shorter than the middle one.

Iora (Ægithina) tiphia, *Lin.*

468.—Jerdon's Birds of India, Vol. II, p. 103; Butler, Guzerat; Stray Feathers, Vol. III, p. 473; Deccan, Stray Feathers, Vol. IX, p. 403; Swinhoe and Barnes, Central India; Ibis, 1885, p. 168.

THE WHITE-WINGED IORA.

Length, 5·3; expanse, 7·5; wing, 2·5; tail, 2·0; tarsus, 0·75; bill at front 0·5; bill from gape, 0·7.

Bill reddish, dusky on culmen; irides dark-brown; legs fleshy-yellow.

Male, above olive-green, beneath yellow; wings black, faintly edged with yellow; greater-coverts broadly tipped with white; scapulars also partly white; tail black.

The female has the tail concolorous with the body, but slightly infuscated, and the wings paler than in the male.

Mr. Hume unites 467—*Iora zeylonica* with *tiphia.* I therefore give Jerdon's description of *zeylonica*:—

Male in full plumage, with the head, back, wings, and tail

deep black, the former with two white bars, caused by the tips of the greater-coverts; scapulars also partly white; the tail tipped with yellowish-white; beneath bright-yellow; abdomen and lower tail-coverts pale-yellow; the flanks have a tuft of white silky feathers, and the bases of the clothing feathers are mostly white.

In non-breeding plumage, and in males not fully adult, the black of the upper plumage is less in extent, and more mixed with green; the white of the quills are faintly edged with pale-yellow externally, and the innermost ones are white internally near the tip; and the pale tips to the tail-feathers are more distinct.

The female is entirely grass-green above, pale-yellow beneath; the wings blackish, with whitish bars and yellow edges; and the tail green pale tipped.

Mr. Hume has gone fully into this question in Stray Feathers, Vol. V, p. 428, *et seq.*

The White-winged Green Bulbul is a permanent resident in the Deccan; it is also common in parts of Rajpootana and at Mhow, Central India; it does not occur in Sind, and in the plains of Northern Guzerat it is replaced by the next species.

They breed from May to September. The nest is generally placed on the upper surface of a horizontal bough, and is very neatly made, deeply cup-shaped, and is composed of grass and fibres, coated outside with spider's webs.

The eggs, two or three in number, are moderately broad oval in shape, slightly pointed towards one end. The ground-color is greyish-white (but occasionally with a creamy tinge), with long streaky blotches of pale-brown or brownish-red. They measure 0·68 in length by 0·54 in breadth.

Iora (Ægithina) nigrolutea, *Marshall.*

468*bis.*—Butler, Guzerat; Stray Feathers, Vol. V, p. 220.

THE WESTERN IORA.

In breeding plumage the male has the forehead, crown, occiput and nape, glossy black, the black terminating in a well defined curved line; the chin, throat, cheeks, ear-coverts, breast, sides of neck, and a broad half-collar occupying the base of the back of the neck and the upper back, intense gamboge-yellow. Rarely this collar is entirely uniform, generally a few of the central feathers are narrowly fringed at the tips with black, occasionally most of the feathers are so fringed. Mid-back glossy-black, rarely unbroken, generally with a little of the yellow (or towards the rump, greenish), bases of the feathers showing through; in one specimen with a great deal of this; rump pale-greenish, the white bases of the feathers often showing through a good deal; upper tail-coverts and tail black, the former with a bluish gloss, the latter with all the feathers tipped white, the white not unfrequently running some distance up the margin of the inner, and in a few cases of the outer webs also; coverts and tertiaries black; both median and greater-coverts broadly tipped with white. In many specimens the tertiaries and the latest secondaries are broadly margined at the tips with white, but in some this is less conspicuous, and in some towards the close of the breeding season it is almost entirely wanting on the tertiaries. The primaries and secondaries hair-brown, more or less of the outer webs towards their bases blackish, and margined on their outer webs very narrowly, in some more, in others less conspicuously with white.

The abdomen is like the breast, but paler; in some with a greenish tinge towards the sides, and on its lower half, and in the other case looking (in skins) nearly white owing to the intermixture of the long silky-white feathers of the flank tufts. Wing-lining and axillaries, and more or less of the inner margins of the quills, satiny-white; a slight primrose tinge at the bend of the wing.

The females and males in non-breeding plumage have the entire under parts a pale mealy-yellow, slightly shaded with olive-green. The head is similar, but not quite so light; the nape and entire back similar, but much more strongly overlaid with olive-green.

The wings and tail are as in the breeding season, except that the wings have the margins, specially of the tertiaries, very conspicuous, and much tinged with pale-yellow; that the greater-coverts often have pale-yellow margins besides the white tips; and that the central tail-feathers are almost entirely greyish-white, tipped purer white, and with the outer webs in many specimens more or less shaded with ashy or occasionally olivaceous ashy. (*Hume*).

The Western Iora is found on the plains at the foot of Mount Aboo, and extends through Northern Guzerat. On Aboo itself the common species alone occurs.

Sub-family, Ireninæ.

Bill stout, of moderate length, somewhat widened at the bases; culmen elevated, and slightly arching from the base; the tip not much hooked, but distinctly toothed; nostrils partially concealed by short plumes; rictus with short but distinct bristles; wings moderate or rather long; fourth quill longest, third nearly as long; tail moderate, even; feet with the tarsus very short; lateral toes very slightly unequal; claws short, well curved.

Genus, Irena, *Horsfield*.

The characters are similar to those of the sub-family.

Irena puella, *Latham*.

469.—Jerdon's Birds of India, Vol. II, p. 105; Butler, Deccan; Stray Feathers, Vol. IX, p. 403.

THE FAIRY BLUE-BIRD.

Length, 10; wing, 5·25; tail, 4; tarsus, 0·5.

Bill black; irides ruby-red; legs black.

Male, the whole upper parts, with the lower tail-coverts, brilliant glistening cobalt-blue; wings, tail, and lower plumage, deep velvet-black.

The female is of a dull, slightly mottled, Antwerp-blue throughout.

The Fairy Blue-bird occurs at Savantvadi, where it is probably a permanent resident, and it has also been procured in the forests southwest of Belgaum.

It does not occur elsewhere within the region.

SUB-FAMILY, Oriolinæ.

Bill Thrush-like, rather long, strong, moderately broad at the base, slightly curving, tolerably hooked, and the tip distinctly notched; wings long, third or fourth quill longest; tail rather short, nearly even; tarsus short; feet small; lateral toes unequal, and the outer one syndactyle; claws well curved.

GENUS, Oriolus, *Linnæus.*

Bill long, slightly broad at the base, somewhat curved at the culmen, which is keeled, slightly hooked at tip, distinctly notched; nostrils basal and lateral, longitudinal, pierced in membrane, nearly apert; wings lengthened, first quill very short, second a little shorter than the third which is longest; tail sub-even, with long coverts; tarsus short; feet moderately strong; anterior scales of tarsus divided; claws moderate, well curved.

Oriolus kundoo, *Sykes.*

470.—Jerdon's Birds of India, Vol. II, p. 107; Butler, Guzerat; Stray Feathers, Vol. III, p. 474; Deccan, Stray Feathers, Vol. IX, p. 403; Murray's Vertebrate Zoology of Sind, p. 137; Swinhoe and Barnes, Central India; Ibis, 1885, p. 68.

THE INDIAN ORIOLE.

Length, 9·5 to 10; expanse, 15 to 16; wing, 5·5 to 5·7; tail, 3·5 to 3·75; tarsus, 0·8 to 0·9; bill at front, 1·0; bill at gape, 1·25.

Bill deep lake-red; irides rich blood-red; legs plumbeous.

Male, bright-yellow; a black stripe from the base of the bill through the eyes for a short distance beyond; wings black, with a yellow bar formed by the primary coverts and the tips and outer edges of the quills; tail with the central feathers black; the next pair black with a broad yellow tip, and the others black at the base, and yellow for the greater part of their terminal length.

The adult female differs from the male in a slightly greenish tint above.

The young bird is yellowish-green above; the rump, vent, the inner webs of the tail-feathers at their tips, and the sides of the abdomen, bright-yellow; wings olive-brown; body beneath whitish, with brown stripes; bill black.

The Indian Oriole occurs generally throughout the district, but is less common in Sind than elsewhere. On the higher ranges it is replaced by *O. melanocephalus.*

It is a permanent resident and breeds during May and June. It seems to have a preference for *neem* trees, as most of the nests I have seen have been built on these. It chooses a fork at the extremity of a slender bough, and between the twigs forming the fork it constructs a purse-like nest, composed of grass stems and roots, vegetable fibre, pieces of rag, &c., all firmly bound at its upper edges to the fork between which it is suspended. The eggs, usually three in number, are moderately long ovals, pure glossy china-white in colour with dark-claret or nearly black specks, spots or blotches, chiefly at the larger end. They vary greatly both in size and shape, but the average is 1·1 inch in length by 0·8 in breadth.

As soon as the eggs are laid, the nest is easy to find, owing to the habit the bird has of attacking any bird, no matter how large, that ventures near the nest.

The nestlings are easily reared by placing them in a cage, accessible to the parent birds, as although naturally shy yet they will attend to, and feed them until long after they are able to fend for themselves.

Oriolus galbula, *Lin.*

470bis.—Murray's Vertebrate Zoology of Sind, p. 136.

THE GOLDEN ORIOLE.

Length, 10; wings, 5·9; tail, 3·6; tarsus, 0·85; bill at front, 0·95.

Bill dull-reddish; irides blood-red; legs lead-grey.

Adult male: Entire plumage, except the wings and tail, rich golden-yellow; a broad stripe from the base of the bill to the eye, covering the lores, deep-black; wings jet-black; the quills tipped and externally narrowly margined with yellowish-white or sulphur-yellow; edge of the wing and under wing-coverts rich yellow, the primary coverts being broadly terminated with the same color; tail black, broadly terminated with yellow; the outer rectrices being more broadly, and the inner ones less marked with this color, the central-rectrices black, only narrowly tipped with yellow.

Adult female: Differs considerably from the male; upper parts (excepting the wings) greenish-yellow or apple-green; the patch in front of the eye dull brownish-black; wings as in the male, but duller and browner, the edgings being pale sulphur-yellow; secondaries and wing-coverts washed with dull greenish-yellow; tail as in the *male*, except that the yellow markings are only on the inner webs, the outer webs of the feathers being blackish; under parts white, on the lower throat, breast, and flanks washed with bright-yellow, the vent and under tail-coverts being entirely yellow; throat, breast, and flanks, more or less distinctly streaked with blackish-brown.

Young male: Closely resembles the female, but is only a little more yellow in tinge of plumage.—*Dresser.*

Occurs in Sind as a somewhat rare visitor during October and November.

Oriolus indicus, *Jerdon.*

471.—Jerdon's Birds of India, Vol. II, p. 109; Butler, Deccan; Stray Feathers, Vol. IX, p. 403; Swinhoe and Barnes, Central India; Ibis, 1885, p. 69.

THE BLACK-NAPED INDIAN ORIOLE.

Length, 10; wing, 6; tail, 3·5; tarsus, 0·87; bill at front, 1·12.

Bill pinky-red; irides rich blood-red; legs plumbeous.

Bright yellow, greenish on the back and coverts; a black horse-shoe mark extending from the base of the bill through the eyes to the nape; tail black; the central feathers barely tipped yellow, the others tipped broadly, the outermost feathers for 1½ inches or so; wings black, the secondaries broadly margined with pale yellow, the tertiaries with the whole outer web, and part of the inner webs, greenish yellow; primaries also tipped with the same; a bright yellow wing-spot formed by the tips of the coverts of the primaries.

Females differ in being slightly greenish above, and in the yellow generally being not quite so vivid.

The young are yellowish-green above, with little or no trace of the occipital crescent; whitish beneath, with dark central lines; bill infuscated.

In a further stage the under-parts are a weaker yellow, with black shafts to the breast-feathers more or less developed.

The Black-naped Indian Oriole is very rare. It has only been procured at Savantvadi and Ratnagiri. Colonel Swinhoe saw it at Manpore, Central India.

Oriolus melanocephalus, *Lin.*

472.—Jerdon's Birds of India, Vol. II, p. 110; Butler, Guzerat; Stray Feathers, Vol. III, p. 474; Deccan, Stray Feathers, Vol. IX, p. 403.

THE BENGAL BLACK-HEADED ORIOLE.

Length, 9·5; expanse, 16; wing, 5·5; tail, 3·5; tarsus, 0·88; bill at front, 1.

Bill pale lake-red; irides rich-red; legs plumbeous.

Whole head, neck and breast in front, deep-black; rest of the plumage rich dark-yellow above, slightly paler beneath, on the lower abdomen and under tail-coverts; wings black, with a small yellow band formed by the primary-coverts; tertiaries with the tips and outer webs pale-yellow; the secondaries also broadly tipped with yellow, gradually diminishing in extent to the last primaries, some of which are tipped and edged with yellow; tail pale-yellow, the two central-feathers with a broad black band about half an inch tipped with yellow, the next pair with barely one inch of black, and the yellow tip nearly half an inch; the next pair with a narrow and sometimes interrupted black band about the terminal third, and the three outer pairs on each side nearly wholly yellow; the outer pair with an occasional smear of black on the outer margin; all the tail-feathers with black shafts diminishing in intensity towards the outermost feathers.

The young bird has the forehead yellow, the head more or less blackish, the neck white with blackish streaks, the belly yellow with longitudinally dark streaks, and the yellow duller in tint.

The Bengal Black-headed Oriole is not very common; it occurs only on the higher ranges, where it replaces *Oriolus indicus*. It is not uncommon on the Sahyadri Range, and again on the Aravellies near Aboo.

Oriolus ceylonensis, *Bonap.*

473.—Jerdon's Birds of India, Vol. II, p. 111; Butler, Deccan; Stray Feathers, Vol. IX, p. 403.

THE SOUTHERN BLACK-HEADED ORIOLE.

Length, 9; expanse, 15·3; wing, 4·9; tail, 3·3; tarsus, 0·87; bill at front, 0·9.

Bill pale lake-red; irides rich-red; legs plumbeous.

Head and neck deep-black; rest of the plumage deep-yellow; wings black; the wing spot formed by the tips of the primary-coverts smaller than in the last; the tertiaries only tipped with yellow; and the black on the tail of greater extent, especially on the central feathers.

The Southern Black-headed Oriole is very doubtfully distinct from *O. melanocephala*. It occurs in the same localities as the last.

FAMILY, Sylviadæ.

Of small size mostly; bill slender; wings usually somewhat lengthened, and tail moderate or short; tarsus long; feet moderate.

SUB-FAMILY, Saxicolinæ.

Bill stouter, more depressed at the base than in the other sub-families; wings moderate, or somewhat long; tail moderate in most, short in some, long in a very few; tarsus moderately long, stout; feet moderate, fitted for terrestrial habits; claws slightly curved.

GENUS, Copsychus, *Wagler*.

Bill moderately long and strong, straight; tip slightly bent, distinctly notched; rictal bristles almost absent; nostrils large exposed basal; wings moderate, fourth and fifth quills longest, third nearly equal to them; tail rather long, graduated, or with the six central feathers equal, the outer ones graduated; tarsus moderately long, stout, nearly entire; feet moderate; middle-toe long; hind-toe and claw moderate; claws slightly curved.

Copsychus saularis, *Lin.*

475.—Jerdon's Birds of India, Vol. II, p. 115; Butler, Guzerat; Stray Feathers, Vol. III, p. 474; Deccan, Stray Feathers, Vol. IX, p. 404; Murray's Vertebrate Zoology of Sind, p. 137; Swinhoe and Barnes, Central India; Ibis, 1885, p. 124.

THE MAGPIE ROBIN.

Length, 7·75 to 8·5; expanse, 11·5; wing, 3·8 to 4; tail, 3·25; tarsus, 1·12; bill at front, 0·68.

Bill black; irides brown; legs black.

Head, neck, breast, body above, and wings, black, glossed blue on all parts except the wings; abdomen, vent and under tail-coverts, white; the four outer tail-feathers on each side white.

The female is duller black than the males and somewhat ashy on the breast.

The young birds have the breast dusky with ruddy spots, the upper surface olive-brown turning to slaty.

The Magpie Robin is distributed generally throughout the district, common in parts of the Deccan, very common in Western Rajputana, and not uncommon in Guzerat. In Sind it occurs but rarely.

I do not think that any remain to breed in Guzerat, but at Poona, at Mhow, and again in Neemuch, I found them breeding plentifully during May, June and July. The nest is generally in a hole in a tree sometimes at a considerable height from the ground, but generally not more than eight or ten feet.

The nest is saucer-shaped, sometimes only a mere pad, and is composed of grass roots, fibres, feathers, &c. The eggs, four or five in number, are typically oval in shape; the ground color is subject to considerable variation.

In some it is greenish or pale-greenish blue, in others greenish-white, or even pale sea-green, streaked and blotched with different shades of reddish-brown, most densely so at the larger end. They average 0·87 inches in length by 0·66 in breadth.

GENUS, Kittacincla, *Gould.* (Cercotrichas.)

Bill more slender than in the last; tail very long, graduated; wings slightly more rounded; tarsus slender, pale; lateral toes very short.

Kittacincla (Cercotrichas) macroura, *Gmelin.*

476.—Jerdon's Birds of India, Vol. II, p. 116; Butler, Deccan; Stray Feathers, Vol. IX, p. 404.

THE SHAMA.
Shama, Hin.

Length, 12; wing, 3·75; tail, 7·9; tarsus, 1; bill at front, 0·75.

Head, neck, back, wing-coverts, breast, and tail, glossy-black; rump white; wings dull-black, outer tail-feathers broadly tipped with white; breast, belly, and under tail-coverts deep chesnut.

The female has the colors less pure and duller than the male.

This splendid songster is only found within our limits on the Sahyadri Range, and in the adjoining forests as far north as Khandalla. It is a permanent resident.

GENUS, Thamnobia, *Swainson.*

Bill slender, very slightly widened at the base; the sides compressed, slightly arched throughout; tip deflected, not notched; gape smooth; wings short, rounded, the fourth and fifth quills longest; the primaries hardly exceeding the tertiaries and secondaries, which are broad; tail moderate, broad, much rounded; tarsus long; the feet moderate; inner-toe much shorter than the outer; hind-toe short; all the claws slightly curved.

Thamnobia fulicata, *Linn.*

479.—Jerdon's Birds of India, Vol. II, p. 121; Butler, Deccan; Stray Feathers, Vol. IX, p. 404.

THE INDIAN BLACK ROBIN.

Length, 6; wing, 3; tail, 2·75; tarsus, 1·1; bill at front, 0·5.

Bill black; irides dark brown; legs blackish.

Male, shining deep black, with a white wing-patch; the middle of the abdomen and the under tail-coverts deep chesnut.

Female dull sooty-brown, darker on the wings and tail; the under tail-coverts chesnut.

The Indian Black Robin is very common in the Deccan, where it is a permanent resident, breeding during April, May and June. The nest, usually a mere pad, is composed of grass roots, vegetable fibre, hair and such like substances. It is generally found in a hole in a wall or tree. The eggs, three in number, are greenish-white in color, spotted and speckled with yellowish-white. They average 0·72 inches in length by about 0·55 in breadth.

Thamnobia cambaiensis, *Lath.*

480.—Jerdon's Birds of India, Vol. II, p. 122; Butler, Guzerat; Stray Feathers, Vol. III, p. 474; Murray's Vertebrate Zoology of Sind, p. 138; Swinhoe and Barnes, Central India; Ibis, p. 124.

THE BROWN-BACKED INDIAN ROBIN.
Kalchuri, Hin.

Length, 6; wing, 2·9; tail, 2·75; tarsus, 1; bill at front, 0·5.

Bill black; irides deep-brown; legs blackish.

The male has the back, wings, and upper tail-coverts dusky

olive-brown; the wings and tail black; the lores, ear-coverts, and lower plumage also black; a white wing-spot, as in the last; the vent and centre of belly deep chesnut.

The female is sooty-brown throughout, except the chesnut beneath.

The Brown-backed or Northern Indian Robin is a common permanent resident throughout the district, excepting the Deccan, where it is replaced by *Thamnobia fulicata.*

Its breeding habits are much like the last, but the eggs are larger, averaging 0·79 in length by 0·59 in breadth.

Genus, **Pratincola**, *Koch.*

Bill short, straight, somewhat wide at base, strongly curving at tip, which is faintly notched; nostrils concealed by tufts of hairs and plumes; strong rictal bristles; wings moderate; fourth, fifth and sixth quills nearly equal and longest; tail moderate, nearly even; tarsus moderate, longish; feet moderate; claws slightly curved, slender.

Pratincola caprata, *Linn.*

481.—Jerdon's Birds of India, Vol. II, p. 123; Butler, Guzerat; Stray Feathers, Vol. III, p. 474; Deccan, Stray Feathers, Vol. IX, p. 404; Murray's Vertebrate Zoology of Sind, p. 141; Swinhoe and Barnes, Central India; Ibis, p. 124.

The White-winged Black Robin.

Length, 5; wing, 2·75; tail, 2·2; tarsus, 0·75; bill at front, 0·38. Bill black; irides deep-brown; legs brown-black.

Male, black; a longitudinal band on the wings, the rump and the upper tail-coverts, and the middle of the lower part of the abdomen, vent, and under tail-coverts, white. When newly moulted, the black is fringed with brown edgings, which gradually get worn away.

Female, dusky-brown, the feathers edged paler with a rufous rump and upper tail-coverts; beneath pale reddish-brown, albescent on the throat and vent; abdomen slightly streaked; vent and under tail-coverts tinged with rufous.

The White-winged Black Robin is a common permanent resident throughout the district; it, however, almost disappears from some parts during the breeding season, which is from March to May. They build flat saucer-shaped or pad-like nests in holes in the sides of wells or banks, occasionally in a bush, but even then the nest rests actually on the ground. The nest is composed of grass, fine roots, vegetable fibres, &c., and usually contains four eggs, but three incubated ones are often found and at times as many as five.

They are moderately broad ovals in shape, of a greenish-white or greenish-blue color, densely but finely speckled with brownish-red. They differ greatly in size, but average 0·67 inches in length by about 0·55 in breadth.

Pratincola indica, *Blyth.*

483.—Jerdon's Birds of India, Vol. II, p. 124; Butler, Guzerat; Stray Feathers, Vol. III, p. 475; *P. maura*, Pall.: Deccan, Stray Feathers, Vol. IX, p. 404; Swinhoe and Barnes, Central India; Ibis, p. 124.

THE INDIAN BUSHCHAT.

Length, 5·25; wing, 2·75; tail, 1·75; tarsus, 0·9; bill at front, 0·38.

Bill black; irides deep-brown; legs black.

The male in summer plumage has the whole head and neck, back, wings, and tail black, the back and wings edged with pale rufous; wing-spot, rump, and upper tail-coverts, white; breast and lower parts bright ferruginous, deep on the breast, paler on the flanks and belly and albescent on the vent and under tail-coverts; a demi-collar of white almost meets on the nape, dividing the back of the head and neck.

In *winter plumage* the black is almost replaced by earthy brown; the rump and tail-coverts are ferruginous-brown; the lores, ear-coverts, and chin, however, are always more or less black; the white wing-spot is less prominent; the whole lower parts are dull ferruginous, albescent on the under tail-coverts, and the demi-collar is deficient or rusty.

The female resembles the male in winter dress, being brown above, margined with paler brown, and rufescent towards the the tail; but the chin and throat are white, and there is a white supercilium. The wing-spot too is a little sullied.

The Indian Bush or Whinchat is a common winter visitant to all parts of the district, appearing about the commencement of September.

Pratincola leucurus, *Blyth.*

484.—Jerdon's Birds of India, Vol. II, p. 126; Murray's Vertebrate Zoology of Sind, p. 140.

THE WHITE-TAILED BUSHCHAT.

Length, 5; wing, 2·5; tail, 2; tarsus, 0·75; bill at front, 0·45.

Bill black; irides brown; legs black.

Male.—Above black, with the usual white wing-patch; the breast bright rufous in the centre; sides of neck, breast, and lower parts pure white; the four outer tail-feathers wholly white on their inner webs, except the tip of the two outermost; and the pair next the centrals (which are wholly black) have the greater portion of the inner web also white.

The *female* is brown above, the feathers edged paler, with a smaller white wing-spot, but no white on the tail; beneath earthy-white, tinged rufous on the breast.

In winter the dorsal feathers are more or less edged with brown.

The White-tailed Bushchat is a winter visitant to Sind; it does not occur elsewhere within our limits.

Pratincola macrorhyncha, *Stol.*

485*bis*.—Murray's Vertebrate Zoology of Sind, p. 138.

STOLICKZA'S BUSHCHAT.

Length, 6; wing, 3; tail, 2·12; tarsus, 0·93; bill at front, 0·7.

Bill black; irides brown; legs black.

Adult male: a broad stripe over the eyes and over the greater portion of the ear-coverts white, with a slight buffy tinge; lower parts of the lores dusky; chin, throat, and entire lower parts, including lower tail-coverts and tibial plumes, white with a yellowish tinge and a very feeble rufescent tinge on breast and flanks; wing-lining and axillaries pure white, the former slightly mottled with dusky; forehead, crown, occiput, nape, back and scapulars light sandy-buff, striated longitudinally with hair-brown; rump and upper tail-coverts white, most of the feathers tinged towards their tip with pale rusty-buff; primaries and secondaries hair-brown, margined on the outer webs with light buff and tipped with yellowish-white, the primaries more narrowly, the secondaries more broadly; tertiary greater-coverts, or perhaps they should be called lower-scapulars, white; tertiaries and greater and median secondary-coverts deep brown, broadly margined with pale, more or less refuscent buff; entire visible portion of lesser-coverts pale sandy-buff; edge of wing and outer webs of earlier greater primary-coverts pure white; tail hair-brown, all the feathers margined on the outer webs with sandy-buff or light yellowish-brown; the outer web of the outermost feather almost entirely of this color; all the feathers, except the central pair, with almost the entire inner webs, white, the outermost pair have an irregular subterminal brown band from 0·2 to 0·3 inch wide on this web, but the rest have only a small patch of brown near the shaft close to the tip, the pair next the centre have the patch rather larger; there are traces of a dark streak from the base of the lower mandible down either sides of the throat, expanding on the sides of the breast; doubtless in breeding plumage this streak and patch are black or blackish.

The female is rather smaller and shows the dark streak and patch much less.

Occurs in Sind, but is not common.

GENUS, Saxicola, *Bechst.*

Bill moderate, straight and compressed, slender, very slightly inflected, with a blunt notch; nostrils apert; rictal bristles feeble or wanting; wing moderately long, pointed; the first short, second half an inch shorter than the third, fourth and fifth, which are equal and longest; tail moderate, even, or very slightly rounded; tarsus long and strong; feet moderate.

Saxicola opistholeuca, *Strick.*

488.—*Saxicola leucoroides*, Guerin.—Jerdon's Birds of India, Vol.

II, p. 130; Butler, Guzerat; Stray Feathers, Vol. III, p. 475; Murray's Vertebrate Zoology of Sind, p. 144; Swinhoe and Barnes, Central India; Ibis, p. 125.

THE INDIAN WHITE-TAILED STONECHAT.

Length, 6·5; expanse, 10·75; wing, 3·75; tail, 2·75; tarsus, 0·9; bill at front, 0·5; bill at gape, 0·75.

Bill black; irides dark-brown; legs black.

Sooty-black; the thigh-coverts, lower abdomen, vent, and under tail-coverts white, and the greater part of the tail also white; the lateral feathers tipped with black for not quite half an inch, the middle feathers for about half an inch.

The female is said to be of a duller and browner hue.

The White-tailed Stonechat occurs sparingly in Sind and Northern Guzerat, more commonly near Mhow in Central India, and at Neemuch in Western Rajpootana. It is a winter visitant only. It is doubtful whether the bird has been found in the Deccan.

Saxicola picatus, *Blyth.*

489.—Jerdon's Birds of India, Vol. II, p. 131; Butler, Guzerat; Stray Feathers, Vol. III, p. 475; Murray's Vertebrate Zoology of Sind, p. 142.

THE PIED STONECHAT.

Length, 6·5; expanse, 11·25; wing, 3·75; tail, 2·75; tarsus, 0·9; bill at front, 0·5; bill at gape, 0·75.

Bill black; irides dark-brown; legs black.

Whole head, neck, and upper breast, back, and wings, black; the rump, upper tail-coverts, and all the lower parts from the breast white; tail white, except the terminal two-thirds of the two central feathers, and the tips of the others, which are black.

The Pied Stonechat is a common winter visitant to Sind and Guzerat, but it is much less common at Mhow and Neemuch, and has not been recorded from the Deccan.

I found it breeding in the vicinity of Chaman, South Afghanistan.

Saxicola alboniger, *Hume.*

489*bis.*—Murray's Vertebrate Zoology of Sind, p. 142.

HUME'S PIED STONECHAT.

Length, 6·5 to 7·75; wing, 3·8 to 4·25; tail, 2·75 to 3; tarsus, 1 to 1·1; bill at front, 0·56 to 0·65.

Bill black; irides dark-brown; legs black.

Head, neck, upper back, and throat black; quills dark brown; under wing-coverts and axillaries black; tail white, with a broad terminal band of dark-brown, broader on the two central feathers; lower back, rump, upper tail-coverts, breast, belly and under tail-coverts white.

Hume's Pied Stonechat is a winter visitant to Sind, but occurs nowhere else within our limits.

Saxicola morio, *Hemp & Ehr.*

490.—*Saxicola leucomela*, Pallas.—Jerdon's Birds of India, Vol. II, p. 181; Murray's Vertebrate Zoology of Sind, p. 143.

THE WHITE-HEADED STONECHAT.

Length, 6·5; wing, 3·6 to 3·9; tail, 2·25 to 2·75; tarsus, 0·85 to 1; bill at front, 0·6 to 0·7.

Bill black; irides dark-brown; legs black.

Crown on the head greyish-white; the rump and upper tail-coverts, and all the lower parts, from the top of the breast, white; rest of the upper parts, neck, and breast, black; tail black, with the base of the central feathers, and all the lateral ones, white; the outermost tipped with black, and part of the outer web also black.

Young birds have the white cap more or less tinged with dingy greyish-brown.

The White-headed Stonechat is a winter visitant to Sind; it does not occur elsewhere within our limits.

Saxicola monachus, *Rupp.*

490*bis*.—Murray's Vertebrate Zoology of Sind, p. 143.

THE HOODED STONECHAT.

Length, 7 to 7·25; wing, 4 to 4·42; tail, 2·75; tarsus, 0·9; bill at front, 0·62.

Bill black; irides brown; legs black.

General color black; quills dark-brown, paler on under surface; head, nape, upper and lower tail-coverts, belly, and flanks, white; tail white, except the terminal half of the two central feathers, and the tips of the others, which are very dark-brown.

The female is similar to the male but browner, and the white parts are tinged with buff.

The Hooded Stonechat occurs as a winter visitant to Sind.

It has not been recorded from any other portion of the region.

Saxicola isabellina, *Rupp.*

491.—*Saxicola œnanthe*, Linn.—Jerdon's Birds of India, Vol. II, p. 132; Butler, Guzerat; Stray Feathers, Vol. III, p. 475; Deccan, Stray Feathers, Vol. IX, p. 404; Murray's Vertebrate Zoology of Sind, p. 146; Swinhoe and Barnes, Central India; Ibis, 1885, p. 125.

THE WHEATEAR.

Length, 6·5 to 7; expanse, 11 to 12; wing, 3·75 to 4; tail, 2·5 to 2·75; tarsus, 1·1; bill at front, 0·45 to 0·5; bill at gape 0·75 to 0·8.

Bill black; irides brown; legs black.

Male, above ashy with a brown tinge; the rump and upper

tail-coverts white, and a white supercilium ; lores and eye-streak black ; wings dusky, edged with brown ; tail with the two central feathers black for the terminal two-thirds, the rest white, the outer feathers black tipped ; under surface pale rusty-brown, albescent on the belly and under tail-coverts ; under wing-coverts blackish with white edgings.

The female is ashy-brown above, wings dusky-brown, tail black-tipped.

In winter the feathers are broadly edged with rufous, most conspicuous on the wing-coverts and tertiaries.

The Wheatear is a common winter visitant to Sind, Guzerat, and Rajputana, but is very rare in the Deccan.

Saxicola tringi, *Hume.*

491*bis.*—*Saxicola chrysopygia,* De Fil.—Murray's Vertebrate Zoology of Sind, p. 145 ; Butler, Guzerat ; Stray Feathers, Vol. III, p. 476.

THE RED-TAILED WHEATEAR.

Length, 6·2 to 6·5 ; expanse, 10 to 11·3 ; wing, 3·7 to 4·4 ; tail, 2·2 to 2·4 ; tarsus, 1 ; bill at front, 0·55 to 0·6.

Bill black ; irides dark-brown ; legs black.

A dark grey line from the gape to and under the eye ; a broad, slightly greyish-white line from the nostrils over the eye, much more conspicuous in some specimens than in others ; ear-coverts silky rufescent-brown ; forehead greyish-brown ; crown, occiput, nape, back and scapulars, nearly uniform grey earthy-brown, as a rule only very slightly tinged with rufescent towards the rump ; but in some specimens more strongly so ; rump and upper tail-coverts bright rufous-fawn, in some specimens pale rufous-buff ; tail-feathers bright, in some pale ferruginous, with a sub-terminal blackish-brown band extending over both webs, and a narrow tipping of rufous-white jets in at the shafts for about the tenth of an inch ; occasionally on the lateral feathers, the black bar is more or less imperfect, the dark band is from 1·1 to 1·4 broad on the central feathers, by about 0·6 or 0·8 on the feathers next the centre, and 0·4 to 0·6 on the external ones. The tertiaries and most of the coverts are hair-brown, broadly margined with pale rufescent ; the winglet, primaries, and secondaries, and primary greater-coverts are slightly darker hair-brown, very narrowly tipped with white, and some of them, the secondaries especially, very narrowly margined with pale rufescent ; the chin and upper throat white, with a faint creamy tinge ; the sides of the neck, behind and below the ear-coverts, grey, greyish-white and greyish-brown, blending on the one side into the color of the throat, and on the other into that of the back of the neck ; the breast and upper abdomen are a very pale rufescent-brown, all the tips of the feathers being paler ; the centre of the abdomen and vent slightly rufescent-white ; flanks rufescent-fawn ; lower tail-coverts a somewhat pale buff ; wing-lining and axillaries pure white.

The Red-tailed Wheatear occurs sparingly as a winter visitant to Sind, and has also been recorded from the base of Mount Aboo

Saxicola deserti, *Ruppell.*

492.—Jerdon's Birds of India, Vol. II, p. 132; Butler, Guzerat; Stray Feathers, Vol. III, p. 476; Deccan, Stray Feathers, Vol. IX, p. 405; Murray's Vertebrate Zoology of Sind, p. 144; Swinhoe and Barnes, Central India; Ibis, 1885, p. 125.

THE BLACK-THROATED WHEATEAR.

Length, 6·5 to 7; expanse, 10·5 to 11; wing, 3·75; tail, 2·5; tarsus, 0·85 to 1; bill at gape, 0·75; bill at front, 0·48.

Bill black; irides brown; legs black.

Above pale isabelline, greyish on the crown and nape, and a whitish eyebrow; rump and upper tail-coverts buffy-white; tail white at base, the rest black; chin, throat, lores, and ears, pure black, extending down the sides of the neck to the shoulder; wing black, with a white patch on the bend of the wing; beneath pale isabelline, the lower tail-coverts buffy-white.

The Black-throated Wheatear occurs in the same localities as *S. isabellinus*, but is perhaps rather more common.

Ædon familiaris, *Mene.*

492*ter*.—Butler, Guzerat; Stray Feathers, Vol. III, p. 476; Murray's Vertebrate Zoology of Sind, p. 163; (*Sylvia familiaris*).

THE GREY-BACKED WARBLER.

Length, 6·5 to 7·5; expanse, 9·75 to 10·75; wing, 3·3 to 3·5; tail, 2·62; tarsus, 1; bill at front, 0·8; bill from gape, 0·9 to 0·95.

Bill, upper mandible and tip of lower a somewhat fleshy but dusky-brown; rest of lower mandible and base yellowish-fleshy; irides dark brown; legs and feet dusky or livid-fleshy.

A broad superciliary stripe, from the nostrils, over the eyes and some little distance behind the eyes, dull white or yellowish-white; a brown stripe from the nostrils to the anterior angle of the eye, continued backwards, though not conspicuous, for some distance from the posterior angle; forehead, crown, occiput, sides of neck, entire back and wings dull earthy-brown, paler and more drabby in some; quills and coverts margined and narrowly tipped with dull yellowish or brownish-white, with usually a slight rufescent tinge on the margins of the primaries; rump brownish-chesnut; upper tail-coverts and tail chesnut; central tail-feathers more or less brown on one or both webs; all the other tail-feathers, with a conspicuous subterminal dark-brown band (which in the outer feathers runs some distance down the outer web), and tipped, the two pairs next the centre narrowly with rufescent, and the other three successively more and more broadly with pure white; chin and throat sordid-white with an indication of a darker line at the angle of the gape; ear-coverts and the rest of the lower parts similar, but tinged with a faint brownish shade usually; wing-lining and axillaries with a very faint yellowish-salmon tint; inner margins of inner webs of quills, on the lower surface, with a decided buffy-tinge.

This is a very uncommon species, and only occurs as an exceptionally rare winter visitant to Sind and Northern Guzerat.

GENUS, Cercomela, *Bon.*

Bill moderate, slender, straight, tolerably curving at the tip and barely notched; rictal bristles small but distinct; wings as in *Saxicola*; second quill a trifle longer; tail somewhat lengthened; feet stout; middle-toe not elongated; hind-toe rather long.

Cercomela melanura, *Rupp.*

493.—Jerdon's Birds of India, Vol. II, p. 133.

THE BLACK-TAILED ROCKCHAT.

Length, 6; wing, 3·12; tail, 2·35; tarsus, 0·88.

Bill blackish; legs black.

Of an uniform ashy-brown tint above, paler on the throat and breast, and passing to whitish below; under tail-coverts white; the tail and upper coverts black.

It is extremely uncertain whether this bird occurs in India or not, but Jerdon says, that " among the drawings of Sir A. Burnes is one of a saxicoline bird, procured in Sind, which Mr. Blyth identifies with Ruppell's bird, which is a native of N. E. Africa and Arabia."

As no other observer has since procured it from thence, it must have been an isolated straggler, that had wandered far from its usual haunts.

Cercomela fusca, *Blyth.*

494.—Jerdon's Birds of India, Vol. II, p. 134; Butler, Guzerat; Stray Feathers, Vol. III, p. 477; Swinhoe and Barnes, Central India; Ibis, p. 125.

THE BROWN ROCKCHAT.

Length, 6·5; expanse, 10·5; wing, 3·5; tail, 2·75; tarsus, 1; bill at gape, 0·8; bill at front, 0·5.

Bill black; irides deep-brown; legs black.

Above light fuscous-brown or rufous-olive, tinged with fawn color on the back; tail dark sepia-brown, obsoletely banded, as seen in a strong light; beneath rufescent-fawn or dull ferruginous.

The Brown Rockchat is very common at Mount Aboo, but does not occur in the plains below; it is also very common at Neemuch, and in the surrounding districts.

It is a permanent resident breeding from March to July or even later, rearing at least two broods in the season. The nest is usually built in holes in rocks, buildings, walls, wells, and banks. Should the site selected not be suitable, they make an embankment of small stones, pellets of dry mud, &c., extending several inches beyond the nest.

The eggs, generally three or four in number, are moderately broad oval in shape, of a pale blue-color, more or less spotted with reddish-brown; these spots occasionally form a nimbus round the large end. They measure 0·82 in length by 0·62 in breadth.

During the time of incubation, and while rearing their young, they are extremely pugnacious, attacking any small bird, squirrel, or lizard that ventures near.

SUB-FAMILY, **Ruticillinæ.**

Bill, slender with tip entire; rictal bristles fairly developed; wings and tail various; tarsi long, slender.

GENUS, **Ruticilla,** *Brehm.*

Bill rather short, straight, slender, slightly notched; rictus nearly smooth; wings moderately long, pointed; first primary about one-third the length of the fourth, fifth and sixth equal and longest; tail moderate, even or slightly rounded; lateral toes nearly equal, hind-toe not much lengthened; claws slender, moderately curved.

Ruticilla rufiventris, *Vieill.*

497.—Jerdon's Birds of India, Vol. II, p. 137; Butler, Guzerat; Stray Feathers, Vol. III, p. 478; Deccan, Stray Feathers, Vol. IX, p. 405; Murray's Vertebrate Zoology of Sind, p. 146; Swinhoe and Barnes, Central India; Ibis, 1885.

THE INDIAN REDSTART.

Length, 6; expanse, 10; wing, 3·5; tail, 2·55; tarsus, 1; bill from gape, 0·6; bill at front, 0·4.

Bill black; irides brown; legs black.

Crown dark ashy-grey; lores, ear-coverts, neck, throat, breast, back and upper wing-coverts, black with greyish edges to the feathers; wings dusky-brown; the primaries margined with pale rufous, the secondaries with dull grey, forming an inconspicuous patch; under wing-coverts, flanks, belly, rump, upper and lower tail-coverts and tail (except half the inner and a little of the outer webs of the two middle tail feathers near the tip, which are brown), bright cinnamon-rufous.

The female is brown above, with the edges of the wings, the abdomen, and under tail-coverts, pale rufous; below, dusky on the throat and breast, changing to clear light rufous on the abdomen and under tail-coverts; rump and tail as in the male.

Mr. Hume, Stray Feathers, Vol. V, p. 36, describes six tolerably distinct stages of plumage, *viz*:—

I. *Winter plumage.*—Black of upper surface entirely veiled

by ashy, rufous-ashy, or brownish-rufous, tips to the feathers. Black of breast more or less ditto.

II. *Early spring stage.*—Tippings of the feathers disappearing first from the breast, next from back, and lastly from the head.

III. *Ante-nuptial stage.*—Whole head, neck, breast and upper breast pure black.

IV. *Nuptial stage.*—Black duller; a greyish-white band across the forehead (dividing off the black of the base of the forehead as a black frontal band), with a grey shade extending backwards on to the crown.

V. *Early autumn stage.*—Broad conspicuous black frontal band; throat, breast, sides of neck, pure black.

Front of head pale blue-grey, growing duller on occiput. Back more or less veiled with grey or rufous-ash tippings.

VI. *Late autumn stage.*—Frontal band not showing out conspicuously; crown and back unicolorous.

Black of breast, &c., more or less veiled with grey or rufous-ashy tippings.

The Indian Redstart is a very common winter visitant to all parts of the district, appearing about the end of September, and leaving towards the end of March, or commencement of April.

GENUS, Larvivora, *Hodgs.*

Bill rather slender, straight, more or less compressed, very feebly notched at the tip, slightly deflected, with the ridge of the upper mandible very slightly elevated between the nostrils, and the gape very feebly bristled; wings moderate, strong; first quill short; third, fourth and fifth quills about equal and longest; tail rather short, and the feathers slightly mucronate at the tip, even, or nearly so; tarsus long, slender, nearly smooth; toes long, slender; claws long, moderately curved, much compressed.

Larvivora superciliaris, *Jerd.*

507.—*Larvivora cyana*, Hodgs.—Jerdon's Birds of India, Vol. II, p. 145; Butler, Deccan; Stray Feathers, Vol. IX, p. 405.

THE BLUE WOODCHAT.

Length, 6; expanse, 10; wing, 3; tail, 2; tarsus, 1·16; bill at front, 0·5.

Bill dusky; irides brown; legs pale fleshy.

Above dusky indigo-blue, with a white superciliary streak; lores and ears black; beneath bright rufous (the feathers all dusky-blue at their bases), albescent towards the vent and under tail-coverts; thigh-coverts cross barred with blue and white.

The female is brown above, white beneath; cheeks, breast and flanks rusty.

The Blue Woodchat is a cold weather visitant to several parts of the Deccan. It is nowhere common.

Genus, Calliope, *Gould.*

Bill of moderate length and strength; wings moderate, first quill very short, second equal to the seventh; tail very slightly rounded; the outer feathers being a little shorter than the penultimate pair; tarsus moderately long, stout; the feet large; hind-toe long; claws long, not much curved.

Calliope camtschatkensis, *Gm.*

512.—Jerdon's Birds of India, Vol. II, p. 150.

THE COMMON RUBY-THROAT.

Length, 6; wing, 3; tail, 2·5; tarsus, 1·12; bill at front, 0·5.

Bill horny-brown; irides dark-brown; legs livid or purplish.

Above olive-brown, beneath dull whitish; a band above and below the eyes whitish; intermediate space black; feathers of the throat somewhat scaly and stiff, light scarlet or ruby-red, with silvery edges, more or less surrounded with black; the breast ashy, flanks bright olive-brown, and belly whitish; axillaries slightly rufescent.

The female has in general no trace of the ruby-throat, which is whitish, and the lores brown; but some old females have a tinge of the ruby color.

Jerdon states that "once on boardship, a little south of Bombay, one took refuge in the month of November." This is the only record of the occurrence of the Common Ruby-throat within our limits.

Genus, Cyanecula, *Brehm.*

Bill rather short, slightly conic, straight; wings moderate; third and fourth quills equal and longest; fifth a little shorter; second equal to sixth; tail rather short, nearly even; tarsus moderately long; claws very slightly curved.

Cyanecula suecica, *Lin.*

514.—Jerdon's Birds of India, Vol. II, p. 152; Butler, Guzerat; Stray Feathers, Vol. III, p. 478; Deccan, Stray Feathers, Vol. IX, p. 405; Murray's Vertebrate Zoology of Sind, p. 147; Swinhoe and Barnes, Central India; Ibis, 1885, p. 125.

THE INDIAN BLUE-THROAT.

Length, 6·2; expanse, 9·25; wing, 3; tail, 2·25; tarsus, 1; bill at front, 0·7.

Bill dusky-horn; gape yellow; irides dark-brown; legs brownish.

Above pale olive-brown, the feathers of the crown slightly centred darker, and with a whitish supercilium; lower parts whitish; the under tail-coverts more or less tinged with rufescent; throat and breast bright shiny azure-blue, the former generally mingled with whitish along the middle, and having a large ferruginous spot in front of the neck; below, and bordering the azure of the breast, is a narrow blackish band, then a narrow whitish band, and below this again a broad ferruginous band; the upper tail-coverts are brown, mingled with ferruginous; tail rufous, the two centre feathers, and the tips of all the others, dark-brown.

Young males have much less blue on the throat, which is often confined to a moustachial streak on each side and a comparatively narrow gorget; they have scarcely any tinge of ferruginous on the throat and breast, the former being chiefly of a dull white.

The females have commonly the throat and foreneck dull white, encircled with dusky spots, which are more developed in old females, and these have sometimes a tolerably broad dusky gorget, mingled with a little blue.

The Indian Blue-throat is a fairly common cold weather visitant to all portions of the district, particularly affecting swampy ground.

Sub-family, Calamoherpinæ.

Bill rather large, depressed and broad at the base; rictal bristles moderately developed; tail rounded; winglet minute.

Genus, Acrocephalus.

Wing moderately long; third and fourth quills longest; rictal bristles short, a few only; claws long; hind-claw curved.

Acrocephalus stentorius, *Hemp & Ehr.*

515.—*Acrocephalus brunnescens*, Jerd.—Jerdon's Birds of India, Vol. II, p. 154; Butler, Guzerat; Stray Feathers, Vol. III, p. 478; Deccan, Stray Feathers, Vol. IX, p. 405; Murray's Vertebrate Zoology of Sind, p. 148; Swinhoe and Barnes, Central India; Ibis, 1885, p. 125.

THE LARGE REED WARBLER.

Length, 8·5; expanse, 10·6; wing, 3·62; tail, 3·25; tarsus, 1·2; bill at front, 0·7.

Bill dark-brown, fleshy at base beneath; irides dull greenish-yellow; legs horny-brown.

Above light olive-brown, darkest on the wings and tail, and lightest on the rump; beneath, and eye-brow, with a tinge of olive-yellow; the chin pure white; wings and tail beneath cinereous; plumage soft and silky.

The Large Reed Warbler is a cold weather visitant to the Deccan, Guzerat and Rajputana portions of our limits, but in Sind it would appear to be a permanent resident, breeding about August.

Acrocephalus dumetorum, *Bly.*

516.—Jerdon's Birds of India, Vol. II, p. 155; Butler, Guzerat;

Stray Feathers, Vol. III, p. 479; Deccan, Stray Feathers, Vol. IX, p. 405; Murray's Vertebrate Zoology of Sind, p. 148.

THE LESSER REED WARBLER.

Length, 6; wing, 2·4; tarsus, 0·9; bill at front, 0·4.

Bill dusky, fleshy at base beneath; irides yellow-brown; legs red-brown.

Above olive-brown, with a pale supercilium; beneath whitish-tinged with pale earthy-brown.

The Lesser Reed Warbler occurs during the winter months in many parts of the district; it is not common, and appears to be locally distributed.

Acrocephalus agricolus, *Jerdon.*

517.—Jerdon's Birds of India, Vol. II, p. 156; Butler, Deccan; Stray Feathers, Vol. IX, p. 406; Murray's Vertebrate Zoology of Sind, p. 149.

THE PADDY FIELD WARBLER.

Length, 5·25; wing, 2·25; tail, 2·25; tarsus, 0·9; bill at front, 0·4.

Bill brown, paler beneath; irides yellow-brown; legs brown.

Above pale rufous-brown, brightest on the rump; wings brown, edged with rufous; tail dull brown; beneath whitish, tinged with fulvous, and brownish on the flanks.

The Paddy Field Warbler occurs as a cold weather visitant to Sind; it is also not uncommon at the same season near Belgaum.

Lusciniola melanopogon, *Tem.*

518*bis.*—Murray's Vertebrate Zoology of Sind, p. 149.

THE MOUSTACHED GRASS WARBLER.

Length, 5·75; expanse, 7·4; wing, 2·45; tail, 2·1; tarsus, 0·85; bill at front, 0·45.

Bill dark-brown, almost black, paler on lower mandible; irides brown to pale-brown; legs dusky-brown, soles pale-yellowish.

A broad conspicuous white stripe from the nostrils over the eyes and ear-coverts; a dark-brown stripe from in front of under and through the eyes, enveloping the upper portion of the ear-coverts, darker in the males than the females; the chin, throat, and lower parts, including the lower tail-coverts, white, faintly tinged rufescent on the breast, more strongly so on the flanks about the vent, and, in some specimens, the lower tail-coverts also; the sides, both of the neck and body, tinged with greyish, or in some olivaceous-brown; the forehead, crown, occiput, and nape, very dark-brown, the feathers tipped and margined with a paler yellowish olive-brown; in some specimens, these tippings entirely obscure the bases, except on a narrow line immediately above the white eye-streak; in others, these parts appear to be very dark-brown, regularly striated with the paler olive-brown, while in some the tippings are almost entirely wanting; the back, scapulars, rump, and upper tail-coverts, the same yellowish olive-brown, becoming more rufescent on the lower back, rump and upper tail-coverts; the feathers of the centre of the back with more or less conspicuous dark central shaft streaks.

In some birds the whole back seems regularly striated with dark lines, in others only a few faint darker streaks are visible in the very centre of the back; in some, again, the lower back is much more decidedly rufous. The wings are hair-brown; the primaries very narrowly margined, and tipped on the outer webs, paler; the secondaries and tertiaries and most of the coverts more distinctly margined with a sort of rufescent-olive; the wing-lining and axillaries pure, or nearly pure white; tail feathers somewhat pale hair-brown, obscurely margined with rufescent-olive; the shafts dull white below.

The Moustached Grass Warbler is a cold weather visitant to Sind; it does not occur elsewhere within our limits.

Lusciniola neglectus, *Hume.*

Murray's Vertebrate Zoology of Sind, p. 150.

HUME'S GRASS WARBLER.

Length, 4 to 4·2; expanse, 6·25 to 6·4; tail from vent, 1·4 to 1·6; wing, barely 2 to 2·15; bill at front, 0·27 to 0·3; tarsus, 0·68 to 0 71.

Bill black, paler or horny-greenish in some at base of lower mandible; irides brown; legs and feet black.

The lores are brownish-white; a comparatively pure and very narrow white streak from the nostrils over the lores and eyes, but not beyond.

The whole upper surface is dull earthy-brown, with, in some, a faintly olivaceous-rufescent tinge on the back, most conspicuous on the rump; the quills and tail are a moderately dark hair-brown, narrowly margined on the outer webs with pale olivaceous-brown, much the same color as the upper parts; the secondaries are very narrowly margined at the tips with albescent, tinged with very pale fulvous-fawn, or earthy-brown, more strongly so in some specimens than in others; the sides and flanks are pale earthy-brown; the wing-lining and axillaries are white, with at times the faintest possible fulvous or brownish tinge.

Hume's Grass Warbler, according to Murray, is a winter visitant to Sind, chiefly affecting acacia groves.

GENUS, Cettia, *Bon.*

Tail rounded, lateral tail feathers short; tarsi robust, scutellated in front.

Cettia cetti, *Marm.*

518*ter.*—Murray's Vertebrate Zoology of Sind, p. 151.

CETTI'S BUSH WARBLER.

Length, 5·8 to 6·5; expanse, 7·5 to 8·4; wing, 2·5 to 2·8; tail, 2·4 to 3; tarsus, 0·8; bill at front, 0·4 to 0·5.

Bill dark horny-brown, but paler on lower mandible; irides brown; legs and feet pale brown or fleshy-brown.

A spot in front of the eyes dusky; a streak from the nostrils over the eye and a circle round the eye fulvous-white; the forehead, crown, and whole upper surface, a warm rufous or ferruginous-brown, more rufous on the rump and upper tail-coverts; the quills and tail hair-brown, margined with rufescent-olive; ear-coverts, sides of neck, body, flanks and vent-feathers, a pale dull greyish or earthy-brown; chin, throat, breast, and abdomen white; lower tail-coverts slighly rufous-brown (webs very lax and much disunited), narrowly tipped with white; axillaries and wing-lining slightly greyish white; the edge of the wing just above the base of the primaries is white; in some few specimens the eye-streak extends beyond the eye, above more than half of the ear-coverts, but in most it ceases just beyond the posterior angle of the eye.

Cetti's Bush Warbler was discovered by Mr. Hume in the mangrove swamps in the Kurrachee Harbour. I am not aware of its having been found anywhere else within our limits.

GENUS, **Locustella,** *Gould.*

Bill of moderate length, slender, straight, compresssd, barely deflected at the tip, which is slightly notched; wings long, with the first quill minute; second nearly equal to the third, which is longest; tail moderate, rounded, or graduated; hind-claw very long, much curved.

Locustella hendersoni, *Cass.*

520.—Jerdon's Birds of India, Vol. II, p. 159; Butler, Guzerat; Stray Feathers, Vol. III, p. 479; Deccan, Stray Feathers, Vol. IX, p. 406.

THE STREAKED REED WARBLER.

Length, 5·5; wing, 2·25; tail, 2·12.

Bill dusky above, paler beneath; irides, hazel; legs fleshy-brown.

Above pale olive-brown, all the feathers centred dark-brown; tail uniform brown, tipped pale, especially as seen from below; beneath white, tinged with earthy-brown on the neck, breast, and flanks; lower tail-coverts fulvescent-white, with narrow longitudinal striæ. In the spring moult the lower plumage is at first a somewhat rich yellow.

The Streaked Wren Warbler occurs sparingly as a seasonal visitant in the neighbourhood of Belgaum, Deesa and Mhow, and must occur in other suitable localities.

It has not been recorded from Sind.

SUB-FAMILY, Drymoicinæ.

Bill moderately long and compressed; wings short, rounded; tail long, more or less graduated; legs and feet moderately strong.

GENUS, Orthotomus, *Horsfield.*

Bill long, slender, rather wide at the base, nearly entire, straight, very slightly deflexed at the tip; a few weak rictal bristles; wing short, feeble, much rounded; fifth and sixth quills equal and longest; tail narrow, feeble, typically short and rounded or graduated, the two centre feathers elongated in some; tarsus moderately long, stout; feet short; hind-toe short; claws moderately curved, compressed.

Orthotomus sutorius, *Forst.*

530.—*Orthotomus longicauda*, Gm.—Jerdon's Birds of India, Vol. II, p. 165; Butler, Guzerat; Stray Feathers, Vol. III, p. 479; Deccan, Stray Feathers, Vol. IX, p. 406; Murray's Vertebrate Zoology of Sind, p. 151; *Sutoria sutoria*, Forst.; Swinhoe and Barnes, Central India; Ibis, 1885, p. 126.

THE INDIAN TAILOR BIRD.
Phutki, Hin.

Length, ♂, 6·5; ♀, 5; expanse, 5 to 6; wing, 1·9; tail, ♂ 3·5, ♀ 2; tarsus, 0·9; bill at front, 0·5; bill at gape, 0·65.

Bill dark horny above, pale-fleshy beneath; irides reddish-yellow or amber; legs fleshy.

Crown rufous; nape somewhat cinereous, with a tinge of rufous; back, scapulars, rump, and upper tail-coverts, yellowish olive-green; wings brown, edged with green; tail narrow, light brown with a green tinge, and the outer feathers on each side with a narrow white tip; beneath white, with a concealed black spot on each side of the throat, formed by the bases of some of the feathers, and only seen at times.

There are four dark-brown hairs arising from the nape, two on each side.

The Tailor Bird is a common permanent resident throughout the district, breeding from the end of June to August. The nests are rather hard to find, although during the time the hen is sitting on the eggs, the cock keeps up a pleasant "tweet" "tweet" on a neighbouring bough, and though one knows that a nest is somewhere near at hand, it requires a careful and persevering search to find it.

When the bird chooses a leaf sufficiently large, it sews the opposite edges together, and in the cavity thus formed, it makes a soft nest of cotton, with a few hairs, just enough to keep it in shape; at times two or more leaves are incorporated into the nest. They lay three (occasionally four) eggs of a rather elongated oval shape, pointed at one end, reddish-white in color, or, I should say, white, suffused with a reddish tinge, blotched, streaked or spotted with red-brown; these markings sometimes form a zone at the large end. Occasionally the eggs are of a greenish-white colour; they measure 0·64 inches in length, by 0·45 in breadth.

GENUS, Prinia, *Horsfield.*

Bill moderately long, very slender, straight, entire; rictal bristles distinct; tail much graduated, rather long, of ten or twelve feathers; feet much as in *Orthotomus*.

Prinia flaviventris, *Deless.*

532.—Jerdon's Birds of India, Vol. II, p. 169; Murray's Vertebrate Zoology of Sind, p. 152.

THE YELLOW-BELLIED WREN WARBLER.

Length, 5·25; expanse, 6·3; wing, 1·87; tail, 2·9; tarsus, 0·75; bill at front, 0·5.

Bill black, fleshy at base beneath; irides reddish-yellow; legs deep yellow.

Head, with lores and ear-coverts, dark ashy; back, wings, and tail, dull olive-green; the quills dusky-brown; chin, throat, and breast, white; the abdomen, vent, and under tail-coverts, bright canary-yellow.

The Yellow-bellied Wren Warbler is a permanent resident in Sind, where it breeds from June to September. The nest is tailor-bird like, but the eggs are bright brick-red without spots.

It has not been recorded from any other portion of the district.

Prinia adamsi, *Jerdon.*

533.—Jerdon's Birds of India, Vol. II, p. 170; Butler, Deccan; Stray Feathers, Vol. IX, p. 406.

THE WHITE-BELLIED WREN WARBLER.

Bill black; legs yellow.

Above greenish, the tail tipped with white; cheeks, throat, and breast, whitish-yellow; belly and vent white, tinged with yellow; tail long, graduated; legs long.

The White-bellied Wren Warbler is not, I believe, a good species. Dr. Adams stated that he found it at Poona in the corn-fields. No one else seems ever to have met with it.

Prinia socialis, *Sykes.*

534.—Jerdon's Birds of India, Vol. II, p. 170; Butler, Guzerat, Stray Feathers, Vol. III, p. 479; Deccan, Stray Feathers; Vol. IX, p. 406.

THE DARK-ASHY WREN WARBLER.

Length, 5·25; expanse, 6; wings, 2; tail, 2·8; tarsus, 0·8; bill at front, 0·45; bill at gape, 0·5.

Bill black; irides orange-buff; legs deep yellow.

Head and back dark ashy; quills and tail reddish-brown, the latter with a dusky band near the tip, and the outer feathers with a small white tip; beneath rufescent-whitish, the flanks rufous.

With the exception of Sind, the Dark-ashy Wren Warbler is a common permanent resident throughout the region, breeding during the monsoons; its nest is very similar to that of the true tailor-bird. The eggs, generally four in number, are bright brick-red in color, generally a shade darker at the larger end.

They measure 0·64 inches in length by about 0·47 in breadth.

Prinia stewarti, *Blyth.*

535.—Jerdon's Birds of India, Vol. II, p. 171; *Burnesia socialis stewarti*, Sykes.—Swinhoe and Barnes, Central India; Ibis, 1885, p. 126.

STEWART'S WREN WARBLER.

Length, 5·2; expanse, 5·5; wing, 1·8; tail, 2·75; tarsus, 0·75; bill at front, 0·45.

Bill black; irides buff; legs deep-yellow.

Above dark-ashy, brown on the wings and rufescent on the tail, with a faint subterminal dark band (as seen from above); throat white; the rest of the body beneath pale rufescent, darker on the flanks, and rusty on the vent and under tail-coverts.

Stewart's Wren Warbler only occurs within our limits in the Mhow Division (which includes Neemuch), it being replaced elsewhere by the closely allied, even if distinct, *P. socialis*, Both forms occur at Neemuch.

It is a permanent resident breeding from the commencement of July to the end of August, and even later. The nest is similar to that of the tailor-bird, but is not quite so neatly made, grass and fibres being used in addition to hair and cotton. The eggs are usually four in number, oval in shape, and of a bright brick-red or chesnut color, with sometimes a darker shade at the larger end, forming an ill-defined cap or zone.

They are highly glossy, and measure about 0·62 inches in length by about 0·46 in breadth.

Prinia gracilis, *Franklin.*

536.—Jerdon's Birds of India, Vol. II, p. 173; Butler, Guzerat; Stray Feathers, Vol. III, p. 480; Deccan, Stray Feathers, Vol. IX, p. 406.

FRANKLIN'S WREN WARBLER.

Length, 4·5; expanse, 5·75; wing, 1·87; tail, 2; tarsus, 0·75; bill at front, 0·3; bill from gape, 0·58.

Bill black; irides deep amber; legs fleshy-yellow.

Slightly rufescent-olive above, tinged greyer on the head and neck; the wing-feathers dusky, edged externally with rufous-brown; under parts silky-white, tinged with yellowish-fulvous on the flanks, and faintly on the sides of the neck; tail brown, albescent-greyish beneath, with a subterminal dark band and whitish tips, most conspicuous on the under surface.

Franklin's Wren Warbler is a common permanent resident all along the Sahyadri Range and in the forests adjoining; it also occurs sparingly on Mount Aboo, and is not uncommon on the Vindhian hills near Mhow. It does not occur in the Sind District.

Prinia hodgsoni, *Blyth.*

538.—Jerdon's Birds of India, Vol. II, p. 173; Butler, Guzerat; Stray Feathers, Vol. III, p. 480; Deccan, Stray Feathers, Vol. IX, p. 406.

The Malabar Wren Warbler.

Length, 4; wing, 1·8; tail, 1·87; tarsus, 0·7; bill at front, 0·4.

Bill black; irides buff; legs yellow.

Above dark ashy-grey, brownish on the wings and tail, the latter with a subterminal dark band, tipped white on the outer feathers; beneath white, slightly tinged with fulvescent, greyish on the edge of the neck and breast.

The Malabar Wren Warbler is only doubtfully distinct from *P. gracilis*; it is thought to be the latter in breeding plumage. If distinct it occurs in precisely the same localities.

Genus, Cisticola, *Lesson.*

Bill rather short, slender, gently curving from the middle, entire at tip; wings short, ample; first quill small, third, fourth and fifth equal and longest, second equal to seventh, shorter than the sixth; tail of twelve feathers, somewhat rounded, short; tarsus long; feet rather large with the lateral toes nearly equal and the hind-toe long; the claws lengthened, especially the hind one only slightly curved.

Cisticola cursitans, *Frankl.*

539.—*Cisticola schœnicola*, Bonaparte.—Jerdon's Birds of India, Vol. II, p. 174; Butler, Guzerat; Stray Feathers, Vol. III, p. 481; Deccan, Stray Feathers, Vol. IX, p. 407; Murray's Vertebrate Zoology of Sind, p. 152.

The Rufous Grass Warbler.

Length, 4·5; wing, 2·12; tail, 1·86; tarsus, 0·75.

Bill dusky-brown above, fleshy beneath; irides pale olive-brown.

Above rufous-brown, all the feathers broadly centred dark-brown; rump plain rufous; quills dusky, narrowly edged with brown; tail with the two central feathers pale brown, darker in the middle, and pale tipped; the others all dark-brown, deeper towards the end, and with a broad whitish tip; plumage beneath rufescent-white, nearly pure white on the chin and throat, and more rufescent on the flanks; tail beneath cinereous at the base, then pale rufous, with a black bar, and a broad white tip, in some uniform dusky-cinereous.

The Rufous Grass Warbler is a common permanent resident in most portions of our limits, and breeds during the monsoon. It makes a long tubular nest, composed of soft white vegetable down, in the centre of a clump of grass, a short distance only from the ground. The eggs, usually five in number, are oval in shape, white or greenish-white in color, thickly speckled with tiny spots of reddish-brown. These spots often show a tendency to form a zone around the larger end.

They measure 0·58 in length by 0·46 in breadth.

Genus, **Drymoipus**, *Bonap.*

(*Drymœca.*)

Bill short or of moderate length, nearly entire, rather deep at the base; culmen moderately curving; rictus bristled; wings very short and rounded; the first three quills nearly equal, graduated, fourth and fifth longest; tail graduated, long, of ten feathers, the feathers obtuse; tarsus long; feet moderate; claws moderately curved.

Drymoipus inornata, *Sykes.*

(*Drymœca.*)

543.—Jerdon's Birds of India, Vol. II, p. 178; 543*bis.*—*D. terricolor*, Hume; Butler, Guzerat; Stray Feathers, Vol. III, p. 481; Deccan, Stray Feathers, Vol. IX, p. 407; Murray's Vertebrate Zoology of Sind, p. 153; *Prinia inornata*, Sykes; Swinhoe and Barnes, Central India; Ibis, 1885, p. 126.

The Common Wren Warbler.

Length, 5 to 5·5; wing, 1·75 to 1·8; tail, 2·75; tarsus, 0·8, bill at front, 0·4.

Bill dusky-brown above, yellowish or fleshy at the base beneath; irides brownish-yellow; legs fleshy-yellow.

Head and back greyish-brown, with an olivaceous tinge on the head and hind-neck; wings brown, edged pale rufous; tail rufous or brownish, with a terminal dark spot, and the centre tail-feathers obsoletely banded; a whitish supercilium and whitish lores and chin; beneath whitish, with a faint fulvescent tinge; thighs pale fulvescent-brown.

It is now generally admitted by ornithologists that the birds described by Dr. Jerdon under Nos. 543 and 544, *viz.*, *D. inornata* and *D. longicaudatus* are the same in different phases of plumage, the principal difference being the longer tail of the latter.

The Common or Earth-brown Wren Warbler is a permanent

resident throughout the distrit, breeding during July and August; it usually constructs a rather pretty nest, composed of fine strips torn from blades of green grass which are plaited together like those of the Baya, but the strips are much finer and the nest altogether neater; it is usually fastened to the thorny twigs of acacia bushes, at no great height from the ground, and the shape depends largely on the position of these twigs. According to my experience the nest is never lined.

Another type of nest is composed of the same material, but is much coarser, and more loosely woven.

Nests of this latter description are built in clumps of sarpat, guinea, or other rank-growing grass, or even in standing corn; they are purse-shaped, with the entrance on one side, the opposite side being prolonged and projecting over, so as to form a canopy. The eggs, four or five in number, are moderately long ovals, of a glossy pale greenish-blue color, boldly spotted and blotched with chocolate and reddish-brown, with a delicate tracery of interlaced hair-like lines at the larger end, but occasionally these lines are absent, the small end being usually spotless. The ground color is also subject to variation, eggs having been taken of a dull olive-green tint, and still more rarely of a clear reddish-white. They measure 0·61 inches in length by 0·45 in breadth. *D. inornata* also equals *D. terricolor.*

Drymoipus rufescens, *Hume.*

544*bis.*—Butler, Guzerat; Stray Feathers, Vol. III, p. 484; Deccan, Stray Feathers, Vol. IX, p. 407.

THE GREAT RUFOUS WREN WARBLER.

Length, 6·45 to 7·2; expanse, 7·1 to 8; tail, 3·3 to 3·9; wing, 2·3; tarsus, 0·9 to 0·95; bill at front, 0·5 to 0·53.

Bill blackish-horny, fleshy at base of lower mandible; irides from brown to deep yellow; legs fleshy to reddish-brown.

Whole upper surface, including tail, and greater median-coverts, tertiaries, and outer webs of primaries and secondaries, rich rufous-brown in full plumage, dull, or earthy-brown, more or less tinged or overlaid with rufous in young birds; tail very distinctly and finely, but obsoletely barred, much less distinctly however in some specimens than in others; all the feathers, except the central ones, narrowly tipped with fulvous-white, with a more or less distinct penultimate dusky bar; the young birds with a good deal of white on the inner webs of the lateral feathers, which is entirely wanting in adults.

In some of the adults, the dark subterminal bar becomes almost obsolete; lores and a stripe over the eye fulvous white; ear-coverts, sides of neck, and breast, and sometimes some of the lesser wing-coverts about the carpal joint, a greenish or greyish-brown; the ear-coverts at times more or less mottled with fulvous-white; lower parts pale fulvous, or buffy, albescent on the chin and throat and middle of abdomen, tinged at times on the breast with grey, more purely buff on lower tail-coverts and wing-lining, and more rufescent on tibial plumes; inner webs of primaries and secondaries hair-brown. The young birds are much paler and more albescent on the lower surface.

The Great Rufous Wren Warbler occurs at Mahableshwar, Ratnagiri, and probably all along the Sahyadri Range; it is not uncommon at Aboo and Deesa. It has not been recorded from any other portion of our limits. *Drymoipus rufescens* equals *D. insignis* in winter plumage.

Drymoipus sylvaticus, *Jerdon.*

545.—Jerdon's Birds of India, Vol. II, p. 181.

THE JUNGLE WREN WARBLER.

Length, 6; wing, 2·4; tail, 2·75; tarsus, 1.

Bill black; irides orange buff; legs dark fleshy-yellow.

Above olive-brown; superciliary streak and beneath white, tinged throughout with yellowish; tail obsoletely barred, with a narrow subterminal dark band, tipped with white, except on the central tail-feathers.

The Jungle Wren Warbler occurs in Central India and Khandeish; it has not been recorded from either the Deccan, Guzerat, or Sind. I found it breeding near Neemuch in July; the nest was purse-shaped, composed of rough grass, and contained three fresh eggs, pale greenish-white in color, thickly spotted with rusty-red, the spots much more dense at the larger end. Mr. Davidson found them to be far from uncommon in Khandeish, and he informs me that the number of eggs is usually four and occasionally five.

Drymoipus neglectus, *Jerdon.*

546.—Jerdon's Birds of India, Vol. II, p. 182; Butler, Deccan; Stray Feathers, Vol. IX, p. 407.

THE ALLIED WREN WARBLER.

Length, 6; wing, 2·4; tail, 2·5 to 3; bill at front, 0·4; tarsus, 0·9.

Bill dusky, fleshy beneath; irides amber; legs dingy-fleshy.

Plumage greenish ashy-brown, but with a decided tinge of rufous throughout; beneath whitish, strongly tinged with olive-rufous; tail very faintly barred.

A single specimen was obtained in Ratnagiri, but Jerdon states it to be common at and near Mhow. I did not meet with it. *D. neglectus* probably equals *D. sylvaticus.*

GENUS, Blandfordius, *Hume.*

Tail of 12 feathers; wings, with the fifth, sixth, and seventh quills, equal and longest; fourth equal to eighth; third nearly equal to ninth.

Blandfordius striatulus, *Hume.*

549*quint.*—Stray Feathers, Vol. I, p. 300; Murray's Vertebrate Zoology of Sind, p. 153.

Length, 6; wing, 1·9; tail, 2·75; bill at front, 0·45; tarsus, 0·7. Bill brown, pale fleshy on lower mandible; legs pale fleshy.

An obscure rufous-white streak from the nostrils to the upper part of the eye; the whole upper parts dull greyish olive-brown (the grey preponderating on the head); all the feathers, except those of the upper tail-coverts, conspicuously centred with dark-brown; wings pale hair-brown, all the feathers margined with rufescent-olive; tail-feathers a sort of olive-brown; the feathers with conspicuously darker, very stiff looking and glistening shafts; all the feathers obsoletely transversely rayed, the central ones most strongly so; all but the central ones narrowly tipped with fulvous-white, and with an obscure subterminal dark band; on the under surface the shafts are white; the ear-coverts mingled fulvous and pale rufous-brown, the sides of the neck streaked like the back; on either side of the throat descends from the gape for about half an inch a band of tiny feathers, white, with minute dark centres, so as to produce the appearance of two or three irregular rows of little spots on each side of the throat; the chin and the centre of the throat, breast, and abdomen, white, tinged buffy on the two latter, and with all the feathers of the throat and breast very faintly and narrowly tipped with brown, so as to produce the appearance of a number of narrow faint transverse bars; the flanks, sides, vent, and lower tail-coverts are tinged with dull olive-brown, mingled with fulvous-buff; the tibial plumes are fulvous-buff; the wing-lining is buffy-white, and so are the inner margins of the inner webs of the quills as seen from below.

The specimen, of which the above is a description, was shot by Mr. Blandford at Kurrachee.

Burnesia gracilis, *Rupp.*

550.—*Burnesia lepida*, Blyth.—Jerdon's Birds of India, Vol. II, p. 185; Butler, Guzerat; Stray Feathers, Vol. III, p. 485; Murray's Vertebrate Zoology of Sind, p. 154.

THE STREAKED WREN WARBLER.

Length, 5·25; wing, 1·75; expanse, 5·5; tail, 0·6; bill at front, 0·4.

Bill plumbeous, fleshy beneath; irides light yellowish-brown; legs pale fleshy-yellow.

General color light olive-grey above, each feather having a medial dusky streak, broader on those of the crown and back; wings light dusky-brown; the feathers margined with olive-grey, and the tail throughout distinctly, but obsoletely, banded above with narrow transverse duskyish lines; below pale, with whitish tips and a subterminal dusky band, or rather spot, on the inner web of each feather; the under parts throughout are greyish-white; the lores, and a slight supercilium, of the same hue.

The Streaked Wren Warbler is a common permanent resident in Sind, frequenting the dense tamarisk thickets that occur so commonly on the *dhunds;* it is somewhat rare in Guzerat, and does not occur at all in the Deccan. It breeds from May to September; the nest, built in low dense tamarisk bushes, is of an oval shape with the entrance at one side near the top, and is composed of small dry tamarisk twigs and fine grass, well lined with vegetable down. The eggs, three in number, are greenish-white in color, profusely streaked, speckled, and spotted with bright brownish-red. The spots are usually more dense at the large end where they not infrequently form au imperfect zone. In shape they are broad ovals, pointed at one end, and measure 0·55 inches in length by about 0·42 in breadth.

Scotocerca inquieta, *Rupp.*

550*bis.*—Murray's Vertebrate Zoology of Sind, p. 154.

THE STREAKED SCRUB WARBLER.

Length, 4·5 to 4·75; expanse, 6·25; wing, 1·9 to 2; tail, 2 to 2·25; tarsus, 0·75 to 0·8; bill at front, 0·35; bill at gape, 0·46.

Bill dark brown, dull brownish-orange at base beneath; irides brownish; legs yellowish-brown.

Above, light brownish-grey, streaked on the head as far as the shoulders, with dark brown narrow-streaks; a pale rufous-brown broad supercilium; the cheeks and ear-coverts are also of this color, which extends down the sides of the neck and breast, becoming very pale and diluted under the wings and on the flanks; wings light brown, the edges of quills and coverts greyish; tail a very much darker or rather blackish-brown; the outer feather on each side is rather lighter, and is tipped with white; the tail-feathers are cross rayed, particularly the outer ones; lower surface of body, except sides of neck, breast and flanks, white, with narrow brown streaks from chin to upper breast; lining of wing, and ridge of the same, reddish-white.

Within our limits the Striated Scrub Warbler has only been procured on the hills that divide Sind from Khelat. It is probable that they are permanent residents, as they breed freely in Southern Afghanistan, commencing about the end of March. The nest is globular in shape, not unlike that of *F. buchanani*, but is somewhat larger; it is usually built in stunted bushes, not more than two feet from the ground. It is well lined with feathers and fine grass, the outer portion being composed of fibres and coarse grass. The maximum number of eggs is six, but five incubated ones are occasionally met with; they are oval in shape, white, with a pinkish tinge when fresh, very minutely spotted and freckled with bright red.

These spots are usually more dense at the large end, but frequently they are speckled equally over the whole surface.

They average 0·64 inches in length by about 0·49 in breadth.

GENUS, Franklinia, *Blyth.*

Bill stout, compressed, deep; culmen moderately curved towards the tip; wings short; tail broad, moderately lengthened and graduated, of twelve feathers, white tipped; tarsi and feet stout.

Franklinia buchanani, *Blyth.*

551.—Jerdon's Birds of India, Vol. II, p. 186; Butler, Guzerat; Stray Feathers, Vol. III, p. 486; Deccan, Stray Feathers, Vol. IX, p. 407; Murray's Vertebrate Zoology of Sind, p. 155; *Cisticola buchanani,* Blyth; Swinhoe and Barnes, Central India; Ibis, 1885, p. 126.

THE RUFOUS-FRONTED WREN WARBLER.

Length, 5·25; expanse, 6·7; wing, 2·2; tail, 2·2; tarsus, 0·9; bill at front, 0·4.

Bill brown, yellowish beneath; irides pale orange-buff; legs fleshy.

Forehead and head pale rufous; plumage above greenish-ashy, beneath white; tail brown, all the feathers, except the two central ones, broadly terminated by white, more broadly so on the outermost feathers.

The Rufous-fronted Wren Warbler is a common permanent resident in Sind and Guzerat, and is not uncommon in Rajputana, but with the exception of Nuggur appears to be altogether absent from the Deccan. It breeds from June to August, building a rather loose, ragged, purse-shaped nest, composed of grass, lined with vegetable down, and is usually placed in a low thorny bush, generally ber or scrub. The eggs, four or five in number, are of a slightly elongated oval shape, and are white in color, thickly spotted and speckled with dingy or purplish-red. In most of the eggs the markings are densest at the large end, and they occasionally form a more or less well defined zone or cap. They average 0·62 inches in length by about 0·48 in breadth.

SUB-FAMILY, Phylloscopinæ.

Mostly of small size; plumage more or less green above, bill in some slightly widened and depressed; wings moderate, or rather long; tail moderate or short; tarsus moderate; feet arboreal.

GENUS, Hypolais, *Brehm.*

Bill slender, wide basally; rictal bristles few; wings moderate ; bastard primary extending beyond or shorter than the primary coverts ; third and fourth quills longest ; tail even or rounded.

Hypolais rama, *Sykes.*

553.—*Phyllopneuste rama,* Sykes.—Jerdon's Birds of India, Vol. II, p. 189 ; Butler, Guzerat ; Stray Feathers, Vol. III, p. 486 ; Deccan, Stray Feathers, Vol. IX, p. 407 ; Murray's Vertebrate Zoology of Sind, p. 157 ; Swinhoe and Barnes, Central India ; Ibis, 1885, p. 126.

SYKES' TREE WARBLER.

Length, 5 ; expanse, 7·5 ; wing, 2·5 ; tail, 2 ; tarsus, 0·75 ; bill at front, 0·4.

Bill dusky, fleshy at base below ; irides dark-brown ; legs light brown.

Above, uniform light greyish-brown ; below pale or albescent, passing into white on the chin, middle of belly, and vent ; lores continued as a slight streak passing over the eye, and the orbital feathers pale.

Sykes' Tree Warbler occurs more or less commonly in all parts of the Presidency. In Sind it is a permanent resident, breeding from March to July. The nest is placed in the centre of a dense stunted tamarisk or other bush, and is composed externally of coarse grass, lined with soft sedges and finer grass. The eggs, four in number, are broadish ovals, white, with brown spots and hair-like lines twined around the large end. They average 0·61 inches in length by 0·49 in breadth.

Hypolais caligata, *Eversm.*

553*bis.*—Murray's Vertebrate Zoology of Sind, p. 158 ; Butler, Deccan ; Stray Feathers, Vol. IX, p. 407.

THE BOOTED TREE WARBLER.

Length, 4·5 to 5 ; expanse, 6·5 to 7 ; wing, 2·22 to 2·32 ; tail, 1·9 to 2·1 ; tarsus, 0·8 ; bill at front, 0·35 to 0·39 ; bill from gape 0·55 to 0·62.

Bill, upper mandible dark-brown, with the edges light ; lower mandible flesh-colored, rather dusky towards the tip ; irides hazel-brown ; legs and feet fleshy-grey, in some tinged yellowish, expecially on the soles, in some glaucous.

Feathers of the head, nape, back, and scapulars, lax hair-brown, tinged towards the margins with a paler, slightly rufous or fulvous-brown (the whole in some specimens with a faint shade of olive) ; rump paler and rather more rufous in tone ; upper tail-coverts hair-brown, with lighter fulvous-brown edges ; tail dark-brown, all but the two outermost rectrices very narrowly margined with pale fulvous or greyish-white ; outermost feather on each side, with the whole of the outer web, dull or greyish-white ; tips and internal margin also greyish-white ; rectrices next to the outermost similar, but with less white on the outer webs and more on the tips.

A conspicuous superciliary streak from the nostril extending over the eye to the ear-coverts of a pale buff, or rich cream-color; lores, cheeks, and ear-coverts the same as the crown of the head, but of a lighter shade; the lower parts buffy, varying in shade and in warmth of tone in different specimens, but always palest, and in some almost white on the chin, the middle of the abdomen, the vent and lower tail-coverts; sides and flanks slightly infuscated; axillaries, wing-lining and edge of wing from carpal-joint, cream-colored varying in warmth of tinge in different specimens; lower surface of remiges and rectrices brownish-grey.

The wings hair-brown, as dark as the tail; the primaries and secondaries very narrowly, and the coverts and tertiaries broadly, margined with rufous or fulvous-brown of the same tone as the rufous of the back.

The Booted Tree Warbler occurs as a cold weather visitant both in Sind and in the Deccan.

Hypolais pallida, *Hemp. & Ehr.*

553*ter*.—Murray's Vertebrate Zoology of Sind, p. 158; Stray Feathers, Vol. VII, p. 398.

THE PALE TREE WARBLER.

Length, 5; wing, 2·63; tail, 2·2; tarsus, 0·83; culmen, 0·62.

Bill horn-brown, dull yellowish at base beneath; irides dark-brown; legs pale horn-brown.

Upper parts pale dull olive-brown, clearer on the back in color, and rather lighter on the rump; from the base of the bill over the eye a rather indistinct yellowish stripe; wing dark-brown; the inner secondaries lighter in color, all the feathers having lighter margins; tail dark-brown, very narrowly edged with lighter brown; under parts buffy-white; the throat and the centre of the abdomen almost pure white; flanks washed with pale brownish.

The Pale Tree Warbler only occurs in Sind as a cold weather visitant.

Hypolais languida, *Hemp. & Ehr.*

553*quat*.—Stray Feathers, Vol. VII, p. 398.

Length, 5·25; wing, 3·1; tail, 2·75; tarsus, 0·9; culmen, 0·75.

Soft parts as in *H. pallida.*

In general coloration of plumage similar to *H. pallida*, but a trifle greyer; bill narrower and more slender; first primary much shorter and narrower. First primary scarcely as long as the primary-coverts, 1·8 shorter than the second, second 0·2 shorter than the third, third and fourth about equal.

This Tree Warbler has been found in Beluchistan, and is somewhat doubtfully recorded from Sind. It occurs in the winter season only.

Hypolais obsoleta, *Severtz.*

Murray's Vertebrate Zoology of Sind, p. 158.

THE DESERT TREE WARBLER.

Wing, 2·4; tail, 2; culmen, 0·8.

The general color of the upper parts is a sandy-brown or pale isabelline-brown; in other respects the coloration is that of the two or three preceding species or sub-species; third and fourth primaries nearly equal and longest; second primary, in a skin from Turkestan, intermediate in length between the sixth and seventh, and in one from Sind between the seventh and eighth; the bastard primary exceeds the primary-coverts by 0·35 inches in both skins.

This Warbler has been procured in Sind, but is very rare.

The following key, originally published in Vol. V, Cat. Br. Mus., may prove useful in discriminating the foregoing:—

A. General color of the upper parts brown or grey; under parts white or pale brown; outside tail-feathers 0·15 to 0·2 inches shorter than the longest.

(*a*) Second primary intermediate between the fifth and sixth; bastard primary falling short of the primary-covert by 0·1 inches, or extending 0·05 beyond them. Lengths of wing, 2·8 to 3·05 inches.

H. LANGUIDA.

B. Bastard primary exceeding the primary coverts by at least 0·1 inch.

(*a*) General color of the upper parts sandy or isabelline-brown.

H. OBSOLETA.

C. General color of the upper parts darkish rufous-brown or grey.

(*a*) Second primary generally intermediate between the fifth and sixth; bastard primary exceeding the primary coverts from 0·1 to 0·3 inches. Length of wing, 2·75 to 2·5 inches.

H. PALLIDA.

(*b*) Second primary generally intermediate between the seventh and eighth, or eighth and ninth; bastard primary exceeding the primary-coverts from 0·2 to 0·4 inches. Length of wing, 2·53 to 2·3 inches; culmen, 0·6 to 0·53.

H. RAMA.

(*c*) Second primary generally intermediate between the sixth and seventh; bastard primary exceeding the primarycoverts 0·15 to 0·26. Length of wing, 2·38 to 2·28 inches; culmen, 0·51 to 0·5.

H. CALIGATA.

GENUS, Phylloscopus, *Bodd.*

Bill very slender, small, straight, shallow, barely deflected at the tip, entire; a few small but distinct rictal bristles; wings as in the last, but the first primary more developed, and the wing somewhat shorter; tail moderate, even, or slightly emarginate in some; tarsus and feet moderate; claws slender.

Phylloscopus tristis, *Bly.*

554.—Jerdon's Birds of India, Vol. II, p. 190; Butler, Guzerat; Stray Feathers, Vol. III, p. 486; Deccan, Stray Feathers, Vol. IX, p. 408; Murray's Vertebrate Zoology of Sind, p. 159.

THE BROWN TREE WARBLER.

Length, 5; expanse, 7·25; wing, 2·45; tail, 2; tarsus, 0·75; bill at front, 0·37.

Bill blackish, yellow beneath and at gape; irides brown; legs brownish-black.

Above uniform dull brown, below albescent, with a faint tinge of ruddy on the pale supercilia; sides of neck, breast, and flanks, axillaries, and fore part of the wing underneath, pure light-yellow.

The Brown Tree Warbler is generally distributed throughout the Presidency, but only as a seasonal visitant.

Phylloscopus neglectus, *Hume.*

554*bis.*—Stray Feathers, Vol. I, p. 195.

HUME'S TREE WARBLER.

Length, 4 to 4·2; expanse, 6·25 to 6·4; tail, 1·4 to 1·6; wing, 2 to 2·15; tarsus, 0·68 to 0·71; bill at front, 0·27 to 0·3.

Bill black, in some paler or greenish-horny at base beneath; irides brown; legs and feet black.

Lores brownish-white; a comparatively pure and very narrow white streak runs from the nostrils over the lores and eyes, but not beyond; the whole upper surface is dull earthy-brown, with in some a faintly olivaceous-rufescent tinge on the back, most conspicuous on the rump; the quills and tail are a moderately dark hair-brown, narrowly margined on the outer webs with pale olivaceous-brown, much the same color as the upper parts; the secondaries are very narrowly margined at the tips with albescent; the whole lower surface is albescent, tinged with very pale fulvous-fawn, or earthy-brown, more strongly so in some specimens than in others; the sides and flanks more strongly so in all; in some specimens the sides and flanks are pale earthy-brown; the wing-lining and axillaries are white, with at times the faintest possible fulvous or brownish tinge.

Mr. Hume, the discoverer of this species, says: "This tiny Leaf Hunter, the smallest of the whole group, is not uncommon along the banks of the Indus and throughout Upper Sind, wherever thick clumps of babool are met with."

Phylloscopus magnirostris, *Bly.*

556.—Jerdon's Birds of India, Vol. II, p. 191 ; Butler, Deccan ; Stray Feathers, Vol. IX, p. 408.

THE LARGE-BILLED TREE WARBLER.

Length, 5 to 5·25 ; expanse, 8·25 ; wing, 2·6 to 2·75 ; tail, 2·12 ; tarsus, 0·75 ; bill at front, 0·5.

Bill dusky-plumbeous, fleshy at base beneath ; irides dusky ; legs pale plumbeous.

Above dusky olive-green, with a faint tinge of tawny on the wings and tail ; medial wing-coverts tipped with greenish-white ; a pale yellow supercilium and the lower ear-coverts partly yellow ; beneath pale, the breast tinged with ashy, mingled with faint yellowish, and the rest of the lower parts more or less pure yellowish-white.

The Large-billed Tree Warbler is a very rare visitant to parts of the Deccan in the cold season ; it has not been recorded from any other portion of our limits.

Phylloscopus lugubris, *Bly.*

558.—Jerdon's Birds of India, Vol. II, p. 192 ; Butler, Deccan ; Stray Feathers, Vol. IX, p. 408.

THE DULL-GREEN TREE WARBLER.

Length, 4·75 ; expanse, 7·5 ; wing, 2·5 ; tail, 1·85 ; tarsus, 0·75 ; bill at front, 0·4.

Bill dusky, beneath amber ; irides dusky-brown ; legs greenish-dusky.

Above dusky olive-green, with a pale yellowish supercilium, and yellowish tips to the medial wing-coverts ; beneath albescent, faintly tinged with yellow medially, and the flanks greenish-yellow.

This is another very rare winter visitant to parts of the Deccan.

Phylloscopus nitidus, *Lath.*

559.—Jerdon's Birds of India, Vol. II, p. 193 ; Butler, Deccan ; Stray Feathers, Vol. IX, p. 408 ; Murray's Vertebrate Zoology of Sind, p. 159.

THE BRIGHT-GREEN TREE WARBLER.

Length, 4·75 ; expanse, 7·25 ; wing, 2 25 to 2·5 ; tail, 1·75 to 2 ; tarsus, 0·7 ; bill at front, 0·4.

Above lively green, below unsullied pale yellowish, brightest about the breast ; a pale wing-band formed by the tips of the larger coverts of the secondaries.

This Tree Warbler is common during the cold weather in the Deccan and occurs again in Sind ; it has not been recorded from Guzerat, where probably it has been overlooked.

Phylloscopus viridanus, *Blyth.*

560.—Jerdon's Birds of India, Vol. II, p. 193; Butler, Deccan; Stray Feathers, Vol. IX, p. 408.

THE GREENISH TREE WARBLER.

Length, 4·75 to 5; expanse, 7·5; wing, 2·25 to 2·5; tail, 1·75 to 2; tarsus, 0·75; bill at front, 0·4.

Above light dull olive-green, beneath greenish-albescent, darker on the flanks; a pale yellow supercilium, and an indication of a slight whitish bar on the wings, the coverts being tipped pale.

Merely a cold weather visitant to the Deccan.

Phylloscopus affinis, *Tickell.*

561.—Jerdon's Birds of India, Vol. II, p. 194; Butler, Deccan; Stray Feathers, Vol. IX, p. 408.

TICKELL'S TREE WARBLER.

Length, 4·75; expanse, 7; wing, 2·38; tail, 1·9; tarsus, 0·74; bill at front, 0·36.

Bill dusky, amber beneath; legs pale brownish-dusky, tinged with yellowish.

Above fuscous olive-green, with an extremely faint tawny tinge; no pale tips to the medial wing-coverts; supercilia, cheeks, and under parts, pale sullied greenish or oil-yellow, brightest on the middle of the belly, with a slight tawny tinge in some, and the breast and flanks a little infuscated.

Within our limits this Warbler has only been recorded as a rare cold weather visitant to parts of the Deccan.

Phylloscopus indicus, *Jerdon.*

562.—Jerdon's Birds of India, Vol. II, p. 193; Butler, Guzerat; Stray Feathers, Vol. III, p. 486; Deccan, Stray Feathers, Vol. IX, p. 408; Swinhoe and Barnes, Central India; Ibis, 1885, p. 126.

THE OLIVACEOUS TREE WARBLER.

Length, 5·25; expanse, 7·25; wing, 2·25; tail, 2; tarsus, 0·75; bill at front, 0·4.

Bill dusky, yellowish beneath; irides dark-brown; legs greenish-brown, yellow on the soles.

Above uniform olive-grey, beneath olivaceous-yellow, purest on the middle of the belly; a clear pale yellow supercilium.

Merely a cold weather visitant to the Deccan.

Phylloscopus sindianus, *Brooks.*

Murray's Vertebrate Zoology of Sind, p. 160.

THE SIND TREE WARBLER.

Length, 4·2 to 4·7; wing, 2·05 to 2·4; tail, 1·75 to 2·09; bill at front, 0·3 to 0·35.

Bill brown, yellow beneath.

Above uniform dull brown, below albescent, with a ruddy tinge on the pale supercilia, sides of face, neck, breast and flanks; axillaries, and edge of wing, yellowish-white, sometimes almost quite white.

This Tree Warbler has only been obtained in Sind.

GENUS, **Reguloides**, *Blyth.*

Bill much as in *Phylloscopus*, or a trifle shorter comparatively; wings moderately long and more pointed, the second primary being very little shorter than the fourth; tarsus and feet rather small.

Reguloides occipitalis, *Jerdon.*

563.—Jerdon's Birds of India, Vol. II, p. 196; Butler, Deccan; Stray Feathers, Vol. IX, p. 409; Murray's Vertebrate Zoology of Sind, p. 160.

THE LARGE CROWNED WARBLER.

Length, 4·75; wing, 2·61; tail, 2; tarsus, 0·7; bill at front, 0·4.

Bill dusky, yellow beneath; irides hazel; legs pale-brownish.

Above mingled green and ashy, the latter prevailing on the back, the former on the rump, wings, and tail; crown dusky, with whitish supercilia, and a conspicuous pale mesial line, broader and tinged with yellow at the occiput; a very pale yellowish wing band; the forepart of the wing brightish-green and its margin and the axillaries pure light yellow; lower parts albescent, mingled with yellowish, and very faintly tinged with ruddy; inner webs of the three outer tail-feathers, on each side, narrowly bordered with white.

This, the largest of the group, is a somewhat rare cold weather visitant to both the Deccan and Sind.

Reguloides superciliosus, *Pallas.*

565.—Jerdon's Birds of India, Vol. II, p. 197; Butler, Deccan; Stray Feathers, Vol. IX, p. 409.

THE CROWNED TREE WARBLER.

Length, 4·25; expanse, 6·5; wing, 2·25; tail, 1·7; tarsus, 0·7; bill at front, 0·3.

Bill dusky, yellow beneath; irides dark-brown; legs pale brown.

Above olive-green, brightest on the rump, wings, and tail; crown dusky, with a pale mesial line, not always very distinct; two conspicuous yellowish-white wing-bars, the hind one the broader of the two, and behind this is a dark patch; tertiaries conspicuously margined with whitish; secondaries and some of the primaries slightly tipped with the same; axillaries with the forepart of the wing underneath pale yellow; supercilia and plumago beneath greenish albescent.

This is another winter visitant to the Deccan.

Reguloides humei, *Brooks.*

565*bis.*—Butler, Deccan; Stray Feathers, Vol. IX, p. 409.

THE BROWN-HEADED WILLOW WARBLER.

Like *R. superciliosus*, but has the supercilium pale brownish-buff to brownish-white, as in *P. tristis*; cheeks strongly tinged with pale ruddy-buff, and seldom having an admixture of yellow; they are mottled as in the affined species with dark-brown; top of head brown, rather inclined to olive; coronal streak very faint, often not visible; color of top of head at all times blended into color of back; back, wings, and tail as in *superciliosus*, but of less bright green, and yellow tips to the wing-coverts not so pure; in other respects the plumage much resembles that of *superciliosus*.

Has been procured in the vicinity of Belgaum.

GENUS, Abrornis, *Hodgson.*

Bill wider than in *Phylloscopus* or *Reguloides*, depressed, moderately deflected, and distinctly notched; nostrils concealed; a few fine rictal setæ; otherwise as in *Phylloscopus*.

Abrornis cantator, *Tickell.*

570.—*Culicipeta cantator*, Tickell.—Jerdon's Birds of India, Vol. II, p. 200.

THE LESSER BLACK-BROWED WARBLER.

Length, 4·25; expanse, 6·25; wing, 2·25; tail, 1·75; tarsus, 0·6.

Bill light dusky above, amber beneath; irides hazel; legs fleshy-yellow.

Bright olive-green above, yellow on the wings and tail; throat, cheeks, supercilia, lower tail-coverts, and margin of the wing, bright yellow; belly and flanks greyish-white; a very narrow yellow bar on the wing; on each side of the crown a broad black band, and an intermediate and narrower greenish one, becoming yellower on the occiput; upper tertiaries slightly margined at the tips with yellowish-white, and the tail feathers have a very narrow-yellowish white internal border.

Central India is one of the localities mentioned by Jerdon as frequented by this pretty little warbler.

SUB-FAMILY, Sylviinæ.

These are a small series of birds, with mostly grey plumage, and frequently marked with black on the head or throat; bill moderately slender; wings rather lengthened; tarsus and feet short, but strong, and with moderately curved claws.

GENUS, **Sylvia**, *Latham.*

Bill moderate or slightly lengthened and slender, with the rictal bristles almost obsolete; wings lengthened and in some pointed; first quill minute, second a little shorter than the third and fourth, which are about equal; secondaries broad; tail slightly rounded; tarsus moderate or short, stout, and scutate; feet strong, short; lateral toes unequal; hind-toe moderate; claws moderately curved.

Sylvia jerdoni, *Blyth.*

531.—*Sylvia orphea*, Tem.—Jerdon's Birds of India, Vol. II, p. 208; Butler, Guzerat; Stray Feathers, Vol. III, p. 487; Deccan, Stray Feathers, Vol. IX, p. 409; Murray's Vertebrate Zoology of Sind, p. 161; Swinhoe and Barnes, Central India; Ibis, 1885, p. 126.

THE LARGE BLACK-CAPPED WARBLER.

Length, 7; expanse, 9·25; wing, 3·2; tail, 2·75; tarsus, 0·9; bill at front, 0·6.

Bill blackish-horny, greyish at base beneath; irides pale whitish-yellow; legs greenish-grey.

Above brownish-ashy, tolerably pure ashy on the nape and rump; cap, lores, and ear-coverts black in the male, dusky or blackish-grey in the female; beneath whitish, pure white on the throat and middle of the belly, tinged albescent on the breast; tail blackish, the outer feathers externally white, for the basal two-thirds, and the next four successively less broadly tipped white; quills dusky-brown with pale edgings.

The Black-capped Warbler is a not uncommon cold weather visitant to all parts of the district.

Sylvia affinis, *Blyth.*

582.—Jerdon's Birds of India, Vol. II, p. 209; Butler, Guzerat; Stray Feathers, Vol. III, p. 487; Deccan, Stray Feathers, Vol. IX, p. 409; Murray's Vertebrate Zoology of Sind, p. 161; Swinhoe and Barnes, Central India; Ibis, 1885, p. 126.

THE ALLIED GREY WARBLER.

Length, 6; wing, 2·65; tail, 2·25; tarsus, 0·75; bill at front, 0·45.

Bill brown; irides brownish-yellow; legs brown.

Head and neck cinereous; ears dusky; the rest of the plumage above reddish cinereous; wing and tail brownish; outer tail feathers nearly all white, the others only tipped with white; throat white; rest of the plumage beneath white with a tinge of reddish.

The Allied Grey Warbler is generally distributed throughout the district during the cold weather.

Sylvia minuscula, *Hume.*

532*bis.*—Murray's Vetebrate Zoology of Sind, p. 161.

HUME'S LESSER WHITE-THROAT.

Length, 5·3; wing 2·3 to 2·4; bill at front, 0·3.

Bill brownish; irides brownish-yellow; legs brown.

Forehead and crown pale bluish-grey; back, rump, and upper tail-coverts isabelline fawn, or pale sandy brown; chin, throat, and under surface, white; second primary equal to the seventh, in some intermediate between seventh and eighth.

Hume's Lesser White-throat is a not uncommon cold weather visitant to Sind and parts of Guzerat and Rajputana.

Sylvia althea, *Hume.*

582*ter.*—Murray's Vertebrate Zoology of Sind, p. 162.

THE HIMALAYAN LESSER WHITE-THROAT.

Upper surface darkish grey, slightly tinged with brown on the back.

Under surface white; second primary intermediate in length between or equal to sixth and seventh, or seventh and eighth; wing, 2·7 to 2·8; culmen, 0·51 to 0·56; tarsus, 0·75 to 0·8.

This species, or race as it may perhaps more properly be called, is a somewhat rare cold weather visitant to most parts of the Presidency.

Sylvia rufa, *Bodd.*

582*quat.*—Butler, Guzerat; (*S. cinerea*), Stray Feathers, Vol. III, p. 488; Murray's Vertebrate Zoology of Sind (*S. cinerea*) p. 162.

THE GREY WARBLER OR WHITE-THROAT.

Length, 6 to 6·25; expanse, 8·5; wing, 2·85 to 2·87; tail, 2·32 to 3; bill at front, 0·44; bill from gape, 0·62.

Bill dusky, fleshy at base below; irides yellowish-brown; legs and feet yellowish-brown.

The entire upper surface is a moderately dark, somewhat reddish sooty, or reddish ashy brown, more cinereous on the head, and with the tertials and their greater coverts rather broadly margined with pale dull ferruginous; the lores are albescent or greyish-white, with traces of a greyer line through them; chin, upper throat, and eyelid feathers pure white; ear-coverts silky brown; lower throat, breast and middle of abdomen, white, tinged with pale vinaceous buff; sides and flanks tinged with brown; first primary very minute, second primary longest, or second and third equal and longest; tail a good deal rounded; exterior feather 0·4 shorter than longest, a paler brown than the rest and margined with white; next feather tipped with brownish-white; quills and greater coverts and tail-feathers all paler margined; axillaries greyish-white; tibial plumes buffy-white; tarsi stout, 0·87 in length.

The Grey Warbler occurs during the cold season both in Sind and Guzerat.

Sylvia nana, *Hemp. & Ehr.*

583*bis.*—Murray's Vertebrate Zoology of Sind, p. 163.

THE DESERT WARBLER.

Length, 4·8 to 4·9; expanse, 7 to 7·2; wing, 2 to 2·2; tail, 1·8 to 2; tarsus, 0·8; bill at front, 0·33.

Bill pale yellow, dusky on culmen and at tip; irides orange-yellow; legs and feet pale yellow.

The lores are greyish-white; from the nostril to the upper margin of the eye runs a very narrow yellowish-streak, whiter and less grey than the lores; this line ceases to be visible in nine out of ten skins, but is sufficiently apparent in the freshly killed bird; a circle of yellowish-white feathers surrounds the eye; forehead, crown, occiput, nape, back, and scapulars, pale fawn-brown; rump and upper tail-coverts pale rufous; central tail-feathers pale rufous, with dark shafts; external lateral feathers wholly white, next pair white on the outer webs, and with a moderately broad white tip to both webs; the rest of the inner webs dark hair-brown; the rest of the feathers dark hair-brown, margined on the outer webs with pale rufous; the whole of the lower parts white, with, in the freshly killed birds, a just perceptible rufous tinge; wing-lining and axillaries pure white; wing pale-brown, narrowly margined and tipped with rufescent-white; the tertiaries pale dingy-rufescent with brown shafts.

Within our limits this Warbler only occurs in the more desert-like portion of Sind and in the Runn of Kutch. It is apparently a permanent resident as Mr. Doig found them breeding in October.

SUB-FAMILY, Motacillinæ.

Bill generally of moderate length, slender, straight, barely deflected at the tip, and indistinctly notched; rictal vibrissæ minute or wanting; wings typically long or pointed, and the tertiaries lengthened; tail long; tarsus moderately long and slender; toes moderate; claws slightly curved; the hind-claw often long and straight.

GENUS, Motacilla, *Lin.*

Bill moderate, straight, slender, compressed at the tip, which is very slightly notched; nostrils apert; rictus almost smooth; wings long, pointed, with nine primary quills, the first two sub-equal and longest; tertiaries lengthened, equal to the primaries; tail long, slender, nearly even; tarsus moderately long, slender, obscurely scutellate; feet moderate; hind-toe short; claws slightly curved; hind-claw small, more curved.

Motacilla maderaspatensis, *Gm.*

589.—Jerdon's Birds of India, Vol. II, p. 217; *M. maderaspatana*, Briss.; Butler, Guzerat; Stray Feathers, Vol. III, p. 489;

Deccan, Stray Feathers, Vol. IX, p. 410; Murray's Vertebrate Zoology of Sind, p. 164; Swinhoe and Barnes, Central India; Ibis, 1885, p. 126.

THE PIED WAGTAIL.

Length, 8·5 to 9; expanse, 12; wing, 3·75 to 4; tail, 4; tarsus, 1; bill at front, 0·6; bill from gape, 0·72.

Bill blackish; irides dark-brown; legs blackish.

Upper plumage, with the chin, throat, and breast black, with a broad white supercilium and a large white wing-spot, formed by the median and greater-coverts, and the edges of some of the primaries; the greater part of the two outermost tail-feathers white, also the edges of the upper tail-coverts; beneath, from the breast, white.

The female has the black less pure. In winter the chin, upper part of the throat, and some feathers just below the eye, are white.

The Pied Wagtail is very generally distributed throughout the Presidency; it is a permanent resident, breeding nearly the whole year through. They have several broods during the season; one pair that frequented a small tank adjoining my compound at Poona had a nest with two young ones and an addled egg on the 3rd March. On the 23rd April I took three incubated eggs from the same nest; they had another nest, built about a yard away from the first one, which contained two eggs on the 9th May. In July, I noticed them feeding a pair of young birds, and towards the end of August they were making preparations for another brood. So that this pair had at least five clutches of eggs in one season. They were the only Wagtails on the tank, and were very pugnacious, and would allow no other bird to remain on the tank; their own young ones, as soon as they were able to forage for themselves, were even driven away.

The nest which is a mere pad, composed of grass fibres, &c., is always near water, and is built upon something solid, such as the ledge of a rock, a niche in a stone bridge, a hole in a bank, or some such similar place.

The eggs, three or four in number, vary much both in size and shape, but are always more or less pointed at one end. The general color is greenish or earthy-white, spotted, speckled, streaked, clouded or smudged with olive, purplish, or earthy-brown.

They average 0·9 inches in length by about 0·65 in breadth.

Motacilla leucopsis, *Gould.*

590.—*Motacilla luzoniensis,* Scop.—Jerdon's Birds of India, Vol. II, p. 218.

THE WHITE-FACED WAGTAIL.

Length, 7·9; extent, 11·25; wing, 3·6; tail, 3·75; tarsus, 0·6; bill at front, 0·6.

Bill black; irides brown; legs black.

In summer plumage, the occiput, nape, and upper parts generally deep black, also a large patch on the breast; a broad frontal band, sides of head (including the eye) and neck, large wing-patch, the two outermost tail-feathers on each side, and the lower parts, white.

In winter plumage, the back, shoulder, and rump are ashy-grey, the occiput, nape, and breast-band alone being black.

The female is a trifle smaller than the male, and the black perhaps is not quite so deep.

The White-faced Wagtail is, I believe, not uncommon at and near Mhow. It is of course a cold weather visitant only.

Motacilla personata, *Gould.*

591.—Jerdon's Birds of India, Vol. II, p. 218; (*M. dukhunensis,* Sykes); Butler, Deccan; Stray Feathers, Vol. IX, p. 411; Murray's Vertebrate Zoology of Sind, p. 165; Swinhoe and Barnes, Central India; Ibis, 1885, p. 127.

THE BLACK-FACED WAGTAIL.

Length, 7·5 to 8; wing, 3·6 to 3·7; tail, 4·5 to 4·75; bill at front, 0·75.

Bill black; irides brown; legs black.

In summer plumage, the back and scapulars, pale grey; occiput, nape, wings, and tail, black; a supercilium, wing-patch, and outermost tail-feathers, white; beneath, the throat, neck, and breast, black, the rest white; primaries are dusky, edged with white, and the upper tail-coverts ashy, edged with black.

In winter dress, the chin, throat, and beneath the eye, are white, leaving only a small patch of black on the breast; the occiput and nape are also grey, the white wing-patch smaller; the coverts and secondaries also grey, edged paler.

With the exception perhaps of Guzerat, the Black-faced Wagtail is generally distributed throughout the district during the cold weather.

Motacilla dukhunensis, *Sykes.*

591*bis.*—Butler, Guzerat; Stray Feathers, Vol. III, p. 489; Deccan, Stray Feathers, Vol. IX, p. 410.

SYKES' GREY AND BLACK WAGTAIL.

Length, 7·5 to 8; wing, 3·6 to 3·7; tail, 4·5 to 4·75; bill at front, 0·75.

Bill black; irides brown; legs black.

Mr. Hume points out, *Stray Feathers, Vol. I, p.* 30, that "the only ready and unfailing diagnosis of the two species," *i.e, personata* and *dukhunensis,* "is that, *in both sexes, and at all seasons, the ear-coverts and whole aural region are in* personata *black, blackish or dark-grey; in* dukhunensis, *pure white or greyish or sordid-white.*" This marked difference, coupled with the conspicuously greater amount of white on the wings of *personata*, as compared with those of *dukhunensis*, ought to render the separation of any specimens of the two species comparatively easy.

This Wagtail is common during the cold season in both the Deccan and Guzerat. It also occurs at Neemuch in Rajputana.

Motacilla alba, *Lin.*

591*ter.*—Murray's Vertebrate Zoology of Sind, p. 166; Swinhoe and Barnes, Central India; Ibis, 1885, p. 127.

The European White-faced Wagtail.

Length, 7·5 to 8; wing, 3·75; tail, 4·75.

Bill black; irides dark-brown; legs black.

Front of the head, lores, all round the eye, ear-coverts, cheeks, and a broad stripe down the sides of the neck, white, as also the belly, vent and under tail-coverts; back of the head and nape, chin, throat and breast, black; back and scapulars darker-grey than in *personata*; upper tail-coverts dark-brown, a few feathers margined white; primaries dusky-brown, the outer webs darker, with a very faint whitish edge; secondaries, tertiaries, and inner webs of the median greater-coverts, dark brown, nearly black, all broadly edged white on their outer webs, and except the primaries, tipped with white; the inner webs of the primaries and secondaries margined for their basal half with white; lesser wing-coverts concolorous with the back; tail black, the two outermost feathers white, except a dark brown margin for nearly three-fourths their length on their inner webs, and in some specimens on the outer web near the shaft; under wing and thigh-coverts white, the latter with some dark streaks.

The European White-faced Wagtail is a common cold weather visitant to Sind. It is by many considered identical with *dukhunensis.*

Genus, Calobates, *Kaup.*

Bill more slender than in *motacilla*; wings slightly shorter, and tertials less elongated; tarsus shorter and pale colored; hind-toe short, with the claw a little longer and moderately curved; otherwise as in *motacilla.*

Calobates melanope, *Pall.*

592.—*C. sulphurea*, Bech.—Jerdon's Birds of India, Vol. II, p. 220; Butler, Guzerat; Stray Feathers, Vol. III, p. 489; Deccan, Stray Feathers, Vol. IX, p. 592; (*C. boarula*, Penn.) Murray's Vertebrate Zoology of Sind, p. 166; *Motacilla melanope*, Pall.; Swinhoe and Barnes, Central India; Ibis, 1885, p. 127.

The Grey and Yellow Wagtail.

Length, 7·5; wing, 2·25; tail, 3·5; tarsus, 0·8; bill at front, 0·45.

Bill black; irides brown; legs pale-brown.

Plumage above pale-grey, with a wash of olivaceous; upper tail-coverts pale-yellow, also the edges of the tertiaries; supercilium, chin and throat, white; rest of the lower parts pale-yellow, greenish on the middle, and laterally pure yellow; a white-wing band; wings and tail brownish-black; the three outer tail-feathers on each side white on the inner web, the outermost wholly so.

In summer the chin and throat become black with a whitish border, and the yellow of the lower parts is darker.

During the cold season, the Grey and Yellow Wagtail is very common throughout the country.

GENUS, **Budytes,** *Cuvier.*

The characters are the same as those of *motacilla,* but the tertials barely so long; the tail shorter; tarsus longer and stouter; hind-toe and claw lengthened, the latter very much so, and but slightly curved.

Budytes cinereocapilla, *Savi.*

593.—*B. viridis,* Gm.—Jerdon's Birds of India, Vol. II, p. 222; Butler, Deccan; Stray Feathers, Vol. IX, p. 410; *Motacilla cinereocapilla,* Savi., Swinhoe and Barnes, Central India; Ibis, 1885, p. 127.

THE SLATY-HEADED FIELD WAGTAIL.

Length, 6·5; expanse, 9·5; wing, 3·13; tail, 2·75; tarsus, 0·8; bill at front, 0·45.

Bill black; irides dusky-brown; legs black.

The usual plumage of adult birds in winter is olive-green above, with a white or occasionally yellow superciliary mark; beneath, the chin and throat whitish, the rest yellow, more or less pure; wings dusky, with two dull whitish-yellow cross bands, formed by the tips of the coverts, and the tertials broadly margined with yellowish; tail black, slightly margined with greenish, and the two outermost feathers on each side chiefly white.

At the spring moult, the whole cap, lores and ear-coverts change to a bluish ash-grey, with or without a white or yellow supercilium, which, however, is not always present, and disappears eventually by the change of color which takes place in the feathers themselves at a later period. The lower parts, too, become more pure and bright yellow; the chin is white, and the throat yellow, with its lateral border white.

A little later in the season, the lores and ear-coverts become darker by a change in the feathers themselves, and finally change to a deep black; and in full breeding plumage, the whole cap, lores, and ear-coverts, are deep black.

Young birds of the year are light brownish-grey, purer on the nape and rump; wings and tail dusky, the former with two whitish cross bands; the tail darker than the wings, with the two outermost feathers on each side nearly white; beneath white, sometimes with a yellowish tinge, and a few brown marks on the breast; a white supercilium always present.

The Slaty-headed Field Wagtail is common in the Deccan and in parts of Rajputana. Of course it only occurs in the cold season.

Budytes melanocephala, *Licht.*

593*bis.*—Butler, Guzerat; Stray Feathers, Vol. III, p. 490; Deccan, Stray Feathers, Vol. IX, p. 410; Murray's Vertebrate Zoology of Sind, p. 168.

THE BLACK-CAP FIELD WAGTAIL.

Length, 6·2 to 6·5; wing, 3·1 to 3·25; tail, 2·75; bill at front, 0·43.

Bill dark-brown; irides brownish; legs dark-brown.

Head, nape, lores, sides of the face and ear-coverts black; back, scapulars, rump, and upper tail-coverts, yellowish-green, the latter lighter, and the feathers edged with yellowish; chin white or buffy-white; rest of under surface pure yellow; primaries and secondaries dull brown, lighter and whitish on the margins at the base of their inner webs; tertiaries dark-brown, edged on lesser wing-coverts yellowish-olive, subterminally dark-brown, and tipped yellowish; median and greater-coverts dark-brown, tipped yellowish, forming two conspicuous wing-bands; tail black margined with greenish; the two outermost feathers on each side white, except a broad dark-brown margin on their inner webs.

During the cold season the Black-capped Field Wagtail is commonly distributed throughout the district.

Budytes flava, *Lin.*

593*ter.*—Butler, Deccan; Stray Feathers, Vol. IX, p. 411; Murray's Vertebrate Zoology of Sind, p. 168.

THE GREY-HEADED FIELD WAGTAIL.

Length, 6 to 6·5; wing, 3·25; tail, 2·95; bill at front, 0·6.

Bill dark-brown; irides dusky-brown; legs dark-brown.

Forehead, crown, nape, and sides of the face, bluish-grey; a dark streak from the base of the bill through the eye, a white, supercilium, and another short white stripe below from under the eye; below the bluish-grey of the face an albescent streak to the chin, which is white; throat, breast, and rest of under surface bright-yellow; neck behind, and back, yellowish-green, tinged brownish; greater and lesser wing-coverts dusky-brown, margined with yellowish-white; primaries, secondaries, and tertiaries, dusky-brown, margined with yellowish-white; tail dark-brown, edged with greenish-yellow, the two outermost feathers white, with a dark-brown margin on their inner webs, broader on the second, and extending over part of the outer web; the next narrowly edged with white; upper tail-coverts like the back.

The female has a white supercilium; the head and crown duller, mixed somewhat with greenish later in the year; the chin is white, and the throat a yellowish or buffy-white; breast and under parts pale-yellow; back greyish-brown.

The Grey-headed Field Wagtail occurs both in the Deccan and in Sind. It has apparently been overlooked in Guzerat and Rajputana.

They are difficult birds to deal with, and Jerdon did not discriminate the two last species.

The following key by Mr. Brooks will assist greatly in helping collectors to discriminate the three species:—

B. flava.—Grey head, broad white supercilium, grey and white cheeks.

B. cinereocapilla.—Dark-grey head, supercilium absent or else very narrow and white; often only half a supercilium behind the eye; cheeks a dark slate color or almost black. This dark cheek is the well marked peculiarity of the species.

B. melanocephala.—Pure black head, with very rarely indeed a supercilium, and then very narrow, like a thin white thread.

The black head is a good distinction.

Budytes calcarata, *Hodgs.*

594.—*B. citreola*, Pallas.—Jerdon's Birds of India, Vol. II, p. 225; Murray's Vertebrate Zoology of Sind, p. 169.

THE YELLOW-HEADED WAGTAIL.

Length, 6·5 to 7; extent, 10·5; wing, 3·25 to 3·5; tail, 3·5; bill at front, 0·48.

Bill black; irides brown; legs black.

Entire head, chin, throat, breast, and under surface, bright yellow; back, rump, and upper tail-coverts dark-brown, nearly black; lesser wing-coverts dark-grey; median and greater wing-coverts dark-brown, margined and tipped with white; the tertiaries broadly margined with white; primaries and secondaries on their outer webs, dusky on their inner, and with whitish margins; tail dark-brown or black; the feathers very narrowly edged with greenish; the four outermost white, except a dusky-brown margin on the inner web for three-fourths their length.

In winter the adult is light ashy-grey above, the nape and sides of the breast darker; head and under surface yellow, olivaceous on the flanks; primaries dusky, edged with greyish-white on their outer webs; secondaries dusky; tertiaries darker, broadly margined with white; wing-coverts brown, broadly tipped with white, forming two conspicuous wing-bands; lower tail-coverts albescent or very pale-yellow; tail as in the breeding plumage.

The Yellow-headed Wagtail is very common during the cold season in Sind, affecting paddy fields, edges of marshes, and banks of rivers and canals.

Budytes citreola, *Pall.*

594*bis.*—Butler, Deccan, Stray Feathers, Vol. IX, p. 411; Murray's Vertebrate Zoology of Sind, p. 169; *Motacilla citreola*, Pall.; Swinhoe and Barnes, Central India; Ibis, 1885, p. 127.

THE GREY-BACKED YELLOW WAGTAIL.

Length, 7·1; wing, 3·18; tail, 2·75; bill at front, 0·4.

Bill pale-brown; irides brown; legs pale brown.

Forehead, crown of head, sides of the face, ear-coverts, chin, throat, breast, and entire under parts bright yellow, paler on the vent, and nearly white on the under tail-coverts; nape, and upper back, black; lower back and scapulars dark-grey; rump and upper tail-coverts pale or dark-brown or yellowish-green, the feathers edged with greenish; primaries and secondaries dusky; tertiaries dark brown; the primaries and secondaries faintly edged and tipped with white, and the tertiaries broadly so, all basally white on their inner webs; lesser wing-coverts like the back and tipped brown; median and greater-coverts brown, edged with white, and forming two conspicuous white or yellowish-white bands; the second band oblique in the closed wing, being formed by the white of the greater coverts, and that of the innermost tertiaries, the longest of which is nearly equal in length with the fourth primary; under wing-coverts white; tail black, the feathers with a faint tinge of whitish on their outer webs; the two outermost tail-feathers on each side white, with a broad margin on their inner webs, to about half an inch from the tip; the next black, with the edge of the outer web and tip white.

The Grey-backed Yellow Wagtail is a common cold weather visitant to the Deccan, Rajputana, and also in a lesser degree to Sind.

GENUS, Limonidromus.

Similar characters to *Budytes*, but with the short hind-claw of *Motacilla*.

Limonidromus indicus, *Gm.*

595.—*Nemoricola indica*, Gm.—Jerdon's Birds of India, Vol. II, p. 226; Butler, Deccan; Stray Feathers, Vol. IX, p. 411.

THE BLACK-BREASTED WAGTAIL.

Length, 6·25; expanse, 10; wing, 3·12; tail, 2·6; tarsus, 0·9; bill at front, 0·48.

Bill dusky, beneath whitish; legs whitish, tinged with purplish-brown.

Plumage above greenish olive-brown, beneath yellowish; supercilium white; a double black band on the breast, the lower one not complete in the centre, which unites laterally with the upper one; wings blackish, with two broad white bands, and a third at the base of the primaries, a fourth near the tips of the secondaries, continued along the edge of the longest tertiary; tail with the middle feathers brown, the next dusky, the outermost white, with generally a brown outer margin and blackish base, the penultimate with white only on its terminal half.

The Black-breasted Wagtail occurs sparingly in the forest tracts of the Deccan during the cold season; it has not been recorded from elsewhere within our limits.

GENUS, Anthus, *Bechst.*

Bill straight, short, and stouter than in *Budytes*; wings, first to third quills longest; plumage spotted; hind-claw short and curved.

Anthus maculatus, *Hodgs.*

596.—*Pipastes agilis*, Sykes.—Jerdon's Birds of India, Vol. II, p. 228; Butler, Guzerat; Stray Feathers, Vol. III, p. 491.

THE INDIAN TREE PIPIT.

Length, 6·5; expanse, 11; wing, 3·5; tail, 2·75; tarsus, 0·8; bill from gape, 0·7.

Bill dusky, fleshy beneath; irides dark-brown; legs pale fleshy-brown.

In winter plumage above fine greenish-olive, with strongly marked dusky streaks on the crown, and some slight dark centres to the dorsal feathers; beneath white, with a faint fulvous tinge, with large dark spots on the throat, breast, and flanks; wing-coverts dark-brown; the median with yellowish-white tips; the greater-coverts broadly edged with olive; the quills brown, edged with olive; tail with the outermost feathers white terminally, and for the greater part of both webs; the penultimate with a white tip; central feathers olive-brown; the intermediate ones brown, with olive edgings.

In summer plumage the upper parts are more brown and less olive, more broadly streaked with dusky centres, and the under parts always pale fulvescent, passing to white on the abdomen and lower tail-coverts.

During the cold season the Indian Tree Pipit is very common in Guzerat and Rajputana; its occurrence in the Deccan has only doubtfully been recorded.

Anthus trivialis, *Lin.*

597.—*Pipastes arboreus*, Bech.—Jerdon's Birds of India, Vol. II, p. 230; Butler, Guzerat; Stray Feathers, Vol. III, p. 490; Deccan, Stray Feathers, Vol. IX, p. 412; *Anthus arboreus*, Bechst.; Murray's Vertebrate Zoology of Sind, p. 170; Swinhoe and Barnes, Central India; Ibis, 1885, p. 127.

THE EUROPEAN TREE PIPIT.

Length, 6·5; wing, 3·5; tail, 2·5; tarsus, 0·8; bill at front, 0·43

Bill dusky, yellowish at base beneath; irides dark-brown; legs pale-brown.

This Pipit is very similar to the last, and a detailed description is therefore unnecessary. The chief points of difference are: the tone of color less deep, less distinctly striated on the body; it is also more tinged with fulvescent on the throat, breast, and under parts generally; and the hind-claw is slightly more curved.

The European Tree Pipit is generally distributed throughout the Presidency during the cold weather.

Anthus spinoletta, *Lin.*

605*ter*.—Butler, Guzerat; Stray Feathers, Vol. III, p. 491; Murray's Vertebrate Zoology of Sind, p. 170.

THE WATER PIPIT.

Length, 6·37 to 7·25; expanse, 9·5 to 11·25; wing, 3·15 to 3·6; tail, 2·75; bill at front, 0·45 to 0·53.

Bill dark horny-brown; irides brown; legs and feet brown or dark-brown.

In the winter plumage the upper surface is a sort of olive-brown, with more or less of a faintly rufous tinge; the rump unstriated; the head and back with dark hair-brown centres to the feathers; there is a well marked dull white stripe from the nostril over the eye; the coverts and the quills are mostly hair-brown, the former broadly margined with brownish or olivaceous-white, purer just at the tips of the coverts, and the latter narrowly margined; the first few primaries with greyish-white, the rest with a sort of greenish or olivaceous-white; the tippings of the coverts form two tolerably well marked wing-bars; the tertiaries, which are somewhat paler than the rest of the quills, are broadly margined with brownish-white; the central tail-feathers, which are the shortest, are a comparatively pale-brown, margined all round with brownish-white; the next pair on either side are very dark-brown, very narrowly margined with pale olivaceous, and the fourth with a tiny whitish spot at the extreme tip; the exterior tail-feathers of all have the whole outer webs white, slightly brownish towards the tip, the whole inner web white for nearly half an inch from the tip, beyond which for another three-quarters of an inch the white occupies (next the shaft) a gradually diminishing portion of the inner web, the rest of the feather being brown; the lower surface is a dull white, in many specimens with a faint vinaceous tinge, in parts with a row of small brown spots down the sides of the neck, with similar spots on the breast, and longer striæ along the sides and flanks.

In the summer plumage the whole upper surface becomes greatly overlaid with an earthy or greyish-brown shade, the striations of the back and head almost disappear, though the edges of the feathers are still somewhat paler than the centres, and the whole lower parts become a nearly uniform pale vinaceous color, without a single spot or streak; in some specimens, which are somewhat less advanced, a few spots still remain on the breast, and one or two streaks on the flanks. In all stages of plumage the axillaries are white; and the greater portion of the wing-lining, and the lower surface of the quills, pale satin-grey.

Within our limits the Water Pipit occurs as a not uncommon winter visitant to Sind, and more rarely to Mount Aboo, but has not been recorded from any other portion of Guzerat.

Anthus blackistoni, *Swinh.*

605*quat.*—Murray's Vertebrate Zoology of Sind, p. 171.

BLAKISTON'S PIPIT.

Length, 6·3; wing, 3·37; tail, 2·7; tarsus, 0·85; bill at front, 0·45.

Bill light brown, darker on culmen and tip; irides brown; legs brown, paler on tarsi.

Upper parts light yellowish-brown, grey on the nape; crown and back with the centres of the feathers deep-brown; lores, eyebrow, and chin, cream-white; under parts cream-white, spotted on the breast, and streaked on the flanks with brown; axillaries pure white; wings brown, feathers edged paler; coverts and tertiaries broadly edged, and tipped with cream-white, forming a double bar across the wing; tail brown, the central feathers yellowish-brown, edged paler; the outer tail-feathers white on the entire outer web, and great part of inner near the apex; penultimate feather edged exteriorly and largely tipped with white.

Within our limits, this Pipit only occurs as a cold weather visitant to Sind. It much affects the large swamps and marshes that are so frequently met with there.

GENUS, Corydalla, *Vigors.*

Bill stout; rictal vibrissæ occasionally present; tarsi moderately long.

Corydalla rufula, *Vieill.*

600.—Jerdon's Birds of India, Vol. II, p. 232; Butler, Guzerat; Stray Feathers, Vol. III, p. 490; Deccan, Stray Feathers, Vol. IX, p. 412; Murray's Vertebrate Zoology of Sind, p. 172; Swinhoe and Barnes, Central India; Ibis, 1885, p. 127.

THE INDIAN TITLARK.

Length, 6·5 to 7; wing, 3 to 3·75; tail, 2·25 to 2·5; tarsus, 1; bill at front, 0·4.

Bill dusky, yellowish at base beneath; irides brown; legs yellowish-brown.

Plumage above pale olive-brown, the feathers centred with dusky-brown; beneath earthy or fulvous white, the fulvous most developed on the breast; chin white; breast and sides of throat marked with dusky-brown striæ; supercilium fulvous-white; outermost tail-feathers almost all white; the penultimate white on the whole outer web, and also a considerable portion obliquely of the inner web.

The Indian Titlark is a common and permanent resident throughout the Presidency, breeding during May and June. The nest, which is a mere pad, is composed of fine roots and fibres, and is usually placed on the ground, under small tufts of grass, which only partially conceal it.

The eggs, three or four in number, are oval in shape, brownish-white in color, profusely speckled with reddish and umber-brown. These spots are more dense at the large end.

They measure 0 8 inches in length by about 0·6 in breadth.

Corydalla striolata, *Bly.*

601.—Jerdon's Birds of India, Vol. II, p. 233.

THE LARGE TITLARK.

Length, 7·5; expanse, 12; tail, 3·25; wing, 3·76; tarsus, 1·05; hind-claw, 0·5; bill from gape, 0·8.

Very similar to *C. rufula*, but larger, the markings more distinct, and the breast much more spotted, the general tinge at the same time being more fulvous.

Jerdon gives Central India as one of the localities frequented by the large Titlark.

GENUS, Agrodroma, *Swainson.*

Hind-claw comparatively short; bill moderately strong; plumage more uniform and less streaked.

Agrodroma campestris, *Lin.*

602.—Jerdon's Birds of India, Vol. II, p. 234; Butler, Guzerat; Stray Feathers, Vol. III, p. 491; Deccan, Stray Feathers, Vol. IX, p. 412; Murray's Vertebrate Zoology of Sind, p. 173; Swinhoe and Barnes, Central India; Ibis, 1885, p. 127.

THE STONE PIPIT.

Length, 7 to 7·25; expanse, 10·75; wing, 3·6; tail, 2·75 to 3; tarsus, 0·95; bill at front, 0·5.

Bill horny, yellowish beneath; irides brown; legs yellowish, with a tinge of fleshy.

General tone of plumage pale rufous-grey, some of the feathers, especially of the head, centred with dusky, those on the back scarcely so at all; beneath, and superciliary stripe, pale fawn-color, whitening on the throat and vent; breast very faintly marked with brown streaks; a brown stripe from the gape below the ears, and another from the lower edge of the under mandible down the throat on each side; wing-coverts brown, broadly edged with pale fawn-color; the two centre feathers of the tail brown, edged with fawn, the outermost nearly all of that color, the penultimate tipped and edged only, and the remainder deep-brown.

During the cold season the Stone Pipit is not uncommon in suitable localities throughout the district. It only occurs in open, stony, and barren places.

Agrodroma similis, *Jerd.*

603.—*A cinnamomea*, Rupp.—Jerdon's Birds of India, Vol. II, p. 235; Butler, Deccan; Stray Feathers, Vol. IX, p. 412.

THE RUFOUS ROCK PIPIT.

Length, 8·25; wing, 3·8; tarsus, 1·1.

Bill dusky, paler at base beneath; irides brown; legs fleshy.

Upper parts dusky olive-brown, the feathers more or less edged with pale ferruginous, deepest on the margins of the wing-feathers; beneath and superciliary stripe ferruginous, with narrow brown streaks on the foreneck and breast; chin and throat dull white; tail with its outermost feathers dark, obliquely tipped for its terminal third with ruddy-whitish, which extends up the narrow outer web to near its base; and the penultimate feather is tipped for about one-quarter of an inch only with the same.

The occurrence of this Pipit within our limits is doubtful, a single specimen only being recorded from the neighbourhood of Ahmednagar.

Agrodroma sordida, *Rupp.*

604.—Jerdon's Birds of India, Vol. II, p. 236; *A. jerdoni*, Finsch; Butler, Guzerat; Stray Feathers, Vol. III, p. 491; Deccan, Stray Feathers, Vol. IX, p. 412; Murray's Vertebrate Zoology of Sind, p. 173; Swinhoe and Barnes, Central India; Ibis, 1885, p. 127.

THE BROWN ROCK PIPIT.

Length, 7·5 to 8; expanse, 12; wing, 4; tail, 3·5; tarsus, 1·25; bill at front, 0·7.

Bill dusky, yellowish beneath, except at tip; irides brown; legs yellowish.

Very similar to the last; colors duller, and not so rufous, being of a dull earthy-brown, darker on the wings and tail, the feathers edged paler; a fawn colored superciliary stripe, and a faint brown mandibular stripe; beneath, the chin and throat whitish, and the rest of the body rufescent-vinous or fawn color, with a few indistinct brown blotches; central tail-feathers dark brown; outer ditto rufescent.

During the cold season the Brown Rock Pipit occurs sparingly throughout the province. It is much addicted to frequenting stony ravines and sandy plains, especially when covered with low stunted bushes, upon which they often alight when disturbed.

Family, Ampelidæ.

Tarsus short or moderate; feet fitted for perching, in some groups strong and scansorial; wings moderate; tail short or moderate; bill various, usually strong, somewhat conic; often of bright, showy, and variegated plumage.

Sub-family, Leiotrichinæ.

Bill usually short, more or less wide at the base, lengthened and slightly curved in a few, entire in some, notched in others; tail short or moderate, even or slightly rounded; tarsi short, stout; feet strong; claws moderately curved, sharp.

Genus, Zosterops.

Bill slightly notched, curved; eyes with a circle of white feathers; nostrils exposed; third and fourth primaries longest.

Zosterops palpebrosa, *Tem.*

631.—Jerdon's Birds of India, Vol. II, p. 265; Butler, Guzerat; Stray Feathers, Vol. III, p. 491; Deccan, Stray Feathers, Vol. IX, p. 413; Murray's Vertebrate Zoology of Sind, p. 174; Swinhoe and Barnes, Central India; Ibis, 1885, p. 127.

The White-eyed Tit.

Length, 4·5; expanse, 6·5; wing, 2·33; tail, 1·7; tarsus, 0·75; bill at front, 0·33 to 0·4.

Bill blackish, horny at base beneath; irides light yellow-brown; legs reddish-horny.

Above light siskin-green, with a circle of close white feathers round the eyes; throat and upper breast canary yellow; belly bluish-white; leg feathers, lower tail-coverts, and some of the feathers on the abdomen, tinged with pale-yellow.

The White-eyed Tit is a common permanent resident in the Deccan, breeding from April to September; the nest is a soft, delicate, little cup, suspended between two twigs, occasionally in a fork, and is composed of fine grass, roots, &c., attached to the twigs from which it is suspended by cobwebs or vegetable fibres.

The eggs, two or three in number, are of a moderately lengthened oval shape, pointed at one end, of a pale blue color, quite unspotted. They average 0·62 inches in length by about 0·47 in breadth.

In other parts of the Presidency it only occurs, I believe, as a cold weather visitant; it is extremely rare in Sind.

Sub-family, Parinæ.

Bill typically rather short, conic, stout, entire, the nares tufted; wings moderate, somewhat rounded; tail short or moderate, long in a few; tarsus and feet short, stout; hind-toe long; claws well curved.

GENUS, **Parus**, *Lin.*

Head uncrested; bill usually stout and moderately short; tail rather short.

Parus nipalensis, *Hodgs.*

645.—*P. cinereus*, Vieill.—Jerdon's Birds of India, Vol. II, p. 278; *P. cæsius*, Tick.; Butler, Guzerat; Stray Feathers, Vol. III, p. 491; Deccan, Stray Feathers, Vol. IX, p. 413; Swinhoe and Barnes, Central India; Ibis, p. 127.

THE INDIAN GREY TIT.

Length, 5·95; wing, 2·8; tail, 2·6; tarsus, 0·6; bill at front, 0·7. Bill black; irides brown; legs blackish.

Head, chin, throat, and breast, and a line along the abdomen, black; large cheek-spot white; plumage above bluish-cinereous; greater-coverts white tipped, forming a conspicuous wing-band; quills dusky-black, edged with pale blue, and the secondaries and tertiaries edged white; beneath albescent, with a tinge of rufescent-ashy, purer white on the under tail-coverts.

The Grey Tit occurs sparingly on Mount Aboo, but does not descend to the plains beneath. It does not occur in Sind, but is common in Southern Afghanistan. It is a common permanent resident in the Deccan, breeding from May to August; the nest (a mere pad composed of moss, hair, fur and feathers), is placed in a hole in a tree, bank, or wall.

The eggs, five or six in number, are slightly elongated ovals, pointed towards one end. The ground color is white, (pinkish before they are blown), blotched, spotted, and streaked, more especially towards the large end, with red or occasionally pale-purple.

They average about 0·71 inches by about 0·54.

Parus nuchalis, *Jerdon.*

646.—Jerdon's Birds of India, Vol. II, p. 279; Butler, Guzerat; Stray Feathers, Vol. III, p. 492.

THE WHITE-WINGED BLACK TIT.

Length, 5; wing, 2·8; tail, 2; tarsus, 0·7; bill at front, 0·4. Bill black; irides red-brown; legs plumbeous.

Above black, with a white nuchal mark; a white band across the wing, and the tertiaries broadly margined and tipped with white; tail with the outer feathers nearly white, the next with the outer web only, and the third with the outer web white only at its base and tip; cheeks, sides of neck, sides of breast, belly, and under tail-coverts, white, with a black mesial stripe from the throat to the vent.

The White-winged Black Tit has been obtained from Cutch and the vicinity of Deesa. It appears to be very locally distributed.

Genus, **Machlolophus**, *Cabanis.*

Head crested; plumage much mixed with yellow and green.

Machlolophus xanthogenys, *Vigors.*

647.—Jerdon's Birds of India, Vol. II, p. 279; Swinhoe and Barnes, Central India; Ibis, 125, p. 127.

The Yellow-cheeked Tit.

Length, 5·25; wing, 2·75; tail, 2·12; tarsus, 0·6; bill at front, 0·33.

Bill black; irides light-brown; legs plumbeous.

Head (fully crested), wings and tail black, the latter tipped white, and the tertiaries laterally edged throughout with white; nape, posterior part of crest, and a small superciliary stripe, bright yellow; back, scapulars, and rump, light olive-green, the scapulars with a few black marks; wing-coverts tipped with pale-yellow; the outer primaries white-edged, and with a white bar near their base, the others bluish externally; tail dusky-grey, white tipped; cheeks, sides of neck, sides of breast and abdomen, and under tail-coverts yellow, passing to greenish on the flanks and under tail-coverts; lores, a stripe on each side of the neck from the eye, chin, throat, and middle of breast, black.

The Yellow-checked Tit occurs on the slopes of the Vindhian hills, near Mhow, and in the woods at their base. It has not been recorded from elsewhere within our limits.

Machlolophus aplonotus, *Bly.*

648.—*M. jerdoni*, Blyth.—Jerdon's Birds of India, Vol. II, p. 280; Butler, Guzerat; Stray Feathers, Vol. III, p. 492; Deccan, Stray Feathers, Vol. IX, p. 413.

The Southern Yellow Tit.

Length, 6; expanse, 10; wing, 3; tail, 2·5; tarsus, 0·7; bill at front, 0·35.

Bill black; irides light-brown; legs plumbeous.

Very similar to the last, but conspicuously larger; has the back less tinged with yellow, being dull green with a slaty tinge; the yellow portion of the plumage not so intense in hue, and the yellow sincipital streak short, and not continued forward over the eye.

This Tit is a permanent resident on the Sahyadri Range, and in the well wooded tracts adjoining; it also occurs on Mount Aboo; it is unknown in Sind.

Jerdon states that he found it common on the Vindhian Range, near Mhow, but a bird that I procured from thence proved to belong to the preceding species.

Tribe, **Conirostres.**

Bill usually entire at the tip, thick, more or less conic, with the lower mandible deeper than in most of the preceding tribe;

wings more generally lengthened; tail usually moderate or short, even or emarginate, rounded in a few; feet fitted for walking on the ground, as well as for perching.

FAMILY, Corvidæ.

Bill strong, more or less compressed, usually entire, rarely notched at the tip; nostrils thickly clad with stiff incumbent bristles; tarsus short; feet strong, and claws well curved; of large size mostly.

SUB-FAMILY, Corvinæ.

Bill very stout, long, straight, with the ridge more or less curved; wings long, somewhat pointed; tail variable; tarsus stout, strongly scutate; claws well curved.

GENUS, Corvus, *Lin.*

Bill long, very strong and thick, straight; the culmen more or less elevated; nares protected by very long and rigid bristles; wing long and pointed, first quill short; second a little shorter than the third and fourth, and the fifth usually subequal to them; tail moderate, even, or somewhat rounded; tarsus very stout, of moderate length, with strong scutæ; feet moderate; lateral toes about equal; claws sharp, and strongly curved.

Corvus lawrencei, *Hume.*

657*bis.*—Murray's Vertebrate Zoology of Sind, p. 175.

THE INDIAN RAVEN.

Length, 23·75 to 24·75; wing, 16·3 to 17·4; tail very much rounded; the outer tail-feathers being always two, and generally 2·5 inches shorter than the central ones; bill at front, 2·8.

Bill black; irides dark or grey-brown; legs black.

Uniform blue-black throughout, with a purplish tinge on the throat and upper breast; feathers of the chin and throat lanceolate; incumbent bristles in front, extend to beyond more than half of the length of the bill, which is much arched.

Within our limits the Indian Raven only occurs in Upper Sind.

Corvus macrorhynchus, *Wagl.*

660.—*C. culminatus*, Sykes.—Jerdon's Birds of India, Vol. II, p. 295; Butler, Guzerat; Stray Feathers, Vol. III, p. 493; Deccan, Stray Feathers, Vol. IX, p. 413; *Corone macrorhyncha*, Wagl.; Swinhoe and Barnes, Central India; Ibis, 1885, p. 128.

THE INDIAN CORBY.

Length, 21; wing, 13·5; tail, 7·75; tarsus, 2·5; bill at front, 2·4.

Bill black; irides dark-brown; legs black.

Above glossy black, dull black beneath ; tail slightly rounded ; wings reach nearly to the end of the tail ; bill straight at the base and high ; culmen raised, curving strongly towards the tip.

With the exception of Sind, the Corby is a common and permanent resident, breeding during March and April and building the usual Corvine stick nest. The eggs, four in number, are moderately broad ovals, somewhat pointed at one end, and are dull sap-green in color, much blotched, streaked, and dashed with brown ; but they vary very much both in size and color.

They average about 1·71 inches in length by 1·18 in breadth.

Corvus umbrinus, *Hedenb.*

660*bis*.—Murray's Vertebrate Zoology of Sind, p. 175.

THE BROWN-NECKED RAVEN.

Length, 21·5 to 23 ; wing, 15 to 16·4 ; tail, 8·6 to 9 ; tarsus, 2·9 ; bill at front, 3.

Bill black ; irides dark-brown ; legs black.

Head and neck glossy umber-brown, also the ear-coverts, sides of the face and sides of the neck, the latter scarcely glossed ; lores, incumbent nasal bristles, feathers round the eye, and at base of bill at the gape, black ; back, scapulars, wing, wing-coverts, upper tail-coverts, and tail, glossy black with a violet-blue gloss ; chin, throat, and breast, dark glossy umber-brown ; rest of under surface brown, glossed with purple on the breast, flanks, abdomen and vent ; under tail-coverts glossy purplish-black ; axillaries and under wing-coverts purplish-black.

The Brown-necked Raven is a not uncommon winter visitant to Upper Sind, but does not occur elsewhere within our limits.

Corvus splendens, *Vieill.*

663.—Jerdon's Birds of India, Vol. II, p. 298 ; Butler, Guzerat ; Stray Feathers, Vol. III, p. 493 ; Deccan, Stray Feathers, Vol. IX, p. 413 ; Murray's Vertebrate Zoology of Sind, p. 176 ; *Corone splendens*, Vieill. ; Swinhoe and Barnes, Central India ; Ibis, 1885, p. 128.

THE COMMON INDIAN CROW.

Kowa, Hin. *Kagra*, Sindi.

Length, 15 to 18 ; wing, 10·75 to 11·25 ; tail, 7 ; tarsus, 1·85 ; bill at front, 2·12.

Bill black ; irides deep-brown ; legs black.

Forehead, sinciput, and lores, glossy black ; occiput, nape, hind-neck, and sides of neck, purplish-ashy ; back, wings, and tail, black, with rich purple and steel-blue reflections ; breast ashy, tinged dark ; middle of abdomen dull black, slightly tinged with steel-blue.

The Common Crow is numerous throughout the district, except on the hills, where it is replaced by *macrorhynchus*. It is a permanent resident, breeding during May and June, making the usual stick nest. The eggs, four or five in number, are broadish oval in shape, pointed at one end, but vary much in color; they are generally greenish-blue or dingy-green, speckled, spotted and dashed with umber-brown.

They measure 1·44 by 1·06. The eggs of the Koel are almost exclusively deposited in the nest of this crow.

SUB-FAMILY, Dendrocittinæ.

Bill short, with the culmen much elevated and curved, quite entire at the tip; gonys straight; commissure curved; nares protected by dense, velvety short feathers; wings short, rounded; tail long, graduated; tarsus short, stout; feet arboreal with the lateral toes slightly unequal.

GENUS, Dendrocitta, *Gould.*

Bill short or moderate, compressed, well curved from the base; nostrils small, basal, concealed by short incumbent feathers; wings short, rounded; fifth and sixth quills longest, fourth subequal; secondaries nearly as long as the primaries; tail elongate, wedge-shaped, with the two central feathers produced; feet moderate or short, arboreal; middle-toe short; lateral toes unequal; hind-toe and claw rather large.

Dendrocitta rufa, *Scop.*

674.—Jerdon's Birds of India, Vol. II, p. 314; Butler, Guzerat; Stray Feathers, Vol. III, p. 494; Deccan, Stray Feathers, Vol. IX, p. 413; Murray's Vertebrate Zoology of Sind, p. 177; Swinhoe and Barnes, Central India; Ibis, p. 128.

THE COMMON INDIAN MAGPIE.

Length, 16 to 18; expanse, 17 to 19; wing, 5·8 to 6·5; tail, 8 to 10·5; tarsus, 1·1 to 1·2; bill at gape, 1·2; bill at front, 1·1.

Bill black; irides blood-red; legs dark-slaty.

Whole head, neck, and breast, sooty-brown or blackish, deepest on the forehead, chin, and throat, and passing into dusky-cinereous; scapulars, back, and upper tail-coverts, dark ferruginous; wing-coverts, and the outer web of the secondaries, light grey, almost whitish in some; rest of the quills black; tail ashy-grey, the feathers all broadly tipped with black, least so on the centre feathers; beneath, from the breast, ferruginous or fulvous.

This Tree Pie is, I believe, a permanent resident throughout the district, but I have only been able to procure eggs in Sind. During part of the hot weather they become very scarce, if not altogether absent, and are then probably engaged in breeding in some near but more suitable locality.

In Sind they breed during May and June, almost always choosing babool trees, placing the nest in a stoutish fork near the top;

li
pusans

they are composed at the bottom of thorny twigs, which form a sort of foundation upon which the true nest is built; the latter consists of fine twigs, lined with grass roots; the nest is frequently of large size. The eggs, four (more rarely five) in number, vary most astonishingly in both ground-color and in the character of the markings. Typically they are longish ovals, a good deal pointed at one end. A common type is a pale salmon or pale greenish-white, thickly splashed and marked with bright or brownish-red; the other type is greenish-white or pale stony color, and the markings are olive and pale purplish-brown, others are intermediate between these two types; some of these eggs are exact counterparts, except in size, of eggs of *Lanius lahtora*. In length they measure from 1·0 to 1·3 inches, and in breadth from 0·78 to 0·95, but the average is about 1·17 inches in length by 0·87 in breadth.

Family, **Sturnidæ**.

Bill straight, or very slightly curved, longish, compressed, subulate, often angulated at the base, slightly notched at the tip or entire; wings long, rather pointed; tail moderate or stout; tarsi short, moderate; lateral toes about equal.

Sub-family, **Sturninæ**.

Bill moderately long, compressed, straight or slightly curved, entire in most; commissure usually angulated, or bent down towards the base; frontal plumes soft, dense, covering the base of the bill, which is prolonged backwards between the plumes; wings with the second primary usually longest; the tail short, even or slightly rounded; tarsus moderately long, stout.

Genus, **Sturnus**, *Linnæus*.

Bill long, straight, subulate, slightly depressed at the base; the culmen convex; tip obtuse, barely deflected; nostrils basal, partly closed by a vaulted membrane; wing with first quill minute; tail even, short; tarsus moderately long; lateral toes nearly equal; hind-toe long.

Sturnus vulgaris, *Lin.*

681.—Jerdon's Birds of India, Vol. II, p. 320; Butler, Guzerat; Stray Feathers, Vol. III, p. 494; Murray's Vertebrate Zoology of Sind, p. 178; Swinhoe and Barnes, Central India; Ibis, 1885, p. 128.

THE COMMON STARLING.

Length, 9; wing, 5; tail, 3; tarsus, 1·6; bill at front, 1·25.

Bill at first brown, but eventually becoming rich yellow; irides brown; legs yellow.

Glossy black, with a pale whitish or brownish tip to each feather, giving the bird a pretty speckled appearance; all the clothing feathers long and lanceolate, becoming longer and more pointed at each moult. In very old birds the specks are said to disappear altogether, or nearly so.

The young bird is dull brown.

The Common Starling of Europe is a not uncommon winter visitant to Sind, Guzerat, and parts of Rajputana. It associates with the Common and Bank Mynas. It does not occur in the Deccan.

Sturnus minor, *Hume.*

681*bis.*—Murray's Vertebrate Zoology of Sind, p. 178.

THE LESSER STARLING.

Wing, 4·3; tarsus, 1; bill at front, 1.

Bill yellow; irides brown; legs yellow.

General character of plumage like that of the Common Starling; but in the first place, the Common Starling has the reflections of the head purple, and of the back green, but in the present species the reflections of the head are green and the back purple.

Secondly the wing is decidedly shorter.

The bills of both are about equal in length, but those of *minor* are more pointed, have a more decided culmen ridge, and are less broad at the base.

The Lesser Starling is a permanent resident in parts of Sind, breeding from March to June. The eggs are similar to those of the Common Starling, but are smaller.

GENUS, Acridotheres, *Vieill.*

Bill rather short, stout, compressed; culmen gently curving and deflected; gonys slightly sloping upwards; nostrils almost concealed by the frontal plumes which extend above them their whole length; tail rounded; tarsus stout; feet strong; toes lengthened; the laterals nearly equal; claws moderately curved.

The head is more or less crested, and some of them have a naked space behind and under the eye.

Acridotheres tristis, *Lin.*

684.—Jerdon's Birds of India, Vol. II, p. 325; Butler, Guzerat; Stray Feathers, Vol. III, p. 494; Deccan, Stray Feathers, Vol. IX, p. 413; Murray's Vertebrate Zoology of Sind, p. 178; Swinhoe and Barnes, Central India; Ibis, 1885, p. 128.

THE COMMON MYNA.

Length, 10; wing, 5·25; tail, 3·5; tarsus, 1·4; bill at front, 0·85.

Bill yellow; irides red-brown with white specks; legs dull-yellow; orbits deep-yellow.

The whole head, with moderate occipital crest, neck and breast, glossy black; the rest of the plumage quaker or snuff-brown, darkest on the back and wing-coverts, and lightest beneath; primaries black, with a white spot at their base, forming a conspicuous wing-spot; tail black with a white tip, successively broader from the centre pair; lower abdomen, vent, and under tail-coverts white.

This Myna is a common permanent resident throughout the district, breeding from June to August. They nest indifferently, in holes, in trees or walls, in deserted crow nests, under the eaves of verandahs, and occasionally, but very rarely, they build a cup-shaped nest in a fork of a tree. The eggs, four or five in number, are rather longish ovals in shape, of a glossy blue-green color, and average 1·19 inches in length by about 0·86 in breadth.

Acridotheres ginginianus, *Lath.*

685.—Jerdon's Birds of India, Vol. II, p. 326; Butler, Guzerat; Stray Feathers, Vol. III, p. 494; Murray's Vertebrate Zoology of Sind, p. 179; Swinhoe and Barnes, Central India; Ibis, 1885, p. 128.

THE BANK MYNA.

Length, 8·5; wing, 5; tail, 3·25; tarsus, 1·25; bill at front, 0·85.

Bill red, yellow at tip; nude eye-spot reddish; irides brown; legs yellow.

Head with rather short occipital crest; lores, ear-coverts, and nape, glossy black; the rest of the plumage dull cinereous or inky-black, paling beneath; wing black, with the wing-spot ferruginous; tail black, tipped dull ferruginous; middle of abdomen, of vent, and the under tail-coverts, pale ferruginous; the frontal feathers are slightly erectile, and those on the side of the head are directed towards the median line.

The Bank Myna is very common throughout Sind and Guzerat; it also occurs in Central India and Rajputana, but is very locally distributed. It does not appear ever to have been noticed in the Deccan. It is a permanent resident wherever found, breeding in holes in river banks, or wells, during June and July; these holes are excavated by the birds themselves. The eggs, four or five in number, are broadish ovals in shape, and glossy greenish-blue in color.

They average 1·05 inches in length by about 0·81 in breadth.

Acridotheres mahrattensis, *Sykes.*

686*bis.*—Butler, Deccan; Stray Feathers, Vol. IX, p. 412.

THE SOUTHERN DUSKY MYNA.

Length, 9·5; wing, 5; tail, 3; tarsus, 1·4; bill at front, 0·7.

Bill orange-yellow; irides pale blue; legs yellow.

The whole head, small frontal crest, and ear-coverts, glossy black; the upper plumage fuscous black, or blackish-brown, with a vinous tinge; primaries black, with a white spot near their base; tail also black, white-tipped, most broadly on the outer feathers; beneath, the throat and breast dull cinereous-blackish; abdomen reddish-cinereous, paling in the centre, whitish on the vent, and the under tail-coverts pure white; the secondaries are glossed with bronze towards their end.

This Myna is a permanent resident in the more hilly districts of the Deccan. The only difference between *mahrattensis* and *fuscus* is that the irides of the former are pale-blue, while those of the latter are yellow.

GENUS, **Sturnia**, *Lesson*.

Bill short, compressed, less stout than in *Acridotheres*, bare, deflected at the tip, often parti-colored; wings moderate, first and second primaries sub-equal; tail nearly even; tarsus short; lateral toes slightly unequal; claws more curved; head usually crested.

Sturnia pagodarum, *Gm.*

687.—*Temenuchus pagodarum*, Gm.—Jerdon's Birds of India, Vol. II, p. 329; Butler, Guzerat; Stray Feathers, Vol. III, p. 494; Deccan, Stray Feathers, Vol. IX, p. 414; Murray's Vertebrate Zoology of Sind, p. 179; Swinhoe and Barnes, Central India; Ibis, 1885, p. 128.

THE BLACK-HEADED MYNA.

Brahmani Myna, Hin.; *Powi*, Hin.

Length, 7·5 to 8·5; expanse, 12·5; wing, 4 to 4·25; tail, 2·5 to 3; tarsus, 1 to 1·2; bill at front, 0·6; bill from gape, 0·9.

Bill greenish-yellow at tip, blue at base; irides greenish-white; legs bright-yellow.

Head and long pendent crest black; body above grey; beneath and ear-coverts bright fulvous-buff, with some mesial pale streaks; wings blackish, with a white edge near the shoulder; tail dull black.

The Black-headed Myna occurs throughout the district, but is somewhat locally distributed; it is somewhat rare in Sind. It is a permanent resident, breeding from June to August, in holes in trees. The eggs, four or five in number, are oval in shape, pale bluish-white in color, and average 0·97 in length by about 0·75 in breadth.

Sturnia malabarica, *Gm.*

688.—*Temenuchus malabaricus*, Gm.—Jerdon's Birds of India, Vol. II, p. 330; Butler, Guzerat; Stray Feathers, Vol. III, p. 494; Deccan, Stray Feathers, Vol. IX, p. 414.

THE GREY-HEADED MYNA.

Powi, Hin.

Length, 7·5; wing, 4; tail, 2·5; tarsus, 1; bill at front, 0·6.

Bill greenish-yellow at tip, bluish at base; irides greyish-white; legs dull yellow.

Upper parts grey; the forehead and throat whitish, the feathers being centred white, and the former occasionally pure white; entire under parts, from the foreneck, ferruginous-buff (some of the feathers of the breast also centred with whitish), deep-colored in old males, faint in young and in females; quills black, the inner web deep-brown, the primaries slightly glossed and faintly tipped with grey, the rest dusky, successively more broadly tipped with deep ferruginous. The colors fade much by abrasion, and become more nearly uniform.

The young birds are nearly all grey, lighter beneath and with rufous tips to the outer tail-feathers.

The Grey-headed Myna occurs during the cold weather in the Deccan. It has also been recorded from Mount Aboo.

Sturnia blythi, *Jerdon*.

689.—*Temenuchus blythi*, Jerd.—Jerdon's Birds of India, Vol. II, p. 331; Butler, Deccan; Stray Feathers, Vol. IX, p. 414.

THE WHITE-HEADED MYNA.

Length, 8·5; wing, 4·2; tail, 3; tarsus, 1; bill at front, 0·7.

Bill greenish, yellow at tip, bluish at base; irides greyish-white; legs reddish-yellow.

Whole head with long crest, neck, throat and breast, silky-white; back and scapulars grey; belly and under tail-coverts deep rufous; wing-coverts and outer web of most of the quills and all the tertiaries also grey; quills black, grey tipped; central tail-feathers dark-grey, blackish at the base, the outer feathers deep ferruginous-brown, dusky towards the base.

The White-headed Myna is common about Belgaum during the rains.

GENUS, Pastor, *Temm*.

Bill short, compressed, curving from the base, very slightly hooked at the tip; gonys straight; nostrils partially concealed by fine frontal plumes; wings long, pointed; first quill longest, second sub-equal, third a little shorter; tail nearly even; tarsus rather short; lateral toes slightly unequal; head adorned with a long pendent occipital crest.

Pastor roseus, *Lin*.

690.—Jerdon's Birds of India, Vol. II, p. 333; Butler, Guzerat; Stray Feathers, Vol. III, p. 495; Deccan, Stray Feathers, Vol. IX, p. 414; Murray's Vertebrate Zoology of Sind, p. 180; Swinhoe and Barnes, Central India; Ibis, 1885, p. 128.

THE ROSE-COLORED STARLING.

Length, 9 to 9·5; expanse, 14; wing, 4·5 to 5·25; tail, 2·75 to 3; tarsus, 1·2; bill at front, 0·7; bill from gape, 1·12.

Bill pinkish, brown at tip, orange-yellow at base; irides deep brown; legs dusky-reddish.

Whole head, with crest, neck, and breast, fine glossy-black, with purple reflections; wings and tail black with a green gloss; rest of the plumage pale-salmon or light rose-color.

Young birds have the salmon or rose-color much dashed with pale-brown and fuscous, and the head not so glossy; and the young of the year are more or less earthy-brown, paler beneath and without a crest.

The Rose-colored Pastor is a common cold weather visitant to all parts of the district. The majority of the birds met with are young birds in imperfect plumage.

SUB-FAMILY, **Lamprotorninæ.**

Bill somewhat stout, the ridge more or less curved and hooked, and the tip notched; nostrils more or less hidden by the close-set frontal plumes; wings long or moderate, and pointed; tarsus short and stout.

GENUS, **Eulabes,** *Cuvier.*

Bill short or moderate, stout, compressed; culmen gradually curved; tip notched; nostrils basal, lateral, placed in a plumed fossa; under mandible with the base broad and dilated; frontal feathers short, velvety, advancing on base of bill; head with naked wattles; wings long, fourth quill longest, first short; tail short, even; feet strong; tarsus equal to the middle-toe; outer-toe slightly longer than inner one; claws well curved; hind-toe and claw large.

Eulabes religiosa, *Lin.*

692.—Jerdon's Birds of India, Vol. II, p. 337; Butler, Deccan; Stray Feathers, Vol. IX, p. 414.

THE SOUTHERN HILL MYNA.

Length, 10; expanse, 18·5; wing, 5·6; tail, 2·8; tarsus, 1·2; bill at front, 1.

Bill orange; wattles deep-yellow; irides dark-brown; legs deep-yellow.

General plumage glossy purplish-black, with green reflections on the lower back and upper tail-coverts; beneath less brightly glossed; wings and tail coal-black without reflections; a white spot on the seven primaries, forming a conspicuous wing-spot.

The wattles on the head commenced below each eye are crossed at the lower posterior angle of the eye, by a triangular patch of minute feathers, passed beyond the ear, where they form a rather large loose flap, or lappet, and then return in a narrow stripe to the top of the head. There is also a small nude patch below the eye.

Is only found in the Deccan (on the Ghâts), and is somewhat rare.

FAMILY, **Fringillidæ.**

Bill short, thick, conic; wings usually long, pointed; tail moderate, even, forked in most; tarsus moderate or short; feet suited both for perching and terrestrial habits; of small size.

SUB-FAMILY, **Ploceinæ.**

Bill strong, conic, slightly lengthened; the culmen arched, and the ridge continued back upon the forehead; wings somewhat rounded, first primary very minute; tail short in most; legs and toes very strong and robust, the latter lengthened, specially the hind-toe, and the claws well developed.

GENUS, **Ploceus,** *Cuv.*

Bill thick at the base, laterally compressed, pointed at the tip; culmen smooth, broad, rounded, and produced backwards on the forehead to a point; commissure nearly straight; nostrils basal, partly concealed; wings moderate or somewhat short, with the first quill small, about one-third of the next four or five, second a little shorter than the third, which is usually longest; tail short, even, or very slightly rounded; feet large; hind-toe and claw strong, all the claws lengthened.

Ploceus philippinus, *Lin.*

694.—*P. baya,* Blyth.—Jerdon's Birds of India, Vol. II, p. 343; Butler, Guzerat; Stray Feathers, Vol. III, p. 495; Deccan, Stray Feathers, Vol. IX, p. 415; Murray's Vertebrate Zoology of Sind, p. 180; Swinhoe and Barnes, Central India; Ibis, 1885, p. 128.

THE COMMON WEAVER-BIRD.

Length, 6; expanse, 9·5; wing, 2·8; tail, 1·9; tarsus, 0·8; bill at front, 0·6.

Bill from pale horny-brown to black; irides dusky-brown; legs brownish-fleshy.

Old males, in breeding plumage, have the crown of the head bright yellow, the rest of the upper plumage with the wings and tail dull brown, edged with pale fulvous-brown, some of the feathers in the middle of the back edged yellow; rump and upper tail-coverts pale rufous-brown; primaries with a narrow edging of pale-yellow; lores, ear-coverts, chin and throat, blackish-brown; breast bright yellow; belly and lower tail-coverts dull white; the flanks, under wing-coverts, and thigh-coverts, pale rusty or buff.

Young males, in the breeding plumage, have the breast pale rusty instead of yellow, and the yellow edging of the inter-scapulars is wanting.

The females and males in winter dress totally want the yellow head, the crown being brown with dark streaks, have pale-rufous supercilia, and the chin and throat are whitish.

The Common Weaver-Bird is generally distributed throughout our limits, but is more abundant in well-wooded districts. It is a permanent resident, breeding towards the end of the rains.

The nest, retort-shaped, is a marvel of skill and ingenuity; it is composed of strips torn from broad-leaved grasses, which are obtained in the following manner; the bird first notches a blade of grass to the required depth, and then after making a similar nip higher up, catches the grass firmly at the lower notch and flies off, taking the strip with it. In Bombay, the nests are generally suspended from the tips of acacia trees, often overhanging a river, tank, or well.

I have never seen a nest composed of any other material than grass, but Jerdon speaks of strips of plantain leaves and strips torn from leaves of cocoanut and date palms being used. After the eggs are laid, and the female has commenced to sit, the male often continues to prolong the tubular entrance, and I have seen nests, having it at least eighteen inches in length. I cannot understand how Jerdon and Hume conclude that two is the normal number of eggs, as I have examined some scores of nests and have never found less than four incubated eggs, and have frequently found five or six. The eggs vary both in size and shape, but are typically longish ovals, pointed at one end, and are dead glossless white in color; they average about 0·82 inches in length by 0·59 in breadth.

Ploceus manyar, *Horsf.*

605.—Jerdon's Birds of India, Vol. II, p. 348; Butler, Guzerat; Stray Feathers, Vol. III, p. 495; Deccan, Stray Feathers, Vol. IX, p. 415; Murray's Vertebrate Zoology of Sind, p. 181; Swinhoe and Barnes, Central India; Ibis, 1885, p. 128.

The Striated Weaver Bird.

Length, 5·8; expanse, 9; wing, 2·75; tail, 1·75; tarsus, 0·75; bill at front, 0·9.

Bill black during the breeding season, at other times pale horny-fleshy; irides light brown; legs fleshy.

The male in full breeding dress has the crown of the head intense yellow; lores, cheeks, ear-coverts, chin, throat, and neck, brownish-black; back, wings, and tail, brown; the feathers of the back with a mesial dark streak, those of the primaries and tail edged with yellowish; rump streaked like the back; upper tail-coverts rufescent; beneath from the throat whitish, tinged with fulvous, and streaked on the breast and flanks with dusky-black.

The male in winter dress is clad like the female, and has the head brown, streaked like the back, a pale yellow supercilium, and a small yellow spot behind the ear-coverts; the chin and throat are whitish, and the streaks on the lower surface less developed.

The Striated Weaver-Bird occurs in suitable localities throughout the Presidency. It is a permanent resident, but only breeds in the vicinity of large tanks or rivers, whose banks are fringed with reeds or rushes, to the tops of which the nests are attached.

They are very similar to those of *P. philippensis*, but are square at the top instead of tapering to a point.

The normal number of eggs, according to my experience, is three, but four are often found; they are exact counterparts of those of *philippensis*, except that they are slightly smaller, averaging 0·79 inches in length by about 0·58 in breadth.

Ploceus bengalensis, *Lin.*

696.—Jerdon's Birds of India, Vol. II, p. 349; Butler, Guzerat; Stray Feathers, Vol. V, p. 210; Murray's Vertebrate Zoology of Sind, p. 181; Swinhoe and Barnes, Central India; Ibis, 1885, p. 128.

THE BLACK-THROATED WEAVER BIRD.

Length, 5·5; expanse, 9·25; wing, 3·75; tail, 1·75.

Bill pearly-white; irides light brown; legs dusky carneous.

The male, in breeding plumage, has the crown brilliant golden-yellow, with, in some instances, a slight inclination to flame color; back dusky brown; rump dingy grey-brown; wings and tail dark brown, the former with very slight pale margins to some of the feathers; the throat white; the cheeks, ear-coverts, and sides of the neck, white, more or less suffused with dusky on the ear-coverts and throat; a broad, brownish-black pectoral band; the rest of the lower plumage sullied or fulvous-white, brownish on the flanks.

In some the pectoral band is broad and entire, in others narrower, and divided along the middle.

The female has the head streakless dusky-brown, the feathers of the back edged with pale rufous-brown; a pale-yellow supercilium, and a spot of the same color behind the ear; also a narrow moustachial stripe; throat white, yellowish in some, and usually separated from the yellow moustache by a narrow black line; pectoral band less developed.

Males after the autumn moult resemble the females, but the breast and flanks are more rufescent; the pectoral band is frequently wanting, or rather concealed, by pale-fulvous deciduary edgings.

With the exception of the Deccan, the Black-throated Weaver Bird occurs throughout the province, but is very locally distributed.

SUB-FAMILY, Estreldinæ.

Of small size; bills large in many and bulged, more slender in others; wings short, rounded; feet large; tail rounded or cuneiform.

GENUS, Amadina. (*Munia.*)

Bill very thick and at the base as deep as long, compressed at the tip; culmen arched, flattened, prolonged backward to a point of the forehead; gape strongly angulated; nares round, sunk and free; wings short; first primary minute, the three next nearly equal; tail moderate or short, rounded or wedged; tarsus stout, moderate; toes long, slender; claws long.

Amadina malacca, *Lin.*

697.—*Munia malacca*, Lin.—Jerdon's Birds of India, Vol. II, p. 352; Butler, Deccan, Stray Feathers, Vol. IX, p. 415.

THE BLACK-HEADED MUNIA.

Length, 4·5; wing, 2·6; tail, 1·5.

Bill bluish, yellowish at tip; irides dark-brown; legs plumbeous.

Whole head, neck, and breast, rich black; back, wings, and tail, pure rich cinnamon-red; upper tail-coverts brighter tinged, and with a glistening lustre; beneath, from the breast, white, with the middle of the abdomen and vent black.

Young birds of the year have the upper parts plain rufescent-brown, and the lower parts pale-buff, the chin and throat being albescent, and the lores dusky.

The Black-headed Munia is a common seasonal visitant about Belgaum, breeding abundantly during the rains, in the sugar-cane fields. The eggs are not distinguishable from those of *A. malabarica.*

Amadina rubronigra, *Hodgson.*

698.—*Munia rubronigra*, Hodgs.—Jerdon's Birds of India, Vol. II, p. 353; Butler, Deccan; Stray Feathers, Vol. IX, p. 415.

THE CHESNUT-BELLIED MUNIA.

Length, 4·5; wings, 2·12; tail, 1·5; tarsus, 0·5; bill at front, 0·5.

Bill plumbeous; irides dark-brown; legs plumbeous.

Head, neck, and breast, black; rest of the plumage deep chesnut or cinnamon, passing to glistening marone on the upper tail-coverts, and tinged with fulvous on the tail; a stripe down the middle of the belly, vent, and under tail-coverts, black.

The Chesnut-bellied Munia is a very rare straggler to parts of the Deccan.

Amadina punctulata, *Lin.*

699.—*Munia undulata*, Lath.—Jerdon's Birds of India, Vol. II, p. 354; Butler, Guzerat; Stray Feathers, Vol. III, p. 495; Deccan, Stray Feathers, Vol. IX, p. 415.

THE SPOTTED MUNIA.

Length, 4·5; wing, 2·2; tail, 1·5; tarsus, 0·75; bill at front, 0·4.

Bill plumbeous; irides brown; legs plumbeous.

Above ruddy-brown, deeper on the head and neck, inclining to whitish on the rump, and the upper tail-coverts and margins of the lateral tail-feathers, glistening fulvous; quills, chesnut externally, dusky within; beneath, the chin and throat, with the face and ear-coverts, rich chesnut; breast and flanks white, with numerous zig-zag cross bars of black; lower abdomen, vent and under tail-coverts, whitish unmarked.

With the exception of Sind, the Spotted or Barred Munia occurs throughout our limits, but is very locally distributed. It is a permanent resident, breeding during July and August. The eggs, five to eight in number, are of the usual glossless, dead-white color. They measure 0·65 in length by about 0·46 in breadth.

Amadina pectoralis, *Jerdon.*

700.—*Munia pectoralis*, Jerd.—Jerdon's Birds of India, Vol. II, p. 355; Butler, Deccan; Stray Feathers, Vol. IX, p. 415.

THE RUFOUS-BELLIED MUNIA.

Length, 4·5; wing, 2·2; tail, 1·7; tarsus, 0·6.

Head, neck, and back, brown; the shafts of the feathers pale; upper tail-coverts dark-brown, the feathers tipped with glistening yellow; wings and tail dark-brown; face, forehead, throat, and breast, dark brown, strongly contrasting with the sides of the neck; lower parts from the breast reddish-fawn color; under tail-coverts dark-brown with pale shafts.

The Rufous-bellied Munia has been procured but very rarely in the jungles west of Belgaum.

Amadina striata, *Lin.*

701.—*Munia striata*, Lin.—Jerdon's Birds of India, Vol. II, p. 356; Butler, Deccan; Stray Feathers, Vol. IX, p. 416.

THE WHITE-BACKED MUNIA.

Length, 4·5; wing, 2·1; tail, 1·6.

Bill bluish; irides brown; legs dark slaty.

Plumage above rich dark brown, deepest on the head, and the feathers white-shafted; rump white; tail almost black; beneath from chin to breast uniform deep blackish-brown; belly, flanks, and vent white; under tail-coverts and thigh-coverts brown.

The middle tail-feathers exceed the outermost by nearly half an inch.

The White-backed Munia is a common permanent resident all along the Sahyadri Range, and in the adjoining forest, but seems to be confined to the Ghats region.

Amadina malabarica, *Lin.*

703.—*Munia malabarica*, Lin.—Jerdon's Birds of India, Vol. II, p. 357; Butler, Guzerat, Stray Feathers, Vol. III, p. 496; Deccan, Stray Feathers, Vol. IX, p. 416; Murray's Vertebrate Zoology of Sind, p. 182; Swinhoe and Barnes, Central India; Ibis, 1885, p. 129.

THE PLAIN BROWN MUNIA.

Length, 5; wing, 2·12; tail, 2.

Bill plumbeous ; irides deep-brown ; legs livid-carneous.

Upper plumage pale earthy-brown, slightly rufescent on the head, and darker towards the forehead ; wings and tail blackish ; the tertiaries slightly bordered with whitish at their truncated tips ; upper tail-coverts white, edged with black externally ; cheeks and lower parts white, tinged with pale earthy-brown on the flanks, which sometimes have some faint cross rays.

The central tail-feathers are much elongated, being three-quarters of an inch longer than the oute most pair.

The Plain Brown Munia is very common throughout the district. It is a permanent resident, and seems to breed the whole year through. The nest is a rather large, loosely constructed sphere, made of grass, lined with fine grass stems. The eggs, from four to ten in number, are rather broad ovals, and are of the usual dead, glossless, white color. They measure 0·6 by about 0·47 inches.

GENUS, **Estrelda,** *Swainson.*

Bill much more slender than *Amadina*; the culmen less arched and flattened at the base, more compressed throughout, deep red in color; tail soft and graduated; feet moderate. Of still smaller size, and more delicate conformation.

Estrelda amandava, *Lin.*

704.—Jerdon's Birds of India, Vol. II, p. 359 ; Butler, Guzerat ; Stray Feathers, Vol. III, p. 496 ; Deccan, Stray Feathers, Vol. IX, p. 416 ; Murray's Vertebrate Zoology of Sind, p. 182 ; Swinhoe and Barnes, Central India ; Ibis, 1885, p. 129.

THE RED WAXBILL.
Lal, Hin.

Length, 4 to 4·25 ; expanse, 5·75 ; wing, 1·8 ; tail, 1·5 ; tarsus, 0·5 ; bill at front, 0·28.

Bill deep red, culmen blackish ; irides crimson ; legs fleshy.

The male, in full summer plumage, is more or less crimson, darkest on the throat, breast, supercilia, cheeks, and upper tail-coverts ; tail black, the outer feathers more or less white tipped ; wings brown ; a range of minute white feathers beneath the eye, and the wings, flanks and sides of breast with numerous round white spots, and a few smaller specks on the back ; abdominal region infuscated ; lower tail-coverts black.

The female is olive-brown above, with the lores blackish, bounded by a whitish semi-circle below the eye ; a few white specks occasionally on the back ; rump and upper tail-coverts tinged with crimson ; beneath paler brown, the abdomen strongly tinged with fulvous-yellow ; the lower tail-coverts dull white.

After breeding the males assume, by moulting, a plumage similar to that of the female.

The young bird is brown above, paler beneath, whitish on the throat and belly; tail blackish, and a few small white specks on the wings.

The Red Waxbill occurs throughout the Presidency, but is locally distributed; it is somewhat rare in the Deccan. It is a permanent resident and breeds during September and October, building a rather large globular nest of grass. The eggs, five or six in number, are dead, glossless, white ovals, measuring 0·55 in length by about 0·43 in breadth.

Estrelda formosa, *Lath.*

705.—Jerdon's Birds of India, Vol. II, p. 361; Butler, Guzerat; Stray Feathers, Vol. III, p. 496; Deccan, Stray Feathers, Vol. IX, p. 416; Swinhoe and Barnes, Central India; Ibis, 1885, p. 129.

THE GREEN WAXBILL.
Harri Lal, Hin.

Length, 4; wing, 1·75; tail, 1·4.

Bill waxy-red; irides pale-brown; feet plumbeons-brown.

Above light olive-green; quills and tail dusky, the former edged with green; beneath very pale-yellow, somewhat darker on the lower belly and under tail-coverts, and with broad transverse dashes of dusky on the flanks and sides of the abdomen.

The Green Waxbill is common on the Vindhian hills near Mhow, also on the Aravalli Range; it occurs but rarely in the Deccan, and has not been recorded from Sind.

It is a permanent resident; both nest and eggs resemble those of *E. amandava*, but are somewhat larger.

SUB-FAMILY, Passerinæ.

Bill stout and strong, somewhat turned, slightly compressed towards the tip; the culmen broad, convex; commissure straight; wings moderate; the first three primaries about equal, the fourth nearly as long; tail moderate, nearly square, or very slightly forked; tarsus moderate; feet formed both for hopping on the ground and perching; lateral toes about equal.

GENUS, Passer, *Brisson.*

The characters are the same as those of the sub-family.

Passer domesticus, *Lin.*

706.—*P. indicus*, Jard. and Selby.—Jerdon's Birds of India, Vol. II, p. 362; Butler, Guzerat; Stray Feathers, Vol. III, p. 496; Deccan, Stray Feathers, Vol. IX, p. 416; Murray's Vertebrate Zoology of Sind, p. 183; Swinhoe and Barnes, Central India; Ibis, 1885, p. 129.

THE HOUSE SPARROW.

Length, 5·5 to 6; expanse, 9; wing, 3; tail, 2·25.

Bill horny-brown; irides light-brown; legs dusky.

Male, head above and nape dark grey; a deep chesnut patch behind the eye, widening on the nape; wing-coverts, scapulars, and mantle, dark chesnut, the scapulars and back with brown stripes or dashes; a white band on the tip of the lesser-coverts; quills dusky, with their outer edges rufous, more broad on the secondaries, and tipped pale; rump and upper tail-coverts ashy-brown; tail dusky, light edged; lores, round the eyes and base of the bill, black; chin, throat, and breast, black; ear-coverts and sides of the neck white; lower parts whitish, ashy on the sides of the breast and flanks.

The *female* is light-brown above, back and scapulars edged with pale-rufous; a pale eye-streak, and the lower parts sullied white; slightly smaller than the male.

The House Sparrow is a common permanent resident throughout the region.

Passer hispaniolensis, *Tem.*

707.—*Passer salicicolus*, Vieill.—Jerdon's Birds of India, Vol. II, p. 364; Murray's Vertebrate Zoology of Sind, p. 183.

THE WILLOW SPARROW.

Length, 5·75; wing, 3; tail, 2.

Male, head and back of neck dark chesnut, the feathers edged paler; the mantle blackish, with creamy-white edgings to the feathers; rump and upper tail-coverts pale brown; shoulder of wing chesnut, with white borders to the lesser-coverts; the rest of the wing dusky, with broad pale rufous-brown edgings, and a whitish bar, formed by the tips of the greater-coverts; secondaries edged and tipped whitish; tail dusky with pale edgings; lores, cheeks, and a narrow supercilium, white, passing into ashy-brown on the ear-coverts; beneath the chin, throat and breast, black, some of the feathers edged whitish; rest of the lower parts sullied white; the flanks and under tail-coverts with dusky longitudinal streaks.

The female resembles that of the Common Sparrow, but the striation of the dorsal feathers is less strongly marked.

This Sparrow very closely resembles the last, chiefly differing in the back of the male more resembling that of the female of the Common Sparrow, and in the black of the breast being less defined, and passing into dashes on the flanks.

The Willow Sparrow, within our limits, only occurs in the more northern parts of Sind.

Passer pyrrhonotus, *Blyth.*

709.—Jerdon's Birds of India, Vol. II, p. 365; Murray's Vertebrate Zoology of Sind, p. 184.

THE RUFOUS-BACKED SPARROW.

Length, 4·62 to 5·37; expanse, 7·5 to 8·5; wing, 2·43 to 2·68;

tail, 1·87 to 2·25; tarsus, 0·62 to 0·68; bill at front, 0·37; bill from gape, 0·43 to 0·5.

Bill dusky to dusky-brown, black in the breeding plumage; irides light-brown; eyelids leaden-slaty; legs pale to dusky fleshy-brown.

Male above: head and ear-coverts grey, with a chesnut stripe from the eye to the nape; the rest of the plumage maroon, the feathers of the back centred dark; wings and tail dusky, the feathers pale edged; beneath sullied brownish-white; throat black.

The females, except that they are everywhere paler, a purer white beneath, a lighter and greyer-brown above, with a slightly redder tinge on the lesser wing-coverts and on the lower back, and a rather more conspicuous white upper wing-bar, formed by the tip of the medial wing-coverts; there is really nothing tangible, except their very much smaller dimensions, by which they can be separated from those of the Common Sparrow.

In the case of the males, in the winter plumage, not only the small size and paler tints and the narrowness of the black throat stripe not descending on to the breast, enable one to separate them from those of the Common Sparrow, but though the chesnut has almost disappeared from the mantle and rump, a trace of it lingers on the lower back, and the patch behind the ear-coverts remains a pure light chesnut instead of a maroon as in the common species.—*Stray Feathers*, Vol. IX, p. 444.

The Rufous-backed Sparrow only occurs in Sind, where it is a permanent resident. It had been lost sight of for years, but has recently been rediscovered by Mr. Doig, who also obtained nests and eggs.

He states that the nests were similar to those of *P. domesticus* but smaller, and were situated in the top of acacia trees, growing in water.

Passer flavicollis, *Franklin.*

711.—Jerdon's Birds of India, Vol. II, p. 368; Butler, Guzerat; Stray Feathers, Vol. III, p 497; Deccan, Stray Feathers, Vol. IX, p. 416; Murray's Vertebrate Zoology of Sind, p. 184; Swinhoe and Barnes, Central India; Ibis, 1885, p. 129.

THE YELLOW-THROATED SPARROW.

Length, 5·5; expanse, 10; wing, 3·4; tail, 2; tarsus, 0·7.

Bill black; irides brown; legs cinereous-brown.

Above ashy-brown; beneath dirty or brownish-white, more albescent on the vent and under tail-coverts, and white on the chin; a yellow spot on the middle of the throat; shoulders and lesser-coverts chesnut; wing with some white marks on the tertiaries, and two white bands formed by the tips of the coverts.

The female merely differs in the yellow neck-spot, and the chesnut on the wings being paler than in the male.

The Yellow-throated Sparrow is a common permanent resident

throughout the region, breeding during the hot season, in holes in trees, &c. The eggs, three or four in number, are greenish-white in color, but so much spotted, smudged, streaked, and clouded with dark sepia-brown as to leave little of the ground-color visible. They measure 0·74 by 0·55.

SUB-FAMILY, Emberizinæ.

Bill with the upper mandible typically smaller and more compressed than the lower, which is broader, equal in a few; a palatal protuberance in many; commissure usually sinuate; tail moderate, even or emarginate.

GENUS, Emberiza.

Bill of varied strength and the mandibles more or less unequal, usually somewhat lengthened; wings moderate or rather long, with the first quill a little shorter than the second and third, which are longest; tail of moderate length; the outermost feathers more or less marked with white.

Emberiza buchanani, *Bly.*

716.—*E. huttoni*, Blyth.—Jerdon's Birds of India, Vol. II, p. 373; Butler, Guzerat; Stray Feathers, Vol. III, p. 497; Deccan, Stray Feathers, Vol. IX, p. 416; Murray's Vertebrate Zoology of Sind, p. 185.

THE GREY-NECKED BUNTING.

Length, 5·75 to 6; wing, 3·5; tail, 3; tarsus, 0·75.

Bill reddish; irides brown; feet fleshy-brown.

Head, neck, nape, and sides of the neck, grey; from the the lower corner of the under mandible on each side a short streak of buffy, between which and the chin, which is also buff, is a streak of greyish, meeting the grey of the sides of the neck; orbital feathers whitish; back grey, with a slight rufescent tinge, the feathers faintly striated; rump and upper tail-coverts greyish-brown or ferruginous, paler on the abdomen and vent, and nearly buff on the under tail-coverts; lesser-coverts ferruginous; median and greater-coverts brown, edged with ferruginous; primaries dull brown, margined narrowly on their outer, and broadly on their inner web with pale-white or rufescent-white; secondaries the same, but the feathers also tipped with pale-rufous; edge of the wing fulvous; tail blackish-brown, the outer web of the outermost feather, except at the extreme base, and half of the inner web, white; the next outermost, blackish-brown on the outer web, and for nearly two-thirds its length on the inner web, blackish-brown; the rest white on their inner web only; centre tail-feathers edged with pale-rufous.

The Grey-necked Bunting is a not uncommon winter visitant to all parts of the district; it is much addicted to frequenting stony hills.

Emberiza stewarti, *Blyth.*

718.—Jerdon's Birds of India, Vol. II, p. 374; Murray's Vertebrate Zoology of Sind, p. 185.

THE WHITE-CAPPED BUNTING.

Length, 6; wing, 3·12; tail, 2·75; tarsus, 0·7.

Bill fleshy-brown; irides brown; legs fleshy-brown.

Male, crown greyish-white; lores, a broad line passing over the eye to the nape, and the throat, black; cheeks and ear-coverts white; back, scapularies, rump, and upper tail-coverts, deep reddish-chesnut; wing-coverts dark-brown, edged with buffy-brown; wings brown, narrowly edged with greyish-white; the central tail-feathers blackish-brown; the two outer on each side blackish-brown at the base, and white for the remainder of their length, with the exception of their outer web, which is brown; the whole under surface creamy-white, crossed on the chest by a broad band of lively chesnut-red.

The female has the whole upper surface, wings, and tail, pale olive-brown, with a streak of dark-brown down the centre of each feather; a slight tinge of rufous on the upper tail-coverts; under surface pale buffy-brown, streaked with dark-brown.

The White-capped Bunting is a seasonal visitant to Sind only.

Emberiza fucata, *Pall.*

719.—Jerdon's Birds of India, Vol. II, p. 375.

THE GREY-HEADED BUNTING.

Length, 6·75; expanse, 10·3; wing, 3·5; tail, 2·5; tarsus, 0·75; bill at front, 0·4.

Bill reddish, dusky on culmen; irides dark-brown; feet, fleshy-orange.

Above, head and neck darkish-grey, with some darker mesial streaks; scapulars, back and rump deep rufous or rufescent-brown, also streaked with black, except on the rump and upper tail-coverts; ear-coverts deep-rufous; a whitish supercilium; wings and tail dark-brown, broadly edged with reddish-fawn color; and the outer feathers of the tail partly white on their inner webs; throat, fore-neck, and breast, greyish-white; a narrow black streak from each corner of the gape, widening as it descends, and forming a gorget with the opposite one; below this white; then an interrupted pectoral band of rufous; and the belly whitish, tinged with rufous on the flanks and sides of vent.

The Grey-headed Bunting is not uncommon during the winter months, on the stony hills in the vicinity of Neemuch. It is also recorded by Jerdon from Mhow, Central India.

Emberiza striolata, *Licht.*

720*bis*.—Butler, Guzerat; Stray Feathers, Vol. III, p. 497; Murray's Vertebrate Zoology of Sind, p. 186.

THE STRIOLATED BUNTING.

Length, 5·5 to 5·97; expanse, 9 to 9·75; wing, 2·87 to 3·1; tail, 2·2 to 2·75; bill at front, 0·35 to 0·39.

Bill, upper mandible brown to blackish-brown, lower waxy, fleshy or dingy-yellow; irides brown; legs pale waxy, dingy or fleshy-yellow, the feet more or less tinged brownish.

The male has the forehead, top of the head, and nape greyish-white, grey or white in different specimens, each feather with a conspicuous linear, median, black streak; a narrow pure white superciliary stripe starting from the base of the bill and extending behind the eye over the ear-coverts; the lores, and a moderately broad stripe directly behind the eye (and immediately under the white stripe), involving the upper portions of the ear-coverts; below this, starting from the base of the lower mandible, a black stripe; below this, from the angle of the lower mandible, a greyish-white stripe, which again is divided from the greyish-white of the chin by a narrow inconspicuous dark streak.

"In the fresh bird in breeding plumage, which I am describing, all these streaks and stripes are as clearly and sharply defined as if painted; but at other seasons, and in stuffed specimens, they are not so clear; the whole of the back, scapulars, and tertials are hair-brown, the former two very broadly, the latter more narrowly, margined with pale, more or less sandy or even rufous brown; in many specimens the darker median streaks of the back feathers are reduced to mere lines, and in some the rufous tinge on the upper back is well marked; the primaries and secondaries and their coverts are a mixture of hair-brown and rich rufous (recalling in color the wings of *Mirafra erythroptera*), the extent of each varying in different specimens, but the brown predominating in the earlier primaries and everywhere at the tips, and decreasing in extent in the hinder part of the wing and towards the bases of the feathers; the second primary, for instance, will be all brown, except a narrow rufous edging for the basal two-thirds of the outer web and a broad rufous stripe on the margin of the inner web for the same distance, while one of the later secondaries will be all rufous except a narrow brown stripe running down the shaft till within one-third of the end of the feather, whence it gradually widens so as to occupy at the tip the whole of both webs; the rump and upper tail-coverts are much the same as the back, but in some specimens slightly more rufous than the lower back; and the longest of the coverts are in some specimens very narrowly tipped with very pale rufous-white; the tail is hair-brown, darker than the brown portion of the quills; all the feathers externally very narrowly margined with pale-rufous, except the external feather on each side which has the whole outer web of that color; the throat and upper breast are greyish white or grey, with more or less numerous and conspicuous black median stripes on the feathers. Specimens differ widely in this respect; in some the greyish-white is a mere edging to dusky black feathers; in others only a few black spots and streaks peep out of an almost unbroken grey, and this among specimens killed at the same time, and of apparently the same age; the lower breast and the whole lower parts of the body are pale greyish-rufous, all the bases of the feathers (only seen if their tips are lifted), being a sort of bluish-dusky; the axillaries, wing-lining, and, in fact, the whole lower surface of the wings, except the points of the quills, a pale delicate salmon-rufous.

"The female only differs in being generally somewhat smaller, in having the white, grey, and black of the head, neck, throat and breast much duller (and in many specimens overcast with a sandy or pale-rufous shade), in the various stripes being less well marked, and in having the dark spots and streaks of the throat almost obsolete."—*Hume, "Ibis,"* 1869.

The Striolated Bunting occurs as a winter visitant to Sind, Rajputana, Kutch and Guzerat. It does not occur in the Deccan.

GENUS, **Euspiza,** *Bonap.*

Bill strong, sub-conic, with the mandibles about equal, and scarcely a trace of a palatal knob; wings and tail rather long, firm.

Euspiza melanocephala, *Scop.*

721.—Jerdon's Birds of India, Vol. II, p. 378; Butler, Guzerat; Stray Feathers, Vol. III, p. 497; Deccan, Stray Feathers, Vol. IX, p. 417; Murray's Vertebrate Zoology of Sind, p. 188; Swinhoe and Barnes, Central India; Ibis, 1885, p. 129.

THE BLACK-HEADED BUNTING.

Length, 7·5 to 8; wing, 3·8 to 4; tail, 3; tarsus, 0·9; bill at front, 0·5.

Bill yellowish-brown; irides light-brown; legs yellowish-brown.

Whole head, including the ear-coverts, black, the feathers generally (*i.e.,* winter) edged light-brown, this disappearing towards spring; back and scapulars rich chesnut, passing to yellowish on the rump and upper tail-coverts, the feathers being edged with bright-yellow, passing behind the ear-coverts to the nape; the side of breast chesnut, continuous with the color of the back.

The Black-headed Bunting is a rather common cold weather visitant to all parts of the region. It is very destructive in the corn fields, when *jowaree, bajri,* and other cereals are ripening.

Euspiza luteola, *Sparr.*

722.—Jerdon's Birds of India, Vol. II, p. 378; Butler, Guzerat; Stray Feathers, Vol. III, p. 498; Deccan, Stray Feathers, Vol.

IX, p. 417; Murray's Vertebrate Zoology of Sind, p. 188; Swinhoe and Barnes, Central India; Ibis, 1885, p. 129.

THE RED-HEADED BUNTING.

Length, 6·75 to 7; wing, 3·5; tail, 3; bill at front, 0·5.

Bill pale fleshy-yellow; irides brown; legs brown.

The whole head, neck, and breast, rich chesnut; back and scapulars yellowish or greenish-yellow, with dark-brown striæ; rump and upper tail-coverts deep-yellow, faintly streaked; quills and tail brown; the coverts and secondaries broadly edged with pale whity brown; quills and rectrices narrowly edged with the same; beneath, from the breast, including the sides of the neck, rich yellow.

The Red-headed Bunting is a not uncommon cold weather visitant to all suitable portions of the Presidency. It is much addicted to frequenting cultivated lands.

GENUS, **Melophus**, *Sws.*

Bill compressed, with the upper mandible slightly notched near the tip; wings rather short; tail even; hind-claw slightly lengthened; head with an erectile frontal crest; otherwise as in *Euspiza.*

Melophus melanicterus, *Gm.*

724.—Jerdon's Birds of India, Vol. II, p. 381; Butler, Guzerat; Stray Feathers, Vol. III, p. 498; Deccan, Stray Feathers, Vol. IX, p. 417; Murray's Vertebrate Zoology of Sind, p. 189; Swinhoe and Barnes, Central India; Ibis, 1885, p. 129.

THE CRESTED BLACK BUNTING.

Length, 6·5; expanse, 10; wing, 3·25; tail, 2·75; bill at front, 0·5.

Bill fleshy-brown; irides dark-brown; legs red-brown.

Male.—The whole body, with crest, glossy blue-black; wings and tail dark cinnamon, with dusky tips; tail-coverts at their base, black and cinnamon.

The female is dusky-brown above, the feathers edged light olive-brownish; beneath rufescent-white, or pale brownish-fulvescent with dusky streaks; quills and tail dull and paler cinnamon than in the male, dusky internally, and on the central tail-feathers. She is a little smaller, and the crest is not so highly developed.

The Crested Black Bunting occurs more or less in suitable localities throughout the region; in many it is a permanent resident breeding during the rains, in banks, under clumps of ferns and grasses. The eggs, three in number, are rather broad ovals in shape, and are of a dull whitish-grey color, with a sprinkling of light-brown spots; the markings are always most dense at the larger end, and sometimes the markings are so closely set as to leave little of the ground-color visible.

They average 0·79 inches in length by nearly 0·63 in breadth.

Sub-family, **Fringillinæ**.

Bill varied in size and form, more or less conical and thick, short and bulged in some, slender and more elongate in others; wing moderate or long; first primary wanting.

Genus, **Carpodacus**, *Kaup*.

Bill distinctly turned and compressed at the tip; commissure sinuated, or with a notch near its base; wings, with the first three primaries, sub-equal and longest; tail distinctly furcate; feet robust; claws well curved.

Bucanetes githagineus, *Licht*.

732*bis*.—Murray's Vertebrate Zoology of Sind, p. 190.

The Desert Bullfinch.

Length, 5·7 to 6; expanse, 10 to 11; wings, 3·2 to 3 6; tail, 2 to 3; tarsus, 0·67 to 0·77; bill at front, 0·35 to 0·41.

Bill orange-yellow, pale-yellow in some, brownish on culmen; irides brown; legs fleshy-brown.

In the male the head is pale bluish-grey, the feathers tipped brown; the chin, throat, breast, cheeks, and ear-coverts a sort of blue-grey, the feathers faintly tinged, most conspicuously so round the base of the lower mandible, with pale rosy; the abdomen, vent, and lower tail-coverts, very pale rosy-white, the longest of the latter with dark shafts; the back and scapulars dull earthy-brown, with, when fresh, a faint rosy tinge, which disappears in the dried skin, and somewhat greyer towards the nape; rump pale-brown, more decidedly tinged with rosy; the visible portion of the upper tail-coverts rosy-white, more strongly tinged with rosy at the margins, the centres and bases of the longest being pale-brown; these, however, are not seen till the feathers are lifted; tail-feathers dark-brown, conspicuously, though narrowly, margined with rosy-white, most rosy towards the bases of the lateral feathers; the wings hair-brown, conspicuously margined and tipped with pale rose-color, or rosy-white; the coverts, secondaries, and tertiaries most broadly so. There is a very narrow, inconspicuous, pale rosy frontal band. The wing-lining and axillaries are pure white; the winglet alone is dark-brown, unmargined with rosy.

The female has the whole upper surface and the sides of the head and body a dull pale earthy-brown, with only a faint rosy tinge upon the rump and upper tail-coverts; the lower parts a still paler earthy-brown with the faintest possible roseate tinge on the breast, and becoming albescent on the vent, lower tail-coverts and tibial plumes; the wings and tail are as in the male; but the margins are narrower and less conspicuous, and are pale brownish instead of rosy-white.

The Desert Bullfinch is a winter visitant to Kutch and Sind; it does not occur elsewhere within our limits.

Carpodacus erythrinus, *Pallas.*

738.—Jerdon's Birds of India, Vol. II, p. 398; Butler, Guzerat; Stray Feathers, Vol. III, p. 498; Deccan, Stray Feathers, Vol. IX, p. 417; Murray's Vertebrate Zoology of Sind, p. 189; Swinhoe and Barnes, Central India; Ibis, 1885, p. 129.

THE COMMON ROSE FINCH.

Length, 5·5; wing, 3·25; tail, 2·25.

Bill yellowish-brown; irides light-brown; feet horny-brown.

Male, in winter plumage, has the head, throat, breast, moustachial stripe, rump, and flanks of abdomen, roseate color, deepest upon the crown, throat, and breast, and paling on the flanks; upper plumage generally brown, more or less ruddy, brightening towards the rump and on the upper tail-coverts; the wing-coverts tipped with ruddy-brown, forming two pale bars on the wing; tertiaries margined with pale-brown; quills and tail-feathers with ruddy edgings. In summer the crown, throat, breast, and rump become brilliant crimson.

The female is pale olive-brown with dark streaks, the tips of the greater and lesser wing-coverts whitish, forming two conspicuous bands on the wings; below paler brown, albescent on the throat, the middle of the belly and the under tail-coverts, and darker and somewhat streaked on the breast and flanks.

The Rose Finch is found during the winter in all suitable localities in the district. It is partial to hilly forest tracts.

SUB-FAMILY, Alaudinæ.

Bill rather long and slender, short and thick in many; wings broad; tertiaries elongated, pointed; claws slightly curved; hind-toe and claw typically long; plumage brown, more or less striated.

GENUS, Mirafra, *Horsf.*

Bill stout, thick, compressed; the culmen curved and convex; the tip slightly deflected; commissure gently curving; wings rather short; first quill short, second shorter than third; fourth, fifth, and sixth, which are nearly equal; tail very short, even; legs rather long; hind-claw moderately long.

Mirafra erythroptera, *Jerdon.*

756.—Jerdon's Birds of India, Vol. II, p. 418; Butler, Guzerat; Stray Feathers, Vol. III, p. 499; Deccan, Stray Feathers, Vol. IX, p. 418; Murray's Vertebrate Zoology of Sind, p. 192; Swinhoe and Barnes, Central India; Ibis, 1885, p. 129.

THE RED-WINGED BUSH LARK.

Length, 5·5; wing, 3·2; tail, 2; tarsus, 0·92; bill at front, 0·4.

Bill fleshy-horny, dusky on culmen; irides dark-brown; legs fleshy.

Upper parts streaked, the centres of the feathers being dusky-brown, and the edges fulvous-brown, rufescent on the head; coronal feathers lengthened; a whitish eye-streak; ear-feathers rufescent-brown; beneath, the throat is pure white, and the rest of the plumage pale fulvescent-whitish; the breast marked with large oval blackish spots; primaries and secondaries ferruginous on both webs, except towards the tip, the dusky portion gradually increasing to the outermost feathers; tail blackish, the four middle feathers brown, and the outermost only whitish on its outer web.

The Red-winged Bush Lark is a common permanent resident in all parts of the Presidency; it is, however, somewhat locally distributed.

It breeds during March and April and again in August and September; the nest, generally domed, is composed of grass stems. The eggs, usually three in number, (occasionally four), are oval in shape, and greenish, brownish or yellowish-white in color, profusely spotted with brownish-red, inky-purple or olive-brown. They average 0·76 inches in length by 0·59 in breadth.

Mirafra cantillans, *Jerd.*

757.—Jerdon's Birds of India, Vol. II, p. 420; Butler, Guzerat; Stray Feathers, Vol. III, p. 499; Swinhoe and Barnes, Central India; Ibis, 1885, p. 129.

THE SINGING BUSH LARK.

Length, 5·5; expanse, 10; wing, 2·9; tail, 2; bill at front, 0·5.

Bill dusky-horny, fleshy beneath; irides dark-brown; legs fleshy-brown.

Above dusky-brown, the feathers laterally margined with rufescent-brown; wings and their coverts strongly margined with rufescent-brown; a pale eye-streak; throat and below the ear-coverts white, and the rest of the under parts pale rufescent, darker on the breast, with a few indistinct small breast spots; outer tail-feathers nearly all white, the penultimate white on the outer web only.

The Singing Bush Lark occurs in Guzerat, near Mhow, in Central India, and in the vicinity of Neemuch, Rajputana, but is very locally distributed.

It is a permanent resident, breeding from March to July; the nest, a domed one, is generally placed on the ground in a tuft of coarse grass.

The eggs, three or four in number, are scarcely distinguishable from those of *M. erythroptera*.

GENUS, Ammomanes, *Cabanis.*

Bill short, thick, compressed, arched at culmen, acute at the tip, which is slightly bent over; gonys ascending; wings long, straight, first quill minute, second not so long as the third and fourth, which are the longest, fifth is nearly equal; tertiaries not elongated beyond the secondaries; tail rather long, slightly emarginate; tarsus and feet moderate; hind-claw large.

Ammomanes phœnicura, *Franklin.*

758.—Jerdon's Birds of India, Vol. II, p. 421; Butler, Guzerat; Stray Feathers, Vol. III, p. 499; Deccan, Stray Feathers, Vol. IX, p. 418; Swinhoe and Barnes, Central India; Ibis, 1885, p. 129.

THE RUFOUS-TAILED FINCH LARK.

Length, 6·5; wing, 4·2; tail, 2·4.

Bill horny-brown, fleshy at base beneath; irides brown; legs fleshy.

Plumage above ashy-brown, with a rufescent tinge; rump, base of tail, the inner webs of the quills, and the tail-feathers, dark rufous or dull ferruginous; the quills and tip of the tail dark-brown, lower parts of the same ferruginous hue, but paler on the throat and lower tail-coverts, and with a few dusky streaks on the breast; extremity of the lower tail-coverts with a dusky spot.

With the exception of Sind, the Rufous-tailed Finch Lark is a common permanent resident throughout the region, breeding during April and May. The nests are placed in deep cavities, formed by clods of earth on ploughed or broken ground, and are mere pads formed of soft grass, occasionally lined with hairs. The eggs, usually four in number (I once found five), are moderately broadish ovals in shape, and vary much in color, but the usual type is yellowish-white, thickly freckled and spotted with reddish or yellowish-brown, with pale underlying spots of inky purple. They average 0·85 inches in length by 0·62 in breadth.

Ammomanes deserti, *Licht.*

759.—*A. lusitanica*, Gm.—Jerdon's Birds of India, Vol. II, p. 422; *A. lusitania,* Gm.; Murray's Vertebrate Zoology of Sind, p. 192.

THE PALE RUFOUS FINCH LARK.

Length, 6; wing, 4; tail, 2·75; tarsus, 0·9.

Bill dusky, yellowish beneath; irides brown; feet pale yellow-brown.

Affined to *A. phœnicura,* but the general hue is less rufescent; upper parts dull sandy grey-brown; the wing-coverts dark shafted; the under parts fulvous-grey, or isabelline, albescent on the throat, and with a few faint dusky striæ on the breast; tail brown, faintly rufescent at its extreme base, and on the outer web of the outermost feathers; broad margins to the inner webs of the primaries and secondaries with the axillaries also pale rufescent.

The Pale Rufous Finch Lark is very common in Sind, frequenting bare stony hills and plains.

Genus, **Pyrrhulauda,** *A. Smith.*

Bill very short, very stout, sides compressed; tip entire; culmen strongly arched; commissure straight; wings moderately long, broad and well developed, and the tertiaries lengthened, first quill very small, the four next equal and longest; tail moderate, slightly forked; tarsus short; toes small; hind-claw slightly lengthened and curved.

Pyrrhulauda grisea, *Scop.*

760.—Jerdon's Birds of India, Vol. II, p. 424; Butler, Guzerat; Stray Feathers, Vol. III, p. 499; Deccan, Stray Feathers, Vol. IX, p. 418; Murray's Vertebrate Zoology of Sind, p. 193; Swinhoe and Barnes, Central India; Ibis, 1885, p. 130.

The Black-bellied Finch Lark.
Dabbak Churi, Hin.

Length, 5; expanse, 10; wing, 3; tail, 1·95; bill at front, 0·36. Bill pale horny; irides dark-brown; legs fleshy.

Male: above pale brownish-grey, the feathers slightly centred darker, somewhat rufescent on the back; forehead and cheeks whitish; wings and tail brown, the feathers all pale edged, and a deep brown or black band from the base of bill through the eyes, continued to the occiput; chin and throat, sides of neck (extending at right angles behind the ear-coverts and thus taking the form of a cross), breast and lower parts deep chocolate-brown or black; sides of breast, of abdomen, and the flanks, whitish, bordering the dark color.

The female wants the black on the lower parts; the plumage is darker, and more rufescent above; the breast faintly streaked with brown, and earthy on the flanks, sides of breast, and neck. She is a rather smaller bird measuring only 4·75 inches in length.

The Black-bellied Finch Lark is a common permanent resident throughout the region, breeding the whole year through.

The nest, which is a mere pad of grass, is placed in a depression on the ground. The eggs, two in number, rarely three, are moderately elongated ovals in shape, of a greenish or yellowish-white color, densely speckled and spotted with various shades of yellowish and earthy-brown. They measure 0·73 by 0·55.

Pyrrhulauda melanauchen, *Cab.*

760*bis*.—Murray's Vertebrate Zoology of Sind, p. 193.

The Black-necked Finch Lark.

Length, 5·4 to 6·1; expanse, 9·6 to 10·1; wing, 3·02 to 3·2; tail, 2·0 to 2·2; tarsus, 0·6 to 0·7; bill at gape, 0·47 to 0·5.

Bill pearly-white to whity-brown; irides brown; legs pale whity-brown to pale fleshy-brown.

"The male has a broad frontal band, cheeks, ear-coverts, and a band from these round the base of the occiput and a large patch on either side of the breast, white ; in the case of the two latter often tinged brownish.

The base of the lower mandible, chin, throat, central portion of breast, abdomen, vent, and lower tail-coverts, axillaries and wing-lining (except lower primary greater-coverts, which are pale grey-brown like the lower surface of the quills) intensely deep, at times somewhat sooty, at times almost chocolate-brown ; the crown and upper part of occiput are deep-brown, never quite so intense as the lower parts, often considerably lighter, and more purely brown ; the anterior portion of the side of the neck behind the lower half of the ear-coverts is always like the breast, sometimes the deep color of these parts extends behind the whole of the ear-coverts, and right round the back of the neck forming a collar immediately behind the white basal occipital band already noticed, sometimes there is not the faintest trace of this, and sometimes again the collar is only represented by a smaller or larger nuchal patch.

"This is perhaps the most common form, and hence the name *melanauchen*.

"The interscapulary region is a pale earthy-brown, sometimes with a sandy tinge; the wings rather darker, but all the feathers margined with a pale whity-brown ; inner webs of quills darker, a sort of pale hair-brown ; central tail-feathers slightly paler than tertiaries; rest of tail-feathers deep-brown, but the outer web of the exterior feather white or nearly so, and the inner half or more of the inner web pale whity-brown ; rump and upper tail-coverts pale earthy or sandy-brown, noticeably paler than the interscapulary region ; flanks much the same color as the rump.

"The female has the chin, throat, abdomen, vent, and lower tail-coverts white, with more or less traces of a very faint tawny tinge; a broad ill-defined pale tawny band, which is sometimes feebly striated darker, covers the breast; the axillaries and lesser lower-coverts about the ulna are deep-brown, sometimes almost as deep as the breast of the male.

"The female also wants the white frontal band and patch on the sides of the head, the white occipital band, the dark crown and dark sides of the neck, and of course the dark collar or dark nuchal patch so common in the males; the whole top of the head is unicolorous or nearly so with the interscapulary region, though the feathers are generally feebly darker centred. The rest of the upper surface is much as in the male, but as a rule sandier, and less earthy in tinge. The males are distinguished at once from those of *grisea* by their dark crowns. Both sexes are distinguished by their somewhat larger size."

Genus, **Calandrella**, *Kaup*.

Bill short, sub-conic, moderately compressed; wing long, straight; first primary minute, the next three primaries about equal; tertiaries elongated; feet small, with shortish toes, and moderately short, but straight hind-claw.

Calandrella brachydactyla, *Leisl.*

761.—Jerdon's Birds of India, Vol. II, p. 426; Butler, Guzerat; Stray Feathers, Vol. III, p. 500; Deccan, Stray Feathers, Vol. IX, p. 418; Murray's Vertebrate Zoology of Sind, p. 198; Swinhoe and Barnes, Central India; Ibis, 1885, p. 130.

THE SOCIAL LARK.

Length, 6·25; wing, 4; tail, 2·25; tarsus, 0·8.

Bill whitish-horny, dusky on culmen; irides dark-brown; legs brownish.

Upper parts pale rufescent-sandy, streaked with dusky, a stripe over the eye, and the whole under parts fulvous-white, tinged with earthy-brown on the breast, which is spotless in some, in a few slightly spotted; wings dusky-brown, with fulvous edgings, broader and deeper colored on the tertiaries, and on the tips of the coverts, and with a whitish edge to the first developed primary; tail dusky, the penultimate feather having the outer web wholly white to near the base, and also some of the inner web. In old or worn plumage the dusky tinge prevails on the back; the breast has some narrow dusky streaks, and a patch of the same appears on each side of the lower part of the foreneck; this is also slightly observable in newly-moulted specimens.

The Social Lark is excessively common during the cold weather, in every portion of the region.

GENUS, Melanocorypha, *Boie.*

Bill thick and convex; tertiaries not elongated; hind-claw moderate, straight.

Melanocorypha bimaculata, *Menet.*

761*ter.*—Murray's Vertebrate Zoology of Sind, p. 195.

Length, 7 to 8; expanse, 13 to 15·25; wing, 4·2 to 4·8; tail, 2·12 to 2·4; tarsus, 1; bill at front, 0·6 to 0·7; bill at gape, 0·7 to 0·9.

Bill horny-brown, beneath yellowish; irides brown; legs yellowish-fleshy.

"Adult male in summer plumage. Above fulvous-brown, the centres of the plumes much darker-brown, giving a somewhat mottled appearance, all the feathers being edged with fulvous, especially on the hinder part of the neck and the centre of the back; wing-coverts colored like the back, but a little more rufous, plainly edged with fulvous, less distinct on the greater-coverts; quills brown with a slight shade of ash-grey on the outer webs; all the feathers more or less narrowly-edged with fulvous, but none of the feathers tipped white; tail dark-brown, with conspicuous white tips to all the feathers except the two central ones; all the rectrices edged more or less broadly with fulvous; lores and a distinct eyebrow whitish; cheeks fulvous-white with a slight mottling with rufous; ear-coverts entirely rufous; throat, breast, and flanks, rufous; a black pectoral gorget extending right across the lower part of the throat; on the upper part of the breast are a few indistinct mottled lines below the black gorget; under tail-coverts whitish; under wing-coverts entirely greyish-brown,

"*Obs.*—Some specimens are much greyer than others; others again are more rufous; some are more white on the belly, and have the breast much obscured, so that the pectoral gorget is scarcely discernible. This last dress seems to be the winter plumage.

"*Young.*—Similar to the adult, but more rufous in the centre; gorget, more obscure, and the stripes on the upper breast more indistinct."—*Sharpe and Dresser, Birds of Europe.*

This fine Lark occurs in Upper Sind, and in the desert east of Oomercot.

GENUS, **Alaudula**, *Blyth.*

Bill more lengthened and slender than in the preceding genera, but still rather short and thick, and slightly curved; wings moderate, with no rudimentary first primary, and the first three quills longest; tail even; feet very small; hind-claw about the length of the toe, nearly straight, of small size.

Alaudula raytal, *Blyth.*

762.—Jerdon's Birds of India, Vol. II, p. 428; Swinhoe and Barnes, Central India; Ibis, 1885, p. 130.

THE INDIAN SAND LARK.
Retal, Hin.

Length, 5·25; expanse, 8; wing, 3; tail, 1·75 to 2; tarsus, 0·7; bill at front, 0·38.

Bill pale horny; irides brown; legs fleshy-yellowish.

General hue of the upper parts light brownish-ashy, with narrow dark centres to the feathers; lower parts white, faintly tinged with fulvous on the breast, where obscurely marked with small spots; wing-coverts and tertiaries margined with pale-rufescent or whitish; the outermost feathers white, except the inner half of the inner web, and the next one is white along the marginal half of its outer web only; a whitish line through the eyes.

The Indian Sand Lark is not uncommon in the neighbourhood of Neemuch, Rajputana, in the cold weather.

Alaudula adamsi, *Hume.*

762*ter.*—Murray's Vertebrate Zoology of Sind, p. 196.

THE LITTLE SAND LARK.

Length, ♂, 5·9 to 6, ♀, 5·6 to 5·7; expanse, ♂, 10·4 to 11, ♀, 10 to 10·5; wing, ♂, 3·3 to 3·5, ♀, 3·05 to 3·2; tail, ♂ & ♀, 2·2; bill at front, ♂, 0·35 to 0·38, ♀, 0·32 to 0·38.

Bill greyish-slate, brownish on culmen and at tip, yellow at base beneath; irides pale-brown; legs fleshy-brown, dusky at joints.

In the winter the whole upper surface is very pale-grey or whity-brown, all the feathers narrowly centred with grey-brown, so as to produce a striated appearance. There is in many specimens a more or less perceptible, but still very faint, rufous tinge on the back; the wings are pale-brown, the outer webs of the first primaries nearly entirely cream-color, the other primaries narrowly tipped and margined white; secondaries more broadly; tertiaries and coverts still more broadly margined with fulvous or slightly greyish-white; the central tail-feathers brown, somewhat conspicuously margined with brownish or fulvous-white; the exterior tail-feathers on either side wholly white, except a dark-brown stripe down the inner margin of the inner web; the next feather with the whole exterior web pure white; interior web dark-brown; other tail-feathers dark-brown, very narrowly margined with dull white; the lores and a stripe over and under the eye white or rufescent-white; a very narrow grey line through the centre of the lores only noticeable in very good specimens or in the fresh bird; ear-coverts mingled grey-brown and fulvous-white, and usually exhibiting a somewhat darker spot just behind and below the posterior angle of the eye; the whole lower parts white, with, in some, a very faint rufescent tinge on the breast, sides, and flanks, and with numerous narrow or linear darkish-brown spots on the breast, very strongly marked, conspicuous in some specimens, reduced almost to speckles in other birds; the flanks and sides are faintly tinged with brown, or in some pale rufescent.

The Little Sand Lark is a permanent resident in Sind. It does not occur elsewhere within our limits.

GENUS, **Spizalauda,** *Blyth.*

Bill as in *Alauda, i.e.*, with the nostrils protected by bristles, but thicker and *Mirafra*-like in its form; wings long, with the first quill minute, the next four about equal and longest, as in the true Larks; tertiaries lengthened; hind-toe and claw moderately developed; claws longer than in *Mirafra;* coronal feathers lengthened, and forming a pointed crest.

Spizalauda deva, *Sykes.*

765.—Jerdon's Birds of India, Vol. II, p. 432; Butler, Deccan; Stray Feathers, Vol. IX, p. 418; Swinhoe and Barnes, Central India; Ibis, 1885, p. 130.

THE SMALL CROWN CREST LARK.

Length, 5·5 to 5·75; wing, 3·4; tail, 2; bill at front, 0·5; tarsus, 0·75.

Bill horny-brown, yellowish beneath; irides dark-brown; feet fleshy-brown.

Upper part, including the crest, isabelline or rufous-brown, with black mesial streaks; upper tail-coverts rufescent without streaks; the first long primary broadly edged with rufescent, and the outermost tail-feathers and most of the penultimate of the same hue, with a few dusky striæ on the breast, and paling on the throat.

The Small Crown Crest Lark is a common permanent resident in the Deccan, and is also common at Mhow and Neemuch, Central India.

It breeds from July to September, making a small cup-shaped nest on the ground, in a slight depression, under a tuft of grass. The eggs, two or three in number, are moderately broad ovals in shape, of a dull white color, profusely spotted, speckled, and blotched with dull yellowish-brown and dingy inky-purple. They measure 0·87 inches in length and about 0·65 in breadth.

Spizalauda malabarica, *Scop.*

765*bis.*—Butler, Guzerat; Stray Feathers, Vol. IV, p. 1; Deccan, Stray Feathers, Vol. IX, p. 418; Swinhoe and Barnes, Central India; Ibis, 1885, p. 130.

THE LARGE CROWN CREST LARK.

Differs from *deva* in being darker in plumage, more rufous above, and whiter beneath, and has larger and more numerous breast spots.

This Lark is not uncommon in parts of the Deccan and Northern Guzerat.

GENUS, Alauda, *Lin.*

Bill moderate, nearly straight, conical or subulate, slender; wings long, the first primary exceedingly minute, and the next four sub-equal, the fifth in some decidedly shorter; tips of the lesser quills emarginated; tail short or moderate, forked; tarsus somewhat lengthened; feet large; hind-claw very long; coronal feathers elongated and forming a full crest.

Alauda gulgula, *Franklin.*

767.—Jerdon's Birds of India, Vol. II, p. 434; Butler, Guzerat; Stray Feathers, Vol. IV, p. 2; Deccan, Stray Feathers, Vol. IX, p. 419; Murray's Vertebrate Zoology of Sind, p. 197; Swinhoe and Barnes, Central India; Ibis, 1885, p. 130.

THE INDIAN SKY LARK.

Length, 6 to 6·5; wing, 3·25 to 3·75; tail, 2 to 2·25; tarsus, 1; bill at front, 0·5.

Bill horny-brown, pale beneath; irides dark-brown; legs fleshy-brown.

Above the feathers are dark-brown, with fulvous margins; beneath fulvescent-white, deeper on the breast, and spotted or streaked with dusky; ear-coverts spotted and tipped dusky; a pale eye-streak; the erectile feathers of the head moderately elongated. Some specimens have a rufous tinge on the upper tail-coverts, and also margining the large quills, more especially the secondaries, while the coverts are edged with grey; the tail has the outermost feather almost wholly fulvescent white, and the penultimate one has its outer web, and sometimes the tip of the inner web of the same tint.

The Indian Sky Lark occurs in suitable places throughout the region. It is a permanent resident, breeding about the commencement of May; the nest, a shallow cup, composed of grass stems, is placed in a depression, scratched by the birds under the shelter of a clod of earth or tuft of grass.

The eggs, four or five in number, are moderately elongated or broadish ovals; they vary much in coloring, but are mostly of two types; the first or commonest has a creamy-white ground, profusely speckled and freckled with excessively fine specks and spots of dull purplish-grey and pale brownish-yellow; in the second type the color is white, and the markings are much darker in shade. They measure 0·8 inches in length by 0·61 in breadth.

GENUS, Galerida, *Boie.*

Bill lengthened, slightly curved; wings with the first primary, moderately developed, the next four sub-equal, the second slightly shorter; toes and hind-claws less elongated than in *Alauda*; an erectile, lengthened and pointed crest on the top the head.

Galerida cristata, *Lin.*

769.—Jerdon's Birds of India, Vol. II, p. 436; Butler, Guzerat; Stray Feathers, Vol. IV, p. 2; Murray's Vertebrate Zoology of Sind, p. 198.

THE LARGE CRESTED LARK.

Length, 7·25 to 7·5; wing, 4 to 4·25; tail, 2·5 to 2·75; tarsus, 1; bill at front, 0·75.

Bill yellowish; irides dark-brown; legs pale-brown.

Pale earthy or sandy-brown, rufescent on the feathers of the upper parts, with pale dusky mesial streaks; the feathers of the crest alone, with dark-brown centres; wings somewhat rufescent; upper tail-coverts the same as are the lower surfaces of the wings and tail; outermost tail-feathers rufescent white, the next with a border on its outer web, the four middle ones colored like the back, and the rest of the tail blackish; supercilia and lower parts sullied white, with a few brown streaks on the breast.

The Large Crested Lark is a common permanent resident

in Sind, and is not uncommon in Northern Guzerat. It breeds during April and May, in much the same way as the other larks. The eggs measure 0·87 inches in length by about 0·65 in breadth.

Genus, **Certhilauda**, *Swainson*.

Bill slender, lengthened, more or less curved; wings very long; nostrils round and naked; wings very long, the first quill short, the second a little shorter than the next three, which are nearly equal; tail moderate or rather long, even; tarsus lengthened; toes short; hinder claw variable, typically short and straight.

Certhilauda desertorum, *Stan.*

770.—Jerdon's Birds of India, Vol. II, p. 438; Murray's Vertebrate Zoology of Sind, p. 199.

The Desert Lark.

Length, 9; wing, 5·25; tail, 2·12; tarsus, 1·38.

Bill horny, darker on culmen, and yellowish-white at base beneath; irides brown; legs sullied china-white.

Light isabella-grey above, more fulvescent on the scapulars, tertiaries, and two middle feathers, which are shaded with pale dusky along the middle; lores, superciliary stripe, throat and belly white; the breast feathers dusky, with broad whitish margins concealing the dark color within; ear-coverts blackish at the tips; wings deep dusky-black; primaries and secondaries pure white at base; the shorter primaries are also white tipped, and the small wing-coverts margined with pale rufescent; tail, except the two middle feathers, deep dusky black, the outermost feathers having their narrow outer web almost wholly white, and the penultimate with a narrow white edge on the outer web. The colors of the female are duller.

The Desert Lark is found in desert and sandy tracts in Sind

Order, **Gemitores**.

Bill moderate or short, straight, compressed; the basal portion weak, and covered with a soft fleshy skin or membrane in which the nostrils are situated; the apical portion arched or vaulted, and more or less curved down at the tip; wings generally long, pointed; tail variable, usually of 12 or 14 feathers; tarsi short and stout; legs feathered to the joint; toes moderately long; hind-toe on the same plane as the anterior ones.

Family, **Treronidæ**.

Bill varied, short and thick in some, slender in others, the tip strong and vaulted; wings long, firm; the tail short or moderate in most, always of 14 feathers; tarsus short, more or less feathered, the bare portion reticulated; inner-toe a little shorter than the outer, which is slightly united at the base to the middle-toe; claws short, well curved.

SUB-FAMILY, Treroninæ.

Bill stronger and thicker than in the other two sub-families; tail typically short; tarsi and feet stout, soft, with very broad soles.

GENUS, Crocopus, *Bonap.*

Bill tolerably short and stout, with the soft basal portion occupying about half the length of the bill; the inner web of the third primary distinctly sinuated; feet yellow.

Crocopus phœnicopterus, *Lath.*

772.—Jerdon's Birds of India, Vol. II, p. 447; Butler, Guzerat; Stray Feathers, Vol. IV, p. 2.

THE BENGAL GREEN PIGEON.

Length, 12·5; expanse, 22; wing, 7·5; tail, 5; bill at front, 0·8.

Bill whitish; irides carmine, with an outer ring of smalt-blue; feet deep-yellow.

Top of the head, and sides of the base of the neck, (forming a demi-collar) ash-grey, contrasting with the yellow-green of the back of the neck; a green tinge on the forehead; the rest of the plumage green; shoulders of the wing lilac in the male, and with a trace of the same in the female; the greater-coverts margined with pale-yellow, forming an oblique bar across the wing; the terminal two-fifths of the tail ash-grey above, deeply tinged with green, albescent beneath, with the medial portion blackish; beneath, the neck and breast are bright yellow-green, with a shade of fulvous, and the abdominal region ash-grey; the lower belly generally more or less mixed with green, but bright yellow in the middle, as are the tibial feathers; vent mingled white and green; under tail-coverts dull vinous-maroon, with white tips, inclining to greenish in the female.

The Bengal Green Pigeon has only doubtfully been recorded from Mount Aboo. It does not occur elsewhere within our limits.

Crocopus chlorigaster, *Blyth.*

773.—Jerdon's Birds of India, Vol. II, p. 448; Butler, Guzerat; Stray Feathers, Vol. IV, p. 2; Deccan, Stray Feathers, Vol. IX, p. 419; Murray's Vertebrate Zoology of Sind, p. 200; Swinhoe and Barnes, Central India; Ibis, 1885, p. 130.

THE SOUTHERN GREEN PIGEON.

Harrial, Hin.

Length, 13; expanse, 22; wing, 7; tail, 4·5; tarsus, 0·8; bill at front, 0·8; bill from gape, 1.

Bill whitish, tinted blue at base and beneath; irides carmine; legs waxy-yellow.

This species differs from the last in having the whole top of the head ashy, devoid in adults, of the slightest tinge of green on the forehead, and the whole under parts are green; the neck and breast, too, are less tinged with yellow, and shade gradually into the green of the belly; there is no trace of green upon the tail, except at its extreme base, which is uniformly ash above.

The Southern Green Pigeon occurs in suitable localities in all parts of the Presidency, but it is very rare in Sind, having only been obtained near the frontier at Jacobabad. It is a permanent resident, making the usual dove-like nest. The eggs, two in number, are oval in shape, and glossy pure white in color. They measure 1·25 inches in length by 0·95 in breadth.

GENUS, Osmotreron, *Bonap.*

Bill as in *Crocopus*, but more slender; legs always red; sexes differ conspicuously in plumage; of small size.

Osmotreron malabarica, *Jerdon.*

775.—Jerdon's Birds of India, Vol. II, p. 450; Butler, Deccan; Stray Feathers, Vol. IX, p. 419.

THE GREY-FRONTED GREEN PIGEON.

Length, 10·5; expanse, 18; wing, 5·75; tail, 4.

Bill glaucous-green; irides red, with an outer circle of blue; legs pinky-red.

Male: forehead pale ashy, or whitish-grey; mantle and wing-coverts maroon; the rest of the upper parts, with the lores, eye-brow, face, and ear-coverts, green; wing-coverts broadly edged with bright yellow, and wing feathers more or less edged with the same; tail green at the base, broadly tipped with ashy-white, and with a medial dark band, and the outermost feathers more or less marked with deep ashy on the inner webs; beneath green, yellowish on the throat and neck, and mixed with pale-yellow on the vent and thigh-coverts; under tail-coverts cinnamon.

The female differs in wanting the maroon color, and in the under tail-coverts being mingled ashy and white.

The Grey-fronted Green Pigeon occurs sparingly all along the Sahyadri Range as far north as Khandalla, extending also to the well-wooded tracts of Ratnagari.

SUB-FAMILY, Carpophaginæ.

Bill lengthened and slender, tolerably depressed at the base, with the terminal third or less of the upper mandible corneous; wings long; tail even, or slightly rounded, longer than in the *Treroninæ;* feet strong, with broad soles; tarsus well feathered.

GENUS, Carpophaga, *Selby.*

The characters are the same as those of the sub-family; plumage glossy metallic-green, or coppery-brown above; of large size.

Carpophaga ænea, *Lin.*

780.—*C. sylvatica*, Tick.—Jerdon's Birds of India, Vol. II, p. 455.

THE GREEN IMPERIAL PIGEON.

Length, 18 to 19 ; expanse, 30 ; wing, 8 to 9 ; tail, 6.

Bill slaty, red at the base above, and bluish-white at the tip ; irides and the nude orbits crimson ; legs lake-red, pale on the soles.

Head, neck, and whole under parts, pearl-grey, purer on the crown and breast, and tinged elsewhere, and sometimes on the crown, with ruddy-vinaceous ; back, rump, wings, and tail, shining coppery-green, brightest on the tail, and the quills slaty-grey without, dark blackish-grey within ; under tail-coverts deep chesnut, with which some of the feathers of the vent and flanks are also sprinkled ; chin, orbital feathers and round the base of the bill, white ; axillaries buff.

Jerdon states in his " Birds of India" that the Green Imperial Pigeon is abundant in Central India, and that he found it breeding there in April and May. I have myself never met with it.

FAMILY, **Columbidæ.**

Bill horny at the apex only; tail, in almost all, of twelve feathers ; tarsus lengthened ; feet more fitted for walking on the ground.

SUB-FAMILY, **Palumbinæ.**

Feet fitted for perching, the tarsus being somewhat shorter, and the feet more arboreal than in the succeeding groups ; tail somewhat longer and more rounded.

GENUS, **Palumbus**, *Kaup.*

Sides of neck adorned with a patch of light-colored feathers.

Palumbus casiotis, *Bonap.*

784.—Jerdon's Birds of India, Vol. II, p. 464 ; Murray's Vertebrate Zoology of Sind, p. 201.

THE HIMALAYAN CUSHAT.

Length, 17 ; expanse, 30 ; wing, 10·25 ; tail, 7 ; bill at front, 0·75.

Bill orange, whitish at base ; irides yellow ; feet red.

Above brownish-grey ; the head, cheeks, rump, and upper tail-coverts, pure ashy ; nape, sides of neck, and shoulders glossed with changeable green and purple ; on each side of the neck a large patch of fulvous or clayey-cream color ; edge of the wing, and a white longitudinal bar, formed by the outer edges of the primaries, white ; winglet and primary-coverts blackish ; tail grey at the base, blackish at the tip ; beneath, the throat is pure ashy, the foreneck and breast vinaceous-ruddy, paling on the belly, and albescent towards the vent; lower tail-coverts ashy; tail with a broad pale band.

Within our limits, the Himalayan Cushat only occurs on the frontier near Jacobabad, and is very rare. I found it very common in Southern Afghanistan where it breeds.

Palumbus elphinstonii, *Sykes.*

786.—Jerdon's Birds of India, Vol. II, p. 465; Butler, Deccan; Stray Feathers, Vol. IX, p. 419.

THE NEILGHERRY WOOD PIGEON.

Length, 15 to 16; expanse, 25; wing, 8 to 8·25; tail, 5·75 to 6.

Bill and orbits deep red, the former with a yellow tip; irides ochre-yellow; legs and feet dull-red.

Above, the head and neck ashy; nuchal patch black, with small white tips; back of neck beyond this, and interscapulars, cupreous-ruddy, with some green reflections; rest of the upper plumage ruddy-brown, becoming dark-ashy on the rump and upper tail-coverts; the wings dusky, the lesser-coverts mostly ruddy-cupreous, and the other coverts and quills, which are dusky-black, more or less edged with the same, and the outer primaries conspicuously pale edged; tail dull black; beneath ashy, albescent on the throat; the neck and breast glossed with green, and the lower abdomen and vent albescent.

The Neilgherry Wood Pigeon is found on parts of the Sahyadri Range; it is not common anywhere, but appears to be well known at Mahableshwar.

GENUS, Palumbæna, *Bonap.*

Feet fitted as much for perching as for walking on the ground. In form, coloring, habits, and nidification intermediate between *Palumbus* and *Columba.*

Palumbæna eversmanni, *Bonap.*

787.—Jerdon's Birds of India, Vol. II, p. 467; Murray's Vertebrate Zoology of Sind, p. 201.

THE INDIAN STOCK PIGEON.

Length, 11·5; expanse, 24; wing, 8; tail, 4.

Bill yellowish; skin round the eye yellowish; irides buff; legs with a yellowish tinge.

Dark-ashy, with a whitish-grey rump; crown and breast tinged with vinaceous; two or three black spots on the wings, forming the rudiments of bands, and the end of the tail black, its outermost feather white for the basal two-thirds of its exterior web, and showing a black, and then a narrow grey band towards its tip; beneath the wings whitish, where dark-ashy in the European bird.

The Indian Stock Pigeon occurs in Sind, towards the frontier; it has not been recorded from any other portion of our limits.

GENUS, Columba, *Lin.*

Feet fitted for walking on the ground, the tarsus being somewhat lengthened; nestle in holes of rocks, buildings, or wells; capable of domestication.

Columba intermedia, *Strick.*

788.—Jerdon's Birds of India, Vol. II, p. 469; Butler, Guzerat; Stray Feathers, Vol. IV, p. 3; Deccan, Stray Feathers, Vol. IX, p. 419; Murray's Vertebrate Zoology of Sind, p. 202; Swinhoe and Barnes, Central India; Ibis, 1885, p. 130.

THE BLUE ROCK PIGEON.

Length, 12 to 13; expanse, 23; wing, 8·75 to 9; tail, 5; bill, 0·75.

Bill black, mealy at base above; irides dull orange; legs dull reddish-pink.

Color slaty-grey, darker on the head, throat, and breast, also on the upper and lower tail-coverts and tail, which last has a blackish terminal band; nuchal-feathers divergent at their tip, and brightly glossed with changeable green and amethystine; two black bars on the wings, formed by the greater-coverts, and the secondaries being tipped with black on the outer web only; and the outermost tail-feather, with its external web, gradually more albescent to the base.

The Blue Rock Pigeon is a very common permanent resident throughout the district, breeding from November to May; a favourite nesting place is a hole or a ledge in a well.

Columba livia, *Bp.*

788*bis*.—Murray's Vertebrate Zoology of Sind, p. 202.

THE ROCK DOVE.

Length, 15; wing, 9; tail, 7·2; tarsus, 0·9; bill at front, 0·75.

Bill blackish; irides orange to dark-brown; legs dull reddish-pink.

Differs from *Columba intermedia* in having a pure white instead of an ash-colored rump.

The Rock Dove occurs on the frontiers of Sind.

SUB-FAMILY, Turturinæ.

Feet fitted for walking on the ground; tail somewhat lengthened (typically), rounded or graduate, and with pale tips to the outer feathers; of delicate make, with small heads; neck usually without the iridescent play of the *Columbinæ*, but frequently adorned with neck spots, as in the *Palumbinæ*, or with rings.

Genus, Turtur.

Bill slender, the tip very slightly arched; the two first quills graduated, second and third longest; tail somewhat long, usually rounded; toes long and slender; the claws slightly curved.

Turtur pulchratus, *Hodgs.*

792.—*Turtur rupicolus*, Pallas.—Jerdon's Birds of India, Vol. II, p. 476; Butler, Guzerat; Stray Feathers, Vol. IV, p. 92; Deccan, Stray Feathers, Vol. IX, p. 420.

The Ashy Turtle Dove.

Length, 12 to 13; expanse, 20·5; wing, 7 to 8; tail, 5 to 5·5; tarsus, 0·75; bill at front, 0·7.

Bill blackish-horny; irides light orange; legs dull purplish.

Head bluish-ashy, with the occiput and nape rufescent; back and rump ashy-brown, more ashy on the latter; wings dusky; the coverts widely margined with dark rufous; tail bluish-black, with a broad white tip; beneath brown, becoming whitish towards the vent; lower tail-coverts white, with a faint tinge of ashy; neck spot black.

The Ashy Turtle Dove is common during the cold weather in many parts of the Deccan; it is also common at Mhow; a single specimen has been recorded from Aboo, but in Sind it does not occur at all.

Turtur meena, *Sykes.*

793.—Jerdon's Birds of India, Vol. II, p. 476; Butler, Deccan; Stray Feathers, Vol. IX, p. 420; Swinhoe and Barnes, Central India; Ibis, 1885, p. 130.

The Rufous Turtle Dove.

Length, 11·5 to 12·5; wing, 7; tail, 4·5.

Bill blackish, tinged lake-red; irides orange; legs dull purple.

General color vinaceous-brown, ashy on the forehead and crown, and whitish towards the base of the bill, and more or less mixed with ashy and dusky above; rump and upper tail-coverts deep grey; wing-coverts and scapulars dusky, broadly margined with rufous; secondary-coverts usually ashy; winglet and primaries, with their coverts dusky, the latter edged with whitish; tail dusky-ash, the outer feathers successively more broadly tipped with deep grey, paling on the outermost feather; beneath the chin and throat whitish; the rest of the plumage pale vinaceous-brown, deepest on the breast, and becoming albescent on the lower abdomen; vent and lower tail-coverts light grey; the neck-patch black, with grey tips, narrower than in the preceding species.

The Rufous Turtle Dove is affined very closely to the last, the principal difference being the color of the under tail-coverts. It is found in the cold weather in parts of the Deccan.

Turtur senegalensis, *Lin.*

794.—*T. cambayensis*, Gm.—Jerdon's Birds of India, Vol. II, p. 478; Butler, Guzerat; Stray Feathers, Vol. IV, p. 3; Deccan, Stray Feathers, Vol. IX, p. 420; Murray's Vertebrate Zoology of Sind, p. 203; Swinhoe and Barnes, Central India; Ibis, 1885, p. 130.

THE LITTLE BROWN DOVE.

Length, 10 to 10·5; expanse, 14; wing, 5; tail, 4·5.

Bill blackish; irides dark-brown; legs lake-red.

Above brown, the head and upper part of the neck pinkish-vinaceous; wing-coverts, except towards the scapulars, pure light-grey; winglet, primaries, and their coverts dusky; the secondaries tinged with grey; tail with the middle feathers brown; the others black at the base, white for nearly their terminal half; beneath the neck and breast pinkish-vinaceous, paling below, and passing to white on the belly and lower tail-coverts; the sides of the neck with a patch on each side, nearly meeting at the base, rufous tipped; the black hardly apparent, except when the neck is stretched.

The Little Brown Dove is exceedingly common throughout the whole region, both on the hills and plains. It is a permanent resident.

Turtur suratensis, *Gm.*

795.—Jerdon's Birds of India, Vol. II, p. 479; Butler, Guzerat; Stray Feathers, Vol. IV, p. 3; Deccan, Stray Feathers, Vol. IX, p. 420; Murray's Vertebrate Zoology of Sind, p. 203; Swinhoe and Barnes, Central India; Ibis, 1885, p. 130.

THE SPOTTED DOVE.

Length, 12; expanse, 16·5; wing, 5·75; tail, 5·5.

Bill dull leaden-black; irides dark hazel; legs dark purplish-red.

Head pale-vinaceous, greyish on the forehead; upper parts generally dusky, each feather with two pale rufous-isabelline terminal spots, enlarging and spreading up each side of the feather upon the wing-coverts; the blackish contracting to a central streak having broad pale vinaceous lateral borders; edge of the wing, with some of the nearest coverts, light grey; tail with the central feathers brown, the outermost ones black at the base, white for the terminal half, and the others intermediate in their coloring; lower parts pale vinaceous, more or less albescent on the throat and passing to white on the vent and lower tail-coverts.

The Spotted Dove occurs more or less abundantly throughout the district. It is a permanent resident, but appears much more commoner at some times than at others.

Turtur risorius, *Lin.*

796.—Jerdon's Birds of India, Vol. II, p. 481; Butler, Guzerat;

Stray Feathers, Vol. IV, p. 3; Deccan, Stray Feathers, Vol. IX, p. 420; Murray's Vertebrate Zoology of Sind, p. 204; Swinhoe and Barnes, Central India; Ibis, 1885, p. 130.

THE COMMON RING DOVE.

Length, 12·5 to 13; expanse, 20; wing, 6·5; tail, 5.

Bill blackish; irides crimson; feet dark pink-red.

Head delicate pale vinous-grey, more or less whitish on the forehead; nape pale vinaceous; a narrow black collar on the nape set off with whitish above, and slightly so below; upper plumage uniform light grey-brown; edge of the wing pure ashy; primaries dusky with slight whitish margins bordering their tips; middle tail-feathers uniform with the back above; the lateral feathers marked with black about the middle, passing to greyish on the basal half, and to white on the terminal, and these successively more pronounced externally; beneath very pale vinaceous, whitish on the throat, passing to light-greyish towards the vent, and the lower tail-coverts pure ashy; wings underneath greyish-white.

The Common Ring Dove occurs abundantly throughout the region, and is a permanent resident.

Turtur tranquebaricus, *Herm.*

797.—Jerdon's Birds of India, Vol. II, p. 482; *T. humilis*, Tem., Butler, Guzerat; Stray Feathers, Vol. IV, p. 3; Deccan, Stray Feathers, Vol. IX, p. 421; *T. humilis*, Tem., Murray's Vertebrate Zoology of Sind, p. 204; Swinhoe and Barnes, Central India; Ibis, 1885, p. 131.

THE RUDDY RING DOVE.

Length, 9·25; expanse, 15; wing, 5·3; tail, 3·3; tarsus, 0·7; bill at front, 0·5.

Bill black; irides dark-brown; legs purplish-red.

Male, head ashy-grey, paler towards the forehead, a black half collar, well set off by whitish above; general color above fine vinous or brick-red; the rump and upper tail-coverts dusky-ash; winglet, primaries and their coverts, and the secondaries, blackish; tail, with the middle feathers, ash-brown, the rest blackish at the base, and broadly tipped with white, successively more broadly from the centre, and spreading up the whole exterior web of the outermost feather; beneath the chin whitish, rest of the lower parts pale vinous-red; vent and lower tail-coverts white, tinged with ashy; wing beneath light-ashy.

The female is a trifle smaller, and of a dull earthy-brown paler below.

The Ruddy Ring Dove is very locally distributed, but is found in all portions of the region with which I am dealing. It is a permanent resident, building the usual frail stick nest, and laying the inevitable two white eggs.

SUB-FAMILY, Phapinæ.

Tarsus much lengthened, not feathered; tail consisting of twelve, fourteen, or sixteen feathers.

GENUS, Chalcophaps, *Gould.*

Bill slender; wings moderately long; second and third quills nearly equal and longest; tail rather short, rounded; tarsus moderately long, not feathered; toes long; hind-toe lengthened; claws moderately curved.

Chalcophaps indica, *Lin.*

798.—Jerdon's Birds of India, Vol. II, p. 484; Butler, Deccan; Stray Feathers, Vol. IX, p. 421.

THE BRONZE-WINGED DOVE.

Length, 10·5; expanse, 17·5; wing, 5·5; tail, 3·75.

Bill bright coral-red, dusky at base; orbits livid-fleshy; irides dark-brown; feet dull purple-red.

Male, forehead white, continued as a supercilium over the eye; crown of the head and the middle of the neck ash-grey; back and wings shining dark emerald-green, slightly glossed with golden; the feathers of the back distinct and scale-like; two broad dusky bars, alternating with two greyish-white ones on the lower back and rump; the feathers with the basal and middle portion of the shaft very broad and flattened; tail dusky, the two outer feathers on each side whitish-grey, with a black sub-terminal band; primaries dusky, and a white bar at the shoulder of the wing; beneath, the whole neck, breast, and lower parts, vinaceous red-brown, paler on the lower abdomen; the lower tail-coverts ashy, the longest being blackish; wing beneath dark reddish-brown.

The female has the forehead greyish-white, and the supercilium narrower; the head rufescent, the lower parts browner, and the under tail-coverts more or less ferruginous; she also wants the white shoulder spot.

The young are more dusky above, with little green, and barred below.

The Bronze-winged Dove is sparingly distributed along the Sahyadri Range; it frequents dense forests.

ORDER, Rasores.

Bill short, vaulted, more or less bent down at the tip; nostrils pierced in a membrane covering the base of the bill, and protected by a cartilaginous scale; wings usually short and rounded, but ample; tail very variable, both in length and form, of from twelve to eighteen feathers; legs and feet strong, feathered to the tarsus, which is frequently spurred in the male; three toes before and one behind; the posterior one typically short, and articulated above the plane of the anterior toes, wanting in a few; nails strong, blunt, and but slightly curved.

FAMILY, Pteroclidæ.

Bill somewhat slender and compressed; wings lengthened and pointed; tarsus short, more or less plumed; feet short; hind-toe rudimentary or wanting; tail of sixteen feathers.

GENUS, Pterocles, *Temm.*

Bill small, slightly arched, the sides compressed; nostrils basal almost concealed by the frontal plumes; wings long and pointed; the first and second quills longest; tail moderate, wedge-shaped or rounded; the central feathers often lengthened; tarsi feathered in front, reticulated posteriorly; the anterior toes bare, united at their base by membrane; hind-toe minute, raised; the claws short, stout, very slightly curved.

Pterocles arenarius, *Pall.*

799.—Jerdon's Birds of India, Vol. II, p. 496; Butler, Guzerat; Stray Feathers, Vol. IV, p. 4; Murray's Vertebrate Zoology of Sind, p. 209; Game Birds of India, Vol. I, p. 47; Swinhoe and Barnes, Central India; Ibis, 1885, p. 131.

THE LARGE SAND GROUSE.

Length, 13·25 to 14·75; expanse, 27 to 30; wing, 9 to 10; tail, 4 to 5; tarsus, 1 to 1·25; bill from gape, 0·6 to 0·7; weight, 15 oz. to 1¼ lbs.

Bill pale bluish-grey to dark plumbeous; irides brown; feet earthy-grey to dark greyish plumbeous.

Male, crown and middle of the nape brownish-grey with a pinkish tinge; rest of the upper parts mingled ashy and fulvous, each feather being bluish-ashy in the middle, edged with fulvous, giving a mottled appearance; greater wing-coverts plain ochreous or orange-buff, and the median-coverts also broadly edged with the same; quills and primary-coverts dark slaty, with black shafts; tail as the back, fulvous with black ashy bands; all the lateral tail-feathers tipped with white; beneath, the chin is deep chesnut, passing as a band under the ear-coverts to the nape, and below this, on the middle of the throat, is a small triangular patch of black; the breast and sides of the neck dull ashy, tinged with fulvous, with a narrow band of black on the breast; abdomen and vent deep black; under tail-coverts black, with white margins to the feathers; tarsal plumes pale yellowish.

The female differs in having the whole head and upper parts with the breast fulvous, banded with brown; the pectoral band is narrower, and between that and the black of the abdomen is unspotted; the chin is fulvous, with a narrow black edging and a few black specks; the under tail-coverts pale fulvous.

The Large or Black-bellied Sand Grouse is found during the winter months, in Sind, Guzerat, and Rajputana. They frequent open sandy plains, and are, if they have been much worried, very difficult to shoot. They go regularly to drink every morning, and native shikaries, taking advantage of this, lie in ambush and often succeed in slaughtering great numbers of them.

They do not breed in India, but at Chaman, Southern Afghanistan, I found them breeding freely during May and June. They lay in slight depressions in the soil, and the eggs, three in number, are similar to those of *P. exustus*, but are of course much larger. They average 1·8 inches in length by about 1·25 in breadth.

Pterocles fasciatus, *Scop.*

800.—Jerdon's Birds of India, Vol. II, p. 498; Butler, Guzerat; Stray Feathers, Vol. IV, p. 4; Deccan, Stray Feathers, Vol IX, p. 421; Game Birds of India, Vol. I, p. 59; Swinhoe and Barnes, Central India; Ibis, 1885, p. 131.

THE PAINTED SAND GROUSE.

Length, 10 to 11·25; expanse, 19·5 to 22·5; wing, 6·4 to 7; tail, 3·25 to 3·75; tarsus, 0·8 to 1; bill from gape, 0·55 to 0·7; weight, 6 to 7½ oz.

Bill brown to dark orange-red; irides brown; feet dirty-yellow to pale orange-brown.

Male, general ground color bright fulvous-yellow, the sides of the head, neck and breast, and shoulder of the wings plain and unspotted; the back, scapulars, tertiaries and tail, banded with deep brown; a narrow white band on the forehead, then a broadish black band, succeeded by another narrow white one, and then a narrow black band, widening behind the eye, and ending in a white spot; the occiput and nape with black streaks; quills brown-black, with narrow pale edgings; the median and greater-coverts of the wings and some of the secondaries broadly banded with inky-black, edged with white; a triple band separates the fulvous of the breast from the abdomen, the first maroon, the second creamy-white, and the third unspotted chocolate-brown, which is the ground color of the abdominal region, vent, and under tail-coverts, each feather being tipped with white.

The female differs in wanting the black and white bands on the head, the pectoral band, and the inky-black and white bars on the wings, the whole upper surface, the sides of the neck, breast, wings, and tail, being fulvous mixed with rufous, and finely barred with black; the chin, throat, ear-coverts, and some of the greater wing-coverts are unspotted fulvous; the lower part of the breast, and the whole abdominal region, very finely barred with chocolate-black and creamy-white.

With the exception of Sind, the Painted Sand Grouse occurs throughout the region, but is very locally distributed; it is a permanent resident, breeding usually in April and May; they make no nest to speak of, but merely scrape a slight depression in the ground, at a spot, sheltered by a tuft of grass or bush. The eggs, two or three in number, (usually three) are of a cylindrical shape, delicate pale salmon-pink in color, with specks and tiny streaks of brownish-red, with a good many spots or clouds of pale inky-purple intermingled.

They measure 1·4 inches in length by 0·98 in breadth.

Pterocles lichtensteini, *Tem.*

800*bis*.—Murray's Vertebrate Zoology of Sind, p. 212; Game Birds of India, Vol. I, p. 65.

THE CLOSE-BARRED SAND GROUSE.

Length, 10·25 to 10·75 ; expanse, 20 to 21 ; wing, 6·5 to 6·75 ; tail, 3·25 ; tarsus, 1·05 ; bill from gape, 0·65 ; weight, 8 oz.

Bill fleshy-brown ; irides brown ; legs orange-yellow.

Frontal zone white, or buffy-white ; a broad black semi-circular band behind it extending from the exterior angle of the eye on each side ; behind this another white or buffy-white band, interrupted on the crown, the feathers of which are buffy white and mesially dark brown ; a buff spot above the hinder angle of each eye ; chin and throat pale buff, their sides the same, with minute black spots ; upper breast, hind-neck, and back, pale or fulvous white, with regular and close barrings of black ; scapulars, wing-coverts and tertiaries the same, the black transverse bars rather broader and deeper in color, the tips of the feathers broadly yellowish-buff ; upper tail-coverts fulvous-white, the black bars more distant and as wide as the fulvous interspaces ; primaries and their coverts hair-brown, the outer web of the first margined with dull white, more conspicuous basally, and some of the inner ones with white margins to the tips ; secondaries dark brown ; lower breast yellowish-buff, with a narrow black band crossing it in the middle and another on the lower part of the breast, formed by the dark termination of the lowest breast feathers ; below this the abdomen, flanks, vent and under tail-coverts are white, with transverse brown bars ; tarsal plumes buffy-white ; tail barred buff and black, the terminal black bar broadest, with a streak running up the shafts of the feathers and partially dividing the broad buffy tips.

The *female* wants the frontal patch and the semi-circular band behind it, also the buff breast and band crossing it in the middle ; the chin and throat are pale buffy, minutely spotted with dark brown ; the upper surface of the body finely, closely, and narrowly barred with pale fulvous and dark brown ; the lower surface the same, but the fulvous interspaces are broader and the dark bars narrower.

The Close-barred Sand Grouse is a cold weather visitant to the trans-indus portion of Sind.

Pterocles alchata, *Lin.*

801.—Jerdon's Birds of India, Vol. II, p. 500; Murray's Vertebrate Zoology of Sind, p. 210; Game Birds of India, Vol. I, p. 77.

THE LARGE PIN-TAILED SAND GROUSE.

Length, 13·5 to 15·5; expanse, 24 to 26; wings, 7·5 to 8·5; tail, ♂ 5 to 7, ♀ 3·75 to 6; tarsus, 1; weight, 8¼ to 12 ounces.

Bill dusky-green to slate color; irides brown; feet dirty or dusky-green.

Forehead and supercilia rusty-fulvous, with a black stripe behind the eye; top of the head and nape fulvous with black bands; the general hue above, including the scapulars and shoulders of the wings, is fulvous or greyish-olive, shaded with fuscous; the scapulars with a few black spots; rump and upper tail-coverts bright pale fulvous with narrow black bars; lesser and median wing-coverts maroon, white tipped; secondary-coverts fulvous with black lunules; greater-coverts and primaries slaty-blue on their outer webs, brown internally; tail banded yellow and black; the median pair blackish on their attenuated portion; the outer feathers greyish white, tipped and edged; beneath, the chin and throat are black, edged with rusty; lores and face rufous-yellow, with a blackish space round the eyes; breast pale fulvous, with a double black band, each of them narrow; abdomen, vent, and lower tail-coverts white, the latter slightly black barred; tarsal plumes whitish.

The female differs in having the upper plumage barred with black and fulvous, with some dusky-ashy spots on the back and scapulars; the lesser and median wing-coverts ashy, with oblique rufous and black lunules; the throat white; a broad blackish demi-collar on the neck, followed by an ashy band tinged with rufous; the median tail-feathers are nearly as long as in the male bird.

It is only in the trans-indus portion of Sind that the Pin-tailed Grouse occurs in any numbers, although stragglers are occasionally procured much further south.

It is only a cold weather visitant.

Pterocles senegalus, *Lin.*

801*bis.*—Murray's Vertebrate Zoology of Sind, p. 207; Butler, Guzerat; Stray Feathers, Vol. IV, p. 4; Game Birds of India, Vol. I, p. 53.

THE SPOTTED SAND GROUSE.

Length, 12·4 to 14·7; expanse, 22 to 24; wing, 7·3 to 8; tail, ♂, 5·3 to 6, ♀, 4 to 4·6; tarsus, 1; bill at front, 0·4 to 0·47; weight, 8 to 12 oz.

Bill pale plumbeous or bluish-white; irides brown; feet pale plumbeous or bluish-white.

The male has the whole chin and throat with a patch extending upwards from the throat, towards, but not quite, meeting on the back of the neck, bright buffy-yellow or orange-buff; lores, forehead, a broad stripe over the eye continued round the nape and the back of the neck, pale blue-grey, dull and tinged fawny in some specimens; crown, occiput, and nape, a sort of dove-color or pale, slightly rufous-fawn; back and rump a somewhat similar, but more sandy color, in many specimens more tinged with fawn; the upper tail-coverts buffy-yellow, all but the longest obscurely tipped with a somewhat pinkish-mouse color. They are more or less pale dove-color at their bases, which color however is not seen till the feathers are lifted. The central tail-feathers have the pointed tips black, in many specimens more or less tinged horny-buffy, and the rest of the visible portion yellowish-buff, but the bases, as may be seen on lifting the feathers, are greyish; the lateral tail-feathers are a greyish-brown at base, dark shafted, with conspicuous white tips, and broad blackish-brown subterminal bands; the primaries are pale isabelline, the shafts conspicuous and black; they have broad ill-defined subterminal brown bands, beyond which there is a narrow paler tipping, and they are pretty conspicuously margined on their inner webs towards the tips with still paler isabelline; the first primary has the outer web browner, the others have the outer webs, especially towards the bases, a brighter isabelline. The whole visible portions of the lesser-coverts and of the primary greater-coverts are yellowish-fawn, or isabelline, varying much in shade in different specimens; these greater-coverts are dark shafted, and with a brownish tinge next the shafts on the inner webs; the scapulars bluish-grey at the bases, tipped broadly, but chiefly on the outer webs, with buffy-yellow, and the lesser ones tinged immediately above the yellow with a somewhat brownish-purple, or dull greyish-vinaceous; the secondary, median, and greater-coverts like the lesser scapulars, but showing more of the vinaceous hue. The secondaries are brown, lighter towards their bases, the lower part of the neck in front and breast are nearly the same blue-grey or greyish-fawn as the back of the neck; the lower breast, abdomen, sides, flanks, axillaries, and wing-lining isabelline or desert color, the upper abdomen often with a faint orange-buffy tinge; a broad deep irregular brown patch runs down the centre of the abdomen to the vent; the lower tail-coverts are greyish-brown at their bases, but are broadly tipped with white (often tinged buffy or isabelline) which is the only color visible until the feathers are lifted; the lower surfaces of the quill shafts are white.

The female has the yellow chin and throat patch like the male, but paler; the lores and feathers immediately encircling the eye pale isabelline white; the whole upper parts and the neck all round pure isabelline, tinged slightly rufous on the occiput, nape, and back, and conspicuously spotted with dull, somewhat greyish-black; the spots on the forehead and front part of the head are small and irregular; on the nape and occiput they are more or less arranged in rows (so as to produce more of a striated appearance) and in a band running from behind the eye round the nape, they are very much more densely set; on the upper tail-coverts they are much larger, while on the scapulars they take the form of double spots or irregular bars; the primaries and their greater coverts are much as in the male, but paler; the central tail-feathers are isabelline dark shafted; the points greyish black, and the rest of the feathers with narrow, transverse, irregular bars of the same color on both webs; the lateral tail-feathers are much as in the male, but have the basal portions more tinged with isabelline, and more or less imperfectly barred; the breast, abdomen, and wing lining are as in the male, bnt somewhat purer and paler; the abdominal patch is narrower and perhaps also somewhat paler.

Within our limits, the Spotted Sand Grouse is only common in Sind, but stragglers occasionally find their way into portions of Guzerat and even Rajputana.

A few apparently remain to breed in Sind, but most of them are mere cold weather visitants.

Pterocles coronatus, *Licht.*

801*ter.*—Murray's Vertebrate Zoology of Sind, p. 206; Game Birds of India, Vol. I, p. 57.

THE CORONETTED SAND GROUSE.

Length, 10 to 11·75; wing, 7 to 7·5; expanse, 22; tarsus, 0·9; bill at front, 0·45; bill at gape, 0·65.

Bill pale slaty; irides brown; legs clayey-slate, with china-white scutæ.

A line on each side of the forehead from the nostrils to above the eye black, and a pale fulvous one between these from the point of the forehead; crown of the head pale chestnut, vinous or rufescent fawn; a pearly grey band from the anterior angle of the eye, continued as a supercilium and extending round to the nape; lores and a narrow band edging the black chin and throat-stripe, white; sides of the face, ear-coverts, and the neck all round orange-buff; base of the neck and upper back isabelline, the feathers edged dusky grey; interscapulars the same, with median buffy spots at the tips; rump and upper tail-coverts a dark or dirty grey, mixed with the fulvous of the base of the feathers; tail with median rectrices of a pale vinous color, dark shafted, with a subterminal dark spot, and very narrowly tipped with white; lateral feathers deeper vinous with also a subterminal dark bar, and broadly tipped with white; all the feathers with a few dusky sprinkles behind the dark band; primaries and their coverts dull grey or dusky brown; all the primaries, except the first three, broadly margined with fulvous-white obliquely towards the tips on their inner webs, and also tipped the same;

secondaries hair-brown; tertiaries vinous on their inner webs and edged on the outer with buffish; scapulars vinous at the base, dark shafted with a subterminal dark band, and mesially tipped with a nearly oval buff spot; median wing-coverts the same, the greater series greyish-buff or buffy-isabelline; abdomen, flanks, under wing-coverts, vent, and lower tail-coverts, white, slightly soiled on the middle of the abdomen, and in some specimens a pale isabelline; tarsal plumes white.

The female has the throat and sides of the neck orange-buff; the chin paler and nearly albescent; the crown very pale cinnamon; entire upper-surface buff, with, in some specimens, a vinous tinge and barred with numerous crescentic and broken bands of dark brown; breast and under parts paler buff, also with crescentic bands; the flanks albescent; scapulars largely blotched with dusky and with buff tips; primaries and secondaries as in the male, but very pale, or hair-brown.

It is only on the confines of Sind that the Coronetted Sand Grouse has been procured and that but rarely. It is of course only a cold weather visitant, but further north in Southern Afghanistan I was so fortunate as to procure two batches of eggs. They measured 1·63 inches in length by 1·07 in breadth.

Pterocles exustus, *Tem.*

802.—Jerdon's Birds of India, Vol. II, p. 502; Butler, Guzerat; Stray Feathers, Vol. IV, p. 4; Deccan, Stray Feathers, Vol. IX, p. 421; Murray's Vertebrate Zoology of Sind, p. 210; Game Birds of India, Vol I, p. 69; Swinhoe and Barnes, Central India; Ibis, 1885, p. 131.

THE COMMON SAND GROUSE.

Length, 11 to 13·75; expanse, 21 to 22·5; wing, 6·5 to 7·5; tail, 4 to 5·9; tarsus, 0·8 to 1; bill from gape, 0·6 to 0·7; weight, 7½ to 10 oz.

Bill pale slaty-grey to pale plumbeous or lavender-blue; irides dark brown; feet same as bill.

Male, general colour fulvous-isabelline, brighter and more yellow about the lores, face, and chin, and mixed with dusky-greenish on the back, wing and upper tail-coverts; primaries black, the tips of all, except the first three, white, broader on the inner web; a longitudinal median line on the wing, formed by some of the coverts and secondaries being brighter buff; tail with the central pair of feathers elongated and highly attenuated, isabelline-yellow, the lateral feathers deep brown; edged and tipped with pale fulvous; a narrow black band on the breast; abdomen deep chocolate brown (burnt or singed color, hence *exustus*), paling on the vent, as are the tarsal plumes.

The female has the whole upper plumage, including the tail feathers (except a plain bar on the wing, formed by the greater-coverts) fulvous, closely barred with deep brown, also the space between the pectoral band and the abdomen; neck and breast unspotted dingy isabelline; abdomen as in the male; the central rectrices are not elongated.

The Common Sand Grouse occurs abundantly throughout the region. It does not affect hilly or rocky districts, nor is it found in forest or swampy places. It is very partial to fallow or ploughed land. It is a permanent resident, breeding pretty near all the year through. The eggs, three in number, are deposited in a slight depression on the ground; they are of the usual shape peculiar to Grouse, long and cylindrical, equally blunt at both ends; in color they are greyish or greenish-white or even light olive-brown, thickly streaked, blotched and spotted equally over the whole surface with darker or lighter shades of olive-brown and with pale underlying clouds of very pale inky-purple.

They average 1·45 inches in length by about 1·03 in breadth.

The following key, published in Stray Feathers, Vol. VII, p. 159, may prove useful:—

Key to the Indian species of PTEROCLES.

A. Without pectoral band.

- *a.* Stripe on each side of forehead from nostril to above the eye, chin and centre of throat, black ... ... 1. *P. coronatus.*
- *b.* Lores and band encircling back of head pearly-grey; cheeks, ear-coverts and throat orange-yellow; centre of abdomen black ... ... 2. *P. senegalus.*

B. With pectoral band.

- *a.* Without black bar on the forehead.
  - *a*' Median rectrices not lengthened much beyond the rest; upper part of throat and sides of neck rufous; lower portion of throat black; band on lower part of breast; abdomen and flanks black ... ... *P. arenarius.*
  - *b*' Median rectrices greatly lengthened beyond the rest.
    - *a*" Throat yellow; black band across breast; abdomen and flanks chesnut ... ... *P. exustus.*
    - *b*" Throat and stripe behind the eye black; sides of throat rufous; centre of breast chestnut, bordered above and below with black; rest of under parts white ... *P. alchata.*
- *b* With black across forehead.
  - *a*' Breast uniform greenish-buff.
    - *a*" Lower part of breast bordered with a chesnut band, succeeded

by a white one; rest of under parts yellowish white, barred narrowly with black; wing-coverts with two black bands, margined on the upper side only with white ... *P. fasciatus.*

b[1] Throat pale buff; upper part of breast buff, crossed with numerous narrow black bars; middle of breast uniform buff, crossed in centre by a narrow black bar, and another of the same hue on its lower edge; rest of under parts yellowish-white, barred narrowly with black ... ... *P. lichtensteini.*

FAMILY, Phasianidæ.

Bill moderate, strong, vaulted; the tip of the upper mandible produced over that of the lower; sides more or less compressed; nostrils apert; wings moderate or short, rounded; tail (typically) lengthened and broad, of from twelve to eighteen feathers; tarsus moderate or long, usually spurred in the males; toes long, anterior ones united by a short membrane at the base; the hind-toe raised, short, sometimes resting on the ground by its point.

SUB-FAMILY, Pavoninæ.

Plumage more or less ocellated.

GENUS, Pavo, *Lin.*

Bill lengthened, slender; the nareal portion large; nostrils linear; head ornamented with an erect crest of feathers of a peculiar structure; orbitar region naked; tail moderate, long, of eighteen feathers; feathers of the back and upper tail-coverts of great length, surpassing the tail and beautifully ocellated; tarsi rather long, spurred in the male.

Pavo cristatus, *Lin.*

803.—Jerdon's Birds of India, Vol. II, p. 506; Butler, Guzerat; Stray Feathers, Vol. IV, p. 5; Deccan, Stray Feathers, Vol. IX, p. 421; Murray's Vertebrate Zoology of Sind, p. 212; Game Birds of India, Vol. I, p. 81; Swinhoe and Barnes, Central India; Ibis, 1885, p. 131.

THE COMMON PEACOCK.

Length, to the end of the true tail, 40 to 48; the long train sometimes measures 50 inches or even more; wings, 18; tail, 24.

Bill horny-brown; naked orbits whitish; irides dark-brown; legs horny-brown.

Male, head, neck, and breast rich purple with gold and green reflections; back green, the feathers scale-like, with coppery edges; the wings with the inner coverts, including the shoulder, white, striated with black; the middle-coverts deep blue; the primaries and tail chesnut; abdomen and vent black, the train chiefly green, beautifully ocellated; the thigh-coverts yellowish-grey; head, with a crest of about twenty-four feathers only, webbed at the tip, and green with blue and gold reflections.

The Peahen is chestnut brown about the head and nape; the neck greenish, edged with pale whity-brown; the upper plumage light hair-brown, with faint wavings, increased on the upper tail-coverts; quills brown, some of the wing-coverts mottled dusky and whitish; tail deep brown with whitish tips; chin and throat white; breast as in the neck; abdomen white, with the lower parts and under tail-coverts brown. Length, 38 to 40; wing, 16; tail, 14. The crest is shorter and duller in its tints.

The Peacock is not indigenous to Sind, but has been introduced, and appears to be in some portions of the country fairly naturalized. In all other places within our limits the Peacock is fairly common or would be if it was not so persecuted by shikaries.

It is a permanent resident breeding during the rains; the hen scratches a depression in the soil which she lines with a few leaves, generally under cover. The eggs, six or eight in number, are broad oval in shape, creamy white or pale pinkish cafe-au-lait color. They are closely pitted over their whole surface with minute pores. They measure 2·74 inches in length by 2·05 in breadth.

SUB-FAMILY, Gallinæ.

Head sometimes furnished with fleshy crest and wattles, or crested, or sub-crested; tail usually of fourteen feathers, compressed, and more or less divaricate, held demi-erect; the upper tail-coverts in the males are (typically) elongated and pendent.

GENUS, Gallus, *Lin.*

Head furnished with a crest of skin; the face nude and also with a loose lappet or wattle; tarsus of the male strongly spurred; the spur long and strongly curved; tail of fourteen feathers, compressed, divaricated, with the median feathers lengthened, curved and drooping, held semi-erect; the backs of the feathers facing each other; the upper tail-coverts lengthened and curved; feathers of the neck hackled, lanceolate.

Gallus ferrugineus, *Gm.*

812.—Jerdon's Birds of India, Vol. II, p 537; Game Birds of India, Vol. I, p. 217.

THE RED JUNGLE FOWL.

♂. Length, 25·0 to 28·2; expanse, 27 to 29·5; wing, 8·12 to 9·5; tail, 11·25 to 14·3; tarsus, 3 to 3·12; bill from gape, 1·19 to 1·37; weight, 1¾ lbs. to 2¼ lbs.

♀. Length, 16·5 to 18·25; expanse, 23 to 25; wing, 7·1 to 7·5; tail, 5·5 to 6·5; tarsus, 2·3 to 2·55; bill from gape, 1·9 to 1·02; weight, $1\frac{9}{16}$ lbs. to $1\frac{10}{16}$ lbs.

Bill slaty-brown; irides orange-red; face, comb, and wattles red; legs slaty-black.

Male, rich golden hackles on the head, neck, throat and breast, paler on the sides of the neck and posteriorly; ear-coverts white; back purplish-brown in the middle, rich orange-brown on the sides; upper tail-coverts lengthened, also bright orange; wings with the lesser and greater-coverts black, glossed with green; median-coverts rich dull maroon; primaries dusky, with pale edges; secondaries chestnut externally, dusky within; tertiaries glossy black; tail with the central feathers rich glossy green-black, the gloss diminishing on the lateral feathers; beneath from the breast unglossed black; thigh-coverts the same.

The Jungle Hen has the general color yellowish-brown, minutely mottled with dark brown; and some of the feathers, especially of the upper back and wing-coverts, having conspicuously pale shafts; the head dusky above, passing into short hackles of dark brown, edged with bright yellow on the neck and sides of the breast; quills and tail dark brown; the central rectrices edged with mottled-brown; ear-coverts yellowish; a line down the throat deep bright red-brown, ending in a point below and passing up in a line behind the ears to join a small supercilium of the same hue; breast pale rufous-brown, with central pale streaks, lighter on the middle of the belly and becoming dull brown on the flanks, vent, thigh-coverts, and under tail-coverts.

I have been assured by a well known sportsman that the Red Jungle Fowl occurs in Central India, but it must be very rare as no one else seems ever to have met with it.

Gallus sonnerati, *Tem.*

813.—Jerdon's Birds of India, Vol. II, p. 539; Butler, Guzerat; Stray Feathers, Vol. IV, p. 5; Deccan, Stray Feathers, Vol. IX, p. 421; Game Birds of India, Vol. I, p. 231; Swinhoe and Barnes, Central India; Ibis, 1885, p. 131.

THE GREY JUNGLE FOWL.

Jangli Murghi, Hin.

♂. Length, 28 to 32; expanse, 27 to 31; wing, 9·35 to 9·65; tail, 14 to 16; tarsus, 2·85 to 3; bill from gape, 1·3; weight, $1\frac{10}{16}$ to $2\frac{1}{2}$ lbs.

♀. Length, 18 to 20; expanse, 26 to 27; wing, 7·8 to 8·3; tail, 6 to 7; tarsus, 2·2 to 2·5; bill from gape, 1·2; weight, $1\frac{9}{16}$ to $1\frac{3}{4}$ lbs.

Bill yellowish-horny; comb, face, and wattles red; irides orange-brown; legs and feet horny-yellowish.

Whole head and neck, with the hackles, blackish-grey, with

yellow spots, each feather being blackish with the shaft white and two spots, the terminal one of somewhat square form, as if a drop of yellow sealing wax; the other whitish, passing on the wing-coverts into oblong spots of glistening wood-brown; ear-coverts pale rufous; the rest of the plumage above and below blackish-grey, the feathers white shafted, and those on the flanks broadly centred and tipped with wood-brown; outermost primaries dusky, with the shaft and narrow edge pale; the others black, faintly glossed; upper tail-coverts glossy purple; central tail-feathers glossy-green, the gloss diminishing on the lateral feathers; vent dirty-brownish; under tail-coverts glossy black with white shafts.

The hen is mottled brown above, with pale shafts on the wing-coverts; beneath blackish-brown, the feathers broadly centred with pure white, passing into plain dull brown on the flanks, thigh-coverts, vent, and under tail-coverts; head and neck rufous-brown, paler on the chin and throat, and somewhat yellowish; primaries dark brown, the secondaries mottled brown; tail blackish-brown, edged with mottled-brown.

The Grey Jungle Fowl is a common permanent resident all along the Sahyadri Range, and in the adjoining forests, including the hilly parts of Ratnagiri and Belgaum; it is also common on Mount Aboo, and indeed all along the Aravelli Range at all events as far as Erinpoora, where I have myself obtained it. It breeds during May and June, the eggs being deposited on the ground under a bush; there is not much nest to speak of, only a few dry leaves. I have never found more than six eggs in a nest; they are oval in shape, pointed at one end, coarse in texture and closely pitted all over like the eggs of guinea fowl. They are creamy or of a rich cafe-au-lait color, most of them spotted or speckled with brownish red. They measure 1·84 inches in length by 1·38 in breadth.

GENUS, **Galloperdix**, *Blyth.*

Bill somewhat lengthened; orbits nude; tail moderately long, broad, of fourteen feathers, held erect and folded as in fowls; tarsus of the male with two or more spurs; females also with one or more spurs, of small size. Sexes differ much in color.

Galloperdix spadiceus, *Gmelin.*

814.—Jerdon's Birds of India, Vol. II, p. 541; Butler, Guzerat; Stray Feathers, Vol. IV, p. 5; Deccan, Stray Feathers, Vol. IX, p. 422; Game Birds of India, Vol. I, p. 247; Swinhoe and Barnes, Central India; Ibis, 1885, p. 131.

THE RED SPUR FOWL.

Length, 13 to 15; expanse, 17 to 20; wing, 5·62 to 6·75; tail, 4·5 to 6; tarsus, 1·6 to 1·75; bill from gape, 1 to 1·2; weight, 9 to 14 oz.

Bill dusky-red, horny at tip; irides from dull yellow to dusky-brown; legs and feet always red but vary in shade, from vermilion-red to dull pink.

Male, head and nape dusky olive-brown; the forehead and round the eye pale whity-brown, somewhat buff in some individuals; chin, throat, and sides of neck, pale brown; the rest of the body, both above and below, rich brown-chesnut or bay, each feather pale edged; primaries brown; the secondaries and tertiaries more or less minutely mottled; tail with the central feathers chesnut, the others dark brown, more or less mottled, this disappearing with age; lower abdomen, vent, and under tail-coverts, olivaceous.

The female has the crown dusky-blackish, the neck olive-brown, and the rest of the upper plumage pale rufous-brown, each feather with two or three blackish bands, and minutely speckled, and the tip pale; the rump and upper tail-coverts are minutely freckled; the tail mostly blackish, with mottled rufous bars, tending to become obsolete; primaries, their coverts, and the winglet, spotless dusky-brown; throat albescent; neck olive-brown, the feathers becoming rufous in the centre, and tipped with black; breast and flanks bright ferruginous, with narrow black tips; belly dusky-brown; under tail-coverts freckled rufous-brown.

The male bird has usually two spurs on each leg, sometimes three on one, and occasionally two on one leg and one on another, usually long and sharp. The hen-bird generally has one on each leg, sometimes absent on one leg; and occasionally two on one leg and one on the other.

The Red Spur Fowl is a permanent resident on the Sahyadri Range, and in the forests adjoining; it is also very common at Aboo.

Since the above was written I found it very abundant at Baroli near Neemuch, extending at least as far as Erinpoora, where I have myself obtained it. It breeds during the hot season, making a slight nest of leaves and grass on the ground, almost exclusively in dense bamboo clumps. The eggs, six to eight in number, vary in shape, but are typically the same shape as those of the common hen.

They also vary in color from pinkish-buff to creamy-white.

They measure 1·65 inches by 1·21.

Galloperdix lunulatus, *Valenc.*

815.—Jerdon's Birds of India, Vol. II, p. 543; Butler, Deccan, Stray Feathers, Vol. IX, p. 422; Game Birds of India, Vol. I, p. 255.

The Painted Spur Fowl.

Length, 12 to 13·6; expanse, 17·5 to 18·5; wing, 5·75 to 6·2; tail, 4·3 to 5; bill from gape, 0·8 to 0·9; weight, 8 to 10 oz.

Bill blackish-horny, paler beneath; irides dark-brown; legs and feet plumbeous.

Male, head, face, and neck variegated black and white, the feathers being black with white streaks and triangular spots, the head mostly black; the upper plumage and wings rich chesnut, with spots on the back, sides of neck, shoulders and wing-coverts; primaries earthy-brown; tail dark sepia-brown, glossed with green in old birds; beneath the throat and neck are variegated black and white, changing on the breast to ochreous-buff, with small triangular black marks, which disappear on the abdomen; the flanks, thigh-coverts, and under tail-coverts dull chesnut.

The female has the top of the head dusky, with the forehead over the eye, and the nape, tinged with chesnut; a pale ruff and moustachial line; the rest of the plumage dull olive-brown, changing to ochreous-olive on the breast and abdomen.

Young males have the general plumage of female, with the tertiaries and tail chesnut brown, with black bands.

Young females have blackish lunulations on part of their plumage.

The male has from one to three spurs on each leg, generally two on each, occasionally three on one and two on the other.

The female has usually at least one spur on each leg, occasionally two, very rarely none at all.

The Painted Spur Fowl is rare in the Deccan; indeed it has only, I believe, been procured once, about 40 miles north-east of Belgaum; one was shot by General Nuttal about 35 miles from Neemuch, Central India, the skin of which is now in my possession, but the Red Spur Fowl is much the commonest of the two species.

FAMILY, **Setraonidæ.**

Bill generally short, stout, and thick; nostrils in many plumed at the base; wings rounded in most, pointed in a few, longer than in the *Phasianidæ*; tail short or moderate, even or very slightly rounded, forked and lengthened in a few; tarsus rather short and stout; face feathered entirely, or with a small patch of nude skin over or round the eye. Plumage of the sexes in general differing but very slightly, sometimes not at all.

SUB-FAMILY, **Perdicinæ.**

Tarsus not feathered; orbits generally plumed, or wanting the nude eyebrow of the grouse; tarsus often spurred.

GENUS, **Francolinus,** *Stephens.*

Bill moderate or somewhat long, stout, slightly curved at the tip; tail of 14 feathers, somewhat lengthened, even, or very slightly rounded; tarsi of the male with strong but blunt spurs.

Francolinus vulgaris, *Step.*

818.—Jerdon's Birds of India, Vol. II, p. 558; Butler, Guzerat;

Stray Feathers, Vol. IV, p. 5; Murray's Vertebrate Zoology of Sind, p. 213; Game Birds of India, Vol. II, p. 9.

THE BLACK PARTRIDGE.

Kala Titar, Hin.

Length, 12·25 to 14·8; expanse, 18·5 to 21·5; wing, 5·7 to 6·7; tail, 3·38 to 4·4; tarsus, 1·5 to 2; bill from gape, 0·9 to 1·25; weight, 8 to 20 oz.

Bill, ♂, black, ♀, horny-brown, the tips of both paler; irides deep brown; legs yellowish or reddish-brown.

Head, cheeks, and throat, deep black; the top of the head and nape edged with rufous, and with some white spots on the sides of the occiput, forming a pale line; ear-coverts pure white; a broad collar of fine chesnut-red passes round the whole neck; upper part of the back black, feathers edged with rufous and white tipped; the middle and lower back, rump, and upper tail-coverts finely barred black, and whitish, or grey; wings with the coverts black, with broad bay or rufous edges, and the quills barred with rufous and black; tail black, the middle feathers barred with black and grey on the upper parts, the lateral feathers being similarly barred at their base only; plumage beneath, from the rufous collar, deep black, more or less banded on the lower part of the abdomen with white, and the flanks of the breast and abdomen spotted with white; thigh-coverts and under tail-coverts chesnut.

The female differs in wanting the black head and neck of the male, which is more or less rufous mixed with brown, the throat and sides of the neck being white, and a dusky band surrounds the white portion of the ear-coverts; the back and wings are dusky, with pale rufous edges, whitish on the wing; the back, rump, and upper tail-coverts are barred pale rufous and dark brown; the tail feathers blackish, with pale bands; the medial pair brown banded; beneath, from the throat, the plumage is white with black spots, longitudinal and arrow-shaped in front, becoming more transverse on the flanks and lower abdomen.

The Black Partridge is very rare in Northern Guzerat; further north it is more frequently met with, and in Sind it is a common permanent resident, breeding during June and July.

The nest, composed of grass, grass roots, &c., is usually untidily put together, but occasionally is more neater. The eggs, six to ten in number, vary greatly in size, but average 1·56 inches in length to about 1·28 in breadth. In color they vary from slightly greenish or brownish-fawn to stone color.

Francolinus pictus, *Jard. & Selb.*

819.—Jerdon's Birds of India, Vol. II, p. 561; Butler, Guzerat; Stray Feathers, Vol. IV, p. 6; Deccan, Stray Feathers, Vol. IX, p. 422; Game Birds of India, Vol. II, p. 19; Swinhoe and Barnes, Central India; Ibis, 1885, p. 131.

THE PAINTED PARTRIDGE.

Length, 11 to 13; expanse, 17 to 19·5; wing, 5·3 to 5·8; tail, 2·6 to 3·55; tarsus, 1·5 to 1·75; bill from gape, 1 to 1·13; weight, $8\frac{1}{16}$ to $12\frac{7}{16}$ oz.

Bill blackish, paler at base beneath; irides deep brown; legs reddish or yellowish-red.

Neither sex have spurs.

Forehead, lores, face, broad supercilium, and ear-coverts ferruginous-chesnut; the top of the head dark brown with pale edgings, the neck all round pale ferruginous; the upper part of the back and scapulars deep brown; the feathers edged laterally with creamy white, and this gradually passing into the markings of the wings, which are chesnut with black bands; the lower back, rump, and upper tail-coverts, are beautifully marked with undulating lines of black and white; tail deep brown, the feathers finely cross-barred at their base; beneath, the throat is white, with longitudinal dark lines; the whole of the rest of the lower surface variegated black and white, each feather being white with two dark cross-bands, and the shaft and tip black; these dark bands gradually narrow towards the vent; under tail-coverts chesnut; feathers of the flanks and sides of the rump are tinged with pale ferruginous.

The female differs in having a somewhat ferruginous tinge beneath, and in the throat being more or less rufous.

With the exception of Sind, the Painted Partridge occurs in all suitable localities throughout our limits. It is a permanent resident, breeding towards the middle of the rains. The eggs, six or eight in number, are somewhat peg-top shape, and are smoky-white in color. They measure 1·4 inches in length by 1·18 in breadth.

GENUS, **Caccabis**, *Kaup.*

Bill somewhat lengthened, stout, red; tarsi of male with a blunt spur, red; tail of 12 or 14 feathers not quite concealed by the upper-coverts; a small nude patch behind the eye; plumage not mottled.

Caccabis chukar, *J. E. Gr.*

820.—Jerdon's Birds of India, Vol. II, p. 564; Murray's Vertebrate Zoology of Sind, p. 213; Game Birds of India, Vol. II, p. 33.

THE CHUKOR PARTRIDGE.
Chukor, Hin.

♂. Length, 14·25 to 15·75; expanse, 21·5 to 23·25; wing, 6·25 to 6·8; tail, 4 to 4·9; tarsus, 1·6 to 1·9; bill from gape, 0·94 to 1·2; weight, 19 to 27 oz.

♀. Length, 13·0 to 14·4; expanse, 20 to 21·3; wing, 5·9 to 6·5; tail, 3·3 to 4·1; tarsus, 1·55 to 1·75; bill from gape, 0·94 to 1·1; weight, 13 to 19 oz.

Bill crimson to deep coral-red, occasionally dusky on the culmen; irides yellowish or reddish-brown; legs and feet pale reddish.

Plumage above pale-bluish or olive-ashy, washed with a rufous tinge; lores black, and a white band behind the eye; ear-coverts rufous; wings reddish-ashy, the coverts tipped with buff, and the primaries narrowly edged with the same; tail ashy on the central feathers, the laterals tinged with rufous; face, chin, and throat, fulvous or rufous, surrounded by a black band which begins at the eye, and forms a sort of necklace round the throat; below this the neck and breast are ashy, changing to buff on the abdomen and under tail-coverts; the flanks of the breast and belly beautifully banded, each feather being ashy at the base, with two large black bands, the terminal one tipped with fine maroon, and the space between the bands creamy-white.

The female closely resembles the male, but is slightly smaller, and wants the spurs.

Within our limits the Chukor only occurs on the rocky hills that divide Sind from Khelat. It is very common both in the Bolan Pass and on the Khoja Amran Range of mountains in Southern Afghanistan.

I found them breeding near Chaman, about the end of March or early in April. There was no nest; the eggs were deposited on the ground, in a depression under a bush. I never found more than eight eggs, but the Afghans asserted that they frequently lay twenty, and I have seen a hen with quite that number of chicks; whether they were all her own or not, I cannot say. The eggs are somewhat peg-topped shape, of a pale stony color, speckled and blotched with lavender-brown. They average 1·61 inches in length by 1·4 in breadth.

Genus, **Ammoperdix.**

Of small-size; bill somewhat lengthened, red; wings long; tarsus wholly devoid of a spur or even of a knob, otherwise as in *Caccabis.*

Ammoperdix bonhami, *Gray.*

821.—Jerdon's Birds of India, Vol. II, p. 567; Murray's Vertebrate Zoology of Sind, p. 214; Game Birds of India, Vol. II, p. 45.

The Seesee Partridge.

Sisi, Hin.

♂. Length, 9·5 to 11; expanse, 16 to 16·75; wing, 4·9 to 5·75; tail, 2 to 2·5; tarsus, 1·1 to 1·2; bill from gaape, 0·67 to 0·77; weight 7 to 8 oz.

♀. Length, 9 to 9·75; expanse, 15 to 16·25; wing, 4·9 to 5·1; tail, 2 to 2·5; tarsus, 1·1 to 1·2; bill from gape, 0·62 to 0·71; weight, 5¾ to 8 oz.

Bill orange or brownish orange-red, inclined to be dusky on culmen; irides from bright yellow to orange-brown.

Male, above pale isabella-brownish, finely freckled with dusky; the crown of the head and cheeks grey; forehead and a narrow line over the eye black; lores and ear-coverts silky-white, rufous posteriorly; beneath this a narrow black line; rump and upper tail-coverts much speckled with black; primaries dusky within, isabella-brown on the outer webs, with dusky pencillings, and all but the first barred on their outer webs with whitish; tail chesnut-brown, paler at the tip, and freckled with black; beneath, the throat is greyish-white, the breast delicate grey, and the sides of the neck grey with numerous white spots, and a few black specks; breast pale rufous isabelline or vinaceous; the feathers of the flanks whitish, tinged with vinaceous, and dashed with rufous and dark-brown; lower tail-coverts pale chesnut.

The female wants the ashy crown of male, and is minutely mottled all over, both above and beneath.

The Seesee is not uncommon in precisely the same localities as those frequented by *C. chukar*.

It breeds at the same time, and in a similar manner to that bird. The eggs are not unlike those of *O. pondiceriana*, but are slightly paler in color. They measure 1·36 inches in length by 1·1 in breadth.

Genus, Ortygornis, *Reich.*

Bill lengthened, tip well turned over; legs red, with one strong and sharp spur, occasionally two; tail rather short, of twelve feathers; wings moderate.

Ortygornis pondicerianus, *Gm.*

822.—Jerdon's Birds of India, Vol. II, p. 569; Butler, Guzerat; Stray Feathers, Vol. IV, p. 6; Deccan, Stray Feathers, Vol. IX, p. 422; Murray's Vertebrate Zoology of Sind, p. 214; Game Birds of India, Vol. II, p. 51; Swinhoe and Barnes, Central India; Ibis, 1885, p. 131.

The Grey Partridge.
Titar, Hin.

♂. Length, 11·6 to 13·4; expanse, 17·4 to 20; wing, 5·3 to 6; tail, 3·35 to 4; tarsus, 1·4 to 1·7; bill from gape, 0·87 to 0·96; weight, 9 oz. to 12 oz.

♀. Length, 10·2 to 11·9; expanse, 16·5 to 18·3; wing, 5 to 5·68; tail, 3·2 to 3·75; tarsus, 1·37 to 1·58; bill from gape, 0·75 to 0·89; weight, 7 oz. to 11 oz.

Bill dusky-brown or blackish, beneath paler; irides dark-brown; legs bright red.

Head above olive-brown, rufous on the forehead over the eyes, and on the nape; lores and face also rufous, with black specks; ear-coverts silky hair-brown; upper plumage, including the wing-coverts, upper tail-coverts, and central tail-feathers, speckled brown, each feather being rich red-brown with three bars of creamy-yellow, and paler and somewhat olive-brown at the tip; primaries pale brown; outer tail-feathers rich chesnut-brown, with a dusky-brown terminal band, pale tipped; beneath, the chin and throat are whitish with small dark-brown spots, forming a triangular mark; the rest of the lower plumage ochreous-white or creamy, most pronounced on the breast, and with numerous minute cross-bars of brown, somewhat broader on the breast and sides of the neck, where it mingles with the upper plumage; lower tail-coverts ferruginous.

The Grey Partridge is common throughout the district, breeding during March, April, and May. Some few birds lay again later in the season, but these are probably birds that have had their previous eggs taken or destroyed.

The eggs are generally six in number, occasionally seven, but I have taken five fully incubated; they are white, more or less tinted with cafe-au-lait, and measure 1·3 inches in length by 1·03 in breadth.

GENUS, Perdicula, *Hodgs.*

Bill short, thick, well curved; tarsus with a blunt tubercle; wings firm, much rounded, outer web of most of the primaries sinuated and moderately firm; tail short, of twelve feathers; of very small size; sexes differ in plumage.

Perdicula asiatica, *Lath.*

826.—*P. cambayensis*, Lath.—Jerdon's Birds of India, Vol. II, p. 581; Butler, Guzerat; Stray Feathers, Vol. IV, p. 6; Deccan, Stray Feathers, Vol. IX, p. 422; Game Birds of India, Vol. II, p. 109; Swinhoe and Barnes, Central India; Ibis, 1885, p. 131.

THE JUNGLE BUSH QUAIL.

Length, 6·3 to 7·2; expanse, 10 to 11·1; wing, 3·0 to 3·5; tail, 1·5 to 1·78; tarsus, 0·94 to 1·0; bill from gape, 0·5 to 0·6; weight, 2 oz. to 2·85 oz.

Bill bluish-black; irides light to reddish-brown; legs and feet light waxy-orange to yellowish-red.

Male, above rich dark reddish-brown, mottled with dull rufous, a long yellowish or rufous-white supercilium, narrowly edged with black, and an indistinct pale line from the gape; between this and the supercilium rufous-brown; the shafts of the feathers of the back of the neck and the back white; many of the feathers of the back with black markings; and the scapulars and wing-coverts richly marked on their inner webs with pale creamy-white and black; primaries red-brown, with fulvous or tawny spots or bars; tail with a few black bars; beneath, the chin is rich chesnut, and the rest of the under surface white, tinged with rufescent on the lower abdomen, flanks, vent, and lower tail-coverts, with numerous cross bars of black, small on the throat and sides of the neck, increasing in size on the breast and abdomen, and disappearing towards the vent.

The female has the lower plumage rufous, with whitish shafts in some specimens, and the black markings of the upper plumage less distinct; the throat is generally darker rufous than the rest of the lower plumage. In some specimens the rufous tinge is more distinct above, and in others less so, and the brown has more of a greenish tinge.

With the exception of Sind, the Jungle Bush Quail occurs in all suitable localities throughout our limits; it is essentially a jungle bird, and does not occur in bare open places like *argoondah.*

It is a permanent resident, breeding on the hills during the rains, the eggs being very similar to those of the next species.

Perdicula argoondah, *Sykes.*

827.—*P. asiatica,* Lath.—Jerdon's Birds of India, Vol. II, p. 588; Butler, Guzerat; Stray Feathers, Vol. IV, p. 7; Deccan, Stray Feathers, Vol. IX, p. 423; Game Birds of India, Vol. II, p. 117; Swinhoe and Barnes, Central India; Ibis, 1885, p. 131.

THE ROCK BUSH QUAIL.
Lowa, Hin.

Length, 6·7 to 7·25; expanse, 10 to 11·2; wing, 3·1 to 3·5; tail, 1·5 to 1·9; tarsus, 0·75 to 1; bill from gape, 0·5 to 0·67; weight, 2¼ to 3 oz.

Bill black, beneath paler; irides vary from brown to light red; feet also vary from dull-red to bright-orange.

Male, upper plumage brownish-rufous, the feathers minutely freckled and lineolated with black and tawny; the feathers of the head and neck tipped with black, and some of the scapulars and wing-coverts with irregular black blotches; primaries dark-brown, with tawny bars on the outer webs; tail with the lateral feathers also barred; a narrow white line passes over the eye from the base of the bill, bordered by dusky and another short line below this from the gape; the rest of the face, chin and throat bright rufous; the whole lower parts, including the sides of the neck, being white with numerous cross-bars of black and tinged with rufous on the flanks, lower belly and thigh-coverts.

The female differs in having the upper surface more uniform rufous-brown, and the whole of the lesser parts pale rufous, albescent on the vent; supercilia barely perceptible. Some specimens of males are more uniformly rufous than in the above description, and want the black markings; these are probably young birds.

The Rock Bush Quail is, with the exception of Sind, generally distributed throughout our limits, never ascending the hills to any great height. It frequents rocky and open ground, whether cultivated or not, more especially if it is studded with low bushes, wherein it can take refuge if disturbed. It is a permanent resident and breeds from August to November, making a loose nest, generally in a slight depression on the ground sheltered by a low bush or tuft of coarse grass. The eggs, six or seven in number, are moderately broad ovals in shape, pointed towards one end; they are white, tinged with excessively pale cafe-au-lait color. They measure 1·02 inches in length by about 0·84 inches in breadth.

The following remarks by Mr. Hume will aid in discriminating this species from the preceding:—

"The adults of both sexes (and, I believe, most of the young also) may be distinguished at a glance by two characters.

"The bright chesnut hue of the chin and throat of the Jungle Bush Quail, which contrasts equally strongly with the white, black-barred, lower surface of the male, and the dull rufous of the same parts in the female. In the Rock Bush Quail, the chin and throat are dull rufous, the chin often being, especially in the females, whitish, and in these latter the throat is unicolorous with the breast.

"The long well marked yellowish-white superciliary stripe which, in the Jungle Bush Quail, begins in males at the nostrils, and in females a little further back, and in both runs over the eyes and ear-coverts right down to the nape, averaging in males 1·15, and in females 0·9 in length. In the Rock Bush Quail the supercilium is by no means well marked, very narrow, and just extends to the ear-coverts; in many specimens it is scarcely traceable. Moreover, the supercilium, such as it is, in the Rock Bush Quail, is immediately above the eye and ear-coverts; whereas in the Jungle Bush Quail, the long supercilium is separated from both eyes and ear-coverts by a narrow band of the same rich chesnut as the throat."

Genus, Microperdix, *Gould.*

Bill red and more slender than in *Perdicula,* and the male wants the tarsal tubercle, otherwise as in *Perdicula.*

Microperdix erythrorhynchus, *Sykes.*

828.—Jerdon's Birds of India, Vol. II, p. 584; Butler, Deccan; Stray Feathers, Vol. IX, p. 423; Game Birds of India, Vol. II, p. 123.

The Painted Bush Quail.

Length, 6·6 to 7·5; expanse, 10 to 11·3; wing, 3 to 3·5; tail, 1·5 to 2; tarsus, 0·97 to 1·1; bill from gape, 0·6 to 0·7; weight, 2¼ to 3$\frac{1}{16}$ oz.

Bill red; irides brown or yellowish-brown; legs and feet red.

Male, forehead, lores and crown of head, black; a white frontal band continued as a supercilium over each eye; upper plumage rich olive-brown, with black lunules; scapulars, wing-coverts and secondaries with large patches of black; the shaft pale yellow, and some faint cross lines of the same; primaries brown, the outer webs barred with dark rufous; tail brown with black spots, and barred with narrow pale yellow lines; beneath, the chin is pure white, bordered by black; the rest of the lower parts are rufous, passing into olive-brown on the sides of the neck, and with a few spots of black on the breast, increasing in size on the sides of the neck and breast; feathers of the flanks with large spots of deep black tipped with white.

The female differs in having the chin, supercilium, forehead, and face rufous in place of white, and the head is brown instead of being black.

The Painted Bush Quail is a common and permanent resident all along the Sahyadri Range, and several other portions of the Deccan; it does not occur in Sind, Guzerat, or Rajputana. Its mode of nidification does not differ from that of the other Bush Quails.

Sub-family, **Coturnicinæ**.

Wings pointed, long; bill moderate; tarsi not spurred; of small size. Sexes differ somewhat in coloration.

Genus, **Coturnix**, *Brisson*.

Bill somewhat slender, straight or slightly curved; tarsi without spurs; tail very short, rounded and soft, concealed by the upper tail-coverts; wings lengthened and pointed, the first and second quills longest.

Coturnix communis, *Bonn*.

829.—Jerdon's Birds of India, Vol. II, p. 586; Butler, Guzerat; Stray Feathers, Vol. IV, p. 7; Deccan, Stray Feathers, Vol. IX, p. 423; Murray's Vertebrate Zoology of Sind, p. 215; Game Birds of India, Vol. II, p. 133; Swinhoe and Barnes, Central India; Ibis, 1885, p. 131.

The Large Grey Quail.

Length, 7·1 to 8·62; expanse, 13·0 to 14·7; wing, 4·0 to 4·55; tail, 1·6 to 2·25; tarsus, 0·9 to 1·15; bill from gape, 0·6 to 0·73; weight, 3·2 to 4·62 oz.

Bill very variable, in color blackish, dusky horny-brown, dull pale bluish, &c.; irides brown; legs and feet pale fleshy.

Male, head brown, with pale edgings to the feathers, and a central pale line; eye-brows, cheeks, and lores whitish, with the ear-coverts partially brown; the upper plumage brown, each feather of the back, scapulars, rump and tail having on one side of the pale yellow shaft, a fine black patch, and some pale cross striæ; wing-coverts greyish-brown, with narrow streaks and bars of the pale yellowish, black bordered; primaries dark-brown, with pale rufous spots and bars on the outer webs; beneath, the chin is dull white; the throat rufous-brown with a double blackish or brown band or collar, separated by some yellowish-white and a few blackish spots on the breast and sides of the neck; the rest of the lower plumage pale rufous, deepest on the lower neck and breast, and becoming earthy on the flanks and vent; the long feathers of the flanks pale chocolate color, with a broad central stripe and some black blotches.

The female chiefly differs in wanting the rufous-brown patches on the throat and breast, which is much spotted with brown; she is larger than the male.

The Grey Quail is a common winter visitant to all portions of our limits. It is much more common in some years than in others. A few pairs do occasionally remain to breed, but these are probably sickly or injured birds.

Coturnix coromandelica, *Gm.*

830.—Jerdon's Birds of India, Vol. II, p. 588; Butler, Guzerat; Stray Feathers, Vol. IV, p. 7; Deccan, Stray Feathers, Vol. IX, p. 423; Murray's Vertebrate Zoology of Sind, p. 215; Game Birds of India, Vol. II, p. 151; Swinhoe and Barnes, Central India; Ibis, 1885, p. 132.

THE BLACK-BREASTED QUAIL.

Length, 6·5 to 7·25; expanse, 7·83 to 12·12; wing, 3·43 to 3·7; tail, 1·2 to 1·56; tarsus, 0·9 to 1·0; bill from gape, 0·5 to 0·6; weight, 2·2 to 3 oz.

Bill blackish, paler at base beneath; irides brown; legs and feet pale fleshy.

Male, upper surface closely resembles that of the Grey Quail, but is somewhat brighter, and the colors more pronounced, the yellow stripes being in greater number; chin and throat pure white; two narrow cross bands of black on the throat, the upper one joined by a longitudinal stripe on each side from the base of the lower mandible; below these the breast is black, breaking up into black blotches on the abdomen, extending along the flanks as far as the vent; lower belly white, tinged with rufous on the flanks and lower tail-coverts; primaries plain unbarred brown.

The female wants the black breast and cross bars, and has the neck and breast spotted dark-brown.

Young males have less of the black on the breast, which is broken up into spots and blotches. During the breeding season, the black breast is more marked, the bill also is darker, and the legs redder.

The Rain Quail is generally distributed throughout the district, and is in most places a permanent resident; in Sind it occurs as a seasonal visitant. It breeds during August, September and October, making a slight nest in a depression on the ground. The eggs, eight or nine in number, are usually broad oval in shape, and vary in color from pale yellowish to rich cafe-au-lait.

" The markings are of three types:—

"First fine specklings and spottings thickly spread over the whole surface of the egg; second bold blotchings and frecklings; third marblings.

"In color the markings equally vary, blackish, purplish, olive, and burnt sienna, all occur."—*Game Birds of India.*

They measure 1·1 inches in length by nearly 0·84 in breadth.

FAMILY, Tinamidæ.

Bill moderate, slender, straight, or slightly curved at tip; wings moderate or short; tail short, occasionally none; the upper tail-coverts lengthened and concealing the tail in many; tarsi unarmed; lateral toes short, hallux small and elevated, or wanting altogether; claws short and blunt.

SUB-FAMILY, Turnicinæ.

Of diminutive size. Three toes in one genus; the hind-toe present in another.

GENUS, Turnix.

Bill slender, of moderate length, straight, much compressed, slightly curved at the tip; nostrils linear; wings of moderate length, with the first quill longest in some, or the first three gently graduated; tail feeble, short, concealed by the upper-coverts, of ten or twelve narrow feathers; tarsus moderate or rather short, separated at the base; no hind-toe.

Turnix taigoor, *Sykes.*

832.—Jerdon's Birds of India, Vol. II, p. 595; Butler, Guzerat; Stray Feathers, Vol. IV, p. 7; Deccan, Stray Feathers, Vol. IX, p. 424; Game Birds of India, Vol. II, p. 169; Swinhoe and Barnes, Central India; Ibis, 1885, p. 132.

THE INDIAN BUSTARD QUAIL.

Length, 5·44 to 6·6; expanse, 10·75 to 12·5; wing, 2·85 to 3·45; tail, 0·9 to 1·38; tarsus, 0·9 to 1·2; bill from gape, 0·6 to 0·78; weight, 1½ to 2¼ oz.

Bill dark slaty; irides pale yellow to straw-white; legs and feet light slaty to plumbeous.

The females are, as a rule, much the largest.

The female is rufous above, with transverse black lines on each feather of the back, scapulars and rump, these having also yellowish-white lateral margins, internally edged with black; the crown of the head rufous, with a series of black and white feathers appearing as white spots, set off with black, along the median line; another and broader series over each eye; a third bordering the throat, which, with the middle of the foreneck to the commencement of the breast (together with the more conspicuous feathers of the wings), is fulvous-white, with tolerably broad black cross-bars; below the breast, light but bright ferruginous.

The male bird differs in wanting the black on the throat and neck, the chin and throat being whitish; the markings on the head are whitish-yellow without black specks; the throat and breast are faintly banded; and the whole tone of plumage is lighter and less pronounced than in the female.

The Indian or Black-breasted Bustard Quail is not common, but, with the exception of Sind, occurs more or less in all parts of the district. It breeds during June, July and August, the nest, if it is worthy of the name, being placed in a depression, sheltered by a tuft of sarpat-grass or stunted bush, and is composed of a few short pieces of grass. The eggs, four in number, are peg-top shape, of a dirty stone color, densely freckled brown and yellow, with a few well defined black blotches, scattered over the shell, and having also a few underlying patches of inky-purple.

They average 0·93 inches in length by about 0·79 in breadth.

Turnix joudera, *Hodgs.*

834.—*T. dussumieri*, Tem.—Jerdon's Birds of India, Vol. II, p. 599; Butler, Guzerat; Stray Feathers, Vol. IV, p. 8; Deccan, Stray Feathers, Vol. IX, p. 424; Murray's Vertebrate Zoology of Sind, p. 216; Game Birds of India, Vol. II, p. 187; Swinhoe and Barnes, Central India; Ibis, p. 132.

THE LARGE BUTTON QUAIL.

Length, 5·87 to 6·12; expanse, 10·0 to 11·0; wings, 3·0 to 3·25; tail, 1·12 to 1·5; tarsus, 0·8; bill from gape, 0·62 to 0·69; weight, $1\frac{3}{16}$ to $1\frac{5}{16}$ oz.

Bill yellow, dusky on culmen and at tip; irides yellowish-white; legs deep yellow.

Crown light brown, with blackish margins to the feathers; a central stripe on the crown; the supercilia and ear-coverts light fulvescent; nape bright ferruginous; back ashy-brown, tending to rufous, the feathers with dark cross bars, most marked on the lower back and rump; scapulars and some of the nearest dorsal plumes with edgings of creamy-yellow; wing-coverts light sandy-brown, with a small black spot near the tip which is margined with pale yellowish; quills earthy-brown, the primaries narrowly edged with yellowish-white; chin and upper part of throat white; the rest of the lower parts ferruginous, deepest on the breast and upper part of the abdomen.

The Large Button Quail is uncommon, but occurs in Sind, Guzerat, Rajputana, Kutch, and portions of the Deccan; it is, however, very rare in the latter. It breeds during July and August; the nest, composed of blades of grass, being partially dome-shaped, and is placed at the foot of a tuft of coarse grass, (I have occasionally found the nest unsheltered). The eggs, four in number, are peg-top shape, yellowish-white in color, thickly speckled, spotted, and blotched with brownish-black, and occasional markings of inky-purple and dingy-yellow, the whole tending to form a cap or zone at the larger end.

They measure 0·87 inches in length by 0·75 in breadth.

Turnix dussumierii, *Tem.*

835.—*T. syksii*, A. Smith.—Jerdon's Birds of India, Vol. II, p. 600; Butler, Guzerat; Stray Feathers, Vol. IV, p. 9; Deccan, Stray Feathers, Vol. IX, p. 424; Murray's Vertebrate Zoology of Sind, p. 217; Game Birds of India, Vol. II, p. 193; Swinhoe and Barnes, Central India; Ibis, 1885, p. 132.

THE SMALL BUTTON QUAIL.

Length, 5·2 to 5·7; expanse, 9·2 to 10·7; wing, 2·76 to 3·0; tail, 1·25 to 1·5; bill from gape, 0·5 to 0·56; tarsus, 0·7 to 0·75; weight, $1\frac{1}{16}$ oz. to $1\frac{1}{4}$ oz.

Bill from leaden-white to plumbeous; irides light yellow to straw-white; legs and feet pale fleshy-white.

Head brown, black barred, with a pale supercilium and central stripe; upper parts chesnut-brown, each feather finely barred with black, and edged with yellowish-white, conspicuously on the scapulars and part of the back and on the wing-coverts so broadly as to appear entirely yellowish-white with chesnut, black-edged spots; quills dusky-brown; rump and upper tail-coverts dark-brown, closely barred with black, and with faint whitish edges to the feathers; throat whitish, with a few blackish specks on the sides; breast pale ferruginous, with the sides of the neck and breast with dark-brown drops and lunules; abdomen whitish.

The Lesser Button Quail is more or less common throughout our limits. It does not appear to ascend the hills to any great height.

ORDER, Grallatores.

Lower part of the tibia bare; tarsus more or less elongated; feet of most, with the hind-toe imperfect and raised, or absent; in a few long, and on the same plane, as the front toes; bill very varied; tail usually short; wings lengthened.

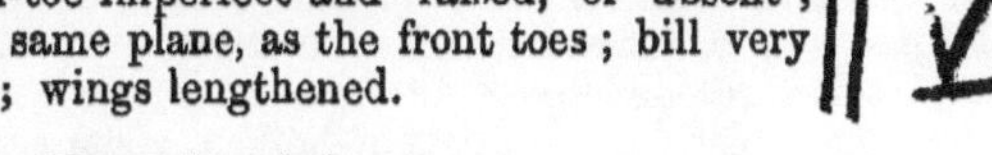

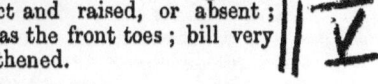

TRIBE, Pressirostris.

Tarsi elongated; hind-toe small or absent; bill moderate or short, thick, moderately depressed at the base, compressed on the side.

FAMILY, Otididæ.

Bill rather short, stout, broad at the base, somewhat compressed towards the tip; upper mandible convex and slightly curved; nostrils in a large membranous groove; legs long, rather stout; tarsi reticulated; three short toes united at the base by a small membrane; hind-toe always absent; claws short and blunt; wings ample, more or less pointed; plumage mottled and game-like.

Genus, Eupodotis, *Lesson.*

Bill long, pointed, nearly straight; legs long and strong; wings lengthened and very ample; male provided with a pouch; sexes alike in plumage or nearly so, but the female about a third smaller; no spring moult; of very large size.

Eupodotis edwardsi, *J. E. Gr.*

836.—Jerdon's Birds of India, Vol. II, p. 607; Butler, Guzerat; Stray Feathers, Vol. IV, p. 9; Deccan, Stray Feathers, Vol. IX, p. 424; Murray's Vertebrate Zoology of Sind, p. 217; Game Birds of India, Vol. I, p. 7.

The Indian Bustard.

♂. Length, 45 to 50; expanse, 86 to 96; wings, 24·5 to 29; tail, 13; tarsus, 7·5 to 8·37; bill from gape, 4·0 to 4·75; weight, 17 to 22 lbs.

♀. Length, 36 to 38; expanse, 72 to 76; wings, 20 to 22; tarsus, 5·5 to 6·8; weight, 8 to 10 lbs.

Bill greyish-brown, dusky at tip; irides vary from pale to bright yellow; legs and feet yellowish-creamy.

Male, top of the head with crest black; face, nape, and the whole neck, white, the feathers somewhat lengthened and hackled in front; the back and upper plumage, including the shoulders of the wings and the inner wing-coverts, pale olive-brown or buff, beautifully mottled and variegated with minute lines of black; outer wing-coverts black, white tipped; greater-coverts slaty-grey, also tipped with white, as in the winglet; primaries dark slaty, more dusky on their outer edges, and white tipped; tail as the back, with a dark subterminal band not always very distinct on the central feathers; a blackish-brown band across the breast; lower parts, with the thigh-coverts, white; the flanks dark olive-brown; vent and lower tail-coverts the same but lighter.

The female is one-third less at least, the white of the neck is less pure, generally, indeed, mottled with olive-brown, and with some rufous about the face and eyes; the pectoral band is incomplete, and consists of broken spots; the abdomen is less pure white, and the flanks paler brown and more spotted.

Young males resemble the females, and it is only the largest old males that have the neck pure white, as described above, in most there being a few brown specks on the neck. In the old male, too, the neck appears very thick, the feathers being well puffed out and full.

The Indian Bustard is fairly common in the more wilder and barren portions of the Deccan, Rajputana, Kutch and Central India. It is also not uncommon in the Thur and Parker districts in Sind.

The Indian Bustard in the true sense of the word is not migratory, yet it wanders much in search of food; at one season of the year it is common in one part of the country, moving to another as the breeding season commences. Most eggs are found in July and August, but occasionally they are to be obtained as early as March and as late as the middle of September. The egg (there is only one) is placed on the ground, at the base of a tussock of grass or bush, in a small depression.

The eggs vary much in size, shape, and color. They are all more or less oval, some are moderately broad ovals, pointed at one end; others are longish ovals, similar at both ends; others again are long and cylindrical.

They vary from 2·75 to 3·42 inches in length, and in breadth from 2·05 to 2·45. The average is 3·11 by 2·24.

The shells are thick and strong, and very commonly exhibit pimples at the large end. In color, they vary from a sort of drab to dingy olive-green. Earthy-brown, pale olive brown, pale reddish-brown, and more rarely pale leaden-blue varieties all occur. The markings also vary in like manner, both in extent and intensity: blotches, clouds, and streaks of a deep reddish-brown, occasionally clearly defined, but more often so faint as to be mere mottlings, are the usual characters; not uncommonly the markings form an irregular cap at the large end, occasionally they are altogether wanting. Some eggs are brilliantly glossy-white, others are dull, and have little or no gloss.

GENUS, **Houbara,** *Bonap.*

Legs rather short; neck of the male furnished with a ruff, and occasionally crested; bill rather lengthened, much depressed at the base.

Houbara macqueeni, *J. E. Gr.*

837.—Jerdon's Birds of India, Vol. II, p. 612; Butler, Guzerat; Stray Feathers, Vol. IV, p. 9; Murray's Vertebrate Zoology of Sind, p. 218; Game Birds of India, Vol. I, p. 17.

THE HOUBARA BUSTARD.
Oobarra, Hin.
Tiloor, Sindi.

♂. Length, 28 to 30·25; expanse, 51·5 to 57·75; wing, 15 to 16; tail, 8·5 to 10·25; tarsus, 3·5 to 4; bill from gape, 2·3 to 2·6; weight, 4 to 5¼ lbs.

♀. Length, 25 to 27·5; expanse, 47 to 51; wing, 14·25 to 15·25; tail, 7·75 to 9·25; tarsus, 3·15 to 3·6; bill from gape, 2 to 2·5; weight, 2$\frac{10}{16}$ to 3¾ lbs.

Bill blackish, paler beneath; irides pale to bright yellow; legs and feet pale dingy-yellow.

Head beautifully crested; the crest consisting of a series of lengthened slender feathers in the centre of the crown, white, with a black tip in front, wholly white behind; upper plumage, including the neck, pale buff, somewhat albescent on the wing-coverts and deeper on the back; upper tail-coverts and tail all delicately and minutely pencilled with black, and each feather with a subterminal black band visible externally, and another at the base of the feathers; upper tail-coverts with the black bands narrower, distant, and more or less ashy; tail banded with bluish-ashy, and all the lateral feathers broadly tipped with creamy-white; greater wing-coverts tipped with white; primaries white at their base, black for the terminal half, and most so on the outer web; lesser wing-coverts and scapulars more or less spotted with black, not barred; the shorter quills and the winglet black, the former tipped with white; the cheeks are white, with black shafts and tips; the throat white; neck fulvous-ashy; belly and lower parts, including the lower surface of the wings, white; under tail-coverts slightly barred; the neck ruff in its full integrity during the breeding season begins from the ear-coverts; the feathers are moderately long, about two inches, and entirely black and silky; on the sides of the neck they are at least six inches long, white at the base and with black tips; and where they terminate are still longer, wholly white, varying in texture, and with more or less disunited webs, very fine and curving downwards below.

The sexes, except as regards length of ruff and crest, are nearly alike in plumage, but the female is lighter in color, and is always considerably smaller.

During the cold weather the Houbara is very common in Sind. It occurs at the same season, but much more rarely in Guzerat and Rajputana.

It does not breed in India, but is supposed to do so in Afghanistan.

Genus, Sypheotides, *Lesson.*

Bill moderately long and broadish; legs lengthened, with a large portion of the tibia bare; in nuptial plumage the male with more or less white wings, and mostly black plumage, highly crested or with ear-tufts, and, in some, the breast plumes greatly developed.

Females larger than the males.

Sypheotides aurita, *Latham.*

839.—Jerdon's Birds of India, Vol. II, p. 619; Butler, Guzerat; Stray Feathers, Vol. IV, p. 10; Deccan, Stray Feathers, Vol. IX, p. 424; Murray's Vertebrate Zoology of Sind, p. 220; Game Birds of India, Vol. I, p. 33; Swinhoe and Barnes, Central India; Ibis, 1885, p. 132.

THE LESSER FLORICAN.
Likh, Hin.
Kermoor, Hin.

♂. Length, 17·25 to 19; expanse, 27·5 to 32; wing, 7·3 to 7·9; tail, 4·1 to 4·5; tarsus, 3·65 to 3·9; bill from gape, 2 to 2·1; weight, 14 oz. to 1 lb.

♀. Length, 18 to 21·3; expanse, 29 to 36; wing, 9 to 9·75; tail, 4·7 to 5; tarsus, 3·9 to 4·4; bill from gape, 2·28 to 2·3; weight, $1\frac{9}{16}$ to $1\frac{10}{16}$ lbs.

Bill pale yellow, fleshy towards gape; irides dull yellow to brownish; legs pale fleshy-yellow.

Male, in full breeding plumage, with the head, neck, ear-tufts, medial wing-coverts, and the whole lower plumage, deep black, the chin alone being white; lower part of the hind-neck and a large patch on the wing, white, the rest of the plumage fulvous, beautifully and closely mottled with dark-brown; the first three primaries plain dusky-brown, the remainder both barred and mottled with brown. The down at the base of all the feathers is a beautiful pale dull rose-color, and the quills, when freshly moulted, have a beautiful bloom, mingled pink and green, which however soon fades. The ear-tufts are about four inches long, and have usually three feathers on each side; with the shaft bare, and a small oval web at the tip, curving upwards. The primaries are much acuminated, sometimes ending in a point almost as fine as a needle.

The female has the prevalent tone of her plumage pale fulvous-yellow; the feathers of the head, back, wings, and tail, clouded and barred with deep brown, those on the head mostly brown, the foreneck with two irregular interrupted streaks increasing on the lower neck and breast, the lower plumage thence being unspotted and albescent; the hind-neck is finely speckled with brown; the chin and throat white; the first three primaries, as in the male, unspotted brown; wing-coverts with only a few bars; axillaries brown.

In both sexes, but it is more marked in the male, the earlier primaries are very sharply pointed, and have the terminal one-third greatly narrowed by a sudden emargination.

The Lesser Florican is generally distributed throughout our limits, but with the exception perhaps of the Deccan only as a seasonal visitant. It appears to be getting scarcer every succeeding year, owing to the merciless manner in which it is shot by sportsmen and others during the breeding season, which lasts from the end of August to the commencement of November, most of the eggs being laid towards the end of September. The eggs, four in number, are placed in a depression sheltered by a tussock of grass or stunted bush (there is no nest to speak of); they are broadish oval in shape, pointed somewhat at one end, of a dark olive-green color, spotted and clouded with light brown. Dark olive-brown, clear, almost sap-green, drab, and stone-colored varieties occur, and the markings vary from brown to reddish or olive-brown; they measure 1·87 inches by 1·6.

FAMILY, Cursoridæ.

Tarsi elevated; bill somewhat slender; three toes only; plumage brown and rufous.

Genus, Cursorius, *Latham.*

Bill moderately long, slender, slightly arched throughout and bent at the tip; nostrils oval, not placed in a groove; wings moderate; the first and second quills longest; tail short, even, of twelve feathers; tarsi long and slender, scutellated; lateral toes short, divided to the base; nails small.

Cursorius coromandelicus, *Gm.*

840.—Jerdon's Birds of India, Vol. II, p. 626; Butler, Guzerat; Stray Feathers, Vol. IV, p. 10; Deccan, Stray Feathers, Vol. IX, p. 425; Murray's Vertebrate Zoology of Sind, p. 221; Swinhoe and Barnes, Central India; Ibis, 1885, p. 132.

THE INDIAN COURIER PLOVER.

Length, 9 to 10; expanse, 19 to 20; wing, 6; tail, 2·4; tarsus, 2·2; bill at front, 0·8.

Bill black; legs creamy or opaque-white; irides deep brown.

Top of head bright ferruginous; lores, continued through the eyes to the nape, black, and a white eyebrow; upper plumage pale ashy or isabella-brown; quills and primary-coverts black; chin white; neck and breast pale isabella-rufous, deepening on the abdomen to chesnut, and terminating in a black bar on the middle of the belly; lower abdomen, vent, and under tail-coverts white.

The Indian Courier Plover occurs more or less commonly throughout the region, excepting, of course, the more hilly tracts.

It is in most places a permanent resident, breeding during April. The eggs (there is no nest), two or three in number, are spherical in shape, of a buff or cream-color, clouded, blotched or smeared with patches of very pale inky-grey, and above this are lines, scratches, and streaks of blackish-brown.

These markings are generally small and closely set, with an occasional inky-black smudge or smear intermingled. They measure about 1·19 inches in length by about 0·97 in breadth.

Cursorius gallicus, *Gm.*

840*bis.*—Jerdon's Birds of India, Vol. II, Appendix, p. 874; Butler, Guzerat; Stray Feathers, Vol. IV, p. 11; Murray's Vertebrate Zoology of Sind, p. 221.

THE CREAM-COLORED COURSER.

Length, 10; wing, 6·5; tail, 2·5; tarsus, 2·2; bill at front, 0·85.

Bill black; legs yellowish-white.

Forehead and upper plumage generally pale isabelline or sandy-yellow; top of the head pale grey; a broad superciliary white band from the eye to the occiput, with a narrower black line beneath it; both widen out at the occiput, which is sub-crested, mixed black and white; quills black; tail concolorous with the upper plumage, with a broad dark-brown terminal band, broadly tipped with white on all, except the central feathers; beneath, as above but paler, and albescent towards the vent and under tail-coverts; lower wing-coverts deep brown.

The Cream-colored Courser is a not uncommon cold weather visitant to Northern Guzerat; it does not occur in the Deccan. In Sind it is a permanent resident, breeding during May and June.

The eggs are barely distinguishable from those of the preceding species.

FAMILY, Glareolidæ.

Bill short, arched; gape very large; wings long; tail even or forked; tarsus rather short, reticulated; hind-toe present, but small.

GENUS, Glareola, *Brisson.*

Bill short, convex, arched from the middle; gape very deeply cleft; nostrils basal, oblique, semi-tubular; wings narrow, very long and pointed, with the first quill longest; tail short and even, or long and forked; tarsi moderate, reticulated, slender; four toes; outer-toe united at the base to the middle one by a short web; middle-claw pectinated; hind-toe not touching the ground; nails pointed.

Glareola orientalis, *Leach.*

842.—Jerdon's Birds of India, Vol. II, p. 631; Butler, Deccan; Stray Feathers, Vol. IX, p. 425; Murray's Vertebrate Zoology of Sind, p. 222.

THE LARGE SWALLOW PLOVER.

Length, 10; expanse, 24; wing, 7·5; tail, 4·5; tarsus, 1·25; bill at gape, 0·98.

Bill black; gape red; irides dark-brown; feet dusky-black.

Upper plumage, including the head, pale hair-brown; orbits white beneath, feathered; quills blackish, the shaft of first primary white externally; upper tail-coverts white; tail with the feathers white at their base, broadly tipped with blackish-brown; beneath, the chin and throat rufous, surrounded by a black line from the gape; below this the breast and abdomen are rufous-earthy, passing into white on the lower abdomen, vent, and under tail-coverts; axillaries and posterior portion of the under wing-coverts chesnut.

The Large Swallow Plover is rare in the Deccan, but is common in Sind. It breeds in the latter district during April and May. The eggs, two or three in number, are deposited on the ground, in a depression, and are broad oval or nearly spherical in shape; they are of a light dirty-green color, or even drab, covered with dark purple blotches and spots, occasionally forming a zone at the large end.

They measure 1·26 inches in length by 0·95 in width.

Glareola pratincola, *Linn.*

842*bis.*—Butler, Deccan; Stray Feathers, Vol. IX, p. 425; Murray's Vertebrate Zoology of Sind, p. 223.

THE COLLARED PRATINCOLE.

Length, 9; wing, 6·75 to 7.

Bill black; gape red; irides red-brown.

Head, nape, back, scapulars and wing-coverts greyish-brown; throat and front of the neck white, slightly tinged ferruginous, encircled by a narrow black band from the base of the bill; lores black; breast whitish-brown; under wing-coverts chesnut; lower surface of the body white, tinged with reddish; upper and under tail-coverts white; tail forked, basally white, tipped with dark-brown.

The Collared Pratincole is not uncommon in Sind, where it breeds, at the same time, place, and in a similar manner to the preceding species. In fact they have been found breeding in company.

A single specimen only has been recorded from Ratnagiri.

Glareola lactea, *Tem.*

843.—Jerdon's Birds of India, Vol. II, p. 632; Butler, Deccan; Stray Feathers, Vol. IX, p. 425; Barnes, Sind, Stray Feathers, Vol. X, p. 166; Murray's Vertebrate Zoology of Sind, p. 223.

THE SMALL SWALLOW PLOVER.

Length, 6·5; expanse, 16·5; wing, 5·75; tail, 2; tarsus, 0·8; bill from gape, 0·56.

Bill black, gape red; irides deep brown; legs dusky-green.

Upper plumage pale brownish-isabella color; upper tail-coverts white; tail white, tipped with dark-brown for about one inch on the centre feathers, diminishing to about one-quarter of an inch on the outer ones; primaries brown, the first four conspicuously white shafted; the inner web white on the last four or five; secondaries all white, tipped with brown; winglet dark-brown; chin, throat, and breast, pale isabella color; belly and under tail-coverts white; axillaries and lower wing-coverts deep brown; feathered orbits white.

The Small Swallow Plover has been recorded from Sholapur by Mr. Davidson, who procured it on the banks of the Bhima. It is not uncommon on the Indus, where I found a colony breeding in April.

The eggs are deposited in slight depressions on sand banks; they are usually four in number, are broadish oval in shape, greenish-white or fawn in color, spotted, streaked and blotched with various shades of olive and reddish-brown, with pale underlying clouds of dull purple. They measure 1·05 inches in length by 0·82 in breadth.

FAMILY, Charadridæ.

Bill straight, stout, and moderately thick in some, slender in a few, more or less raised and swollen at the tip; nostrils placed in a long groove; wings moderately long, and pointed; tail usually short; tarsi long, reticulated in most, or scutellate near the feet only; toes usually short, connected at the base by a membrane; hind-toe minute or wanting.

SUB-FAMILY, **Charadrinæ.**

Bill short, somewhat weak, slightly enlarged above at the tip; tarsi shorter than in the next two families and more reticulated; wings long and much pointed; first quill usually longest; tail short, nearly even; hind-toe generally wanting. 3 toes

GENUS, **Squatarola,** *Cuvier.*

Bill enlarged at the tip, both above and below; nasal groove short; a very minute hind-toe present, provided with a rudimentary claw; otherwise as in *Charadrius.*

Squatarola helvetica, *Lin.*

844.—Jerdon's Birds of India, Vol. II, p. 635; Butler, Guzerat; Stray Feathers, Vol. IV, p. 11; Deccan, Stray Feathers, Vol. IX, p. 425; Murray's Vertebrate Zoology of Sind, p. 224.

THE GREY PLOVER.

Length, 12; wing, 8; tail, 3·25; tarsus, 2; bill at front, 1·25.

Bill black; irides dusky-brown; feet blackish-grey.

In winter plumage, forehead and chin white; streak over the eyes, forepart of the neck, sides of the breast and flanks, white, variegated with spots of brown and ash color; head and all the upper parts of the body dusky-brown, the feathers edged and tipped with greyish-white; belly, abdomen, thighs and upper tail-coverts, pure white; beneath the wing some long black feathers arising from the axillæ; tail white, towards the tip reddish, with transverse brown bars which become paler and less numerous on the lateral feathers.

In summer plumage the forehead, lores, throat, and whole lower surface become deep black, edged white on the forehead and sides of the neck, and the upper plumage is brown, more or less barred with black and white.

The young birds differ from the winter plumage only in having the spots on the breast and flanks larger and paler, and the upper parts greyish with white spots.

The Grey Plover is a cold weather visitant all along the sea-coast, and is particularly abundant about the Kurrachee Harbour.

GENUS, **Charadrius,** *Lin.*

Bill straight, short, compressed, swollen at the tip; legs moderate; wings long, pointed, first quill longest; tail short.

Charadrius fulvus, *Gm.*

845.—*C. longipes*, Tem.—Jerdon's Birds of India, Vol. II, p. 636; Butler, Guzerat; Stray Feathers, Vol. IV, p. 11; Deccan, Stray Feathers, Vol. IX, p. 425; Murray's Vertebrate Zoology of Sind, p. 224; Swinhoe and Barnes, Central India; Ibis, 1885, p. 132.

THE ASIATIC GOLDEN PLOVER.

Length, 10; expanse, 20; wings, 6·75; tail, 2·75; tarsus, 1·75; bill at front, 0·85.

Bill black; irides deep brown; legs and feet dark plumbeous.

In winter plumage the general color above is dull blackish-grey, the edges of all the feathers with triangular spots of gamboge-yellow; the primaries blackish; tail feathers banded whitish and dull black; the chin white, front of neck and breast white, tinged with dusky and spotted with dull yellow; the rest of the lower plumage dull whitish; the flanks somewhat spotted with ashy and yellowish.

In summer plumage the upper plumage becomes darker, the ground color being somewhat deeper, and the yellow spots diminished in extent; the forehead is white; the cheeks, throat, neck, and middle of breast and abdomen, deep black, edged with white on the sides of the neck, breast and flanks of the abdomen; lower tail-coverts white; primaries black, the stem of the first white towards the tip, and the secondaries tipped with white, as are the median-coverts; tail brown, banded with black; bill and feet deeper black than in winter.

The young have the colors somewhat as in winter plumage, but the yellow spots above are less marked, the breast is more dusky-grey, and they do not become so black the first summer as they subsequently do.

The Eastern Golden Plover is a cold weather visitant to most portions of the region, but occurs much more commonly in some places than in others.

Charadrius pluvialis, *Lin.*

845*bis*.—Murray's Vertebrate Zoology of Sind, p. 225.

THE EUROPEAN GOLDEN PLOVER.

Length, 10·5 to 11·5; wing, 7·5.

Bill black; irides deep brown.

Forehead yellowish-white, streaked and spotted with pale brown and grey; head on the sides greyish-brown; the crown, back of neck and nape, greyish-brown with purple reflections and yellow angular spots on the edges and tips of the feathers; chin and throat whitish; breast dusky greyish-white, tinged yellow, and spotted with darker grey; axillary plumes white; greater and lesser wing-coverts greyish-black, the spots paler and the feathers of the greater-coverts tipped with white; the tail is deep brown, and barred obliquely with yellowish or yellowish-white; upper tail-coverts like the back.

Pluvialis is at once distinguished by its pure white axillary plumes, which in *fulvus* are brownish or smoke-grey.

The European Golden Plover has been recorded from Sind; but it is a very rare cold weather visitant.

GENUS, Ægialitis, *Boie.*

Bill much as in *Charadrius*, but more slender; wings long of small size.

Ægialitis asiatica, *Pall.*

845*quat.*—Butler, Deccan; Stray Feathers, Vol. IX, p. 426.

THE CASPIAN SAND PLOVER.

Length, 7·5; wing, 5·5; tarsus, 1·5; bill at front, 0·8.

Bill black; legs and feet greenish-yellow.

Crown, nape, the whole of the back and wings above hair, brown; forehead, eyebrows, eyelids, sides of the face and throat pure white; across the breast a broad rufous band, the lowest feathers of which, in some specimens, are terminated by dark umber-brown; thence to the extremities of the under tail-coverts, pure white; primaries brownish-black; the shafts of all mesially white; secondaries long, extending nearly to the end of the primaries; axillaries white; tail moderately long; the outer feathers on each side smoke-grey, the others darker in color, as they approach the middle.

The Caspian Sand Plover was obtained by Mr. Vidal in Ratnagiri. It is an exceedingly rare cold weather visitant.

This is the first authentic instance of its occurrence within Indian limits.

Ægialitis geoffroyi, *Wagler.*

846.—Jerdon's Birds of India, Vol. II, p. 638; Butler, Guzerat; Stray Feathers, Vol. IV, p. 12; Deccan, Stray Feathers, Vol. IX, p. 426; Murray's Vertebrate Zoology of Sind, p. 226.

THE LARGE SAND PLOVER.

Length, 8·5; expanse, 17·5; wing, 5·5; tail, 2; tarsus, 1·5; bill at front, 1.

Bill blackish; irides dark-brown; orbits blackish; legs greyish-green.

Winter plumage; greyish-brown on the upper parts, ear-coverts, and beneath the eyes, and sides of the breast; the rest of the under parts, with the feathers immediately above the bill, and a streak over the eye, white; primaries darker, and the secondaries partly white on their outer web.

In summer dress, the forehead, lores, ear-coverts and beneath the eye, are black, having a white mark on each side of the forehead; the neck and breast are bright rufous, contrasting with the pure white throat; the head is more or less deeply tinged with rufous, and the back, and especially the scapularies, are partially banded with the same.

The Large Sand Plover is a more or less common cold weather visitant to all parts of the coast.

Ægialitis mongola, *Pall.*

847.—*O. pyrrhothorax*, Tem.—Jerdon's Birds of India, Vol. II, p. 639; Butler, Guzerat; Stray Feathers, Vol. IV, p. 12; Deccan, Stray Feathers, Vol. IX, p. 426; Murray's Vertebrate Zoology of Sind, p. 226.

THE LESSER SAND PLOVER.

Length, 7·25; expanse, 15·75; wing, 5; tail, 1·9; tarsus, 1·25; bill at front, 0·75.

Similar to the last, both in winter and summer plumage, only differing in size, being considerably smaller, and the bill differs slightly in shape.

The Lesser Sand Plover occurs as a cold weather visitant all along the sea coast, ascending the rivers also, for a short distance.

Ægialitis cantiana, *Latham.*

848.—Jerdon's Birds of India, Vol. II, p. 640; Butler, Guzerat; Stray Feathers, Vol. IV, p. 12; Deccan, Stray Feathers, Vol. IX, p. 426; Murray's Vertebrate Zoology of Sind, p. 226; Swinhoe and Barnes, Central India; Ibis, 1885, p. 132.

THE KENTISH RINGED PLOVER.

Length, 6·75; expanse, 13 to 14, wing, 4·3; tail, 2; tarsus, 1·1; bill at front, 0·6.

Bill black; irides brown; feet dusky-grey to blackish.

Crown of the head and nape light brownish-red, the rest of the upper parts ashy-brown; primaries brown, the shafts white; tail with the central feathers as the back, the two outermost white, and the next partially white; forehead, a broad streak over the eye, and a ring round the neck, white; lores and ear-coverts black, and a black stripe on the forehead; lower parts white, with a large patch of black on each side of the breast.

The Kentish Ringed Plover is a common cold weather visitant all along the coast, and occurs inland on the banks of all the larger rivers and lakes.

Ægialitis dubia, *Scop.*

849.—*Æ. philippensis*, Scop.—Jerdon's Birds of India, Vol. II, p. 640; *Æ. curonicus*, Gmel.; Butler, Guzerat; Stray Feathers, Vol. IV, p. 12; Deccan, Stray Feathers, Vol. IX, p. 426; *Æ. philippensis*, Lath.; Murray's Vertebrate Zoology of Sind, p. 227; Swinhoe and Barnes, Central India; Ibis, 1885, p. 132.

April

THE INDIAN RINGED PLOVER.

Length, 7·25; expanse, 13·5; wing, 4·5; tail, 2·5; tarsus, 1; bill at front, 0·56.

Bill black, yellowish at the base; irides deep brown; orbits yellow; legs yellow.

Frontal zone white, followed by a black band edged with white, which passes over the eyes as a superciliary mark; lores black, passing under the eyes through the ear-coverts; chin, throat, and lower face, passing as a collar round the hind-neck, white, succeeded by a broadish black zone or ring which borders the white ring, gradually narrowing behind; upper plumage cinereous brown; quills brown; tail, with the central feathers ashy-brown, tipped dark-brown, the outermost feathers nearly all white, with a brown spot on the inner web, gradually increasing in extent and becoming ashy at the base; lower plumage and under wing-coverts white.

The Indian Ringed Plover is a common permanent resident throughout the region. It breeds during March and April; the eggs are deposited in a depression, scraped in the sand, near the waters' edge; they are usually four in number, and are moderately elongated ovals, pinched at the small end; the shell is fine and compact, but without gloss. They are of a fawn or buffy-stone color, spotted and marked with lines and figures of blackish-brown, with a few underlying markings of pale inky-purple.

They measure 1·14 inches in length by 0·84 in breadth.

Ægialitis minuta, *Pall.*

850.—Jerdon's Birds of India, Vol. II, p. 641; Butler, Deccan; Stray Feathers, Vol. IX, p. 426; Swinhoe and Barnes, Central India; Ibis, 1885, p. 132.

THE LESSER RINGED PLOVER.

Length, 6·75; expanse, 12·25; wing, 4·08; tail, 2·1; tarsus, 0·92; bill from gape, 0·56.

Bill blackish, intense yellow at base beneath and gape; irides dark-brown; legs bluish-grey; eyelids yellow.

Very similar to the last but smaller altogether, and with proportionally much smaller legs and feet. The upper plumage is of a somewhat darker shade; the quills are also blacker; the lateral tail-feathers have more white; the base of the lower mandible is more yellow (this at once serves to distinguish the two), and the tertiaries are less lengthened.

The distinctness of this species from the last is disputed by many, but Mr. Hume has in "Stray Feathers," at various times, clearly pointed out the differences. It has not been recorded from Sind. Its mode of nidification resembles that of the preceding species in all respects.

SUB-FAMILY, **Vanellinæ.**

Of moderate or largish size; legs lengthened; bill moderately strong; a short hind-toe frequently present.

GENUS, **Vanellus**, *Lin.*

Bill moderate, straight, compressed at the base; nostrils linear in a cleft occupying two-thirds of the upper mandible; wing pointed, fourth and fifth quills longest; shoulder of wing with a tubercle; tail nearly even; a very short hind-toe; head crested.

Vanellus vulgaris, *Bechst.*

851.—*V. cristatus*, Mey.—Jerdon's Birds of India, Vol. II, p. 643; Murray's Vertebrate Zoology of Sind, p. 228.

THE CRESTED LAPWING.

Length, 12; wing, 9; tail, 4; tarsus, 2.

Bill black; irides hazel-brown; legs orange-brown.

Head with lengthened slender crest black; behind the eye, ear-coverts, nape, and sides of neck, white; upper plumage green, glossed with purple and coppery, becoming golden-green on the lower back and rump, and with a golden fulvous tinge on the scapulars; primaries black, the first three greyish-white at the tip; tail white at the base with a broad black terminal band, broadest on the medial feathers; lores, chin, throat, and breast glossy blue-black; lower breast, abdomen, and vent white; lower tail-coverts chesnut.

In winter, the chin and throat are white.

The female only differs in having a shorter crest than the male.

The Peewit is a cold weather visitant to Northern Sind; it does not occur elsewhere within our limits.

GENUS, **Chettusia**, *Bonap.*

Bill stronger than in restricted *Vanellus*; head not crested; plumage ashy; tarsi moderately long, otherwise as in *Vanellus.*

Chettusia gregaria, *Pall.*

852.—Jerdon's Birds of India, Vol. II, p, 644; Butler, Guzerat; Stray Feathers, Vol. IV, p. 12; Deccan, Stray Feathers, Vol. IX, p. 426; Murray's Vertebrate Zoology of Sind, p. 229.

THE BLACK-SIDED LAPWING.

Length, 13; wing, 8·5; tail, 3·5; tarsus, 2·3; bill at front, 1·2.

Bill black; irides dark-brown; legs dull black.

Forehead and superciliary band passing round to the occiput white; top of the head black; back of neck and upper plumage generally of an olivaceous-brown, tinged with grey; primaries black; secondaries white; tail white with a subterminal black band, wanting in the outermost feathers; a narrow band from the lores through the eyes, black; sides of head and neck, both in front and on the sides above, pale rufous, passing to brownish on the lower part of the neck, and to brownish-ashy on the breast; middle of the abdomen deep black, bordered posteriorly by deep chesnut; lower belly, vent, and under tail-coverts white.

The Black-sided Lapwing occurs as a cold weather visitant more or less commonly throughout the region.

Chettusia villotœi, *Aud.*

853.—*C. leucura,* Licht.—Jerdon's Birds of India, Vol. II, p. 646; *C. flavipes,* Sav.; Butler, Guzerat; Stray Feathers, Vol. IV, p. 13; Murray's Vertebrate Zoology of Sind, p. 229; Swinhoe and Barnes, Central India; Ibis, 1885, p. 132.

THE WHITE-TAILED LAPWING.

Length, 11; expanse, 23; wing, 7; tail, 2·75; tarsus, 2 6; bill at front, 1.

Bill black; irides brownish-red; legs bright yellow.

General color above brownish-grey, with a reddish-purple gloss on the mantle, extending over the tertiaries; head and neck browner and glossless; the throat and around the bill white; breast more ashy; the feathers margined paler; rest of the under parts, with the tail and its upper-coverts, white; the belly and flanks conspicuously tinged with dull rosy, or a roseate-cream hue; primaries and their coverts black; the secondaries and their coverts largely tipped with white, and having a black bar above the white; rest of the wing-coverts like the back.

With the exception of the Deccan, the White-tailed Lapwing is a not uncommon winter visitant throughout the region.

It is by no means so rare as Jerdon states.

Chettusia cinerea, *Bly.*

854.—*C. inornata,* T. and Schleg.—Jerdon's Birds of India, Vol. II, p. 646; Swinhoe and Barnes, Central India; Ibis, 1885, p. 132.

THE GREY-HEADED LAPWING.

Length, 14 to 15; expanse, 30·5 to 32·5; wing, 9·5 to 10; tail, 4·5 to 5; tarsus, 3 to 3·3; bill at front, 1·5; bill at gape, 1·5.

Bill bright yellow, terminal one-third deep black; irides light crimson; eyelids plumbeous; edges of eyelids and lores bright yellow; legs and feet yellow.

General color of the upper parts pale greyish-brown; the head, neck, and breast, pure light grey, passing into black on the lower part of the breast, and terminating abruptly, contrasting with the white belly; primaries, their coverts, and the winglet, black; the secondaries and their coverts chiefly white, and the tertiaries concolorous with the back; upper tail-coverts white, slightly tinged with brownish; and tail pure white, having a black subterminal band, broad on its medial feathers, nearly obsolete on the penultimates, and quite so on the outermost.

The Grey-headed Lapwing is very rare. A single specimen was obtained by Colonel Swinhoe at the Depalpore Lake in January 1882. This appears to be the only recorded instance of its occurrence within our limits.

Genus, **Lobivanellus**, *Strickland.*

Bill moderately long and stout, the horny tip not much elevated; a lappet of nude skin at the base of the bill in front of the eye; shoulder of the wing furnished with a tubercle which in some becomes developed at the breeding season into a short horny spur; tail even; wings long; a very small hind-toe and rudimentary claw.

Lobivanellus indicus, *Bodd.*

855.—*L. goensis*, Gm.—Jerdon's Birds of India, Vol. II, p. 648; Butler, Guzerat; Stray Feathers, Vol. IV, p. 14; Deccan, Stray Feathers, Vol. IX, p. 427; Murray's Vertebrate Zoology of Sind, p. 229; Swinhoe and Barnes, Central India; Ibis, 1885, p. 133.

THE RED-WATTLED LAPWING.

Tituri, Hin.

Length, 12·8; expanse, 30; wing, 9·5; tail, 4·5; tarsus, 3; bill at front, 1·4.

Bill red, tipped black; eyelids and wattles lake-red; irides red-brown; legs bright yellow.

Head, back of neck, face, chin, throat, and breast, glossy black; ear-coverts white, continued in a stripe down the sides of the neck and round to the nape; back, scapulars, wing-coverts, and tertiaries, pale brownish-green, the wing-coverts glossed with purple; a white band on the wing formed by the greater-coverts and partly by the secondaries; primaries and most of the secondaries black; winglet black; tail white with a black band near the tip, the central feathers tipped brown; beneath from the breast white.

The Red-wattled Lapwing is a common permanent resident throughout the region.

It breeds from March to August, but April, May, and June are the favorite months. The eggs are laid in a small depression on the ground, are always four in number, and are of the typical Plover type, broad at one end, and much pointed towards the other. The ground color varies from a pale olive-green to a reddish-buff; the markings are deep brown or black, and there are spots, clouds and blotches, distributed more or less thickly over the whole surface, and besides this, there are often underlying clouds and spots of pale inky-purple.

They average 1·64 inches in length by about 1·2 in breadth.

GENUS, **Lobipluvia.**

Wattles yellow; bill rather slender; hind-toe absent.

Lobipluvia malabarica, *Bodd.*

856.—*Sarciophorus bilobus,* Gm.—Jerdon's Birds of India, Vol. II, p. 649; Butler, Guzerat; Stray Feathers, Vol. IV, p. 14; Deccan, Stray Feathers, Vol. IX, p. 427; Murray's Vertebrate Zoology of Sind, p. 230; Swinhoe and Barnes, Central India; Ibis, 1885, p. 133.

THE YELLOW-WATTLED LAPWING.

Length, 11·75; expanse, 27; wing, 8·25; tail, 3·25; tarsus, 2·5; bill at front, 1.

Bill yellow, black at tip; lappet pale-yellow; irides pale-yellow; legs yellow.

Head and nape black; rest of the upper plumage, including wing-coverts and tertiaries, chin, throat, and upper part of breast, pale ashy-brown; a white streak from behind the eye bordering the black head all round; winglet and primaries black; secondaries white at their base, brownish-black for the greater part of their length, the white increasing in extent towards the last, and with the tips of the greater wing-coverts forming a not very conspicuous white wing-band; upper tail-coverts white; tail white with a broad blackish subterminal band, evanescent on the outer feathers; beneath, from the breast, pure white.

The Yellow-wattled Lapwing is a more or less common permanent resident throughout our limits. It affects dry uplands and sandy plains, and does not evince that partiality for damp localities shown by the other members of this group. The eggs, four in number, are deposited in a depression scratched in the bare ground, without any attempt at concealment. They are similar in shape to those of *L. indicus,* but are considerably smaller, averaging 1·45 in length by 1·07 in width. The ground color varies from buffy to olive-green, and they are thickly blotched, spotted and streaked with pale olive-brown and dingy inky-purple.

GENUS, **Hoplopterus,** *Bona.*

Wings furnished with a long and stout, slightly curved horny spur, present at all seasons; no hind-toe; otherwise as in *Vanellus.*

Hoplopterus ventralis, *Cuv.*

857.—Jerdon's Birds of India, Vol. II, p. 650; Murray's Vertebrate Zoology of Sind, p. 231; Swinhoe and Barnes, Central India; Ibis, 1885, p. 133.

THE SPUR-WINGED LAPWING.

Length, 12; expanse, 25; wing, 8; tail, 4; tarsus, 2·5; bill at front, 1·12.

Bill black ; irides deep-brown ; legs reddish-black.

Head, including the long crest, face as far as the middle of the eye, and a broad band from the base of the lower mandible down the chin and throat, glossy black; a white line from behind the eye, bordering the black and meeting its fellow behind ; sides of the back and neck pale-ashy, gradually passing into the brownish-ashy of the back, scapulars and wing-coverts, and forming a pectoral band, between which and the black throat is a broad white space ; quills black, white at their base, the white increasing in extent to the last secondary, which is merely black-tipped; primary and secondary-coverts white ; the shoulder black ; winglet white ; tail-feathers white, with a broad black tip ; upper tail-coverts white ; abdomen white, with an interrupted black band in the centre.

The occurrence of the Spur-wing Lapwing within our limits is doubtful; a specimen is recorded from Upper Sind.

SUB-FAMILY, **Esacinæ.**

Of large size ; bill very strong and thick, dilated both above and below, and compressed; gonys more or less strongly angulated ; no hind-toe ; legs long.

GENUS, **Esacus,** *Less.*

Bill long, sub-recurved, strong, convex above, considerably compressed ; the base thick and rounded ; edges sharp, notched towards the tip ; nares broad, linear, advanced, in a wide groove that extends from the base to the tip of the culmen ; otherwise as in *Œdicnemus.*

Esacus recurvirostris, *Cuv.*

858.—Jerdon's Birds of India, Vol. II, p. 652 ; Butler, Guzerat ; Stray Feathers, Vol. IV, p. 14 ; Deccan, Stray Feathers, Vol. IX, p. 427 ; Murray's Vertebrate Zoology of Sind, p. 231 ; Swinhoe and Barnes, Central India ; Ibis, 1885, p. 133.

THE LARGE STONE PLOVER.

Length, 19 to 20 ; expanse, 36 ; wing, 11 ; tail, 4·5 ; tarsus, 3·25 ; bill at front, 2·75 ; bill from gape, 3·5.

Bill greenish-yellow, black at tip ; irides bright pale-yellow ; legs yellow.

General color above brownish sky-grey ; forehead white ; eye-brow, ear-coverts, and moustaches blackish ; shoulders, winglet, some of the outermost wing-coverts, quills, and tip of tail, blackish ; wings and tail irregularly but broadly banded with white ; beneath, with the lower surface of wings and tail, white.

The Large Stone Plover is a common permanent resident in Sind ; it occurs much more rarely in the other portions of our district. It breeds about March. The eggs, two in number, are deposited in a depression in the sand in river beds ; they are broad oval in shape, very slightly pointed towards one end, and the ground color varies from an earthy-drab color to a pale olive-brown. The markings consist of blotches, streaks, lines, spots, &c., of various shades of olive and umber-brown, in some becoming almost black.

They measure 2·15 inches in length by about 1·6 in breadth.

Genus, **Œdicnemus**, *Cuv.*

Bill very stout, thick, straight, compressed; culmen raised, the tip inflated both above and below; lower mandible with a strongly marked angular gonys; nostrils long, median, in a groove about half the length of the bill; wings moderately long, second quill longest; tail of twelve feathers, somewhat lengthened, much rounded; tarsus long, reticulated; three toes only, united at the base by a short membrane; nail of the middle-toe dilated, trenchant, hollowed out beneath.

Œdicnemus scolopax, *S. G. Gm.*

859.—*Œ. crepitans*, Tem.—Jerdon's Birds of India, Vol. II, p. 654; Butler, Guzerat; Stray Feathers, Vol. IX, p. 427; Murray's Vertebrate Zoology of Sind, p. 232; Swinhoe and Barnes, Central India; Ibis, 1885, p. 133.

The Stone Plover.

Length, 16 to 17; wing, 9; tail, 4·5; tarsus, 3·4; bill at front, 1·5.

Bill yellow, black at tip; irides and orbits yellow; legs and feet yellow.

Upper parts reddish-ashy with a longitudinal dusky stripe down the middle of each feather; a pale bar on the wing formed by the tips of the coverts; quills black, the first with a large and conspicuous white spot near the middle, the second with one somewhat smaller; tail with all the feathers, except the central ones, tipped with black; lores, cheeks, throat, belly, and thigh-coverts, white; the neck and breast tinged with reddish-earthy, and marked with fine longitudinal streaks; under tail-coverts reddish-ashy.

The Stone Plover is not uncommon in suitable localities throughout our limits; it is a permanent resident, breeding from February to June, but the majority lay in April. The nest is a mere hollow scraped out by the birds, unlined, or with at most a few blades of grass or dead leaves. The eggs, two in number, occasionally three, are broadish oval in shape, the ground color, varying from yellowish-white to pale buffy-brown, and the markings from olive to blackish-brown, and consists of spots, specks, streaks, blotches, and clouds, thickly or thinly spread over the whole surface.

They measure 1·9 inches in length by 1·39 in breadth.

Family, **Hæmatopodidæ**, *Bonap.*

Feet with three toes, and with a small hind-toe raised above the others; plumage variegated; bill varied, stout; legs long or moderate.

SUB-FAMILY, Strepsilinæ.

Bill short, conical, with the culmen flattened, the tip compressed and truncated; upper mandible slightly turned upwards; nostrils basal; wings long, very pointed; the first primary longest; tail rounded, of twelve feathers; tarsus short; tibia barely denuded; toes divided to the base; a moderate hind-toe; claws short and pointed.

GENUS, Strepsilas, *Lin.*

The characters are those of the family, of which it is the sole genus.

Strepsilas interpres, *Lin.*

860.—Jerdon's Birds of India, Vol. II, p. 656; Murray's Vertebrate Zoology of Sind, p. 233.

THE TURNSTONE.

Length, 8·25; wing, 6; tail, 2·5; tarsus, 1; bill at front, 0·75.

Bill black; irides deep brown; legs orange-yellow.

Head and neck white; the crown of the head with some black stripes; a narrow black frontal band, continued behind the eye and meeting another narrow stripe of the same color from the base of the lower mandible; shortly beyond these unite into an incomplete collar, extending back along the sides of the neck, and in front expanding and forming a broad gorget covering the breast, and which, at its termination below, sends up another incomplete band towards the shoulder of the wing; mantle and wings chesnut-brown mixed with black, especially on the scapulars; coverts edged with grey and whitish; primaries black, stem of the first white; secondaries tipped greyish; back, rump, and upper tail-coverts white, crossed on the rump by a black band; tail white, with a broad subterminal band of black; lower parts white.

The female differs in having the colors not so distinct, and the white on the head and neck less pure.

In winter plumage the colors are not so pure and rich in tint as in summer.

The young have the upper plumage and sides of the neck and throat dark ashy-brown, the feathers edged paler and the lower parts white.

The Turnstone is a cold weather visitant to the sea-coast. It is common about the Kurrachee Harbour, but is somewhat rare lower down the coast.

SUB-FAMILY, Dromadinæ.

Bill lengthened, compressed, smooth, barely grooved, very strong, with the culmen gently arching towards the tip, which is pointed; lower mandible strongly angulated; gonys long, commencing near the chin; bill slightly descending at first from the chin; nostrils oval, lateral, near the base, pervious; wings long, equal to the tail, first primary longest; tail even or barely rounded; tarsus very long, as also the bare portion of the tibia; feet much webbed, especially the outer and middle toes.

GENUS, **Dromas**, *Payk.*

The characters are the same as those of the sub-family.

Dromas ardeola, *Payk.*

861.—Jerdon's Birds of India, Vol. II, p. 658; Murray's Vertebrate Zoology of Sind, p. 234.

THE CRAB PLOVER.

Length, 15; wing, 8·75; tail, 2·95; tarsus, 3·6; bill, 2·5.

Bill black; irides brown; legs plumbeous.

Whole head, neck, wing-coverts, lengthened tertiaries, scapulars and lower parts, white; mantle, interscapular region, greater wing-coverts and primaries, black; some of the tertiaries and the tail reddish-ashy, paling on the inner webs.

The Crab Plover is not uncommon on the sea-coast near Kurrachee and at Mandavee.

It is only of late years that any authentic information in regard to its nidification has been obtained. It has now been ascertained beyond any possibility of doubt, incredible as it may appear, that they burrow in sandhills (on small islands in the Persian Gulf), to the depth of about four feet or so, and lay a single white egg, similar to a duck egg, measuring 2·54 inches in length and 1·77 in breadth.

SUB-FAMILY, **Hæmatopodinæ.**

Bill lengthened, strong, and truncated; tarsus short; plumage black or pied.

GENUS, **Hæmatopus**, *Lin.*

Bill straight or slightly bent upwards, very long, robust, compressed, ending in a truncated point; nostrils in the middle of a long and deep oblique cleft; wings moderate or long, nearly reaching the end of the tail, pointed; first quill longest; tail moderate, nearly even, of twelve feathers; tarsi short, strong, reticulated; hind-toe wanting; anterior toes short, thick, edged with callosities; the outer-toe joined at the base to the middle one by a web.

Hæmatopus ostralegus, *Lin.*

862.—Jerdon's Birds of India, Vol. II, p. 659; Butler, Guzerat; Stray Feathers, Vol. V, p. 212; Deccan, Stray Feathers, Vol. IX, p. 427; Murray's Vertebrate Zoology of Sind, p. 234.

THE OYSTER CATCHER.

Length, 16 to 17; wing, 10; tail, 4; tarsus, 2; bill at front, 4.

Bill orange-yellow, dusky on culmen; irides crimson-red; eyelids orange, with a small space of the lower eyelid plumed and white.

Whole head and neck, upper back, wings and tail, black; lower back, rump, upper tail-coverts, and lower plumage from the breast, white; a broad wing-band formed by the greater-coverts also white.

Young birds are less pure black, with pale edges to the feathers, and after the first moult they are said to have a white collar all round the neck.

The Oyster Catcher is a cold weather visitant, and occurs all along the coast, but is not found inland.

FAMILY, Gruidæ.

Bill short, stout, straight, slightly cleft, somewhat like that of the Bustards; legs scutellated; wings ample; of large size, with pale grey or white plumage, and with a long neck.

GENUS, Grus, *Lin.*

Bill moderately long, straight, somewhat thick; mandibles nearly equal, compressed, with the tip subulate; nostrils apert, placed near the middle of the bill in a broad and deep groove closed posteriorly by membrane; wings long, ample; third quill longest; tail short; tibia much denuded; tarsi lengthened, scutellated in front; toes short, strong; nails blunt; hallux short, raised.

Grus antigone, *Lin.*

863.—Jerdon's Birds of India, Vol. II, p. 662; Butler, Guzerat, Stray Feathers, Vol. IV, p. 14; Murray's Vertebrate Zoology of Sind, p. 235; Game Birds of India, Vol. III, p. 1; Swinhoe and Barnes, Central India; Ibis, 1885, p. 133.

THE SARUS.

Length, 52; expanse, 96; wing, 26; tail, 9·25; tarsus, 12 to 13; bill at front, 6·25; weight, 17 to 18lbs.

Bill pale sea-green, brownish at tip; irides orange-red; legs and feet pale rosy-red.

Head and neck naked and covered for three or four inches with numerous crimson papillæ, clad with a few scant black hairs, which accumulate into a broad ring on the neck and form a sort of mane down the nape of the neck; ear-coverts white; below this the neck is whitish-grey, which gradually passes into the pale blue or French-grey, which is the color of the whole plumage, the quills and inner webs of the tail-feathers being slaty.

At the breeding season they assume a pure white collar, immediately below the crimson papillose skin of the neck, which also becomes brighter in color; and in old birds, the tertiaries and some of the scapulars become white and more lengthened, hanging over gracefully and exceeding the tail.

The young have the head and neck dull ferruginous.

The Sarus is a common permanent resident throughout Rajputana and Guzerat, but is very rare in Sind and does not occur at all in the Deccan.

They breed towards the middle of the rains; the nest, a huge heap of rushes and straw, is placed generally on some spot surrounded by water; occasionally it is commenced in the water itself, in which case the egg cavity is about 8 or 10 inches above the surface of the water. The eggs, two in number, are elongated ovals, a good deal pointed towards one end; the shell is hard and strong, pitted with small pores, is generally somewhat glossy, and frequently exhibit creases or wrinkles. The ground color varies from pure white to pale sea-green and pinky-cream color; occasionally they are spotless and quite devoid of markings, but generally they are more or less blotched and clouded with pale yellowish-brown and purplish-pink.

The eggs vary greatly in size; in length from 3·6 to 4·48, and in breadth from 2·35 to 2·75. They average 3·96 in length by 2·56 in breadth.

The Sarus occasionally breeds in the cold weather, as on the 5th February 1885, while shooting with General Nuttall at Gangrar about 60 miles from Neemuch, I found a nest containing two fresh eggs, and again on the 30th March at Jeerun I found two incubated eggs.

Grus leucogeranus, *Pall.*

864.—Jerdon's Birds of India, Vol. II, p. 663; Murray's Vertebrate Zoology of Sind, p. 236; Game Birds of India, Vol. III, p. 11.

THE SNOW WREATH OR SIBERIAN CRANE.

Length, 48 to 56; expanse, 83 to 99·5; wing, 22·5 to 26; tail, 7·75 to 9·5; tarsus, 10·5 to 12; bill from gape, 6·75 to 8; weight, 12½ to 19 lbs.

Bill umber-brown; membrane of nasal groove, skin of forehead, lores and cheeks, red, duller colored in less mature birds; irides bright but very pale-yellow; legs and feet dull pale reddish-pink.

Plumage wholly white; quills black; tertiaries lengthened.

The Snow Wreath is a very rare cold weather visitant to the northern portion of Sind.

Grus communis, *Bechst.*

865.—*G. cinerea* Bechts.—Jerdon's Birds of India, Vol. II, p. 664; Butler, Guzerat; Stray Feathers, Vol. IV, p. 15; Deccan, Stray Feathers, Vol. IX, p. 427; Murray's Vertebrate Zoology of Sind, p. 237; Game Birds of India, Vol. III, p. 21.

THE COMMON CRANE.

Kullum or *Kulang*, Hin.

Length, 43 to 48 ; expanse, 79 to 91 ; wing, 20·5 to 24 ; tail, 7·0 to 9·12 ; tarsus, 8 25 to 9·9 ; bill from gape, 4·3 to 4·8 ; weight, 9 1/16 to 13 lbs.

Bill dingy horny-green, yellowish at tip ; irides deep reddish or dingy-orange ; legs and feet black.

Forehead and cheeks nude, with black bristly hairs ; crown nude, dull orange-red ; occiput, throat, and fore part of the neck, of a deep blackish-grey ; between the eyes, sides of the head and upper part of the neck, white ; as is the greater part of the back of the neck, but the color impure and with a reddish. tinge. All the upper part of the body and the lower plumage dark ashy-blue ; quills and greater-coverts dull black ; secondaries and tertiaries grey, black tipped, the latter narrowing to a point with the barbs of the uppermost feathers disunited, and all arching down and forming an elegant tuft of floating plumes, which it is able to erect at pleasure.

The Common Crane occurs abundantly in suitable localities, (wherever there are large tanks) throughout the region, but only during the cold season. The Kulung or Kullum is one of the finest game birds in India, as it is one of the wariest. It is almost impossible to stalk them while feeding, as they leave some of their number as sentinels, and on the slightest symptom of danger they give the alarm, and the whole flock rises, and is soon out of danger.

GENUS, **Anthropoides**, *Vieill.*

Bill shorter than *Grus*, depressed at the base, and slightly swollen at the tip ; tarsus lengthened ; head and neck densely feathered ; the feathers of the neck and breast lanceolate and hackled. Of smaller size, and the neck less lengthened than in the previous species.

Anthropoides virgo, *Lin.*

866.—Jerdon's Birds of India, Vol. II, p, 666 ; Butler, Guzerat ; Stray Feathers, Vol. IV, p. 15 ; Deccan, Stray Feathers, Vol. IX, p. 427 ; Murray's Vertebrate Zoology of Sind, p. 237 ; Game Birds of India, Vol. III, p. 31.

THE DEMOISELLE CRANE.

Karonch or *Karkarra*, Hin.

Length, 31 to 35·5 ; expanse, 66 to 73 ; wing, 18 to 21 ; tail, 6 to 7·5 ; tarsus, 6·25 to 7·5 ; bill from gape, 2·7 to 3·5 ; weight, 5 to 6¾ lbs.

Bill greenish, reddish at tip ; irides rich red ; legs and feet black.

Forehead, face, sides of head, neck, and the lengthened breast plumes, black ; a tuft of white decomposed feathers extending backwards and outwards from the eye; the general plumage fine purplish-grey; quills black; the greatly elongated tertiaries and scapulars dusky-slaty, drooping.

Young birds have no black and want the white ear-tuft.

The Demoiselle Crane is a common cold weather visitant to all suitable portions of the region. It is perhaps more sought after by shikaries than even the preceding.

Tribe, Longirostris.

Bill more or less lengthened, slender, and feeble; wings usually long and pointed; tail short; tarsus moderately long; toes moderate, the exterior one generally joined to the middle-toe by a short web, and the hallux short and raised, absent in a very few.

Family, Scolopacidæ.

Bill typically long, slender, in many somewhat soft towards the tip, in others hard throughout; wings lengthened, as are the tertials; tail short; tarsus moderately long; toes slightly united by a very short web; plumage brown, of various shades, above white, more or less tinged brown or ashy beneath.

Sub-family, Scolopacinæ.

Bill long, straight, rather soft, swollen at the tip, which is gently bent over the lower mandible; tarsus rather short; tail varying in the number of feathers.

Genus, Scolopax, *Lin.*

Bill long, thin, more or less rounded, of soft texture, swollen at the tip, and obtuse; upper mandible channelled for the greater part of its length, slightly bent downwards at the tips; lower mandible channelled only in the middle; nostrils basal, longitudinal; wings moderately long, very pointed; first quill longest; tail short, of twelve soft uniform feathers; tibia plumed to the joint; toes free to the base; tarsus short, stout; hind-toe short.

Scolopax rusticola, *Lin.*

867.—Jerdon's Birds of India, Vol. II, p. 670; Butler, Deccan; Stray Feathers, Vol. IX, p. 428; Murray's Vertebrate Zoology of Sind, p. 238; Game Birds of India, Vol. III, p. 309.

The Woodcock.

Length, 13·0 to 15·0; expanse, 23·0 to 25·5; wing, 7·2 to 8·0; tail, 3·0 to 3·85; tarsus, 1·35 to 1·57; bill from gape, 2·8 to 3·3; weight, 7 to 12½ oz.

Bill fleshy-grey, dusky at tip; irides dark-brown; legs fleshy-plumbeous.

Forehead and crown ashy-grey, tinged rufous; a dusky streak from gape to eyes; occiput, with four broad transverse bars of blackish-brown; the rest of the upper part variegated with chesnut brown, ochre-yellow and ash-grey, with zigzag lines and irregular spots of black; throat white; rest of the underparts yellowish white, passing into rufous on the breast and forepart of neck with cross wavy bars of dusky-brown; quills barred ferruginous and black; tail black; the outer webs edged rufous; tips ash-grey above, silvery-white beneath.

The Woodcock only occurs within our limits as a rare cold weather visitant.

Genus, **Gallinago**, *Stephens.*

Tibia bare for a small space above the joint; tail with 16 to 28 feathers, the outer ones often narrowed; otherwise as in *Scolopax.*

Gallinago nemoricola, *Hodgs.*

868.—Jerdon's Birds of India, Vol. II, p. 672; Butler, Deccan; Stray Feathers, Vol. IX, p. 428; Game Birds of India, Vol. III, p. 325.

THE WOOD SNIPE.

Length, 11·0 to 12·5; expanse, 18·0 to 19·75; wing, 5·4 to 5·7; tail, 2·5 to 2·9; tarsus, 1·41 to 1·49; bill from gape, 4·9 to 6·1.

Bill varies from drab to reddish-fleshy, tipped blackish-brown; irides hazel to deep brown; legs bluish-grey to greenish.

Top of the head black, with rufous-yellow longish markings; upper part of back black, the feathers margined with pale rufous-yellow, and often smeared bluish; scapulars the same, some of them with zigzag markings; long dorsal plumes black with zigzag markings of rufous-grey, as are most of the wing-coverts; winglet and primary-coverts dusky-black, faintly edged whitish; quills dusky; lower back and upper tail-coverts barred reddish and dusky; tail with the central feathers black at the base, chesnut with dusky bars towards the tip; laterals dusky with whitish-bars; beneath, the chin white, the sides of the neck ashy, smeared with buff and blackish; breast ashy, smeared with buff and obscurely barred; the rest of the lower plumage, with the thigh-coverts, whitish, with numerous dusky bars; lower tail-coverts rufescent, with dusky marks, and the under wing-coverts barred black and whitish.

The Wood Snipe is an extremely rare cold weather visitant to parts of the Deccan.

Gallinago sthenura, *Kuhl.*

870.—Jerdon's Birds of India, Vol. II, p. 674; Butler, Guzerat; Stray Feathers, Vol. V, p. 212; Deccan, Stray Feathers, Vol. IX, p. 428; Murray's Vertebrate Zoology of Sind, p. 239; Game Birds of India, Vol. III, p, 339; *S. stenura*, Kuhl.; Swinhoe and Barnes, Central India; Ibis, 1885, p. 133.

THE PIN-TAILED SNIPE.

♂. Length, 9·75 to 10·9; expanse, 15·5 to 17·4; wing, 4·95

to 5·42 ; tail, 2·0 to 2·57 ; tarsus, 1·19 to 1·27 ; bill from gape, 2·12 to 2·25 ; bill at front, 2·2 to 2·6 ; weight, 3·3 oz. to 4·75 oz. ; average, 3·91 oz.

♀. Length, 10·0 to 11·17 ; expanse, 16·1 to 18·25 ; wing, 5·0 to 5·58 ; tail, 2·0 to 2·67 ; tarsus, 1·2 to 1·35 ; bill from gape, 2·38 to 2·62 ; bill at front, 2·45 to 2·7 ; weight, 3·75 oz. to 5·1 oz. ; average, 4·2 oz. ; average of both sexes, 4·06 oz.

Bill blackish-horny at tip ; deep brown in the centre, greenish-horny at base ; irides deep brown ; legs and feet leaden-greenish.

Very similar to the Common Snipe in color ; but the under wing-coverts and axillaries richly barred with dusky and white.

Such is Dr. Jerdon's description, which is very meagre. Mr. Hume in the "Game Birds of India" has fully discussed the differences.

1st.—The bill of the Fantail is more or less spatulate, that of the Pintail never so.

2nd.—In the Pintail the axillaries and the entire wing-lining, except the lower greater-coverts, are invariably strongly and distinctly barred with blackish-brown. This is never the case with Common Snipe ; the median secondary lower-coverts are always unbarred, forming a white unbarred patch in the centre of the upper portion of the lower surface of the closed wing.

3rd.—In the Common Snipe, the tail consists of fourteen ordinary shaped soft feathers, occasionally sixteen, rarely twelve. In the Pintail there are only ten such feathers, but on either side of these are from five to nine very narrow, rather rigid, feathers, making up a total of twenty to twenty-eight feathers.

There ought not to be the slightest difficulty in discriminating this species from the next, but sportsmen and others constantly overlook the differences, hence the difficulty in ascertaining even approximately the relative proportions they bear to each other in any one given district.

The Pintail Snipe is of course only a cold weather visitant, and occurs throughout the region. In Sind the Fantails are much the commonest, in fact, I ought to say that the Pintail is decidedly uncommon ; further south, they occur in greater numbers, until at Bombay they are just as common as the Fantails.

Gallinago gallinaria, *Gm.*

871.—Jerdon's Birds of India, Vol. II, p. 614 ; (*G. scolopacinus*, Bon.) ; Butler, Guzerat ; Stray Feathers, Vol. IV, p. 15 ; Deccan, Stray Feathers, Vol. IX, p. 428 ; Murray's Vertebrate Zoology of Sind, p. 240 ; *G. cœlestis*, Fren. ; Game Birds of India, Vol. III, p. 359 ; Swinhoe and Barnes, Central India ; Ibis, 1885, p. 133.

THE COMMON OR FANTAIL SNIPE.

Chaha, Hin.

♂. Length, 9·0 to 11·3 ; expanse, 15·0 to 17·5 ; wing, 4·9 to

5·9; tail, 2·5 to 2·9; tarsus, 1·2 to 1·34; bill from gape, 2·39 to 2·7; bill at front, 2·43 to 2·75; weight, 3·3 to 5·1 oz.; average, 4·15 oz.

♀. Length, 9·2 to 12·5; expanse, 16·0 to 18·25; wing, 4·87 to 5·71; tail, 2·3 to 3·0; tarsus, 1·25 to 1·33; bill from gape, 2·5 to 2·9; bill at front, 2·62 to 3·0; weight, 3·1 oz. to 5·5 oz.; average, 4·27 oz.; average of both sexes, 4·2 oz.

Bill horny-brown, tip blackish, brownish-green at base; irides deep blackish-brown; legs and feet greenish.

Crown black, divided longitudinally by a yellowish-white line; a dusky brown eyestreak, and a yellowish superciliary one; back and scapulars velvet-black, crossed with chesnut-brown bars, and with longitudinal streaks of ochre-yellow; wing-coverts dusky-brown, edged with reddish-white; quills blackish; chin and throat white; cheeks, neck and breast above mottled black and ferruginous; flanks barred white and dusky; the lower part of the breast and abdomen pure white; tail black with the terminal third red-brown, barred black and tipped whitish; lower wing-coverts white, very faintly barred.

The Fantail Snipe is a common cold weather visitant throughout the region.

Gallinago gallinula, *Lin.*

872.—Jerdon's Birds of India, Vol. II, p. 676; Butler, Guzerat; Stray Feathers, Vol. IV, p. 15; Deccan, Stray Feathers, Vol. IX, p. 428; Murray's Vertebrate Zoology of Sind, p. 241; Game Birds of India, Vol. III, p. 373; Swinhoe and Barnes, Central India; Ibis, 1885, p. 133.

The Jack Snipe.

Length, 7·75 to 9·0; expanse, 13·25 to 14·89; wing, 4·1 to 4·67; tail, 1·87 to 2·5; tarsus, 0·89 to 0·95; bill from gape, 1·5 to 1·7; bill from front, 1·54 to 1·74; weight, 1·53 oz. to 2·48 oz.

Bill blackish-brown at tip, paling towards base; irides deep brown; legs and feet pale-greenish.

Crown divided by a black band slightly edged with reddish-brown, extending from the forehead to the nape; beneath this and parallel to it are two streaks of yellowish-white, separated by another of black; a dusky line between the gape and the eye; back and scapulars black, glossed with green, and with purple reflections; the scapulars with the outer webs creamy-yellow, forming two conspicuous longitudinal bands extending from the shoulder to the tail; quills dusky; wing-coverts black, edged with pale brown and white; throat white; neck in front and upper breast pale yellow-brown tinged with ashy, and with dark longitudinal spots; lower breast and belly pure white; tail dusky, edged with pale ferruginous.

The Jack Snipe is generally distributed throughout the region during the cold weather. It is, however, much less common than either of the other two, arriving later, and departing earlier than they do. It is much addicted to remaining in one spot, generally a corner, and if often disturbed or even shot at, returns to the same spot. In some seasons considerable numbers are met with ; at others they occur more rarely.

GENUS, Rhynchœa, *Cuvier*.

Bill shorter than in *Gallinago*, slightly curved downwards at the tip ; wings rather short, broad, slightly rounded, beautifully ocellated ; second quill longest, first and third sub-equal ; tail of 14 or 16 feathers, slightly rounded, short ; tarsus long ; tibia much denuded.

Rhynchœa bengalensis, *Lin*.

873.—Jerdon's Birds of India, Vol. II, p. 677 ; Butler, Guzerat ; Stray Feathers, Vol. IV, p. 15 ; Deccan, Stray Feathers, Vol. IX, p. 428 ; Murray's Vertebrate Zoology of Sind, p. 242 ; Game Birds of India, Vol. III, p. 381 ; Swinhoe and Barnes, Central India ; Ibis, 1885, p. 133.

THE PAINTED SNIPE.

♂. Length, 9·25 to 10·0 ; expanse, 16·8 to 18·0 ; wing, 4·9 to 5·2 ; tail, 1·5 to 1·8 ; tarsus, 1·65 to 1·83 ; bill at front, 1·65 to 1·85 ; weight, 3·5 to 4·9 oz.

♀. Length, 9·75 to 10·89 ; expanse, 18·0 to 19·25 ; wing, 5·25 to 5·6 ; tail, 1·6 to 2 ; tarsus, 1·75 to 1·96 ; bill at front, 1·8 to 2·05 ; weight, 4·4 to 6·42 oz.

The bill is very variable, typically it is a pale fleshy-brown, darker or purer brown towards the tip and with a greenish tinge towards the base ; irides vary from hazel to deep brown ; legs and feet usually greenish, but are also subject to variation.

Upper plumage more or less olivaceous, the feathers finally marked with zigzag dark lines, and the scapulars and inner wing-coverts with broad bars of black, edged with white ; a median pale buff line on the head, and another behind and round the eye ; scapulars with a pale buff stripe as in the snipe ; wing-coverts mottled and barred with pale olive and buff ; quills olivaceous-grey, with dark narrow cross lines, blackish towards base on the outer web, and with a series of five or more buff ocelli on the outer web ; the inner web with white cross bands alternating with the ocelli, and gradually changing to buff on the tertials ; tail olivaceous-grey, with four or five rows of buff ocelli on both webs and tipped with buff ; chin whitish ; neck, throat, and breast olivaceous-brown, with whitish spots or bars ; the lower parts from the breast white, passing on the sides of the breast towards the shoulder, and becoming continuous with the pale scapulary stripe.

The female is darker and plainer colored above ; the wing-coverts and tertials dark olive with narrow black cross lines, the outermost tertiaries white, forming a conspicuous white stripe ;

lores, sides of face, and whole neck, deep ferruginous chesnut, gradually changing on the breast into dark olive, almost black beneath; this is bordered on the sides (as in the male) by a pure white line passing up to the scapular region; lower part white, a dark band on the flanks bordering the white ascending line posteriorly.

The Painted Snipe is a fairly common permanent resident in suitable localities throughout the region, but they necessarily vary their quarters a good deal, as the tanks and jheels dry up or otherwise. They appear to breed at various periods throughout the year, but the majority lay during the middle of the rains. The nest is a more or less compact pad of sedge or grass, usually sheltered by a tussock of grass, but occasionally it is quite exposed. The eggs, four in number, are moderately broad ovals, pointed or pinched in at one end. They are hard in texture, faintly glossy. The ground color is a pale buff or warm cafe-au-lait color, thickly and boldly blotched and streaked with rich brown almost black.

They measure 1·4 inches in length by about 1 in breadth.

Sub-family, Limosinæ.

Bill much lengthened, soft at the tip, straight or slightly turned upwards; mostly of somewhat large size; a distinct web between the outer toes.

Genus, Limosa, *Brisson.*

Bill very long, slender, soft, straight or slightly sub-recurved at the tip, cylindrical at the base, obtuse at the point; nostrils basal; wings moderately long, the first quill longest; tail short, even; tibia bare for a considerable extent; tarsus long, slender, scutellate in front; feet with the middle-toe very long; a web between the outer and middle-toes; hind-toe short; nail of middle-toe dilated internally, with a cutting or finely toothed edge.

Limosa ægocephala, *Lin.*

875.—Jerdon's Birds of India, Vol. II, p. 681; Butler, Guzerat; Stray Feathers, Vol. IV, p. 16; Murray's Vertebrate Zoology of Sind, p. 243; Swinhoe and Barnes, Central India; Ibis, 1885, p. 133.

THE BLACK-TAILED GODWIT.

♂. Length, 16·0 to 18·1; expanse, 25·0 to 29·8; wing, 7·5 to 8·81; tail, 3·12 to 3·5; tarsus, 2·85 to 3·35; bill, 3·65 to 4·5; weight, 7½ to 12 oz.

♀. Length, 18·3 to 20·2; expanse, 28·0 to 31·3; wing, 8·4 to 9·25; tail, 3·25 to 3·94; tarsus, 3·3 to 3·7; bill, 4·5 to 5·1; weight, 9 to 15 oz.

Bill livid-fleshy, gradually passing to blackish-brown at tip; irides dark-brown; legs and feet blackish-green to dull greyish-

Winter plumage; all the upper parts uniform ashy-brown, with the shafts of the feathers of a somewhat deeper tint; superciliary stripe and rump white; quills dusky; the basal part of some of the primaries white; greater wing-coverts ashy-grey, broadly edged with white; tail white at the base, the terminal two-thirds black; the two middle feathers tipped with white; beneath, the throat, neck, breast, and flanks greyish-white; the abdomen and under tail-coverts white.

In summer the head becomes black, the back and scapulars black, edged and tipped with ferruginous, and the lower parts bright ferruginous, the middle of the abdomen alone being white.

Young birds have the feathers edged with reddish, and the tail tipped with white.

The Black-tailed Godwit is a common cold weather visitant to Sind and Northern Guzerat; it occurs also in Central India. I have myself shot it near Mhow, and Mr. Hume obtained it at the Kunkrowli Lake, Oodeypore, but it is not common there. It does not appear to have been recorded from the Deccan. They are excellent birds for the table at all times, but when fat and in good condition, they are simply delicious.

Limosa laponica, *Lin.*

875*bis.*—Murray's Vertebrate Zoology of Sind, p. 244.

THE BAR-TAILED GODWIT.

♂. Length, 14·5 to 14·8; expanse, 27·0 to 27·5; tail, 2·7 to 3·3; wing, 7·8 to 8·4; tarsus, 2; bill, 2·8 to 3·1; weight, 8·1 oz.

♀. Length, 15·75; expanse, 28·0; wing, 8·4; tail, 3; tarsus, 2; bill, 3·65; weight, 9 oz.

Bill pinkish for about the basal half, rest black or dusky; irides brown; legs and feet black, in some dusky-plumbeous.

In the winter plumage there is a broad indistinct white superciliary band, and the feathers immediately below the eye are also white; the chin and throat are pure white; the forehead, the whole top, back and sides of the head, and neck all round brownish-white, closely streaked with darker brown, the streaks very minute on the sides of the head, somewhat larger on the front of the neck, and darker and stronger on the head and back of the neck, where but little of the white remains visible. The upper back pale earthy-brown, each feather with a narrow dark-brown central shaft-stripe, and mostly margined somewhat paler.

The breast pale greyish-brown, more or less obscured by the albescent tippings to the feathers, and some of the feathers, with, inconspicuous darker shafts; the feathers of the central portion of the breast, if raised, will be found to be not merely tipped whitish, but to be also obscurely barred with white; the abdomen, vent, and lower tail-coverts are pure white, as are also the axillaries and wing-lining; the rump is white with a few cuneiform or heart-shaped blackish-brown spots; upper tail-coverts white, with narrow irregular arrow-head bars; tail feathers grey-brown, with dark shafts tipped white, and mottled with white on the inner webs of the exterior ones, in some with traces of darker transverse bars; the primaries and their greater-coverts black; the shafts of the first two or three white, subsequent ones brownish-white; scapulars and tertiaries pale brown, darker shafted, margined paler, and many of them more or less tinged with ashy; the lesser and median-coverts like the scapulars, but margined whitish; secondaries brown, paler on their inner webs, and margined on both webs and on the tips with white, as indeed are also, so far as the tips are concerned, the later primaries, though less conspicuously so; the greater secondary-coverts are more ashy-brown, narrowly margined with white. In one specimen, which appears to be further advanced, the lateral tail-feathers are distinctly barred brown and white; the cuneiform barrings on the rump and upper tail-coverts are more marked; the axillaries are all strongly barred; the feathers of the sides and flanks, and also the lower tail-coverts, exhibit numerous arrow-head bars; and one or two rufous or chesnut feathers with black bars have begun to show themselves on the breast.

The summer plumage is thus described by Temminck:—

Male.—Upper parts of the head and occiput blackish-brown, mixed with streaks of reddish-yellow; a band of the latter color over the eyes; lores blackish-brown; cheeks and throat of a yellowish-red; all the lower parts of the body, including the under tail-coverts, pale yellowish-red; upper part of the back and scapulars blackish-brown, marbled with reddish-yellow and whitish-grey; lower part of the back and rump white, marked with longitudinal yellowish-red spots; the tail marked with brown and white bars, those of the latter tint irregularly distributed and disposed more or less longitudinally; quills black from their tip, the remaining part towards the bases blackish-brown, with their inner webs whitish-grey, marbled with pale brown; the secondaries grey, with the shafts and margins white.

Female.—The head and lores, as in the male; the throat white, marked with reddish-grey; cheeks and neck very light reddish, with numerous brown streaks, which become broader, and form small transverse brown and white bars on the sides of the breast; the latter and the belly marbled with white and very pale reddish; the abdominal part white; the lower tail-coverts reddish-white with light brown bars.—*Hume, Stray Feathers,* Vol. I, p. 236.

The Bar-tailed Godwit is a not uncommon cold weather visitant to Kurrachee Harbour, and also occurs further east at the mouths of the Indus.

GENUS, **Terekia,** *Bona.*

Bill very long, slender, recurved; tarsus rather short; feet with the front toes joined by a web, narrow and short between the inner and mid-toes, of small size.

Terekia cinerea, *Gm.*

876.—Jerdon's Birds of India, Vol. II, p. 682; Butler, Guzerat; Stray Feathers, Vol. IV, p. 16; Murray's Vertebrate Zoology of Sind, p. 246.

THE AVOCET SAND-PIPER.

Length, 8·9; expanse, 16·25; wing, 5; tail, 2; tarsus, 1·1; bill at front, 1·8.

Bill orange-yellow at the base, dusky at tip; irides brown; legs pale orange.

Upper plumage bluish-ashy, the stems of the feathers dark, with some broadish dark streaks; forehead and cheeks white, with ashy striæ; shoulder of wing, edge of wing, and quills blackish-brown, the first primary with a white stem; secondaries tipped with white; throat whitish; neck in front and top of breast pale-ashy, with streaks of reddish-brown; lower breast, belly, and under tail-coverts white.

The Avocet Sand-piper is a not uncommon cold weather visitant to Sind, Kutch, and Northern Guzerat. It does not occur in the Deccan.

SUB-FAMILY, Numeninæ.

Bill very long, curved downwards.

GENUS, Numenius, *Lin.*

Bill very long, moderately slender, curved, almost round; upper mandible channelled, the tip hard, obtuse, slightly produced beyond the lower; nostrils basal, linear, apert; wings moderately long, the first quill longest; tail short, even, or slightly rounded; tarsus moderately long, scutate inferiorly; anterior toes short, basally connected by web, and bordered by a narrow membrane; hind-toe short, with the nail rudimentary.

Numenius lineatus, *Cab.*

877.—*N. arquata*, Lin.—Jerdon's Birds of India, Vol. II, p. 683; Butler, Guzerat; Stray Feathers, Vol. IV, p. 16; Deccan, Stray Feathers, Vol. IX, p. 429; Murray's Vertebrate Zoology of Sind, p. 247; Swinhoe and Barnes, Central India; Ibis, 1885, p. 134.

THE CURLEW.

Length, 21 to 26; expanse, 34 to 38; wing, 11·0 to 12·25; tail, 4·5; tarsus, 3·25; bill at front, 4·0 to 6·25.

Bill dusky-brown, beneath fleshy; irides dark-brown; legs and feet pale bluish-grey.

Head, neck, and breast, pale ashy, tinged with rufous, the shafts and middle of the feathers dusky; upper back and scapulars blackish-brown, the feathers broadly edged with rufous-brown; lower back white, with dusky spots; tail yellowish-white, with transverse brown bars; abdomen white, with dusky spots.

The Curlew is a not uncommon cold weather visitant to suitable localities throughout the region ; it is much more common on the sea-coast than it is inland, where it only affects the larger jheels.

Numenius phæopus, *Lin.*

878.—Jerdon's Birds of India, Vol. II, p. 684 ; Butler, Guzerat ; Stray Feathers, Vol. IV, p. 16 ; Deccan, Stray Feathers, Vol. IX, p. 429 ; Murray's Vertebrate Zoology of Sind, p. 247.

THE WHIMBREL.

Length, 16 to 18 ; expanse, 29 ; wing, 9·5 to 10 ; tail, 3·75 ; bill at front, 3·0 to 3·5.

Bill dusky, reddish at base ; irides brown ; legs dark bluish-grey.

Forehead and crown cinereous-brown, the latter divided by a longitudinal pale streak ; over each eye a broad streak of white mixed with brown ; sides of the head, neck, and breast, pale-ashy with brown streaks ; upper back, scapulars, and wing-coverts deep brown, the feathers with pale edgings ; lower back white ; rump white, barred with ashy-brown ; tail cinereous brown with dark oblique bars ; abdomen and under tail-coverts white, the flanks barred with brown.

The Whimbrel is common all along the sea-coast during the cold season ; it is much more rare inland.

SUB-FAMILY, Tringinæ.

Bill short or moderate, soft, and somewhat flexible, occasionally dilated or curved ; wings long ; tail short ; legs moderate, short ; the toes usually divided to the base, or with a very rudimentary web.

GENUS, Philomachus, *Mœhring.*

Bill, wings, and tail, as in *Tringa ;* tarsus somewhat more lengthened ; the outer-toe joined to the middle one by a short web.

Philomachus pugnax, *Lin.*

880.—Jerdon's Birds of India, Vol. II, p. 687 ; Butler, Guzerat ; Stray Feathers, Vol. IV, p. 17 ; Deccan, Stray Feathers, Vol. IX, p. 429 ; Murray's Vertebrate Zoology of Sind, p. 248 ; *Machetes pugnax*, Lin. ; Swinhoe and Barnes, Central India ; Ibis, 1885, p. 134.

THE RUFF.

Length, 12 to 13 ; wing, 7·25 ; expanse, 22·5 ; tail, 2·5 ; tarsus, 2 ; bill at front, 1·3 ; weight, 6 oz.

In winter plumage, the male has the upper plumage variable, generally rich brown, with black central spots, and reddish or whitish edges, the head and neck usually somewhat paler ; the greater-coverts barred black and reddish-brown; primaries dusky; tail with the middle feathers barred black and reddish-brown; the throat, forepart of the neck, and the lower parts pure white, sometimes mottled with blackish; the breast reddish or ashy-brown, with or without darker spots.

The female is much smaller, has more of an ashy tint throughout, and the feathers more or less dark centred.

Length, 9·5 to 10·5; wing, 6; tail, 2·2; tarsus, 1·6; weight, 3·5 to 4 oz.

The Ruff is a very common cold weather visitant to Guzerat, Kutch, and Jodhpore; it is rather less common in Sind, and in the Deccan it is rare. It is one of the earliest of our winter visitants. It is excellent eating when in good condition.

Genus, **Tringa**, *Lin.*

Bill moderate or short, soft, flexible, straight, or bent down at the tip, which is depressed and obtuse, channelled through almost to the tip; wings long with the first quill longest; tail short, even; tarsus rather short, scutellate anteriorly; toes free, or barely united by a small web.

Tringa crassirostris, *Tem. & Schleg.*

881*bis.*—Murray's Vertebrate Zoology of Sind, p. 249.

Temminck's Knot.

Length, 11·35 to 12·0; expanse, 23·5 to 24; wing, 7·1 to 7·3; tail, 2·7 to 2·8; tarsus, 1·4 to 1·55; bill at front, 1·6 to 1·85.

Bill black, occasionally paler at base beneath; legs and feet vary from dusky to pale plumbeous.

In the winter plumage the upper surface reminds one not a little of that of *Totanus stagnatilis.* The whole lower parts are white, but the base of the neck in front, and the sides, are marked with numerous small brown striæ, and the upper breast, besides more or less of these striations, is mottled with larger pale brown spots, here and there interspersed with conspicuous heart-shaped blackish-brown spots, which are the first traces of the coming summer plumage.

Lores, top, back, and sides of the head and neck very pale greyish-brown, all the feathers narrowly streaked along the shaft with dark-brown; the upper back and whole mantle is a mixture of pale brown and ashy, most of the feathers with blackish shafts, more or less darkly centred, and all conspicuously, though narrowly, margined and tipped with white; lower back and rump brown, the feathers narrowly and regularly margined with white; upper tail-coverts similar, but the white margins much broader and the brown more or less obsolete on many of them; tail feathers greyish-brown, greyer and somewhat darker on the central one, and paler and browner on the external ones, all are excessively narrowly, in fact almost obsoletely, bordered with white; the primaries and their greater-coverts are hair-brown, most of the latter tipped white; the secondaries and their greater-coverts are a pale somewhat greyish-brown, all of them narrowly, but the coverts less narrowly of the two, margined with white; the wing-lining (except just at the margin of the wing which is mottled with brown), pure white; the axillaries white with traces of irregular, wavy, pale brown bars; there are a few elongated triangular pale brown dashes on the flanks, and in some specimens one or two larger blackish-brown spots pertaining to the summer plumage.

According to Schlegel, the summer plumage is as follows:—

Feathers of the head and neck, each with a large dark-brown longitudinal streak or spot on an albescent ground, which is tinged with brownish-rufous on the nape. Feathers of the breast and nape, brownish-black, each with a whitish transverse band about the middle, often tinged with brownish-red towards the middle. The rest of the lower parts and the rump pure white, spotted, except towards the middle of the abdomen, with broader or narrower dark brown-spots.

Back and wings brownish-black, lighter on the wing-coverts; all the feathers spotted and bordered with a bright brownish-rufous, gradually disappearing towards the edge of the wing. Lower wing-coverts white, becoming black at the base.—*Hume, Stray Feathers*, Vol. 1, p. 240.

This species was found by Mr. Hume to be not uncommon in the Kurrachee Harbour during the cold season.

Tringa subarquata, *Gm.*

882.—Jordon's Birds of India, Vol. II, p. 689; Butler, Deccan; Stray Feathers, Vol. IX, p. 429; Murray's Vertebrate Zoology of Sind, p. 250.

THE CURLEW STINT.

Length, 8; wing, 5; tail, 1·75; tarsus, 1·16; bill at front, 1·6. Bill black; irides brown; legs dusky-grey.

In winter plumage, the face and supercilium white; a brown streak from the gape to the eye; upper part of head, back, scapulars, and wing-coverts, ashy-brown, the shafts of the feathers somewhat darker; feathers of the nape streaked with brown, and edged whitish; upper tail-coverts white; tail ashy-grey, edged with white; throat and beneath pure white; the feathers of the neck in front and of the breast streaked with pale brown.

The Curlew Stint is common during the cold weather along the sea coast, but does not seem to penetrate far inland. It has been procured at Sholapore.

Tringa alpina, *Lin.*

883.—*T. cinclus*, Lin.—Jerdon's Birds of India, Vol. II, p. 690; Murray's Vertebrate Zoology of Sind, p. 251.

THE DUNLIN.

Length, 7·5; wing, 4·5; tail, 1·9; tarsus, 1; bill at front, 1·25.

Bill black; irides deep brown; legs greenish-dusky.

In winter plumage, above, with the lores and cheeks ashy-brown, the shafts of the feathers dark, and those of the upper parts edged paler; supercilia and sides of the forehead whitish-ashy; lesser and median-coverts brown, edged with ashy; quills deep brown, with a pale edging; middle tail-feathers dark-brown, the laterals ashy and edged with white; throat white; breast whitish-ashy with a few brown streaks; abdomen and under tail-coverts pure white.

In summer the head is black, the upper plumage much mixed with ferruginous and brown; the abdomen pure black; and the breast white and spotted.

The Dunlin occurs as a fairly common cold weather visitant to the Kurrachee Harbour.

Tringa minuta, *Leisl.*

884.—Jerdon's Birds of India, Vol. II, p. 690; Butler, Guzerat; Stray Feathers, Vol. IV, p. 17; Deccan, Stray Feathers, Vol. IX, p. 429; Murray's Vertebrate Zoology of Sind, p. 251; Swinhoe and Barnes, Central India; Ibis, 1885, p. 134.

THE LITTLE STINT.

Length, 6; wing, 3·8; tail, 1·5; tarsus, 0·9; bill at front, 0·7.

Bill black; irides deep brown; legs black.

All the upper parts ashy-brown, the shafts dusky; a broad streak from the gape to the eye, and a whitish supercilium; the two central tail-feathers brown, the outer ones ashy-brown, edged with whitish; throat, foreneck, middle of the breast, and all the under parts pure white; the sides of the breast ashy-brown.

In summer, the head, and upper parts, with the two central tail-feathers become black, broadly edged and tipped with rufous brown; and the cheeks, sides of neck, and breast reddish.

The Little Stint is more or less common in suitable localities throughout the district. It only occurs as a cold weather visitant.

Tringa temmincki, *Leisl.*

885.—Jerdon's Birds of India, Vol. II, p. 691; Butler, Guzerat; Stray Feathers, Vol. IV, p. 17; Deccan, Stray Feathers, Vol. IX, p. 429; Murray's Vertebrate Zoology of Sind, p. 251.

THE WHITE-TAILED STINT.

Length, 6 to 6·25; wing, 3·8; tail, 1·9; tarsus, 0·75; bill at front, 0·7.

Bill black, irides deep brown; legs blackish.

In winter plumage, all the upper parts brown, with dusky streaks in the centres of the feathers, the four central tail-feathers ashy-brown, the others whitish, and the two outermost ones pure white; throat white; front of neck and breast ashy brown, belly and under tail-coverts pure white.

The White-tailed Stint is somewhat rare in the Deccan, but is not uncommon in the remaining portion of our limits. Of course it only occurs as a cold weather visitant.

Genus, Limicola, *Kaup*.

Bill broad and depressed.

Limicola platyrhyncha, *Tem*.

886.—Jerdon's Birds of India, Vol. II, p. 692; Murray's Vertebrate Zoology of Sind, p. 252.

The Broad-billed Stint.

Length, 6·25; wing, 3·9; tail, 1·75; tarsus, 0·75; bill at front, 1·1.

Bill blackish; irides deep brown; legs dusky.

In winter plumage, above ashy-brown, with a rufous tint; cheeks white, spotted with brown; quills brown; tail brown, edged with pale reddish-ashy; neck white with brown spots: the rest of the lower parts white, tinged with rufous on the sides of the breast, the flanks, and under tail-coverts.

The bill is rather long, broad, and flattened, and slightly bent down at the tip.

In summer the upper plumage is more or less black, edged with rufous and buffy-white, the quills with black shafts; the breast whitish with black spots and tinged with rufous; the rest of the lower surface white.

The Broad-billed Stint occurs not uncommonly in the Kurrachee Harbour and along the adjacent coast during the cold season.

Genus, Calidris, *Cuvier*.

Hind-toe wanting, otherwise as in *Tringa*; the web at the base of the toes very small.

Calidris arenaria, *Tem*.

888.—Jerdon's Birds of India, Vol. II, p. 694; Butler, Deccan; Stray Feathers, Vol. IX, p. 429; Murray's Vertebrate Zoology of Sind, p. 252.

The Sanderling.

Length, 8; wing, 4·75; tail, 2; tarsus, 0·9; bill at front, 1.

Bill black; irides deep brown; legs black.

In winter plumage, all the upper parts cinereous, with the shafts of the feathers blackish-brown; forehead and cheeks pure white; head and edge of the wing blackish-grey; wing-coverts broadly edged white; primaries dusky, with the edges and tips brownish; tail deep grey, the feathers edged with white, the two middle ones the darkest, all the lower parts pure white.

The Sanderling is more or less common along the coast during winter.

SUB-FAMILY, Phalaropinæ.

Feet with toes bordered by a free membrane cut into lobes as in the Coots; otherwise much as in *Tringa*.

GENUS, Lobipes.

Bill slender and pointed; the feet lobed; otherwise as in *Tringa*.

Lobipes hyperboreus, *Lin.*

890.—Jerdon's Birds of India, Vol. II, p. 696; Murray's Vertebrate Zoology of Sind, p. 253.

THE RED-NECKED PHALAROPE.

Length, 6·5; wing, 4·4; tail, 2·25; tarsus, 0·75; bill, 0·75.

Bill dusky; irides brown; feet yellowish-green.

Forehead white; crown, occiput, and nape dusky-brown; the back, scapulars, and two middle tail-feathers the same, but the feathers broadly edged with whitish; all the lower parts white, passing into pale-ashy on the sides of the breast and flanks.

In summer plumage the back and scapulars are deep black, with reddish edges; the wing-coverts black with a white band and the neck ferruginous.

The Coot-footed Stint or Red-necked Phalarope occurs in the cold weather in the Kurrachee Harbour and adjacent sea-coast.

I met with it at Chaman, South Afghanistan, where it must have been migrating.

SUB-FAMILY, Totaninæ.

Bill moderately long, slender, with the tip hard and pointed, slightly ascending in some; tarsi slender, rather long; feet elongate; outer-toe joined by web to the middle one.

GENUS, Actitis.

Bill moderate or rather long, slender, straight, compressed, and acuminate, with the tip hard; the groove of the bill extending quite to the tip; wings moderately long, with first quill longest; tail slightly lengthened; tarsus rather short or moderate; toes, rather long.

Actitis (Rhyacophilus) glareola, *Gm.*

891.—Jerdon's Birds of India, Vol. II, p. 697; Butler, Guzerat; Stray Feathers, Vol. IV, p. 17; Deccan, Stray Feathers, Vol. IX, p. 429; Murray's Vertebrate Zoology of Sind, p. 253; Swinhoe and Barnes, Central India; Ibis, 1885, p. 134.

THE SPOTTED SAND-PIPER.

Length, 8·5 to 9·0; wing, 5; expanse, 16·5; tail, 2; tarsus, 1·5; bill at front, 1·2.

Bill greenish, dusky-black at tip; irides deep brown; legs pale-greenish.

In winter, the plumage is deep brown on the forehead, crown, back, and wings, with white and greyish spots on the back, a dusky streak between the gape and the eye, and a white supercilium; cheeks and nape dirty-white with ashy-brown spots; upper tail-coverts pure white, tail narrowly barred black and white, the two outer feathers on each side entirely white; throat white; foreneck and breast dirty white, with spots and streaks of ashy-brown; flanks barred with the same; abdomen and under tail-coverts pure white.

In summer the feathers of the crown and nape are distinctly streaked brown and white; the feathers of the back have a large black spot as well as the white spots, and the white of the lower parts is purer.

The Spotted Sand-piper is a common cold weather visitant to all parts of the region; it is perhaps less common in Sind than elsewhere.

GENUS, **Totanus**, *Bech.*

Bill slightly curved at tip, groove half the length of the bill; tarsi with narrow scales in front; otherwise as in *Actitis.*

Totanus ochropus, *Lin.*

892.—Jerdon's Birds of India, Vol. II, p. 698; Butler, Guzerat; Stray Feathers, Vol. IV, p. 18; Deccan, Stray Feathers, Vol. IX, p. 430; Murray's Vertebrate Zoology of Sind, p. 254; Swinhoe and Barnes, Central India; Ibis, 1885, p. 134.

THE GREEN SAND-PIPER.

Length, 9·75 to 10·5; expanse, 18 to 19; wing, 5·5 to 6; tail, 3; tarsus, 1·5; bill at front, 1·4.

Bill dusky green, blackish at tip; irides brown; legs dingy-green.

Crown, nape, and upper parts ashy-brown, tinged with olive-green; all the feathers of the back, scapulars and wing-coverts with an edging of small white spots; quills deep brown; upper tail-coverts pure white; tail with the basal third white; the rest white with brown bars, the two outermost feathers entirely white; a brown streak from the gape to the eye, and a white supercilium; all beneath pure white, a few of the feathers on the neck and breast with dusky streaks.

In summer, the upper parts are darker, greener, and more spotted, and the streaks on the neck more distinct.

The Green Sand-piper is a very common cold weather visitant to all parts of the Presidency.

It is one of the earliest of our winter visitors, arriving soon after the commencement of the rains.

Tringoides (Actitis) hypoleucus, *Lin.*

893.—Jerdon's Birds of India, Vol. II, p. 699; Butler, Guzerat; Stray Feathers, Vol. IV, p. 18; Deccan, Stray Feathers, Vol. IX, p. 430; Murray's Vertebrate Zoology of Sind, p. 254; Swinhoe and Barnes, Central India; Ibis, 1885, p. 134.

THE COMMON SAND-PIPER.

Length, 7·75 to 8·25; expanse, 13·5; wings, 4·25 to 4·5; tail, 2·4; tarsus, 1; bill at front, 1.

Bill dusky; irides brown; legs pale green.

All the upper parts ashy-brown, glossed with green, and the shafts darker; back and wing-coverts with fine transverse brown lines; a white supercilium; quills brown with a large white spot on the inner webs of all except the first two; the four central tail-feathers like the back; the two next tipped with white, the outer one tipped with white, and barred on the outer web with brown and white; beneath pure white, streaked with brown on the neck and breast.

This Sand-piper is more or less common during the cold season throughout the whole region.

Totanus glottis, *Lin.*

894.—Jerdon's Birds of India, Vol. II, p. 700; Butler, Guzerat; Stray Feathers, Vol. IV, p. 18; Deccan, Stray Feathers, Vol. IX, p. 430; Murray's Vertebrate Zoology of Sind, p. 255; Swinhoe and Barnes, Central India; Ibis, 1885, p. 135.

THE GREEN SHANKS.

Length, 14 to 15; expanse, 25; wing, 8; tail, 3·75; tarsus, 2·75; bill at front, 2·2.

Bill dusky greenish; irides brown; legs yellowish green.

In winter plumage, the head, cheeks, sides and back of neck, cinereous-white with brown streaks; upper back, scapulars, and wing-coverts, dusky brown, the feathers edged with yellowish-white; the lower back and upper tail-coverts pure white; quills dusky, some of them spotted with white on their inner webs; tail white with cross bars of brown, the outer feathers entirely white with the exception of a narrow streak on the outer web; throat, foreneck, middle of the breast, and lower parts pure white; the sides of the breast streaked with brown, and somewhat ashy.

The Green Shanks is more or less common throughout the region during the cold season.

Totanus stagnatilis, *Bech.*

895.—Jerdon's Birds of India, Vol. II, p. 701; Butler, Guzerat; Stray Feathers, Vol. IV, p. 18; Deccan, Stray Feathers, Vol. IX, p. 430; Murray's Vertebrate Zoology of Sind, p. 225; Swinhoe and Barnes, Central India; Ibis, 1885, p. 134.

THE LITTLE GREEN SHANKS.

Length, 10·5; wing, 5·5; tail, 2; tarsus, 2·25; bill at front, 1·6.

Bill dusky-green; irides brown; legs pale green.

Above pale ashy-brown, the nape streaked with dark-brown; the top of the head and neck, and the scapulars edged with whitish; eye brows and cheeks white, spotted with brown; greater wing-coverts pale ashy, edged whitish; the lesser-coverts ashy-brown, with paler edges, and the stem black; quills brown black, the shafts white; lower back white; tail white, with brown bands; beneath pure white; the sides of the neck, of the breast, and the flanks spotted with brown.

The Lesser Green Shanks is not uncommon during the cold weather in all parts of the region.

Totanus fuscus, *Lin.*

896.—Jerdon's Birds of India, Vol. II, p. 702; Butler, Guzerat; Stray Feathers, Vol. IV, p. 18; Murray's Vertebrate Zoology of Sind, p. 255; Swinhoe and Barnes, Central India; Ibis, 1885, p. 134.

THE SPOTTED RED SHANKS.

Length, 13; expanse, 22·5; wing, 6·75; tail, 2·5; tarsus, 2·8; bill at front, 2·4.

Bill blackish, orange at base beneath; irides brown; legs orange-red.

In winter plumage, the crown, nape, and back ashy-grey, with fine dusky streaks; a blackish patch between the bill and the eyes, and a white streak above; cheeks and neck variegated white and ashy; wing-coverts and scapulars grey, edged with white; rump pure white; central tail-feathers uniform ash-grey, narrowly edged with white; rump pure white; outer tail-feathers with white and brown bars; throat, breast, abdomen, and under tail-coverts pure white.

In summer, the head, neck and under parts become dusky or blackish-grey, and the vent and lower tail-coverts are barred white and brown.

During the cold season the Spotted Red Shanks is common in Sind, occurs sparingly in Guzerat and Rajputana, but has not been recorded from any part of the Deccan.

Totanus calidris, *Lin.*

897.—Jerdon's Birds of India, Vol. II, p. 702; Butler, Guzerat; Stray Feathers, Vol. IV, p. 18; Deccan, Stray Feathers, Vol. IX, p. 430; Murray's Vertebrate Zoology of Sind, p. 256; Swinhoe and Barnes, Central India; Ibis, 1885, p. 134.

THE RED SHANKS.

Length, 10·5 to 11·5; wing, 6; tail, 2·4; tarsus, 1·8; bill, 1·1.

Bill dusky, reddish at base; irides brown; legs pale red.

In winter, the crown, lores, back of neck, upper back, scapulars, and wing-coverts, cinereous-brown, darker on the shafts; supercilium white; sides of the head greyish-white; lower back white; primaries and their coverts dusky brown; the secondaries white for the greater portion of their length; upper tail-coverts and tail barred with white and dark-brown; throat white; foreneck and breast greyish-white; abdomen and lower tail-coverts white.

During the cold season the Red Shank occurs more or less commonly throughout the whole region.

FAMILY, Himantopidæ.

Of black and white plumage, not changing in summer; the legs very much lengthened; bill long and very thin, and in one genus recurved.

GENUS, Himantopus, *Brisson.*

Bill long, twice the length of the head, very slender, somewhat rounded, pointed, channeled on the sides as far as the middle; tip of the upper mandible very slightly bent over the under one; nostrils linear; wings long, pointed, first quill longest, tail short, even, of twelve feathers; tibia bare for the greater part of its length; legs very long, thin reticulated; toes short; outer-toe joined to the middle one by a broad web; inner one with a very small web; nails short, flat; hind-toe wanting.

Himantopus candidus, *Bona.*

898.—Jerdon's Birds of India, Vol. II, p. 704; Butler, Guzerat; Stray Feathers, Vol. IV, p. 18; Deccan, Stray Feathers, Vol. IX, p. 430; *H. intermedius,* Blyth.; Murray's Vertebrate Zoology of Sind, p. 258; Swinhoe and Barnes, Central India; Ibis, 1885, p. 134.

THE STILT.

Gaj-paun, Hin.

Length, 14·5 to 15·5; expanse, 26 to 30; wing, 8·5 to 9; tail, 3; tarsus, 4·5 to 5·5; bill at front, 2·75.

Bill black, reddish at base; irides blood-red; feet lake-red.

Back of the head black or dusky, more or less mixed with whitish, in some nearly all white, in others with only the nape black; back and sides of neck grey; interscapulars and wings glossy green-black; tail pale ash-grey; rest of the plumage, including the back and rump, pure white, sometimes tinged with rosy on the breast.

The Stilt or Long-legs is common throughout the whole region, but only occurs during the cold weather in Guzerat and the Deccan. In Sind it appears to be a permanent resident, breeding freely in the Narra District during June. The eggs, four in number, are deposited on the bare ground; they are oval in shape, pinched in at one end; the ground color varies from olive-brown to greenish stone, and the markings consist of spots, streaks, and blotches of black, blackish-brown and rich umber-brown. They measure 1·64 inches in length by about 1·21 in breadth.

GENUS, Recurvirostra, *Lin.*

Bill very long, thin, flexible, turned up towards the tip, which is very thin and pointed, channeled both above and below; nostrils long linear; wings long, pointed; tail somewhat wedged; tarsi moderately long, and slender; front toes united by a web, which is notched in the middle; hind-toe very minute; nails short, curved.

Recurvirostra avocetta, *Lin.*

899.—Jerdon's Birds of India, Vol. II, p. 786; Butler, Guzerat; Stray Feathers, Vol. IV, p. 18; Murray's Vertebrate Zoology of Sind p. 258; Swinhoe and Barnes, Central India; Ibis, 1885, p. 134.

THE AVOCET.

Length, 18; wing, 8·5; tail, 3; tarsus, 3·25; bill at front, 3·5.

Bill black; irides red-brown; legs pale bluish-grey.

Crown of the head, nape, most of the hind-neck, scapulars, lesser wing-coverts, and primary quills, deep black; all the rest of the plumage pure white.

The Avocet is common during the winter in Sind, rare in Guzerat, and does not occur at all in the Deccan. I have myself seen it at Gungrar, near Neemuch, but it is very rare.

TRIBE, Latitores.

Feet very long; anterior toes usually free to the base, edged by a web in a few; hind-toe large; beak usually short or moderate, stout, compressed; wing short or moderate, generally armed with spurs or tubercles near the flexure; tail generally short.

FAMILY, Parridæ.

Feet enormous; claws much lengthened; bill moderate, compressed; wings spurred or tubercled.

SUB-FAMILY, Parrinæ.

Of small or moderate size; feet and claws enormously long, thin.

GENUS, Parra (METOPODIUS.)

Bill moderate, stout, compressed, thick at the base; culmen curved at the tip; forehead with a lappet of skin; tail short; nostrils small, ovate, in the middle of the bill; wings moderate or short, second and third quills longest, first sub-equal, spurred at the shoulder; tarsus long; feet enormous, the toes long and thin, and the claws very long and pointed: hind-claw especially long.

Parra indica, *Lath.*

900.—Jerdon's Birds of India, Vol. II, p. 708; Butler, Guzerat; Stray Feathers, Vol. IV, p. 19; Deccan, Stray Feathers, Vol. IX, p. 430; Swinhoe and Barnes, Central India; Ibis, 1885, p. 134.

THE BRONZE-WINGED JACANA.

Length, ♂, 10, ♀, 12; expanse, ♂, 20·5, ♀, 24; wing, ♂, 6, ♀, 7·5; tail, ♂, 1·6, ♀, 1·75; tarsus, ♂, 2·4, ♀, 3; bill, ♂, 1·12, ♀. 1·25; middle-toe, ♂, 3·6, ♀, 4; hind-toe, ♂, 3·25; claw alone, 2·5.

Bill greenish-yellow, tinged red at base; frontal lappet livid; irides brown; legs dull green.

Head, neck, and all the under parts rich dark green, glossed on the head, neck, and breast, and with purple reflections on the back of the neck and upper back; a broad white supercilium beginning just over the eye; interscapulars, wing-coverts, (except the primary), scapulars, and tertiaries, pale shining bronze; the lower back maroon, with a beautiful purple gloss; tail dark cinereous, the lateral feathers bordered with black, tipped white, and with a white shaft; primary-coverts and quills black, faintly glossed with green; lower abdomen and thigh-coverts dull blackish-green; under tail-coverts deep chesnut.

The young bird has the crown chesnut, with a pale eyebrow; the face white; back of the head and hind neck purple, with a lake and coppery gloss; the back cupreous olive-green; the upper tail-coverts and tail dull coppery; quills and primary-coverts black; tertials as the back, partly edged with white; throat white; neck and breast pale buff with a median white stripe, and the belly white with the flanks blackish; thigh-coverts mixed black and white.

Bill yellowish-green, darker on the upper mandible; the front lappet is also wanting.

With the exception of Sind, the Bronze-winged Jacana occurs in suitable localities throughout our limits, but is nowhere common; in fact it is only found on the larger reed-grown tanks, and never on rivers or the smaller tanks, which are generally free from weeds. It is a permanent resident, breeding at the commencement of the rains, or about July.

The nest is composed of rushes and weeds, and is a rather large circular pad, with a depression in the centre; it is placed generally on a bed of lotus leaves, surrounded more or less by rushes. The eggs, four in number, are moderately broad ovals, a good deal pointed at one end; they are highly glossy, of a rich warm stone or cafe-au-lait color, the whole surface of the egg being covered with a mass of finer or coarser brownish-black or almost black lines, intermingled and entangled in inextricable confusion; sometimes these markings are paled down here and there to a rich red brown, with an occasional large spot or blotch of the same color as the markings.

They measure 1·47 inches in length by about 1·03 in breadth.

Genus, **Hydrophasianus**, *Wag.*

Bill more slender than in *Metopodius;* forehead without a lappet; tail very long, the four central feathers especially greatly lengthened at the breeding season; wings long, with the first and second quills equal, and longer than the third; first and fourth primaries with a lancet-shaped portion of web, as it were, appended to the tip; hind-claw not so long as in *Metopodius*, otherwise similar to that genus.

Hydrophasianus chirurgus, *Scop.*

901.—Jerdon's Birds of India, Vol. II, p. 709; Butler, Guzerat; Stray Feathers, Vol. IV, p. 20; Deccan, Stray Feathers, Vol. IX, p. 431; Murray's Vertebrate Zoology of Sind, p. 258; Swinhoe and Barnes, Central India; Ibis, 1885, p. 134.

THE PHEASANT-TAILED JACANA.

Length, ♂, 18, ♀, 20; expanse, ♂, 24, ♀, 30; wing, ♂, 8, ♀, 9·5; tail, ♂, 10, ♀, 11; tarsus, ♂, 2·12, ♀, 2·4; bill at front, ♂, 1·12, ♀, 1·25.

Bill pale leaden-blue, greenish at tip; irides dark brown; legs pale bluish-green.

In summer plumage, the forehead, top of the head, face, chin, throat, and neck white, a broad black mark on the top of the head; hind neck pale shining yellow, edged by a dark line; upper plumage, including the scapulars and tertiaries, shining dark olive-brown with purple reflections; wings with the coverts white, first primary black, the second nearly so, and the third black on the outer webs and a broad tip; the rest white, all tipped with black, as are the greater wing-coverts; upper tail-coverts bronzed-black; tail black; beneath from the breast deep brownish-black, dull on the thigh-coverts; the under tail-coverts deep chesnut.

In winter plumage, the upper parts, including the lesser wing-coverts and tertiaries, are pale hair-brown, the former more or less barred with white, and the greater-coverts pure white; the top of the head and back of the neck brown, with a white supercilium, and the feathers of the forehead white spotted; a pale golden-yellow line from behind the eye down the sides of the neck, bordered by the black line from the gape, which crosses the lower part of the breast, forming a more or less broad pectoral gorget; first primary (only) with an appendage, fourth attenuated and prolonged; tail with the central feathers as the back, pale brown, slightly lengthened.

Length, 12 to 13; tail, 3 to 4.

In young birds the superciliary line is ferruginous, passing into a less marked yellow neck-stripe, and the brown band is also less distinct.

The Pheasant-tailed Jacana occurs commonly throughout the district. It is a permanent resident, breeding about the middle of the rains, or a little later.

The nest is a heap of weeds, placed in the water in the midst of grass or rushes. The eggs, invariably four in number, are peg-top shape; the shell is compact and hard and is highly glossy; the ground color varies from greenish-bronze to rufous-brown bronze; they are unspotted.

They measure 1·46 in length by 1·12 in breadth.

Family, Rallidæ.

Bill more or less compressed, short, pointed, and wedge-shaped; nostrils median, in a short groove, pervious; legs stout; tarsus short, or moderately long; feet large; wings moderate or short, and rounded, usually with a tubercle or small spur on the flexure; tail short or almost wanting.

Sub-family, Gallinulinæ.

Bill with the keel advancing on the forehead, where there is usually a casque; toes long and slender or bordered by a scolloped web; wings short and rounded; hind-toe long.

Genus, Porphyrio, *Brisson.*

Bill very strong, thick, conic, depressed; base prolonged into a thick horny casque covering the forehead and the top of the head; upper mandible very thick, curving from the base, pointed; lower mandible less thick; gonys ascending; gape gently curving; nares apert, oval in the middle of the bill; wings moderate, ample; tail short; tarsus lengthened, strong; toes very, long, free, bordered by a narrow web; claws long, very slightly curved.

Porphyrio poliocephalus, *Latham.*

902.—Jerdon's Birds of India, Vol. II, p. 713; Butler, Guzerat; Stray Feathers, Vol. IV, p. 20; Deccan, Stray Feathers, Vol. IX, p. 431; Murray's Vertebrate Zoology of Sind, p. 260; Swinhoe and Barnes, Central India; Ibis, 1885, p. 135.

The Purple Coot.

Keim, Hin.

Length, 18 to 19; expanse, 30 to 32; wing, 10; tail, 4; tarsus, 3·5.

Bill red, culmen darker, a blood-red spot at base of each mandible; casque cherry-red; irides dull red; legs dull pale brick-red.

Lores, round the eyes, cheeks, head, and nape, purple tinged with grey on the sides, and gradually passing into the purer purple of the hind-neck, back, and upper tail-coverts; wing-coverts pale blue; the quills dull Antwerp-blue, dusky on their inner webs; tail black, the feathers slightly edged dull blue; beneath, the lower parts of the checks, chin, and throat, pale cœrulean-blue, more or less edged with purplish-grey, and passing into the purer blue of the lower neck and breast; abdomen, sides of the body and vent abruptly deep purple; the thigh-coverts dull blue; under tail-coverts pure white; lower wing-coverts dull pale blue; quills and tail beneath glossy blackish.

The Purple Coot occurs abundantly in all suitable localities, throughout the region. It is a permanent resident, breeding from July to September; the nest is composed of grass and weeds, heaped together, with a central depression; it is generally floating, but occasionally it is found on the ground, in a dense patch of grass or reeds.

The eggs, eight or ten in number, are oval in shape, but they vary somewhat. The ground color of the egg, when fresh, is a pure salmon or pinkish-stone color, but they rapidly fade. The markings consist of spots, streaks, and blotches of rich red color, with underlying clouds of pale purple. They have no gloss.

They measure 1·93 inches in length by about 1·39 in breadth.

GENUS, **Fulica**, *Lin.*

Bill moderate or short, thick; the upper mandible gradually deflected, compressed, extending backwards into a horny shield on the forehead; nostrils small, placed in the middle of the bill; wings short, concave, with a tubercle at the flexure; second and third quils longest; tail very short; tarsus moderate, compressed; toes very long, bordered by a wide lobed membrane; claws short, curved and sharp.

Plumage dense, soft, but open in texture.

Fulica atra, *Lin.*

903.—Jerdon's Birds of India, Vol. II, p. 715; Butler, Guzerat; Stray Feathers, Vol. IV, p. 20; Deccan, Stray Feathers, Vol. IX, p. 431; Murray's Vertebrate Zoology of Sind, p. 261; Swinhoe and Barnes, Central India; Ibis, 1885, p. 135.

THE BALD COOT.

Length, 15 to 16; wing, 7·75; tail, 2; bill at gape, 1·4.

Bill dead white in winter, tinged slightly with rosy in the breeding season; frontal disc white; irides blood-red; feet dull green, with a garter of yellow green and red above the joint in summer.

Head and neck deep black; upper plumage greyish-black; below the same, with an ashy tinge.

The Common Coot occurs abundantly throughout the region.

It is a permanent resident, making a large nest of reeds and rushes, in water a foot or so deep; the nest is based upon the ground, but rises several inches above the water level. Occasionally they are built upon the ground close to the waters edge, and occasionally they are more or less floating. The eggs, seven to ten in number, are broadish ovals, slightly compressed towards one end; they have no gloss and are of a pale buffy-stone-color, closely and evenly stippled with black or blackish-brown specks with an occasional spot of somewhat larger size scattered sparingly about the surface.

The eggs average 1·98 in length by 1·4 in breadth.

Genus, Gallicrex, *Blyth*.

Bill much as in *Gallinula*, but with the base (in the male) prolonged over the forehead and rising into a fleshy carbuncle or horn on the top of the head, which is only developed at the time of breeding; feet large; hind-toe with the claw short, more curved than the others; otherwise as in *Gallinula*.

Gallicrex cinereus, *Gm.*

904.—*G. cristatus*, Latham.—Jerdon's Birds of India, Vol. II. p. 716; Murray's Vertebrate Zoology of Sind, p. 261.

THE WATER-COCK.

♂. Length, 16 to 17; expanse, 23; wing, 8·5; tail, 3·5; tarsus, 3; bill from gape; 1·23.

♀. Length, 14; expanse, 22; wing, 7; tail, 2·5; tarsus 2·5; bill from gape, 1·25.

Bill greenish-yellow, red at the base; irides, ♂, red, ♀ brown; legs, ♂, dull red, ♀, dull green.

Male in breeding plumage dull black; the feathers of the back, wing-coverts, rump, and upper tail-coverts, more or less edged with pale brown; tertials dark-brown, edged with pale whity-brown; edge of the wing white; quills dusky, the shaft of the first quill thick, white; tail blackish-brown, the outer feathers edged pale brown; lower wing-coverts dusky, with whitish edges.

The female has the crown of the head and a pale streak over the eye unspotted brown; the rest of the body above dark brown; all the feathers edged with pale fulvous, most broadly so on the back, scapulars, and wing-coverts; edge of the wing and outer web of first quill white; quills dusky-brown; lores, cheeks, and sides of neck fulvous-brown; the chin and throat whitish; the rest of the lower part brownish-fulvous; the feathers barred transversely with brown, darkest on the flanks, outer thigh-coverts, and under tail-coverts, and whitish on the belly; wings beneath dark cinereous.

Within our limits the Kora or Water-Cock has only been; recorded from Sind.

Genus, Gallinula, *Brisson*.

Bill moderate, compressed, rather thick at the base, slightly curved at tip, expanding into a small shield on the forehead;

nostrils longitudinal, in a groove in the middle of the bill; wings moderate, second, third, and fourth quills sub-equal, with a small sharp tubercle or spur; tail short; tarsus moderately long, narrow, edged by a very narrow membrane.

Gallinula chloropus, *Lin.*

905.—Jerdon's Birds of India, Vol. II, p. 718; Butler, Guzerat; Stray Feathers, Vol. IV, p. 20; Deccan, Stray Feathers, Vol. IX, p. 431; Murray's Vertebrate Zoology of Sind, p. 262; Swinhoe and Barnes, Central India; Ibis, 1885, p. 135,

THE WATER HEN.

Length, 12 to 13; expanse, 20; wing, 6·75; tail, 2·95; tarsus, 1·8; bill from gape, 1·1.

Bill red, yellow at tip; irides red; legs pale olive-green, with an orange garter above the knee.

Head dusky-grey; the upper plumage deep olive; the wing dusky; edge of the wing white; throat, neck, and breast, dusky-grey, the rest of the under parts deep bluish-grey; the feathers edged with whitish, and the flanks with large streaks of white; under tail-coverts pure white, with a few black feathers intermixed.

The young has the head and under parts olivaceous-brown; the throat, neck in front, and a spot beneath the eye whitish; breast and beneath pale grey.

The Water Hen is a common permanent resident throughout the district, breeding from July to September. The nest varies much according to the situation in which it is placed; when built in low bushes (always overhanging water), the nest is neat and carefully made, but when placed among reeds and flags, it is a much less pretentious affair. The eggs, seven to nine in number, are moderately broad ovals in shape, and in color they are pale stone or drab, more or less thickly sprinkled with spots, streaks and blotches of red, or reddish-brown. The larger markings are frequently surrounded by a reddish halo.

They measure 1·62 inches in length by 1·21 inches in breadth.

GENUS, Erythra.

Intermediate between *Gallinula* and *Porzana*.

Erythra phœnicura, *Penn.*

907.—Jerdon's Birds of India, Vol. II, p. 720; Butler, Guzerat; Stray Feathers, Vol. IV, p. 21; Deccan, Stray Feathers, Vol. IX, p. 431; *Gallinula phœnicura*, Penn.; Murray's Vertebrate Zoology of Sind, p. 263.

THE WHITE-BREASTED WATER HEN.

Length, 12·75; expanse, 21; wing, 6·5; tail, 2·5; tarsus, 2·5; bill at front, 1·5.

Bill greenish-yellow; culmen orange; irides blood-red; legs greenish.

Above black with greenish reflections, especially on the wing-coverts; chin, throat, and breast, pure white; lower abdomen, vent, and under tail-coverts, deep chesnut.

The White-breasted Water Hen occurs in suitable localities throughout our limits; it is a permanent resident, breeding about August. The rest is placed in a variety of situations. In bamboo clumps, amongst reeds and rushes, upon the ground, and even upon trees. The eggs, four or five in number, are oval in shape, pointed somewhat at one end; in color they are pale pinkish-stone, more or less profusely streaked and blotched with pale reddish-purple. They measure 1·6 inches in length by about 1·18 in breadth.

SUB-FAMILY, **Rallinæ.**

Base of the bill not prolonged over the forehead; beak much compressed; feet somewhat shorter than in *Gallinula*; body still more compressed.

GENUS **Porzana,** *Vieill.*

Bill about the length of the head, compressed throughout, moderately slender, very slightly deeper at the base, and somewhat narrowed in the middle; wings moderate, rounded; tail very short; tarsus moderate; toes rather long, slender, smooth; claws compressed, sharp.

Porzana akool, *Sykes.*

908.—Jerdon's Birds of India, Vol. II, p. 722; Butler, Guzerat; Stray Feathers, Vol. IV, p. 21; Deccan, Stray Feathers, Vol. IX, p. 431; Swinhoe and Barnes, Central India; Ibis, 1885, p. 135.

THE BROWN AND ASHY CRAKE.

THE BROWN RAIL.

Length, ♂, 10·87 to 12·0, ♀, 10·0 to 11·3; expanse, ♂, 15·75 to 17·0, ♀, 15·0 to 15·82; wing, ♂, 4·9 to 5·3, ♀, 4·4 to 4·9; tail, ♂, 2·4 to 2·8, ♀, 2·3 to 2·62; tarsus, ♂, 1·9 to 2·1, ♀, 1·7 to 1·8; bill from gape, ♂, 1·3 to 1·68, ♀, 1·2 to 1·4; weight, ♂, 4 to 6 ozs., ♀, 3·7 to 4·9 oz.

Bill green, dusky on culmen; lower mandible tipped lavender blue; irides vary from reddish-brown to crimson; legs and feet dull lake-red in adults in breeding season, darker in cold season; young birds reddish-brown.

Above olive-brown, ashy-brown on rump; wings and tail dusky; wing-coverts deep brown; chin white; throat, breast, and belly ash-brown; flanks olive-brown; lower tail-coverts deep brown.

The Brown and Ashy Crake is a common permanent resident in Guzerat and parts of Rajputana; it does not occur in Sind, and is decidedly rare in the Deccan. They breed twice during the rains, once in July and again in September. The nest is similar to, but smaller than, that of the Water Hen. The eggs vary from four to eight in number; they are oval in shape, slightly compressed at one end; the texture of the shell is fine, but they have scarcely any gloss; the ground color is white, with a scarcely noticeable tinge of salmon-pink, which is very evanescent; the markings consist of streaks and spots of purplish or brownish-red, with occasional underlying blotches of pale purple. They measure 1·49 inches in length by 1·09 in breadth.

Porzana maruetta, *Leach.*

909.—Jerdon's Birds of India, Vol. II, p. 722; Butler, Guzerat; Stray Feathers, Vol. V, p. 215; Deccan, Stray Feathers, Vol. IX, p. 432; Murray's Vertebrate Zoology of Sind, p. 264.

THE SPOTTED CRAKE.

Length, 8·7 to 9·2; expanse, 14·5 to 15·7; wing, 4·3 to 4·8; tail, 1·85 to 2·1; tarsus, 1·21 to 1·43; bill from gape, 0·77 to 0·9; weight, 3 to 4 oz.

The tip of the lower and the greater part of the upper mandible dusky olive-green; the basal two-thirds of lower mandible and a band at base of the upper one wax-yellow with an orange tinge on culmen, and a red spot at the base of the maxilla on either side; irides reddish-brown; legs and feet generally bright olive-green. This is Mr. Hume's description of the soft parts. Jerdon's is much shorter, as follows: Bill greenish-yellow, orange, at the base; irides red-brown; legs and feet bright yellowish-green.

Crown, back, scapulars, and rump, olive-brown, blotched with dusky, and all the feathers, except those of the head, elegantly spotted and streaked with white; forehead and eyestreak ash-grey, the latter speckled with white; nape thickly spotted with black and white; cheeks cinereous, speckled with black; wing-coverts olive-brown, sparingly spotted with white; quills brown; throat ash-grey; forepart of the neck and breast pale olivaceous, tinged with ashy-grey and spotted with white; belly and vent ashy-white; flanks with transverse bars of white, black, and olivaceous-brown.

The Spotted Crake occurs as a more or less common cold weather visitant to all parts of the district.

Porzana bailloni, *Vieill.*

910.—*P. pygmæa,* Naum.—Jerdon's Birds of India, Vol. II, p. 723; Butler, Guzerat; Stray Feathers, Vol. V, p. 215; Deccan, Stray Feathers, Vol. IX, p. 432; Murray's Vertebrate Zoology of Sind, p. 264; Swinhoe and Barnes, Central India; Ibis, 1885, p. 135.

BAILLON'S CRAKE.

Length, 6·62 to 7·75; expanse, 10 to 11·75; wing, 3·12 to 3·7; tail, 1·75 to 2·2; tarsus, 1·05 to 1·25; bill from gape, 0·68 to 0·78; weight, 1·1 to 1·8 oz.

Bill green ; culmen and tip dusky ; irides vary from red to carmine, in some, probably young birds, they are reddish-brown ; legs and feet brownish-olive.

Crown and neck above wood-brown ; back, scapulars, and wing-coverts, yellow-brown, tinged with olive and with numerous white, black-edged, irregular-spots ; cheeks, throat, and neck, and under parts, bluish-grey ; the sides of the abdomen and under tail-coverts black with white cross bars.

The following remarks by Mr. Hume in his "Game Birds of India" may prove useful :—

"This species and the Little Crake are so much alike that it may be well to point out how they may be distinguished.

"Baillon's Crake may be recognized by its smaller size, shorter, and in proportion, deeper bill, and by having the back, scapulars, and greater wing-coverts, all more or less profusely variegated, with a somewhat bluish-white ; whereas in the Little Crake the corresponding markings, which are rather coarser and of a purer white, are confined, as a rule, to the centre of the back, though occasionally there is a trace of these on some of the longer scapulars. In Baillon's Crake the outer web of the first primary is nearly entirely white or yellowish-white ; in the Little Crake it is brown, only slightly yellower and paler than the inner web. Moreover, in the Little Crake there is much less barring on the flanks and under tail-coverts.

"Again, though possible, this is only seasonal (on this point I cannot speak with certainty) ; the Little Crake has the base of the bill bright red. Lastly the adult females of the Little Crake have the entire breast and upper abdomen uniform fulvous-fawn, while those of Baillon's Crake have these parts an albescent-grey, often only very slightly intermingled or fringed on the breast with brownish-fawn."

Baillon's Crake appears to be a not uncommon bird in most parts of the district, but appears to be very locally distributed, and most of the birds we meet with are merely seasonal visitants. Some few, however, remain to breed, notably so at Milana, near Deesa. The nest is not unlike that of the Water Hen. The eggs, five or six in number, are oval in shape, slightly pointed at one end ; the ground color is a pale stone or slight greenish-drab, with faint dusky clouds and streaks, mostly at the larger end. They measure about 1·2 inches in length by 0·87 in breadth.

Porzana parva, *Scop.*

910bis.—*P. minuta*, Pall.—Murray's Vertebrate Zoology of Sind, p. 265.

THE LITTLE RAIL.

Length, 7 to 8 ; wing, 3·8 ; tail, 1·5 to 1·75 ; bill, 0·7.

Bill yellowish-green ; irides red ; feet and legs yellowish-green.

Crown of the head deep brown ; sides of the head, both above and below the eye, ash or slate color ; cheeks and throat dull or greyish-white, the forepart of the neck pale ash; under parts ashy or grey-blue in the males, light rufous buff in female; lower abdomen and vent deep or olive-brown, spotted with white; neck behind and shoulder of the wing olive-brown; back deep olive-brown, the feathers with broad dark mesial stripes, their inner margins pale with some white linear spots and streaks; primaries and secondaries deep brown with paler edges; lesser wing-coverts plain dull olive-brown; tail dusky olive-brown; under tail-coverts slaty-grey with spots and bars of white.

Within our limits the Little Rail only occurs in Sind.

Porzana fusca, *Lin.*

911.—Jerdon's Birds of India, Vol. II, p. 724.

THE RUDDY RAIL.

Length, 8·4 to 8·7; expanse, 13·25 to 14·5; wing, 3·75 to 4·25; tail, 2·2; tarsus, 1·4 to 1·55; bill at front, 0·8 to 0·9; bill at gape, 0·9 to 1.

Bill blackish-horny to greenish-brown; irides red; legs red, dusky at joints and on toes.

Forehead, cheeks, and sides of the head, neck, throat, breast, and abdomen, vinous chesnut, albescent on the chin and throat; upper plumage dull olive-brown, darker on the wings and tail; lower abdomen, vent, and under tail-coverts, darker olivaceous with white bars.

The young want the rufous tint and have the entire chin and throat white, and the the rest of the lower surface dull earthy olive-brown, mottled or imperfectly barred with brownish-white.

According to Jerdon the Ruddy Rail is found throughout India. I cannot find any record of its occurrence within our limits, but probably owing to its skulking habits, it has been overlooked.

GENUS, Hypotænidia, *Reich.*

Bill somewhat lengthened, straight, or slightly turned down at the tip, slender, grooved for two-thirds of its length; nostrils linear; wings with the first quill much shorter than the second or third, and a small spur on the shoulder; tarsus and toes as in *Porzana*. The feathers of the forehead somewhat spiny.

Hypotænidia striata, *Lin.*

913.—Jerdon's Birds of India, Vol. II, p. 726, Butler, Deccan; Stray Feathers, Vol IX, p. 432.

THE BLUE-BREASTED BANDED RAIL.

Length, 9·8 to 11·5; expanse, 14·25 to 17·5; wing, 4·5 to 5·0; tail, 1·5 to 2·25; tarsus, 1·35 to 1·62; bill from gape, 1·35 to 1·82; weight, 3·6 to 5 oz.

The colors of the soft parts are extremely variable.

Top of head and hind-neck dark chesnut; upper plumage

(including the quills and tail) olivaceous throughout, with narrow white, black-edged bars; beneath, the chin and throat whitish; the neck, breast, and upper abdomen, bluish-grey; the lower abdomen, vent, under tail-coverts, and thigh-coverts, dull olivaceous, with white bands.

The Blue-breasted Banded Rail is a not uncommon seasonal visitant to portions of the Deccan; it breeds during August and September. It does not occur in Sind, neither has it been recorded from Guzerat.

Genus, **Rallus**, *Lin.*

With longer bills than *Hypotænidia*.

Rallus indicus, *Blyth.*

914.—Jerdon's Birds of India, Vol. II, p. 726; Swinhoe and Barnes, Central India; Ibis, 1885, p. 135.

The Indian Water Rail.

Length, 10·5 to 12; expanse, 15 to 16·75; wing, 4·5 to 5; tail, 2 to 2·8; tarsus, 1·55 to 1·75 ; bill at front, 1·5 to 1·75; bill from gape, 1·6 to 1·9.

Bill horny-brown; basal half of upper mandible and basal two-thirds of lower mandible orange-red; irides red to red-brown; legs brownish-pink to fleshy-brown.

Above olive-brown, with black central streaks; a dark streak below the eye, continued back over the ear-coverts; lesser-coverts with a few white marks; throat whitish; cheeks, foreneck, breast, and upper abdomen, brownish-ashy; lower belly reddish-brown; flanks black with white bands; lower tail-coverts mixed white, rufous, and black; quills and tail dusky-brown, the feathers of the last edged paler.

The Indian Water Rail is, I believe, a very rare and uncertain winter visitant to Central India. I have seen it twice at the Panghur Lake, and I think I saw it once at Gungrar. I cannot find any record of its occurrence within our limits.

Tribe, **Cultirostres.**

Bill thick, stout, pointed, slightly curved in some; tarsus elongated; feet moderately large; hind-toe large, on the same plane as the anterior toes; wings ample; tail short, mostly of large or moderate size.

Family, **Ciconidæ.**

Bill very large and stout, lengthened, straight, or slightly ascending, and with the lower mandible sub-recurved, smooth, without a groove, less cleft than in the Herons; nostrils linear, near the base of the culmen; wings long, second and third or third and fourth quills longest; tail short; tarsus usually reticulate with hexagonal scales; all the anterior toes joined at the base by membrane; hallux resting on the ground for part of its length; claws blunt.

Genus, Leptoptilus, *Lesson.*

Bill enormous, much thickened; head more or less nude; wing-coverts long, broad; under tail-coverts long, soft, and somewhat decomposed, of very large size.

Leptoptilus argalus, *Lin.*

915.—Jerdon's Birds of India, Vol. II, p. 730; Butler, Guzerat; Stray Feathers, Vol. IV, p. 21; Deccan, Stray Feathers, Vol. IX, p. 432; Murray's Vertebrate Zoology of Sind, p. 266; Swinhoe and Barnes, Central India; Ibis, 1885, p. 135.

THE ADJUTANT.

Length, 60; wing, 30; tail, 11; tarsus, 10·5; bill at front, 12

Bill pale dirty-greenish; irides greyish-white; legs greyish-white.

Adult in breeding plumage; whole head, neck, and gular pouch bare, with a very few scattered short hairs, yellowish red mixed with fleshy, and varying much in tint in different individuals; a ruff of white feathers bordering the upper part of the back, lengthened and somewhat loose in texture on the shoulder; upper plumage, including the lesser and median wing-coverts, slaty black, ashy or slaty in fresh moulted birds, with a slight green gloss; the greater-coverts silvery-grey; primaries and secondaries black, slightly glossed externally; tertiaries silvery-grey, gradually passing into the greater-coverts, and with them forming one long conspicuous wing-band; two or three of the innermost feathers, slightly decomposed in structure; scapulars with a tinge of grey; lower plumage white.

In non-breeding plumage the silvery-grey wing-band is wanting, the whole plumage is more dull, and the nude skin of the head and neck less mixed with red.

The Adjutant is not uncommon during the rainy season in Central India and Guzerat; it is much more rare in the Deccan, and in Sind it is seldom met with.

Leptoptilus javanicus, *Horsf.*

916.—Jerdon's Birds of India, Vol. II, p. 732; Butler, Deccan; Stray Feathers, Vol. IX, p. 432; Swinhoe and Barnes, Central India; Ibis, 1885, p. 135.

THE HAIR-CRESTED STORK.

Length, 54; wing, 26; tail, 11; tarsus, 10; bill, 10.

Bill dirty-yellowish; bare top of head dirty-green; nude face and neck much tinged with yellow, and at seasons with red; irides whitish; legs dusky-black.

Top of the head entirely bald, horny; the rest of the head, face and neck bare, with a few longish hair-like feathers on the occiput; the face and the rest of the neck more or less thickly covered with hairs, some long, others short, collected into a thin mane on the back of the neck, and a small tuft on the lower part of the neck; a large white neck-ruff covering the sides of the neck and breast; plumage above glossy greenish-black; all the body feathers and the lesser wing-coverts faintly barred with several narrow bars; scapulars, the uppermost tertiaries, and the last of the greater-coverts more brightly green glossed and edged with white; plumage beneath white.

Jerdon states that the Hair-crested Adjutant is found in small numbers throughout India, but as a matter of fact within our limits it has very doubtfully been recorded from the Deccan, and a single specimen was obtained by myself in Central India.

GENUS, **Xenorhynchus**, *Bona.*

Bill very long, stout, solid, compressed, slightly ascending to the tip; tarsus much elongated.

Xenorhynchus asiaticus, *Lath.*

917.—*Mycteria australis*, Shaw.—Jerdon's Birds of India, Vol. II, p. 734; Butler, Guzerat; Stray Feathers, Vol. IV, p. 22; Deccan, Stray Feathers, Vol. IX, p. 432; Murray's Vertebrate Zoology of Sind, p. 266; Swinhoe and Barnes, Central India; Ibis, 1885, p. 135.

THE BLACK-NECKED STORK.

Length, 52 to 56; wing, 23 to 24; tail, 9; tarsus, 12 to 13; bill at front, 11 to 13.

Bill black; irides brown; legs red.

Head and neck rich dark glossy-green, beautifully glossed with purple on the hind-head and occiput; middle and greater-coverts, scapulars, and a portion of the interscapulars, tertiaries, and tail glossy green; the rest of the plumage pure white.

The Black-necked Stork is fairly common in Sind; further south in Guzerat it becomes less common, and in the Deccan it is rare. It is a permanent resident, building a large platform nest of sticks about September in some high tree. The eggs, three or four in number, are moderately broad ovals, compressed towards one end; they are unspotted sullied white in color. The shell is smooth to the touch, but rather coarse in texture. The eggs vary from 2·65 to 3·13 inches in length, and from 1·98 to 2·3 in. breadth, but they average 2·91 by 2·12.

GENUS, **Ciconia**, *Linnæus.*

Bill straight, moderately robust, acute; upper mandible convex above; lower mandible inclining a little upwards at the tip; nostrils pierced in the horny substance of the bill; orbits more or less naked; tarsi long; a considerable part of the tibia nude; wings moderate, ample, third and fourth quills longest; toes strongly webbed at the base; hind-toe moderately long; claws short, depressed, blunt, not pectinated.

Ciconia nigra, *Lin.*

918.—Jerdon's Birds of India, Vol. II, p. 735; Butler, Guzerat; Stray Feathers, Vol. IV, p. 22; Deccan, Stray Feathers, Vol. IX, p. 433; Murray's Vertebrate Zoology of Sind, p. 267; Swinhoe and Barnes, Central India; Ibis, 1885, p. 135.

THE BLACK STORK.

Length, 42; expanse, 72; wing, 24; tail, 10; tarsus, 8; bill at front, 7·9.

Bill blood red; irides dark-brown; legs dark-red.

Whole plumage deep blackish-brown, with violet, purple, and green reflections, except the lower part of the breast and the abdomen, which are pure white.

With the exception of Sind where it is common the Black Stork is only a somewhat rare seasonal visitant to suitable portions of the region.

Ciconia alba, *Bechst.*

919.—Jerdon's Birds of India, Vol. II, p. 736; Butler, Guzerat; Stray Feathers, Vol. IV, p. 22; Deccan, Stray Feathers, Vol. IX, p. 433; Murray's Vertebrate Zoology of Sind, p. 267.

THE WHITE STORK.

Length, 42; expanse, 78; wing, 24; tail, 10; tarsus, 8·5; bill at front, 7·5.

Bill fine blood-red; irides brown; naked orbits black; legs red.

Head, neck, and all the body pure white; greater-coverts, scapulars, and quills black.

The White Stork is a not uncommon winter visitant to all suitable places within the district.

Ciconia (Dissura) episcopa, *Bodd.*

920.—*C. leucocephala,* Gm.—Jerdon's Birds of India, Vol. II, p. 737; Butler, Guzerat; Stray Feathers, Vol. IV, p. 22; Deccan, Stray Feathers, Vol. IX, p. 443; Murray's Vertebrate Zoology of Sind, p. 267; Swinhoe and Barnes, Central India; Ibis, 1885, p. 135.

THE WHITE-NECKED STORK.

Length, 36 to 37; expanse, 68; wing, 20; tail, 7; tarsus, 7; bill at front, 6.

Bill dusky, reddish on culmen and beneath; the nude front, face, throat, and patch behind the ear dusky-plumbeous; irides red; sclerotic black with an anterior patch of red, and a posterior one of yellow; tarsus dull red; naked skin of the ulna exposed bright blood-red.

Top of the head black; the whole neck white; the rest of the body black, beautifully glossed with purple on the back of neck, upper back and breast, and upper part of abdomen; quills and upper tail-coverts glossed with green, as is part of the lower back; tail white.

The White-necked Stork is tolerably common throughout the region. It is a permanent resident.

FAMILY, Ardeidæ.

Bill typically more slender than in the Storks, very sharp, deeply cleft; legs long, scutellated; toes long, slender; outer-toe only joined by web to the middle one; hind-toe long, on the same plane as the others; middle-toe with the inner edge of the claw dilated and pectinated; nostrils narrow, at the basal extremity of a long furrow.

GENUS, Ardea, *Linn.*

Bill elongate, straight, thick, compressed, pointed; the upper mandible with a groove from the nostrils, evanescent towards the tip; nostrils near the base narrow, longitudinal, partially concealed by membrane; wings moderately long, the second, third, and fourth quills usually sub-equal and longest; tail short, even; tarsus lengthened, usually scutellate in front; toes long; outer-toe connected to the middle one by a web; claws long, that of the middle-toe with the inner margin produced, and pectinated, of large size, usually grey above, with the neck moderately long and slender, and the feathers of the lower neck and breast lengthened and pendent.

Ardea cinerea, *Lin.*

923.—Jerdon's Birds of India, Vol. II, p. 741; Butler, Guzerat; Stray Feathers, Vol. IV, p. 23; Deccan, Stray Feathers, Vol. IX, p. 433; Murray's Vertebrate Zoology of Sind, p. 269; Swinhoe and Barnes, Central India; Ibis, 1885, p. 135.

THE BLUE HERON.

Length, 39; expanse, 66; wing, 18; tail, 8; tarsus, 5·75; bill at front, 5.

Bill dark yellow, brownish on culmen; irides gamboge-yellow; lores and naked orbitar skin greenish; legs and feet brown.

Adult: forehead and crown pure white; occiput black, and a pendent crest of narrow, long, black feathers at the back of the head; neck white; back and wings fine bluish-grey; quills black; scapulars silvery-grey, long and pointed, forming graceful plumes; tail bluish-ashy; forepart of the neck with longitudinal black spots, the feathers drooping down on the top of the breast, loose, and elongated, and forming a fine pectoral plume; lower breast and the rest of the under parts pure white.

The young bird has the head and neck ashy, with dusky-grey streaks in front; the upper plumage tinged with brown; and the lengthened occipital feathers as well as the breast plumes absent.

The Common Heron occurs plentifully throughout the region.

They are permanent residents, but disappear from many places during the breeding season, when they in company with other Herons and Egrets, form immense breeding colonies. Such colonies occur on the *dhunds* along the Eastern Narra Canal in Sind, and other places in the district. They all build platform nests, composed of sticks, and the eggs are very similar, only differing somewhat in size.

Further on a table will be found giving dimensions of the eggs of the various species.

They breed usually during the rains.

Ardea purpurea, *Lin.*

924.—Jerdon's Birds of India, Vol. II, p. 743; Butler, Guzerat; Stray Feathers, Vol. IV, p. 23; Deccan, Stray Feathers, Vol. IX, p. 433; Murray's Vertebrate Zoology of Sind, p. 269; Swinhoe and Barnes, Central India; Ibis, 1885, p. 135.

THE PURPLE HERON.

Length, 36 to 42; expanse, 58; wing, 15·5; tail, 5·75; tarsus, 5·25; bill at front, 5·4.

Bill deep yellow, brownish above; orbitar skin greenish-yellow; irides yellow; tarsus reddish-brown, yellowish behind and on the soles of the feet.

Adult in full plumage: crown and occipital crest black with green reflections; throat white; cheeks and sides of the neck reddish-brown, with three longitudinal narrow black bands, two lateral ones from the eyes to the breast, and the third from the nape down the back of the neck; neck in front variegated with rufous black and purple, the feathers on the top of the breast long and acuminated, purplish-white; back, wings, and tail, reddish-ash; the scapulars purple, long, and subulate, forming a brilliant plume on each side; breast and flanks deep brownish-red; belly and thigh-coverts the same, but paler and mixed with white.

The immature bird has the crest, scapulars and neck plumes deficient; the forehead black; the nape and cheeks pale rufous; the throat white; the forepart of the neck and the sides of the breast yellowish-white, with black spots; back, wings, and tail, dusky-ash, the feathers edged with reddish-ash; lower parts whitish.

The Purple Heron is common in suitable places throughout the district. The remarks concerning breeding apply to this species also.

GENUS, Herodias, *Boie.*

Bill moderately long and slender, straight and much compressed; plumage white; the neck very long and slender; tibia naked for nearly half its length; tarsus long, thin.

Herodias alba, *Lin.*

924*bis*.—Murray's Vertebrate Zoology of Sind, p. 270.

THE LARGE WHITE HERON.

Wing, 17·2 ; tarsus, 7·91 ; bill at front, 5.

Bill, yellow.

Plumage, pure white ; in the breeding season it developes a long dorsal train of decomposed feathers, extending about five inches from the end of the tail ; at this season the bill is black.

This Large White Heron occurs in Sind.

Herodias torra, *B. Ham.*

925.—*H. alba*, Lin.—Jerdon's Birds of India, Vol. II, p. 744 ; Butler, Guzerat ; Stray Feathers, Vol. IX, p. 433 ; Murray's Vertebrate Zoology of Sind, p. 270 ; Swinhoe and Barnes, Central India ; Ibis, 1885, p. 135.

THE LARGE EGRET.

Length, 36 ; expanse, 54 ; wing, 13·2 to 15·2 ; tail, 6·5 ; tarsus, 5·25 to 7 ; bill at front, 3·72 to 4·6.

Bill black, changing to yellow in winter ; naked skin at base of bill and round the eyes pea-green to verditer ; irides pale yellow ; naked part of tibia pale livid ; tarsus black, more or less suffused with vinous red.

Plumage pure white ; in the breeding season an elongated dorsal train of fine decomposed feathers, which pass the tail sometimes by 4 or 5 inches ; no crest or breast plumes.

The Large Egret is very common in Sind ; it occurs more sparingly in other places, but is nowhere rare.

The remarks about breeding apply to this species also.

Herodias intermedia, *Hass.*

926.—*H. egrettoides*, Tem.—Jerdon's Birds of India, Vol. II, p. 745 ; Butler, Guzerat ; Stray Feathers, Vol. IV, p. 23 ; Deccan, Stray Feathers, Vol. IX, p. 433 ; Murray's Vertebrate Zoology of Sind, p. 270 ; Swinhoe and Barnes, Central India ; Ibis, 1885, p. 136.

THE SMALLER EGRET.

Length, 27 to 28 ; expanse, 46 ; wing, 11·15 to 12·65 ; tail, 5 ; tarsus, 4·1 to 4·6 ; bill at front, 2·68 to 3·09.

Bill black ; irides yellow ; legs black ; facial skin greenish.

In summer, plumage pure white, like the last ; a long dorsal train reaching nearly to the ground, and a beautiful long pectoral tuft of similarly formed feathers, but no crest.

In winter, the dorsal and pectoral trains are wanting, and the bill is yellow.

The Smaller Egret is very common throughout the region except perhaps in Ratnagiri.

Breeds similarly to the others.

Herodias garzetta, *Lin.*

927.—Jerdon's Birds of India, Vol. II, p. 746; Butler, Guzerat; Stray Feathers, Vol. IV, p. 23; Deccan, Stray Feathers, Vol. IX, p. 433; Murray's Vertebrate Zoology of Sind, p. 270; Swinhoe and Barnes, Central India; Ibis, 1885, p. 136.

THE LITTLE EGRET.

Length, 24 to 25; wing, 9·8 to 11·4; tail, 3·9; tarsus, 3·7 to 4·6; bill at front, 3·1 to 3·6.

In breeding plumage, as in the others, white; a pendent occipital crest of two or three long feathers; dorsal train of decomposed feathers long, and in fine specimens curving upwards at the extremity, some lengthened pectoral feathers also.

The bill is always black.

In non-breeding dress the occipital crest and the dorsal and pectoral plumes are wanting.

The Little Egret is very common throughout the district.

The remarks about breeding apply to this species also.

GENUS, Demi-egretta, *Blyth.*

Bill long, slender, otherwise much as in *Herodias*, but the adult plumage is dark, the young birds alone being white.

Demi-egretta gularis, *Boie.*

928.—*D. asha*, Sykes.—Jerdon's Birds of India, Vol. II, p. 746; Butler, Guzerat; Stray Feathers, Vol. IV, p. 23; Deccan, Stray Feathers, Vol. IX, p. 434; Murray's Vertebrate Zoology of Sind, p. 271.

THE ASHY EGRET.

Length, 24; wing, 10·25; tail, 3·25; tarsus, 3·95; bill at front, 3·5.

Bill reddish-yellow, dusky above; orbitar skin yellow-green; irides yellow; legs blackish; the feet and lower part of the tarsus yellowish.

Adult in breeding season has the whole plumage dusky-slaty; the chin and throat white; an occipital crest; a dorsal train of decomposed feathers not reaching to the end of the tail; and a pectoral plume of narrow and pointed not decomposed feathers.

In the cold season entirely of a slaty color, the throat alone white.

Young birds are pure white throughout, or, according to Layard, have some of the wing-coverts edged with grey. At the first breeding season they assume the dark slaty color, with traces of white on the winglet and lower surface in some; specimens in a state of change are, of course, much varied with white.

The Ashy Egret or White-throated Reef Heron is fairly common along the coast, but does not seem to occur far inland, unless on very large sheets of water.

GENUS, **Bubulcus**, *Pucheran.*

Bill somewhat short, stout, slightly curved along the culmen, smooth; feet longer, otherwise as in *Egretta*; assumes golden-yellow, hair-like plumes on the head, breast, and back during the breeding season.

Bubulcus coromandus, *Bodd.*

929.—Jerdon's Birds of India, Vol. II, p. 749; Butler, Guzerat; Stray Feathers, Vol. IV, p. 23; Deccan, Stray Feathers, Vol. IX, 434; Murray's Vertebrate Zoology of Sind, p. 271; Swinhoe and Barnes, Central India; Ibis, 1885, p. 136.

THE CATTLE EGRET.

Length, 21; expanse, 37; wing, 10·25; tail, 4; tarsus, 3·5; bill at front, 2·5.

Bill deep orange-yellow; orbitar region yellowish-pink; irides pale yellow; legs whitish-green on the tibia and to a little below the knee; rest of the tarsus blackish-green, with a reddish tinge on the toes, which are greenish below.

In summer dress, the whole head, which is crested, neck, and breast, rich golden-buff, except the chin, and a narrow median line on the neck; dorsal plumes of the same hue, very filamentose and decomposed, about eight or nine inches long; elongated feathers of the breast white at base, yellow at tip; the rest of the plumage pure white.

In non-breeding dress the plumage is entirely white; the bill yellow in place of orange, and the orbitar skin yellow.

The Cattle Heron is common throughout the district. In its breeding habits it resembles the other members of the family, but occasionally a colony of them may be found breeding alone or in company with the Pond Heron. Their eggs may be distinguished from those of all other herons by their excessive paleness.

GENUS, **Ardeola**, *Boie.*

Bill moderately long, straight, pointed; tarsus short, stout; feet moderately large; tibia feathered nearly to the knee; neck short, densely feathered; the feathers long and lax; toes long; dorsal plumes in the breeding season hair-like, dark; wing white.

Ardeola grayi, *Sykes.*

930.—*A. leucoptera*, Bodd.—Jerdon's Birds of India, Vol. II, p. 751; Butler, Guzerat; Stray Feathers, Vol. IV, p. 23; Deccan, Stray Feathers, Vol. IX, p. 434; Murray's Vertebrate Zoology of Sind, p. 272; Swinhoe and Barnes, Central India; Ibis, 1885, p. 136.

THE POND HERON.
Andhe bagla, Hin.

Length, 18·5; expanse, 28; wing, 8·5; tail, 3; tarsus, 2·4; bill at front, 2·5.

Bill yellowish, blue at base, black at tip; orbits greenish-yellow; irides bright yellow; legs and feet dull green.

Adult in full breeding plumage has the head crested, with long occipital white plumes; head and neck greyish yellow; the back with the feathers decomposed, dark maroon; wings, rump and upper tail-coverts, tail, and all beneath, white.

In non-breeding dress, the head, neck, and breast, are fulvous with brown stripes, darkest on the head; the upper plumage pale ashy-brown; wings, (except the uppermost tertials) white, and the lower parts from the breast white; thigh-coverts fulvous.

The Pond Heron is a common permanent resident throughout the district.

GENUS, **Butorides**, *Blyth.*

Bill rather long, straight, moderately stout; neck short, thickish; tibia feathered nearly to the joint; tarsus short; inner-toe short; head crested; feathers of the back and scapulars highly lanceolate; plumage dull blue.

Butorides javanica, *Horsf.*

931.—Jerdon's Birds of India, Vol. II, p. 752; Butler, Guzerat; Stray Feathers, Vol. IV, p. 24; Deccan, Stray Feathers, Vol. IX, p. 434; Murray's Vertebrate Zoology of Sind, p. 272; Swinhoe and Barnes, Central India; Ibis, 1885, p. 136.

THE LITTLE GREEN HERON.

Length, 16 to 17; wing, 7; tail, 2·25; tarsus, 1·9; bill, 2·5.

Bill black, pale yellow beneath; lores yellowish-green; irides bright yellow; legs pale yellow-green; the soles dark yellow.

Head, with lengthened occipital crest, glossy black; a short black line from below the eye, between which and the black head the ear-coverts are greyish-white; back and sides of neck ashy-grey; feathers of the back, including the scapulars and feathers covering the tertials, lengthened, lanceolate, dull green; the upper ones with an ashy tinge; rump reddish-ashy; upper tail-coverts greenish; wing-coverts glossy green, edged with pale fulvous; quills dark slaty, narrowly tipped with white, and passing into green on the tertials, edged with fulvous; tail dark slaty, and the lower plumage, with the thigh-coverts, ashy, with a central line down the neck to the breast whitish; the feathers being white at the base and becoming albescent on the vent and under tail-coverts.

The Little Green Heron or Bittern is a common permanent resident throughout the district, breeding in a similar manner to the other members of the family.

The following table may be of some use as it gives the average dimension of the eggs; but they are so much alike, that it is advisable always to shoot a bird off the nest to avoid mistakes.

Jerdon's Number.	Names.		Dimensions.		Color.
			Length.	Breadth.	
923	Ardea cinerea...	...	2·27	1·66	Delicate bluish or sea-green.
924	Ardea purpurea	...	2·17	1·56	Do. do. do.
925	Herodias torra	...	2·11	1·55	Do. do. do.
926	Herodias intermedia	...	1·9	1·44	Do. but rather paler.
927	Herodias garzetta	...	1·73	1·32	Do. do. do.
928	Demi-egretta gularis	...	1·68	1·3	Do. but still more pale.
929	Bubulcus coromandus	...	1·71	1·32	White, faintly tinged greenish or bluish.
930	Ardeola grayi ...	...	1·48	1·17	Rather deep sea green or greenish or bluish.
931	Butorides javanica	...	1·62	1·21	Greenish.
937	Nycticorax griseus	...	1·92	1·35	Do.

GENUS, **Ardetta,** *Gray.*

Bill slender, straight; tibia feathered nearly to the joint; tarsus short; toes lengthened and strong; claws long, of small or moderate size; plumage of neck more or less lengthened, as in the Bittern; of nocturnal habits.

Ardetta flavicollis, *Latham.*

932.—Jerdon's Birds of India, Vol. II, p. 753; Murray's Vertebrate Zoology of Sind, p. 273.

THE BLACK BITTERN.
Kala Bagla, Hin.

Length, 23 to 24; expanse, 30; wing, 8·5; tail, 3; tarsus, 2·5; bill at front, 3·5.

Bill livid red-brown; culmen dusky; cere livid purple; irides yellow; legs pale brown, with a tinge of green in some, reddish-brown in others.

Plumage above (in breeding season) dull cinereous black; chin and throat with the feathers white, tipped with red-brown; the large feathers of the neck mixed with white, red-brown, and dusky-black; each feather having some black at the base and tip, and more or less red-brown on one web only; a stripe of golden-yellow down the side of the neck, widening inferiorly; feathers of the back lengthened, but not decomposed, forming a dorsal plume; the feathers of the breast dark ashy, slightly lengthened; abdomen dusky, mixed with whitish; inner wing-coverts dusky-reddish.

The young bird has the feathers slightly edged with rufous, and the throat and neck less richly colored than in the adult.

The Black Bittern, within our limits, has only been recorded from Sind. Mr. Doig found them breeeding on the Narra Canal in the month of May. He says the nests are formed of tamarisk twigs and occasionally a few aquatic weeds, and that the eggs, always four in number, are broad ovals, pointed at both ends, and are nearly white in color.

They measure 1·7 by 1·22.

Ardetta cinnamomea, *Gm.*

933.—Jerdon's Birds of India, Vol. II, p. 755; Butler, Deccan, Stray Feathers, Vol. IX, p. 434; Murray's Vertebrate Zoology of Sind, p. 274.

THE CHESNUT BITTERN.
Lal Bagla, Hin.

Length, 16; expanse, 22; wing, 6; tail, 1·75; tarsus, 2; bill at front, 2.

Bill yellow; culmen dusky; cere yellow; irides yellow; legs greenish yellow, with yellow soles.

Above, fine chesnut color, with a tinge of cinereous on the crown; beneath fulvous, whitish on the throat, and with a pectoral gorget of feathers, dark brown in the centre; thigh-coverts cinnamomeus; lower surface of the wings dull ashy.

The young bird has the plumage streaked, the feathers being reddish-brown in the centre with pale yellowish margins.

The Chesnut Bittern occurs both in Sind and in the Deccan. I have not heard of its occurrence in Guzerat, but most probably it will be found to occur there.

It is probably only a seasonal visitant.

Ardetta sinensis, *Gm.*

934.—Jerdon's Birds of India, Vol. II, p. 755; Butler, Guzerat; Stray Feathers, Vol. V, p. 216; Deccan, Stray Feathers, Vol. IX, p.434; Murray's Vertebrate Zoology of Sind, p. 274.

THE YELLOW BITTERN.

Length, 14 to 15; wing, 5·25; tail, 1·75; tarsus, 1·75; bill at front, 2·25.

Bill pale yellow; culmen brownish; irides yellow; legs and feet pale green.

Adult, top of head black; back of neck cinnamon rufous; face, sides of neck and breast pale fulvous yellow, white on the chin; back and scapulars pale earthy or sandy brown; wing-coverts and tertiaries pale isabelline-fulvous, the latter verging to pale brownish; quills and tail black; sides of the breast deep brown, edged with pale yellow, passing to white on the vent and under tail-coverts; back of neck and rest of lower plumage yellowish-white, passing to white.

The young bird has the upper plumage more or less cinnamon-brown, mixed with pale fulvous, and some of the occipital feathers blackish brown.

The Yellow Bittern is not very common in Sind; it occurs also in Guzerat, but is rare in the Deccan. Captain Butler found it breeding at Milana, about 18 miles east of Deesa. The nest, composed of sedges, was built in a dense clump of bulrushes. The eggs, three in number, were of a pale skim-milk blue color and were about 1·25 inches in length.

Ardetta minuta, *Lin.*

935.—Jerdon's Birds of India, Vol. II, p. 756; Murray's Vertebrate Zoology of Sind, p. 274.

THE LITTLE BITTERN.

Length, 14; wings, 5·75; tail, 2; tarsus, 1·5; bill at front, 1·75.

Bill bright yellow, dusky above, round the eyes yellow; irides yellow; feet yellowish-green.

Top of head, occiput, back, scapulars, and tail, glossy black; small wing-coverts and the upper three-fourths of the other coverts pale sienna-yellow, the lower fourth more or less white; quills ashy-black; cheeks, neck, and all the lower surface of the body pale rufescent, tinged with purplish yellow on the neck, and with brown streaks on the flanks.

Within our limits the Little Bittern has only been recorded from Sind, where Mr. Doig obtained the eggs.

GENUS, Botaurus, *Brisson.*

Bill rather short, stout, higher at the base than broad; the upper mandible curved towards the point; tarsi short; tibia feathered for the greater portion of its length; feet very long; claws long, moderately curved; neck short, densely feathered and thick.

Botaurus stellaris, *Lin.*

936.—Jerdon's Birds of India, Vol. II, p. 757; Butler, Guzerat; Stray Feathers, Vol. IV, p. 24; Deccan, Stray Feathers, Vol. IX, p. 436; Murray's Vertebrate Zoology of Sind, p. 275.

THE BITTERN.

Length, 26 to 30; expanse, 46; wing, 13; tail, 4·5; tarsus, 3·75; bill at front, 3.

Bill brown, below pale yellow; orbits pale yellow; irides bright gamboge-yellow; legs greenish-yellow.

Crown of head and a broad moustache black; neck ochre-yellow, with brown zigzag lines on the sides, and long streaks and spots of brown in front; upper plumage ochre-yellow with a tinge of reddish, each feather marked with a dusky spot; primaries and secondaries dark ferruginous, with bars of blackish-brown; all the coverts (except the primary) and the scapulars, mottled yellow and dusky; beneath, the same, but paler, and with large dusky streaks.

The Bittern is a rare bird; it occurs in Sind, and has been recorded from one or two localities in the Deccan. It is a cold weather visitant only.

Goisakius melanolophus, *Raffl.*

936*bis.*—Butler, Deccan; Stray Feathers, Vol. IX, p. 435.

THE MALAYAN TIGER BITTERN.

Length, 17 to 19·62; expanse, 29·5 to 37; wing, 9·12 to 10·37; tarsus, 2·3 to 2·69; bill at front, 1·8; bill from gape, 2·4.

Bare skin at base of bill green; bill horny-brown, greenish-horny beneath; irides greenish-yellow; legs and feet greenish-olive.

Crown of head and nape black; the feathers of the occiput lengthened into a full crest, and each irregularly marked with a white spot across its centre, and a smaller white tip; the feathers of the forehead and above the eyes black, with ochreous instead of white spots, forming an obscure bar above the eye; cheeks and sides of throat pale ochreous, with narrow zigzag lines of black across the feathers; the mantle chesnut, freckled and irregularly barred with narrow zigzag lines of black; upper tail-coverts dull black, with white dots.

Tail, above, dark slaty or bluish-black; quills black, tipped with white; the base of the white tinged with chesnut and mottled with black; greater-coverts of first three primaries black, broadly tipped white; the base of the white on the outer webs tinged with chesnut, which is closely freckled with black blotches and spots, and replaced at the extreme tip by white less densely freckled; two or three small feathers at the angle of the wing pure white.

Under primary-coverts pale ochreous, closely barred with black, and the larger feathers broadly tipped white; rest of under wing-coverts barred black and white.

Chin and throat white, faintly tinged with ochreous, and with an obscure central streak of black dots; throat rich chesnut, minutely banded with black bars; centre of the breast like the throat, with two lateral streaks of ochreous (one on either side) formed by some of the feathers continuously being paler chesnut and free from all black but a few dots.

Abdominal feathers pale ochreous-chesnut, with small dots and obscure bars of black, but mostly with a white central streak; elongated feathers of the abdominal train paler ochreous, very faintly and sparsely dotted with black, and with the central streak of white more apparent; coverts of tibia ochreous, mottled with dull black; under tail-coverts white, tinged on their outer margins with ochreous and speckled with black dots.—*T. W. Bourdillon, Stray Feathers,* Vol. VII, p. 525.

The Malayan Tiger Bittern is extremely rare; the only specimen recorded from our district was obtained by Mr. Laird in the forests west of Belgaum.

GENUS, Nycticorax, *Steph.*

Bill short, stout; culmen curved; wings with third quill

longest; tarsus short, reticulated in front, with large hexagonal scales; feet moderate; claws short, curved; head crested; tail broad, even.

Nycticorax griseus, *Lin.*

937.—Jerdon's Birds of India, Vol. II, p. 758; Butler, Guzerat; Stray Feathers, Vol. IV, p. 24; Deccan, Stray Feathers, Vol. IX, p. 435; Murray's Vertebrate Zoology of Sind, p. 276; Swinhoe and Barnes, Central India; Ibis, 1885, p. 136.

THE NIGHT HERON.

Wak, Hin.

Length, 21 to 23; wing, 12·5; tail, 3·75; tarsus, 3; bill at front, 2·8.

Bill black, yellowish at base; lores and orbits yellowish-green; irides blood-red; feet yellowish-green.

Forehead and a narrow streak above the eye white; crown of the head, upper part of back, and scapulars, black, glossed with green; occiput with a crest of three (or more) narrow long white feathers, six to seven inches long, channeled, and fitting into each other; lower back, wings, and tail fine blue-grey; all beneath pure white.

The young bird wants the occipital plumes; the upper plumage is brownish ashy, with whitish spots; and the lower plumage whitish with brown streaks.

The Night Heron is a common and permanent resident in most parts of our district. It breeds during the rains, making a large loose stick nest, generally associating in colonies, with other species of herons, &c.

FAMILY, **Tantalidæ.**

Bill long, more or less thick, arched in many; the culmen rounded and bent; nostrils usually basal; wings long; tail rather short; tarsus long or moderate; feet moderate; anterior toes joined at the base by web; hind-toe moderate, or rather short, resting on the ground.

SUB-FAMILY, **Tantalinæ.**

Bill very large, thick, rounded, smooth; legs long.

GENUS, **Tantalus**, *Lin.*

Bill lengthened, straight; culmen rounded; the tip bent down, slightly emarginated; nostrils basal, superior; head, cheeks, and throat bare; legs lengthened; tibia nude for half its length; tarsus long, reticulated; toes moderately long, with a web between the front toes; hind-toe moderately long, slightly raised.

Tantalus leucocephalus, *Forster.*

938.—Jerdon's Birds of India, Vol. II, p. 761; Butler, Guzerat;

Stray Feathers, Vol. IV, p 24; Deccan, Stray Feathers, Vol. IX, p. 435; Murray's Vertebrate Zoology of Sind, p. 276; Swinhoe and Barnes, Central India; Ibis, 1885, p. 136.

THE PELICAN IBIS.

Length, 42; expanse, 72; wing, 20; tail, 7; tarsus, 7·75; bill at front, 9 to 10.

Bill deep yellow, tip greenish, as also are the naked orbits, head and gular skin; irides pale yellow-brown; legs fleshy-red.

Plumage white; the quills and tail richly glossed green-black; tertiaries white, beautifully tinged with rosy, with a darker band near the end, and a white tip; the feathers loose and decomposed; lesser and median-coverts glossy green, with white edges; greater-coverts pure white.

In summer the tertiaries acquire a deeper rosy tint, and the bill and nude parts become of a brighter and deeper yellow.

The young bird has the plumage generally brown, paler on the back and rump, dark on the wing-coverts; beneath more or less albescent, with a broad brown patch on the sides of the abdomen; bill pale greenish-yellow.

The Pelican Ibis, or Painted Adjutant, is generally distributed throughout the region. It is a permanent resident. I found a colony of these birds breeding in March, at Hir, about ten miles from Neemuch; the nests, considering the size of the birds, were very frail; they were composed of twigs, and the eggs could be seen from below; there were fifty or sixty nests, and none contained more than four eggs, but they were all fresh, and possibly they may lay more. The eggs are elongated ovals, much compressed at one end; the shell is fine and compact, of a dull white color.

They measure 2·76 inches in length by about 1·9 in breadth.

SUB-FAMILY, Plataleinæ.

Bill very broad, flat, and depressed.

GENUS, Platalea, *Lin.*

Bill long, very broad, depressed and thin, dilated, and rounded at the extremity like a spatula; nostrils basal, oblong, apert; wings moderate, second quill longest; tibia bare for nearly half its length; tarsus moderately long, reticulated; the three anterior toes united at the base by a deeply cut web; head and face more or less nude.

Platalea leucorodia, *Lin.*

937.—Jerdon's Birds of India, Vol. II, p. 763; Butler, Guzerat; Stray Feathers, Vol. IV, p. 24; Deccan, Stray Feathers, Vol. IX, p. 433; Murray's Vertebrate Zoology of Sind, p. 277; Swinhoe and Barnes, Central India; Ibis, 1885, p. 136.

THE SPOONBILL.

Length, 31 to 36; wing, 14·5 to 16; tail, 6·5; tarsus, 5 to 6; bill at front, 7·8 to 8·5.

Bill black, (more or less mottled with yellowish undulations during the winter), ochry-yellow at the tip; irides blood-red; naked skin of face and gular skin orange-yellow; legs black.

Plumage pure white, with a patch of buffy-yellow on the upper part of the breast, extending up the sides towards the back; the crest composed of long subulate and canaliculate feathers placed on the occiput.

The young wants the crest, has the shafts of the quills and the tips of the primaries black, the naked orbits dingy-white, and bill dark ashy, soft and flexible. The patch of buff is said not to appear till the second or third year.

The Spoonbill is more or less common throughout the region. It breeds in Sind during October and November in company; the nests are large platforms, composed of sticks. The eggs, four or five in number, are elongated ovals in shape, a good deal pointed at one end; they are white in color, more or less spotted with brown or yellowish-brown. They measure 2·7 by 1·81.

SUB-FAMILY, Anastomatinæ.

Bill very thick, stout, coarse, gaping in the middle.

GENUS, Anastomus, *Illiger*.

Bill moderately long, not deeply cleft, very thick, solid, nearly straight; mandibles nearly equal, not meeting in the middle, but leaving a greater or lesser space gaping; upper mandible notched at the tip; nostrils basal, superior; wings moderately long, with second or third quills longest, sub-equal; tail moderate, nearly even; tibia naked for a considerable space; tarsi long, reticulated; feet rather short; the front toes joined at the base by web.

Anastomus oscitans, *Bodd.*

940.—Jerdon's Birds of India, Vol. II, p. 765; Butler, Guzerat; Stray Feathers, Vol. IV, p. 24; Deccan, Stray Feathers, Vol. IX, p. 435; Murray's Vertebrate Zoology of Sind, p. 277; Swinhoe and Barnes, Central India; Ibis, 1885, p. 136.

THE SHELL IBIS.

Length, 29 to 32; expanse, 50 to 54; wing, 16·5 to 17; tail, 7; tarsus, 5·5; bill at front, 6·25.

Bill dull greenish, tinged with reddish beneath; nude orbits and gular skin blackish; irides grey or pale brown; legs pale fleshy.

General color of the plumage pale ashy-grey, tinged with reddish on the head and neck; the winglet, primaries, secondaries, tertials, scapulars, and tail, black.

The Shell Ibis occurs sparingly throughout the province; in most places it is only a cold weather visitant, but in Sind it breeds during August. The nests are platforms composed of twigs. The eggs, four or five in number, are of an oval shape, of a creamy-white color when fresh, but soon get stained as incubation proceeds.

They measure 2·24 by 1·6.

SUB-FAMILY, Ibisinæ.

Bill long, thin, curved.

GENUS, Ibis, *Bonap.*

Bill very long, moderately stout, thickened at the base, somewhat square, arched more or less throughout; the upper mandible with a long lateral groove produced to the tip; nostrils basal, narrow; wings long, the second quill longest, or the third and fourth sub-equal to it; tail short, even, of twelve feathers; tarsus moderate; toes long, hallux resting on the ground; head and neck of the adult devoid of feathers; scapulars and tertials decomposed, lengthened; feathers of the breast elongated; plumage white.

Ibis melanocephala, *Lath.*

941.—Jerdon's Birds of India, Vol. II, p. 768; Butler, Guzerat; Stray Feathers, Vol. IV, p. 25; Butler, Deccan, Stray Feathers, Vol. IX, p. 435; Murray's Vertebrate Zoology of Sind p. 278; Swinhoe and Barnes, Central India; Ibis, 1885, p. 136.

THE WHITE IBIS.

Length, 29; expanse, 45; wing, 14; tail, 5·75; tarsus, 4; bill at front, 6.

Bill black; irides red-brown; legs black.

Head and neck nude, black; rest of the plumage white, the quills black with green reflections; scapulars and tertials with the barbs disunited and open, lengthened, of a dull inky-purple or quaker-grey; winglet, primary coverts, under wing-coverts and axillaries, creamy-white.

The young have the head and neck more or less clothed with short white feathers, which gradually fall off, and they want the lengthened scapulars.

The White Ibis is more or less common throughout the district. It is probably a permanent resident in most places; it breeds in Sind during October, November, and December.

GENUS (Geronticus) Inocotis.

Bill more slender and longer than in the last; tarsi robust, covered anteriorly with hexagonal scales; toes somewhat short, stout; top of the head only nude; plumage dark; wings long ample.

Inocotis papillosus, *Tem.*

942.—Jerdon's Birds of India, Vol. II, p. 769; Butler, Guzerat; Stray Feathers, Vol. IV, p. 24; Butler, Deccan, Stray Feathers, Vol. IX, p. 435; Murray's Vertebrate Zoology of Sind, p. 278.

THE BLACK OR WARTY-HEADED IBIS.

Length, 25 to 30; expanse, 48; wing, 14 to 15; tail, 7; tarsus, 3; bill, 6.

Bill greenish-leaden; irides dull orange-red; legs and feet brick-red.

Head nude, black, with a triangular patch of bright red papillæ or warts on the back of the head, the point of the triangle just above the eyes; neck and body above fuscous brown, nearly black on the upper tail-coverts; wings glossy steel-blue, mixed with purple, and a large white patch on the innermost lesser coverts; quills dusky black; lower parts dark blackish-brown; under tail-coverts glossed with blue.

The Black Ibis is fairly common throughout the region; it is a permanent resident, breeding during the monsoon. The nests are more often solitary than otherwise. The eggs, three or four in number, are moderately long ovals, more or less pointed at one end, and are of a beautiful sea-green, but are somewhat coarse in texture. They are occasionally spotted.

They measure 2·43 inches in length by about 1·7 in breadth.

The nests are usually found on the tops of high trees, and are composed of twigs and fine sticks. Occasionally the deserted nest of some other species is appropriated.

GENUS, Falcinellus, *Bechst.*

Bill long, slender; tarsi lengthened, scutellated anteriorly; toes long and slender, otherwise as in the last; wings with the second and third primaries longest; face nude.

Falcinellus igneus, *Gmelin.*

943.—Jerdon's Birds of India, Vol. II, p. 770; Butler, Guzerat; Stray Feathers, Vol. IV, p. 24; Deccan, Stray Feathers, Vol. IX, p. 436; Murray's Vertebrate Zoology of Sind, p. 279.

THE GLOSSY IBIS.

Length, 22; expanse, 38; wing, 10·75; tarsus, 4·5; bill at front, 6.

Bill dull pale greenish; irides brown; lores and nude orbits pale green; legs blackish-green, with a blue garter above the knee.

Adult: head, neck, breast, upper back, and all the under parts fine chesnut-red, tinged with brown on the head; lower back, rump, wing-coverts, quills and tail dark green, with bronze and purplish reflections.

The young birds of the year are ashy-brown, with white markings on the head and breast. After the moult they are brown on the head and neck, the feathers whitish edged; the back greenish-brown; wings and tail as in the adult, but less glossed; the lower neck, belly, breast, and thigh-coverts, dusky black, with more or less greenish reflections on the breast; lores whitish.

The Glossy Ibis is somewhat rare in the Deccan; it is rather more common in Guzerat, but in Sind it is a common permanent resident.

Mr. Doig found them breeding in some numbers in June, in high trees on the borders of lakes inside the sand hills along the banks of the Narra Canal.

He says they build a stick nest, and that the eggs, usually three in number, are oval in shape, pointed at each end. They are of a beautiful green color, and measure about 2 inches in length by 1·4 in breadth.

Order, **Natatores.**

Feet more or less fully webbed, the legs placed far backwards on the body, and the tarsi compressed, adapting them for swimming; bill and wings varied; plumage very thick and close, with a quantity of down next the skin, in some families impregnated with oil; the hind-toe is occasionally absent, and always small. In one family the toes are free, only bordered by a wide web.

Tribe, **Lamellirostres.**

Bill thick, depressed, broad, covered with a soft skin, the tip alone being horny; the edges in most furnished with numerous laminæ; wings moderately long, first and second quills sub-equal, or second longest.

Family, **Phænicopteridæ.**

Neck and legs of enormous length; bill suddenly bent down.

Genus, **Phænicopterus,** *Lin.*

Bill high at the base, suddenly bent down; the margin lamellate and dentate; legs very long; tibia bare to a considerable extent; tarsus scutellate; feet short; wings moderate, first and second quills sub-equal, longest; neck very long.

Phænicopterus antiquorum, *Tem.*

944.—*P. roseus*, Pall.—Jerdon's Birds of India, Vol. II, p. 775; Butler, Guzerat; Stray Feathers, Vol. IV, p. 25; Deccan, Stray Feathers, Vol. IX, p. 436; Murray's Vertebrate Zoology of Sind, p. 280.

THE FLAMINGO.

Length, 52; wing, 16·5; tail, 6; bill, 4; tarsus, 12; mid-toe, 3·5; weight, 10 lbs.

Bill rosy, black at tip; irides pale golden-yellow; legs and feet pale rosy-red.

Throughout of a rosy-white, the rose color more marked on the head, back, and tail; wing-coverts (except the primary coverts, which are white) and the tertiaries, fine rosy-red; quills black, the last of the secondaries white; lower wing-coverts black.

The female is smaller, and the young birds have the upper plumage, especially the wing-coverts, mixed with brown and dusky spots, and hardly any rosy tinge.

The Flamingo occurs as a cold weather visitant throughout the district. It is very common on all the larger lakes in Sind, becoming less so further south.

In the Deccan it is somewhat rare.

Phænicopterus minor, *Geoff. St. Hill.*

944*bis.*—Murray's Vertebrate Zoology of Sind, p. 281; Butler, Guzerat; Stray Feathers, Vol. IV, p. 25; Deccan, Stray Feathers, Vol. IX, p. 436.

THE LESSER FLAMINGO.

Length, 33 to 35; wing, 12·5 to 13·75; tail, 4·5 to 4·75; tarsus, 7·5 to 8·5; bill from gape, 3 5.

Bill bright crimson-lake, deep vinous-red at base, black at tip; irides yellow; legs and feet deep brilliant red.

In winter plumage the head, neck, and the whole body above and below is a delicate pale rose color; on the back little more than white, tinged with rosy; the scapulars are almost white, with a pale rosy streak down the centre; the quills are black, except the tertials, which are like the scapulars, but slightly pinker; the wing-coverts are pale rosy-white, the lesser and median broadly centred at the tip with a bright rather pale cerise; the feathers of the upper portion of the back are many of them similarly centred, and over the broad rosy-white scapulars a number of comparatively narrow, elongated, intensely cherry colored plumes (which reach as far down as the end of the closed wing) have been thrown out; the whole visible portion of the secondary, lesser and median-coverts have become the most brilliant cherry color with only narrow white tips; and the lower tail-coverts, flanks and vent feathers are bright rosy, tinged with cherry color, with only narrow white tips.

The Lesser Flamingo is far less common than *P. antiquorum* with whom it associates.

FAMILY, Cygnidæ.

Neck very long; legs moderate; front toes broadly webbed; hind-toe not lobed; keel long; bill high at the base, with a fleshy or callous tubercle.

SUB-FAMILY, Cygninæ.

Bill long as head, with a soft cere; bill equally broad throughout; front toes with large web.

GENUS, Cygnus.

Cere extending to eye, tip horny; wings, second and third quills longest; tail short and rounded.

Cygnus olor, *Gm.*

944*ter.*—Murray's Vertebrate Zoology of Sind, p. 282; Game Birds of India, Vol. III, p. 41.

THE MUTE SWAN.

Length, 60; expanse, 82; wing, 22·5; tail, 10; tarsus, 4; bill from gape, 3·75.

Bill reddish-orange, edges and tip black; irides dark brown; legs and feet black; callous tubercle at base of upper mandible and cere black.

Entire plumage white.

The Mute Swan was obtained on the Munchur Lake during an exceptionally severe winter by Mr. Watson in 1878. Dr. Stoliczka records that he noticed several Swans on the Runn of Cutch, but at too great a distance for it to be possible to identify them. The Mute Swan must be considered a very rare and uncertain cold weather visitant to Sind.

FAMILY, Anseridæ.

Bill moderate or short, narrower in front than behind, more or less raised at the base; legs rather long, set more forward on the body than the ducks; plumage of the sexes differing but slightly.

SUB-FAMILY, Anserinæ.

Bill short, high at the base, conical; nail large, convex; laminar teeth more or less exposed, short; nostrils median, large; tarsus thick, lengthened; feet of moderate or rather small size; wings ample, moderately long, first and second quills longest; tail short, of 16 or 18 feathers; legs nearly central; tibia feathered nearly to the joint; neck moderately long; trachea simple.

GENUS, Anser, *Brisson.*

Bill very high at the base, about the length of the head; the lamellæ tooth-like, very apparent externally; nostrils a little behind the middle; toes moderately long; claws short and curved; neck moderately long; of large size and grey plumage, the bill pale, and legs usually reddish.

Anser cinereus, *Mey.*

945.—Jerdon's Birds of India, Vol. II, p. 779; Butler, Guzerat; Stray Feathers, Vol. IV, p. 26; Murray's Vertebrate Zoology of Sind, p. 283; Game Birds of India, Vol. III, p. 55; Swinhoe and Barnes, Central India; Ibis, 1885, p. 136.

THE GREY GOOSE.

Length, 30 to 35; expanse, 58 to 68; wing, 15·75 to 19·0; tail, 5·75 to 7·0; tarsus, 2·5 to 3·2; weight, 5¾ to 8⅞ lbs.

Bill creamy-white to pale livid fleshy-pink or dingy livid purplish-red; nail sullied white; irides brown.

Legs and feet vary in color, similar to the bill.

Head and neck clove-brown, tinged with grey, the forehead whitish; back, scapulars, greater and middle wing-coverts, clove-brown, the feathers broadly edged with greyish-white; lower back and upper tail-coverts bluish-ashy; lesser wing-coverts and base of the primaries bluish-grey; primaries black, shaded with grey, with the shafts white; secondaries black, edged with white; rump and sides of the upper tail-coverts white; tail brown, edged with white, the outermost one almost wholly white; breast and upper belly greyish white, undulated with bars of a deeper tint; lower abdomen and under tail-coverts white.

The Grey or Lag Goose of England is very common in Sind, occurring in all the larger lakes, and on the river; it is far from being uncommon in Guzerat, Central India and Rajputana; it does not occur in the Deccan.

It is a cold weather visitant only. It is very variable in plumage, scarcely two birds being found alike.

Anser albifrons, *Scop.*

947.—Jerdon's Birds of India, Vol. II, p. 780; Murray's Vertebrate Zoology of Sind, p. 284; Game Birds of India, Vol. III, p. 73.

THE WHITE-FRONTED GOOSE.

Length, 26 to 28; expanse, 52 to 56; wing, 15 to 15·75; tail, 5·2 to 6; tarsus, 2·45 to 2·75; bill from gape, 1·87 to 2; weight, $4\frac{5}{16}$ to $5\frac{9}{16}$ lbs.

Bill pale livid-fleshy; nail whitish or pale yellowish-white; irides pale brown; legs and feet bright orange.

Head and neck brownish, shaded with reddish; forehead and part of the cheeks white, surrounded by a dark brown band; body above dull ashy-brown, with reddish-white margins to the feathers; upper tail-coverts dark ashy, the longest white; lesser wing-coverts dull brown, slightly edged rufous; middle-coverts ashy-bluish, tipped white; primaries ashy-grey, black at the tip; secondaries black; tail ashy; the feathers edged and broadly tipped with white; plumage beneath brownish on the breast and flanks, passing into whitish-grey with spots and wide cross bands of black on the lower part of the breast, the upper abdomen and flanks; lower abdomen and under tail-coverts pure white.

Within our limits the White-fronted Goose is a comparatively rare cold weather visitant to Sind alone.

Anser indicus, *Lath.*

949.—Jerdon's Birds of India, Vol. II, p. 782; Murray's Vertebrate Zoology of Sind, p. 285; Game Birds of India, Vol. III, p. 81.

THE BARRED-HEADED GOOSE.

Length, 27·25 to 33·5; expanse, 56 to 66; wing, 16 to 19; tail, 5 to 7; bill from gape, 1·8 to 2·3; weight, 4 to $6\frac{4}{16}$ lbs.

Bill orange-yellow to orange; nail blackish; irides deep brown; legs and feet bright orange.

Head white, with two blackish bars on the occiput and nape; back of neck hair-brown, sides of neck white; upper plumage very pale ashy, the feathers edged with whitish and tinged with pale reddish brown; lower back and rump pure pale ashy-grey; sides of the rump and upper tail-coverts whitish; tail grey, white tipped; wing-coverts pure ashy; quills grey, dusky towards the tip, and gradually becoming darker on the secondaries; tertials brownish-grey; beneath, the chin and throat white; neck brownish-ashy, passing gradually into cinereous on the breast, whitish on the abdomen; vent and under tail-coverts white; flanks cinnamon-brown with pale edgings.

The Barred-headed Goose is very common in Sind during the cold season.

It only occurs occasionally in other parts of the district.

FAMILY, Anatidæ.

Bill flat, broad, laminated at the sides.

SUB-FAMILY, Plectropterinæ.

Wings generally with one or more spurs on the shoulder; bill, in most, furnished with a boss or protuberance at the base; legs in general long; plumage glossed black and white.

GENUS, Sarcidiornis, *Eyton*.

Bill lengthened, of nearly equal width throughout; that of the males usually furnished with a naked, compressed, fleshy protuberance on the culmen; wings with one or more tubercles or blunt spurs at the shoulder; first and second primaries subequal and longest; legs lengthened; feet large; tarsus with subquadrate scales of large size; plumage glossy black above; sexes nearly alike in color, but the males much larger than the females.

Sarcidiornis melanonotus, *Penn*.

950.—Jerdon's Birds of India, Vol. II, p. 785; Butler, Guzerat; Stray Feathers, Vol. IV, p. 27; Deccan, Stray Feathers, Vol. IX, p. 436; Murray's Vertebrate Zoology of Sind, p. 286; Game Birds of India, Vol. III, p. 91; Swinhoe and Barnes, Central India; Ibis, 1885, p. 136.

THE BLACK-BACKED GOOSE, OR COMB DUCK.

Nukta, Hin.

Length, ♂, 31·5, ♀, 26·4; expanse, ♂, 55, ♀, 46; wing, ♂, 15·37, ♀, 11·3; tail, ♂, 6·5, ♀, 4; tarsus, ♂, 2·87, ♀, 2·2; bill from gape, ♂, 2·8, ♀, 2·21; weight, ♂, 5¾ lbs, ♀, 3 lbs.

Bill and comb black; irides dark brown; legs greenish-plumbeous.

Head and neck white, spotted with glossy black; the top of the head and back of the neck mostly black; interscapulars and scapulars black, glossed with purple; back ashy-grey, becoming dusky on the rump; the upper tail-coverts glossy-green; wing-coverts glossed green; quills black; tail black; all the lower parts pure white. The female is much smaller, less brightly colored, more spotted on the neck, and she wants the fleshy boss at the base of the bill.

The Nukta or Comb Duck is more or less generally spread throughout the district. In Sind it is a mere straggler, and in the Deccan it is a far from common seasonal visitant, but in Guzerat, Central India, and Rajputana it is a permanent resident, breeding towards the end of the rains, in holes in trees. The eggs, usually twelve in number, (Mr. Anderson speaks of finding forty in a nest) are oval in shape, and are close and compact in texture, and resemble polished ivory both in color and appearance.

They measure 2·3 by 1·7.

SUB-FAMILY, Nettapodinæ.

Of small size; bill small, high at the base.

GENUS, Nettapus, *Brandt.*

Bill small, high at the base, gradually narrowing in front; the lamellæ short, distant concealed; nostrils small near the base; wings rather short; tail short, rounded, of twelve feathers; tarsus short; feet long; hind-toe short; claws short and curved.

Nettapus coromandelianus, *Gm.*

951.—Jerdon's Birds of India, Vol. II, p. 786; Butler, Deccan; Stray Feathers, Vol. IX, p. 436; Guzerat, Stray Feathers, Vol. IV, p. 27; Swinhoe and Barnes, Central India; Ibis, 1885, p. 137.

THE COTTON TEAL.

♂. Length, 12·62 to 13·5; expanse, 20·5 to 24; wing, 6·25 to 6·75; tail, 2·82 to 3·25; tarsus, 1; bill, 1 to 1·25; weight, 8 to 11 ozs.

♀. Length, 12·5 to 12·75; expanse, 21 to 22; wing, 6·25 to 6·37; tail, 2·8 to 3; bill from gape, 1 to 1·2; weight, 6·2 to 9 ozs.

Bill black; irides crimson; legs and feet from light yellowish to dirty sap-green.

Top of the head black; back, scapulars and wings richly glossed with purple and green, the purple prevailing on the back and scapulars; the wing-coverts and base of the quills green; rump blackish in the middle, white at the sides; upper tail-coverts cinereous brown with pale mottlings; tail blackish-brown; primary quills with a large white patch tipped with black on their terminal half, the white gradually diminishing in extent; the secondaries only tipped with white; tertials pure black, glossed green externally, purplish within; face, back of head, and whole neck and under parts pure white, with a black collar round the lower part of the neck; flanks white, with fine zig-zag brown lines; vent and under tail-coverts mottled, dusky and white.

The female is duller and more brown, above faintly glossed; the primaries want the white patch; the sides of the rump and upper tail-coverts are pale brown; the top of the head is dusky, and there is a dark stripe through the eyes; the neck is mottled with dusky lines, the under parts are dirty white, the flanks pale brown, and under tail-coverts whitish.

This miniature Goose is not uncommon in suitable localities (weed-grown tanks and jheels) in the Deccan; it is far more common in Central India and parts of Rajputana, but I cannot find any record of its occurrence in Guzerat, neither does it occur in Sind.

It is a permanent resident, breeding in July and August.

The eggs, ten or twelve in number, are generally placed in holes in trees; they are oval in shape, of a delicate ivory-white color, and measure 1·7 inches in length by about 1·29 in breadth.

SUB-FAMILY, Tadorninæ.

Bill more or less raised at the base, and flattened towards the tip; plumage more or less rufous.

GENUS, Dendrocygna, *Sws.*

Bill rather large, lengthened, of uniform width, slightly elevated at the base; wings short, broad, rounded; second, third, and fourth primaries sub-equal and longest; secondaries long; tarsus long and stout; feet large; hind-toe rather long.

Dendrocygna javanica, *Horsf.*

952.—*D. awsuree*, Sykes.—Jerdon's Birds of India, Vol. II, p. 789; Butler, Guzerat; Stray Feathers, Vol. IV, p. 27; Deccan, Stray Feathers, Vol. IX, p. 436; Murray's Vertebrate Zoology of Sind, p. 287; Game Birds of India, Vol. III, p. 110; Swinhoe and Barnes, Central India, Ibis, 1885, p. 137.

THE WHISTLING TEAL.

Length, 16 to 17·45; expanse, 27·25 to 30·3; wing, 7 to 8·04; tail, 2·3 to 3·02; tarsus, 1·6 to 1·92; bill from gape, 1·7 to 2·06; weight, 1 to 1¼ lbs.

Bill blackish; irides brown; orbits bright-yellow; legs and feet dark plumbeous.

Head and occiput dull wood-brown; face, ears, and neck, pale whity-brown, becoming darker on the back of the neck and upper back, and faintly edged with pale rusty; back and scapulars dusky-black, broadly edged with rusty-brown; rump glossy black; upper tail-coverts chesnut; tail brown with slightly paler edges; lesser and median wing-coverts fine rich maroon-red; greater-coverts and all the quills dusky-black; beneath, the chin and throat albescent; the neck whity-brown, passing into brown, yellowish on the lower neck, and gradually merging into the deep ferruginous or light chesnut of the whole of the lower surface; vent and under tail-coverts albescent.

The Whistling Teal is very common in Sind, fairly common in Central India and Rajputana, and not uncommon in Guzerat; in all these places, I believe, it to be a permanent resident; in the Deccan, where it is more or less rare, it only occurs as a seasonal visitant. The nest is usually placed on the lower limb of a largish tree, but occasionally old crow nests are utilized. The eggs, ten to fourteen in number, are of a broad oval shape, and are nearly pure white in color.

They measure 1·86 inches in length by 1·48 in breadth.

Dendrocygna fulva, *Gm.*

953.—*D. major*, Jerd.—Jerdon's Birds of India, Vol. II, p. 790; Butler, Guzerat; Stray Feathers, Vol. IX, p. 487; Murray's Vertebrate Zoology of Sind, p. 288; Game Birds of India, Vol. III, p. 119.

THE LARGER WHISTLING TEAL.

Length, 19·5 to 20·1; expanse, 36 to 36·75; wing, 8·75 to 9 2; tail, 3; tarsus, 2·5; bill from gape, 2·4; weight, 1 10/16 to 1 12/16 lbs.

Bill dusky-leaden, bluish at base; irides brown; legs and feet pale leaden or lavender-blue.

Head and neck chesnut, darker on the top of the head, whence a dark line extends down the back of the neck; chin, throat, and foreneck pale; in the centre of the neck there is a broad patch of small, whitish somewhat hackled feathers; upper part of the back and scapulars deep brown; the feathers edged with chesnut; lower part of the back black; lesser wing-coverts dark maroon; the other wing-coverts, wings, and tail, dusky black; lower plumage chesnut; under tail-coverts (and a few of the upper tail-coverts also) yellowish-white; the feathers of the flanks much lengthened, chesnut on one side, and yellowish-white on the other.

The Larger Whistling Teal is a rare seasonal visitant to the Deccan, and occurs also in Sind. I can find no record of its occurrence in any other portion of our limits.

GENUS, Casarca, *Bonap.*

Bill moderate, slightly raised at the base, depressed anteriorly, of uniform width; nail large; laminæ slender, very apparent; wings moderately long, when closed reaching to the end of the tail, which is short and slightly rounded, of fourteen or sixteen feathers; tarsus moderate, stout; toes long; hind-toe lobed.

Casarca rutila, *Pall.*

954.—Jerdon's Birds of India, Vol. II, p. 791; Butler, Guzerat; Stray Feathers, Vol. IV, p. 27; Deccan, Stray Feathers, Vol. IX, p. 437; Murray's Vertebrate Zoology of Sind, p. 288; Game Birds of India, Vol. III, p. 122; *Tadorna casarca*, Pall.; Swinhoe and Barnes, Central India; Ibis, 1885, p. 137.

THE RUDDY SHIELDRAKE.

♂ *Chakwa*, ♀ *Chakwi*, Hin.

♂. Length, 24·5 to 27·0; expanse, 48·0 to 52·5; wing, 14·25 to 15·5; tail, 5·4 to 6·3; tarsus, 2·3 to 2·7; bill from gape, 2·2 to 2·4; weight, 3 to $4\frac{1}{4}$ lbs.

♀. Length, 21·75 to 24·0; expanse, 42·5 to 47·75; wing, 12·36 to 14·0; tail, 5·06 to 6·0; tarsus, 2·12 to 2·4; bill from gape, 2·0 to 2·3; weight, $2\frac{1}{16}$ to $3\frac{5}{16}$ lbs.

Bill black; irides dark-brown; legs and feet black.

Male, forehead and cheeks pale ochreous-yellow or ferruginous; the region of the eyes, crown and nape, greyish-white; the rest of the neck ochreous-yellow, tinged with orange, surrounded by a glossy black collar nearly half an inch wide; the back and scapulars orange-fulvous, some of the feathers edged paler; upper tail-coverts glossy green black; lesser and middle wing-coverts white; greater-coverts green, glossed with purple; primaries black; secondaries glossy green; tertials bright fulvous; chin pale yellowish; breast and lower parts orange-fulvous, deepest on the breast.

The black collar is only seasonal and is never assumed by the female.

The Shieldrake or Brahminy Duck is a common cold weather visitant to all parts of the region; it is generally seen in pairs or small parties. It is an extremely wary, difficult bird to approach, and takes a pleasure in putting every bird within hearing on the *qui vive*, by keeping in front of the sportsman, but just out of range and uttering its warning note just at a critical moment. The best way to get rid of them is to indulge in a little rifle practice at their expense.

GENUS, Tadorna, *Leach.*

Bill short, high, and gibbous at the base, concave in the middle; the tip flattened and turning upwards, of nearly uniform breadth; the nail abruptly hooked; marginal lamellæ not projecting; wing tuberculated; tarsus moderate; feet rather short; tail of 16 feathers.

Tadorna cornuta, *S. G. Gm.*

956.—*T. vulpanser*, Flem.—Jerdon's Birds of India, Vol. II, p. 794; Murray's Vertebrate Zoology of Sind, p. 290; Game Birds of India, Vol. III, p. 135.

The Shieldrake.

♂. Length, 23·5 to 25·25; expanse, 41 to 46; wing, 12·5 to 13·6; tail, 4·75 to 5·5; tarsus, 2·1 to 2·3; bill from gape, 2·2 to 2·4; weight, $2\frac{1}{16}$ to $2\frac{14}{16}$.

♀. Length, 20·8 to 22; expanse, 39 to 42; wing, 11·75 to 12·4; tail, 4·2 to 4·9; tarsus, 1·95 to 2·07; bill from gape, 2·1 to 2·2; weight, 2 to $2\frac{5}{16}$ lbs.

Bill deep red; nail dusky; irides brown; legs and feet fleshy-pink to fleshy-red.

Male, head and upper part of neck deep blackish-green, with glossy reflections; lower part of the neck, back, and wing-coverts, rump, and base of the tail, white, the latter black tipped; scapulars black; primaries black; greater-coverts, forming the speculum, rich bronzed-green, three or four of the secondaries next the black, with their outer webs, rich orange-brown; lower plumage white; a broad band of ferruginous-brown across the breast, the ends passing upwards and uniting between the shoulders; a mesial line on the abdomen, widening at the vent, black; under tail-coverts pale reddish-brown.

The male is rather brighter in color than the female, and during the breeding season acquires a large fleshy knob at the base of the upper mandible.

The Shieldrake, within our limits, has only been recorded from Sind, where it occurs as a cold weather visitant. It affects the sea coast principally, but is occasionally found on the larger lakes.

Family, Anatidæ.

Bill broader at the base than high, shallow, depressed, of nearly equal width throughout, or wider at the tip; both mandibles with numerous transverse lamellæ; nostrils sub-basal or nearly median; tarsus moderately short, set far back on the body.

Sub-family, Anatinæ.

Hind-toe not bordered by a membrane; head of moderate size; neck long and more or less slender; bill usually of even width throughout, or wider at the tip, not raised at the base; lamellæ numerous, fine; legs set a little more forward than in the next group, and they can walk tolerably well; the wings of most are long, and they fly rapidly.

Genus, Spatula, *Boie*.

Bill long, the upper mandible wide, flattened in front of the nostrils and much dilated at the tip, or spatulate; the nail small; lamellæ very fine, like cilia, and projecting; tail slightly cuneate, of 14 feathers; tarsus short, cosmopolite.

Spatula clypeata, *Lin.*

957.—Jerdon's Birds of India, Vol. II, p. 796; Butler, Guzerat;

Stray Feathers, Vol. IV, p. 27; Deccan, Stray Feathers, Vol. IX, p. 437; Murray's Vertebrate Zoology of Sind, p. 290; Game Birds of India, Vol. III, p. 141; Swinhoe and Barnes, Central India; Ibis, 1885, p. 137.

THE SHOVELLER.

♂. Length, 19·7 to 21·75; expanse, 29·75 to 32·5; wing, 9 to 9·8; tail, 3·6 to 4; tarsus, 1·2 to 1·5; bill from gape, 2·95 to 3·05; weight, 1$\frac{3}{16}$ to 1$\frac{4}{16}$ lbs.

♀. Length, 18 to 19; expanse, 27 to 29·5; wing, 8 to 8·9; tail, 3·5 to 3·85; tarsus, 1·2 to 1·4; bill from gape, 2·65 to 2·87; weight, 1 to 1$\frac{7}{16}$ lbs.

Bill black, or leaden-dusky; in the female dark brown; irides vary from yellow to brown and reddish-orange; legs and feet vary from orange to Indian-red.

Male, head and upper part of the neck deep brown, with glossy green reflections; back dark umber-brown; scapulars white; rump and upper tail-coverts brown, glossed with blackish-green; the sides of the rump white; tail brown, the feathers edged with white, and the outer one wholly white; lesser wing-coverts pale greyish-blue; median, tipped with white; greater-coverts, forming the speculum, brilliant green; primaries umber-brown; tertials rich purplish-black; lower neck and breast white; abdomen brownish-red; lower tail-coverts brown, glossed with blackish-green.

The female has the head pale reddish-brown with fine dusky streaks; the rest of the upper parts dark brown, the feathers edged with reddish-white; lesser wing-coverts slightly tinged with pale blue; speculum not so bright as in the male; under parts reddish, with large round spots.

Towards the end of summer the male puts on a peculiar livery, something like that of the female, but with the head black.

The Shoveller is very common throughout the district, but it does not appear in such immense flocks as so many of the other ducks do, preferring to form small parties; it affects the edges of tanks in preference to open water. It is not a nice eating duck, and is not much sought after by sportsmen.

GENUS, Anas, *Lin.*

Bill of moderate length, depressed throughout, not so deep at the base as wide, nearly of uniform width; the lamellæ short, projecting very slightly; the tip rounded; nostrils near the base; tail short, of 16 feathers, the middle tail feathers of some more or less curled upwards.

Anas boschas, *Lin.*

958.—Jerdon's Birds of India, Vol. II, p. 798; Butler, Guzerat; Stray Feathers, Vol. IV, p. 27; Deccan, Stray Feathers, Vol. IX, p. 437; Murray's Vertebrate Zoology of Sind, p. 292; Game Birds of India, Vol. III, p. 151; Swinhoe and Barnes, Central India; Ibis, 1885, p. 137.

THE MALLARD.

♂. Length, 22·5 to 24·5; expanse, 35 to 38; wing, 10·45 to 11·3; tail, 4·2 to 4·8; tarsus, 1·6 to 1·85; bill from gape, 2·5 to 2·75; weight, 2½ to 3 lbs.

♀. Length, 20 to 21·75; expanse, 33 to 35; wing, 9·2 to 10·8; tail, 4·1 to 4·7; tarsus, 1·5 to 1·7; bill from gape, 2·47 to 2·63; weight, 1$\frac{10}{16}$ to 2$\frac{10}{16}$ lbs.

Bill dingy greenish-yellow; nail black; irides brown; legs and feet reddish-orange to vermilion-red.

Male, head and upper half of neck deep emerald-green, approaching to black on the cheeks and forehead; a white collar round the neck, hind-neck brown, with fine transverse grey lines; mantle chesnut-brown, with pale margins to the feathers; rump and upper tail-coverts blackish-green, the sides of the rump greyish-white, with fine transverse undulating line of clove-brown; scapulars greyish-white, with cross wavy brown marks, and some of the outer ones chesnut, with darker cross lines; wing-coverts and primaries brown; speculum deep Prussian-blue, with purple and green reflections, bounded on each side by a double border, the inner one velvet-black, the outer white; tail greyish-brown, all the feathers bordered with white; the four central feathers curled upwards; lower-neck and breast dark chesnut; abdomen and flanks greyish-white, with transverse undulating lines of brown; under tail-coverts blackish-green.

The female has the upper plumage brown, of different shades, the feathers edged with pale reddish-brown; the head and neck creamy-white or yellowish with dusky streaks; speculum much as in the male; throat buff or whitish; breast and under-parts yellowish-brown, obscurely spotted and streaked with darker brown, the central tail-feathers not turned up.

The Mallard is a common cold weather visitant to Sind; it is occasionally met with in Guzerat, but in Central India and the Deccan it is extremely rare, only occurring as a straggler. It is one of the very best ducks for the table.

Anas pœcilorhyncha, *Forst.*

959.—Jerdon's Birds of India, Vol. II, p. 799; Butler, Guzerat; Stray Feathers, Vol. IV, p. 29; Deccan, Stray Feathers, Vol. IX, p. 437; Murray's Vertebrate Zoology of Sind, p. 292; Game Birds of India, Vol. III, p. 165; Swinhoe and Barnes, Central India; Ibis, 1885, p. 137.

THE GREY OR SPOT-BILLED DUCK.

Length, 22 to 25·9; expanse, 32·5 to 38·5; wing, 9·2 to 11·2; tail, 4·9 to 5·8; tarsus, 1·7 to 1·93; bill from gape, 2·3 to 2·75; weight, 1$\frac{14}{16}$ to 3¼ lbs.

Bill black, red at base, yellow at tip; irides brown; legs and feet coral to vermilion-red, in young birds inclining to orange.

Top of the head and nape dark sepia-brown, with some pale

brown edgings; a dark brown line from the upper mandible through the eye ending in a point; supercilium, whole face, and neck dingy fulvous with small brown streaks, enlarging on the lower neck; upper plumage, including the lesser and median wing-coverts and scapulars, hair-brown; greater-coverts white, edged with deep black; primaries brown; secondaries, forming a conspicuous speculum, glossy green, with a black tip, narrowly edged with white on the innermost feathers; tertiaries white externally (forming a continuous line with the white coverts), hair-brown internally; lower back and rump black; tail deep brown; beneath, from the breast, pale earthy or dingy-white, with numerous brown spots, increasing in size on the abdomen and flanks; vent and under tail-coverts deep blackish-brown.

The Grey Duck is a more or less tolerably common permanent resident throughout the district. It is a very good eating bird, almost when in good condition rivalling the Mallard in flavor and delicacy. It breeds towards the close of the rains, making a nest amongst sedges and rushes. The eggs, six or seven in number, are broad ovals, white or greyish-white in color, measuring 2·16 inches in length by about 1·71 in breadth.

Anas (Rhodonessa) caryophyllacea, *Latham.*

960.—Jerdon's Birds of India Vol. II, p. 800; Butler, Deccan; Stray Feathers, Vol. IX, p. 437; Game Birds of India, Vol. III, p. 173; Swinhoe and Barnes, Central India; Ibis, 1885, p. 137.

The Pink-headed Duck.

Length, 24; wing, 10·75; tail, 4·75, expanse, 34·5; bill at front, 2·37; weight, 2 lbs.

Bill reddish-white, rosy at base, and faintly bluish at tip; irides deep orange-red; legs and feet dark slate or blackish.

Male, with the head, cheeks, sides of neck, and hind-neck, beautiful pale rosy-pink, with, in the breeding season, a small tuft of still brighter rosy on the top of the head; the rest of the plumage fine glossy dark chocolate-brown, paler and less glossed beneath; speculum and the inner webs of many of the quills pale reddish-fawn or dull salmon color; edge of the wing white; uppermost tertiaries rich glossy green; lower wing-coverts and quills beneath pale dull pink color, with a satiny lustre.

The female has the pink of the head somewhat more dull and pale, and the vertex has a brownish spot in some, which is continued faintly down the back of the neck.

Young birds have the head and neck pale vinous-isabella color, with the top of the head, nape, and hind-neck, brown; the whole plumage lighter brown, in some mixed with whitish beneath.

Colonel Swinhoe found the Pink-headed Duck very plentiful at the Depalpore Lake near Mhow. It does not appear to have been recorded from elsewhere within our limits.

GENUS, Chaulelasmus, *Gray*.

Bill equal to the head, depressed throughout, of nearly uniform width, but slightly narrowing towards the tip, which has a small nail; the lamellæ long, projecting; wings lengthened; tail rather long; the central feathers slightly lengthened.

Chaulelasmus streperus, *Linn*.

961.—Jerdon's Birds of India, Vol. II, p. 802; Butler, Guzerat; Stray Feathers, Vol. IV, p. 27; Deccan, Stray Feathers, Vol. IX, p. 438; Murray's Vertebrate Zoology of Sind, p. 293; Game Birds of India, Vol. III, p. 181; Swinhoe and Barnes, Central India; Ibis, Vol. III, p. 137.

THE GADWALL.

♂. Length, 19·4 to 21·5; expanse, 33 to 36·75; wing, 10·75 to 11·6; tail, 3·9 to 4·3; tarsus, 1·4 to 1·5; bill from gape, 2 to 2·22; weight, $1\frac{7}{16}$ to $2\frac{2}{16}$ lbs.

♀. Length, 18 to 20·1; expanse, 30 to 33·75; wing, 9 to 10·2; tail, 3·7 to 4·5; tarsus, 1·37 to 1·43; bill from gape, 1·94 to 2·1; weight, $1\frac{1}{16}$ to $1\frac{10}{16}$ lbs.

Bill brownish-black, tinged reddish beneath; irides dark-brown; legs yellowish brown to dull orange.

Male, head and neck greyish-white, speckled with brown; back dark clove-brown, with white crescentic lines; scapulars undulated with white and blackish-brown; rump and upper tail-coverts glossed with purplish-blue; tail cinereous-brown, edged and tipped with white; lesser wing-coverts grey, mixed with white; median wing-coverts rich brownish-chesnut; greater-coverts glossy black, speculum white above, black beneath; quills brown; tertials brownish-grey; lower part of the neck and breast dark brown with white crescentic lines; abdomen white, minutely speckled with greyish-brown, and the flanks with brown and white undulations; lower tail-coverts glossy-black.

The female has the head black mixed with whitish, a pale superciliary streak, the upper parts deep brown, the feathers edged with buff; the lesser wing-coverts hair-brown, margined paler; the speculum as in the male; the tail marbled with brown and whitish; the chin and throat whitish; breast pale buff, with brown spots, and the rest of the lower parts white; the bill paler and the margins reddish.

The female is very like that of the Mallard, but is smaller, and the speculum is white, opposed to the metallic purplish one of the Mallard.

The Gadwall is one of the commonest of the ducks, and occurs during the cold season throughout the district.

It is fairly good eating but not equal to either the Mallard or the Spot-bill.

Chaulelasmus angustirostris, *Men*.

961*bis*.—Butler, Guzerat; Stray Feathers, Vol. IV, p. 30; Murray's

Vertebrate Zoology of Sind, p. 294; Game Birds of India, Vol. III, p. 237.

THE MARBLED TEAL.

♂. Length, 18·3 to 19; expanse, 28·5 to 29·5; wing, 8·1 to 8·5; tail, 3·6 to 4; tarsus, 1·44 to 1·52; bill at front, 1·77 to 1·85; weight, 1 3/16 to 1 6/16 lbs.

♀. Length, 16·9 to 17·5; expanse, 27 to 28; wing, 7·9 to 8·1; tail, 2·8 to 3·7; tarsus, 1·4 to 1·5; bill at front, 1·6 to 1·75; weight, 1 to 1 3/16 lbs.

Bill dusky plumbeous, darker on culmen; irides dark brown; legs and feet greenish-plumbeous.

"The male has the forehead, crown, occiput, and nape brownish-white, with numerous narrow, close-set, wavy, irregular, dark brown bars, which become more speckly on the occiput, where also the ground color is a more rufescent-brown; feathers immediately round the eye very dark brown; a broad irregular stripe over the eye, and a large patch on the side of the head behind the eyes moderately dark brown, shading into the very dark brown immediately surrounding the eyes; the whole sides of the head below the dark eye and ear-patch, the whole chin, throat and front of neck, slightly greyish or brownish-white, very narrowly, regularly and closely streaked with brown; the lower parts a slightly brownish-white; the breast feathers with greyish-brown subterminal transverse bars, mostly more or less concealed by the pale tippings of the superincumbent feathers, and only clearly seen when the feathers are lifted; the sides and flanks similar, but the subterminal bars much broader, and some of the flank feathers with several bars; the vent-feathers and under tail-coverts, generally, with a slightly more rufescent tinge, and with two or more narrow, widely separated, transverse brown bars; the tibial plumes browner, and with numerous narrow, closely set, but ill marked, transverse brown bars; the abdomen more or less obsoletely mottled with pale grey-brown, which, on lifting the feathers, is found to arise from more or less faint, irregular, transverse, subterminal, brownish bars.

"The barrings above described are very much more marked in some specimens than in others, in some in fact they are almost entirely obsolete on the abdomen, and can hardly be traced.

"The upper back greyish-brown, the feathers with a subterminal richer brown bar; scapulars brown, each feather with a yellowish-white terminal spot, and of a much richer brown, the larger ones especially, just above the spot; the tertiaries and secondary greater coverts are greyish-brown, the former obsoletely barred paler; the secondaries are pale grey; the primaries their greater-coverts, and the winglet pale ashy, the primaries with a silver-grey tinge on the outer webs towards the tips, where they are much darker, and where the shafts also are conspicuously darker; the middle-back, rump, and upper tail-coverts the same grey-brown as the upper part of the back; the feathers of the middle back narrowly and obscurely tipped with yellowish-white, those of the rump and upper tail-coverts more broadly and conspicuously so, and with a subterminal dark brown spot; the longest of the upper tail-coverts are very broadly and conspicuously so tipped, and have a subterminal dark band; the tail-feathers pale grey-brown broadly tipped and narrowly margined with yellowish-white, the two central tail-feathers darker on the inner webs and dark shafted, and the lateral tail feathers paling as they recede from the centre.

"The female is similar, but smaller, with the eye-patch and generally all the markings and tints duller and less conspicuous." —*Stray Feathers*, Vol. I, p. 562.

The Marbled Teal is a common cold weather visitant to Sind, and occurs sparingly in Northern Guzerat, whence I have myself obtained it.

It is a most indifferent bird for the table and is not much sought after, when other species are obtainable.

GENUS, **Dafila**, *Leach.*

Tail long, of 16 feathers, with the central feathers much lengthened and narrow; neck very long; bill slightly narrower than in the preceding forms, and elevated at the base, equal to the head of uniform width; lamellæ not projecting; wings long, the first primary longest.

Dafila acuta, *Lin.*

962.—Jerdon's Birds of India, Vol. II, p. 803; Butler, Guzerat; Stray Feathers, Vol. IV, p. 27; Deccan, Stray Feathers, Vol. IX, p. 438; Murray's Vertebrate Zoology of Sind, p. 297; Game Birds of India, Vol. III, p. 189; Swinhoe and Barnes, Central India; Ibis, 1885, p. 137.

THE PINTAIL DUCK.

♂. Length, 22 to 29; expanse, 32 to 37·75; wing, 10·3 to 11·75; tail, 4·8 to 9·4; tarsus, 1·5 to 1·8; bill from gape, 2·0 to 2·45; weight, $1\frac{0}{16}$ to $2\frac{2}{16}$.

♀. Length, 20 to 22·5; expanse, 32 to 34·5; wing, 9·3 to 10·2; tail, 4·2 to 5·5; tarsus, 1·45 to 1·7; bill from gape, 2·1 to 2·35; weight, $1\frac{3}{16}$ to $1\frac{4}{16}$ lbs.

Bill black, sides of upper mandible bluish; irides dark-brown; legs greyish plumbeous.

Male, forehead and crown umber-brown, the feathers with paler edges; the rest of the head, chin, and throat, dark hair-brown, slightly glossed behind the ears with purplish-green; forepart of the neck and two lateral streaks, passing upwards to the occiput, white; neck above deep blackish-brown; the whole of the back beautifully marked with transverse undulating lines of black and greyish-white; scapulars black; upper tail-coverts and tail dark cinereous-brown, the edges of the feathers paler, and the two central elongated tail feathers black; wing-coverts and primaries hair-brown; lesser wing-coverts smoke-grey; the speculum blackish-green, glossed with purple, bordered above by a pale ferruginous bar, and below by a white one; tertiaries long and acuminate, velvet-black, with a broadish edging of greyish or yellowish-white; breast and abdomen white, the sides of both with transverse black and whitish lines, and the latter minutely speckled with grey towards the vent; under tail-coverts black.

The female has the head and neck reddish-brown, speckled and streaked with dusky; the upper plumage umber-brown, the feathers edged with reddish-white; wing-coverts brown, edged white; lower parts pale fulvous, obscurely spotted with brown; speculum dull without the green gloss; tail, with the two medial feathers, scarcely longer than the others.

The Pintail is common in Sind during the cold season; fairly common in Guzerat, and Central India; but is somewhat less common in the Deccan. The Pintail is a very excellent bird for the table and is much sought after in consequence.

Genus, **Mareca**, *Stephens.*

Bill short, raised at the base, narrowing towards the tip; nail moderate; lamellæ distant, projecting in the middle of the bill; tail short, cuneate, of fourteen feathers; hind-toe small with a narrow web.

Mareca penelope, *Lin.*

963.—Jerdon's Birds of India, Vol. II, p. 804; Butler, Guzerat; Stray Feathers, Vol. IV, p. 30; Deccan, Stray Feathers, Vol. IX, p. 438; Murray's Vertebrate Zoology of Sind, p. 299; Game Birds of India, Vol. III, p. 197; Swinhoe and Barnes, Central India; Ibis, 1885, p. 137.

The Wigeon.

♂. Length, 19 to 19·5; expanse, 32·75 to 34·5; wing, 10 to 10·6; tail, 4 to 4·6; tarsus, 1·4 to 1·6; bill from gape, 1·7 to 1·82; weight, 1 $\frac{5}{16}$ to 1 $\frac{10}{16}$ lbs.

♀. Length, 17·8 to 19·25; expanse, 31·5 to 34; wing, 9·3 to 10·2; tail, 3·5 to 5·0; tarsus, 1·4 to 1·6; bill from gape, 1·68 to 1·8; weight, 1 $\frac{3}{16}$ to 1 $\frac{12}{16}$ lbs.

Bill pale delicate greyish-lavender or leaden, rarely a slaty-blue, with the nostrils, tip of upper, and all but the basal portion of the rami of the lower mandible, black, and often with a narrow black line along the margins of the upper mandible also. Sometimes only the tip of the lower mandible is black, the rest of the same blue as the upper one, but dingier; irides vary from hazel to deep brown; the legs and feet vary from pale drab-brown with a faint olive tinge, through dusky-leaden to light plumbeous; in all cases the webs are dusky, occasionally almost black, and very often with a dusky shade over the joints.

Male, forehead and crown creamy-yellow; rest of the head and upper part of the neck chesnut-red; the cheeks speckled with black; back minutely barred with transverse wavy lines of black and white; scapulars black, edged with white; tail blackish-grey; wing-coverts pure white; the greater-coverts with velvet-black tips, some of the lesser ones, near the body, pale greyish; quills cinereous-brown; speculum of three bars, the middle one glossy green, the upper and under ones black; chin and throat black; lower part of the neck and breast vinaceous-red; abdomen white; the flanks with black and white wavy lines; under tail-coverts black, glossed green.

The female has the head and neck fulvous-brown, speckled with dusky; the back and scapulars dusky brown with reddish edges; wing-coverts brown, edged with whitish; the speculum without the dark green gloss; the breast and belly much as in the male; the flanks rufous-brown with ashy tips; bill and legs more dusky than in the male.

During the cold season, the Wigeon is more or less common throughout the district; on its first arrival and for some weeks after it is good eating, but afterwards acquires a muddy flavor.

Genus, Querquedula, *Stephens.*

Bill of moderate length and of uniform width, slightly raised at the base; the lamellæ not apparent; the nail small, and the tip obtuse; wings long and pointed; tail wedge shaped, of 14 or 16 feathers.

Querquedula crecca, *Linn.*

964.—Jerdon's Birds of India, Vol. II, p. 806; Butler, Guzerat; Stray Feathers, Vol. IV, p. 30; Deccan, Stray Feathers, Vol. IX, p. 438; Murray's Vertebrate Zoology of Sind, p. 300; Game Birds of India, Vol. III, p. 205; Swinhoe and Barnes, Central India; Ibis, 1885, p. 137.

THE COMMON TEAL.

♂. Length, 14·5 to 15·85; expanse, 23·0 to 25·25; wing, 7·2 to 8·0; tail, 3·0 to 3·6; tarsus, 1·1 to 1·3; bill from gape, 1·65 to 1·8; weight, 10½ to 15 ozs.

♀. Length, 13·5 to 14·9; expanse, 22·5 to 25·0; wing, 6·5 to 7·4; tail, 2·9 to 3·5; tarsus, 1·0 to 1·2; bill from gape, 1·5 to 1·77; weight, 7 7/16 to 12 ozs.

Bill blackish; irides hazel-brown; legs and feet greyish-brown.

Male, crown of head, cheeks, front and sides of the neck, ferruginous-brown; on the sides of the head, enclosing the eye, a large patch of deep glossy green, passing off backwards to the nape in the form of a black band; back and scapulars beautifully marked with transverse undulating lines of black and white, some of the longer scapulars creamy-yellow with a portion of their outer webs velvet-black; tail hair-brown, the feathers edged

Pitasi

18 Jan

with white; wing-coverts brown, tinged with grey; the speculum, formed by the tips of the secondary-coverts, deep green in the middle, velvet-black at the sides, bordered above by a broad yellowish-white bar; chin black; lower part of the neck in front and breast reddish or creamy-white, with round black spots; abdomen white; lower tail-coverts blackish-brown, bordered at the sides with yellowish-white.

The female has the head, neck, and all the upper parts, dusky-brown, the feathers more or less broadly edged with pale reddish-brown; the throat, cheeks, and a band behind the eyes, yellowish-white, spotted with black; the speculum as in the male, and the under parts yellowish-white.

The Common Teal is most abundant throughout the entire region; it is one of the earliest ducks to arrive. It is excellent eating.

Querquedula circia, *Lin.*

965.—Jerdon's Birds of India, Vol. II, p. 807; Butler, Guzerat; Stray Feathers, Vol. IV, p. 30; Deccan, Stray Feathers, Vol. IX, p. 438; Murray's Vertebrate Zoology of Sind, p. 301; Game Birds of India, Vol. III, p. 215; Swinhoe and Barnes, Central India; Ibis, 1885, p. 137.

THE BLUE-WINGED TEAL.

♂. Length, 15·9 to 16·25; expanse, 25·0 to 27·25; wing, 7·4 to 8·1; tail, 3·3 to 3·8; tarsus, 1·0 to 1·3; bill from gape, 1·75 to 1·92; weight, $\frac{10}{16}$ to 1 lb.

♀. Length, 14·8 to 15·5; expanse, 23·0 to 25·5; wing, 7·0 to 7·5; tail from vent, 2·9 to 3·5; tarsus, 1·0 to 1·15; bill from gape, 1·7 to 1·85; weight, $\frac{8}{16}$ to $\frac{11}{16}$ lbs.

Bill blackish-brown; irides hazel; legs and feet dusky.

Male, crown, occiput, and a line down the back of the neck, umber-brown; over each eye a band of pure white, prolonged down the sides of the neck; cheeks and upper part of the neck chesnut-brown, with fine longitudinal streaks of white; back brown, glossed with green, the feathers edged with ashy and yellowish-brown; scapulars long and acuminate, black, with a broad central white streak; wing-coverts bluish-ash; speculum greyish-green, bordered above and below by a white bar; tail dusky-grey, the feathers edged lighter; upper tail-coverts yellowish-white, spotted with black; chin black; lower part of the neck and breast pale fulvous, with crescent-shaped black bars; abdomen white; the flanks with transverse wavy lines of black; vent and under tail-coverts yellowish-white, spotted with black.

The female has the head, neck, and upper parts, dusky-brown, the feathers with whitish edges; the eye-streak faint; wing-coverts dark ashy-grey; speculum dull, the greenish tinge almost wanting; chin and throat white; the lower part of the breast and belly white, spotted with brown on the flanks and lower abdomen.

The Garganey or Blue-winged Teal, although very common throughout the district, scarcely occurs in such immense numbers as the Common Teal. It is good eating, equal if not superior to *Q. crecca.*

Querquedula formosa, *Geor.*

966.—*Q. glocitans*, Pall.—Jerdon's Birds of India, Vol. II, p. 808; Murray's Vertebrate Zoology of Sind, p. 302; Game Birds of India, Vol. III, p. 225.

THE CLUCKING TEAL.

♂. Length, 15·8; wing, 8·15; tail, 3·9; tarsus, 1·3; bill at front, 1·5; bill from gape, 1·92; weight, 1 lb.

Bill dusky; irides chesnut-brown; legs dusky.

Male: forehead, top of the head, and occiput, rich purple-brown, banded by a narrow white line from the eye; face, cheeks, and sides of cheeks fawn color; a black streak from below the eye, meeting a black patch on the throat; nape and hind-neck glossy green, ending in a black stripe down the back of the neck, separated from the fawn color of the side of the neck by a narrow white line; upper plumage finely marbled-grey, edged with rufous on the back; upper wing-coverts hair-brown; the median-coverts the same, with an edging of rufous forming the anterior margin of the speculum, which is glossy-green, ending in velvet-black, and bordered posteriorly by silvery-white; primaries brown; scapulars lengthened, deep black in the centre, white on their upper side, and rufous externally; upper tail-coverts brown, white on either side; tail of 16 feathers dark brown; beneath the throat black; the neck and breast vinous-purple, with a few black spots, paling below; abdomen white; flanks mottled-grey; under tail-coverts black.

The female wants the rich markings on the head and face, which are mottled grey and brown; the scapulars are not lengthened; the upper plumage is dusky, with rufous edgings; the chin and throat white; the breast rufous, largely spotted with dark brown, as are the flanks; the tail-coverts white, with brown spots.

The Clucking Teal is a very rare straggler within our limits, but a specimen has been recorded from the Muncher Lake in Sind.

SUB-FAMILY, Fuligulinæ.

Hind-toe short, bordered by a more or less wide web; wings shorter than in the last sub-family; tarsus short, more compressed, set further backwards; feet large, the web reaching to the very end of the toes, and wide; tail generally short, rounded, or somewhat wedged.

GENUS, Fuligula, *Steph.*

Bill nearly as long as the head, moderately wide; tip

depressed; nail large; lamellæ distant; wings moderate, first quill longest.

Fuligula rufina, *Pallas.*

967.—*Branta rufina*, Pall.—Jerdon's Birds of India, Vol. II, p. 811; Butler, Guzerat; Stray Feathers, Vol. IV, p. 30; Deccan, Stray Feathers, Vol. IX, p. 438; Murray's Vertebrate Zoology of Sind, p. 313; Game Birds of India, Vol. III, p. 253.

THE RED-CRESTED POCHARD.

Length, 20·1 to 22·1; expanse, 33·75 to 38·2; wing, 9·6 to 10·75; tail, 3·0 to 4·2; tarsus, 1·5 to 1·75; bill from gape, 2·25 to 2·42; weight, 1 $\frac{10}{16}$ to 2 $\frac{14}{16}$ lbs.

Bill bright vermilion-red; nail brownish-white; irides vary from brown to red; legs from dingy salmon color to orange-red.

Male: head, cheeks, throat, and the upper part of the neck reddish-bay; the feathers on the crown elongated, and of a silky texture, forming a crest somewhat paler than the rest of the head; back, wings, and tail, yellowish-brown; the band of the wing, a large spot on the sides of the back, the speculum, and the base of the primary quills, white; lower part of the neck, breast, and abdomen, deep black; the flanks white.

The female has the upper parts pale yellowish brown, darker on the head and neck, and the crest less developed; speculum half greyish-white, half pale brown; base of the quills white, tinged with brown; breast and flanks yellowish-brown; belly grey; bill and feet reddish-brown.

The Red-crested Pochard is common in Sind, less so in Guzerat and Rajputana, and rare in the Deccan. It affects only the larger tanks and jheels, keeping in the middle; it is a very wary bird, taking wing at the first sign of danger, and flying up and down well out of shot, and is consequently not often found in the sportsman's bag. In tanks and jheels not much shot over; of course, it is much less wary.

Fuligula ferina, *Lin.*

968.—*Aythya ferina*, Lin.—Jerdon's Birds of India, Vol. II, p. 812; Butler, Guzerat; Stray Feathers, Vol. IV, p. 30; Deccan, Stray Feathers, Vol. IX, p. 438; Murray's Vertebrate Zoology of Sind, p. 306; Game Birds of India, Vol. III, p. 247; Swinhoe and Barnes, Central India; Ibis, 1885, p. 138.

THE RED-HEADED POCHARD.

Length, 17·25 to 18·5; expanse, 28·75 to 32·2; wing, 7·9 to 8·5; tail, 2·2 to 3·2; tarsus, 1·4 to 1·5; bill from gape, 2 to 2·27; weight, 1 $\frac{5}{16}$ to 2 $\frac{5}{16}$ lbs.

Bill bluish-grey, the tip and base black; irides orange-yellow; legs and feet bluish-grey.

Male, head and neck bright chesnut-red; upper part of the back black; middle and lower back, wing-coverts, and scapulars, white, with numerous fine undulating black lines; rump and upper tail-coverts black; tail dark ashy-brown; primaries deep dusky-brown; secondaries bluish-grey; breast black; abdomen whitish, faintly undulated like the back, the lines becoming darker towards the vent; under tail-coverts black.

The female has the crown, nape, and sides of the neck, and the upper part of the back, reddish-brown; the back as in the male, but the lines less distinct; throat and forepart of the neck white, mixed with reddish; breast reddish-brown, mottled with white; the middle of the abdomen greyish-white.

The Pochard or Dun-bird is common in Sind during the cold weather; it is not uncommon in Guzerat and Rajputana, but is less so in the Deccan. When in good condition the Pochard is not bad eating; if not disturbed much, they are by no means shy, but when often fired at they soon become wary.

Fuligula nyroca, *Guld.*

969.—*Aythya nyroca,* Guld.—Jerdon's Birds of India, Vol. III, p. 813; Butler, Guzerat; Stray Feathers, Vol. IV, p. 30; Deccan, Stray Feathers, Vol. IX, p. 439; Murray's Vertebrate Zoology of Sind, p. 301; Game Birds of India, Vol. III, p. 263; *Nyroca ferruginea,* Gmel.; Swinhoe and Barnes, Central India; Ibis, 1885, p. 138.

THE WHITE-EYED POCHARD.

Length, 16 to 17; expanse, 24 to 27·5; wing, 6·75 to 7·5; tail, 3 to 3·5; tarsus, 1 to 1·25; bill from gape, 1·9 to 2·1; weight, $1\frac{2}{18}$ to $1\frac{9}{18}$ lbs.

Bill bluish; irides white; legs grey.

Male, head and neck deep ferruginous, with a narrow collar of blackish-brown on the lower part of the neck; back, scapulars and wing-coverts, dusky brown, somewhat glossed with green and purple, and the whole finely powdered with pale reddish-brown; upper tail-coverts and tail dusky-brown, with a dash of ferruginous; primaries dusky; speculum white, edged with black in the lower part; chin whitish; lower part of the neck and breast bright ferruginous; abdomen and under tail-coverts pure-white; the lower portion and vent blackish grey.

The female differs from the male in the head and neck being brown, the feathers edged with ferruginous; the upper parts are glossy umber brown, the feathers edged with pale brown; the irides are less pure white, and the bill and feet are dusky-grey; otherwise as in the male. The White-eyed Pochard occurs more or less abundantly throughout the region.

It is by no means wary, but is not sought after by sportsmen, as it is at the best of times but indifferent eating.

Fuligula marila, *Lin.*

970.—Jerdon's Birds of India, Vol. II, p. 814; Murray's

Vertebrate Zoology of Sind, p. 305; Game Birds of India, Vol. III, p. 271.

THE SCAUP POCHARD.

Length, 18 to 20; expanse, 28 to 32; wing, 8 to 9; tail, 2·5 to 2·75; tarsus, 1·33 to 1·42; bill at front, 1·6 to 1·9.

Bill, ♂, bluish, beneath dusky, black at tip; ♀, deep grey; irides brilliant yellow; legs bluish-ashy; webs dusky.

Male, head and neck, black, glossed with green; top of the back and scapulars whitish, with zigzag black lines; lower back and upper tail-coverts black; tail brown; wing-coverts black, marbled with ashy; speculum white; quills brown; lower neck and breast deep black; abdomen and sides pure white, with brown zigzag markings on the lower portion; under tail-coverts black.

The female has the head and neck blackish brown, with a large white space round the eye; back, scapulars, and wings, with brown and white zigzag markings; lower back and upper tail-coverts smoky black; lower neck and breast deep brown; abdomen white, marked with brown posteriorly.

The Scaup Pochard occurs in Sind. It is usually passed over as a White-eye.

Fuligula cristata, *Ray*.

971.—Jerdon's Birds of India, Vol. II, p. 815; Butler, Guzerat; Stray Feathers, Vol. IV, p. 31; Deccan, Stray Feathers, Vol. IX, p. 438; Murray's Vertebrate Zoology of Sind, p. 304; Game Birds of India, Vol. III, p. 277; Swinhoe and Barnes, Central India; Ibis, 1885, p. 138.

THE CRESTED POCHARD.

Length, 15·2 to 17·2; expanse, 26·7 to 30·3; wing, 7·6 to 8·5; tail, 2·5 to 3·25; tarsus, 1·2 to 1·4; bill from gape, 1·81 to 2; weight, 1$\frac{5}{16}$ to 2½ lbs.

Bill dark bluish-grey, black at tip; irides golden yellow; legs leaden; webs dusky.

Head and neck, including the long pendent, silky crest, glossy black with green and purple reflections; back, wings, and rump, black, slightly glossed and powdered with greyish white; breast glossy black; rest of the lower parts pure white; the vent black; speculum, formed by the secondaries, white, with a narrow greenish-black edge; tertials glossy-green.

The female has the colors somewhat duller and more brown; the crest not so long; speculum smaller; and the lower parts spotted with brown.

The young want the crest, and have the base of the bill and region of the eyes varied with white.

The Tufted Pochard is more or less common throughout the whole region, less in Sind, perhaps, than elsewhere. It is quite abundant in Central India. It is not a particularly good bird for the table, but at times it is eatable.

GENUS, Clangula.

Clangula glaucium, *Lin.*

971*bis*.—*C. glaucion*, Lin.—Murray's Vertebrate Zoology of Sind, p. 296; Game Birds of India, Vol. III, p. 285.

THE GOLDEN-EYE OR GARROT.

♂. Length, 16·5 to 19; expanse, 28 to 32; wing, 8·6 to 9·35; tail, 3·3 to 4·1; tarsus, 1·41 to 1·65; bill from gape, 1·2 to 1·4; weight, 2 to $2\frac{10}{16}$ lbs.

♀. Length, 15·7 to 16·5; expanse, 26·3 to 28; wing, 7·5 to 8·25; tail, 3 to 3·4; tarsus, 1·22 to 1·35; bill from gape, 1·12 to 1·19; weight, $1\frac{7}{16}$ to $1\frac{14}{16}$ lbs.

Bill, in old males, bluish or greenish-black, duskier and duller colored in old females and young; nail black; irides vary from orange-yellow to pale yellow.

Male: Head and upper part of the neck deep glossy green, in some lights purple; throat brownish-black; a patch of white between the upper mandible and cheek; lower neck all round, breast, forepart of the abdomen, sides, and lower tail-coverts, white; axillary feathers and lower wing-coverts blackish-brown; edges of posterior elongated feathers on the sides black; back, inner and posterior scapulars, black; outer scapulars white with black margins; tail deep brown, tinged with grey; the sides of the rump and tibia dusky-grey; feathers on the hind-part of the abdomen, dusky at the base.

Female: Head and upper neck umber-brown; lower neck all round dull ash-grey, the feathers terminally edged paler; lower parts white, but sides of the body, rump, and part of the abdomen, grey; axillaries and lower wing-coverts brownish-grey; back and scapulars deep ashy-grey, shading to black on the hind-back; tail dark-brown, tinged with grey; smaller wing-coverts deep grey, many of them tipped pale grey; primaries, their coverts, four outer secondaries, and five inner, with their coverts, brownish-black; the other secondaries pure white, as on their coverts, except at the base.

Two specimens only have been recorded from India; one of them was obtained 45 years ago by Sir A. Burnes, on the Indus.

FAMILY, Mergidæ.

Bill straight, narrow, cylindrical, the tip well bent over; the edges of the mandibles armed with strong teeth pointing backwards; nostrils median, longitudinal; tarsus short, set far backwards; feet large, hind-toe lobed; wings moderate; tail wedge-shaped, of 16 or 18 feathers; form lengthened and flattened; head more or less crested.

GENUS, Mergus, *Lin.*

The characters are the same as those of the family.

Mergus merganser, *Lin.*

972.—*M. castor*, Lin.—Jerdon's Birds of India, Vol. II, p. 817; Murray's Vertebrate Zoology of Sind, p. 309; Game Birds of India, Vol. III, p. 299.

THE MERGANSER.

Length, ♂ 25·0 to 28·1, ♀ 22·9 to 25·0; expanse, ♂ 35·6 to 40·8, ♀ 34·5 to 37·8; wing, ♂ 10·95 to 12·1, ♀ 9·8 to 10·95; tail, ♂ 4·8 to 5·9, ♀ 4·6 to 5·65; tarsus, ♂, 2, ♀ 1·75; bill, ♂ 2·8, 2·5; weight, 2 to $3\frac{5}{16}$ lbs.

Bill deep blood-red, black on culmen, edges paler; irides red; feet orange-red.

Male: Head (with a short thick crest) and upper part of the neck, glossy blackish-green; lower part of the neck white; upper back and scapulars next the body deep black; the rest of the back and upper tail-coverts ashy; the tips of the feathers whitish here and there; tail ashy-grey; breast, abdomen, and under tail-coverts, white, tinged with orange-buff; wing-coverts and outermost scapulars rich buff-orange, and the latter edged with black.

The female (and young males till the second moult) have the head and neck reddish-brown; the throat white; the upper plumage ashy; beneath yellowish-white; the sides of the breast, and the flanks pale ashy; a white speculum; primaries black; tail ashy-brown.

The Goosander is believed to occur in Sind.

Mergus serrator, *Lin.*

972*bis*.—Murray's Vertebrate Zoology of Sind, p. 308; Game Birds of India, Vol. III, p. 305.

THE RED-BREASTED MERGANSER.

♂, Length, 24 to 26; expanse, 29 to 32·5; wing, 9 to 10; tail, 3·1 to 4·2; tarsus, 1·8 to 2·05; bill at front, 2·4 to 2·5.

In the male the bill varies from orange-red to deep vermilion, is more or less dusky on the edge, and has the nail varying from pale yellowish-grey to almost black. In young females there is more dusky on the upper mandible, where the red is often only a lateral band.

The whole head, chin, throat and the neck all round, for about one inch, black, glossed with metallic green on the sides of the head and a bluer sheen elsewhere; along the middle of the crown and occiput runs a comparatively narrow line of excessively narrow, more or less disintegrated, webbed, elongate feathers, of which the longest are over three inches in length, forming a conspicuous crest; the rest of the neck all round, to just the base, pure white, with a conspicuous narrow black line down the centre of its hinder aspect; at the base of the neck a light brownish-rufous, or pale brownish-chesnut band, extends all round, narrower behind and broadening into a crop-patch. This band is streaked longitudinally with blackish-brown. The interscapulary region and upper back, the extreme sides of the breast and scapulars, velvet-black; outside the scapulars and between these and the wing there is a conspicuous patch of long white feathers; the primaries and their coverts (which latter are darkest), the shoulder of the wing and lesser-coverts just above the carpus, blackish-brown; the rest of the lesser and median-coverts pure white; the secondary greater-coverts black, all, except the first three, very broadly tipped with white, but leaving a portion of their black bases visible below the white median-coverts, thus forming the first black bar across the white of the wing; the secondaries are black, all, except the first three, very broadly tipped with white; tertiaries white, conspicuously margined with black, except the last three, which are black; axillaries pure white; rest of the lower parts white, with, in life, a beautiful salmon or buffy tinge which disappears in the skin; flanks white, vermiculated with greyish-black; middle and lower back, rump and upper tail-coverts, white, with very delicate and close vermiculations of dull black, producing a grey effect; tail dull brown; lower wing-coverts white.

The female has the entire crown, occiput and crest brown, with more or less of a dull rufous or chesnut tinge, and rather ashy towards the forehead; sides of the head and neck all round pale dull brownish chesnut; chin white; throat albescent; breast and entire lower parts white or pinkish-white in life, only at the base of the throat and crop the grey-brown bases of the feathers show through to a certain extent like hidden bars; interscapulary region, mantle, lower back, rump and upper tail-coverts brown; most of the feathers with paler margins; quills dusky-black; secondaries and their greater-coverts black, all but the first three broadly tipped with white; tertiaries blackish-dusky, paling anteriorly, whitish towards the tip; the innermost mostly white, with a black outer margin; tail like the back.

Both sexes from the above description resemble the Goosander, but may be distinguished by their small size, and in proportion to their length much thinner bills.—*Hume's Stray Feathers*, Vol. IX, p. 268.

The Red-breasted Merganser is a very rare cold weather visitant to the Mekran and Kurrachee Coast.

GENUS, **Mergellus.**

Bill shorter and somewhat wider than in *Mergus*, the tip much less hooked; teeth numerous and prominent in the lower mandible; of small size; pied, black and white; tail of 16 feathers.

Mergellus albellus, *Lin.*

973.—Jerdon's Birds of India, Vol. II, p. 818, Butler, Guzerat; Stray Feathers, Vol. IV, p. 31; Murray's Vertebrate Zoology of Sind, p. 310; Game Birds of India, Vol. III, p. 293.

THE SMEW.

♂. Length, 17·0 to 18·1; expanse, 26·3 to 28·7; wing, 7·55 to 8·32; tail from vent, 3·3 to 4·1; tarsus, 1·2 to 1·31; bill from gape, 1·63 to 1·72; weight, $1\frac{1}{4}$ to $1\frac{3}{4}$ lbs.

♀. Length, 15·5 to 16·75; expanse, 23·75 to 26·25; wing, 7·01 to 7·3; tail, 3·3 to 3·9; tarsus, 1·11 to 1·19; bill from gape, 1·48 to 1·6; weight, 1 to $1\frac{6\frac{1}{2}}{16}$lbs.

The bill is as a rule a delicate pale plumbeous, sometimes a clearer and bluer tint, sometimes duskier, and in some almost black.

The irides vary from brown to red-brown or even red.

The legs and feet vary from pale blue-grey to plumbeous and dark lavender; webs vary from dusky to black; there is often an olive tinge on the tarsi, and occasionally both these and the toes exhibit small dusky spots and patches.

Male: A large patch on each side of the base of the bill enclosing the eyes, and another longitudinal one on the occiput, black, glossed with green; the rest of the head, occipital crest, and neck white; back, some of the lesser wing-coverts, and the primaries, black; scapulars white, edged with black on the outer webs; secondaries and greater wing-coverts black, tipped with white; some of the lesser wing-coverts white; upper tail-coverts and tail bluish-grey; all the lower parts white, with two crescentic bands of black advancing from the shoulders, one nearly encircling the lower part of the breast, the other the upper part of the breast, flanks, and thigh-coverts with wavy black lines.

The female has the crown, cheeks, and occiput, reddish-brown; the crest shorter than in the male; back, upper tail-coverts, and tail, deep ashy-grey; wings as in the male, but the dark parts grey instead of black; the throat, sides, and front of the upper-neck, and the abdomen, white; and the lower-neck, breast, and flanks, clouded with ash-color.

The Smew is a cold weather visitant to Sind, and has been recorded from Northern Guzerat. It is an exceedingly wary bird, keeping in the middle of rivers where the water is deepest.

FAMILY, **Podicipidæ.**

Tarsus compressed; primaries short; feet lobed; tail very short, almost wanting; bill slightly curved above at the tip.

GENUS, **Podiceps**, *Latham.*

Bill straight, compressed, moderately stout; nostrils oblong, lateral; wings short, concave; tarsus moderate, compressed, with large scutellæ, serrated posteriorly; hallux bordered by a web; claws flat, depressed.

Podiceps cristatus, *Lin.*

974.—Jerdon's Birds of India, Vol. II, p. 821; Butler, Guzerat;

Stray Feathers, Vol. V, p. 224; Murray's Vertebrate Zoology of Sind, p. 311.

THE CRESTED GREBE.

Length, 22; wing, 7·5; bill at front, 2·37; tarsus, 2.

Bill brown, tip white, beneath and at the sides reddish; irides crimson-red; naked lores red; feet plumbeous externally, within greenish-yellow.

Head (with a double occipital crest) shining-back, which color descends along the back of the neck; lower neck above ashy-brown; back and wings, including scapulars and middle-coverts, brown, with a blackish-green lustre; lesser wing-coverts and secondaries white; cheeks and throat fulvous-white, succeeded by a wide frieze or collar, chesnut above, shining black below; lower neck, breast and abdomen silky-white, tinged with rufous and ashy on the sides of the breast and abdomen.

The young bird has the head brown; the crest undeveloped; face and ears white, bordered with a rusty collar and a much smaller bill.

The Crested Grebe is a not uncommon cold weather visitant to the Kurrachee Coast, and has been obtained on some of the larger tanks in Guzerat.

Podiceps nigricollis, *Sund.*

974*bis.*—Murray's Vertebrate Zoology of Sind, Vol. II, p. 311.

THE BLACK-NECKED GREBE.

Length, 12 to 13; expanse, 22·5 to 24·5; wing, 5·2 to 5·6; tarsus, 2·9 to 3·2; bill at gape, 3·6 to 4.

Bill black; irides vermilion; legs and feet greenish-plumbeous, blackish exteriorly.

Male: Whole of the top of the head, together with the rest of the upper part, the chin, throat, and neck all round, blackish-brown, very glossy on the head; back and wings duller and browner on the neck all round; the chin and throat almost quite black, but a good deal speckled with white; this white speckling extending as a stripe at the sides of the neck behind the ear-coverts; two short thick tufts on either side of the occiput, which, though scarcely noticeable in the dried skin, are erected at pleasure in the live bird; behind the eye for about 1·4 inches a broad streak of orange and reddish-yellow silky glistening feathers; the inner web of the sixth primary, and almost the whole of the subsequent primaries and secondaries, pure white; tertiaries and wing-coverts unicolorous with the back; the whole breast, abdomen and vent, satin-white, a little tinged with greyish-brown about the vent; tail unicolorous with the back, and on either side of it, and of the tail-coverts a good deal of white appears; sides and flanks mottled with blackish-brown, with traces of a rufous or orange striation.

In full breeding plumage the sides and flanks are very strongly streaked with orange-red, and the parts indicated as speckled with white are entirely black; in the winter plumage the colors are duller, and the front of the neck is an earthy-brown; and the whole of those portions indicated as speckled with white are pure white; the orange-red tuft behind the eye is entirely wanting.—*Stray Feathers*, Vol. I, p. 267.

The Black-necked Grebe is common about the Sind and Mekran Coasts. It has not been recorded from elsewhere within our limits.

Podiceps minor, *Gm.*

975.—*P. philippensis*, Gm.—Jerdon's Birds of India, Vol. II, p. 822; Butler, Guzerat; Stray Feathers, Vol. IV, p. 31; Deccan, Stray Feathers, Vol. IX, p. 430; Murray's Vertebrate Zoology of Sind, p. 312; Swinhoe and Barnes, Central India; Ibis, 1885, p. 138,

THE LITTLE GREBE OR DABCHICK.

Length, 8 to 9; wing, 4; tarsus, 1·25; bill at front, 0·75.

Bill blackish, paler at base; irides red-brown; legs greenish-black on the outside, livid tinged with fleshy within.

Head, above, and the back of the neck, dark sepia-brown, or black tinged with green; upper plumage generally glossy brown-black tinged with green; the sides of the rump fulvous; quills more or less white at the base; the first six quills almost all pale brown; secondaries with only a little brown on the outer webs; chin and base of the lower mandible glossy black; cheeks, ear-coverts, and sides of the neck, bright chesnut; breast brown, mixed with whitish or glossy blackish-grey; belly silky-white, the flanks brown.

Young birds want the chesnut red on the neck, which is mostly white, the brown above is paler, and the chin and throat are pure white.

The Little Grebe or Dabchick is a common permanent resident throughout the region, breeding towards the end of the monsoon.

The nest is a mass of weeds and rushes, resting on the water. The eggs when fresh are pure white, but soon become discolored, owing to the habit the bird has of covering them with wet weeds every time she leaves the nest. The eggs are moderately broad ovals, pointed at each end. They are slightly chalky in texture and have rarely much gloss. They measure 1·39 inches in length by about 1 inch in breadth.

FAMILY, Procellaridæ.

Bill long, straight, compressed, very deeply grooved; tip strong, arched, and much hooked; nostrils tubular, situated at the base of the bill, and exposed.

SUB-FAMILY, Procellarinæ.

Nostrils at base of keel divided by a septum; hind-toe generally present; bill slender, compressed; tarsus moderate.

GENUS, **Oceanites**, *Keys and Blas.*

Bill short and slender, curved at the tip; tail forked; wings long, second quill longest; tibia partially naked.

Oceanites oceanica, *Kuhl.*

976.—Murray's Vertebrate Zoology of Sind, p. 313.

WILSON'S PETREL.

Length, 7·12; wing, 6·25; tarsus, 1·4; bill at front, 0·5.

Bill dull black; irides blackish; legs and feet polished black.

General plumage deep sooty-brown, or brownish-black, blackish on the primaries, tertiaries, occiput, nape and tail; secondary greater-coverts and latest secondaries wood-brown or pale hair-brown, narrowly margined towards the tips with yellowish-white; upper tail-coverts, flanks and bases of some of the external under tail-coverts pure white; a few of the feathers of the lower abdomen narrowly fringed with white.

Wilson's Petrel is not uncommon along the coast.

GENUS, **Puffinus**, *Briss.*

Bill longer than head, slender, compressed at point; lower mandible deflected at tip; nostrils in a double tube, extending along the upper surface of the bill; tarsus moderate, compressed; toes three in front, rather long; hind-toe rudimentary; first quill longest.

Puffinus persicus, *Hume.*

976*bis*.—Murray's Vertebrate Zoology of Sind, p. 313.

THE PERSIAN SHEARWATER.

Length, 13; wing, 7; tarsus, 1·5; bill from forehead, 1·3.

Bill dusky-brown, bluish at base; irides brown; legs and feet white, tinged with pink and lavender, with claws, margin of web, exterior of foot, and outer-toes, and part of ridge of mid-toe, black.

Female: The head and nape deep sooty-brown, the whole of the rest of the upper parts blackish-brown, almost, if not quite, black on the primaries, rump, upper tail-coverts and tail; upper portion of the lores mingled dusky-brown and whitish; lower portion of the lores, and the whole of the chin and throat, as far as the eyes on either side, breast, abdomen, vent and shorter central lower tail-coverts, pure white; a white line about 0·06 wide encircles the eye, and extends backwards from the posterior angle as a narrow white streak for a distance of 0·35 to 0·4 inches; below this the ear-coverts are dusky-brown, slightly mingled with whitish; the white line below the eye is only separated from the white of the throat by a hair line of greyish-brown; the sides of the neck and breast where the brown of the upper meets the white of the lower parts, are somewhat paler brown, slightly intermingled with white;

the sides, axillaries, flanks and the lesser under wing-coverts next the body, and the whole of the exterior and longer tail-coverts are deep brown; the rest of the lower wing-coverts, except just at the edge of the wing, are white, here and there slightly mottled, especially at the edge of the wing with dusky brown; the longer axillaries are mottled white along their bases.

Within our limits the Persian Shearwater is found along the Sind Coast and at the mouths of the Indus.

FAMILY, Laridæ.

Bill straight, compressed; wings long and pointed; tail long; tarsi with transverse scutæ in front; hind-toe usually short.

SUB-FAMILY, Stercorariinæ.

Base of bill covered with a cere, tip hooked; first quill longest; nostrils median.

GENUS, Stercorarius, *Brisson.*

Keel of bill covered with a bony or membraneous cere; first quill longest.

Stercorarius asiaticus, *Hume.*

977*ter.*—Murray's Vertebrate Zoology of Sind, p. 314.

THE SKUA.

Length, 19; expanse, 45; wing, 13; tail, 6·4; tarsus, 1·8; bill from gape, 2·02.

Bill brown; cere pale greenish brown; irides brown; legs and feet dull black.

I extract the following from Murray's Vertebrate Zoology of Sind:—

"This is not uncommon off the Manora headland, and along the Sind and Mekran Coasts. There is some difference of opinion in regard to the identity of this bird. Mr. Hume, in Vol. I, p. 268 (Stray Feathers) refers it to *L. parasiticus,* but in his observations on the species states it may not improbably hereafter turn out that both his specimens and those of Major Tickell's belong to a distinct species intermediate between *pomarinus* and *parasiticus,* in which case he says it may stand as *Stercorarius asiaticus, nobis.* In Vol. V of the same journal he points out the differences between *L. parasiticus* and his *Stercorarius asiaticus.*

The following is the description of the species obtained by him at Pusnee on the Mekran Coast:—

"The central tail feathers are manifestly imperfectly developed, one projects 0·75 and the other 0·25 beyond the rest of the tail; the bird is obviously in a state of change of plumage, as the two first primaries in each wing are old, and comparatively pale brown with conspicuous white shafts only tinged brownish for about 0·5 immediately above the tips, while all the other primaries are new and very dark brown, almost black, with only the basal half of the shafts white, and even that slightly tinged brown ; some of the secondaries, scapulars, coverts and feathers of the back are brown ; the same dull pale umber as the first two primaries, and so are two of the tail feathers, while the whole of the rest of the wings and tail are of the same deep blackish brown as the third to the tenth primaries. What is noticeable is, that on the back and scapulars the paler brown feathers have no white tippings, which most probably have worn off, these feathers being the old ones, but all the dark feathers of these parts have narrow brownish white margins. The upper tail-coverts are conspicuously tipped with white, and the longer ones have two very broad slightly rufous or fulvous-white bars ; the forehead, crown, and occiput are dull pale wood-brown, here and there faintly tinged rufescent ; the feathers with pretty broad blackish brown central streaks ; the lores are greyish-white ; the feathers narrowly dark centred ; the cheeks, ear-coverts and nape are white, more or less tinged with fulvous or buffy, with very narrow dark brown shaft-stripes ; the chin and throat white ; the feathers of the base of the neck all round and the breast white, tinged in places fulvous, in places slightly rufescent, with a broad dark brown subterminal transverse band ; the sides, flanks and lower tail-coverts are white, with broad brown transverse bars, which in some of the lower tail-coverts have a slight rufescent aureola ; the abdomen and vent are white, but on the sides of the abdomen there are faint traces of barrings similar to those of the breast and flanks ; the axillaries are broadly barred, with somewhat greyish-brown and greyish-white ; the tibial feathers pure brown."

SUB-FAMILY, **Larinæ.**

Bill long, straight above, and slightly curved at tip.

GENUS, **Larus,** *Lin.*

Bill moderate, strong, compressed, cultrated, bent down at tip ; lower mandible angled beneath ; nostrils linear, lateral, longitudinal, pervious ; tibia naked ; tarsi moderate ; toes palmated ; hind-toe free, short and high on the tarsus ; wings long.

Larus cachinnans, *Pall.*

978*bis*.—Murray's Vertebrate Zoology of Sind, p. 316.

THE YELLOW-LEGGED HERRING GULL.

Length, 23·0 to 25·75 ; expanse, 58 to 60 ; wing, 16·75 to 18 ; tarsus, 2·5 to 2·78 ; bill at front, 1·9 to 2·35.

Bill yellow, red at tip beneath in summer ; in winter it is dull, yellow, whitish at tip, with a dark spot on both mandibles near the tip and an orange spot at the tip of the lower one.—*Stray Feathers,* Vol. I, p. 270.

Summer plumage.—Entire head, neck all round, entire lower parts, upper tail-coverts and tail pure white ; entire mantle and back, tertiaries and secondaries, a delicate pale bluish-grey; the tertiaries and secondaries, and longer scapulars broadly tipped with white; the earlier secondaries, especially with the major portion of the inner webs, also white; edge of the wing about the carpal joint white; primaries—the first with the whole outer web black—tipped with white and with a broad white band across both webs near the tip; above this band a considerable portion of the inner web is black, and the rest pale grey; second primary similar, but the white band often entirely wanting or reduced to a spot on the inner web only; the black on the inner web of less extent than in the first, and the basal portion of the outer web the same pale blue-grey as the coverts and the rest of the wing; the third and following primaries have only the white tips and no white band, the outer webs become more grey as they recede from the second, and the black diminishes on the inner webs proportionally, so that on the seventh or eighth it is generally reduced to a narrow black band across both webs, or in some cases on the outer web only, and in others entirely wanting on the last three quills.

In the winter plumage the nape and the back of the neck are striated with pale brown, in some specimens thinly on the crown also; legs and feet lemon yellow.

This Gull is numerous during the winter in the Kurrachee Harbour and along the adjacent coast.

Larus affinis, *Rein.*

978*ter*.—Butler, Deccan; Stray Feathers, Vol. IX, p. 439; Murray's Vertebrate Zoology of Sind, p. 316.

THE LESSER HERRING GULL.

♂. Length, 24·2; wing, 17·2; tarsus, 2·6; bill at front, 2·25.

♀. Length, 22·3; wing, 16·8; tarsus, 2·6; bill at front, 2·1.

Bill yellow, angle of lower mandible red; irides pale yellow; eyelids yellowish-red.

Head, crown, neck, and nape white in summer; in winter streaked with dusky brown, and with a dusky eye-spot; chin, throat, and breast white; back dark slaty-grey also the greater and lesser wing-coverts; primaries dark slaty-grey; the first six tipped with white; the first with a broad bar and the extreme tip white, the rest only tipped white; secondaries like the back, and tipped with white; some of the tertials also tipped with white; under wing-coverts white; upper and under tail-coverts and tail white.

The Lesser Herring Gull occurs in immense numbers all along the coast.

Larus ichthyætus, *Pall.*

979.—Jerdon's Birds of India, Vol. II, p. 831; Butler, Deccan, Stray Feathers, Vol. IX, p. 439; Murray's Vertebrate Zoology of Sind, p. 319.

THE GREAT BLACK-HEADED GULL.

Length, 28·5 to 29; wing, 19 to 20; tail, 7·5; bill, 2·6.

Bill red, yellow at tip, with a black bar across both mandibles; the extreme tip orange-yellow.

In summer plumage, the whole head and upper neck black; the feathered orbits white; the back and wings blue-grey; the upper tail-coverts and the tail pure white, with a black band; primaries with a black band increasing in width to the outermost one, which has the whole of the outer web and half of the inner web black; the rest of the first five primaries white; the others grey, white tipped; rest of the plumage pure white.

In winter the head and neck are white, with a few dusky markings down the nape and on the back of the neck; and the central tail-feathers are sometimes grey.

The young bird has the head white with brown streaks, the back and wings grey with brown marks, the tail mottled with brown at its base.

Occurs more or less sparingly all along our coast.

Larus brunneicephalus, *Jerd.*

980.—Jerdon's Birds of India, Vol. II, p. 832; Butler, Guzerat; Stray Feathers, Vol. IV, p. 31; Deccan, Stray Feathers, Vol. IX, p. 439; Murray's Vertebrate Zoology of Sind, p. 318.

THE BROWN-HEADED GULL.

Length, 16 to 17; expanse, 40; wing, 13; tail, 5·5; bill at front, 1·5.

Bill red, tip darker; irides white; legs and feet fine red.

In summer, the whole head and neck sooty-brown, darker where it terminates; orbital feathers white posteriorly; back and wings light grey; nape, hind-neck, upper tail-coverts, and tail, white; first primary black, inner web white at base, and with a white subterminal band; the next has both webs white at the base, and a smaller terminal spot; the third is grey with still less black, and no white, and so on, lessening to the seventh; the other quills are all grey.

In winter the head is white, generally somewhat soiled, often with a few faint dusky marks, and there is always a dark spot behind the ear-coverts.

The young bird is colored like the adult in winter plumage, but the tail has a dark band, and the irides are yellow-brown.

The Brown-headed Gull occurs all along the coast and in suitable places (large lakes) inland throughout the region.

Larus ridibundus, *Lin.*

981.—Jerdon's Birds of India, Vol. II, p. 832; Butler, Deccan; Stray Feathers, Vol. IX, p. 439; Murray's Vertebrate Zoology of Sind, p. 319.

THE LAUGHING GULL.

Length, 15 to 17; wing, 13; tail, 5; tarsus, 1·75; bill at front, 1·75.

Bill deep red; irides dark brown; legs and feet deep red.

Head and upper part of neck deep reddish-brown, more extended in front and on the sides; lower neck white; eyelids white; upper plumage ashy; upper tail-coverts and tail white; first four primaries white, tipped and edged with black within, and the first with the outer web black; fifth and sixth nearly all black; the rest of the quills grey; beneath, from the breast white, faintly tinged rosy.

In winter plumage, the head is white with some dusky markings on the occiput and ears.

The Laughing Gull is common all along the coast, and has been frequently observed on the larger lakes inland.

Larus hemprichi, *Bp.*

981*ter.*—Butler, Deccan, Stray Feathers, Vol. IX, p. 439; Murray's Vertebrate Zoology of Sind, p. 318.

THE SOOTY GULL.

Length, 17·5 to 18·5; wing, 13·25 to 13·7; tarsus, 2; bill at front, 1·8 to 2.

Bill greenish-drab, tipped yellow, with a subterminal black bar; irides dark brown; legs and feet greyish-yellow.

In summer, forehead, crown, nape, chin, and throat, chocolate-brown; neck in front darker, nearly blackish-brown, forming a sort of "bib" on the upper breast, the edges of the brown of the back of the neck margining the broad white demicollar of the same color; upper back, scapulars, lesser, median, and greater-coverts, also the secondaries and tertials, deep chocolate-brown, all the secondaries broadly tipped with white; primaries dark brown, nearly black, all, except the first three, tipped with white; edge of the wing white; breast and sides of the breast paler brown than the back; abdomen, vent, under tail-coverts, flanks, upper tail and thigh-coverts, white.

In winter the forehead and lores are a pale brown, also the crown of the head and cheeks, the feathers here and there margined with greyish-white; breast pale brown, the feathers margined greyish-white; chin and throat white, the feathers of the latter tipped with brown, otherwise as in the summer plumage, the color of the mantle and wings being paler.

The Sooty Gull occurs in the Kurrachee Harbour and all along the Coast as far south at least as Bombay, where Mr. Hume observed a specimen.

Larus gelastes, *Licht.*

981*quat.*—Murray's Vertebrate Zoology of Sind, p. 317.

Length, 17 to 18·5; wing, 11·5 to 12; tarsus, 2 to 2·12; bill at front, 1·6 to 1·82.

Bill red, occasionally with a blackish tinge; irides pale yellow; eyelids bright red; legs and feet deep red.

Summer plumage.—Entire head, neck, upper back, rump, upper tail-coverts, entire lower parts and tail, white, tinged with rosy, except on the head, when the rosy tint is scarcely perceptible; mantle, secondaries, tertiaries, lesser and median wing-coverts, and the upper greater-coverts, also the wing-lining, pale bluish french-grey, rather pearly-grey on the back and tertiaries; four or five of the primary-coverts and edge of the wing white; primaries, the first white, except the outer web, tip and margin of the inner web; secondaries to fourth primaries white, the margins of their outer webs narrower and decreasing in extent terminally, and broadening and running up basally on their inner webs, with the black tips broader successively; fifth and sixth primaries tipped white; the outer web of the fifth greyish, and that of the sixth slightly darker with a subterminal dark band.

Very common during winter in the Kurrachee Harbour and adjoining coast.

GENUS, **Hydrochelidon,** *Boie.*

Bill rather long, slender, very gently arched on the culmen; gonys with the ascending portion short; tail short, slightly forked; tarsus moderate; feet not fully webbed.

Hydrochelidon hybrida, *Pall.*

984.—*H. indica*, Steph.—Jerdon's Birds of India, Vol. II, p. 837; Butler, Guzerat; Stray Feathers, Vol. IV, p. 32; Deccan, Stray Feathers, Vol. IX, p. 440; Murray's Vertebrate Zoology of Sind, p. 323.

THE SMALL MARSH TERN.

Length, 10 to 11; expanse, 29; wing, 8·5 to 9; tail, 3·5; tarsus, 1; bill at front, 1·12.

Bill lake-red; irides brown; feet dull red.

In summer plumage, the head and nape black; lores and a broad line through the eyes, white; back of neck, mantle, wings and tail, darkish-grey; chin, cheeks, and sides of neck, very pale grey, deepening on the breast; abdomen dull black; under tail-coverts white.

In winter plumage, the forehead and round the bill white; top of head and nape more or less black, or dusky, edged with white; the whole lower parts white; bill dusky lake; feet dingy lake.

The young have the head brownish, dusky on the occiput, and the usual mottled plumage above; primaries dark ashy; the bill dark brown, reddish at the base; feet fleshy brown.

The Whiskered or Small Marsh Tern is not uncommon during the cold season.

SUB-FAMILY, **Sterninæ.**

Bill long or moderate, entire, straight, compressed and pointed; the lower mandible angled; nostrils longitudinal; wing long and pointed; tail short and even, or long and forked; tarsus short and slender; toes short, webbed.

GENUS, Sterna, *Lin.*

Nostrils with plumes reaching to the opening; first quills longest; tail forked; tarsus rather long; bill moderate; culmen slightly curved, and with a projecting angle.

Sterna caspia, *Pall.*

982.—Jerdon's Birds of India, Vol. II, p. 855; Butler, Deccan; Stray Feathers, Vol. IX, p. 439; Murray's Vertebrate Zoology of Sind, p. 322.

THE CASPIAN TERN.

Length, 18 to 20; expanse, 49; wing, 16; tail, 4·5 to 5; tarsus, 1·75; bill at front, 2·75.

Bill coral red; irides brown; legs and feet black.

In summer, head above, nape, and ear-coverts, pure black; mantle, wings, and tail, pearl-grey; some of the first primaries dark-edged and tipped; back of neck and lower plumage white.

In winter, the head is white, the occiput marked with numerous black streaks.

The Caspian Tern is not uncommon during the cold weather on the Sind coast; it is much less common further south, but extends as far as Bombay, whence Mr. Hume records a specimen.

It is also found inland on some of the larger lakes and jheels.

Sterna anglica, *Mont.*

983.—Jerdon's Birds of India, Vol. II, p. 836; *S. nilatica*, Hass.; Butler, Guzerat; Stray Feathers, Vol. IV, p. 31; Deccan, Stray Feathers, Vol. IX, p. 440; Murray's Vertebrate Zoology of Sind, p. 320.

THE GULL-BILLED TERN.

Length, 14 to 16; expanse, 38 to 40; wing, 13 to 14·5; tail, 5 to 6; tarsus, 1·5; bill at front, 1·5.

Bill black; irides dark brown; legs black.

In summer, the forehead, crown, and nape, deep black; mantle, wings, and tail, light grey, paling on the tail; quills hoary-grey; the first five primaries tipped with dusky on their inner webs; sides of the head and plumage beneath pure white.

In winter, the head is white with grey streaks, the ear-coverts and (more or less) round the eyes dusky.

The young is somewhat similar to the adult in winter plumage, but has the primaries all dusky grey.

The Gull-billed Tern is very common during the cold season in suitable places throughout the region. It is very doubtful whether any of them remain to breed.

Sterna seena, *Sykes.*

985.—*Seena aurantia*, Gray.—Jerdon's Birds of India, Vol. II, p. 838 ; Butler, Guzerat ; Stray Feathers, Vol. IV, p. 32 ; Deccan, Stray Feathers, Vol. IX, p. 440 ; Murray's Vertebrate Zoology of Sind, p. 323 ; Swinhoe and Barnes, Central India ; Ibis, 1885, p. 135.

THE LARGE RIVER TERN.

Length, 15 to 16 ; expanse, 34 ; wing, 11 ; tail, 7·5 ; tarsus, 1 ; bill at front, 1·5.

Bill bright deep yellow ; irides brown ; legs red.

Whole head above glossy-black ; upper plumage pale grey ; tail with the lateral feathers white ; whole lower plumage white, the flanks tinged with ashy.

The Large River Tern (with the exception perhaps of the Deccan, where its occurrence appears doubtful), occurs more or less commonly in the cold season throughout the district. A few at all events remain to breed, as I have found eggs, both in Sind and Central India, during April and May. They are deposited in slight depressions in the sandy bed or banks of rivers ; there is no nest. The eggs, four in number, are broadish ovals in shape, and are of a buffy or greenish stone color, spotted and streaked, more especially at the larger end, with deep brown and underlying spots of pale inky-purple.

They measure 1·65 inches in length by about 1·25 in breadth.

Sterna melanogastra, *Tem.*

987.—*S. javanica*, Hors.—Jerdon's Birds of India, Vol. II, p. 840 ; Butler, Deccan ; Stray Feathers, Vol. IX, p. 440 ; Murray's Vertebrate Zoology of Sind, p. 323 ; Swinhoe and Barnes, Central India ; Ibis, 1885, p. 138.

THE BLACK-BELLIED TERN.

Length, 12 ; expanse, 26 ; wing, 9 ; tail, 6 ; tarsus, 1 ; bill at front, 1·48.

Bill orange-yellow ; irides brown ; legs and feet vermilion red.

Head and nape black ; neck, mantle, wings and tail, light-grey ; face, lores and ear-coverts, white ; chin and throat white ; neck and breast light pearl-grey ; abdomen, vent, and under tail-coverts brown-black.

In winter plumage the head is mixed with dusky, and the abdomen is pearly-grey instead of black.

The Black-bellied Tern is a more or less common permanent resident throughout the region. Major Butler does not appear to have met with it in Northern Guzerat, but I cannot help thinking that he has passed over it. They breed during March and April, depositing their eggs in mere depressions in the sand, close to the water. The eggs, three or four in number, are moderately oval in shape, of a buffy ground color, spotted and streaked with purplish-brown. They measure 1·33 by 0·99.

Sterna albigena, *Licht.*

987*bis.*—Murray's Vertebrate Zoology of Sind, p. 324; Butler, Deccan, Stray Feathers, Vol. IX, p. 440.

THE WHITE-CHEEKED TERN.

Length, 12·5 to 14·5; expanse, 29·5; wing, 9·8; tail, 4 to 6·5; tarsus, 0·75; bill from gape, 2·15.

Bill blackish, tipped whitish-horny; irides brown; legs and feet Indian-red, tinged dusky.

The lores and point of the forehead white, the latter with a few black speckles; a patch in front of the eye black, speckled with white; the anterior half of the crown white, tinged earthy or brownish-grey, and with spots and blotches of brownish-black; feathers immediately above the eye, all the feathers behind it, the sides of the head, occiput and nape, black; the posterior half of the crown blackish-brown, a little mingled with greyish-white; an imperfect white band from the lores beneath the eyes, with another imperfect black one below it; the back of the neck is whitish, the feathers suffused with grey towards the tips; the whole of the back, scapulars, wings and tail, a moderately dark French-grey, darker than in *S. bengalensis*, but not so dark as in some specimens of *bergii*; the upper tail-coverts slightly paler; the wings more silvery, but the outer web of the first primary and of the exterior elongated tail-feathers much darker; the inner webs of the primaries darker; the first primary with a considerable portion of the inner web white to the margin; the other primaries also with white on their inner web, but with a grey band on their margin; the second and third tail feathers also a rather darker grey on their outer webs towards the points; the rest of tail feathers, inner and outer webs, pretty well concolorous with the rump and upper tail-coverts; the chin, throat, and sides of neck, almost pure white, with only a few faint dusky grey patches; the breast and abdomen a dusky bluish-grey, with many large patches of white; the lower tail-coverts greyish-white; the wing-lining white.

In breeding plumage, according to Heuglin, the upper surface is a full bluish-grey; the front and sides of the neck, breast and abdomen, a somewhat paler and more purplish-grey; the entire upper surface of the head and nape intensely black; the chin and upper part of the throat, the lores, and an oblique band below the eyes, conspicuously snowy-white; the beak coral-red, blackish towards the base of the culmen and tip; the feet bright coral-red.

The White-cheeked Tern occurs along the Sind and Mekran coasts, and is not uncommon in the Kurrachee Harbour.

Sterna saundersi, *Hume.*

988*ter.*—Murray's Vertebrate Zoology of Sind, p. 325; Butler, Deccan, Stray Feathers, Vol. IX, p. 441.

SAUNDER'S LITTLE TERN.

Length, 9·12; expanse, 19·25; wing, 6·43; tail, 3; tarsus, 0·6; bill from gape, 1·5.

Bill yellow, tipped dusky; irides blackish brown; legs and feet dusky yellowish-olive.

A triangular frontal patch, the angles reaching to within 0·12 of the eyes, white; a very broad stripe through the lores to the eye black; a narrow white line intervenes between this stripe and the upper mandible; the whole crown, occiput, short occipital crest and sides of occiput as low as the lower margin of the eye, velvet-black, the central two-thirds of the lower eyelid white, and no black below this; all the rest of the sides of head and neck, chin, throat, entire under parts, wing-lining and exterior tail-feathers, pure white; the first three primaries black with black shafts and broad white margins on their inner webs; their greater coverts dusky black; the whole of the rest of the upper surface, including wings and tail, and excepting parts and feathers already described, a most delicate satin-grey, contrasting in the strongest manner with the early black primaries.

Saunder's Little Tern is very abundant at Kurrachee and along the adjacent coast. It is a permanent resident, breeding during April and May. The eggs, two in number, are deposited in a small depression in the sand. They are rather longish ovals pointed at one end; the ground color is drab or stone, and the markings consist of spots, streaks, and blotches of a dark or reddish-brown color.

They measure 1·3 inches in length by 0·9 in breadth.

Sterna bergii, *Licht.*

989.—*T. cristatus*, Steph.—Jerdon's Birds of India, Vol. II, p. 842; Butler, Deccan, Stray Feathers, Vol. IX, p. 441; Murray's Vertebrate Zoology of Sind, p. 322.

THE LARGE SEA TERN.

Length, 17 to 18; wing, 13 to 14; tail, 7; tarsus, 1·25; bill at front, 2·5.

Bill pale yellow; irides dark brown; legs black.

Head, with the longish occipital crest, deep glossy-black; forehead, lores, ear-coverts, nape, and all the lower parts silky-white; back, wings and tail, rather darkish silvery-grey; edge of the wing and tips of the secondaries white; quills dark at the base and tip, hoary or silvery toward the terminal portion, with the inner web and shafts white internally, diminishing in quantity from the first.

The Large Sea Tern is very common at Kurrachee and all along the sea coast. It breeds during April and May, on islands in the Persian Gulf, in company with many other species of Terns. Boat loads of eggs are annually brought into Kurrachee. The eggs are broad ovals, much pointed at one end;

the ground color varies from pale buff to warm salmon color; the markings are of two colors—dark burnt sienna and pale inky-purple. They measure 2·45 by 1·7.

Sterna media, *Horsf.*

990.—*T. bengalensis*, Less.—Jerdon's Birds of India, Vol. II, p. 843; Butler, Deccan; Stray Feathers, Vol. IX, p. 441; Murray's Vertebrate Zoology of Sind, p. 321.

THE SMALLER SEA TERN.

Length, 15 to 16; wing, 12; tail, 6·5; tarsus, 1·23; bill at front, 2·25.

Bill yellow; irides deep brown; legs black.

Whole head, including the forehead and occipital crest, glossy-black; lores, face, sides of neck, and all the lower parts, white; upper plumage light silvery-grey, paling slightly on the tail; quills dark grey, white on the inner portion of the inner webs.

In winter plumage the entire forehead and lores are pure white, the crown white, the feathers centred dusky; occiput dusky, the feathers slightly margined with white; a spot in front of the eye, and a line behind it, black.

The Smaller Sea Tern is most abundant in the Kurrachee Harbour and all along the coasts.

It breeds on islands in the Persian Gulf.

Sterna cantiaca, *Gm.*

990*bis*.—Murray's Vertebrate Zoology of Sind, p. 321.

Length, 17·5 to 18; wing, 11·5 to 12·5; tail, 6 to 6·2; bill at front, 2 to 2·4.

Bill black, tipped yellowish-white; irides brown; legs and feet black.

Forehead, crown, back of neck, and nape, occipital crest and ear-coverts, glossy black; sides of the face, chin, throat, neck in front and behind, breast and entire lower parts, white, tinged with rosy; mantle and wings pale silvery-grey; the first primary is slightly darker than the rest, with more than half of the inner webs near the shaft white; the next two or three paler, also the succeeding ones, till they shade away into the color of the wing-coverts; their inner webs greyish-white or white; under wing-coverts white; tail forked, white; the external feathers on each side slightly greyish on their outer webs; upper tail-coverts white.

In winter plumage the whole of the head is white or mottled with white and black, and there is a crescentic narrow black spot in front of the eye; mantle and wings as in the summer plumage.

This Tern is common in the Kurrachee Harbour and on the Sind and Mekran Coasts. It breeds in the Persian Gulf.

Sterna anaetheta, *Scop.*

992.—*O. anasthætus*, Scop.—Jerdon's Birds of India, Vol. II, p. 844; *S. anasthætus*, Scop.; Murray's Vertebrate Zoology of Sind, p. 325; Butler, Deccan; Stray Feathers, Vol. IX, p. 441.

THE BROWN-WINGED TERN.

Length, 14; wing, 10; tail, 6·75; tarsus, 0·7; bill at front, 1·6.

Bill dusky reddish, red at base of lower mandible; irides brown; legs coral-red.

Forehead white, top of the head black; nape pure silky-white; plumage above ashy-grey, with white margins to the feathers of the back; wings dusky brown, black along the margin, over the radius, and edged in front with white; quills blackish, paler internally; face and lower plumage white.

The Brown-winged Tern occurs on the Sind and Mekran Coasts.

Sterna fuliginosa, *Gm.*

992*bis.*—Butler, Deccan, Stray Feathers, Vol. IX, p. 441; Murray's Vertebrate Zoology of Sind, p. 326.

THE SOOTY TERN.

Length, 17; wing, 11; tail, 7; tarsus, 1; bill at gape, 2·2.

Legs and feet black; irides brown.

Forehead and a streak from the base of the bill to the eye white; sides of the face, chin, throat, neck in front, breast and entire under parts, white; top of head, nape, neck behind, back, scapulars and wings, sooty-black; under wing-coverts white; tail forked; external feathers on each side white on their outer web; rest are white at the base.

The Sooty Tern occurs all along the coast.

GENUS, Anous, *Leach.*

Bill long, slender, straight, very slightly curved towards the tip; gonys well marked, short; nostrils in a large groove; wings very long; tail slightly rounded; tarsus short; feet large, fully webbed; toe serrated.

Anous stolidus, *Lin.*

993.—Jerdon's Birds of India, Vol. II, p. 845; Murray's Vertebrate Zoology of Sind, p. 326.

THE NODDY.

Length, 14·5 to 16; wing, 10·25 to 11·5; tail, 5·5 to 6; tarsus, 1; bill, 1·5 to 1·75; middle-toe, 1·75.

Legs and feet black; irides brown.

Entirely sooty-brown, with a darker band along the radius, and the quills and tail blacker, somewhat paler on the head and neck; lores dark brown, with a narrow white line dividing this from the hue of the head, which at times appears to assume a delicate purplish-ash color as far as the crown, gradually shading into the brown of the occiput; lower parts slightly lighter than above.

The young bird has the feathers blackish, edged with white.

The Noddy occurs on the Sind and Mekran Coasts.

GENUS, Rhynchops, *Lin.*

Bill with the upper mandible much shorter than the lower one, exceedingly compressed, long, straight; the tip of both mandibles truncated; wings long; feet short; webs excised.

Rhynchops albicollis, *Sws.*

995.—Jerdon's Birds of India, Vol. II, p. 847; Butler, Guzerat; Stray Feathers, Vol. IV, p. 32; Deccan, Stray Feathers, Vol. IX, p. 441; Murray's Vertebrate Zoology of Sind, p. 327.

THE INDIAN SKIMMER.

Length, 16·5; expanse, 44; wing, 16; tail, 4·75; tarsus, 1·25; bill, upper mandible, 2·9; lower mandible, 3·75.

Bill deep orange, yellowish at tip; irides brown; legs bright vermilion-red.

Crown of the head, back and scapulars, rump and the two central tail-feathers, sooty-brown or black; the quills somewhat darker, edges of the secondaries and tertials white; forehead, face to the eyes, the back of the neck, and the whole lower parts, with the sides of the lower back and rump, and the lateral tail-feathers, white; wing beneath glossy-cinereous.

The young bird has the feathers edged with creamy-white, and the bill and legs dusky-yellow.

The Scissors-bill or Skimmer is very common on the Indus, and occurs, but more rarely, in Guzerat, the Deccan and Central India.

It affects the larger rivers, rarely visiting tanks or *jheels*. The only one I obtained in Central India was hawking over the surface of a tank during the rains, but this is most exceptionable.

FAMILY, Phætonidæ.

SUB-FAMILY, Phætoninæ, *J. E. Gr.*

Bill as long as the head, sharp, and gently curved above; margins finely serrated; two central feathers of tail long and narrow; tarsus short.

GENUS, Phæton, *Lin.*

The characters are the same as those of the sub-family.

Phæton indicus, *Hume.*

996*bis.*—Murray's Vertebrate Zoology of Sind, p. 327.

THE INDIAN TROPIC BIRD.

Length, including elongated central tail-feathers which project from 3 to 5·9 inches beyond the rest of the tail, 20 to 23; expanse, 37 to 40; tail, 7·5 to 10·5; wing, 10·75 to 11·75; tarsus, 1; bill at front, 2·4.

Irides deep brown; legs and hind-toe with web white, tinged bluish and creamy-yellow; rest of feet and claws black.

A broad conspicuous black crescent in front of the eye, and a narrow black line, from the gape to nostrils, and nostrils to culmen, dividing the feathers from the bill; the whole forehead, front part of the crown, ear-coverts, and entire lower parts, including wing lining and axillaries, pure white; a black line from the posterior angle of the eye, running round the back of the nape, where it forms a more or less conspicuous half-collar; hind-crown and nape inside the half-collar white, each feather with a triangular black bar near the tip; carpal joint of wing, four or five posterior primaries, all the secondaries, the primary coverts except those of the first five quills, the greater and median coverts pure white; winglet, greater-coverts, shafts and outer webs of the first five primaries, together with a narrow stripe along the shaft of the inner web, black; the extreme tips and inner webs of these feathers white; tertiaries and their greater-coverts black, narrowly margined on the exterior webs and tipped with white; the lesser secondary-coverts similar; the entire back, rump, scapulars and upper tail-coverts white, closely barred with black, the bars being slightly cuspidate on the upper back, and the longest scapulars almost devoid of barring; tail-feathers white, their bases black shafted, and the lateral feathers mostly with an arrow-head bar or spot near the tips.

The above description is reproduced from "Stray Feathers." It still remains doubtful whether this is an immature phase of *P. œthereus* or a new species.

Several specimens have been obtained at different times on the Mekran Coast.

TRIBE, **Piscatores.**

Feet entirely webbed, the hind-toe articulated on the inner side of the tarsus, directed inwards, and in some slightly forwards joined to the inner front-toe by web, forming a most powerful oar; legs short; wings long or moderate; bill varied.

FAMILY, **Sulidæ.**

Bill stout, straight; wings long; tail moderate, wedged; feet fully webbed; size large; of oceanic habits.

GENUS, **Sula,** *Brisson.*

Bill lengthened, compressed, straight, thick at base, acute and compressed at tip; margin serrated; culmen convex; upper mandible furrowed; nostrils minute, almost impervious, in a long groove, supposed to be wanting; wing very long; tail moderately long, wedge-shaped; tarsus short; claw of the middle-toe pectinated externally.

Sula cyanops, *Sund.*

999*bis.*—Murray's Vertebrate Zoology of Sind, p. 328.

THE WHITE BOOBY.

Length, 32·5; wing, 16·5; tail, 8; tarsus, 2·25; bill at front, 4.

Bill horny-blackish at base; irides lemon-yellow; legs and feet bluish-grey.

Face to behind the eyes and throat nude; entire head, neck, back, rump, upper tail-coverts, and entire lower parts white with a slight fulvous tinge; primaries, secondaries and tertials, also the tail, black.

The White Booby occurs on the Sind Coast.

SUB-FAMILY, Pelecaninæ.

Bill long, flattened, compressed and hooked at tip; tail short; lower mandible and throat with a membraneous pouch; orbits nude.

GENUS, Pelecanus, *Lin.*

The characters are the same as those of the sub-family.

Pelecanus crispus, *Bouch.*

1004*bis.*—Murray's Vertebrate Zoology of Sind, p. 328.

THE WHITE PELICAN.

♂. Length, 70 to 74·5; expanse, 114 to 122; wing, 26·25 to 29·28; tail, 9·5 to 10; bill at front, 15·4 to 16·6.

♀. Length, 66 to 68; wing, 25 to 28.

In the adult in spring plumage, excepting the quills, primary coverts and winglet, the whole plumage is white, with more or less of a pearly-grey tinge on both the upper and under surfaces according to the light in which it is looked at; there is a broad band at the base of the neck in front and at the sides, faintly tinged with very pale straw color; there is not the faintest tinge of rosy anywhere; the whole of the feathers of the head and neck are very narrow, long, soft, and silky, much curled, and twisted on the head, especially behind and just above the eye; and the feathers of the back of the head are much elongated, so as to form a dense, full crest, some 4·25 inches long; a line of feathers, about 1·5 inches wide, down the whole back of the neck, is of a more snowy and less pearly-white than the rest of the neck; the scapulars, rump, and upper tail-coverts and median and greater wing-coverts are conspicuously black shafted, and all these, except the longest of the scapulars, are very long and lanceolate. A few of the longest scapulars are broad and round or mucronate at the end; back, scapulars and tail with a beautiful satiny gloss; the two exterior tail feathers with nearly the whole shafts black, and generally with a decided grey tinge on the outer web to near the tip; the rest of the tail feathers with only the terminal third of the shafts black; primaries (all of which are white at the base) and their coverts and winglet very dark brown, almost black; the second to the fifth primary emarginate on the outer web and silvered with grey on the last above the emargination, which in the second is hidden by the coverts; there is more or less silvery or grey on the outer webs of all the other primaries, their coverts and winglets; the first five primaries are faintly notched on the inner web, and more pale or greyish-white on the latter above the notches, while the rest of the primaries have the inner portions of the inner webs white; this is still more conspicuous in the secondaries, most of which have their whole outer webs a silver-grey; the tertials are pure white; the feathers of the base of the neck and breast thickly set, very narrow and pointed, the filaments along the margin a good deal separated.

The young bird wants the linear lanceolate feathers. It has the whole head, neck, and upper and lower surface white; the back of the neck more or less shaded with grey; tips of the quills and a row of small coverts near the margin of the wing pale wood-brown; the feathers of the head shorter and more fur-like than in the adult; crest small; scapulars and shoulder feathers broadly tipped with pale brown, with dark shafts; tail feathers white at the base on both webs; greater part of the rest of the inner web white; primaries and secondaries white at their bases; a large portion of their inner webs white; the rest a darkish brown.

Adult: irides white, in the young pale yellow; legs and feet pale plumbeous; edges of upper and lower mandibles for the terminal two-thirds yellowish, and in the young a horny white-brown, or yellowish-grey; the nail orange or pale orange.

In the breeding plumage the pouch is a deep orange-red, with a black patch on either side, just at the base of the lower mandible; in the non-breeding plumage a dirty primrose, or pale fleshy, tinged with lemon-yellow.

The White Pelican occurs on the river Indus in Sind.

Pelecanus javanicus, *Horsf.*

1003.—Jerdon's Birds of India, Vol. II, p. 857; *P. onocrotalus*, Lin.; Butler, Guzerat, Stray Feathers, Vol. IV, p. 32; Murray's Vertebrate Zoology of Sind, p. 330.

The Lesser White Pelican.

Length, 56; wing, 25; tail, 6·5; tarsus, 4; bill, 12 to 13.

Bill bluish, red and yellow on the sides, tip blood-red; lower mandible bluish posteriorly, yellow in front; pouch yellow, veined with purplish-red; irides blood-red; legs fleshy pink.

White, in fresh plumage with a highly roseate tint; primaries dusky; secondaries grey externally; tertiaries whitish with broad black margins on each side, internally greyish; tail white.

With the exception of the Deccan the Lesser White Pelican is more or less common throughout the district.

It only occurs as a visitant, and does not remain to breed.

Pelecanus philippensis, *Gm.*

1004.—Jerdon's Birds of India, Vol. II, p. 858; Butler, Guzerat, Stray Feathers, Vol. IV, p. 33; Deccan, Stray Feathers, Vol. IX, p. 442; Murray's Vertebrate Zoology of Sind, p. 330.

THE GREY PELICAN.

Length, 62; expanse, 96; wing, 24; tail, 18; tarsus, 3; bill at front, 12 to 14.

Bill pale bluish, tinged with carneous, yellow at tip; naked face and gular pouch pale livid fleshy, the latter varied with reddish lines, and faintly tinged with yellow; irides pale brown; legs fleshy.

Head and neck greyish-white, the feathers rather scant and somewhat fur-like; a short occipital crest of slightly recurved feathers brownish, tipped with greyish-white; upper plumage greyish-white, the feathers of the back, rump, and upper tail-coverts being dingy whitish, tinged with grey; scapulars grey with black shafts, and the feathers white at the base; lesser and median-coverts greyish-white; greater coverts grey, with black shafts; primaries dusky-grey with black shafts, white at the base with white shafts; secondaries and tertiaries much the same; the tail grey, the feathers also black shafted, and the basal half or two-thirds of the inner webs white, as well as the base of the shaft; lower plumage greyish-white, the feathers lanceolate, pure white, in the centre and tip, with grey margins and brownish at the base; under tail-coverts greyish-white, slightly mottled with brownish; under wing-coverts whitish.

With the exception of the Deccan, where it is somewhat rare, the Grey Pelican is a common seasonal visitant throughout the region.

FAMILY, Graculidæ.

Bill moderately long, cylindric, hooked at the tip, grooved; wing moderate, tail-feathers stiff; upper tail-coverts exceedingly short; lower tail-coverts also short.

GENUS, Phalacrocorax, *Brisson.*

Bill moderately long, slightly raised at the base, the tip well hooked; nostrils, a small narrow line, apparently not pervious; upper mandible truncated, orbits and throat more or less nude; tail moderate or rather long, of fourteen stiff feathers, cuneate; wings rather short.

Phalacrocorax carbo, *Lin.*

1005.—Jerdon's Birds of India, Vol. II, p. 861; Butler, Guzerat,

Stray Feathers, Vol. IV, p. 33; Murray's Vertebrate Zoology of Sind, p. 330.

THE LARGE CORMORANT.

Length, 32 to 34; expanse, 60; wing, 14; tail, 7·5; tarsus, 2·25; bill at front, 2·5.

Bill brownish; irides sea-green; facial skin pale greenish; gular pouch deep yellow; feet black.

Back, the feathers of the back, scapulars and wing-coverts, bronze-color with black edges; face, sides of the head, and chin, white and a white spot on the thigh-coverts.

In breeding plumage the male bird assumes a lot of white hair-like feathers on the neck, very conspicuous in some examples, less so in others.

With the exception of the Deccan, whence it has not been recorded, the Large Cormorant is generally spread throughout the region. It is a permanent resident in Sind, breeding in the Eastern Narra.

Palacrocorax fuscicollis, *Steph.*

1006.—*G. sinensis*, Shaw.—Jerdon's Birds of India, Vol. II, p. 862; Butler, Guzerat, Stray Feathers, Vol. IV, p. 331; Deccan, Stray Feathers, Vol. IX, p. 442; Murray's Vertebrate Zoology of Sind, p. 33; Swinhoe and Barnes, Central India, Ibis, 1885, p. 138.

THE LESSER CORMORANT.

Length, 24 to 27; expanse, 36 to 40; wing, 11; tail, 5·25 to 6; tarsus, 1·7; bill at front, 2·25.

Bill dusky brown, reddish beneath; gular skin yellow; irides bluish-green; nude orbits black; feet black.

Adult, head and neck shining black; feathers of the back and wing-coverts bronze color as in the last; throat white; this color extending towards the eye, and passing into a pale brown on the cheeks; lower plumage deep black.

In breeding plumage this Cormorant assumes some white specks on the forehead and above the eyes, and a white tuft behind each ear; the chin, however, is then black.

The young birds are more or less brown above, and white beneath.

The Lesser Cormorant is more or less common throughout the district; it is a permanent resident and breeds in company during the rains.

The eggs are similar to those of the snake bird.

Phalacrocorax pygmæus, *Pall.*

1007.—*G. javanicus*, Horsf.—Jerdon's Birds of India, Vol. II, p. 863; Butler, Guzerat, Stray Feathers, Vol. IV, p. 34; Deccan, Stray Feathers, Vol. IX, p. 442; Murray's Vertebrate Zoology of Sind, p. 332; Swinhoe and Barnes, Central India, Ibis, 1885, p. 138.

THE LITTLE CORMORANT.

Length, 19 to 20; expanse, 32; wing, 8·5; tail, 5·5 to 6; tarsus, 1·25; bill at front, 1·25.

Bill brown, livid-purple during breeding season; gular skin and orbits blackish, livid in summer; legs blackish, dusky-livid at the same season.

In winter, the plumage is more or less black, the feathers brown-edged on the neck, breast and back, and the chin, white.

In full breeding plumage, in June or July, the whole body is glossy black; the head with a short occipital crest; the wing-coverts, scapulars, secondaries and tertiaries, as it were glossed with silvery, with a black margin, and the interscapulars with a narrow silvery centre; a white triangular spot on the top of the head; lores white, and a broad line through the eyes with white hairs, and several also on the nape and sides of the neck; chin black.

The young have the upper plumage brown, mixed with blackish, and the lower parts reddish brown, white posteriorly, and the throat whitish.

The Little Cormorant is abundantly spread throughout the entire region.

It is a permanent resident and breeds in company towards the end of the rains.

The nests, composed of sticks, are placed on trees, standing well out into the water. The eggs, three or four in number, are long ovals, more or less pointed at one end, with a chalky coating, white or bluish-white in color when fresh laid, but becoming soiled as incubation proceeds.

This coating is easily removable, and frequently becomes detached in the nest, leaving the hard greenish-blue shell visible. They measure 1·75 inches in length by 1·16 in breadth.

SUB-FAMILY, Plotinæ.

Bill elongate, slender, straight, subulate, very acute, the margin obliquely toothed towards the tip; nostrils very small, basal; tail long, rounded; neck very long and slender; body and feet as in the Cormorants.

GENUS, Plotus, *Lin.*

The characters are the same as those of the sub-family.

Plotus melanogaster, *Penn.*

1008.—Jerdon's Birds of India, Vol. II, p. 865; Butler, Guzerat, Stray Feathers, Vol. IV, p. 34; Deccan, Stray Feathers, Vol. IX, p. 442; Murray's Vertebrate Zoology of Sind, p. 332; Swinhoe and Barnes, Central India, Ibis, 1885, p. 138.

THE INDIAN SNAKE BIRD.

Length, 32; wing, 14; tail, 9; tarsus, 1·5; bill at front, 3·5.

Bill dusky above, yellowish on the sides; irides yellow; legs black.

Forehead, nape, and neck, mottled brown, each feather being dark-brown with a pale edging, the median line of the head, nape, and hind neck being darker than the rest, and the median line below paler; a minute white line from the base of the bill over the eye; the cheeks, chin, and throat, white, continued in a line from below the eye down the side of the neck for nearly half its length, and gradually overcome on the sides of the fore-neck by the brown feathers which run along the sides of the neck, and form a narrow line passing up through the white to the gape; upper back gradually changing from the brown of the hind-neck into the brownish-black of the rest of the dorsal region, and on the sides spotted with white, the spots commencing at first as small oval drops, and gradually increasing in size and shape to the scapulars, which are long and lanceolate, and deep black with the central portion silvery-white; wing-coverts black, spotted with silvery-white; tertiaries and the last secondaries also with a silvery streak on their outer webs; quills and tail deep raven black; the feathers of the tail with a barred appearance on their outer webs, caused by a series of transverse elevated ridges which are gradually lost on the outermost feathers; lower portion of the neck, breast, and all the lower parts, glossy brownish-black.

The female has the head and neck pale whity-brown, lightest on the lower sides, and albescent on the chin, face, and throat, and a fulvous patch on the sides of the neck, continued from the paler median line of the lower side of the neck and extending to the shoulder; back browner than in the male, becoming black on the rump; wing-coverts more or less brown; otherwise as in the male.

The young birds are colored somewhat as the female, and the nestlings have white down, with the wings and tail blackish.

The Snake Bird is very common throughout the district.

It is a permanent resident breeding from the commencement until long after the rains. They construct a flat stick nest on some tree, growing well into the water. The eggs, four in number, are elongated ovals, pointed more or less at one end, with a whitish or greenish-white chalky covering, which is easily removed by scraping. The real shell is of a greenish-blue color. They measure 2·13 inches in length by about 1·37 in breadth.

APPENDIX.

---o---

Owing to the kindness of Mr. J. Davidson, I am enabled to add a list of the birds collected or observed by him in Khandesh during the past four years. Many of these are rare and some of them have not previously been recorded from the Presidency; of these latter I append descriptions.

Aquila nipalensis, *Hodgs.*

27*bis*.—Jerdon's Birds of India, Vol. I, p. 57 (young); Stray Feathers, Vol. VII, p. 338.

Dimensions much as in *A. mogilnik.*

This species has two very distinct stages of plumage: First, the leading character of this first stage is to have two conspicuous white, or fulvous-white, wing-bands; the whole of the head, neck, chin, throat, back, lesser-scapulars, lesser wing-coverts, breast, abdomen, sides, leg-feathers, axillaries, wing-lining, except the greater lower wing-coverts, are a nearly uniform brown; the upper tail-coverts are clear, slightly yellowish-white; the tail dark-brown, more or less conspicuously tipped with fulvous-white, and with or without narrow, transverse, irregular grey-bands; the quills and greater wing-coverts are pure white, or white mingled with brown, slightly darker than the rest of the wing-lining.

The specimens in this stage vary greatly in the prevailing shade of brown; some are very pale, almost whitey-brown, others moderately pale hair-brown; some are entirely destitute of bars on the tail, others exhibit them conspicuously, and in the specimens before me the very lightest bird, and one of the darkest have no bars whatsoever on the tail; the lower tail-coverts, in almost all the specimens, are white, or slightly fulvous-white; but in one specimen they are mottled with the same brown as the rest of the lower parts.

In some, the pale tippings to the tail feathers are obsolete, in others conspicuous; the lesser and median lower wing-coverts, in one or two specimens, are narrowly tipped with white; generally they are of the same uniform brown, as the breast, abdomen, etc. In both these forms, the lower surface of the primaries are but faintly mottled with greyish-white.

Some specimens again are met with, changing to the next form; in these the wing-bands have nearly disappeared; the tail feathers show the irregular, narrow bars more strongly than in any of the others; the whole of the crown is darker, the pale tipping of the tail is almost obsolete; many of the median lower wing-coverts are rufous-buff, and the longer scapulars, and a few of the feathers of the back, are a deep chocolate brown.

The second stage is characteristically of a dark hair, or even at times umber-brown, darkest above, and chocolate-brown on the scapulars, with no pale bands on the wings or tips to the tail feathers, and with numerous narrow, transverse, irregular grey bars on the latter; and with much brown mingled with the lower tail-coverts.

Some specimens show traces of the wing-bars, characteristic of the preceding stage, but the more adult of them show more or less of a reddish buff patch on the nape and pale margins to the lesser wing-coverts.

A good many which I suppose to be those nearest to the first form, besides showing traces of the wing-bars, have all the feathers of the lower abdomen narrowly tipped with dingy fulvous-white.

That this is really the adult stage there can be no doubt; but even here the changes are most confusing, because one bird, for instance, having a most conspicuous orange-buff patch on the nape, has the whole of the upper tail-coverts a clear fulvous-white, as in the first stage; while another, though of a deeper brown, shows no trace of buff upon the nape, and has the upper tail-coverts uniform blackish-brown, as in the adult.

The wing-lining also varies very much in this stage. In some—and these by no means the most advanced—it is altogether deep brown, as in the perfect adult, while in others, by no means the least advanced, it is a rufous-buff, or a rufous-buff mingled with dark brown; in one, and that a bird showing the incipient orange-buff head, they are precisely as in the second stage; the lesser and median lower wing-coverts being uniform pale hair-brown, and the larger lower wing-coverts white.—*Hume*, "*Rough Notes.*"

Scops sunia, *Hodgs.*

74*bis.*—*Ephialtes pennatus*, Hodgs. (Rufous phase) Jerdon's Birds of India, Vol. I, p. 137.

Dimensions same as *S. pennatus*, Hodgs.

Upper parts uniform bright golden chestnut red, with black shafts, inconspicuous on the back, more distinct on the forehead, ear-plumes, and shoulders of the wings; outer edge of scapulars whitish; disc rufous, with some of the feathers white shafted; ruff deep brown, with the outer feathers black tipped, or black; beneath, deeply tinged with the hue of the back, but with more or less white on the belly, and under tail-coverts; the breast and sides of the belly with central brownish black streaks, the latter with transverse pencillings; four faint bars on the inner webs of the tail feathers, and the primaries also indistinctly barred with dusky or mottled brown. The young bird has all the feathers duller red, more black shafted, and there is much white on the lower surface, and the disc has a good deal of white; the scapulars are white externally with black tips; and the bars on the quills and tail feathers are more distinct brown and mottled.

I obtained a specimen of this bird at Khandalla, but I identified it as *E. pennatus*, in the rufous phase.

Heteroglaux (Carine) blewitti, *Hume.*

76*quint.*—Stray Feathers, Vol. I, p. 468.

♂. Length, 8·8; wing, 5·8; tail, 2·75; tarsus, 1; bill from gape, 0·65.

♀. Length, 9·5; expanse, 22·5; wing, 5·8; tarsus, 0·91; tail 2·9.

The lores, a line over the eye, a broad line under the eye, and a triangular patch immediately behind the eye, white; the bristles of the lores, with the terminal halves, black; the longest bristles reach just to the tip of the bill. From the gape, runs a stripe backwards, enveloping the whole of the ear-coverts, in color a rather dark earth-brown, obsoletely barred with albescent; chin and throat, and the sides of the lower mandible, below the stripe above mentioned, pure white; across this from the base of the lower mandible, on one side to the base on the other runs a conspicuous, transverse, dark-brown band. Forehead, top, and back of the head, back, and sides of the neck, scapulars, and interscapulary region an uniform rather dark earth brown; on lifting the feathers of the back of the neck and on lifting the scapulars, each feather is found to have a white bar about midway between base and tip, or in some cases nearer the tip, but these are not visible when the feathers are in repose. The wings are hair-brown, darkest on the primaries, secondaries and their greater coverts, and more nearly concolorous with the scapulars, on the lesser and median coverts, and tertiaries. All the quills have four or five conspicuous white spots on the outer webs, and corresponding imperfect bars (not quite reaching to the shafts) on the inner webs, which bars are pale brown towards the tips, and higher up pure white. The winglet, which is almost blackish brown, is similarly marked. The primary greater coverts similar, the rest of the greater, and some of the median-coverts, with very large conspicuous white spots near the tips on the outer webs. The lesser-coverts and most of the median unspotted; rump and upper tail-coverts, uniform brown, rather darker than the interscapulary region, some of them exhibiting, when lifted, a concealed white bar as in the scapulars. Tail hair brown, tipped white, and with three conspicuous transverse white bars, a fourth, a less perfect one, concealed by the upper tail-coverts. The breast feathers are mostly white, but are broadly tipped with hair-brown, which, owing to the overlapping of the feathers, is what is chiefly seen. The sides of the breast of this same color, but with traces of white bands well inside the tips, and not noticeable till the feathers are lifted.

Centre of abdomen, tibial, and tarsal plumes, toe-feathers, and lower tail-coverts pure white; sides of abdomen, sides and flanks, broadly banded with hair-brown.

Erythrosterna hyperythra, *Cab.*

323*ter.*—Stray Feathers, Vol. VII, p. 376.

Length, 5·33; wing, 2·88; tail, 3·3; tarsus, 0·78.

Bill dusky above, yellow beneath; irides dark brown; feet purplish brown.

The upper surface is brownish-grey, turning to a purer grey on the rump and upper tail-coverts; tail black, with the basal halves of the lateral rectrices white; the upper tail-coverts, especially the longest, are blackish in parts, especially on the outer webs. The lower surface is a bright red-brown or rusty-red, except on the middle of the abdomen, which is pure white. The red-brown color is most intense on the throat and breast, lighter on the contrary and mingled with albescent on the sides of the abdomen and lower tail-coverts. The prevailing hue of the tibial plumes is grey; the loral region is somewhat dotted with white; the sides of the head and neck contrast in pure, and not brownish grey with the upper surface, and are divided from the red-brown of throat and breast by an irregular blackish line; the under wing-coverts are tinged with rusty yellow.

The distinguishing characters of the species are the rich orange-brown of the throat and breast, and the black stripe running from the bill down the sides of the neck to the breast, and terminating below the bend of the closed wing. The specimens I obtained were both males, adult and immature; and the above characters are distinct in both, but much more so in the older bird.—*Stray Feathers,* Vol. VII, p. 376.

Megalurus palustris, *Horsf.*

440.—Jerdon's Birds of India, Vol. II, p. 70.

THE STRIATED MARSH BABBLER.

♂. Length, 9·9 to 10·62; expanse, 12 to 13; tail, 4·75 to 5·12; wing, 3·8 to 4·15; tarsus, 1·3 to 1·5; bill from gape, 0·95 to 1.

♀. Length, 8·8; expanse, 10·5; tail, 4·37; wing, 3·62; tarsus, 1·2; bill from gape, 0·9.

Bill, upper mandible dark brown, lower fleshy-white; irides wood brown; legs and feet dark horny, pink or pale brown.

Upper parts bright olive-brown, with a mesial black stripe to each feather of the back and scapulars; the edges of the wing-feathers also brown; tail pale dusky-brown, with light edges to the feathers; crown rufescent, with mesial dark lines, obsolete towards the front, and the feathers small, rigid and oppressed; a pale whitish streak over the eye; beneath, the chin and throat are white, the rest whitish, tinged with earthy-brown; the breast and flanks slightly speckled with brown.

Sturnopastor contra, *Lin.*

683.—Jerdon's Birds of India, Vol. II, p. 323.

THE PIED STARLING.
Ablak, Hin.

Length, 9; wing, 4·75; tail, 2·75; tarsus, 1·25; bill at front, 1·13.

Bill red at base, yellow at tip; irides brown; nude skin and orbits orange-yellow; legs yellowish.

Head, neck, and upper part of breast, glossy black; ear-coverts white, extending in a narrow line to the nape; back, wings, and tail, black, slightly glossed; upper tail-coverts white, as also an oblique bar on the wing, caused by the lesser coverts and outer portion of the scapulars; beneath, from the breast, white, tinged with reddish-ash; under tail-coverts pure white.

The young bird is more brown than black, and the colors are less defined.

I am not sure that I am correct in including the Pied Starling in the Birds of Bombay, but soon after leaving Khundwa, my attention was attracted to a bird strange to me. I noticed the bird at intervals until I left the train at Jubbulpore, when I found it to be the Pied Starling. It is quite common at Saugor, and I feel sure that specimens must straggle to the presidency.

Otocorys pencillata, *Gould.*

763.—Jerdon's Birds of India, Vol. II, p. 429.

THE HORNED LARK.

Length, 8; wing, 4·5; tail, 3; tarsus, 1; bill from gape, 0·8.

Bill and feet black.

Head, neck, and back, streakless vinaceous-ashy, passing to purer grey on the wings; narrow frontal band, lores, ear-coverts, and the sides of the neck, meeting as a gorget across the breast, purple black; the crown and the pointed sincipital tufts also black; forehead, supercilia, continued round the ear-coverts posteriorly, throat, and below the breast, white, the latter tinged with yellow; primaries fuscous-ashy, the first externally, white; the tail blackish, except the medial feathers, which are colored like the back, and the outermost and penultimate, which have white margins.

List of Birds obtained by Mr. J. Davidson at Khandesh.

2. Otogyps calvus, *Scop.*
3*bis* Gyps fulvescens, *Hume.*
4*bis* „ pallescens, *Hume.*
5. Pseudogyps bengalensis, *Gm.*
6. Neophron ginginianus, *Lath.*
9. Falco peregrinator, *Sund.*
11. „ jugger, *J. E. Gr.*
16. „ chiquera, *Daud.*
17. Cerchneis tinnunculus, *Lin.*
23. Astur badius, *Gm.*
24. Accipiter nisus, *Lin.*
27*bis* Aquila nipalensis, *Hodgs.*
28. „ clanga, *Pall.*
29. „ vindhiana, *Frankl.*
31. Hieraëtus pennatus, *Gm.*
33. Nisaëtus fasciatus, *Vieill.*
35. Limnaëtus cirrhatus, *Gm.*
38. Circaëtus gallicus, *Gm.*
39. Spilornis cheela, *Lath.*
40. Pandion haliaëtus, *Lin.*
45. Buteo ferox, *S. G. Gm.*
48. Butastur teesa, *Frankl.*
51. Circus macrurus, *S. G. Gm.*
52. „ cineraceus, *Mont.*
54. „ æruginosus, *Lin.*
55. Haliastur indus, *Bodd.*
56. Milvus govinda, *Sykes.*
57. Pernis ptilorhynchus, *Tem.*
59. Elanus cæruleus, *Desfr.*
60. Strix javanica, *Gm.*
65. Syrnium ocellatum, *Less.*
68. Asio accipitrinus, *Pall.*
69. Bubo bengalensis, *Frankl.*
70. „ coromandus, *Lath.*
72. Ketupa ceylonensis, *Gm.*
74*bis* Scops sunia, *Hodgs.*
75*ters* „ bakkamuna, *Forst.*
76. Carine brama, *Tem.*
76*quint* Heteroglaux blewitti, *Hume.*
77. Glaucidium radiatum, *Tick.*
81. Ninox lugubris, *Tick.*
82. Hirundo rustica, *Lin.*
84. „ filifera, *Steph.*
85. „ erythropygia, *Sykes.*
86. „ fluvicola, *Jerd.*
87. Cotyle riparia, *Lin.*
89. „ sinensis, *J. E. Gr.*
90. Ptyonoprogne concolor, *Sykes.*
91. „ rupestris, *Scop.*
92. Chelidon urbica, *Lin.*
98. Cypsellus melba, *Lin.*
100. „ affinis, *J. E. Gr.*
102. „ batassiensis, *J. E. Gr.*
104. Dendrochelidon coronata, *Tick.*
107. Caprimulgus indicus, *Lath.*
111. „ atripennis, *Jerd.*
112. „ asiaticus, *Lath.*
113. Caprimulgus mahrattensis, *Sykes.*
114. „ monticolus, *Frankl.*
117. Merops viridis, *Lin.*
118. „ philippinus, *Lin.*
120. „ persicus, *Pall.*
123. Coracias indicus, *Lin.*
125. „ garrula, *Lin.*
127. Pelargopsis gurial, *Pear.*
129. Halcyon smyrnensis, *Lin.*
134. Alcedo bengalensis, *Gm.*
136. Ceryle rudis, *Lin.*
144. Ocyceros birostris, *Scop.*
147. Palæornis eupatria, *Lin.*
148. „ torquatus, *Bodd.*
149. „ purpureus, *P. L. S Muller.*
160. Picus mahrattensis, *Lath.*
164. Yungipicus nanus, *Vig.*
167. Chrysocolaptes festivus, *Bodd.*
175. Chrysophlegma chlorigaster, *Jerd.*
180. Brachypternus aurantius, *Lin.*
188. Yunx torquila, *Lin.*
193*bis* Megalæma inornata, *Wald.*
194. „ viridis, *Bodd.*
197. Xantholæma hæmacephala, *P. L. S. Mull.*
199. Cuculus canorus, *Lin.*
201. „ poliocephalus, *Lath.*
202. „ sonnerati, *Lath.*
205. Hierococcyx varius, *Vahl.*
208. Cacomantis passerinus, *Vahl.*
212. Coccystes jacobinus, *Bodd.*
214. Eudynamis honorata, *Lin.*
217. Centrococcyx rufipennis, *Ill.*
220. Taccocua sirkee, *J. E. Gr.*
226. Æthopyga vigorsi, *Sykes.*
232. Cinnyris ceylonica, *Lin.*
234. „ asiatica, *Lath.*
238. Dicæum erythrorhynchus, *Lath.*
240. Piprisoma agile, *Tick.*
246. Salpornis spilonota, *Frankl.*
250. Sitta castaneiventris, *Frankl.*
254. Upupa epops, *Lin.*
255. „ ceylonensis, *Reich.*
256. Lanius lahtora, *Sykes.*
257. „ erythronotus, *Vig.*
260. „ vittatus, *Valenc.*
261. „ cristatus, *Lin.*
265. Tephrodornis pondicerianus, *Gm.*
267. Hemipus picatus, *Sykes.*
268. Volvocivora sykesi, *Strickl.*
270. Graucalus macii, *Less.*
272. Pericrocotus flammeus, *Forst.*
276. „ peregrinus, *Lin.*
277. „ erythropygius, *Jerd.*
278. Buchanga atra, *Herm.*
280. „ longicaudata, *Hay.*
281. „ cærulescens, *Lin.*

285. Dissemurus paradiseus, *Lin.*
288. Muscipeta paradisi, *Lin.*
290. Hypothymis azurea, *Bodd.*
292. Leucocerca aureola, *Vieill.*
293. „ leucogaster, *Cuv.*
295. Culicicapa ceylonensis, *Sws.*
297. Alseonax latirostris, *Raffl.*
301. Stoporala melanops, *Vig.*
304. Cyornis rubeculoides, *Vig.*
306. „ tickelli, *Bly.*
307. „ ruficaudus, *Sws.*
310. Muscicapula superciliaris, *Jerd.*
323*bis* Erythrosterna parva, *Bechst.*
323*ter* „ hyperythra, *Cab.*
342. Myiophoneus horsfieldi, *Vig.*
345. Pitta brachyura, *Lin.*
351. Cyanocinclus cyaneus, *Lin.*
353. Petrophila cinclorhyncha, *Vig.*
354. Geocichla cyanotis, *Jard. & Selb.*
359. Merula nigropilea, *Lafr.*
385. Pyctoris sinensis, *Gm.*
389. Alcippe poiocephala, *Jerd.*
397. Dumetia hyperythra, *Frankl.*
398. „ albogularis, *Bly.*
399. Pellorneum ruficeps, *Sws.*
404*ter* Pomatorhinus obscurus, *Hume.*
434. Malacocercus malabaricus, *Jerd.*
436. Argya malcolmi, *Sykes.*
438. Chatarrhœa caudata, *Dum.*
440. Megalurus palustris, *Horsf.*
452. Ixus luteolus, *Less.*
460*bis* Otocompsa fuscicaudata, *Gould.*
462. Molpastes hæmorrhous, *Gm.*
463. Phyllornis jerdoni, *Bly.*
464. „ malabaricus, *Gm.*
468. Iora tiphia, *Lin.*
468*bis* „ nigrolutea, *Marsh.*
470. Oriolus kundoo, *Sykes.*
472. „ melanocephalus, *Lin.*
475. Copsychus saularis, *Lin.*
479. Thamnobia fulicata, *Lin.*
481. Pratincola caprata, *Lin.*
483. „ indicus, *Bly.*
488. Saxicola opistholeuca, *Strickl.*
491. „ isabellinus, *Rüpp.*
492. „ deserti, *Rüpp.*
497. Ruticilla rufiventris, *Vieill.*
507. Larvivora superciliaris, *Jerd.*
512. Calliope pectoralis, *Gould.*
514. Cyanecula suecica, *Lin.*
515. Acrocephalus stentorius, *Hemp & Ehr.*
516. „ dumetorum, *Bly.*
530. Orthotomus sutorius, *Forst.*
535. Prinia stewarti, *Bly.*
538. „ hodgsoni, *Bly.*
539. Cisticola cursitans, *Frankl.*
543. Drymœca inornata, *Sykes.*
545. „ sylvatica, *Jerd.*
551. Franklinia buchanani, *Bly.*
553. Hypolais rama, *Sykes.*
553*bis* „ caligata, *Licht.*
554. Phylloscopus tristis, *Bly.*
556. „ magnirostris, *Bly.*
559. „ nitidus, *Bly.*
560. „ viridanus, *Bly.*
561. „ affinis, *Tick.*
562. Phylloscopus indicus, *Jerd.*
563. Reguloides occipitalis, *Jerd.*
565*bis* „ humii, *Brooks.*
581. Sylvia jerdoni, *Bly.*
582. „ affinis, *Bly.*
582*ter* „ althœa, *Hume.*
589. Motacilla maderaspatensis, *Gm.*
591*bis* „ dukhunensis, *Sykes.*
592. Calobates melanope, *Pall.*
593. Budytes cinereocapilla, *Savi.*
593*bis* „ melanocephala, *Licht.*
594*bis* „ citreola, *Pall.*
597. Anthus trivialis, *Lin.*
600. Corydalla rufula, *Vieill.*
601. „ striolata, *Bly.*
602. Agrodroma campestris, *Lin.*
604. „ sordida, *Rüpp.*
631. Zosterops palpebrosa, *Tem.*
645. Parus nipalensis, *Hodgs.*
648. Machlolophus aplonotus, *Bly.*
660. Corvus macrorhynchus, *Wagl.*
663. „ splendens, *Vieill.*
674. Dendrocitta rufa, *Scop.*
684. Acridotheres tristis, *Lin.*
685. „ ginginianus, *Lath.*
687. Sturnia pagodarum, *Gm.*
688. „ malabarica, *Gm.*
690. Pastor roseus, *Lin.*
694. Ploceus philippinus, *Lin.*
699. Amadina punctulata, *Lin.*
703. „ malabarica, *Lin.*
704. Estrelda amandava, *Lin.*
705. „ formosa, *Lath.*
706. Passer domesticus, *Lin.*
711. Gymnoris flavicollis, *Frankl.*
716. Emberiza buchanani, *Bly.*
721. Euspiza melanocephala, *Scops.*
722. „ luteola, *Sparrm.*
724. Melophus melanicterus, *Gm.*
738. Carpodacus erythrinus, *Pall.*
756. Mirafra erythroptera, *Jerd.*
757. „ cantillans, *Jerd.*
758. Ammomanes phœnicura, *Frankl.*
760. Pyrrhulauda grisea, *Scop.*
761. Calandrella brachydactyla, *Leisl.*
763. Otocorys pencillata, *Gould.*
765. Spizalauda deva, *Sykes.*
773. Crocopus chlorigaster, *Bly*
788. Columba intermedia, *Strickl.*
792. Turtur pulchratus, *Hodgs.*
793. „ meena, *Sykes.*
794. „ senegalensis, *Lin.*
795. „ suratensis, *Gm.*
796. „ risorius, *Lin.*
797. „ tranquebaricus, *Herm.*
800. Pterocles fasciatus, *Scop.*
802. „ exustus, *Tem.*
803. Pavo cristatus, *Lin.*
813. Gallus sonnerati, *Tem.*
814. Galloperdix spadiceus, *Gm.*
819. Francolinus pictus, *Jard. & Selb.*
822. Ortygornis pondicerianus, *Gm.*
826. Perdicula asiatica, *Lath.*
827. „ argoondah, *Sykes.*
829. Coturnix communis, *Bonn.*
830. „ coromandelica, *Gm.*

832. Turnix taigoor, *Sykes*.
834. „ joudera, *Hodgs*.
835. „ dussumieri, *Tem*.
836. Eupodotis edwardsi, *J. E. Gr*.
839. Sypheotides aurita, *Lath*.
840. Cursorius coromandelicus, *Gm*.
843. Glareola lactea, *Tem*.
845. Charadrius fulvus, *Gm*.
848. Ægialitis cantiana, *Lath*.
850. „ minuta, *Pall*.
852. Chettusia gregaria, *Pall*.
853. „ villotæi, *And*.
855. Lobivanellus indicus, *Bodd*.
856. Lobipluvia malabarica, *Bodd*.
858. Æsacus recurvirostris, *Cuv*.
859. Œdicnemus scolopax, *S. G. Gm*.
863. Grus antigone, *Lin*.
865. „ communis, *Bechst*.
866. Anthropoides virgo, *Lin*.
870. Gallinago sthenura, *Kuhl*.
871. „ gallinaria, *Gm*.
872. „ gallinula, *Lin*.
873. Rhynchæa bengalensis, *Lin*.
875. Limosa ægocephala, *Lin*.
877. Numenius lineatus, *Cuv*.
880. Machetes pugnax, *Lin*.
884. Tringa minuta, *Leisl*.
885. Tringa temmincki, *Leisl*.
891. Rhyacophila glareola, *Lin*.
892. Totanus ochropus, *Lin*.
893. Tringoides hypoleucus, *Lin*.
894. Totanus glottis, *Lin*.
895. „ stagnatilis, *Bechst*.
896. „ fuscus, *Lin*.
897. „ calidris, *Lin*.
898. Himantopus candidus, *Bonn*.
899. Recurvirostra avocetta, *Lin*.
901. Hydrophasianus chirurgus, *Scop*.
902. Porphyrio poliocephalus, *Lath*.
903. Fulica atra, *Lin*.
905. Gallinula chloropus, *Lin*.
907. Erythra phœnicura, *Penn*.
908. Porzana akool, *Sykes*.
909. „ maruetta, *Leach*.
910. „ bailloni, *Vieill*.
911. „ fusca, *Lin*.
915. Leptoptilus argalus, *Lath*.
918. Ciconia nigra, *Lin*.
919. Ciconia alba, *Lin*.
920. Dissura episcopa, *Bodd*.
923. Ardea cinerea, *Lin*.
924. „ purpurea, *Lin*.
925. Herodias torra, *B. Ham*.
926. „ intermedia, *Hass*.
927. „ garzetta, *Lin*.
929. Bubulcus coromandus, *Bodd*.
930. Ardeola grayi, *Sykes*.
931. Butorides javanica, *Horsf*.
933. Ardetta cinnamomea, *Gm*.
936. Botaurus stellaris, *Lin*.
937. Nycticorax griseus, *Lin*.
938. Tantalus leucocephalus, *Forst*.
939. Platalea leucorodia, *Lin*.
940. Anastomus oscitans, *Bodd*.
941. Ibis melanocephala, *Lath*.
942. Inocotis papillosus, *Tem*.
943. Falcinellus igneus, *S. G. Gm*.
944. Phœnicopterus antiquorum, *Tem*.
950. Sarcidiornis melanonotus, *Penn*.
951. Nettopus coromandelianus, *Gm*.
953. Dendrocygna fulva, *Gm*.
954. Casarca rutila, *Pall*.
957. Spatula clypeata, *Lin*.
959. Anas pœcilorhyncha, *Forst*.
961. Chaulelasmus streperus, *Lin*.
962. Dafila acuta, *Lin*.
963. Mareca penelope, *Lin*.
964. Querquedula crecca, *Lin*.
965. „ circia, *Lin*.
968. Fuligula ferina, *Pall*.
969. „ nyroca, *Guld*.
971. „ cristata, *Lin*.
975. Podiceps minor, *Gm*.
981. Larus ridibundus, *Lin*.
982. Sterna caspia, *Pall*.
984. Hydrochelidon hybrida, *Pall*.
985. Sterna seena, *Sykes*.
987. „ melanogastra, *Tem*.
988.* „ minuta, *Lin*.
995. Rhynchops albicollis, *Sws*.
1004. Pelecanus philippensis, *Gm*.
1005. Phalacrocorax carbo, *Lin*.
1006. „ fuscicollis, *Steph*.
1007. „ pygmæus, *Pall*.
1008. Plotus melanogaster, *Penn*.

* This was probably 988*ter S. saundersi*, Hume.

INDEX.

www.ingramcontent.com/pod-product-compliance
Lightning Source LLC
Chambersburg PA
CBHW021425300426
44114CB00010B/644

* 9 7 8 3 3 3 7 7 3 1 8 9 2 *